SAUNDERS BOOKS IN PSYCHOLOGY

LEWIS F. PETRINOVICH
ROBERT D. SINGER
Consulting Editors

ROBERT D. SINGER, Ph.D.
Professor of Psychology
University of California at Riverside

ANNE SINGER
Lecturer in Psychology
University of California at Riverside

PSYCHOLOGICAL DEVELOPMENT IN CHILDREN

W. B. SAUNDERS COMPANY
PHILADELPHIA, LONDON, TORONTO

W. B. Saunders Company: West Washington Square
Philadelphia, Pa. 19105

12 Dyott Street
London, WC1A 1DB

1835 Yonge Street
Toronto 7, Ontario

Psychological Development in Children

©1969 by W. B. Saunders Company. Copyright under the International Copyright Union. All rights reserved. This book is protected by copyright. No part of it may be duplicated or reproduced in any manner without written permission from the publisher. Made in the United States of America. Press of W. B. Saunders Company. Library of Congress catalog card number 73-81828.

Print No.: 2   3   4   5   6   7   8   9

Dedication

To Pearl Singer and her grandchildren, Susan and Elizabeth. Also to the staff of the Pediatrics and Surgical Departments of St. Vincent's Hospital, New York City, for unselfish dedication, kindness, and highest professional competence.

Acknowledgments

It is not easy to give credit to all those people who in our lifetime have contributed directly or indirectly to making this book possible. They are many, and are certainly not responsible for any of its shortcomings but only for whatever merit it may contain.

However, we would like to thank the marvelous staff of the Center for Advanced Study in the Behavioral Sciences, Palo Alto, California, who were of such great help during the most stimulating and pleasant year we spent there. Also we must express our great appreciation to Professor Justin Aronfreed of the University of Pennsylvania who presided over the exciting seminars on developmental psychology at the Center and who was kind enough to make detailed comments on early forms of the manuscript which evolved into this book.

We also owe a great deal to a number of people who have stimulated our thinking. In addition to Professor Aronfreed, they include Professors Norma and Seymour Feshbach of the University of California at Los Angeles, Professors Albert Bandura and Walter Mischel at Stanford University and Professor Robert Pace of the University of California at Los Angeles.

We would also like to pay tribute to two great teachers who have inspired us, and we are certain many others, to pursue a life of teaching and scholarship. They have done much more in their lives than teach, but to us they are people who have given of themselves unsparingly to motivate others to carry on a life of dedication to education. They are people of character in the finest sense of the term, persons of quality and understanding who were able to communicate the rewards and excitement of the life of the mind and spirit. To Josephine Britton of the Chaffee School in Windsor, Connecticut and Professor Malcolm Preston of the University of Pennsylvania, our thanks.

ROBERT D. SINGER
ANNE SINGER

New York, June, 1969

Preface

There are many textbooks available in the field of child psychology. What is this book like and how does it differ from the others?

We have approached child psychology from a developmental point of view. More than a description of what children feel, think, or do at various ages, our viewpoint concentrates on developmental processes for explanations of how and why the child's emotional, cognitive, and overtly behavioral capacities undergo systematic changes over time.

We have attempted a rather unique approach in that the book is both chronological and topical. Some texts follow children, over the course of time, through developmental or age periods. Others, ignoring chronology, treat topics like intelligence, emotions, and social behavior. This book combines both approaches. Psychological development is followed from conception to late adolescence. However, chapters are interspersed explaining the developmental principles and processes which make more meaningful the behavior of children at any given age. These chapters deal with topics such as maturation, behavior genetics, Piaget's theory of cognitive development, principles of social learning, patterns of child rearing, and the role of family and social class variables in development.

We have been selective in the materials included. We have stressed the importance of early and continued optimal stimulation, the crucial role of the social bond to others, the acquisition of language, and the development of various levels and types of thinking. Also emphasized are the nature of imitation, identity, and sex typed behaviors, as well as the roles of reward and punishment in the development of social behavior.

A principle theme of the book is socialization, the way in which the child acquires the feelings, thoughts, and social behaviors which make him a functioning member of the part of the culture in which he lives. Stress, therefore, is given to internalization, to the principles which explain how a child develops the ability to regulate his own behavior. Under internalization, the development of moral judgment, empathy, vicarious responding, anxiety, guilt, shame, and altruistic behavior are discussed.

This book is purposefully theoretical: we have tried to explain as much of the child's life as possible by utilizing the principles of social learning theory and cognitive theory. We believe that psychological theory can be presented clearly and meaningfully to students so that, rather than learning a multitude of isolated facts about childhood, they can understand explanatory principles and the scientific viewpoint.

We have relied heavily on research findings and, throughout the book, have presented a number of studies which give the student a representative sample of the variety of methods and approaches used to understand child development. These studies, chosen for their potential interest to students as well as for comprehensiveness, cover longitudinal and cross-sectional approaches, interview methods, case studies, anthropological field study, and, of course, the experimental method.

Finally, this book is relatively short. There was greater effort placed on being pertinent, to the point, and on covering what is vital than in being encyclopedic. Consequently, the instructor may wish to assign additional readings of his own choice or to lecture in a way which will expand on or supplement what we have written. We feel, however, that the book is sufficiently inclusive to stand on its own as a complete basic text on child development. It is compact rather than chatty, but we hope that it is interesting and illuminating.

ROBERT D. SINGER
ANNE SINGER

Contents

CHAPTER 1
INTRODUCTION 1

PART 1—UNDERSTANDING CHILDREN

Child Development 1
The Child as an Object of Study 3
Child Behavior and Child Development 4
The Child as a Person 5
Understanding from the Scientific Viewpoint 6
Evaluating the Scientific Approach 7
Applications of Developmental Psychology to the
   Question of Values and Action 7
Social Change and Child Rearing 9
Abnormality 10
Education 11
Child Development and the Science of Psychology 11
Contributions to General Psychology 12

PART 2—BASIC AIMS AND ORGANIZATION

Development and Psychological Processes 14
Changes in Child Psychology 14
Beginning with Phenomena 15
From Phenomena to Explanation and Understanding 16
Explanatory Approaches to the Child 16
Stage Theories 17
Social Learning Theories 17
Approaches and Methods 18
Theoretical Limitations 19
Chronology 20
Nonchronological Approaches 21
Child Development, Science, and Methodology 22
Research Presentation 23
References 23

ix

CHAPTER 2
Development Before Birth 26

- Genetic Factors in Behavior 26
- Genetics and Culture 27
- The Process of Heredity 27
- Cell Reproduction 29
- The Embryo 31
- The Fetus 33
- Response Processes of the Premature Infant 34
- Genotypes and Phenotypes 38
- What is Inherited? 38
- Summary 39
- References 40

CHAPTER 3
Processes of Early Development: I

- The Neonate 42
- Early Response Processes 42
- Individual Differences 46
- Emotional Processes in Infancy 48
- Emotional Responses in Infancy 52
- The Process of Social Attachment 54
- Stimulation and Response Processes 61
- Levels of Stimulation 65
- Summary 70
- References 71

CHAPTER 4
Processes of Early Development: II

- Socialization 77
- The Learning Process 82
- The Process of Early Cognitive Development 89
- Summary 98
- References 99

CHAPTER 5
Maturation and Learning 103

- Processes of Behavioral Acquisition and Development 103
- Maturation 104
- Maturation and Psychology 104
- Maturation and Experience 105

Practice and Privation 106
Maturation and Experience — Different Processes? 109
Summary 111
References 112

CHAPTER 6
Motivational and Cognitive Processes 114

PART 1 — SOCIALIZATION OF MOTIVES

Socialization of Sexual Motivation 114
Socialization of Dependency Motivation 119
Socialization of Aggressive Motivation 121
Socialization of Motivated Behavior 123
Positive Aspects of Socialization 125
Summary — Part 1 129

PART 2 — COGNITIVE PROCESSES 130

Intelligence 130
The Meaning of Intelligence 131
Intellectual Development 133
The Process of Language Acquisition 134
Language and Learning Processes 138
Development of Mediation 143
Break from Chronology 146
Summary — Part 2 147
References 148

CHAPTER 7
Inheritance and Psychological Processes 153

Introduction 153
Innate Factors 154
Sensory and Motor Processes 156
Environmental Effects 158
Inheritance and IQ 160
Study of Children in Foster and Adoptive Homes 160
Effect of Environment 162
The Study of Twins 163
Understanding Heredity and Environment in Relation
    to Intelligence 165
Mental Retardation 166
Inheritance of Mental Disorders 169
Inheritance and Social Values 172
Summary 174
References 175

CHAPTER 8
STAGE THEORIES 178

Stage Theory in Child Development 178
Freud's Psychosexual Stages of Development 178
Interpersonal Relations... 180
Childhood Activities 182
Jean Piaget 182
Experimental Tests of Piaget's Theory of Intellectual
  Development... 184
Generality of Stages 186
Stages and Special Experience 187
Resemblance Sorting 187
Piaget and the Development of Moral Judgments 188
Piaget and Learning Theory.. 190
Piaget's Contribution to Child Development and Stage
  Theories... 193
Is the Stage Concept Dispensable?................................. 193
Summary.. 195
References.. 196

CHAPTER 9
The Processes of Social Learning in Children 198

PART 1—REINFORCEMENT AND IMITATION 198

Introduction 198
The Vocabulary of Social Learning................................. 199
Social Nature of Learning 202
The Process of Imitation... 206
Observational Learning and Imitation............................. 208
Conditions Affecting Imitation 211
Power, Control, and Imitation 212
The Reinforcement Process... 214
Reinforcement and "Abnormal" Behavior....................... 219
The Effects of Negative Reinforcement 220
Non-Reward 221
Summary—Part 1 222

PART 2—DYNAMIC PROCESSES IN SOCIAL LEARNING............. 223

Suppression 223
Approach-Avoidance Conflict 227
Avoidance-Avoidance Conflict....................................... 228
Displacement.. 230
Frustration.. 230
Cognitive Processes 231

Summary—Part 2 232
References 233

CHAPTER 10

ACHIEVEMENT: THE CHILD FROM SIX TO EARLY ADOLESCENCE 237

School and Achievement Motivation 237
Training in Achievement 240
Achievement and Risk Taking 245
Children's Achievement and Social Class 247
Family Structure, Social Structure, and Achievement 248
School Days—The Ability to Delay Gratification 250
School Days and Anxiety 255
School and Social Life 258
School Days and Social Ties 261
The Inner World of Preadolescence 265
The School and Social Acceptance 267
Determinants of Acceptance and Interpersonal
  Behavior 269
The Teacher and Social Classroom Behavior 269
Summary 270
References 271

CHAPTER 11

THE PROCESS OF CHILD REARING 274

PART 1—SPECIFIC PARENTAL BEHAVIORS 274

Dimensions of Child Rearing 275
Measuring Dimensions of Child Rearing 280
The Child Rearing Process and Problem Children 280
Summary of Child Rearing Dimensions 285
Disciplinary Processes 286
Summary—Part 1 287

PART 2—EFFECTS OF CHILD REARING PROCEDURES 288

The Experimental Method 290
Discipline and Aggression 293
Effects of Warmth vs. Coldness (Hostility) and Child
  Behavior 293
Restrictiveness-Permissiveness and Child Behavior 294
Interaction of Warmth with Other Dimensions 295
Summary—Part 2 296
References 297

CHAPTER 12

FAMILY AND SOCIAL CLASS IN THE SOCIALIZATION PROCESS 299

- The Function of the Family 299
- The Nuclear Family 300
- Extended Families 301
- Generality Despite Diversity 308
- The Current State of the American Family 308
- Social Class and the Child Rearing Process 313
- Negro Migration and Male Status 315
- The Convergence of Child Rearing Patterns 316
- Divergences Between the Working and Middle Classes 317
- Differential Treatment of Boys and Girls by Social Class 319
- Differences in Mother-Father Roles and Social Class 321
- Changing Role Assignments 322
- Summary 323
- References 324

CHAPTER 13

EARLY ADOLESCENCE 326

PART 1 — GENERAL OVERVIEW OF ADOLESCENCE 326

- Cognitive Processes in Adolescence 326
- Physical Processes — Puberty 327
- Social and Interpersonal Process 327
- Adolescence as a Social Phenomenon — Role and Status 330
- Conformity to Behavioral Demands — the Peer Group 332

PART 2 — DEVELOPMENTAL ISSUES IN EARLY ADOLESCENCE 336

- Cognitive Development in Early Adolescence 336
- Understanding the Roles and Perspectives of Others in Early Adolescence 341
- Moral Judgments and Early Adolescence — Cognitive Aspects 343
- Sexual Maturation and Early Adolescence 346
- Sex and Interpersonal Processes 348
- Early Adolescence and the Need for Independence 350
- Summary 353
- References 354

CHAPTER 14

THE INTERNALIZATION PROCESS 356

PART 1 — INTERNALIZATION AND IDENTITY 356

Adolescence 356
Socialization Processes 357
The Process of Internalization 358
Identification.. 360
Sex Gender and Identity.. 362
Sex Preferences and Social Class 364
Sex Preferences and Age 365
The Dimension of Similarity.. 366
Perceived Attributes of Males and Females 369
Aggression and Competition — Sex Typed Behaviors 370
Sex Typing and Intellectual Functioning 371
Social Learning Interpretation of Sex Typed Behavioral
    Processes 373
The Internalization of Conscience and Moral Behavior 374
Moral Values and Moral Behavior — Generality and
    Specificity 376
Freudian Approach to Morality.. 378
Summary — Part 1 379

PART 2 — INTERNALIZATION AND EMOTIONAL PROCESSES 380

Punishment and Suppression.. 380
Observation of Models and Affective Change 383
Importance of Cognitive Activities in Internalization 384
Internalization and Patterns of Child Rearing 385
The Sensitization Processes and Internalization 389
Fear, Guilt, and Shame.. 389
Internalization and Freedom 390
Summary — Part 2 390
References.. 391

CHAPTER 15

Later Adolescence... 394

The Adolescent Subculture 394
Sexuality in Later Adolescence... 400
Adolescence and Antisocial Behavior 408
A Review of the Causes of Adolescent Delinquency............ 415
Adolescence and Orientation Toward the Future............... 416
Self and Identity.. 421
Methodological Note and Conclusion 422
Summary.. 423
References.. 424

Index... 425

CHAPTER 1

INTRODUCTION

PART 1 — UNDERSTANDING CHILDREN

CHILD DEVELOPMENT

Developmental psychology represents an approach to understanding children through a description and explanation of the psychological changes which children undergo in the course of time. As children grow older they form attachments to people, acquire language, and learn to behave in ways which are rewarding. They become able to think and to regulate some of their own behavior. The adolescent about to go for a ride in the family car certainly has psychological abilities and capacities which he lacked as an infant. In what important ways do children change over time and how can these changes be described and understood? These are the questions to which developmental psychology addresses itself.

The changes which children undergo, while building upon and preserving aspects of previous ways of behaving, produce new types of behavior which differ in important ways from previous forms. At birth the child can make sounds; later he can babble, then articulate words and sentences, and finally engage in prolonged conversations. At first the infant, unable to differentiate one person from another, will let anyone care for him; later he may tolerate only his mother, crying if she goes away or if strangers try to comfort him. When somewhat older, the child learns to like a variety of caretakers if they are rewarding to him. He will learn to object to those people, however, who treat him in ways which he dislikes. Developmental psychology is concerned with describing and explaining such sequences of change.

Psychological changes can be either *quantitative* or *qualitative* in nature. A *quantitative change* is a change in amount or frequency. For

1

example, as time goes on a child acquires more and more words and may say them aloud more frequently than before. The difference between babbling and saying "I would like some milk please," is, however, a *qualitative change*, one in quality rather than quantity. Regardless of the precise relationship between babbling and speech, the difference between them is certainly a qualitative one. The child has changed from babbling to using language to ask someone else for what he wants. A qualitative change is a change in the type or kind of behavior which is occurring. A qualitative psychological change is said to have taken place when new forms of behavior, often indicative of new capacities or abilities, can be recognized.

To give a more extended example: the development in the child of the ability to use language as a way of solving problems is an instance of a qualitative change from his earlier forms of nonverbal, trial and error behavior.[9] Roughly between the ages of four and five and a half, children learn to think in terms of words when confronted with a problem. The use of language in this way does more than just enable the child to solve old problems faster than he could before. Without the development of this new process, which psychologists call "verbal mediation," the child might never be able to solve certain kinds of problems at all.[26] One of the reasons that a child from a "culturally deprived" background does not do well in school is that he fails to adequately develop the ability to mediate verbally; he does not use language to represent to himself various aspects of a problem or various, possible, correct answers to the problem. First of all, he often does not learn to use verbal labeling (either audible or, later, silent use of words) to represent enough features of the problem situation. Secondly, even if he does have the words for parts of the problem situation, the child doesn't seem to be able to use them well enough to think about what a correct solution would be.[26] The eventual emergence of the ability to think silently in terms of words when confronted with difficulties adds a new psychological dimension to the child. It gives him a powerful new tool for coping with his environment and it represents a large step in his development.

Verbal mediation is a specific *psychological process*, a method or way of behaving. Developmental changes come about as a result of the operation of various processes such as perception, learning, or thinking (cognition). Verbal mediation, although a process, is acquired and involves thinking. Consequently, it can be conceptualized as part of the more general processes of learning and cognition. Processes are equivalent to psychological operation; the ways, methods, or modes by which different behaviors emerge, become established, and change. Verbal mediation, once mastered by the child, gives him a new way of operating in the world; it enables him to use the symbols of language to solve complex problems or to engage in learning involving the skill of abstracting. It represents a new *quality*, a new *process*, and therefore, the development of a new way of behaving.

Verbal mediation and many other behavioral processes do not emerge spontaneously and are not functioning at birth; they usually develop over time. They often have antecedents in more general processes, such as perception or the ability to profit from experience, which can partly function at birth. Additional changes in processes emerge in quantitative and qualitative steps from birth. The course and adequacy of development, the appearance of changes dependent on the functioning of various psychological processes, depend partly on genetic factors and certainly on the nature of repeated experiences, the many interactions with social and nonsocial stimuli which the child encounters in his environment. It is the task of the developmental psychologist to clarify such processes as learning, for instance, and to describe how they influence development to produce the psychological changes involved in becoming an adult. These changes, the results of the operation of various psychological processes, are often gradual and it is seldom easy to state when a distinct qualitative change has occured.

THE CHILD AS AN OBJECT OF STUDY

So far very little has been said about children. Someone might inquire whether the developmental psychologist is interested in the changes caused by psychological processes emerging and operating in interaction with the environment over time, or whether he is interested in children. Such a question, however reasonable it might seem, would be misleading. The goal is to understand children, and the issue, if any, is merely how to best proceed in trying to understand them.

One approach involves trying to describe what children actually do, think, or feel at various ages. This is the "child psychology" approach and was the most common one until recently. It is primarily *descriptive* in nature in contrast to the "child development" approach, which as we shall see, is more *explanatory* or conceptually oriented. If one stresses child psychology rather than child development in trying to understand children, it is sufficient to construct categories representative of various behaviors in childhood and to tabulate the frequency with which children of various ages engage in them. Inferences can then be made about the feelings, traits, conflicts, and motives of the child at various ages. Techniques can be used which include observing and questioning children, testing them, or working with them in therapy. Interviews may be conducted with parents and teachers about the children. Using these methods, children at various age levels can be compared with each other or with adults. The principal tendency in such an approach is to describe what the average or abnormal child does, feels, thinks, or is interested in at ages 1, 2, 3, 5, 12, or any age with which the investigator is concerned.[34]

Unfortunately, only to describe inner and outer behaviors relating to feelings, thought, or actions is not really to understand them. To understand a child psychologically, it is not enough only to describe what he is like. It is also imperative to know why and how he came to be that way, to understand how he has changed. The aim of developmental psychology is to approach children through a sound theoretical understanding of the wide scope of human developmental processes which produce quantitative and qualitative changes.

Description in the form of categorization, simple enumeration, and averages is essential, but it is only the beginning. To understand development and to discover the principles and laws of development are indispensable aims in the study of children. Granted that the 5- or 14-year-old boy and girl are the way they are described, one wants to know why they are that way.[3] If a particular child behaves in a certain way at a certain age, what brought him to that point? What processes made that behavior possible?

It is in children that we can study some of the most basic and fundamental phenomena and processes of human development. Although it is not entirely clear how soon after conception psychological change can be spoken of, it may be earlier than many suspect. There is reason to believe that some types of learning, such as classical conditioning, may take place before the child is born.[13] The fetus of about six to seven months may already be capable of some learning. Certainly there is evidence for simple adaptation within the first few minutes after birth.[52] The study of development implies the advantages of identifying phenomena at their start, noting their changes and transformations, and actively looking for and tracing the emergence of the psychological processes which account for them.

CHILD BEHAVIOR AND CHILD DEVELOPMENT

It is possible to become interested in some of the behavior which children display without being interested in psychological development. The child is often used as an experimental subject. This does not need to mean, however, that studying him will shed light on a developmental process. Children are sometimes studied in order to prove some point about perception or learning. The chief interest of the experimenter may be to show that children perform similarly to some lower form of organism, thus demonstrating phylogenetic validity for a certain theory or model of learning.[50] If a psychological theory or model is developed from the study of animals, demonstrating that it holds for children too lends it validity as an interpretation of human behavior. This is, for some purposes, a legitimate and worthwhile enterprise. However, it is not always useful for the person interested in developmental child psychology. He studies children in order to understand their psychological development.

The developmental psychologist seeks to comprehend children by constructing the laws that are descriptive of their psychological growth. Understanding the child means that one is able to trace the course of his development; how, for instance, he becomes able to perceive, to think, or to feel empathically. This means understanding how these and other abilities undergo both the quantitative and particularly the qualitative transformations, which change the child from a helpless infant to an independent adult. Taking our departure from this broader viewpoint, in this book we will examine the child's psychological processes from the time of conception and his emergence at birth. We will then follow his psychological growth and the nature of the processes involved through his initial attempts within the family to perceive, explore, manipulate, and comprehend the world. Next, development and related processes will be traced from his entrance into the peer group and school through the time of partial independence from the family and possible entrance into higher education.

THE CHILD AS A PERSON

One of the chronic complaints about psychology as taught in colleges and universities is that it deals with almost everything except whole people as seen by themselves and others. It is sometimes alleged that in psychology courses the student learns chiefly about rats, cats, and monkeys. At other times the student learns about experimental methods or statistical tests. Some students of psychology feel that they are often hard put to catch a glimpse of a feeling, thinking, behaving human being. It seems that the attempt to comprehend the person meaningfully somehow eludes the psychologist. If one were to ask a student to name some people who really understand human nature, his list might well include many individuals who have had little to do with the science of psychology. Novelists, politicians, historians, philosophers, or even relatives might be mentioned more often than psychologists. There are reasons for this, and neither the students nor the psychologists are at fault. To most individuals, understanding people has to do with a full understanding of a specific person with whom they come into contact. They want to know what that person is "like" and what he is "up to." They are concerned with the behavior of *individuals* and not with *processes* or general laws.

Parents are most concerned with experiencing their particular children from day to day and trying to cope with their behavior. Another way of saying this is that parents deal mostly with the concrete experienced phenomena and problems of their family. For example, when an older male child hits his younger sister, his mother is concerned. The boy hits the sister and the sister screams. The mother shouts, "No, no!," and slaps the boy's hands. Now the boy has a tantrum, kicking and yelling on the floor while the sister yells, "Bad, bad!" The mother may be upset by such behavior, feeling it emotionally. She may strongly dislike it but feels powerless to prevent it. The psychologist, however, may be concerned with questions such as: What specific phenomena are involved? What has caused this sequence of events? How does such behavior develop? How can one in terms of laws comprehend, predict, and change such behavior?

UNDERSTANDING FROM THE SCIENTIFIC VIEWPOINT

There are various ways of answering such questions. It is clear, regardless of any other considerations, that a recognizable common phenomenon is occurring. Most broadly, psychologists call this phenomenon aggression. Aggression has been analyzed into various components such as anger, hostility, and overt aggressive behavior. Anger has been classified as an emotion, hostility as a learned attitude, and overt aggressive behavior as a class of largely learned responses. There are various types of aggression, and aggression has various causes. The emergence of aggressive behavior has a developmental history which can be traced. But now haven't we begun to lose the previously described, vivid behavior of these particular children and their mother? They already seem a bit far away. We are well down the road to a general and somewhat abstract analysis.

What has happened is an illustration of the inevitable nature of scientific psychological investigation. It is inevitable whether one likes it or not. In order to understand the behavior of individual children, psychologists must *first* understand how behavior develops in children in general. This is the way of science. To understand children involves being able to analyze objectively phenomena and processes, like fighting, asking for help, learning, or thinking, in such a way that their development or modes of operation can be described in terms of scientific laws. It is true that to accomplish this aim psychologists often study the behavior of only one child. But the general rules or laws that we can depend on must often be derived, not from the behavior of one child, family, or school but from the systematic study of many. Only after success is met in this scientific endeavor do we usually have the basis for hoping to reliably understand a given child. Opinions based on one case or instance may sometimes be misleading and unreliable, although the objective study of one case may be an important or even crucial starting place for analysis. There is certainly a gap between limited, subjective personal experience and a tightly formulated and tested objective scientific theory of child development. However, this does not mean that child development can not have two goals: the formulation of general laws, and the comprehension of any given child.

EVALUATING THE SCIENTIFIC APPROACH

The success of the scientific enterprise aimed at the study of child development may be evaluated in a number of ways. One of the tests of the adequacy of a scientific formulation in child development is whether it helps us understand a particular child or a specific family. Description, enumeration, the analysis of phenomena and processes, as well as experimentation, abstraction, and the positioning of laws and theories, may be the chief activities of the developmentalist. However, it is fair to ask that one be able to use the results of this abstract work to help understand the behavior of a given child. It is, in addition, also fair to ask that the different parts or pieces of scientific developmental analysis ultimately fit together. This is really tantamount to saying that the goal of the developmental psychologist should be the formulation of an integrated theory of child development.

In a good theory there should be a meaningful route from the specific to the general and from the general to the specific. If we can go from children to laws of development and back from the laws to given children, it might be possible to explain, almost exactly, why a boy hit his sister. We might even come to understand how and why the sister came to shout, "Bad, bad!" In addition, if the parents decided that they wanted less aggression in their midst, developmental psychology might provide them with the guidelines for producing more peace and harmony. Developmental psychologists, then, are interested in comprehending the child as a person by formulating a general theory of behavioral processes in childhood, which should be applicable to individual children.

APPLICATIONS OF DEVELOPMENTAL PSYCHOLOGY TO THE QUESTION OF VALUES AND ACTION

If anyone doubts the interest the American public has in the practical art of the care and raising of children, he needs only to observe the great popularity of works like Dr. Spock's *Pocket Book of Baby and Child Care*.[48] It would seem that these days many parents are rather uncertain about how to raise their children. In addition, child rearing seems to have undergone changes among different social classes during the past few decades.³¹ Parents today, it may be suspected, often look to experts to tell them how to raise their children or how to handle certain problems of their children. Common sense or tradition no longer seems to suffice. Women's magazines are full of columns by psychologists, psychiatrists, psychoanalysts, and pediatricians with many pages devoted to explanations, discussions, and advice about the proper psychological treatment of children. Behind this advice, implicitly or explicitly, lie views or theories about child development. Parents' questions, however, also involve issues of values as well as issues of facts. "What do I want my child to be like?" is often the question lurking behind "Oh, doctor, what should I do?"

"How can I do it?" may be simpler to answer than "What should I do?" How to act may sometimes be deduced fairly readily from a given theory of child development. How might a mother make her children less aggressive? A mother who had read *Social Learning and Personality Development*, by Albert Bandura and Richard Walters, might act in the following ways: she would not hit, yell at, or be otherwise aggressive in front of her children; if she did she would be providing examples of aggression; she would then be a model of aggressive techniques that the children might imitate. When the children fought she would calmly separate them, distract them, and give them something else to do. In this way she would halt the aggression and be a model of nonpunitive behavior. She would try to make certain that the children never received rewards for aggression, since the aggressor, if allowed to get any benefits for "tough" behavior, would tend to behave this way even more often than in the past. The mother would find out which situations tended to evoke aggressive behavior in her children and would try to prevent their occurrence; that is, she would try to remove some of the causes of aggression. Finally, she would attempt to teach her children to respond with nonaggressive behaviors even in the situations which usually provoked them to aggression. Rewarding peaceful classes of behaviors would make the occurrence of aggressive behaviors less probable than before. The mother would be well advised to act nonaggressively herself while rewarding nonaggressive alternatives.³

All of this, of course, assumes that the mother *wants* to have less aggressive children. She could just as well try to utilize the Bandura and Walters theory to produce an even more assertive or aggressive child. She would merely reverse the principles outlined above. One must realize, however, that many parents may be unable to follow advice on child rearing since they may find it hard to voluntarily control their behavior toward their children. Parents, as other people, may be very strongly influenced by their own psychological needs and habits and may find them hard to change.

Parents are often interested in "what to do" so that their children, as we have stated, will turn out in a certain way. However, they may be uncertain, these days, about exactly how they want their children to turn out. At least they may be unsure of what they are willing to put up with. Matters of fact in child rearing, therefore, are sometimes inseparable from questions of value. It is not within the jurisdiction of applied science to tell people what they should do; it may only tell them how to do it once they have a goal in mind. Even when they know what they want to do, parents may need special help so that they can actually do it.

SOCIAL CHANGE AND CHILD REARING

We live in a society which is undergoing great changes. There are rapid changes in technology, modes of life, values, and attitudes. These changes may be occurring faster than they used to. Parents cannot be certain what human qualities will be useful in life 15 or 20 years from now. As a result of increased mobility, speedy transportation, mass media, and mass higher education, groups with divergent views on child rearing are now often aware of each other's *general* practices.[39] At the same time, the tendency of just a mother and father to live with their children in a private house or apartment makes it harder for people to observe *precisely* what other parents are really doing with their children.[4] There is both increased exposure to diverse ideas due to the mass media and mobility and less chance to learn and observe actual child rearing due to the relative isolation of the family.[30, 4] What are the neighbors up to? Uncertainty about child rearing seems to be an almost inevitable consequence of modern American life. Parents are quite concerned over whether they are raising their children properly and seem to want guidance.

Perhaps we have less to worry about in this regard than we suspect. Cultures, some believe, tend to be functional and adaptive. It sometimes looks as though those practices which help produce individuals who will get along well in a particular culture tend to become predominant, and practices which produce maladaptation may drop out in time. American culture may now need a different sort of person than it did 50 years ago. Consequently, child rearing practices may change to produce people more in line with what is needed. Unfortunately, how such transformations come about is not well understood. The types of parental practices which will bring the child satisfaction and reward in his future life may somehow tend to persist, and those which will not may possibly tend to vanish.[31] However, there is no smoothly functioning system to bring about changes in child rearing; no one is directing a plan and cultural demands may change faster than the parent's ability to sense them. Even sensing them, the parent may not know what to do. How is the mother to know what effects it will have on her child ten years later if she does A rather than B? The faster the culture alters in terms of changing the types of behavior which lead to satisfaction and success, or to failure, the greater the parent's uncertainty. All, however, is not confusion.

Parents do have some knowledge of the basics which the world expects of their children. This is clear since boys are put in trousers rather than dresses and given toy guns and steam shovels rather than doll carriages and tea sets to play with. All children get toilet trained and are taught to wear clothes in public. However, parents do not have all the information about child development and behavior they need. Laws of child development, as they are discovered, can aid parents in raising their children. This is true whether they wish to fit their children to the environment as they see it, or whether they prefer them to be agents of change or examples of self-directed individuality. Whether children are directed toward conformity or independence, acting from knowledge should be preferred to acting from ignorance. It may even turn out that a knowledge of developmental principles, if parents are able to use them, may help in making decisions about questions of value. Of course parents also need to know what sorts of environment their children will have to live in and what sorts of behavior will be useful in these environments. Such knowledge could make for happier individuals and a more satisfactory society.

ABNORMALITY

Children do not always behave in ways that make themselves, their parents, or society satisfied and happy. In some cases only the parents and society are very dissatisfied with the way the child is behaving. In other cases, however, the child is also, or even exclusively, the dissatisfied one.[3, 2, 12] This is an age of concern about mental illness or mental health, mental illness for those who dwell on the question of personal or social maladaptation, and mental health for those who seem to be looking for a criterion of optimal psychological growth, the way the ideal child or adult should be.[25] There is an extensive list of types of maladaptations, psychological disorders, mental illnesses, or socially unsatisfying and unsanctioned types of behaviors found in childhood. These include childhood schizophrenia, neuroses, mental retardation, behavior disorders and juvenile deliquency, as well as speech, reading, and learning problems.[2] These abnormalities have in common only the consequence that they are not rewarding to somebody but instead bring about an undesired state of affairs. They are ways of acting or feeling that the child, or some other person or group, would greatly prefer altered.

Persons who want to prevent these conditions or who want to remedy them once they occur look more and more to the science of child development for help. Child development deals with the ways in which various behavior is acquired, often through learning, and how this behavior consequently undergoes qualitative changes. Therefore, developmental psychology is equally pertinent to understanding the acquisition and change of both desired and undesired behaviors.[3] It is, at least, a reasonable supposition that the same principles of development that account for normal behavior in children will also account for those personally or socially undesirable ones termed abnormal. It is in this way that developmental psychology contributes knowledge to those interested in the treatment of abnormality.[3] A thorough understanding of how some emotional states and ways of thinking or acting develop, together with an understanding of how psychological change takes place, can help parents or professional therapists alter the child. What is considered normal and what is deemed abnormal, however, is often a matter of social values. Although it may be easier to change a child than society, it might often be helpful to change the child's environment since different environments produce different behaviors.

EDUCATION

Another area in which values and the applications of developmental psychology meet is that of education.[6] Values such as the emphasis placed on achievement and success and the need to outdo other countries have put a premium on the educated person. (Values, of course, are always subject to dispute and possible change.) The chief road to status and satisfaction in our culture is through education. Few people praise the school dropout. Questions about the precise nature of learning, and how it develops in the child, have recently become subjects of prime concern to developmental psychologists.[10] Developmental psychology may, therefore, have contributions to make to the school system and, even before that, in preparing the child to benefit optimally from the school. Developmental psychology can help to define the processes by which learning takes place and the nature and operation of these processes at various age levels.[36] In this way, society, the parent, and the school system can move intelligently to plan the way in which education should take place. Knowledge about the laws of development can help them take maximum advantage of the child's potentials and capacities. Developmental psychologists can aid the culture to transmit or change values, information, and modes of thinking more efficiently.

CHILD DEVELOPMENT AND THE SCIENCE OF PSYCHOLOGY

Developmental psychology today is in the mainstream of general psychology, drawing heavily on knowledge from the areas of learning, perception, motivation, personality, and social psychology. The psychologists who have pointed this out feel that we cannot understand the child's behavior without an understanding of the fundamental principles discovered in these fields of psychology. We believe that this is a fair and accurate appraisal, particularly since it has been demonstrated that findings from fields like perception, learning, and cognition do help to illuminate the behavior and development of children.[34]

Some psychologists have also emphasized that developmental psychology itself can contribute to the various areas of psychological knowledge. Developmental psychology has borrowed heavily in the past from other fields of psychology under the assumption that what was true about learning in adults or rats was likely to be true of learning in the child. Similar assumptions were made about motivation and group formation. However, many psychologists were slower to see that the study of child development could contribute to knowledge in other areas as well as borrow from them. They began to see this when certain psychological assumptions were questioned, at least partly on the basis of findings from the field of developmental psychology.

CONTRIBUTIONS TO GENERAL PSYCHOLOGY

Processes such as learning or motivation have been illuminated by the study of child development. For instance, findings from the study of animals and children indicate that reward or reinforcement, either positive or negative, may sometimes be dependent on factors other than drive reduction. We will discuss some evidence from the study of children. Previously some psychologists assumed that all learning began with the reduction of primary drives like strong hunger, thirst, or pain.[32] It has been shown that children born with a disorder which prevents them from feeling any pain, nevertheless develop the emotions of fear or anxiety as other children do. This complicates certain assumptions of primary drive reduction theory, which maintains that fear or anxiety (negative reinforcers) are fundamentally consequences of the primary drive state of pain. In addition, observations of children's curiosity and exploratory and manipulative behavior (the tendencies to seek out, scrutinize, and handle things) show that these activities are reinforcing, although they do not serve to reduce any primary drive as such a drive is usually conceived. Neither does it appear clear that these are secondary drives derived from their association with primary ones.[53]

Since various incentives, such as candy or praise, are often used in work with children, child studies have helped learning theorists to clarify their understanding of the nature of reinforcement. For instance, lower-class children work well for concrete rewards like candy, but less well for praise. On the other hand, social approval is a powerful source of reinforcement for middle-class children.[49] Why should this be so? Do middle-class parents simply give social approval more often, or is it that they more often pair social approval with candy or toys so that praise derives greater value from this association? Is it that middle-class parents are somehow warmer and more affectionate, so that approval comes to mean more to their children? Such questions raise issues about the general nature of reinforcement.

It has been demonstrated that children who have just had a lot of attention from an adult are less likely in the ensuing period to be influenced by the positive things an adult says than children who have been deprived of attention. Deprivation of attention increases its reinforcement power.[22] This finding, unlike some others, seems to fit drive reduction theory. The analogy would be that a hungry person is more likely to do things for food than a full one; a child starved for attention will do more for approval than one "full" of attention. A somewhat different interpretation has been given to these results by claiming that they are due to the frustration induced in the children by depriving them of attention.[23]

It is not the intent here to try to settle these complex issues and questions, or, in this particular section, to explore them in depth or with precision. We want to suggest that the study of children's development can lead to asking challenging and provocative questions in various fields of human psychology. Potentially, it can lead to solving problems in fundamental psychological areas such as learning and motivation. The study of psychological development in childhood can become, and is becoming, a basic tool in molding theories within psychology in general. The psychological study of children is helping to illuminate the life of the adult as well as of the child. It is helping us to choose among some of the alternate answers that have been proposed to some perplexing psychological questions. In addition, it is opening up relatively unexplored or incompletely studied areas, such as, how language is learned, the nature of cognitive (thinking) activity, the way in which punishment functions, how behavior can come under internal control to the extent that it is fairly independent of its immediate consequences, and how people seem to acquire new ways of behaving rather quickly through imitation. All of these rather basic and general psychological problems, originally not chiefly in the domain of child psychology, have received important illumination from the field of development psychology.

PART 2 — BASIC AIMS AND ORGANIZATION

DEVELOPMENT AND PSYCHOLOGICAL PROCESSES

This book is about the psychological development of the human child. To understand this development, often consisting of qualitative changes, we must study the child's most important psychological processes from their beginnings until their maturity. Since the child is born into a world of people, to whose expectations and demands he must adapt, this book stresses the component processes of socialization which enable the child to learn the behaviors needed to live in society.[3] Our main theme is the developmental history of the child from conception to adolescence. This is equivalent to the history of the acquisition and functioning of psychological processes producing changes in a context of other human beings.

Perhaps the most fundamental fact of development is that the child becomes attached to his parents and others with whom he comes into close contact. These attachments motivate much of his social behavior. As part of cognitive learning, or thinking, the child becomes able to anticipate the possible consequences of his actions. This acquisition of the ability to consider future consequences is an important qualitative change. It helps him to control his own behavior by including the probable reactions of other people in his plans. Gaining such controls is part of the process known as internalization. The acquisition of language and mastering the use of language as a tool are also parts of this complex learning process. Language acquisition helps bring about internalization, the ability to regulate one's own behavior. The child also acquires large repertoires of social behavior through imitation. This is part of the process of observational learning. Most psychological processes such as perception, learning, or thinking are accompanied and influenced by emotional reactions to the people and things the child encounters. The child experiences excitement, joy, distress, anxiety, anger, and other feelings, and these emotions influence what he does.

Most of the psychological processes which are acquired in childhood have a clear development history and can be partly explored by studying growing children over several years.[35] To comprehend the child means to be knowledgeable about the functioning of these psychological processes which usually arise in a context of other people.

CHANGES IN CHILD PSYCHOLOGY

A generation ago, child psychology, as we have already noted, consisted chiefly of descriptions of children's behavior at various ages. It was gists strive to comprehend, and it is by observing the relationships among such phenomena that psychologists can infer the nature of the underlying psychological processes.

FROM PHENOMENA TO EXPLANATION AND UNDERSTANDING

Since developmental psychology is a scientific study, it is necessary to proceed from the observed phenomena of the child's activities to an understanding of them. To accomplish this goal the psychologist must find explanations for the important aspects of the child's behavior and development. Inevitably, therefore, there is a need for explanatory concepts or principles, which describe the nature of developmental processes. These concepts or principles must come to grips with the development of external and internal behavior of the child. The processes in which heredity plays a large part influence development through the interaction of genetically controlled biological factors with most environments.[5] Unless conditions are extreme or physiology defective, all children will see and hear, walk and run. However, other processes are not as biologically determined and almost inevitable; they are more strongly affected by the experiences to which the child is exposed. The psychologist must often look for principles of development that will explain how the child acquires important new behavior chiefly through environmental experiences. These developmental principles must take into account processes such as learning and thinking. Such processes, however, always involve an interaction between a living, biological organism and its environment. What changes are occurring as a child acquires the increasingly complex types of behavior of which he gradually becomes capable? What accounts for these changes? These are the most important questions the developmentalist tries to answer.[3]

EXPLANATORY APPROACHES TO THE CHILD

There are several, contemporary, explanatory approaches to the psychological aspects of developmental change which are important. They all seem to agree that developmental processes depend on an interaction between the child's innate dispositions and his experiences.[6, 17, 20] His experiences take place in a social environment. This environment is composed of parents and other people, plus a world of inanimate objects, most of which are there because people have put them there. Cribs, blankets, high chairs, and feeding bottles exist because people exist and it is with these people and objects that the child actively interacts. It is in this context that both his physiological and psychological processes develop.

considered important to give the student such facts as the age at w the average child was able to walk, how many words the averag month old was capable of saying, or what ten-year-old boys ch worried about.[15, 44, 45] This book will present many such facts, but no purely descriptive purposes. They are included when they contribu the understanding of development in childhood, that is, when convey information about the acquisition and functioning of the ch psychological processes.

The reader, we assume, is interested in children, perhaps in a pa ular child. He will understand any child better if he knows, for ample, how children acquire their anxieties, and not just what chil tend to be afraid of. It is also important for the reader to underst how children acquire language and under what conditions they dev the ability to use it as a tool in solving problems. This is more impor than knowing how many words the average two year old can utter. more important to understand why some ten-year-old children con most of their misdeeds and others become masters of evasion, tha know which social rules ten year olds were most likely to brea 1966.[1, 8, 11] Consequently, large portions of the text are devoted t explanation of such major psychological processes as learning and nition and how they account for development in childhood.

BEGINNING WITH PHENOMENA

Although the chief concern of the text is with understanding of processes which cause change rather than with simple descriptio behavioral phenomena, the starting place must often be with the p nomena. There are various kinds of phenomena and they can be scribed, classified, and measured.

What are some of the important phenomena of childhood? behavior that comprises the formation of an attachment or b between the child and the mother constitutes a group of p nomena.[40, 47] The infant's actions, such as crying or thrashing about which the mother or others respond by helping the infant, are also portant phenomena.[43] The behavioral components of aggression, hurting of others for the satisfaction of seeing another injured, others.[16] So is the behavior from which the presence of the child's fe and anxieties are inferred.[19] Curiosity, exploration, manipulation, a locomotion, that is, looking, listening, touching, handling things, a moving about, are also vital phenomena in the child's life and wor The child's behavior in the face of difficulty, his problem solving act ties, his willingness or unwillingness to give up pleasures of the mome his attention to the behavior of others, are all phenomena to be und stood. These are some of the psychological realities which psycho

STAGE THEORIES

Some psychologists consider the nature of development to be relatively sequential and fixed. They believe in stages of development. In their view, the course of acquisition of intelligence, thinking, moral behavior, or other psychological abilities and processes is quite similar for most children. They believe that each of these develops in some invariant order.[20] Each stage of thinking, for instance, must be gone through in the same fixed order by every child, from the first stage to the last one reached. They also stress the generality or similarity of ways of thinking or behaving in children who are roughly in the same age period, such as one to two years, two to seven years, or 12 to 15 years.[17] Children are believed to reach each stage at roughly the same age. Psychologists of this persuasion are likely to use explanatory concepts such as "psychosexual stages of development," "developmental period," or "critical period."

SOCIAL LEARNING THEORIES

Psychologists who stress social learning believe that the acquisition of psychological processes is much less sequential or fixed. Some of them stress the effects of individual physiological differences or differences in prenatal or early sensory experience. More of them emphasize the influence of variations in learning, variations in the patterns of social rewards and punishments experienced by each child. They also point to the dissimilarities in the people who are available for various children to imitate. Because the types of models to imitate vary so much, as do the nature, amount, and timing of rewards and punishments from child to child, social learning theorists stress the variety of individual behavior which is possible in children of the same age. At the same time they seek to discover the general principles or processes of development which will account for the uniformities in development which do exist.

These psychologists consider the behavior of parents and the effects of genetic variation heterogeneous enough so that development would not, in fact, be highly stereotyped or invariant in order in all children. "Positive reinforcement," "negative reinforcement," "anxiety reduction," and "symbolic model" are explanatory concepts likely to be used by this group of developmental psychologists.[3] They are interested chiefly in finding general processes and laws, but they caution that the existence of these does not mean that all children behave similarly at the same age or that they acquire their behavior in exactly the same order.

APPROACHES AND METHODS

Although they view development quite differently in several regards (only some of them briefly mentioned here), most developmental psychologists respect systematic empirical methods of studying children. They tend to refer to the interaction between the child and the environment as the basis of developmental processes, and they believe in studying interactions objectively if possible. Those stressing fairly fixed stages of development are chiefly identified with the work of either Sigmund Freud or Jean Piaget, both Europeans.[21, 38] The followers of Piaget are interested largely in the principles by which cognitive structures, including intelligence and thinking, are acquired. However, they are also interested in the interpersonal aspects of social behavior. For instance, they are concerned with such matters as the acquisition of moral rules, perceptions about friendliness, and the process of imitation.[28] The followers of the Freudian view are concerned both with aspects of abnormal development and the more general problem of the internal emotional and motivational life of the child.[37] Social learning theorists are chiefly concerned with the laws of behavior, with what children do and what causes them to do it.[3]

As for methods of studying children, some developmental psychologists, following Piaget, often interview children and ask them questions in a systematic way and record their answers. Sometimes they pose problems to children or give them tests in order to understand how children think or to discover what they believe to be socially right or wrong. Although they often observe overt behavior they seldom carry out statistically analyzed systematic experiments in which variables are altered to see what specific effects they will have on behavior. However, there is currently a tendency among certain followers of Piaget to do more experimental work. Followers of Freud or other contemporary psychoanalysts, rely mostly on case studies, psychotherapy records, projective tests, and similar clinical methods to gather their empirical information. But there are some psychoanalytically oriented psychologists who use the experimental method in an attempt to test and to extend psychoanalytic theory more objectively.

Developmental psychologists who are not stage theorists are often interested in the overt, observable social behavior of the child or in his motivational and cognitive processes. They base their conceptualizations of what is going on inside the child on inferences made from directly observable behavior. They are often busy studying how a change in certain aspects of the environment, such as what the child sees or is rewarded for, will alter his actions. For example, they will usually not ask a child what he considers to be honest if they are studying the issue of moral behavior in childhood, but they will probably observe the conditions under which the child will actually cheat. Social learning theorists, for example, are concerned with doing experiments varying the conditions surrounding the child and noting the change in behavior. Such developmental psychologists often follow the tradition of experimental psychology and derive much of their methodological orientation from American behaviorism.[51] Of course, this is not always the case. Developmentalists who are not stage theorists use other methods than the experimental method.

There are many developmental psychologists who work in several traditions and use a multiplicity of approaches to sutdy behavioral processes. These methods may include interviewing parents or giving children personality tests. Many psychologists are concerned with a specific problem and would view some of the distinctions made earlier as somewhat artificial. The choice of the type of investigation used by them is often dictated by the nature of the problem at hand. The experimental method, or any other method, is not always the easiest or best one to use for studying all psychological phenomena or processes. Consequently, there has been a tendency in recent years to concentrate on specific questions to be answered about child development. Many modern developmentalists are not rigid about adhering to specific methods of investigation and, also avoid adherence to specific theoretical positions.

THEORETICAL LIMITATIONS

All broad points of view and methods enumerated above have made major contributions to understanding children. At some points these positions merge, and at others they diverge. No one, however, can supply all the explanatory principles we need, nor is there a general comprehensive theory of child development. A great need of developmental psychology is a general theory. At present, there is no inclusive theory. The theories of the psychologists devoted to the area of learning and those who concentrate on motivation or cognition are often quite different. Although most developmental psychologists speak of the acquisition of certain behaviors, some use the concept of learning and others the broader concept of experience to explain how acquisition occurs. It is probably asking too much of psychologists, at this stage of the science, to expect them to subsume all of the vital elements of a child's life under one cohesive explanatory structure. Certainly the authors of this book do not feel able to do so. Although a framework constructed from social learning and cognitive development will cover much of psychological development, it will not encompass all the vital elements of psychological experience and life in childhood. Behavior genetics, the study of the influence of heredity on psychological development, and the study of the development of perception, for instance, do not easily fall under the theoretical approaches just discussed. In this text we will try for as much integration as possible under a general viewpoint of current social learning theory plus cognitive development. However, it is important not to sacrifice reality and accuracy in a zeal for premature theoretical closure. For instance, very little is yet known about emotional development or about the motivational forces involved in imitation. The science of developmental psychology still has much to accomplish.

CHRONOLOGY

One way to look at children and their development, regardless of theoretical orientation, is to study changes in their behavior as they grow up.[34] When a child is six or seven years old, he can solve problems he was incapable of solving at three years. He can talk with reasonable intelligence to an adult at 12 years of age although he was unable to say a word at five months. The child will certainly break out in many cries of distress from the day of his birth on. However, he can't really be said to be anxious until he has some capacity, however crude, to realize that something undesirable may happen to him. Distress is a response to something unpleasant. Anxiety is the *anticipation* of something unpleasant. Whether one believes in general stages of development in childhood or in the specificity of acquisition in each child, the dimension of time is involved. The acquisition of certain processes like the ability to use language, enables the child to learn more quickly and to learn more complex things.[18] This means that, however they come about, certain aspects of a child's behavioral abilities often precede others. The ability to delay gratification, to give up the pleasure of the moment for greater later rewards, may be seen as desirable by adults and may be related to the motive to achieve, but no one expects such behavior from a hungry baby.[33] He wants to eat when he is hungry and he wants to eat right away. It takes time to learn to wait patiently.

The description of how any group of children is behaving, at any age, can lead naturally to the question of how they developed the ability to behave that way. The concept of "critical periods" is useful in this approach.[24, 41] There is some reason to believe that if children do not have particular experiences or do not develop certain abilities at specified broad points in their life, it may be more difficult for them to do so later.[46] To put it conversely, learning certain things or having some experiences at certain age periods may make some kinds of behavior more likely in future years. Similarly, the same experiences, depending on when they happen and what has gone on before, may have quite different effects. For instance, separating a four-month-old, a ten-month-old, a two-year-old, or a 14-year-old child from his parents, for the identical period of six months, will have quite different effects.[55]

Therefore, it is useful at times to take a generally chronological approach to child development. This means studying the development of the child's psychological processes sequentially over time. Behavior does take time to be acquired and to change. One need not be a stage theorist to make this assumption. The proposition that behavioral capacities change over time is compatible with a variety of approaches to child development.

NONCHRONOLOGICAL APPROACHES

Nevertheless, dividing the child's life into any sort of age periods is partly arbitrary from the developmental point of view. Developmental time is not the same as chronological time. Parts of development occur quickly and other aspects take many years. Children may develop various behaviors in different orders or at different ages. Despite some stage-like or periodic aspects to development, much of development begins early and goes on for many, many years. When aspects of development have a seeming periodic of stage-like character, we still have to explain why this is so. The reasons for different, so-called stages or orderly sequences may differ. Moreover, there are effects on a child's life which the student should know about which do not seem to fit best into a chronological approach.

For instance, the study of families, and their various methods of raising children, deserves some attention. The American child, in most cases, is born into a family consisting only of a husband and wife living together with their one or two other children, if any. This unit is referred to as the "nuclear" family and is vastly different from family units in some other cultures.[17] The genetic endowment inherited from the mother and father and their behavior toward the child determines many aspects of the child's development.[14] The parents, through their methods of child rearing, and as models for the child, continue to be important influences on his behavior for many years and, to some extent perhaps, his whole life. The subjects of the family and the methods of child rearing used by parents deserve independent treatment since they influence so many psychological processes.[42]

Learning, its nature in children of varying backgrounds, and the related issues of socialization, internalization, and achievement also need analysis, sometimes independent of age. Some children have nursery school experience as early as two and one-half years of age, followed by a year of kindergarten at about five.[39] The child can be studied in terms of the development of learning and performance from conception to age six, before the question of formal institutional education arises. Obviously, the nature of social learning experiences before age six will influence the child's performance in educational institutions. However, learning in the school and interaction with other children there introduces important experiences into the life of the child which can change him in important ways.

It is also helpful to depart from a predominantly chronological approach in order to present some of the basic theoretical constructs which clarify human psychological development. It is important to explain some of the basic principles of inheritance, maturation, and environmental experience. It may, in certain chapters, be helpful to deal with some of the theoretical aspects of developmental psychology independent of chronology. Facts are sometimes meaningless without a theoretical explanation, just as theories are empty without corresponding facts. Theoretical constructs may often be applicable at almost any age. That reinforcing (rewarding) a behavior will lead to the more frequent occurrence of that behavior is true, no matter how old the child.

Certain topics, such as how the child gains control over his own behavior, how he learns to react to transgression, or how one explains the presence of guilt, do involve chronological considerations. There seems little point, for instance, in differentiating between guilt and shame when the child is only ten months old and incapable of comprehending social rules.[3] By the time he is five or six years old a child may be able to experience both shame and guilt. However, shame and guilt, as emotional reactions, can be acquired at different ages by different children. We shall, therefore, partly follow the child's development chronologically as he grows older, develops new functions and processes, changes, and becomes both more complex and differentiated. But we will depart from this procedure when it seems best to present theoretical constructs or topics relating to the processes which explain that development.

CHILD DEVELOPMENT, SCIENCE, AND METHODOLOGY

This text aims to present objective, reliable information about child behavior gathered by competent investigators, under reasonably well controlled conditions. The information has been made public in journals and books and the investigators have usually described how they went about studying the aspect of child development that interested them. Consequently, others can repeat their work to see if it is reliable.[35] Their conclusions and interpretations have, for the most part, been made explicit and clear so that others may scrutinize their logic and either agree with them or offer alternate explanations for their findings.

Facts, or data, as they are often called, about children and developmental processes have been gathered in a wide variety of ways. It is often helpful for the student to know how psychologists and other social scientists go about gathering information about children and how they construct explanations and theories from their observations. Sometimes, of course, a concept or even a theory can come first, before many facts are known. Psychologists may then look for supporting or confirming data.[7] The research methods which psychologists use are often discussed as a separate part of a textbook, sometimes at the beginning. Some texts say little about method or may refer the student to a book that deals exclusively with research methods in child development.[35] In this text the methods of research will be discussed as they arise in the course of the information presented about the development of the child. Methodology, the various ways in which the developmental psychologists study children, will be embedded in the context of the book. When a good example of the method of interviewing, the method of experiment, or the method of observation arises, it will then be discussed to the extent that it seems helpful in understanding the nature or validity of the material under consideration.

RESEARCH PRESENTATION

Throughout the book will be found a series of "studies," each containing a description of one of the investigations on which the conclusions of the text are based. The first of these studies will appear in Chapter 3. By reading these studies, the student will sometimes get an understanding of the method of fact-finding used. At other times the results obtained will be stressed, or the reasons why the investigators developed the hypotheses they did. Occasionally the material in a study will deal with the theoretical bases or implications of the investigations presented.

We hope that this is a fruitful and interesting way to absorb the empirical, scientific basis of child development. The materials chosen to be in the studies cover a wide range of both approaches and subject matter. Their function is to expose the reader to the multiplicity of fascinating work being done in child psychology and to make more real and vivid the methods, findings, and theories on which the science of developmental psychology is based.

Where useful, particularly in early chapters, illustrative figures, diagrams, pictures, or tables will be included to help clarify the text.

REFERENCES

1. Aronfreed, J. The origins of self criticism. *Psych. Rev.*, 71, 1964, 193-218.
2. Bakwin, H., and Bakwin, R. M. *Clinical Management of Behavior Disorders in Children.* W. B. Saunders, Philadelphia, 1963.
3. Bandura, A., and Walters, R. H. *Social Learning and Personality Development.* Holt, Rinehart and Winston, New York, 1963.
4. Benedict, R. The family: Genus Americanus. (In) *The Family, Its Functions and Destiny*, Anshen, R. N. (Ed.). Harper Brothers, New York, 1959.

5. Bliss, E. L. (Ed.), *Roots of Behavior: Genetics, Instinct and Socialization in Animal Behavior.* John Wiley, New York, 1962.
6. Bloom, B. S., et al. *Compensatory Education for Cultural Deprivation.* Holt, Rinehart and Winston. New York, 1966.
7. Bronfenbrenner, U. Freudian theories of indentification and their derivatives. *Child Develpm., 31,* 1960, 15-40.
8. Brown, R. W., and Berko, J. Word association and the acquisition of grammar. *Child Develpm. 31,* 1960, 1-14.
9. Brown, R. W., and Lennenberg, E. H. A study of language and cognition. (In) *Psycholinguistics: A Book of Readings,* Saporta, S. (Ed.). Holt, Rinehart and Winston, New York, 1961.
10. Bruner, J. The new educational technology. (In) *Revolution in Teaching.* de Grazia, A. and Sohn, D. A. (Eds.). Bantam Books, New York, 1962.
11. Canton, G. N. Effects of three types of pretraining on discrimination learning in children. *J. Exp. Psychol., 49,* 1955, 339-343.
12. Caplan, G. (Ed.) *Prevention of Mental Disorders in Children.* Basic Books, New York, 1961.
13. Daragassies, S. S.-M. Neurological maturation of the premature infant of 28 to 41 weeks gestation age. (In) *Human Development,* Falkner, F. (Ed.). W. B. Saunders, Philadelphia, 1966.
14. Dobzhansky, T. *Mankind Evolving.* Yale University. Press, New Haven, 1962.
15. England, A. D. Nonstructured approach to the study of children's fears. *J. Clin. Psychol., 2,* 1964, 363-368.
16. Feshbach, S. The function of aggression and the regulation of aggressive drive. *Psych. Rev., 71,* 1964, 257-272.
17. Flavell, J. H. *The Developmental Psychology of Jean Piaget.* D. Van Nostrand, New York, 1963.
18. Flavell, J. H. Spontaneous verbal rehearsal in a memory task as a function of age. *Child Develpm., 37,* 1966, 283-299.
19. Freud, S. *The Problem of Anxiety.* W. W. Norton, New York, 1936.
20. Freud, S. Three contributions of the theory of sex. (In) *The Basic Writings of Sigmund Freud.* Random House, New York, 1938.
21. Freud, S. *An Outline of Psychoanalysis.* W. W. Norton, New York, 1949.
22. Gewirtz, J. L., and Baer, D. M. Deprivation and satiation of social reinforcers as drive conditions. *J. Abnorm. Soc. Psychol., 57,* 1958, 165-172.
23. Hartup, W. W., and Himeno, Y. Social isolation versus interaction in relation to aggression in preschool children. *J. Abnorm. Soc. Psychol., 59,* 1959, 17-22.
24. Hess, E. H. Imprinting. *Science, 130,* 1959, 133-141.
25. Jahoda, M. *Current Concepts of Positive Mental Health.* Basic Books, New York, 1958.
26. Jensen, A. R. Social class and verbal learning. (In) *Social Class, Race, and Psychological Development,* Deutsch, M., et al. (Eds.). Holt, Rinehart and Winston, New York, 1967.
27. Kephard, W. M. *The Family, Society, and The Individual.* Houghton-Mifflin, Boston, 1966.
28. Kohlberg, L. A cognitive-developmental analysis of children's sex-role concepts and attitudes. (In) *The Development of Sex Differences,* Maccoby, E. E. (Ed.). Stanford University Press, Stanford, 1966.
29. Lazarus, A. A. The elimination of children's phobias by deconditioning. (In) *Behavior Therapy and The Neuroses,* Eysenck, H. J. (Ed.). Pergamon Press, New York, 1960.
30. Linton, R. The natural history of the family. (In) *The Family, Its Function and Destiny,* Anshen, R. N. (Ed.). Harper, New York, 1959.
31. Miller, D. R., and Swanson, G. E. *The Changing American Parent.* John Wiley, New York, 1958.
32. Miller, N. E. Studies of fear as an acquirable drive. I. Fear as motivation and fear-reduction as reinforcement in the learning of new responses. *J. Exp. Psychol., 38,* 1948, 89-101.
33. Mischel, W., and Metzner, R. Preference for delayed gratification as a function of age, intelligence, and delay of interval. *J. Abnorm. Soc. Psychol., 64,* 1962, 425-431.
34. Mussen, P. H., Conger, S. C., and Kagan, J. *Child Development and Personality.* Harper and Row, New York, 1963.

35. Mussen, P. H. (Ed.)   *Handbook of Research Methods in Child Development.* John Wiley, New York, 1960.
36. Palermo, D. S., and Lipsitt, L. P. (Eds.)   *Research Readings In Child Psychology.* Holt, Rinehart and Winston, New York, 1963.
37. Pavenstedt, E.   A Study of Immature Mothers and Their Children. (In) *Prevention of Mental Disorders in Children,* Caplan, G. (Ed.). Basic Books, New York, 1961.
38. Piaget, J.   *The Origins of Intelligence in Children.* International Universities Press, New York, 1952.
39. Read, K. H.   *The Nursery School.* W. B. Saunders, Philadelphia, 1966.
40. Schaffer, H. R., and Emerson, R. E.   Patterns of response to physical contact in early human development. *J. Child Psychol. Psychiat., 5,* 1964, 1-13.
41. Scott, J. P.   Critical periods in the development of social behavior in puppies. *Psychosom. Med., 20,* 1958, 42-54.
42. Sears, R. R., Alpert, R., and Rau, L.   *Identification and Child Rearing.* Stanford University Press, Stanford, 1965.
43. Sears, R. R., Maccoby, E., and Levin, H.   *Patterns of Child Rearing.* Row Peterson, Evanston, 1957.
44. Shirley, M. M.   The first two years, a study of 25 babies. *Ins. Child Welf. Monograph,* Series No. 8, University of Minnesota Press, Minneapolis, 1933.
45. Smith, M. E.   An investigation into the development of the sentence and the extent of vocabulary in young children. *Univ. of Iowa Stud. Child Welf., 3,* No. 5, 1926.
46. Spitz, R. A.   Hospitalism. An inquiry into the genesis of psychiatric conditions in early childhood. *Psychoanal. Stud. Child., 1,* 1945, 53-74.
47. Spitz, R. A., and Wolf, K.   Anaclitic depression. *Psychoanal. Stud. Child., 2,* 1946, 313-342.
48. Spock, B.   *The Pocket Book of Baby and Child Care.* Pocket Books, New York, 1950.
49. Terrell, G., and Durkin, K.   Social class and the nature of human discrimination learning. *J. Abnorm. Soc. Psychol., 59,* 1958, 270-272.
50. Warren, A. B., and Brown, R. H.   Conditioned operant phenomenon in children. *J. Genet. Psychol., 28,* 1943, 181-207.
51. Watson, J. B.   Behaviorism. Norton, New York, 1924.
52. Wenger, M. A.   An investigation of conditioned responses in human infants. *University of Iowa Stud. Child Welf., 12,* No. 1, 7-90.
53. White, R. W.   Motivation reconsidered: the concept of competence. *Psych. Rev., 66,* 1959, 297-333.
54. Williams, C. D.   The elimination of tantrum behavior by extinction procedures. *J. Abnorm. Soc. Psychol., 59,* 1959, 269.
55. Yarrow, L. J.   Separation from parents in early childhood. (In) *Review of Child Development Research,* Hoffman, M. C., and Hoffman, L. W. (Eds.). Russell Sage Foundation, New York, 1964.

CHAPTER 2

DEVELOPMENT BEFORE BIRTH

GENETIC FACTORS IN BEHAVIOR

The first contribution of the parents to the development of the child is genetic, occurring at the moment of conception. From the time that the male sperm encounters and fertilizes the female ovum, or egg cell, the genes begin to control the processes which regulate biochemical, and, consequently, physiological growth and development. In many ways each new child resembles its parents, without being identical to them or to its siblings. Family characteristics vary greatly in the degree of their genetic origin. Certain inherited biochemical and physiological factors, in interaction with the environment, produce physical maturation, the orderly growth of physical structures like arms and legs, and the related behavioral abilities like crawling and walking. There is certainly a qualitative difference between an immobile infant and a running three year old. Of cource, protection from extreme environmental deprivation is necessary for such changes to occur, and maturation is dependent not only on the pattern of development produced by the genes, but also on such environmentally supplied necessities as food, oxygen, water, plus certain forms of stimulation. Physiological processes, however, are the foundation of behavioral development. The psychological response capacities of the child, how he can or cannot respond, ultimately depend on his physiological composition.

The human infant has a high degree of organization and plasticity, being a highly modifiable and adaptable biological creature.[6, 25] His specifically human genetic composition produces an organism which has a highly developed ability to learn. Despite a fairly wide range of genetic and, consequently, physiological differences, the behavior of many children can, nevertheless, turn out to be similar. Children can mold

26

themselves to the requirements of similar environments and thus, under some conditions, be quite alike in spite of some differences in physiological functioning. This capacity of human biological structures to allow for systematic behavorial variations appropriate to environmental conditions is the hallmark of the child, as contrasted to the young of many other species.[3, 7] The child is an organism with a considerable capacity to learn. However, we should continually keep in mind that some genetic differences can impose severe limitations on learning and adaptability.[4] These genetic combinations can produce feeble-mindedness and organic brain deterioration, and may contribute to insanity.[15, 17, 19, 20, 22]

GENETICS AND CULTURE

The real uniqueness of human development lies in the fact that the human species alone has evolved the capacity to learn and to store knowledge by using symbols to the degree that makes it possible to maintain a culture.[6] Once a form of learned behavior, like the ability to read and write, has been acquired by people in a culture, it may be taught by them to a child. It can be learned by him and later he may teach it to others. It is on this process of symbolic storage and transmission that culture depends. Usual human genetic composition is such that the child, under normal circumstances, will possess the capacity to learn reading and writing. However, he does not inherit reading and writing; it must be taught to him. Consequently, in comparison with other young animals, the specific importance of genetic variation is often less for the child. His genetic endowment, even if differing in some ways from that of other children, will usually allow for considerable learning, which tends to reduce the effects of largely inherent differences. Socialization, the acquisition of the behavior considered appropriate in any given part of a culture, is made possible by this ability to learn. Genetic variation influences the amount or efficiency of learning; of course, so do environmental influences. Genetic action probably also has indirect regulatory effects on all aspects of learning and may be important as a determinant of the complexity and abstractness of the learning which the child can master with relative ease.[6, 7, 8, 21, 22] That is to say, some children are born with a greater potential for being able to learn than others, but environmental circumstances will determine the extent to which the potential will be fulfilled.

THE PROCESS OF HEREDITY

It has been observed quite correctly that no other concept in biology has been so misunderstood as heredity.[6, 7] A psychologist might add that perhaps no concept in his field has been so misunderstood as the relationship between heredity and environment in the development of psychological characteristics in the child (and adult). Before dealing with this perplexing issue, it will be helpful to examine the process of heredity so that later discussion may be based on an understanding of its mode of operation. Heredity, first of all, depends on the genes.

The genes, located in the chromosomes, are provided by the parents' reproductive cells at the moment of conception and are structurally complex molecules of deoxyribonucleic acid (DNA).[28] Figure 2-1 represents a model of such a molecule.

Genes are biochemical substances which control enzymatic and other biochemical reactions in the body. These biochemical reactions

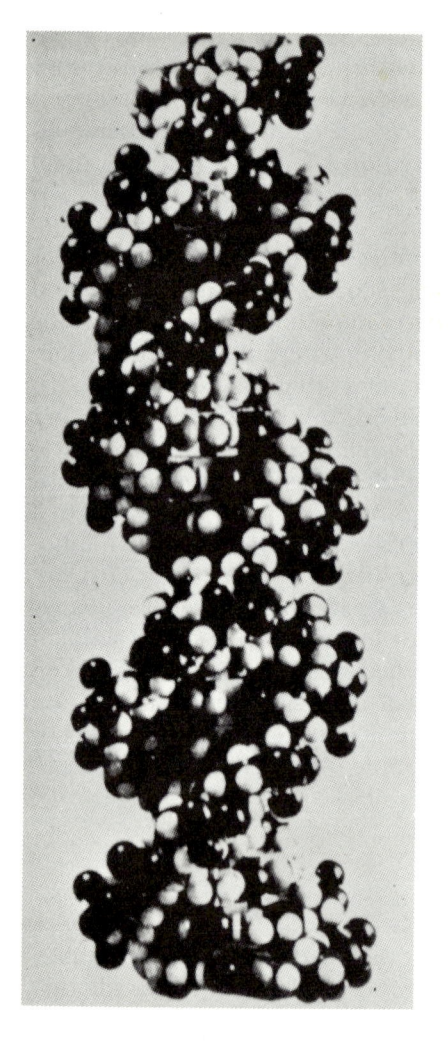

Figure 2-1. Photograph of a molecular model of deoxyribonucleic acid (through the courtesy of Dr. M. H. F. Wilkins. From Villee, C. A.: Biology.)

(along with environmental factors such as nutrition, oxygen supply, and so forth) control, in turn, the composition and specialization of cells. As cell specialization proceeds, the formation of the various structures and organs of the body, such as the eye, takes place.[2] The structures and organs which are formed have capacities to respond in characteristic ways to a variety of environmental stimuli. The eye, for instance, can respond to a variety of different wavelengths of light, and this particular type of responding, once it is integrated into other bodily systems of response, is called vision.

It is important to remember that the actions of genes are always dependent on the nature of the environment in which they are situated. Cell development and the growth of bodily structures are always a joint outcome of an interaction between genetically controlled biochemistry and the nature of the internal and external environment. The genes and biochemical reactions which they produce can generate their effects only from nutritional elements under proper conditions. The process of inheritance, consequently, consists of a series of chiefly biochemical reactions which are encoded (stored) in the genes, but whose expression depends on the internal and external supportive environment.

Under a relatively normal range of circumstances, heredity controls body structure. Except under quite unusual conditions, members of any given species share common physical characteristics and children show resemblances to their parents.[8] This tendency of individuals, because of genetic factors, to resemble their parents in physical characteristics and sometimes in behavior, is called heredity.[29] In some cases resemblances to parents may be quite simple and probably predictable. In some regards, however, children vary enormously from their parents. Psychologists are often particularly interested in variations in behavior, from the parents or among the offspring, which are largely due to differences in environmental experiences.[1, 3]

CELL REPRODUCTION

In order that biological growth may proceed, genes and cells must be able to duplicate themselves. The genes are located in larger structures called chromosomes which occur in pairs. Almost every human being has 46 chromosomes (23 pairs) in every cell, except for the reproductive cells which have only 23 unpaired chromosomes. Figure 2-2 shows this diagrammatically, along with one or two of the types of abnormal exceptions.

When a male sex cell, called the sperm, combines with a female sex cell, called the ovum, a cell is formed, which again has 23 pairs of, or 46, chromosomes. After fertilization, the cell divides as each chromosome reproduces itself, forming a new cell identical with the original one.

Figure 2-2. Human chromosomes. *A*, Normal male. *B*, Normal female. *C*, XO condition—gonadal dysgenesis. *D*, XXXY—an unusual example of Klinefelter's syndrome; the typical individual with Klinefelter's syndrome has an XXY pattern of chromosomes. (Photographs courtesy of Dr. Melvin Grumbach. From Villee, C. A.: Biology.)

DEVELOPMENT BEFORE BIRTH 31

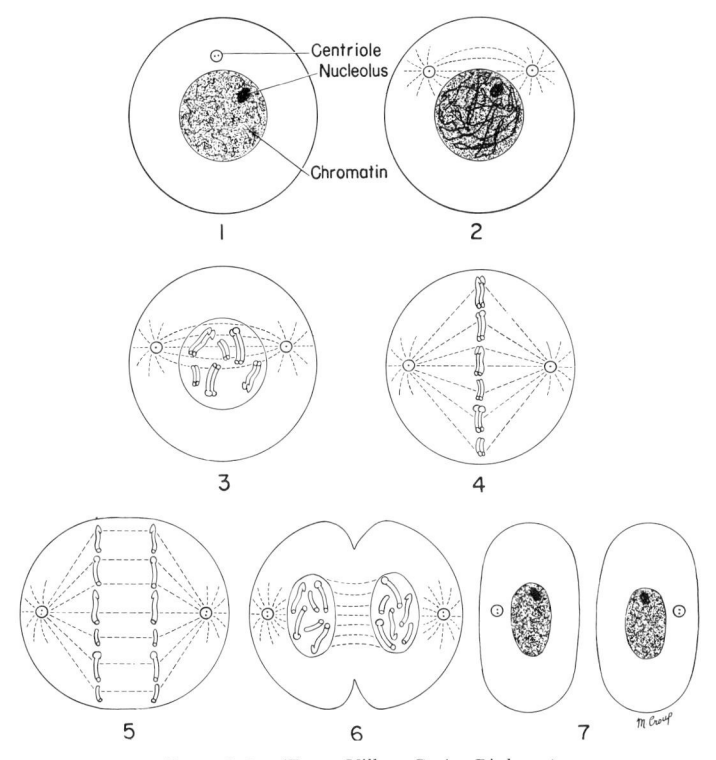

Figure 2-3. (From Villee, C. A.: Biology.)

Further cell division then proceeds. Figure 2-3 shows this process of cell division. It pictures the splitting of one cell in seven stages, with the two cells, each having the same number and kind of chromosomes, presented in the seventh stage. Even though every cell in an individual body has identical chromosomes, cells obviously differ from one another, forming such variations as bone, muscle, or nerves. This specilization takes place through an interaction between encoded genetic reactions and environmental forces acting on the cell.

THE EMBRYO

The fertilized egg first splits down the center to form two cells. The next split runs at right angles to the first, dividing the two cells into four. At this point an embryo is said to have been formed. As cells continue to cling together, the four divide into eight cells, eight into 16, then 32, 64, 128, and upward.[28] In this manner of continual division, the development of the embryo proceeds.

The two-week-old embryo looks like a flat disc. Among the first

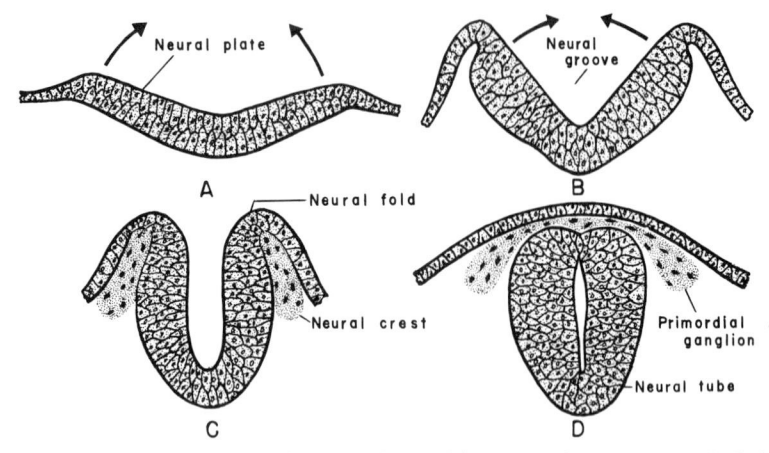

Figure 2-4. Cross sections of the ectoderm of human embryos at successively later stages to illustrate the origin of the neural tube and the neural crest, which forms the dorsal root ganglia and the sympathetic nerve ganglia. (From Villee, C. A.: Biology.)

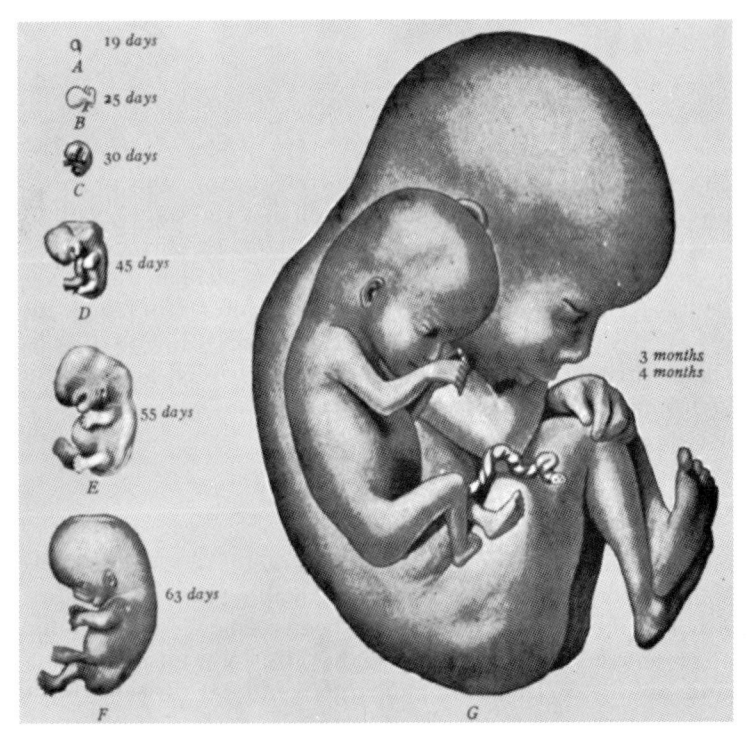

Figure 2-5. A graded series of human embryos. Note the characteristic position of the arms and legs in the four month fetus. (From Arey, L. B.: Developmental Anatomy.)

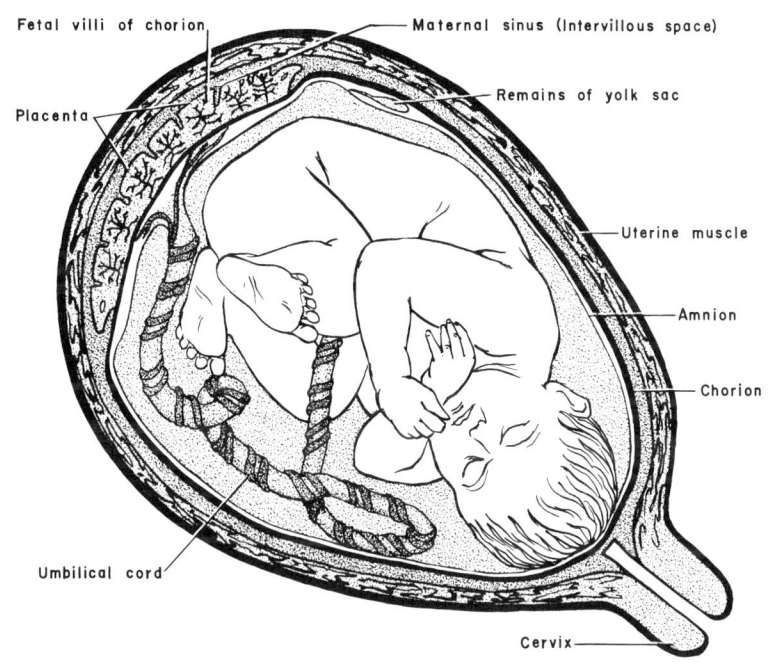

Figure 2-6. A diagrammatic section through the uterus, showing the placenta and the fetus shortly before birth. (From Villee, C. A.: Biology.)

organs to appear are the embryonic brain and the spinal cord, which will form the central nervous system. At three weeks the brain and head region begin to form, with the spinal cord following slightly later.

Early in this process, a structure, called the neural plate, develops a groove and then a fold, which turns up and joins to produce the neural tube. This eventually develops into the brain as we usually think of it.[29] This can be seen in Figure 2-4.

The front part of the neural tube grows rapidly. Consequently, the brain is established by the fifth week of development. The head grows so rapidly in the early development of the embryo that it dwarfs the other structures. Figure 2-5 shows the disproportionate size of the head of the embryo at three and four months after conception. At birth, the other organs and structures have caught up in their rate of growth to a fair extent, although not completely, as can be seen in Figure 2-6.

THE FETUS

When the embryo is about three months old it is referred to as a fetus. By the time the embryo is two months past conception, it begins to

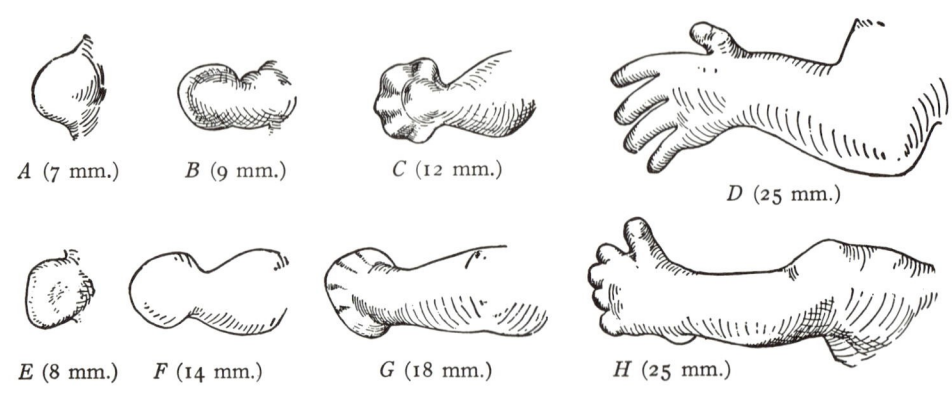

Figure 2-7. Stages in the development of the human arm (upper row) and leg (lower row), between the fifth and the eighth weeks. (From Arey, L. B.: Developmental Anatomy.)

look human.[29] The face is evident now, as are the arms and legs and the internal organs have also begun to form. Development in the next seven months consists not in the beginning of new structures, but in the completion of details and growth in size of the ones already present in rudimentary form. Figure 2-7 shows aspects of the development of the human arm and leg.

Villee describes the development of the embryo two months after conception as follows: "The embryo is about 3 inches long after three months of development, 10 inches long after five months, and 20 inches long after nine months. During the third month the nails begin forming and the sex of the fetus can be distinguished." A three-month embryo, as we have stated, is called a fetus. Villee continues: "By four months the face looks quite human; by five months, hair appears on the body and head. During the sixth month eyebrows and eyelashes appear. After seven months the fetus resembles an old person with red and wrinkled skin. During the eighth and ninth months fat is deposited under the skin, causing the wrinkles to partially smooth out; the limbs become rounded, the nails project at the finger tips, the original coat of hair is shed, and the fetus is 'at full term' ready to be born. The total gestation period, or time of development, for human beings is about 280 days from the beginning of the last menstrual period before conception, until the time of birth.[29] The fetus when it emerges at birth is called the neonate, or newborn.

RESPONSE PROCESSES OF THE PREMATURE INFANT

As important as the genetically controlled physical development of the embryo and fetus are in themselves, the psychologist is chiefly concerned with the physical capacities for behavior that arise as a result of that development. He wants to know the course of development of qualitatively new behavior abilities. The growing capacity of the fetus for behavior is closely correlated with its neurological maturation. It is difficult to know the behavioral possibilities of the fetus, since it is developing in a closely confined area within the mother. Some fetuses, however, are born prematurely, before full term. If at about 28 weeks — that is, at about seven months after the first day of the mother's last menstrual period, the fetus is born, it is called a premature infant. It is possible, and useful, to study the behavioral capacities of premature neonatal (newborn) infants.[5]

The premature infant has periods of wakefulness even at 28 weeks of age. There are some body movements in response to intense lights but no pupillary reflex and no movements of the eye to follow a light. There is a diffuse movement to sound waves. Taste is already partly developed, and repulsion or attraction to the taste of various substances exists. Touch may possibly be differentiated from pain; but this is in doubt. Many of the reflexes to be discussed in the next chapter are present, but in a very weak and only partly organized state. Some bodily movements take place and are well established in some areas, but are still flaccid and immature in others.[5] Figures 2-8, 2-9, and 2-10 show aspects of movements or mobility in the 28-week-old premature baby.[5]

By 35 weeks after the first day of the mother's last menstruation, the premature baby has shown marked changes in muscle tone, which has become quite like that of the full term baby. Flexion of the limbs, however, is still poor. Nevertheless, the head can now be straightened by the infant. He pulls up his head, if held in a sitting position, and can for a short time get it into line with the trunk of his body. The infant pulls his head away from a pinch on the ear. This and other such responses may possibly be reactions to pain. If held upright, the infant can straighten his legs. The pupillary light reflex is established; the pupil

Figure 2-8. At 28 weeks the automatic walking reflex is clearly present and operates with the lower extremities more or less flexed, since their alignment is still unstable. (From Dargassies, S. Ste-A. *In* Human Development, Falkner, F. [Ed.].)

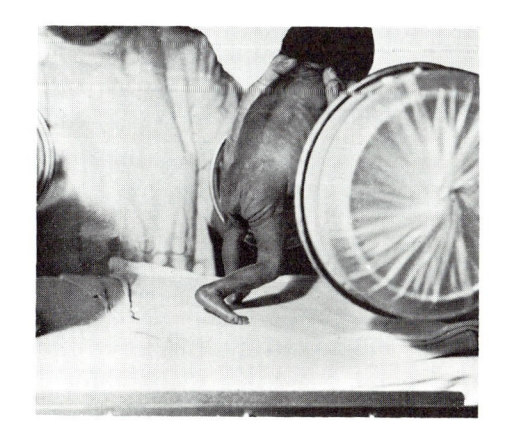

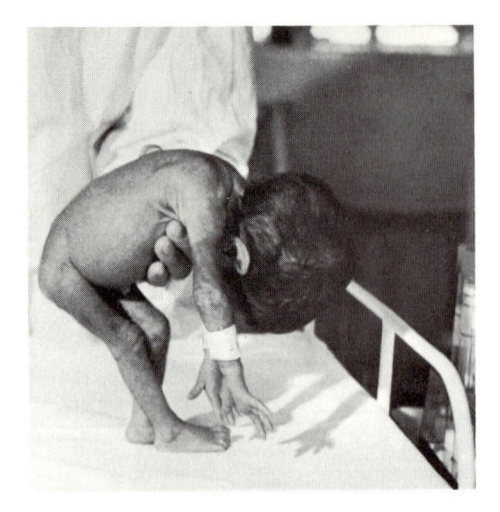

Figure 2-9. At 28 weeks the reflexive straightening of the entire body in an erect position is still impossible (the extension of the lower extremities does not produce extension of the trunk and the head), but there is active extension of the knee. (From Dargassies, S. Ste-A. *In* Human Development, Falkner, F. [Ed.].)

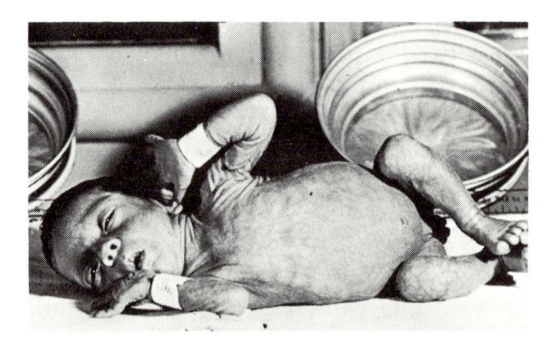

Figure 2-10. Good spontaneous motility in the 28 week premature infant testifies to the quality of active tonus which contrasts with the looseness of the passive tonus. (From Dargassies, S. Ste-A. *In* Human Development, Falkner, F. [Ed.].)

contracts in bright light and expands in dim light. The premature newborn has been able to ingest liquid food since the age of 32 weeks and will grasp strongly at anything placed in his palm. Vigilance is strong; he is awake more often, and can move his eyeballs without moving the rest of the head. Although they are probably stronger at 35 weeks, these reactions are clearly present at 32 weeks of age.[5]

At 37 weeks, the premature baby is qualitatively much like a full term one. He can flex his arms and legs and straighten his entire body. Grasp is strong. He will turn his eyes and head toward a soft light. The premature baby now cries fairly strongly. Certain reflexes are still partly weak and muscle tone as well as certain kinds of flexion and extension, as of the neck, are still not quite up to the level of a full term infant.

At 41 weeks the premature infant is almost, but not quite, the behavioral equal of the full term baby, demonstrating the continuity of neurological and sensory development.[5] These sequences of neurological and sensory development are under the control of the genes interacting with environmental influences. Their sequence of development is roughly the same for almost all human infants. Figures 2-11, 2-12, and 2-13 illustrate aspects of physical capacities in the 37-week-old premature new born.[5] These observable physical characteristics of the infant depend largely on the underlying genetic structure.

Figure 2-11. The grasp reflex is so strong at 37 weeks that the infant can be lifted from the bed by means of it. (From Dargassies, S. Ste-A. *In* Human Development, Falkner, F. [Ed.].)

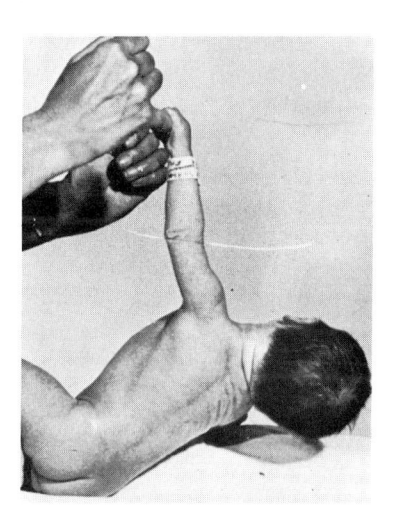

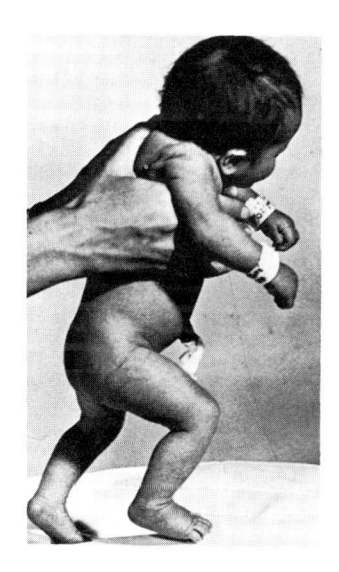

Figure 2-12. At 37 weeks, the infant uses the whole sole of the foot in reflexive walking, as does the full term newborn. The newborn, however, places the heel first. (From Dargassies, S. St.-A. *In* Human Development, Faulkner, F. [Ed.].)

Figure 2-13. At 37 weeks, the tonus of the neck muscles is sufficient to hold the head in alignment with the trunk for a few seconds. This results from the strength of the extensor muscles (the flexors of the neck are less developed). (From Dargassies, S. Ste-A. *In* Human Development, Falkner, F. [Ed.].)

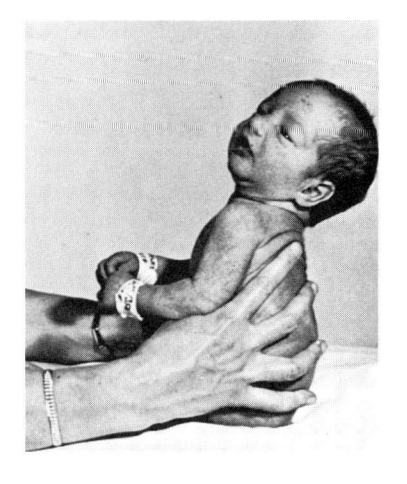

GENOTYPES AND PHENOTYPES

The specific aggregate of all the genes which a person possesses is referred to as his genotype. Even under the best of conditions, with electronic microscopes, genes are generally not clearly observable in the human cell. What we are usually able to observe are a person's characteristics which are the results of the interaction of the genotype with the environment. These observable or measurable characteristics are called phenotypes. Eye, hair and skin color, body size, and body weight in the child and the adult are all phenotypes. Some phenotypes are almost entirely determined by genetic action, although others, like body weight and height, are only partly determined. Type of diet, amount eaten, or even climatic conditions may influence height and weight considerably but won't change blood type.[13] Although some phenotypes may be the result of reactions involving only a single pair of genes, this is the exception rather than the rule. Most of the phenotypes (observable or measurable characteristics of human composition) depend on a number of genes. We seldom know which *underlying* genotype is responsible for a given phenotypic characteristic in the child, although there are a few cases in which we do know.[18, 23]

WHAT IS INHERITED?

An important question must be raised as to whether human behavior can be inherited. That is, can we say that the baby's crying, the infant's crawling, a child's fear of dogs, or the adolescent's fighting is inherited? Or to move to the abstract level: is the communication, exploration, emotionality, or aggression of the child inherited? It is reasonably clear that the answer is No. Behaviors are not inherited. It is physical structures which are inherited, with their accompanying capacities to respond to a range of environments.[17, 25] Insofar as genetic composition helps to produce physical structures which play a determining role in the acquisition or expression of behavior, behavior may be said to be influenced by heredity. It is with the behavior, however, that the psychologist is concerned. For instance, a child does not inherit fear or anxiety from his parents. However, he may inherit a type of nervous system which leads to sensitivity to noise and pain and which tends, in general, to be overreactive.[10, 11] Such a child is clearly more likely to acquire fears and anxieties than a child who has inherited a passive or less sensitive nervous system.[12, 13] The actual fear and anxiety responses, however, are learned, not inherited.

Although only physical structures, like nervous systems, are inherited, variations in physical structure may obviously influence the number of behaviors learned or the speed and ease with which they are acquired.[16, 24] It is important to note, however, that the consequences of having one variation in physical structure rather than another may be made irrelevant, or may even be reversed, by the environment. If a child with a physiological predisposition to experience fear lives in a calm, benign, secure home with quiet, supportive parents, he may grow up fearing little. Conversely, a child with a nervous system normally rather impervious to assault can be made a neurotic wreck by years of living with ambivalent, conflict-ridden, irresponsible, inconsistent, hostile, and physically abusive parents.[3] Children do not inherit bodily temperatures, the healing of wounds, intelligence, or aggressive behavior. They inherit physical structures and patterns of physiological processes, largely genetically determined and selected through evolution, which interact with environmental variables in producing the particular behaviors or capacities in question.

Inheritance, therefore, can influence the probability that a certain behavior will arise in a particular child. The behavior itself, however, is never inherited. Behavior must mature, be elicited, acquired, or learned. Even reflexive behavior or unconditional responses must be evoked by something in the environment. If a stimulus does not evoke them, they will not occur. At most one can say either that the predisposition to perform certain behaviors is strongly enhanced by hereditary factors, or that inherited physiological factors limit behavioral possibilities.

Such enhancements or limitations may be quite strong. To illustrate: a child may be born with a hereditary defect which will produce a nervous system rendering him almost incapable of any significant learning.[21, 26, 27] What the child inherits from his parents, then, is a set of chromosomes containing genes which will strongly influence the development of his bodily organs, their structure and their functioning. These, in turn, will influence what he experiences or learns, and how others will react to him.

SUMMARY

In many ways the psychological development of children is influenced by their biochemical and physiological characteristics. For instance, some children may have autonomic nervous systems which react to environmental stimuli in ways that produce fear or anxiety more frequently than is the case for other children. There are children who are innately more sensitive to stimulation of certain types than other children who are less responsive to the same levels of stimulation. It also appears, that in ways not yet understood, the biochemical and physiological composition of a child may make it easier or harder for him to learn in comparison to others. Further, height, weight, eye or hair color, which are physical characteristics, may become factors in psychological development because of social preferences which people have, such as admiration for tallness in boys or for blond hair in girls. Consequently, physical characteristics, that is, biochemically or physiologically produced ones, can be determining factors in psychological change.

Physical characteristics develop as a result of genetic action interacting with external environmental conditions. In fact, it is possible to think of two environments, a genetic one and a nongenetic one in mutual contact, operating to produce physical growth and functioning. The child's behavioral dispositions, his emotional, cognitive, and social behaviors, are the joint outcome of the interaction of physical structures, produced largely by the genetic environment, and his experiences, produced largely by the external environment. However, the genetic environment could not function without external support and there could be no experience without physical structures for stimuli to effect.

From their parents children inherit their genetic composition, which is determined at the moment of conception. The genetic composition of the child will be more like that of his parents than of people not related to him. Consequently, there will be similarity between the physical characteristics of the child, the child's parents, and the child's brothers and sisters.

It should be stressed again that behavior is not inherited; inheritance influences the nature of biochemical and physiological functioning and the consequent capacities of organs and physical structures. However the physical differences which exist among children as a result of genetically transmitted inheritance affect the acquisition of behavior and the course of behavioral change in psychological development. Behavior, however, must be elicited (evoked), acquired, or learned as a result of contact with stimuli in the environment. The effect of environmental stimuli in establishing, maintaining, or changing behavior, however, will depend partly on the physical attributes of the child. So, although behavior is never inherited, its nature may be influenced by heredity through differences in physical characteristics and modes of biochemical and physiological functioning.

REFERENCES

1. Anastasi, A. *Differential Psychology.* Macmillan, New York, 1937.
2. Arey, L. B. *Developmental Anatomy.* W. B. Saunders, Philadelphia (6th Edition), 1954.
3. Bandura, A., and Walters, R. H. *Social Learning and Personality Development.* Holt, Rinehart, and Winston, New York, 1963.
4. Chess, S., et al. Characteristics of the individual child's behavioral responses to the environment. *Amer. J. Orthopsychiat.,* 29, 1959, 791-802.
5. Dargassies, S. S.-A. Neurological maturation of the premature infant of 28 or 41 weeks gestational age. (In) *Human Development,* Falkner, F. (Ed.). W. B. Saunders, Philadelphia, 1966.
6. Dobzhansky, T. The biological concept of heredity as applied to man. (In) *The Nature and Transmission of the Genetic and Cultural Characteristics of Human Populations,* Milbank Memorial Fund, New York, 1957.

7. Dobzhansky, T. *Mankind Evolving.* Yale University Press, New Haven, 1962.
8. Dodson, E. A. *A Textbook of Evolution.* W. B. Saunders, Philadelphia, 1956.
9. Eysenck, H. J. Conditioning and personality. *Brit. J. Psychol. 53,* 1962, 299-305.
10. Eysenck, H. J. The biological basis of personality. *Nature, 199,* 1963, 1031-1034.
11. Eysenck, H. J. *Experiments in Behavior Therapy.* Pergamon Press, Oxford, 1964.
12. Eysenck, H. J., and Rachman, S. *The Causes and Cures of Neurosis.* Knapp, San Diego, 1965.
13. Fuller, J. L., and Thompson, R. W. *Behavior Genetics.* John Wiley, New York, 1960.
14. Galton, F. *Hereditary Genius.* Appleton, New York, 1883.
15. Garrod, A. E. *Inborn Errors of Metabolism.* Froude, Hodder, and Stoughton, London (2nd Edition), 1923.
16. Grossman, H. J., and Greenberg, N. H. Psychosomatic differentiation in infancy. *Psychosom. Med., 19,* 1957, 293.
17. Jacobs, P. A., et al. The somatic chromosomes in Mongolism. *Lancet., 1,* 1959, 710.
18. Jervis, G. A. Genetic factors in mental deficiency. *Amer. J. Hum. Genet., 4,* 1952, 260-271.
19. Jervis, G. A. Phenylpyruvic oligophrenia (phenylketonuria) *Proc. Assoc. Res. Nerv. Ment. Dis., 53,* 1954, 259-282.
20. Kallman, J. F. *Heredity in Health and Mental Disorder.* Norton, New York, 1953.
21. McClearn, G. E. The inheritance of behavior. (In) *Psychology in the Making,* Postman, L. J. (Ed.). Knopf, New York, 1962.
22. McClearn, G. E. Genetics and behavior. (In) *Review of Child Development Research,* Hoffman, M. L., and Hoffman, L. W. (Eds.). Russell Sage Foundation, New York, 1964.
23. Penrose, L. S. *The Biology of Mental Defect.* Sidgwick and Jackson, London, 1954.
24. Richmond, J. B., and Lustman, S. L. Autonomic function in the neonate. *Psychosom. Med., 17,* 1955, 269.
25. Singer, R. D. Organization as a unifying concept in schizophrenia. *A.M.A. Arch. Gen. Psychiat., 2,* 1960, 61-74.
26. Sorsby, A. (Ed.), *Clinical Genetics.* Butterworth, London, 1953.
27. Sutton, H. E. *Genes, Enzymes and Inherited Diseases.* Holt, Rinehart and Winston, New York, 1961.
28. Vandenberg, S. G. The hereditary abilities study: hereditary components in a psychological test battery. *Amer. J. Hum. Genet., 14,* 1962, 220-237.
29. Villee, C. A. *Biology.* W. B. Saunders, Philadelphia, (4th Edition), 1964.

CHAPTER 3

PROCESSES OF EARLY DEVELOPMENT: I

THE NEONATE

Figure 3-1 shows what a healthy newborn baby looks like. It was taken six hours after birth.

The length of the average newborn male is 20 inches; of the female, 19.6 inches. The normal range for both sexes is from 19 to 21½ inches. About two-thirds of all full-term infants weigh between 6 and 8½ pounds. Five to 10 percent of this weight is lost during the first few days after birth. Let us now turn to the behavioral abilities which this newborn infant has and begin to trace the quantitative and qualitative changes which he will undergo.

EARLY RESPONSE PROCESSES

Reflexes

The nervous system of the newborn is not yet mature. Responses to both internal and external stimuli consist largely of reflexes depending largely on the midbrain and spinal cord. Reflexes consist of relatively automatic (innate) responses to certain types of stimulation. Many functions of the infant nervous system are performed by simple reflexes. These require only three basic units, the *receptor,* the *transmitter,* and the *effector.* The receptor is a sensory nerve that can detect an internally or externally produced stimulus activating a neural impulse. The neural impulse, activated by a stimulus, is then carried by the *transmitter,* a nerve

A deep flush spreads over the entire body if baby cries hard. Veins on head swell and throb. You will notice no tears as tear ducts do not function as yet.

The skin is thin and dry. You may see veins through it. Fair skin may be rosy-red temporarily. Downy hair is not unusual. Some *vernix caseosa* (white, prenatal skin covering) remains.

Head usually strikes you as being too big for the body. It may be temporarily out of shape — lopsided or elongated — due to pressure before or during birth.

The feet look more complete than they are. X-ray would show only one real bone at the heel. Other bones are now cartilage. Skin often loose and wrinkly.

The trunk may startle you in some normal detail: short neck, small sloping shoulders, swollen breasts, large rounded abdomen, umbilical stump (future navel), slender, narrow pelvis and hips.

Eyes appear dark blue, have a blank stary gaze. You may catch one or both turning or turned to crossed or wall-eyed position. Lids, characteristically, puffy.

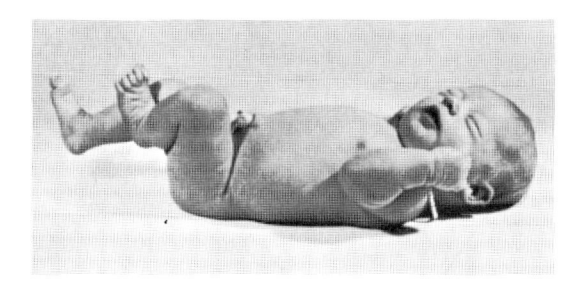

The legs are most often seen drawn up against the abdomen in pre-birth position. Extended legs measure shorter than you'd expect compared to the arms. The knees stay slightly bent and legs are more or less bowed.

Genitals of both sexes will seem large (especially scrotum) in comparison with the scale of, for example, the hands to adult size.

The face will disappoint you unless you expect to see: pudgy cheeks, a broad, flat nose with mere hint of a bridge, receding chin, undersized lower jaw.

Weight unless well above the average of 6 or 7 lbs. will not prepare you for how really tiny newborn is. Top to toe measure: anywhere between 18" to 21".

The hands, if you open them out flat from their characteristic fist position, have: finely lined palms, tissue-paper thin nails, dry, loose fitting skin and deep bracelet creases at wrist.

On the skull you will see or feel the two most obvious soft spots or *fontanels*. One is above the brow, the other close to crown of head in back.

Figure 3-1. What a healthy newborn baby looks like. This unretouched photograph taken 6 hours after birth at Lawrence Memorial Hospital. (From *Baby Talk*, January 1964.)

which may consist of one or several neurons. The *effector* may be a muscle or a gland, or any organ activated by impulses from the transmitters.[57]

Certain terms, like *stimuli* and *responses,* often found in the vocabulary of learning theory, have been used in the preceding paragraph. Some readers may be quite familiar with such terms and the other learning concepts utilized in this chapter. For those who are not, Chapter 9, The Processes of Social Learning in Children, includes a glossary of these terms and discusses some of them at length.

Reflexes involving breathing, feeding, and so on, include transmission of impulses to and from excitatory and inhibitory centers in the midbrain. These need not include either conscious or voluntary control over behavior. Nor do they have to be learned. Certain ongoing functions of the body adjust themselves without ordinarily coming to conscious attention even in the adult with a fully mature nervous system. Breathing and digestion, for instance, operate in most cases without our awareness. The baby's cortex hardly functions at all in the first few hours of life, but he is the efficient possessor and user of a great many reflexes (as enumerated in the following paragraphs) which developed while he was still in the uterus. These reflexes have been built in, through the process of evolution, and are elicited by certain stimuli. Reflexes are innate, and ensure to a fair degree that the infant will survive if he receives a minimal amount of care. Survival in infancy cannot depend on a gradual process of complex social learning.

A bright light makes an infant *blink; coughing* and *sneezing* clear the respiratory tract. *Yawning* draws in oxygen. In feeding, the infant shows the *rooting* reflex, which causes his head to turn toward anything that touches his cheek, such as the mother's breast, and the *sucking* reflex which occurs when his lips are touched. *Swallowing* and *gagging* are also reflexive in nature.

An infant will briefly *grasp* anything put in his hands. At birth one may be able to lift him to a standing position by inserting a finger or a stick into his fists. This is called the grasping or *Darwinian* reflex. His toes will also curl around to get hold of an object if they, or the sides of his feet, are touched. Figure 3-2A illustrates the grasp, or Darwinian, reflex, along with some of the other reflexive behaviors of the infant.

If the newborn is held upright with his feet touching a flat surface, his legs will prance up and down, in the *dancing* reflex. The well known *startle,* or *Moro,* reflex is shown in Figure 3-2B. A sudden stimulus, such as jarring the crib, will cause the legs to draw up with soles almost touching as the arms fly out to the sides. The absence of this reflex in the first eight weeks of life may be an indication of brain damage. The Moro reflex starts to wane after eight weeks probably because of increased control by the later-developing cortex.[100] The *tonic neck* reflex, or "fencing position," refers to the usual posture of the infant when lying

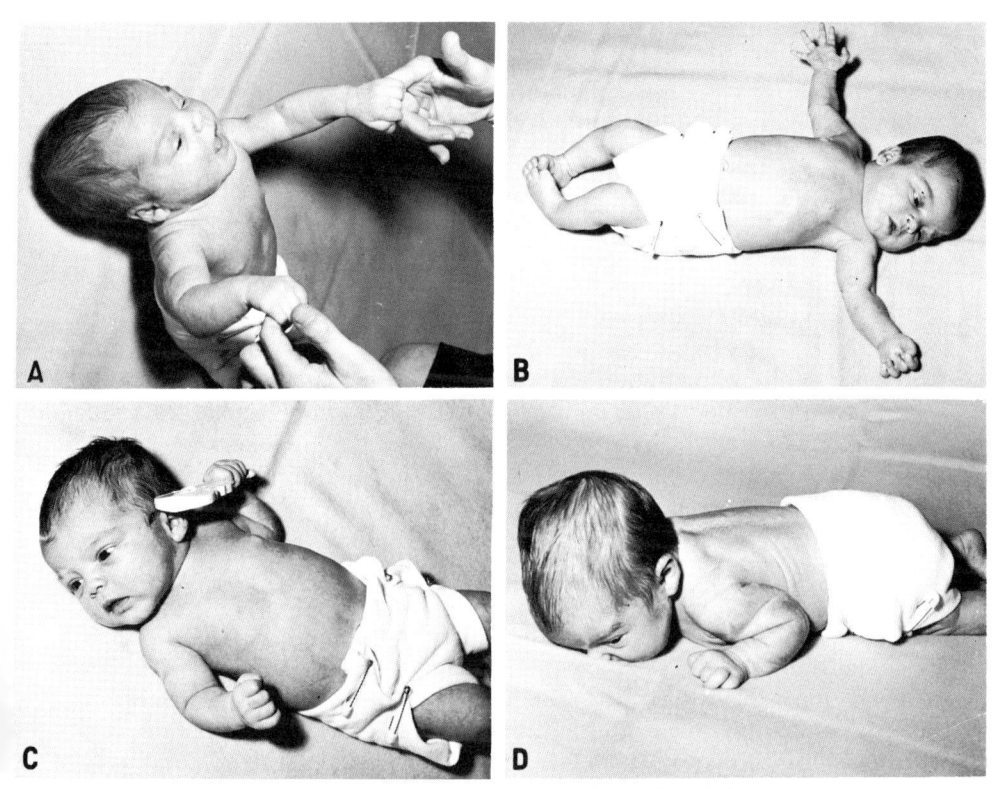

Figure 3-2. Reflexes and motor development of the newborn infant. *A*, Grasp reflex. *B*, Startle reflex (Moro reflex). *C*, Tonic neck reflex. *D*, Lifts head slightly from the bed. (From Marlow, D. R.: Pediatric Nursing.)

on his back; his head turns to one preferred side, and he extends the arm and leg on that side while flexing the other arm and leg. It first occurs in the fetus between 20 and 28 weeks after conception and continues until the eighteenth or twentieth week after birth. (See Figure 3-2C.)

At birth the infant can raise his head somewhat when on his stomach (Figure 3-2D), but not when on his back. He can make crawling and kicking movements, and active infants may move about a good bit in their cribs. In addition to these motoric reflexes, the child is born with a vast and complex system of ongoing autonomic regulatory processes or reflexes for control of internal bodily processes. The autonomic nervous system helps to control bodily temperature, breathing rate, excretory functions, hunger, digestion, and so on, all of which are essential for survival. The cerebrospinal or central nervous system chiefly controls motoric (bodily) movements, and the autonomic nervous system mainly regulates internal physiological functions.

INDIVIDUAL DIFFERENCES

There are large individual differences among children even before they are born, as shown by the wide variation which has been recorded in the amount of activity of the fetus in the uterus.[137] These differences continue through the first few days of life and keep up with some consistency for at least several months and probably much longer.[93, 116, 131]

Early individual differences are sometimes measured in terms of responsiveness of the autonomic nervous system and related indices.[4, 56, 79, 108, 149] Indices of autonomic nervous system activity correlate highly with ratings of wakefulness.[16, 89] Some restless and hyperactive newborns find little or no comfort in body contact, and develop into noncuddling babies.[115] Although not much is known about the reasons for such variations. McGrade and his coworkers found that infants born following a long labor are more responsive to stimulus change than those born following a short labor.[97]

Activity Level

By the age of three months the infant has usually established a fairly regular daily cycle of sleeping and waking.[101] Shortly after birth the baby spends most of his time in sound sleep, but his state varies enormously with the amount and strength of internal and external stimulation he is undergoing at any one time. His activity level ranges from minimal, as in deep sleep, to complete arousal, when he may be screaming and thrashing around. He will seldom show extreme arousal, since most babies are attended to before hunger or pain or any other strong stimulus has acted on them very long.

Sleep

During sound sleep the newborn is completely relaxed. There is little or no diffuse muscle activity. The eyelids are closed, and no eye movements can be observed. The infant breathes regularly at about 36 respirations per minute, on the average.[48]

As the infant's sleep becomes more irregular and less completely relaxed, his muscle tone feels firmer to the touch. Motor activity appears, running from gentle limb movements to spontaneous startles, alternating with relatively inactive periods. Grimaces occur oftener and include smiling, frowning, and rhythmical mouthing. The face may become flushed during active periods. Breathing may be irregularly rapid and shallow, with 48 or more respirations per minute being about average. The eyes are closed but may be squinted, and movements may be observed through the closed lids. These rapid eye movements (REM) resemble in part those observed in adults during dreaming, and tend to occur during periods of high motor activity in the sleep cycle.[110] Rather than believing that newborns dream like adults, investigators conclude that the rapid eye movements do not require cortical activity for their occurrence, as dreams probably do, but may originate in the midbrain, which is an older and more primitive part of the brain, compared to the cortex.

Wolff suggests that much of the disorganized mass activity shown by Western babies in their isolated cribs might be totally inhibited if they remained in physical contact with their mothers, since it is not reported in animal infants, where such contact is almost continual.[148]

Drowsiness

In the drowsy state the infant is more active than in deep sleep but less active than in irregular or periodic sleep. He is likely to show bursts of wriggling while he is waking up but not while falling asleep. The eyes open and close; they appear dull, glazed, and unfocused, and the eyelids appear heavy. Just before closing, the eyes may roll upward and outward, and breathing may become irregular. The duration of drowsiness varies among infants, and usually is longer while going to sleep than while awaking.

Alert Inactivity and Waking Activity

This is a relaxed but attentive state; the infant's eyes are open and appear bright and shining. Many babies can pursue an object with coordinated movements of both eyes within two hours after delivery. After 24 hours almost all can make these eye movements, and by the third day can coordinate head and eye movements. Newborns respond readily to visual stimuli and to sounds, to touch, and to a painful tickle.[16, 148] The average age of first response to smells is about 50 hours, or two days. It is during periods of alert inactivity that the baby is most responsive to all kinds of stimuli.

The proportion of time an infant spends in waking activity—that is, with his eyes open, babbling, or wriggling, or manipulating objects, shows a definite increase at about eight weeks, but varies widely among babies from birth onward.[33]

Crying

Characteristic patterns of crying may be identifiable even during the first five days of life.[148, 149] Vocalization is accompanied by vigorous movements of the arms and legs, the face is screwed up in a grimace, and the skin becomes bright red. In some babies tears can be observed as early as 24 hours after delivery.

Crying, whimpering, and whining occur from birth on, and are considered indicators of distress. They may be elicited by a variety of stimuli including sudden intense auditory or visual changes.[72, 132] That is, startle and distress may occur to stimuli not physically painful, but which interrupt an ongoing state of some sort.[78]

Certain stimuli seem to be innate or early learned inhibitors of distress. Contact with the mother, nonnutritive sucking, and the sight of the adult face are examples of such distress inhibitors. All such stimuli also act as elicitors of the first social smiles.[19, 58, 80]

EMOTIONAL PROCESSES IN INFANCY

Pleasure

So far we have described many attributes of the child in the first few days, weeks, or months after birth, but not much has been said about emotional responses. The organism is an ongoing system; in addition, it experiences pleasure and displeasure from various processes within the system, or from those resulting from outside events impinging upon the system.

Tactual and kinesthetic stimuli, such as light touches on sensitive areas, blowing on the body, tickling under the chin, and gentle jogging or rocking will elicit from an infant a "non-social" smile, judged to be an indication of pleasure.[139] As we will show later, this kind of moderate arousal influences both the utilization of environmental cues and perceptual organization. Smiling, vocalization, exploration, and imitation are all linked with variations in arousal.[13] On the other hand, an already existing, moderate range of arousal makes a truly "social" smile possible; during intense hunger or deep sleep the infant will ignore most cues and events. Usually mild variations in stimulation are pleasant for the child but large variations are unpleasant.

The Smiling Response

Considerable controversy has arisen over whether smiling responses are conditioned (learned) or innate (nonlearned). As has already been observed, tactual and kinesthetic stimuli, such as those experienced by the infant when handled by the mother, cause smiling. This smiling is considered innate. Very early in life the sight of a human face will cause a smiling response, the so-called "social" smile. A number of experiments have been done to determine whether this is also innate, or whether the child has already learned to associate the facial stimulus, probably his mother's, with pleasant tactual and kinesthetic stimulation experienced during "mothering" or caretaking activities. See Study 3.1 for a typical experiment.

Between the third and sixth weeks Wolff could elicit no smiles with tactual and kinesthetic stimuli, but by the third week infants smiled differentially to various kinds of external stimuli.[150] If smiling to stimuli involving touch is innate, it is an innate behavior which takes some weeks to appear. While awake, infants smiled most frequently to a high-pitched voice; shortly afterwards, a nodding human head plus voice elicited more smiles than the voice alone. By the fourth or fifth weeks a silent human face evoked a smile if eye-to-eye contact was maintained or if the face was moving.[1, 5, 148] Wolff found that the smile waned gradually, but could be reinstated if the observer moved his tongue or put on sunglasses. He emphasizes the role of certain auditory or visual stimuli as "releasers" of the smile, classifying it as an innate response akin to the imprinting and the following response in birds.[94] (A "releaser" is a configuration of stimuli that will evoke a certain behavior not previously observed or performed by the organism.) The study below demonstrates one way in which a psychologist investigated the smiling response. It is based on the observation of only one child. However, it involved changing environmental conditions fairly systematically to see how the child would respond. Such studies may pave the way for experiments with larger numbers of children.

THE SMILING RESPONSE

STUDY 3.1

This study combines observational and rudimentary experimental techniques. Salzen, the experimenter, states that he observed one baby, whose first smile occurred when she was seven weeks of age. He distinguishes this from the "gastric smile" which had previously occurred, but which bore no apparent relation to external events. The new smile was in response to external stimuli, and is reported as quite distinct from the other smile, though no details are given.

At eight weeks the infant's smiles were "quite distinct and definite," and occurred when she appeared to be looking out a window in daylight, when looking at lighted electric lamps, and once when looking at the white interior of her carrying cot. She also smiled at a human face, especially if it was moving from side to side. Up to this point, the investigator was largely reporting the infant's rather naturally occurring behavior. He then proceeded to a more controlled part of the study.

Salzen presented the baby with three cardboard ovals about 13 inches long; they were white, black, and white with a black rim. The baby smiled at all of them, indicating to Salzen that brightness in itself made no difference, since the black was as good a smile-producer as the others. Oscillation of the ovals appeared more effective, as with the human face. A flashlight with a diameter of two inches was also effective in eliciting smiles, more so if it was turned on and off repeatedly.

The experimenter tried to eliminate as many random variations in procedure as possible. All stimuli were presented at similar times and in the same way; by hand, 2 to 3 feet above the baby when she was lying quietly, either after feeding or after waking but before feeding cries started. The observer stayed out of sight as much as possible, and presented the stimuli when the baby was looking up and was not aware of him. All stimuli were presented several times and in varied order on several occasions during the eighth week.

The most effective stimulus proved to be another cardboard oval with eight black sectors radiating from the center and approximately equal in areas to the white sectors in between. This also was more effective when rotated. The baby would stop crying for food or actually feeding, and watch it, with smiles, for several minutes. No other stimulus, "including the human face emitting any manner of coaxing noises," would stop the same food cries when this stimulus was removed.

These stimuli continued to elicit smiling during the ninth to eleventh weeks. In the eleventh week talking helped to produce a smile in response to the human face. In the twelfth week no cardboard oval produced a smile, even when accompanied by talking. Another sight-sound combination, like a rattle, would cause a smile, and by the thirteenth week so did a loudly ticking clock.

Salzen concludes that the smiling response may be evoked by any form of contrast or any change in brightness and speculates on the relation of the visual following response to the classical following response in chicks, which we will discuss later in this chapter.

Salzen, E. A. Visual stimuli eliciting the smiling response in the human infant. *J. Genet. Psychol.*, 102, 1963, 51-54.

When a face is stationary and immobile, and so less arousing and less of a contrast, investigators find that the infant must be about two months old before he is able to respond to it with a smile.[5] Comparing children reared at home and in an institution, Ambrose found that home-reared children smiled in response to the immobile face about three weeks earlier than the institution-reared, whose first response occurred at about 11 weeks of age. He advanced this difference as evidence that the social smile is learned as a conditioned response; it is more frequently elicited and rewarded in the home than in an institution. This position is also taken by Brackbill, who eliminated the smiling response in four infants three and a half to four and a half months old by ceasing to smile, pick up, pat, or talk to these infants when they smiled in the experimental situation.[19] As smiling decreased, crying and fussing increased. White confirmed Ambrose's findings.[144] On the other hand, although Watson obtained results similar to those of Ambrose with an upright face, when he used faces turned 90 degrees or upside down they were relatively ineffective in eliciting smiles.[140] Many mothering activities take place at a 90 degree facial angle. The baby gets used to seeing its mother at this angle. Watson found that the smile waned at around 13 to 14 weeks to both the mother's familiar face and the unfamiliar experimenter's face. The infant reacted similarly to both of them. This seemingly argues against Ambrose's statement that discrimination of the mother from strangers is being achieved at this time. However, since the mothers in this study were required to be unresponsive, perhaps this also was "unfamiliar" to the babies.

Cross-cultural studies tend to support the learned nature of the social smiling response. In Israel, Gewirtz compared the development of the smile in four different child rearing environments.[50] He found that many infants smiled at a stationary human face by the eighth or ninth week after delivery. The speed at which the smile and other responses developed was influenced by the caretaking arrangements; it was fastest when there was the most sensory stimulation and a variety of social interactions. Two different investigators studied the Ganda tribe in Africa and found the infants to be precocious in their social development.[3, 17] They attribute this to the great amount of visual and auditory stimulation they receive, being constantly carried on the mother's back. Other investigators have also argued that learning strongly effects the social smile.[31, 133, 138]

Spitz argues that since the baby will smile at any vaguely human configuration of stimuli, such as a mask or scarecrow, it cannot originally be a learned response.[128] Another investigator found that a blind and deaf child showed a smiling response, even though unable to learn it the way most infants might.[54] The traditional view supports the innate nature of the smile.[21]

In summary, it seems likely that Watson's "nonsocial" smile comprises the innate basis for a response that can be developed, altered, and eliminated by reinforcing components of learning. Any form of mild stimulation, including visual stimulation, is pleasant as are sensations as touch, rocking, and so on. Although smiling to certain stimuli several weeks after birth may be innate, conditioning (learning) seems to determine to what new stimuli smiling will occur, as well as how often.

EMOTIONAL RESPONSES IN INFANCY

Displeasure

From birth on, crying is considered an indicator of distress in the baby. It occurs at birth and may be elicited by a variety of stimuli, including sudden intense auditory or visual changes.[72, 132]

For many years it was thought that pain was the only innate cause of distress, and that any other stimuli must be associated with pain, either internal or external, to cause distress and crying.[34, 45] More recently, however, it has been found that even children born with absolutely no sense of pain (congenital analgesia) show a normal development of fear and anxiety at other, nonpainful events.[37, 142] When one such child was spanked by her mother, she cried as much as or more than her normal sister, although spanking couldn't have hurt the analgesic child physically. Study 3.2 presents this inquiry in detail. This investigation, like Study 3.1, involved only one child. However, it is instructive and its general conclusions have proven valid.

ANXIETY WITHOUT PAIN

STUDY 3.2

L. J. West and I. E. Farber studied a girl who was born apparently without any sense of pain. No peculiarities were noticed until she began to teethe, when she started to chew on her fingers until they bled. Around the age of two years she broke a toe. This went unremarked by her, and remained untreated until her mother noticed the swelling and discoloration. She was hospitalized, and a cast put on her right foot. She attempted to use the cast to scratch an itch on her other leg and broke her left leg in the process. This kind of accident became increasingly frequent. By the age of seven she carried numerous scars and deformities; for instance, she was almost blind because she repeatedly rubbed her eyes without closing them, creating scratches on the corneas. She retained such senses as heat, touch, cold, and vibration, and her scores on the Stanford-Binet intelligence test were slightly above average.

She showed some personality disturbances, but the investigators felt that these could readily be accounted for by the very real frustrations and deprivations of the various accidents and protective restrictions resulting from her insensitivity to pain.

She showed no emotional response to a hypodermic needle, since she had never been hurt by one, although she had been given numerous injections. On the other hand, the sight of a wooden tongue depressor caused marked emotional reactions. Tongue depressors had often made her gag, and she both hated and feared them.

When she was disobedient her mother spanked her, which made her cry. Her crying was not caused by the pain of spanking, but rather by her mother's display of anger and rejection.

The conclusion follows that nonpainful stimuli, symbolic of unpleasant or threatening experiences, can produce the characteristic responses of the autonomic nervous system usually associated with fear or anxiety.

West, L. J., and Farber, I. E. The role of pain in emotional development. (In) Explorations in the physiology of emotions. L. J. West and M. Greenblatt (Eds.), *Psychiatric Research Reports of the American Psychiatric Association*, 12, 1960, 119-126.

Current theory holds that there is no archetypal event or class of events, causing pain, which is the exclusive source of crying in infants.[78] Startle and distress occur to events not physically painful, such as the visual and auditory stimuli mentioned above. The interruption of any highly practiced and well organized responses can also lead to distress. A variety of events which are startling, disturbing, unexpected, or somehow threatening, can cause distress or related unpleasant emotional states.

Distress and the more complicated phenomenon of anxiety may be brought under control by certain specific inhibitors that either are innate or develop their effectiveness to reduce distress soon after birth. These include non-nutritive sucking, physical contact with the mother, or the mother's heartbeat.[58, 80, 115] (A "specific inhibitor" is a stimulus that will cause certain behaviors to cease the very first time the organism perceives that stimulus; the cessation response is innate and specific to the animal species involved.)

Crying is believed to have a considerably innate element, but it soon becomes modifiable by learned stimuli. Children may cry and smile for inborn reasons, but soon learn to cry and smile in situations different from the original ones. Children learn to be upset or pleased by new environmental conditions associated with rewarding or distressing experiences.

THE PROCESS OF SOCIAL ATTACHMENT

Imprinting in Animals

The discussion of smiling and crying included the terms "releasers" and "inhibitors." These terms can be found in the literature on animal behavior, specifically, in the explanation of the phenomenon known as "imprinting".[67, 68, 69, 70, 94] We will first take up imprinting in animals, and then the aspects of the concept that can be applied to human infants. Imprinting in animals may tell us *something* about how infants become attached to their mothers.

Imprinting is usually defined by the phenomenon of the "following response." Broadly, it refers to a relatively quick and strong attachment of one organism to another organism. A gosling, after one or two hours of being with the mother, will follow her wherever she goes.[65] If the mother is not present the gosling may follow something else that moves. The time required to establish the following response indicative of attachment varies with the species; in deer and buffalo two or three days' contact is necessary to establish the following response.[28, 64] On the other hand, if contact with the mother is prevented, certain emotional consequences follow. For instance, if lambs are kept from any perceptual contact with the mother for as long as two weeks after birth, they become loners, with no gregarious attachment to the herd.[118]

The period during which imprinting must take place if it is to be effective is called the critical period. It is usually a brief period early in life before the animal becomes fearful. Lorenz gives a number of examples of fear responses in animals, elicited by a first encounter with certain stimuli.[94] The onset of the fear response often marks the end of the critical period for imprinting, with animals showing little ability to imprint once they become frightened by the movements of other organisms.

The effectiveness of imprinting varies under different conditions.[55] The length of the critical period, when imprinting is possible, is not invariant. It is initiated by central arousal of some kind, from novelty, movement, or color of the stimulus, and is probably terminated by a learned increase in fear.[83] Apparently imprinting is proportional to the effort expended by the imprinted animal during acquisition of the response. Study 3.3 illustrates an investigation demonstrating the role of effort in acquisition of the following response in chicks.

IMPRINTING

STUDY 3.3

Two experiments were run on the imprinting of three groups of chicks, using a circular runway. The object used for imprinting was a blue and yellow rubber doll. (Two substitute or surrogate objects were also used in the experiments; in Experiment I it was a doll of cheesecloth and rags made to resemble a hen, and in Experiment II it was a blue and yellow cellulose duck.)

The chicks were trained (imprinted) as follows: all chicks were trained at around three hours post-hatch. Chicks from the first group were placed one by one in the runway, and allowed to *follow* the training object around for six revolutions at a rate of one revolution per minute. The second group was placed one at a time in a plastic box, which was *pulled* one foot behind the stimulus object. Whenever the chick turned away, the box was turned until the chick again faced the object. Chicks from the third group were placed in the runway and *exposed* to a stationary object for six minutes.

After training the chicks were tested for strength of imprinting at 24 and 48 hours of age, in the circular runway. The imprinting object was moved through three complete revolutions of one per minute. (This was repeated with the nonimprinting surrogate, either the "hen" or the "duck.") "Following" was scored whenever the chick moved to within one foot of the object as it revolved. Amount of following was the measure of the strength of imprinting.

The results came out as follows: chicks who originally had followed the imprinting object by themselves showed a much greater following response in the later test phase than chicks who were originally pulled around in a box. The chicks which were pulled, however, showed greater imprinting than chicks who had been exposed only to a stationary object. From these two experiments and a third, similar one, it is not clear whether the walking chicks were, strictly speaking, more strongly imprinted or simply acquired a strong tendency to follow any similar moving object. But in either case the imprinting score, counted as the amount of time the chicks followed the test object, decreased with the decrease in the amount of movement by chicks in each group. The greater the original effort, the more following.

Thompson, W. R., and Dubanoski, R. A. Imprinting and the "Law of Effort." *Anim. Behav.*, *12*, 1964, 213-218.

Sound and color influence the approach of chicks to a stimulus, but form is irrelevant: that is, if it is hen-colored, the chick will approach; if it also clucks like a hen, the approach tendency is stronger; but it makes no difference if the clucking, hen-colored object is hen-shaped or merely a rectangle.[124] Some investigators believe imprinting phenomena are best viewed as perceptual preferences or instances of perceptual learning since they are somewhat modifiable.[82] The role of prior learning in the appearance of critical periods has also begun to be emphasized.[9, 44, 62, 82, 109, 117] This would mean that each age period is critical for the development of certain responses, in a complex, successive program of development. Successive critical periods, therefore, may vary depending on earlier experiences.

The Social Attachment Process in Higher Animals

The concept of critical periods has a number of implications for the treatment of human infants. One aspect will be taken up under the heading of Maternal Deprivation later in the chapter. To anticipate somewhat, it has been found that children deprived of certain stimulation at a particular age do not develop normally, but show characteristic behavior deficiencies.[7, 18, 51, 52, 95, 129] At a given age period they may be qualitatively inferior to children of the same age, not being able to do the same things.

Philip Gray has summarized evidence for what he calls imprinting in human infants as follows.[55] The infant's first social response (according to Gray) is learning to distinguish its parent. This process may be analogous to what is known as imprinting in lower animals. After the parent is distinguished from strangers, the child learns to be afraid of strange stimuli; this can become traumatic and remain so. Siblings, says Gray, can and do imprint on each other, and may influence each other to a great extent. One may consider a qualitative change to have occured when the child has formed specific attachments to certain people.

Gray believes that the smiling response is the child's equivalent of the following response.[55] It is accompanied by movement and vocalization.[8] The smiling response appears at three to six weeks of age, and until the sixth month it occurs to more than the human face.[74, 84, 102, 103, 114, 128] Gray believes the critical period for human imprinting must lie roughly between six weeks and six months, beginning with the onset of learning ability, continuing with the smiling response, and ending with the fear of strangers.

Caldwell would date the onset of the critical period for the human analogue to imprinting in babies considerably earlier than the sixth week.[23] She theorized that the oculomotor (visual) following response of infants may be the human equivalent of the locomotor (walking) following response in birds. This response, as we have seen, begins shortly after birth. However, it is possible that imprinting cannot be said to occur until the child can distinguish its own mother from other stimuli that it may also have been watching.

During the first six months the attachment behavior of infants seems indiscriminate.[115, 116] The baby objects to the withdrawal of attention by anyone, not just his mother. Even later, the mother is not always the sole principal object of attachment. Many children are attached to several people right from the beginning. Specific attachments are formed to persons who never performed any caretaking activities (which seems rather unfair, somehow), arguing against the classical view that children learn to love others only because they associate them with primary need reduction, such as feeding. The child's principal object, according to some psychologists, is intense interaction with another specific person, not necessarily the most available person, or the caretaker. However, the child is completely dependent on the caretaker for survival. What does the mother or mother surrogate do to protect and nurture the infant?

Early Maternal Behavior

All animals show certain behaviors in common; the infant is always highly dependent on certain species-specific patterns; the mother must perform essential successive caretaking activities if the baby is to survive.[104] These activities include caretaking of various sorts, feeding, grooming, and so on. Critical periods can be modified (accelerated and extended) by early enriched stimulation,[62, 99] and future development can be altered by the ommission of certain stimuli at particular stages in the infant's development.[30, 66]

The imprinting-like phenomenon discussed previously is part of a pattern of mother-infant attachment shown by many animals early in the development of the young. Puppies must live with human caretakers from the age of three and a half to 13 weeks if they are to become "man's best friend" and the age of seven weeks seems to be the culmination of the critical period for social development.[119] If puppies do not have contact with people in this age period they will not be friendly to humans at later ages.

Animals become fearful of certain stimuli at a particular age also. A previous positive tie may be a precondition to the opposite reaction of flight from the unknown. Babies strongly attached to their mothers will be more afraid of strange people.[129] Harlow has done much research on the social attachment behavior of infant monkeys.[58, 59, 60] Study 3.4 presents a summary of some of his research in this area.

SUBSTITUTE MOTHERS

STUDY 3.4

In Harlow's mother-infant experiments, infant monkeys are provided with terrycloth and wire mother-substitutes, which look vaguely monkey-like and may or may not be equipped with a nursing bottle in their chests to provide nutritional support to the young one. They are separated from their real live mothers.

Comparing the effects of live vs. inanimate mothering on the baby monkeys, Harlow reports a number of findings:

1. Monkey infants develop strong attachments to inanimate cloth surrogate mothers. These bonds are to a large degree independent of nutritional support.

2. The infants approach the cloth surrogate mothers for attachment and comfort, and for security and protection in strange or frightening situations.

3. It becomes clear, when the infants with cloth surrogate mothers grow up, that they have deficiencies in sexual and other spheres and that the surrogate mother does not adequately replicate the contributions of a real, live mother.

4. Cloth-surrogate-raised monkey infants show a significantly higher level of oral exploration directed at themselves and at playmates than monkeys with real mothers. (A two-hour period of social interaction with other infants was allowed each day.) This greater orality lasted throughout the three months this behavior was studied. (Excessive orality, as found in many test situations with humans, is a mark of social inadequacy and infantilism.)

5. Even in early social contacts, mother-raised babies interact more freely and subtly (with other infants) and have more social awareness than the cloth-surrogate-raised monkeys.

6. Facial expressions, probably learned from the live mother, such as the facial threat pattern (retracted lips, exposed teeth, and flattened hair on top of the head) as well as social frowning, occur earlier and happen more often in the live-mother-raised infants.

7. At first the live-mother-raised infants spend less time in the area where they can play with other infants, because their mothers often keep these infants near themselves. From 90 days on, this protectiveness disappears and they spend as much time in this area as the cloth-surrogate-reared infants.

8. The live-mother-raised infants show more complex play patterns that appear earlier than surrogate-raised infant play patterns. They engage in more rough-and-tumble play, and more mutual chasing with reduced physical contact, which is the next play to develop.

9. At about one year an integrated play pattern involving all available animate and inanimate objects develops, which includes vigorous activity, and which Harlow calls "mad activity play." This pattern is almost nonexistent for surrogate-raised monkeys, but very vigorous and frequent for live mother-raised monkeys.

10. Monkeys separated from their mothers at the age of one day and put with another infant spend most of their time clinging together face to face with their arms around one another. However, if members of pairs raised this way are reassigned partners, they immediately cling to the new partner with no sign of disturbance. They are not personally attached; the behavior is nonspecific.

Harlow draws a number of conclusions from these findings:

1. The live mother plays an active role in the subsequent personal and social development of the infant.

2. The early live mother-and-infant contact stimulates the formation and differentiation of facial and probably total bodily postural expressions, which may later make social interaction easier.

3. The surrogate cloth mother does not provide any reciprocity of behavior. The baby does not have to adjust its response to those of the mother, and of course, the mother does not adjust to the infant.

4. The live mother intensively grooms the infants in a

way that seems pleasurable to both, and she provides some sexual stimulation.

These multiple postural, physical interactions may impart an acceptance of, and seeking for, reciprocal physical contact with age-mates. It may be easier to form affectional bonds through play patterns with other monkeys because of the preceding mother-infant interactions.

These experiments illustrate the method of comparing "normal" and other ways of rearing infants, observing differences, and drawing logical inferences about possible reasons for the differences. Of course, normal monkey mothering could be said to occur only in the jungle, and not in the primate cage, but the two conditions studied are obviously enough different from each other in important ways to create widely different infant behaviors. The reasons inferred from the differences are not necessarily the ones that will eventually prove to be the most correct; only further experimentation will demonstrate exactly what particular maternal behavior leads to a particular result in the infant.

Harlow, H. F. The maternal affectional system. (In) *Determinants of Infant Behavior, Vol. 2* B. M. Foss (Ed.). John Wiley, New York, 1963, pp. 3-33.

There tends to be a general, qualitative developmental pattern of change in the mother-infant interactions of monkeys and apes, over time, as follows:

1. The infant clings closely to the mother.
2. The infant ventures away from the mother and may interact with other monkeys, but keeps returning; the mother also draws the young one to her.
3. The mother becomes neutral; she tolerates the young one seeking her but makes no effort to get hold of him.
4. The mother actively discourages the young one and forces him to stay away.
5. The young monkey establishes a pattern of behavior with other young monkeys.

This may be a difficult, fluctuating period, with temporary contacts between mother and young, and attempts to reestablish contact with the mother. Some primate species seem to have an easier transition than others, but the same sequence of qualitative changes occurs in most of them. Sooner or later severance of mother-infant contact and increased contact with peers becomes established.[32] It seems that both monkey and human mothers are gradually obligated to dissolve the intense physical bonds characterizing the early mother-child relationship. In the lower primate world, at least, it is the mother who initiates separation, forcing independence on her offspring.

Human children cannot differentiate between adults until they are somewhere between three and six months old. Separation from the mother before three months has little effect, and up to six months the disturbance is slight.[122] During the first six months, maternal behavior is likely to include feeding, including extensive opportunities for sucking, fondling, rocking, and other contact, human auditory verbal stimulation (humming, small talk), and other sensory stimulation. The following section takes up the visual and auditory functioning of the infant. This presentation sets the stage for differentiating between deficits in stimulation and other types of deficits to which the infant may be subjected which may affect his behavior, including aspects of the process of social attachment.

STIMULATION AND RESPONSE PROCESSES

Response to Visual Stimuli

Babies see best at a distance of eight or nine inches during the first few weeks, and cannot focus sharply on objects closer or farther away.[61] Most mothering activities take place with mother's and infant's faces about that distance apart, providing a good opportunity for the development of social responsiveness to visual stimuli.

For the first two or three weeks the infant shows "obligatory attention" to objects that catch his eye, he will stare at stimuli for long periods of fixation. During the first week he becomes quiet during fixation, but by the third week he will show rhythmic limb movements, panting, sporadic smiles, vocalizations, and other evidences of what looks like increased excitement during fixations, as the obligatory fixation period wanes.[130] The infant's form perception is developed more than was generally supposed a few years ago, but is nevertheless restricted during the first weeks of life.[17, 38, 41]

At about five weeks, when presented with a stimulus, the infant may pay no attention to it, or will focus beyond it, but by ten weeks he fixates the object and may take an unco-ordinated swipe at it. By three and a half months the baby's visual accommodation approaches that of the adult, and he brings both hands up to grasp the stimulus. By five or five and a half months he can lift both hands and grasp the stimulus in one quick motion.[145]

Response to Auditory Stimuli

Infants can discriminate pitch; low tones are more soothing.[141] Soothing tones, often made by the mother, will quiet some active babies only 36 to 96 hours old. Movements are reduced, and some will stop crying. In one study, tones of long duration interrupted sucking behavior whereas two-second tones did not.[77] Leventhal and Lipsitt produced differential changes in breathing and leg movement with certain tones.[88]

The Orienting Response

As seen just previously, the capacity for visual and auditory responses, however rudimentary, is present soon after birth. The fixation of attention to such stimuli is known as the "orienting reaction" or "orienting response." Often this orientation is toward the mother. The orienting response is accompanied by both changes in arousal level and modification of attention.[13, 14] These modifications of attention are the forerunners of responses labeled "curiosity" and "exploration," of which attention is an essential component. Thus the orienting response may be the primary foundation for the infant's social development. It brings him into contact with agents of society, whether his mother or others.[29, 48, 75, 105]

Infants as young as three months can be caused to explore new objects more extensively if they are given visual and auditory feedback; that is, if sights and sounds appear as a result of their own efforts.[104] Children like to make things happen. The nature of their responses can be shaped or changed by providing perceptual reinforcement as a result of certain of their activities. Infants like to look and hear, and many will work to produce a visual or auditory stimulus.[17, 46] Monkeys also respond to this kind of reinforcement.[22] Study 3.5 provides an example of the influence of visual and auditory feedback on infant activity.

EXPLORATORY BEHAVIOR IN INFANTS

STUDY 3.5

Investigators devised an experimental crib for use in studying the effect of visual feedback on the exploratory behavior of infants. It holds the baby in a suitable position, permits measurement of certain behaviors, and provides the sensory feedback from that behavior. The drawing (Fig. 3.3) illustrates the arrangement of the various parts of the apparatus. Every time the baby touches the stainless steel sphere (b) the response is recorded in another room. Visual stimuli are presented on the screen and auditory stimuli come from a speaker behind the screen. Both can be controlled by the baby's touch on the sphere, or by the experimenter. The infant's behavior is monitored by closed-circuit TV and earphones and can be photographed from the TV screen. Most babies around six months old will perform for at least eight minutes without fussing.

The curves below show performances (frequency of touching the sphere) of two infants under contingent (CRF) and noncontingent (NC) conditions. In the CRF condition, the movie appeared for one and a half seconds only when the infant touched the sphere, in the NC conditions, the music turned on and off for alternate one and a half-second periods no matter what the infant did. A steep curve indicates a fast rate of response and a flat curve indicates a slow rate of response. The steep CRF curve for infant A shows that infant A touched the sphere often to turn on the movie.

Rheingold, H. L., Stanley, W. C., and Cooley, J. A. Method of studying exploratory behavior in infants. *Science, 136,* 1962, 1034-1055.

Behavior such as this is more adequately maintained if the sensory feedback is complex and varied than if it is simple and unvarying. This is true whether the stimulus is visual or auditory. Relatively complex light patterns attract the attention of six-month-old infants better than simple patterns. Human voices, especially those of strange females, cause cardiac deceleration, quieting, then vocalization in the six month olds.[73] Cardiac deceleration is one of the newer measures of the orienting reflex or attention; the slowing of heart rate may have reinforcing properties in itself, which would make it a rewarding result of increased attention, and an effective reinforcer of such behavior.[98]

The studies cited so far have emphasized the rewarding qualities of certain kinds of stimulation, especially visual and auditory. There seem to be constitutional or early established differences in the extent to which infants develop and maintain social attachments by looking and listening.[115, 116] However, since mothers who provide frequent distance-receptor stimulation (visual and auditory) also tend to give much physical contact and to encourage their children to touch things, children in

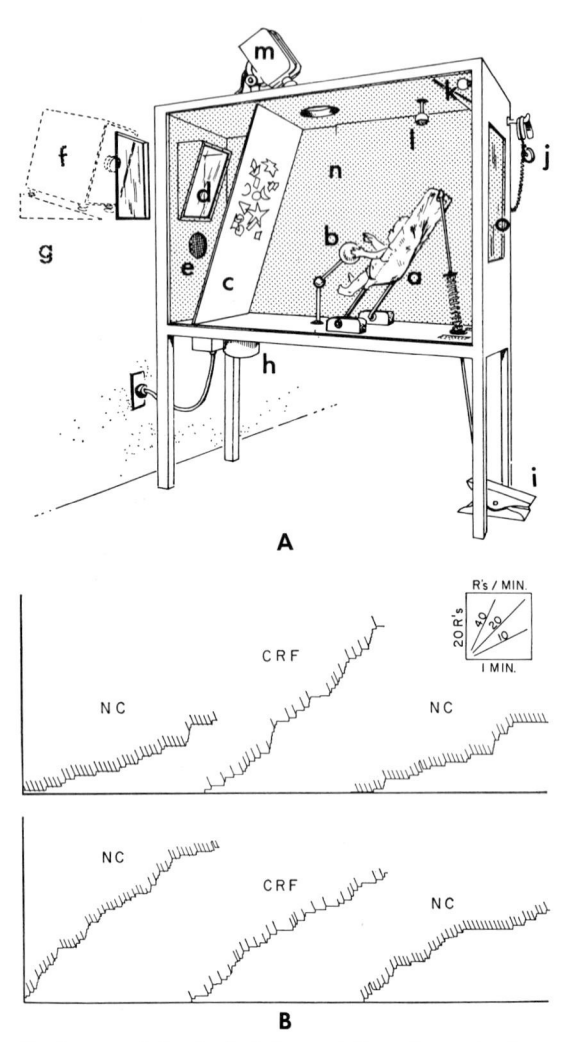

Figure 3-3. Exploratory behavior in infants. *A*, Experimental crib: *a*, seat; *b*, manipulandum; *c*, screen; *d*, projection opening; *e*, sound source; *f*, projector; *g*, control room; *h*, ventilator; *i*, rocker; *j*, intercom; *k*, crib lights; *l*, microphone; *m*, television camera; *n*, doors of crib; *o*, window. *B*, Cumulative response curves for two infants. (From Rheingold, H. L., Stanley, W. C., and Cooley, J. A.: Science *136*, 1962, 1054-1055, Copyright 1962 by the American Association for the Advancement of Science.)

such homes have maximal social stimulation in all sensory modes.[91] They are probably likely to form strong social attachments.

The withdrawal of certain kinds of external stimulation may be associated with heightened arousal.[6, 85] Babies will persist in orienting toward a source of stimulation longer if its location keeps changing.[27] The babies seem to desire the stimulation. However, infants tire of very familiar stimuli. Although before three weeks there is little habituation to a repeatedly exposed pattern, after eight weeks the infant becomes habituated much faster.[40] He stops paying attention to over-repetition. Recent experiments show that the speed of habituation to simple stimuli in infants three months old is suggestive of future intelligence. Infants who habituate fast attain relatively high scores on intelligence tests at later ages.

Role of the Mother

During the first six months, it is normally the mother who furnishes most of the various stimuli to the infant; she not only performs caretaking activities, but also determines his general level of stimulation. She may either keep him isolated in a dim, quiet room, or take him to the supermarket. There may be music, talking, bright colors, and shifting light-patterns around him, or his surroundings may be hushed and uniform.

It is becoming evident that a certain amount of varied stimulation is good for a baby, that is, such stimulation speeds development. Normal development is assumed to proceed by a gradual process of paced advances in responding to the complexity of the environment.[112] This leads us directly to the fields of stimulus complexity and novelty, and then back to stimulus deprivation and the child in the orphanage.

LEVELS OF STIMULATION

Novelty and Complexity

From a very early age, infants will look longer at or interrupt other activity longer to attend to stimuli that keep changing or are complex in nature. They will attend less intently to unchanging, monotonous, or simple patterns of lines or sound.[12, 24, 25, 38, 39, 111, 114, 127] Cantor explains this in terms of the eliciting of attention by the stimuli rather than a preference on the part of the child. Study 3.6 presents a typical experiment of this type using various visual patterns as stimuli.

VISUAL PERCEPTION IN THE INFANT

STUDY 3.6

In order to determine whether young infants preferred one visual pattern over another, Fantz constructed an ingenious baby-testing apparatus. Infants from one to 14 weeks old were placed face up in a form-fitting crib. A uniform gray structure above the infant's head held the stimuli and excluded vision of other objects or people. The patterns were presented side by side, and the experimenter observed the baby through a small hole midway between the test stimuli. Lighting was so arranged that the surface of the baby's eyeballs reflected the pattern at which he was looking. The image of the pattern coincided with the pupil of the eye, providing a simple and reliable criterion of fixation. Between exposures the patterns were hidden by a gray shield containing a 4-inch hole overhead. A test exposure was begun only when the baby was looking at the hole, making it equally likely that he would glance at either pattern when it was suddenly exposed.

In total scores for all weekly sessions, 19 infants fixated a checkerboard pattern more than a plain square, and only three favored the square. Twenty subjects showed higher time scores looking at a bull's-eye pattern than at a pattern of stripes. An increase in the checkerboard and the bull's-eye preference was shown at eight weeks. The infants who were first tested at an early age reversed from a preference for stripes to the bull's-eye at around eight weeks, suggesting the possibility of early visual maturation or learning. By eight weeks of age infants may like more *complex* and more *novel* stimuli.

The author draws the following conclusions:

1. Visual patterns are discriminated by infants during the first six months, as evidenced by the differences in fixation times.

2. Changes in the strength or duration of the pattern preferences occur around two months of age, independently of amount of testing.

3. Consistent visual preferences are present as early as the first two months, thus arguing against an extreme learning theory view of the development of visual organi-

zation and pattern discrimination. (These experiments show that they are not learned by trial and error, from a start of complete confusion.)

4. The determination of natural visual preferences among different stimuli is a powerful method of studying early visual development which can provide data of importance to theories of perception, learning, and neural functioning.

This was a pioneer study, the methods of which have indeed been used repeatedly since then. Various explanations have been advanced to account for the resulting data, such as preferences for complex stimuli, novel stimuli, or stimuli incorporating a relatively great amount of contour, relative to stimulus area, and the area opened up here is still an active one in research on vision in infants.

Fantz, Robert L. Pattern vision in young infants. *Psychol. Rec. 8*, 1958, 43-47.

Once the child starts to look at a highly interesting pattern, his attention tends to remain fixated upon it. Patterns rated as less interesting evoked several short fixations; the infant looked awhile, glanced away, and looked back again. At around six months, girls tend to watch faces longer than boys do.[92] When shown a flat form outline of a human head and a life-size model, infants preferred the flat form for the first two months, but shifted preference to the three-dimensional model in the third month, even when viewing the stimuli with only one eye.[41]

Most stimuli that elicit the smiling response will also inhibit distress caused by other stimuli. These distress inhibitors are most often some kind of complex and novel stimuli.[114]

Optimal Arousal vs. Stimulus Privation

We have mentioned the fact that moderate stimulation is necessary for the normal appearance of qualitative behavioral changes in animal species, including humans. The organism tends to seek and maintain an optimal level of stimulation, which in turn maintains an optimal level of arousal.[13, 14, 43, 63, 71, 86, 87, 126] Stimulus deprivation during rearing results in rhesus monkeys that are inactive, prefer quite simple visual and manipulatory stimuli, show little exploration of the environment, are sexually and maternally abnormal, and withdraw from social contact.[112] This is believed to be caused not by any intellectual deficiency, but rather by increasingly serious response deficits; the animals are simply not equipped, through practice, to deal with stimuli. Not stimulated enough, they do not learn which response to produce. It has also been shown that certain changes in arousal level influence cue utilization and perceptual organization.[20, 35, 76, 125]

Stimulation may occur through handling and other tactual events, through the distance receptors (eyes and ears), or through the infant's own exploratory activities. Kittens handled a lot learned to approach strange objects and humans, and also to solve mazes as well as the kittens that had been given experience in a complex environment but not handled.[147] Reasonable arousal and stimulation is needed if development is to proceed normally.

The absence of most stimuli creates what Gewirtz has called a state of *privation*.[49] The functional stimuli needed for earliest learning are missing. Very few stimuli that evoke responses or require the child to make a discrimination are presented. Very few potentially reinforcing (rewarding or punishing) stimuli are provided, or presented in a way that will direct the behavior of the infant so that learning occurs. Few social stimuli are available to be paired with rewards so that social responses may develop. In the absence of stimuli to which the infant can react, there will be no habituation of innate or early-learned startle, avoidance, or emotional responses.

A less serious condition than that of the *total* privation just described is that of *functional* privation. Here there may be a lot of noise and social stimulation, but the number and pairing of evoking and reinforcing stimuli may be too few to establish caretakers as sources of pleasure themselves. Instead of regular patterns being established, there is a great deal of confusion. People care for the child only sporadically and at odd times. Children reared under these conditions will not respond to attention, affection, or smiles, and will seem asocial or autistic. That is, they do not seem attached to people and do not respond to them in most cases.

Gewirtz distinguishes between privation and deprivation. *Deprivation* refers to an abrupt and continuing change away from a relatively satisfying state of affairs. Deprivation means the termination of already formed associations or attachments. Deprivation is frustrating; learning contingencies already established are now ended, and previous attachments terminated. This may lead to anger or other irrelevant emotional responses. In the absence of the previous controlling stimuli the child may show more primitive, less complex behavior than before. Unless new attachments are formed, the child may become listless, withdrawn, and irreversibly depressed.[129] This state of lethargy, sometimes leading to death, has been called "anaclitic depression."

Maternal Deprivation or Stimulus Deprivation: Children in Institutions

This section must include some materials on ages beyond infancy. Other related aspects of mother-toddler interaction, pre-school learning, and so forth, will be discussed at length in subsequent chapters.

Under three months of age, infants in foundling homes smile readily and are otherwise responsive, but then undergo progressively worse withdrawal. When infants institutionalized from birth to six months are compared with family-reared infants, the former are often found to be deficient in both frequency and types of sounds produced. Children tested at six months who were institutionalized from the second month on showed a small but significant decline in their developmental level, when compared with children in foster homes.[90] The drop of developmental level was precipitous in foundling home infants between the third and six month; and was more gradual beyond the sixth month.[129] In eight case histories of problem children from an orphanage, six had been committed under the age of four months, and one under five and a half months. When tested at age three and a half they were very maladapted. They were called "extremely wild" children and were sent from the institution to Belleview Hospital, and then to state incarceration. Other such findings are numerous.[18, 51, 52]

On the other hand, children who had been removed from institutions to foster homes under the age of six months showed no great emotional disturbances.[123] When institutionally-reared infants were given 20 minutes of daily handling over the normal caretaking, they showed accelerated development of visual exploration. Infants given much visual stimulation *plus* handling slowed down at first, but after several weeks their activity increased well beyond that of the infants who were handled (but not visually stimulated) and infants who were given the usual care.[143] This brings us to a point of very great interest.

The malfunctioning of children in many institutions has often been attributed to the deprivation of maternal love. As we have seen, before three to six months of age, children cannot differentiate between adults. The deprivation of maternal love can only create trouble after the child has learned to associate her with reinforcements of various sorts. This leads to the conclusion that the ill effects produced in children taken from their mothers before they are six months old must be due to some other cause than deprivation of mother love. This cause is probably *stimulus privation* or *stimulus deprivation*, the absolute or relative absence of tactile, visual, or auditory stimulation. Institutions may be bad for children simply because they do not provide enough stimulation. In the average home, however, it is the mother that provides much of the stimulation that a child needs. Institutions, if they are to be beneficial, must have sufficient staff to provide the stimulation that the young children need.

These necessary forms of stimulation can clearly be provided within an institutional setting. When they are provided, they seem to have positive results.[143] The findings on stimulus complexity, arousal level, and so on provide a theoretical support to the proposition that visual, auditory and tactual stimulation is important for the normal qualitative development of human capacities.[26, 123] The processes of learning depend on the presence of levels of stimulation which provide arousal and the formation of orderly associations between stimuli and responses. In addition, attachment to other human beings, a vital factor in normal socialization, depends on regular meaningful interaction between the child and one or more caretakers, starting at an early age. This caretaker is often the mother, but need not be. The formation of social bonds or attachments to other human beings is one of the most important qualitative features of human development.

SUMMARY

The newborn's survival depends on reflexes which are present at birth and on his being cared for. The infant is unable to care for himself and is dependent on being sheltered, kept clean, and fed by others, and his reflexes enable him to breathe, suck, and swallow. The infant is capable of a wide variety of reactions despite his inability to care for himself. He can see, hear, wriggle, cry, smell, taste, feel, yawn, grasp, cough, and show signs of distress and pleasure.

Perhaps the most important developmental change which the infant undergoes, particularly in terms of its implications for socialization, is his alteration from a detached newborn to an infant emotionally attached to his mother and other family members. The infant, in time, learns to identify his mother and other principal caretakers and to differentiate them from strangers. He becomes socially attached to these persons and to those with whom he interacts, such as the father and brothers and sisters. This process of social attachment or formation of social bonds has been compared by some of the process of imprinting in some animals.

Normal development seems to require a good deal of stimulating, interaction between the infant and a caretaker, usually the mother. Interaction with a stimulating nonsocial environment also seems vital. Infants need to see, hear, feel, and manipulate. They demonstrate curiosity and tendencies to explore their environment. They like variety and respond more to stimuli which are somewhat more complex than ones they have been exposed to previously. They like interesting, novel occurrences, particularly ones they can manipulate themselves.

Moderate, varied, and increasingly complex stimulation, seems to benefit developmental change. The deprivation of stimulation or complete privation of stimulation can cause developmental retardation. Since stimulation is often provided by the mother, her absence in the early months can be harmful unless other people provide what she is not present to give. Once the infant has become attached to the mother however, her absence means more than a possible reduction in stimulation. It represents a break in an established social bond and is quite emotionally disturbing. If an infant must be separated from his mother at about six to eight months of age, disturbance may be expected due to a break in the social (emotional) tie with the mother. In such cases it may still help to provide a concerned substitute caretaker.

REFERENCES

1. Ahrens, R. Beitrag zur Entwicklung des Physionomie und Mimikerkennens. *Z. f. exp. u. angew. Psychol.*, 2, 1954, 599-633.
2. Ahrens, R. Das Verhatten des Sauglings in der Zeit Zwischen erstem und siebentem Monat. *Z. f. exp. u. angew. Psychol.*, 2, 1954, 412-454.
3. Ainsworth, M. D. The development of infant-mother interaction among the Ganda, (In) *Determinants of Infant Behavior*, Vol. 2. Foss, B. M. (Ed.), John Wiley, New York, 1963.
4. Aldrich, C. A., Sung, C., and Knop, C. The crying of newly born babies: II. The individual phase. *J. Pediat.*, 27, 1945, 89-96.
5. Ambrose, J. A. The development of the smiling response in early infancy, (In) *Determinants of Infant Behavior*, Vol. 1, Foss, B. M. (Ed.). John Wiley, New York, 1961.
6. Amsel, A. The role of frustrative nonreward in noncontinuous reward situations. *Psychological Bulletin*, 55, 1958, 102-119.
7. Bakwin, H. Loneliness in infants. *Amer. J. Dis. Child.*, 63, 1942, 30-40.
8. Banham, K. M. The development of affectionate behavior in infancy. *J. Genet. Psychol*, 76, 1950, 283-389.
9. Bateson, G. The message: "This is play." Group processes. (In) *Transactions of the Second Conference*, Schaffer, B. (Ed.). Josiah Macy Foundation, New York, 1955.
10. Bateson, P. P. G. Relation between conspicuousness of stimuli and their effectiveness in the imprinting situation. *J. Comp. Physiol. Psychol.*, 58, 1964, 407-411.
11. Bateson, P. P. G. Changes in chicks' responses to novel moving objects over the sensitive period for imprinting. *Animal Behav.*, 12, 1964, 479-489.
12. Berlyne, D. E. The influence of the albedo and complexity of stimuli on visual fixation in the human infant. *Brit. J. Psychol.*, 49, 1958, 315-318.
13. Berlyne, D. E. *Conflict, Arousal, and Curiosity*. McGraw-Hill, New York, 1960.
14. Berlyne, D. E. Exploratory and epistemic behavior. (In) *Psychology: The Study of a Science*, Vol. 5, Koch, S. (Ed.). McGraw-Hill, New York, 1963.
15. Berlyne, D. E., and Frommer, F. D. Some determinants of the incidence and content of children's questions. *Child. Develpm.*, 37, 1966, 177-189.
16. Birns, B. Individual differences in human neonates' responses to stimulation. *Child Develpm.*, 36, 1965, 249-256.
17. Bower, T. G. R. The visual world of infants. *Sci. Amer.*, 134, 1966, 80-92.
18. Bowlby, J. *Maternal Care and Mental Health*. World Health Organization, Geneva, 1951.
19. Brackbill, Y. Extinction of the smiling response in infants as a function of reinforcement schedule. *Child Develpm.*, 29, 1958, 115-124.
20. Bruner, J. S., Matter, J., and Papaneck, M. Breadth of learning as a function of drive level and mechanization. *Psychol. Rev.*, 62, 1955, 1-10.
21. Buhler, C. *The First Year of Life*. Day, New York, 1930.
22. Butler, R. A. Incentive conditions which influence visual exploration; *J. Exp. Psychol.*, 48, 1954, 19-23.
23. Caldwell, B. M. The usefulness of the critical period hypothesis in the study of filiative behavior. *Merrill-Palmer Quart. Behav. Develpm.*, 8, 1962, 229-242.
24. Cantor, G. N. Responses of infants and children to complex and novel stimulation. (In) *Advances in Child Development and Behavior*, Vol. 1, Lipsitt, L. P., and Spiker, C. C. (Eds.). Academic Press, New York, 1963.
25. Cantor G. N., Cantor, J. H., and Ditrichs, R. Observing behavior in pre-school children as a function of stimulus complexity. *Child Develpm.*, 34, 1963, 683-689.

26. Casler, L. Maternal Deprivation: A critical review of the literature. *Monogr. Soc. Res. Child Develpm.* Ser. No. 8, *26*, No. 2, 1961.
27. Charlesworth, W. R. Persistence of orienting and attending behavior in young infants as a function of stimulus uncertainty. Presented at meeting of Soc. Res. Child Develpm., Minneapolis, March, 1965.
28. Darling, F. *Wild Country.*, London, 1938.
29. Dember, W. N., and Earl, R. W. Analysis of exploratory, manipulatory, and curiosity behaviors. *Psychol. Rev. 64*, 1957, 91-96.
30. Denenberg, V. H., and Bell, R. W. Critical periods for the effects of infantile experience and adult learning. *Science, 131*, 1960, 227-228.
31. Dennis, W. An experimental test of two theories of social smiling in infants. *J. Soc. Psychol., 6*, 1935, 214-223.
32. De Vore, I. Mother-infant relations in free-running baboons. (In) *Maternal Behavior in Mammals*, Rheingold, H., (Ed.). John Wiley, New York, 1963.
33. DiHirichova, J., and Lapackova, V. Development in the waking state in young infants. *Child Develpm., 35*, 1964, 365-370.
34. Dollard, J., and Miller, N. E. *Personality and Psychotherapy.* McGraw-Hill, New York, 1950.
35. Easterbrook, J. A. The effect of emotion on cue utilization and the organization of behavior. *Psychol. Rev. 66*, 1959, 183-201.
36. Eisenberg, R. B., et al. Auditory behavior in the human neonate: a preliminary report. *J. Speech Hear. Res., 7*, 1964, 245-269.
37. Franconi, G., and Ferrazzini, J. Kongenitale Analgie: Kongenitale generalisiente Schmerzin differenz. *Helv. Pediat. Acta, 12*, 1957, 79-115.
38. Fantz, R. L. Pattern vision in young infants. *Psychol. Rec. 8*, 1958, 43-47.
39. Fantz, R. L. The origin of form perception. *Sci. Amer., 204*, No. 5, 1961, 66-72.
40. Fantz, R. L. Visual experience in infants: decreased attention to familiar patterns as relative to novel ones. *Science*, 146, 1964, 668-670.
41. Fantz, R. L. Pattern discrimination and selective attention as determinants of perceptual development from birth. (In) *Perceptual Development in Children*, Kidd, A. H., and Rivoire, J. L. (Eds.). International Universities Press, New York, 1965.
42. Fantz, R. L., Ordy, J. M., and Udelf, M. S. Maturation of pattern vision in infants during the first six months. *J. comp. Physiol. Psychol., 55*, 1962, 907-917.
43. Fiske, D. W. and Maddi, S. A. Conceptual framework (In) *Functions of Varied Experience*, Fiske, D. W. and Maddi, S., (Eds.). Dorsey, Homewood, Ill., 1961.
44. Freedman, D. G., King, J. A., and Elliot, O. Critical periods in the social development of dogs. *Science, 133*, 1961, 1016-1017.
45. Freud, S. *Problems of Anxiety*, Norton, New York, 1936.
46. Friedlander, B. Z. Techniques for attended and unattended studies of human infant's operant play for perceptual reinforcement. *Mental Development Center*, Western Reserve University Press, Cleveland, 1964.
47. Geber, M. Problemes poses par le developpement du jeune enfant Africain en fonction de son milieu social. *Travail Hum., 23*, 1960, 97-111.
48. Getell, A., and Amatruda, C. S. *Developmental Diagnosis: Normal and Abnormal Child Development.* Hoeber, New York, 1941.
49. Gewirtz, J. L. Deprivation. (In) *Determinants of Infant Behavior*, Vol. 1, Foss, B. M. (Ed.). John Wiley, New York, 1961.
50. Gewirtz, J. L. The course of infant smiling in four child-rearing environments in Israel. (In) *Determinants of Infant Behavior.* Vol. 3, Foss, B. M. (Ed.). John Wiley, New York, 1965.
51. Goldfarb, W. The effect of early institutional care on adolescent personality. *J. Exp. Educ., 12*, 1943, 106-129.
52. Goldfarb, W. Infant rearing as a factor in foster home replacement. *Amer. J. Orthopsychiat., 14*, 1944, 162-167.
53. Goldfarb, W. Variations in adolescent adjustment of institutionally-reared children. *Amer. J. Orthopsychiat., 17*, 1947, 449-457.
54. Goodenough, F. L. Expression of the emotions in a blind-deaf child. *J. Abnorm. Soc. Psychol., 27*, 1932, 328-333.
55. Gray, P. H. Theory and evidence of imprinting in human infants. *J. Psychol., 46*, 1958, 155-166.

56. Grossman, H. J., and Greenberg, N. H. Psychosomatic differentiation in infancy: I. Autonomic activity in the newborn. *Psychosom. Med., 19*, 1957, 293-306.
57. Guyton, A. C. *Function of The Human Body.* W. B. Saunders, Philadelphia, (2nd Edition), 1964.
58. Harlow, H. F. The nature of love. *Amer. Psychologist, 13*, 1958, 673-685.
59. Harlow, H. F., and Zimmerman, R. R. Affectional responses in the infant monkey. *Science, 130*, 1959, 421-432.
60. Harlow, H. F. The maternal affectional system. (In) *Determinants of Infant Behavior;* Vol. 2., Foss. B. M. (Ed.). John Wiley, New York, 1963.
61. Haynes, H. M., White, B. L., and Held, R. Visual accommodation in human infants. *Science, 148;* 1965, 528-530.
62. Haywood, H. C., and Zimmerman, D. W. Effects of early environmental complexity on the following response in chicks. *Percept. Mot. Skills, 18*, 1964, 653-658.
63. Hebb, D. O., and Thompson, W. R. The social significance of animal studies. (In) *Handbook of Social Psychology.* Vol. 1., Lindzey, G. (Ed.). Addison-Wesley, Reading, 1954.
64. Hedeger, H. *Wild Animals in Captivity.*, London, 1950.
65. Heinroth, O. Beitvage zur Biologie, namentlich Ethologie un Physiologie der Anatiden. *Verhandl. V. Int. Ornithol. Kongr.* 1910, 589-702.
66. Hershev, Leonard., Richmond, J. B., and Moore, A. U. Modifiability of the critical period for the development of maternal behavior in sheep and goats. *Behaviour, 20*, 1963, 311-321.
67. Hess, E. H. Imprinting. *Science, 130*, 1959, 133-141.
68. Hess, E. H. Imprinting in animals. *Sci. Amer., 148*, 1958, 81-90.
69. Hess, E. H. Two conditions limiting critical age for imprinting. *J. Comp. Physiol. Psychol., 52*, 1959, 515-518.
70. Hess, E. H. Ethology. (In) *New Directions in Psychology*, Brown, R., et al. (Eds.). Holt, Rinehart and Winston, New York, 1962.
71. Hunt, J. McV. Motivation inherent in information processing and action. (In) *Motivation and Social Interaction*, Harvey, O. J. (Ed.). Ronald Press, New York, 1963.
72. Illingsworth, R. S. Crying in infants and children. *Brit. Med. J., I*, 1955, 75-79.
73. Kagan, J., and Lewis, M. *Studies of attention in the human infant.* Fels Research Institute, Yellow Springs, 1964.
74. Kaila. E. Die realstonen des Sauglings auf das menschichs Geschict. *Ann. Univ. Aboensis., 17*, 1932, 1-114.
75. Kasatkin, N. I., and Levilsova, A. M. The formation of visual conditional reflexes and their differentiation in infants. *J. Gen. Psychol., 12*, 1935, 416-435.
76. Kausler, D. H., and Trapp, E. P. Motivation and cue utilization in intentional and incidental learning. *Psych. Rev., 67*, 1960, 373-379.
77. Keen, R. Effects of auditory stimuli on sucking behavior in the human neonate. *J. Exp. Child Psychol., 1*, 1964, 348-354.
78. Kessen, W., and Mandler, G. Anxiety, pain, and the inhibitors of distress. *Psych. Rev. 68*, 1961, 396-404.
79. Kessen, W., Williams, E. J., and Williams J. P. Selection and test of response measures in the study of the human newborn. *Child Develpm., 32*, 1961, 7-24.
80. Kessen, W., and Lentzendorff, A. M. The effect of non-nutritive sucking on movement in the human newborn. *J. Comp. Physiol. Psychol., 56*, 1963, 69-72.
81. Klopfer, P. H. Imprinting: a reassessment. *Science, 147*, 1965, 302-303.
82. Klopfer, P. H., and Hallman, J. P. Perceptual preferences and imprinting in ducks. *Science, 145*, 1964, 1333-1334.
83. Kovach, J. K. Effects of autonomic drugs on imprinting. *J. Comp. Physiol. Psychol., 57*, 1964, 183-187.
84. Laroche, J. L., and Tcheng, F. *Le Sourire des nourissons.* Univ. Louvain, Belgique, 1963.
85. Lawrence, D. H., and Festinger, L. *Deterrents and Reinforcements: The Psychology of Insufficient Rewards.* Stanford University Press, Stanford, 1962.
86. Leuba, C. Towards some integration of learning theories: The concept of optimal stimulation. *Psychol. Rep., 1*, 1955, 27-33.
87. Leuba, C. Relation of stimulus intensities to learning and development. *Psychol. Rep., II*, 1962, 55-65.

88. Leventhal, A. S., and Lipsitt, L. P. Adaptation, pitch discrimination and sound vocalization in the neonate. *Child Develpm.*, *35*, 1964, 759-767.
89. Levin, S. R., and Kaye, H. Nonnutritive sucking by human neonates. *Child Develpm.*, *35*, 1964, 749-758.
90. Levy, R. T. Effects of institutional vs. boarding house care on a group of infants. *J. Pers.*, *15*, 1947, 233-241.
91. Lewis, M. *Exploration and distance receptors.* Fels Research institute, Yellow Springs, 1964.
92. Lewis, M., Kagan, J., and Kalafor, P. Patterns of fixation in the young infant. *Child Develpm.*, *37*, 1966, 331-341.
93. Lipton, E. L., and Steinschneider, A. Studies on the psychophysiology of infancy. *Merrill-Palmer Quart. Behav. Develpm.*, *10*, 1964, 103-117.
94. Lorenz, K. Z. *King Solomon's Ring.* Methuen, London, 1952.
95. Lorenz, K. Z. Comparative behaviourology. (In) *Discussions on Child Development,* Tanner, J. M., and Inhelder, B. (Eds.). Tavistock Publication, International Universities Press, N.Y., 1956.
96. Lowery, L. G. Personality distortion and early institutional care. *Amer. J. Orthopsychiat.*, *10*, 1940, 576-585.
97. McGrade, B. J., Kesser, W., and Lentzendorff, A. M. Activity in the newborn as related to delivery difficulty. *Child Develpm.*, *36*, 1965, 73-79.
98. Malmo, R. B. Slowing of heart rate after septal self-stimulation in rats. *Science*, *66*, 1961, 367-386.
99. Marr, J. N. Varying stimulation and imprinting in dogs. *J. Genet. Psychol.*, *104*, 1964, 351-364.
100. Parmelee, A. H., Werner, W. H., and Schultz, H. R. infant sleep patterns: from birth to 16 weeks of age. *J. Pediat.*, *65*, 1964, 576-582.
101. Polak, P. R., Emde, R. N., and Spitz, R. A. The smiling response to the human face: I. Methodology, quantification, and natural history. *J. Nerv. Ment. Dis.*, *139*, 1964, 103-109.
102. Polak, P. R., Emde, R. N., and Spitz, R. A. The smiling responses: II. Visual discrimination and the onset of depth perception. *J. Nerv. Ment. Dis.*, *139*, 1964, 407-415.
103. Rheingold, H. L. (Ed.) *Maternal Behavior at Mammals.* John Wiley, New York, 1963.
104. Rheingold, H. L. The effect of environmental stimulation upon social and exploratory behavior in the human infants. (In) *Determinants of Infant Behavior.* Foss, B. M. (Ed.). John Wiley, New York, 1961.
105. Rheingold, H. L., Stanley, W. C., and Cooley, J. A. Method for studying exploratory behavior in infants. *Science*, *136*, 1962, 1054-1055.
106. Rheingold, Harriet, L. Controlling the infant's exploratory behavior. (In) *Determinants of Infant Behavior*, Foss, B. M. (Ed.). John Wiley, New York, 1963.
107. Richmond, J. B., and Lipton, E. L. Some aspects of the neurophysiology of the newborn and their implications for child development. (In) *Dynamic Psychopathology in Childhood*, Jessner, L., and Pavenstadt, E., (Eds.). Grune and Stratton, N.Y. 1959.
108. Riesen, A. H. Plasticity of behavior: Psychological aspects. (In) *Biological and Biochemical Bases of Behavior*, Harlow, H. F., and Woolsey, C. N. (Eds.). University of Wisconsin Press, Madison, 1958.
109. Roffwarg, H. P., Dement, W. C., and Fisher, C. Preliminary observations of the sleep-dream pattern in neonates, infants, children, and adults. (In) *Problems of Sleep and Dreams in Children*, Harms, E. (Ed.). Macmillan, New York, 1964.
110. Saayman G., Ames, E. W., and Woffett, A. Response to novelty as an indicator of visual discrimination in the human infant. *J. Exp. Child Psychol.*, *1*, 1964, 189-198.
111. Sackett, G. P. Effects of rearing conditions upon the behavior of rhesus monkeys (Macaca Mulatta). *Child Develpm.*, *36*, 1965, 854-868.
112. Salk, L. Mothers' heartbeat in an imprinting stimulus. *Trans. N.Y. Acad. Sci.*, *24*, 1962, 753-763.
113. Salzen, E. A. Visual stimuli eliciting the smiling response in the human infant. *J. Genet. Psychol.*, *102*, 1963, 51-54.
114. Schaffer, H. R., and Emerson, P. E. The development of social attachments in infancy. *Monogr. Soc. Res. Child Develpm.*, *29* No. 3, 1964.

115. Schaffer, H. R., and Emerson, P. E.   Patterns of response to physical contact in early human development. *J. Child Psychol. Psychiat.*, 5, 1964, 1-13.
116. Schneirla, T. C., and Rosenblatt, J. S.   Critical periods in the development of behavior. *Science*, 134, 1963, 110-116.
117. Scott, J. P.   Social behavior, organization and leadership in a small flock of domestic sheep. *Comp. Psychol. Monogr.*, 18, 1945, 1-29.
118. Scott, J. P.   Critical periods in the social development of puppies. *Psychosom, Med.*, 1958, 42-54.
119. Scott, J. P.   Critical periods in behavioral development. *Science*, 138, 1962, 949-958.
120. Seay, B., Hansen, E., and Harlow, H. F.   Mother-infant separation in monkeys. *J. Child Psychol. Psychiat.*, 3, 1962, 123-132.
121. Skard, A., G.   Maternal deprivation: The research and its implications. *J. Marr. and Fam.*, 27, 1965, 333-343.
122. Skodak, M., and Skeds, H. M.   A final follow-up study of one hundred adopted children. *J. Genet. Psychol.*, 75, 1949, 85-125.
123. Smith, T. L., and Meyer, M. E.   Preference of chicks in the original stimulus situation of imprinting *Psychonom. Sci.*, 2, 1965, 121-122.
124. Smock, C. D.   Effects of motivational factors on perceptual-cognitive efficiency of children who vary in intellectual levels. *Co-operative Research Project, No. 790.* Purdue University Studies, West Lafayette, 1962.
125. Smock, C. D., and Holt, B. J.   Children's reactions to novelty: An experimental study of curiosity motivation. *Child Develpm.*, 33, 1962, 631-642.
126. Spears, W. C.   The assessment of visual discrimination and preferences in the human infant. Unpublished Ph.D. thesis. Brown University Press, Providence, 1962.
127. Spitz, R. A.   The smiling response: a contribution to the ontogenesis of social relations. *Genet. Psychol. Monogr.*, 34, 1946, 57-125.
128. Spitz, R. A., and Wolf, K.   Anaclitic depressions. *Psychoanal. Stud. of Child.*, 2, 1946, 313-342.
129. Stechler, G.   Attention and arousal in the infant. Presented at meeting of Soc. Res. Child Develpm., Minneapolis, March, 1965.
130. Thomas, A., et al.   A longitudinal study of primary reaction patterns in children. *Comprehensive Psychiat.*, 1, 1960, 103-112.
131. Thompson, G. G.   *Child Psychology.* Houghton Mifflin, New York, 1952.
132. Thompson, J.   Development of facial expression of emotion in blind and seeing children. *Arch. Psychol.*, No. 264, 1941, 1-47.
133. Thompson, W. R., and Dubanoski, R. A.   Imprinting and the law of effort. *Anim. Behav.* 12, 1964, 213-218.
134. Thorpe, W. H.   *Learning and Instinct in Animals.* Methuen, London, 1956.
135. Trygg, L., et al.   Olfactory responses and adaptation in the human neonate. *J. Comp. Physiol. Psychol.*, 56, 1963, 71-81.
136. Walter, E. C.   Prediction of postnatal development from fetal activity. *Child Develpm.*, 36, 1965, 801-808.
137. Washburn, R. W.   A study of the smiling and laughing of infants in the first year of life. *Genet. Psychol Mongr.*, 6, 1929, 397-537.
138. Watson, J. B.   *Behaviorism.* University of Chicago Press, Chicago, 1924.
139. Watson, J. S.   Visual angle of mother's face and the smiling response. Unpublished study. Merrill-Palmer Institute of Human Development and Family Life; Detroit, 1964.
140. Weiss, LaB. A.   Differential variations in the amount of activity of newborn infants under continous light and sound stimulation. *University of Iowa Stud. Child Welf.*, 9, 1934, 9-74.
141. West, L. J., and Farber, I. E.   The role of pain in emotional development. (In) Explorations in the Physiology of Emotions, *Psychiat. Res. Rep.*, No. 12, 1960, 119-126.
142. White, B. L.   The development of perception during the first six months of life. Paper presented at the Annual Meeting of The American Association for the Advancement of Science, Cleveland, 1963.
143. White, B. L., and Castle, P. W.   Visual exploratory behavior following postnatal handling of human infants. *Percept. Mot. Skills*, 18, 1964, 497-502.

144. White, B. L., Castle, P. W., and Held, R. Observations on the development of visually directed reaching. *Child Developm. 35*, 1964, 349-364.
145. White, R. W. Motivation reconsidered: The concept of competence. *Psych. Rev., 66*, 1959, 297-333.
146. Wilson, M., Warren, J. M., and Abbott, L. Infantile stimulation, activity, and learning by cats. *Child Develpm., 36*, 1965, 843-853.
147. Wolff, P. H. The causes, controls, and organization of behavior in the neonate. *Psychol. Issues,* Monograph 17, Vol. 5. 1966.
148. Wolff, P. H. Observations on newborn infants. *Psychosom. Med., 21,* 1959, 110-118.
149. Wolff, P. H. Observations on the early development of smiling. (In) *Determinants of Infant Behavior,* Vol. 2, Foss, B. M. (Ed.). John Wiley, New York, 1963.

CHAPTER 4

PROCESSES OF EARLY DEVELOPMENT: II

SOCIALIZATION

Mother-Infant Attachment

The child is becoming socialized when he learns to behave in the ways expected of him by the people who raise him. He learns to behave in ways that are typical of children of his age in his own part of the general culture. The child will master these expected ways of functioning only if he becomes sufficiently attached, in the ways described in Chapter 3, to some caretaking figure or figures. Most often this is the mother, who supervises his early problem-solving activities. Eating the foods given to him when they are presented, and learning to eliminate his waste products in the approved manner are two of the first major tasks that the surrounding adults in the family expect the child to master. Weaning and toilet training represent important events or demands with which every child must cope.

As we saw in Chapter 3, by the age of six months, the child can distinguish his mother from other people. Around this age, long separation from the mother can produce some undesirable behavioral effects. The baby has begun to form his first truly social attachment. The intensity of this attachment will vary from child to child. It will cause a number of behavioral responses such as clinging or crying to which the mother and others in the home will respond in a characteristic way, further affecting attachment behavior. The eventual intensity of the emotional bond depends upon both the "need" of the child and the extent to which the people around him are prepared to satisfy it.[80] The child's emotional attachment to people becomes a vital factor in his mastering the developmental tasks with which he is faced. If the child has weak attachments to others he is less likely to do things they want.

Before one year of age most infants become attached to more than one person in the family, although normally the mother is the favorite. Before six months the baby wants company and will cry if left alone, no matter who leaves; the seven month old may cry only if a certain individual leaves; at ten months, a child who cries when his mother leaves will cry only harder if a stranger tries to comfort him. He becomes suspicious of the doctor, whom he previously tolerated or even smiled upon.

The intensity of the child's attachment may originate in his innate level of preference for different amounts or types of stimulation. Some infants dislike cuddling, hugging, and kissing, and prefer to use visual and auditory means of social interaction. The mother finds that she must adjust her behavior to the child, even though she may have her own, different, and preferred level for body contact with the baby. In any case, the infant begins to form a social attachment when he discovers that another person is a much more accommodating and interesting source of stimulation than any other object.[78, 79, 80] No matter to what extent affectionate behavior is determined by the nature of the child, it is interesting to note that sons with highly affectionate mothers had lower scores on developmental tests at one year, but higher intelligence scores during the school years than sons with less affectionate mothers. On the other hand, the mothers' behavior was only minimally related to the daughters' later intelligence scores.[6]

There is little doubt that the cold, detached, withdrawn behavior of a child called autistic starts almost at birth, and, whatever its initial cause, heavily influences the reactions of his parents. This early withdrawal from contact takes away a good deal of the exclusive blame that some direct at the parents of such children because of their supposed "rejection" of the child. It seems quite possible that the child may first "reject" the parent. At the least a mutual process may be involved; parents may reject such children since they are unresponsive, and this rejection may then lead to even greater withdrawal by the child.

Feeding and Weaning

There is a great deal of overlap between measures of "orality" (the tendency to suck, nibble, or mouth objects, or to eat a lot, and so on) and measures of dependency.[62] (Dependency refers to the behavior of the child which has the effect of having others come and help him.) The infant shows a great deal of dependency associated with feeding. Over the years there has been a decline in breast-feeding. In 1927, 77 percent of infants still breast fed at three months. This rate dropped to 36 percent in 1949 and to only 21 percent or less in 1957.[39, 58] For a long time there was a controversy over the effect of breast- versus bottle-feeding on the development of thumbsucking and other oral behaviors which were thought to be indicative of dependency.[43, 83] Experts counseled mothers to breast-feed for the good of the child. Nowadays research indicates that, if anything, there seems to be an advantage to feeding children formulas from bottles. Formula-fed babies at three months (where mothers had abandoned breast-feeding within the first month) gained weight more rapidly, cried less, and were as healthy as breast-fed infants.[33, 37, 51] No clear adjustment patterns involving dependency (or other psychological dimensions) appear as a direct consequence of any aspect of the infant feeding experience, including breast versus bottle, early versus late weaning, or the amount of sucking provided.[15] Qualitative differences in development are not a simple function of such practices.

On the issue of thumbsucking, two opposing theories were advanced. Levy maintained that it was the result of deprivation or frustration of the oral sucking drive.[43] Sears and Wise said it was due to the overgratification of the sucking drive; much practice and reward of sucking led to a stronger drive.[83] Yarrow reconciled these views by saying that if the oral sucking drive is frustrated during early infancy while the drive is strong, it can lead to thumb sucking; but on the other hand, if weaning is delayed and sucking continues too long, it can become an overly strong habit, through repeated reinforcement, which thumbsucking will gratify.[99] Thus either previous theory can be correct depending on the timing of weaning. This may be a more precise explanation and may prove valid in spite of the results citing no clearcut effects of different sucking experiences in children.[15] Although sheer amount of sucking may not be the most meaningful measure of orality or dependency, examination of the timing of the activity (when and under what circumstances it occurs) may reveal a pattern.

There are wide differences in the age at which mothers feel their babies should be weaned, and great variations in weaning methods. Recently the different social classes in America have become more similar in feeding and weaning practices; feeding schedules are more permissive in the middle class, and weaning takes place later than it used to. This may be partly due to wide dissemination of information about infant care.[86] Most of the differences occur within social classes, rather than between them, and are related to the general characteristics of the parent.[82] As noted above, no clearly distinguishable personality differences result from wide variations in feeding and weaning practices alone; it is the general nature of patterns of child rearing in the family which matters. Especially important are such matters as how and when the child is punished and rewarded, and what sorts of people are on hand for the child to imitate.

Toilet Training

Many parents have strong opinions about toilet training, and find it impossible to separate from sex in their minds.[82] If you start asking a mother about bowel training it is likely that she will soon be talking about modesty or masturbation.

A number of factors influences the timing and success of toilet training efforts. Such training has a special importance because it creates the first occasion when the child has considerable control over the situation, at least at the later training periods; he can "go" where and when he likes, within limits. The eating situation is different. A child has little control over eating, except to refuse foods. Any baby who is fairly normal (not psychotic) for instance, will eat long before his health is seriously impaired. He gets too hungry to keep refusing food and comes to enjoy many of the new ones given to him. On the other hand, a small but significant percentage of babies will become severely constipated during a battle of wills over going to the "potty," enough so to require medical intervention. Toilet training provides the child with a chance to demonstrate both mastery of a task and some autonomy. Both weaning and toilet training provide opportunities for many positive experiences as well as negative ones.

Since children are constitutionally different from one another, identical child rearing practices may have somewhat different effects on them. Infants who dislike being wet, perhaps due to greater skin irritability, toilet train earlier and may find it a relief.[17, 18] Some children are more regular in all their physiological patterns; some are more irritable, or more distractible. These factors also affect the ease with which they will become toilet trained.

Some parents begin training before the baby is six months old, but many others wait until around 11 months or until much later. Some children respond to toilet training in a matter of weeks and others take more than a year. Accidents may still be common among two and a half year olds, even three year olds have occasional mishaps such as wetting at night. In the last 25 years fewer parents have been starting to train before six months, and in general, the trend seems to be for middle-class mothers to be more permissive and supportive. Perhaps they are accepting more quickly than working-class parents the popular parent education literature. There is a great deal of overlap between the social classes, however, and the degree of difference is small, even though fairly consistent.[15]

In a study of about 1000 mothers who were induced to wait until the child was about two years old before starting to toilet train, it was found that less than 2 percent of the children showed enuresis (urinary accidents), encopresis (bowel accidents), or chronic constipation after five years of age, compared to the figure of 10 to 20 percent reported in normal pediatric practice. The children's bowel and bladder training were completed on the average at 28.5 months of age by day and 33.3 months of age by night. Constipation and fecal incontinence have been shown to be partly associated with early toilet training and coercive training.[75] However, neglectful or overly lenient training can have the same effects. The best approach seems to be firm but nonpunitive training at about 19 to 24 months.

Several studies shows that a certain group of personality traits, tending to occur together, have been associated with the label of "anal character." These traits include obstinacy, orderliness, and parsimony. Freudians believe these characteristics to result from too severe (or too lenient) toilet training. The occurrence of these traits in a child seems to have little to do directly with toilet training, however. The mothers of children displaying these traits usually have the same traits themselves. The cluster, or any part of it, may be learned by the child through imitation, direct reward or punishment, secondary reward or punishment, or any combination of these. Orderliness is probably due to direct teaching of orderliness, of which toilet training neatness or regularity is only a part.[7, 34, 82] Many other types of behavior of the mother, such as being cold and restrictive, rather than toilet training practices as such, seem to encourage so-called "anal characteristics." As in the case of weaning, toilet training practices, in themselves, do not seem to effect later adjustment.

Study 4.1 provides an example of the prompt response shown by a 19-month-old girl to a particular technique of toilet training. It shows how rewards can be used to socialize the child's toilet training related behavior.

A CRASH PROGRAM OF TRAINING

STUDY 1.1

At the time the training program was started, this 19-month-old girl had begun to cry when placed on the potty chair (about four times a day). Her mother was most anxious to train her, since the family was planning a long automobile trip in about 30 days, and diapers would be an enormous nuisance.

The little girl was told she would be given a piece of candy and that her mother would praise her when she "went" on the potty, though the candy was also given casually after meals with no reward connotation. On the second trial she "went," received candy, and was praised. On the fourth day she volunteered "urinate a toto, get candy." On the fifth day she asked to be taken to the pot. She was fully trained by the twelfth day. After this she was given candy only on demand, and after 60 days she made no more requests for it. She underwent a short relapse after an illness, but was retrained in one week. The car trip was a completely dry success.

This method of training is called "positive reinforcement." It involves only rewards for the desired behavior, and no specific punishment for lapses, although the reward is withheld for lapses, and, probably in this case, the child could detect the disappointment of her mother.

Madsen, C. H. Positive reinforcement in the toilet training of a normal child: A case report. (In) *Case Studies in Behavior Modification*, Ullman, L. D., and Krasner, L. (Eds.). Holt, Rinehart, and Winston, New York, 1965, pp. 305-306.

THE LEARNING PROCESS

Socialization depends on learning. The child must learn to behave in certain ways expected of him. It is important, therefore, to examine the various types of learning which psychologists have described, and which make weaning and toilet training, for example, possible. Although some psychologists make a sharp distinction between conditioning and other forms of learning, we will not. For the purposes of the present text we will merely consider conditioning as a form of learning. In Chapter 3 we saw that the baby arrives in the outside world with many well developed reflexes, relatively good visual and auditory perception, and other remarkable abilities. These innate potentials for response are immediately influenced by external events and form the basis for the earliest learning. A number of experiments have been done to determine just what and how early an infant can learn. Some learning has been demonstrated before the baby leaves the uterus; this was reviewed in Chapter 3 and will not be taken up here. Certainly the ability to become toilet trained and other such complex behaviors depend on learning.

Infant learning has been demonstrated in puppies, monkeys, guinea pigs, and albino rats, among other animals.[16, 20, 27, 30, 32, 57, 87] This ability in lower mammals leads one to suspect a considerable range of positive results for even the youngest human infants, and this proves to be the case.

Learning During the First Three Weeks After Birth

Aversive Conditioning

Aversive conditioning involves learning either to avoid or to escape an unpleasant event. If the infant learns to respond properly to a preliminary signal, the unpleasant event may not take place. Some studies find no such avoidance conditioning before 45 days of age, others find nothing under six months. However, using different procedures, some may have established such conditioning within the first five days of life.[93, 97] A conditioned response to avoid ammonia vapor has been demonstrated as early as the age of four weeks premature, but these results are hard to duplicate.[73] Lipsitt concludes that special apparatus and carefully controlled conditions are necessary to remove the uncertainties in this area.[48]

Aversive conditioning includes both avoidance and escape learning. In learning to avoid, the child can prevent the unpleasant event altogether, if he makes the right response after the warning signal is given that such an event is coming. In escape learning, the child always experiences the unpleasant event but learns to terminate it after it has begun.

Classical Appetitional Conditioning

Most newborns will adjust to being fed only at certain times within ten days of birth.[38] They no longer cry excessively between feedings. They actually seem to learn to become hungry at regular intervals. When nine-day-old infants are shifted from a three-hour feeding schedule to a four-hour one, they become more active during the fourth hour than infants accustomed to a four-hour schedule, perhaps because they are hungrier, but they eventually settle down to the new schedule of feeding.[55] When a buzzer signaled that a bottle of milk was on the way, in five days, eight out of ten infants showed sucking and mouth opening responses to the buzzer, along with a decrease in crying and body movement. Originally such responses were made only to the presentation of the bottle of milk to the mouth. Four babies who were not trained to associate the buzzer with the bottle of milk showed no special response to the buzzer alone.[56] Within the first few days of life, when a low-frequency loud tone is paired with the insertion of a nipple in the mouth, a classical conditioned response to the tone can be produced.[97] Classical conditioning involves the attachment of an established response to a stimulus which did not previously elicit it. In this case, the sucking response originally made to the bottle of milk presented to the mouth is now made to the loud tone.

Adaptation and Habituation

Newborns are known to stop responding to stimuli which were initially effective elicitors of response, after a number of similar presentations. Actually, this may be considered the earliest and most primitive precursor, or form, of learning. There have been many studies on lower animals demonstrating this "adaptation" phenomenon.[35, 44, 68, 74] The human fetus will soon stop responding to tonal stimuli.[25, 69] Infants also learn to ignore odor after a few trials.[22]

Wertheimer performed an adaptation study on what may be the youngest human newborn ever studied; the baby was ten minutes old at the *end* of the investigation. Study 4.2 summarizes the method and results.

AN EXAMPLE OF EARLY HABITUATION

STUDY 4.2

The subject was born with drug anesthesia, by natural childbirth. The experiment was started only three minutes after birth. On each trial a click was made with a toy "cricket" next to the right or left ear of the subject (in predetermined order). The subject was lying on her back. Two observers independently recorded whether the eyes (whose movements were fully co-ordinated) moved to the infant's left, to the infant's right, or not at all, in response to each click.

As soon as the first click occurred, the baby, who had been crying with closed eyes, stopped crying, opened her eyes, and "looked" in the direction of the click. Fifty-two successive trials were run, at a rate of about eight per minute. The series was terminated because the subject "lost interest," adapted or satiated; no further eye movements occurred in response to the clicks. When the experiment was over, the subject was only ten minutes old.

In the 22 trials in which both observers reported eye movement in the same direction, 19 responses were in the direction of the click and three were in the opposite direction. The difference between this distribution and chance (where the infant would be expected to look to the left 11 times and to the right 11 times) is statistically significant. In the remaining trials, for 23 there was no movement at all, and in six trials one observer recorded an eye movement whereas the other recorded none. In only one trial did the observers disagree about the direction of the movement.

Wertheimer concludes from this experiment that within ten minutes after birth, rudimentary directional location of sounds is possible, and that eye movements are at least roughly coordinated with hearing. This finding is not compatible with the view that space perception, and particularly cross-modal spatial coordination, is based upon a long and difficult learning process.

Wertheimer, M. Psychomotor coordination of auditory and visual space at birth. *Science, 134*, 1961, p. 1692.

Other investigators have also used habituation techniques to assess the capacity of the newborn to discriminate between stimuli.[8, 10, 12, 23, 46] In general, the technique is to habituate a baby to a certain stimulus through repeated presentations. When response to that stimulus has disappeared, a slightly different stimulus is introduced. If the baby now shows a response, it means he can tell that the stimulus is different from the preceding ones. If he makes no response, it means that he cannot tell the new stimulus from the ones to which he had habituated.

Habituation may not be conditioning or learning. It is not certain whether there is an association being weakened between a stimulus and a response. Rheingold and Stanley caution the student that "...any suggestion that neonatal habituation is similar to extinction, Pavlov's internal inhibition, or Hull's inhibition would be premature indeed." The cessation of attention, rather than learning or unlearning may be involved. However, this is still an open issue within learning theory.

Learning After The First Weeks

Classical Aversive Conditioning

The most famous case of this kind of learning after the first weeks was reported by Watson and Rayner.[92] A nine-month old boy named Albert was shown several furry animals he had never seen before, including a rat and a rabbit. He showed no fear, and even reached out to touch them. A loud noise was produced behind Albert's head the next time the rat was presented. Children are frightened (unconditioned response) by unexpected loud noises. Albert was frightened by the noise (the unconditioned stimulus) and soon became frightened when the rat (conditioned stimulus) was shown by itself. The rat became the conditioned stimulus for the fear response, so the fear response to the rat is called the "conditioned response." This conditioned fear response was subsequently shown to the rabbit and to other furry objects; the fear response spread (generalized) to these other objects. Other investigators have produced comparable results.[1, 40, 54]

Appetitional Conditioning

The Czechoslovakian investigator, H. Papousek, has done a great deal of work in the area of appetitional learning.[63, 64, 65, 66] As a measure of learning, he used general body movements and head-turning responses rather than the sucking response itself, which he found too complex to measure accurately. His method is unusual, combining as it does both operant and classical conditioning methods. In operant methods, partly established responses are strengthened by rewarding them. "Strengthening" means causing the desired response to occur more frequently by rewarding it. In Papousek's design, a bell was sounded as the conditioned stimulus for ten seconds. If the child turned his head to the left he received the nipple, and the bell was turned off. If he didn't turn, he was stimulated by a touch of the nipple to the left corner of his mouth. If he still didn't turn, the experimenter gently turned the baby's head with his hand, and milk was then given. This is operant reinforcement to strengthen the response. These steps were continued until the baby learned to turn his head in response to the bell alone. Later, a different sound, a buzzer, was introduced to study differentiation following conditioning. The infant was fed on the *right* side when the buzzer was sounded. Papousek used children from one to 20 weeks old, and found stable learning at about four to six weeks of age. Differentiation between bell and buzzer could be learned at three months, and a reversal (turning *right* to the bell and *left* to the buzzer) could be mastered at about four months.

In this series of experiments on appetitional conditioning, the correct response does not occur at once; an operant type of procedure is used to evoke the response desired. After training, the bell and buzzer are used in the discrimination techniques which also employ operant principles.

Operant Conditioning

The purpose of operant conditioning is often to get the child to do one thing more frequently than other things. The desired behavior is rewarded; the others are not. Of course, the rewarded behavior is then performed more frequently by the child.

Many operant learning studies have been conducted on the child of four weeks and older. A typical operant study ran as follows: two different shaped objects on a tray were presented to infants aged six to

15 months; one of the two objects held a sweet substance and could be lifted to the mouth; the other was stuck to the tray and could not be lifted. By the age of six months, children could learn to respond only to the movable object.[47] Drinking the sweet substance from the movable object reinforced the infants.

At a more complicated level, Simmons and Lipsett presented different colored lights in two six-inch wooden panels as stimuli to be discriminated by infants.[85] Chimes sounded when the correct panel was pressed. The chime sounds were reinforcing to the children. By the age of ten to 12 months, infants tended to respond more to the chime-associated color, and less when no chimes occurred to either color. They could also resume responding to the different colors when chimes were again associated with them. This is called "putting the infant under stimulus control" (the presence or absence of the chimes).

Learning by Imitation in Early Childhood

In everyday life, at home, learning is not induced by placing closely observed infants in carefully controlled experimental situations. Such experiments, which are done by psychologists, are vital to the demonstration of principles of learning, to show exactly how the child can learn, and what he can master at various ages. But usually, for the child at home, in the family, learning of various sorts is going on almost all the time, in a great variety of ways, whether the adults intend it or not. Not only does classical and operant conditioning occur in children, their observations also play a role in the learning process.[2]

The young child watches people around him and soon begins to reproduce their actions and verbal utterances, as far as his capabilities permit. This process is called imitation; the person imitated is called a model. The child, as he gets older, may be observed to imitate larger and larger segments of behavior. Some theorists say that the child has *identified* with one or more persons around him. They say that he has taken over some of their behavior so completely that that behavior is now a part of himself. In a later chapter we shall discuss whether the term "identification" is really useful in helping to explain how or why the behavior of children can become very similar to that of other people.[2]

Imitation Before Attachment or Attachment Before Imitation?

For a long time it was thought that the baby only imitated people whom he liked, who were familiar to him, and who were distinguished from others by him. Freud stated that the relationship between the child and the person who cares for and protects him (whom he labeled the "anaclitic object choice") provides the foundation for both the development of imitative behavior and the establishment of subsequent socioemotional attachments.[26] This viewpoint influenced the thinking of many psychologists.[60, 61, 81, 96] It ignores the possibility that imitative behavior may occur before the formation of specific attachments and may in itself contribute to the child's responsiveness or attachment to others.

The age at which the baby first shows imitation is disputed. Some records have been filmed and otherwise recorded of imitative tongue protrusions by babies less than one month old.[99, 100] An experimenter sticks his tongue out at a baby and the baby then sticks out his own tongue. Others have reported imitative vocalizations and mouth and hand movements within the first six months of life.[19, 88] The cry of a child in response to another child has been called by Piaget the earliest precursor of imitation.[72] However, the crying of another infant rapidly becomes ineffective as an eliciting stimulus for imitative crying, and it may be that such crying is merely a response to an unpleasantly loud noise.[13] The stringency of the criteria used to define imitation affect the conclusions drawn. When the criterion was exact copying of complex manipulative or verbal behavior, no imitation was found in infants from 54 to 74 weeks of age.[84] However, precise and detailed copying of a model is the exception, not the rule, even among older children and adults.[41]

The level of arousal of the infant plays a large part in the development of imitative behavior. Changes in arousal influence cue utilization and perceptual organization. The child is unlikely to notice things unless he is alert. There are marked individual differences in arousal state, stable over the first few months of life. In most cases, however, all mild stimulation appears pleasurable, within certain limits. Imitation is used very early between child and adult as a means of playful communication. The mother imitates some of the child's vocalizations or movements and vice versa. In this way mild stimulation and arousal are maintained. Both mother and child enjoy such imitative play and so learn to attend to each other.

Early Acquisition of Vocal Behavior

Parental influences affect the amount of vocalization produced by very young babies. A baby will vocalize more if the parents vocalize a lot to the baby and if they reward the baby's vocalization. Not much is known about the earliest acquisition of language. Limited work has been done, recording with tapes and movies the behavior of children from birth on.[14] By about the age of one year, responses to words can be conditioned about four times faster than to other, nonverbal sounds. Considerable work has been done on the phonetic analysis of babbling.[11] At least one investigator regards speech as a motor skill, and also notes that the early vocalizations of the infant are not the same as meaningful speech.[45] According to this view, language comprehension should be regarded as distinct from language expression, such as babbling, and therefore requires different assessment techniques. Social class differences affect parental practices and the resultant use of speech by the child. Children who have had a single mothering agent were found to speak better than children who had six to eight substitute mothers. Fewer lower-than-middle-class children have a single mother-child relationship in their early years. Lower-class mothers read less to their babies than middle-class mothers. When lower-class mothers were instructed to read aloud to their children at least ten minutes a day from the age of one year, their children significantly exceeded other comparable children in all phases of speech by the age of 20 months.

O. H. Mowrer uses the concepts of imitation and identification to explain the acquisition of speech.[60] He believes that the young child soon learns to associate speech with various gratifications provided by the mother while she takes care of him. Mothers tend to chat with the baby while changing him, feeding him, and playing with him. When the mother goes away and the baby is alone, if he accidentally produces something vaguely like speech, it is reinforcing to him; it provides some comfort by recalling the mother's company and activities. Furthermore, when he makes speech-like sounds in the presence of another person, that person is quite likely to respond with smiles, attention, imitative sounds, and other forms of social reinforcement. These responses are quite gratifying to the infant. Thus gradually, the baby learns sounds by imitation and derives satisfaction from practicing them both by himself and in the company of others. Finally, of course, the production of a recognizable word, such as "mama" or "cup," may produce the desired object, and "instrumental learning" has begun. Instrumental learning refers here to the child's learning to use language as an instrument to get what he wants. For instance, he can ask for milk and get it. In general, instrumental learning refers to the acquisition of behavior which can be used to get the organism desired goal objects, like food or attention. As we shall see later, the acquisition of language may be the most important, qualitative, psychological change in the life of the child.

THE PROCESS OF EARLY COGNITIVE DEVELOPMENT

Perceptual Development

By the age of six months, the child has mastered his native tools to some extent. He makes fine visual and auditory discriminations, begins to know individual members of his family besides his mother, and has even begun to look fairly co-ordinate in his grasping and other large motor movements. Generally speaking, these abilities continue to show improvement with age. Interestingly enough, this is not true of all his perceptions.

The sensory discrimination of tonal pitch, weight, hue, and color saturation improve with age. High and low pitch thresholds do not, and neither does the two-point skin sensitivity threshold—these show a decrease in acuity as the child gets older. The discrimination of visual extents (size and length) increases from 12 months to four years, and can be trained with practice at four to 12 months. After four years, there is little change in discriminations of size or length.[98]

The gross differentiation of depth perception develops from six to 14 months.[29, 89, 90] Finer differentiation is well developed in four year olds. Stereoscopic perception appears to improve with age, but this may be accounted for by the methods of assessment, in which the younger child is asked to perform tasks too complex for his comprehension. Form discrimination and form constancy are well developed in infants, and no great changes occur in the first two years.

Motor Recognition and Imitation

A child's earliest behavior consists of reflex-like activities, including sucking, swallowing, crying, and so on. Learning quickly leads to the modification of such behaviors. A hungry baby will reject a finger or blanket offered him to suck on, but a full baby may suck on a number of objects. He has learned that only a particular object will satisfy a particular need.[42, 72] Learning involves not only the acquisition of observable responses but learning about the nature of the environment.

By the age of three or four months a sated (nonhungry) infant will apply each of the responses in his repertoire to an object offered him; he puts it in his mouth, rubs it, shakes it, hits with it, and so on. As new responses develop, he applies them to any object on which he can get his hands.

By eight to 10 months, he may pick up an unfamiliar object, throw it down, squeeze it, scratch it, pat it, swing it around, or splash with it.[70, 71] By seven or eight months, if a child sees a familiar object out of reach, he will "recognize" it by performing the appropriate response in fractional form; upon seeing a doll he may move his hand in a grasping motion.[91] These fractional responses become increasingly schematic, and become useful in problem solving as they become transferable from one stimulus situation to another. Piaget gives an example of a child faced with the problem of a small object inside an only partly open matchbox.[70] The infant could not get the object out with her finger. While looking at the box intently, she opened her mouth widely several times, and then unhesitatingly poked a finger into the box and pulled out the drawer, thereby obtaining the trinket.

By about 18 months, *imitative* or *representational* behavior may be deferred to a time when the person being imitated is no longer present. This is certainly an important qualitative change; before, the stimulus had to be present to be imitated. This development in imitation first appears in advance of much real language. For instance, the 18 month old may watch another boy do something on one day and then be seen running through a fractional set of elements of that behavior the next day, before he is at all capable of telling about either what he saw or what he is doing.[72] The child is learning to remember and to think. This is cognitive learning, a form of learning qualitatively different from classical or operant conditioning.

Means-End Behavior: Problem Solving

The ability to solve problems begins to appear at about eight months of age. The child becomes capable of categorizing objects in terms of their uses, as defined by his past experiences with the objects. The child learns that he must grasp the object to produce effects; the object becomes an extension of the hands. He can then use a stick to push or pull objects within manual reach, and then learns that he can use other things for the same purpose, such as a book or a doll. A generalization has occurred. He can categorize any object as a possible grasp-extender, in addition to its usual functions. He has now clearly begun to think.

Similarly Piaget's experiments (hiding objects under a pillow, placing objects on something that can be pulled toward the child, or moving objects from one concealment to another) show that the child can conceptualize objects even if they are out of sight.[70, 71] When he is about ten months old, he will look for an object where it is *usually* hidden even if he saw it hidden somewhere else. By about 18 to 24 months he learns that the object is underneath the cover where it was last seen. The child is led by experience to postulate a world of enduring objects that can be explored by different senses. The child's world is changing from a series of fleeting experiences to one of some stability and conservation. Thus, before the age of two, the child develops the "assignment of meaning" to objects in terms of their response-defined uses, prior to the development of language, through repeated perceptual experience learns to use means-objects in problem solving, and develops a concept of the conservation or invariance (permanence) of objects despite changes either in location or the sense with which they are experienced.

To recapitulate, it appears that thinking does not emerge suddenly at a particular point in the child's development, but rather that it can be traced to the progressive influence of experience on sensorimotor functioning. Behavior is modified by its results. Thus, there is no sharp division between sensorimotor functioning, conditioning, learning, and intellect. Development results in an increasing mastery of actions performed on objects, first, a partial copy of actions performed by others, stored in the child's repertoire, but later, more complex combinations of actions observed or performed previously, resulting in new actions not previously existent.[91] From this we can conclude that it is partly arbitrary to state at which point a qualitative change has taken place. Qualitative changes appear often as a result of gradual quantitative changes. It is often a matter of judgment at what point a distinctly new psychological mode of functioning has occurred.

Exploratory Behavior

Closely tied in with the development of perceptual and sensorimotor functions is the concept of an impelling or motivating force of some sort that makes reinforcing to the infant the exploration and mastery of his environment. If the child is to understand the world, he must explore it. Much of this exploration takes the form of play, as he builds up a representation or "cognitive map" of his surroundings.

The young infant's interest in objects has no plausible relationship to the primary drives of hunger, thirst, sexual stimulation, and so on. The warm, dry, wakeful, sated baby is the one who will most actively explore the properties of anything within reach. Once he can crawl he is "into everything," as many an exasperated mother will testify. Infants possess a tendency to be curious, to explore, learn, act upon, and master external objects and stimuli. These tendencies can be grouped under the heading of "effectance" "competence," or "intrinsic" motivation.[36, 95]

There seem to be three easily distinguished stages in the development of this motivation. In the first stage, according to Hunt, the infant is *attentive* and *responsive to changes in ongoing stimulation*, whether visual, auditory, tactile, or kinesthetic. This corresponds to Piaget's first and second stages of intellectual development and occurs from birth to around four or five months. The attention response serves as a motivational basis for the *co-ordination* of relatively independent systems of sucking, looking, listening, vocalizing, wiggling, and grasping. This corresponds to Piaget's second stage of sensorimotor development.[70]

Repeated, familiar, sensory inputs lead to apathy and retardation in infants, as explained in Chapter 3 in the section on institutionalized infants. When there is a lack of variation in receptor input, the child cannot learn to produce changes in input by his own actions. He also cannot encounter well organized and orderly sensations following a recurrent pattern which he can learn to recognize and predict. The child needs order in his experiences but he also needs new orderly experiences as he loses interest in the old ones.

At Hunt's second stage, infants begin acting to regain perceptual contact with experienced events. As they begin to recognize objects and people, children become attached to them, as shown by smiles at their presence and distress at their disappearance. It is after this stage, at about six months, that the fear of strange objects sets in. These recognitions and the accompanying emotional attachments lead to what has been called "autogenic responses."[21] These include babbling because the familiar sound is pleasant to him, both in its own properties and because of the association described by Mowrer between vocal stimulation and the presence of the mother. Similarly, the baby engages in hand- and foot-watching; a convenient familiar object can appear and disappear and be viewed from different angles. This is an early form of playing.

Imitation starts with activities already in the child's behavioral repertoire; the adult must imitate what the baby already does. The infant's response is a pseudo-imitation of the familiar, and at first, variations from known vocalizations will cause a drop in interest.[36, 72] At first the baby only likes to imitate the mother's approximation of his own "vocabulary."

Repeated encounters with the familiar lead to "learning sets." The child acquires the cognition that one should be able to recognize objects that are heard and seen; he acquires some kind of mental "plan" of how things are and a notion of object constancy.[70] Also, he comes to realize that if one acts, interesting events will follow. The element of purpose emerges. This corresponds to Piaget's description of means-end processes.

At stage three in Hunt's schema, an *interest in novelty* begins to emerge. This interest in novelty corresponds to Piaget's fifth and sixth stages of sensorimotor development, and provides motivation for the developmental transitions of the first and second year. It involves a continuing process of growth.

The transitions that occur include the following:

1. A shift of attention from vivid events and actions per se to objects and their manipulation; the baby begins "letting go," and engaging in other actions which increase the variety of sensory input.

2. The child discovers new means of doing things through active experimentation; actions irrelevant to the goal are eliminated, relevant ones are progressively modified. The repetition of success experiences, such as obtaining with a stick an out-of-reach object, probably lies behind the child's behavior perceived by adults as independence, confidence, or competence.

3. The interest in novelty motivates imitation. In turn, new actions, gestures, and vocalizations play a central role in socialization, as they are rewarded or punished by adults important to the child.

Motor Processes

Although the most striking aspect of the baby from six months to two years may be his emergence from ordinary animal status to that of a thinking human animal, his increasing motor skills are what make it all possible. Cognition would be minimal if the child were unable to move himself or other objects. A brief summary of motor events follows. Detailed accounts can be found in Spock, Gesell and Amatruda, and McGraw.[28, 52, 86]

Locomotion

Head and torso control are good enough by five or six months to enable most babies to sit up with some support and is usual by about seven months. By nine or ten months most babies can sit without support as long as they want to. Most babies can stand with help at nine or ten months (see Fig. 4-1).

Babies begin to turn over from side to back or front by three or four months, and can go from back to front or vice versa by six or seven

Figure 4-1. *A*, 26 weeks. Sitting with hands forward for support. *B*, 44 weeks. The creep position. *C*, 48 weeks. Walks with two hands held. *D*, 13 months. Walks without any help. (From Illingworth, R. S.: The introduction into Developmental Assessment in the First Year. With permission of Messrs. E. and S. Livingstone, Ltd., 1962.)

months if unimpeded by clothing. Crawling or hitching along at six to eight months precedes creeping on hands and knees in most babies. Babies learn to pull themselves to a standing position at about the same time they learn to creep. They then begin a cautious sideways locomotion while hanging on to some support. Forward walking while holding someone's hands develops next, and finally walking alone is begun.[28, 84, 86] The average age for independent walking is 13 to 14 months, but some children may walk as early as nine or as late as 18 months, and an occasional child walks at seven or eight months. Time of walking is closely tied to general rate of development, which may vary widely and still be well within the normal range.

As the widespread legs straighten up, the wobbly gait of beginning walkers gradually becomes smoother, and trotting or running develops next. Most babies can climb stairs about the time they have mastered walking. Most children master the adult manner of ascending and descending with alternate feet by three and a half or four years of age. Once children can get about fairly well they utilize locomotion in their play. Two year olds are skillful with kiddie cars and perform complicated maneuvers with them. Most children of three can climb on playground equipment, and most can manage tricycles and even two-wheel scooters. About half of the three year old group can manage slides well.[31] We should remember that children not only enjoy play, but learn from it, as they practice and perfect their newfound skills.

Finer Motor Skills

By six months, visual control is well established, and the baby can see, and put in his mouth, tiny dust specks or hairs from the floor. Most babies from about the age of one year like to look at, pat, and feel picture books, especially those with some texture in the design.

At six to seven months most babies can grasp efficiently. Study 4.3 gives a listing of approximate development of manual skills from about four months to one year.

DEVELOPMENT OF MANUAL SKILLS

STUDY 4.3

16 weeks: Hands come together in play. Pulls dress over face. Tries to grasp object. Plays for long time with rattle place in hand.
24 weeks: Holds bottle, Palmar grasp of cubes (Figure 4-2A). Drops cube when given another.

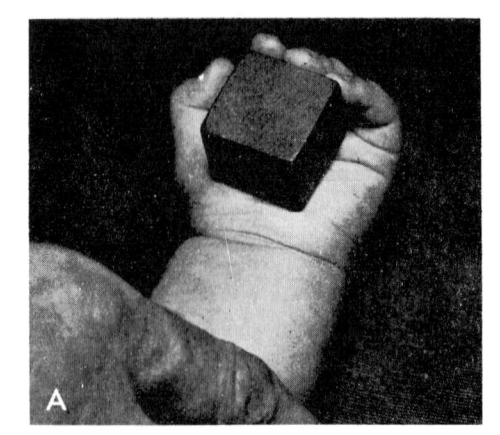

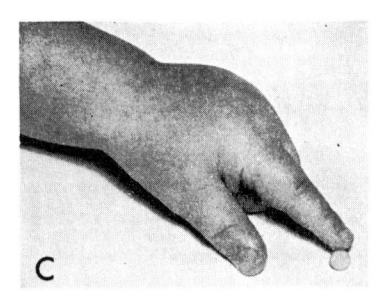

Figure 4-2. Manual skills. (From Illingworth, R. S.: The Introduction into Developmental Assessment in the First Year. With permission of Messrs. E. and S. Livingstone, Ltd., 1962.)

28 weeks: Transfers object from hand to hand. Unidextrous. Feeds self with biscuit. Bangs blocks on table. Holds one cube when given another.

40 weeks: Finger-thumb opposition. Can pick up pellet between finger and thumb. Offers block to mother, but won't let it go. Index finger approach to an object (Fig. 4-2C).

44 weeks: Places one block after another into a box.

48 weeks: Gives block to mother.

52 weeks: Mouthing nearly stopped. Beginning to throw objects on floor.

1 year: Mature grasp of cube (Fig. 4-2B).

Breckenridge, M. E., and Vincent, E. L. *Child Development.* W. B. Saunders, Philadelphia, 1965, p. 243.

Other Motor Skills.

During the second and third years, most motor activities show advances in smoothness and dexterity. Many babies are feeding themselves part of their meals by one year of age. Figure 4-3 shows a sample of activities mastered by the average child of 18 months. By three children can do a reasonable job of feeding themselves the whole meal, with little or no gobbling, gulping, smacking, or smearing. Many children can go to the toilet by themselves by the age of three, if their clothes are easy to manage. They can also perform at least part of the task of dressing themselves, with some help in telling back from front and unfastening buttons.

Figure 4-3. Early mastered activities. (From Gesell, A. and Amatruda, C. S.: Developmental Diagnosis: Normal and Abnormal Child Development. Hoeber, New York, 1941.)

Consolidation of Motor and Language Processes

So far as perceptual and motor development is concerned, the two to three year old is mostly consolidating gains, learning to make finer discriminations, and becoming proficient in his various skills, as seen above. Many children are weaned from the bottle and toilet-trained by their second birthday. The major area of advancement for the two year old is likely to be in his speech; from a score or two of words, and an occasional two-word sentence, he progresses to a fairly sophisticated grammatical level, and a great proliferation of vocabulary, both in words recognized and produced. It often seems that he is only silent when asleep. This can be a problem to the mother, both from the sheer volume of responses she is required to make and from the still uncertain pronunciation of the two year old, who easily becomes infuriated if she cannot fathom what he is trying to tell her. Language development will be taken up in detail in Chapter 6.

SUMMARY

Socialization, the mastering by the child of the kinds of behavior required to live adaptively among people, depends partly on his becoming attached to others. Once such attachments are formed, approval or disapproval positive or negative psychological reactions by others to the child, become important and are effective in regulating his behavior. Two aspects of socialization which almost all children in our culture have to master in approximately the first two years of life are learning to consume semisolid and solid foods (weaning) and becoming toilet trained. Although the child may have to give up comfortable past habits, he is reinforced by new rewards, including feelings of mastery, parental approval, and chances for a more varied diet. In any event, when and how parents wean or toilet train their children does not alone seem to have any major effects on development. Parental attitudes, like coldness or restrictiveness, may, however, be part of more general patterns of behavior, which certainly will effect the psychological changes the child will undergo.

Socialization involves learning. The learning process accounts for the child's ability to alter his feeding schedule, to change substantially from one class of foods to another, and to control his urinary and bowel habits. The simplest form of learning is adaptation or habituation, that is, essentially ceasing to respond to stimuli which previously evoked behavior. Perhaps of greatest importance in bringing about psychological changes through learning are classical and operant conditioning. In classical conditioning the child learns to give a response which is already established to a new stimulus. In operant conditioning the reinforcement of a response causes it to occur more frequently. Imitation may well account for how certain responses occur in the first place so that they may either become associated with new stimuli or strengthened by reinforcement. The child learns through observation; if he performs what he has observed, the child is said to be imitating.

An important class of responses acquired by children beginning sometime in the first year of life can be called "vocal behavior." Learning becomes much easier once the child begins to acquire words and to master speech. Paralleling language acquisition and other forms of development is the mastery of cognitive abilities; the child begins to think and to solve problems. It should be remembered that as children pass from infants, to being toddlers, to being able to walk and run, they are mastering motor skills which enable them to get around and explore their environment more fully. Cognitive (thinking) and related psychological abilities depend partly on the child's increased ability to move physically and so to extend the possibilities of interaction with the environment.

REFERENCES

1. Aldrich, C. A. A. A new test for learning in the newborn: The conditioned reflex. *Amer. J. Dis. Child.*, 1928, 36-37.
2. Bandura, A., and Walters, R. H. *Social Learning and Personality Development*. Holt, Rinehart, and Winston, New York, 1963.
3. Bartoshuk, A. K. Human neonatal cardiac acceleration to sound: habituation and dis-habituation. *Percept. Mot. Skills*, 15, 1962, 15-27.
4. Bartoshuk, A. K. Response decrement with repeated elicitation of human neonatal cardiac acceleration to sound. *J. Comp. Physiol. Psychol.*, 55, 1962, 9-13.
5. Bayley, N. The development of motor abilities during the first three years. *Monogr. Soc. Res. Child Develpm.*, No. 1, 1935.
6. Bayley, N., and Schaefer, E. S. Correlations of maternal and child behaviors with the development of mental abilities: Data from the Berkeley Growth Study. *Monogr. Soc. Res. Child Develpm.*, 29, No. 97, 1964.
7. Beloff, H. The structure and origin of anal character. *Genet. Psychol. Monogr.*, 55, 1957, 141-172.
8. Brackbill, Y. Research and clinical work with children. (In) *Some Views on Soviet Psychology*, Bauer, M. (Ed.). American Psychological Assn. Washington, 1962, 99-164.
9. Brazelton, T. B. A child oriented approach to toilet training. *Pediatrics*, 29, 1962, 121-128.
10. Bridger, W. H. Sensory habituation and discrimination in the human neonate. *Amer. J. Psychiat.*, 117, 1961, 991-996.
11. Brodbeck, A. J., and Irwin, D. C. The speech behavior of infants without families. *Child Develpm.*, 17, 1946, 145-156.
12. Bronstein, A. I., et al. On the development of the functions of analyzers in infants and some animals in the early stage of ontogenesis. (In) *Problems of evolution of Physiological Functions*, Acad. Sci. U.S.S.R. Dept. of Health, Education and Welfare Translation Service, Washington, 1958.
13. Buhler, C., and Hetzer, H. Das erste verstandnis fur Ausdruck im eisten Labensjahr. *Z. f. Psychol.*, 107, 1928, 50-61.
14. Bullowa, M., Jones, L. G., and Beuer, T. J. The development from vocal to verbal development in children. (In) The Acquisition of Language. *Monogr. Soc. Res. Child Develpm.*, No. 92, 29, 1964, 101-114.
15. Caldwell, B. M. The effect of infant care. (In) *Review of Child Development. Vol. 1,*

Hoffman, M. L., and Hoffman, L. W. (Eds.). Russell Sage Foundation, New York, 1964.
16. Caldwell, D. F., and Werboff, J. Classical conditioning in newborn rats. *Science, 136*, 1962, 1118-1119.
17. Chess, S., et al. *Your Child is A Person.* Viking, New York, 1965.
18. Brazelton, T. B. Observation of the neonate. *J. Amer. Acad. Child Psychiat., 1*, 1962, 38-58.
19. Church, J. *Language and the Discovery of Reality.* Random House, New York, 1961.
20. Cornwell, A. C., and Fuller, J. L. Conditioned response in young puppies. *J. Comp. Physiol. Psychol., 54*, 1961, 13-15.
21. Dennis, W. Infant development under conditions of restricted practice and minimum social stimulation. *Genet Psychol. Monogr., 23*, 1941, 143-191.
22. Disher, D. R. The reaction of newborn infants to chemical stimuli administered nasally. *Ohio State Stud. Inf. Behav., 52, No. 12*, Ohio State Press, Columbus, 1934.
23. Engen, T., Lipsitt, L. P., and Kaye, H. Olfactory responses and adaptation in the human neonate. *J. Comp. Physiol. Psychol., 56*, 1963, 73-77.
24. Erwin, S., and Miller, W. R. Language development. (In) *Child Psychology*, Stevenson, H. W. (Ed.). N.S.S.E., Chicago, 1963.
25. Forbes, H. S., and Forbes, H. B. Fetal sense reaction: hearing. *J. Comp. Psychol., 7*, 1927, 353-355.
26. Freud, S. On Narcissism: An introduction. (In) *Collected Papers Vol. 4*, Jones, E. (Ed.). Hogarth, London, 1925.
27. Fuller, J. L., Easler, C. A., and Baker, E. M. Formation of conditioning avoidance responses in young puppies. *Amer. J. Physiol., 160*, 1950, 462-466.
28. Gesell, A., and Amatruda, C. S. *Developmental Diagnosis: Normal and Abnormal Child Development.* Hoeber, New York, 1941.
29. Gibson, E., J., and Walk, R. D. "The visual cliff." *Sci. Amer., 202*, 1960, 64-71.
30. Golubeva, E. L. Conditioned reflexes of the newborn guinea pig. *Psychol. Abstr., 13*, No. 6113, 1939.
31. Gutteridge, M. A study of motor achievements of young children. *Arch. Psychol.*, 1939, 244.
32. Harlow, F. The development of learning in the rhesus monkey. *Amer. Scient., 46*, 1959, 459-479.
33. Heinstein, M. I. Behavioral Correlates of Breast-Bottle Regimes Under Varing Parent-Infant Relationships. *Monogr. Soc. Res. Child Develpm., 28, No. 4*, 1963.
34. Hetherington, E. M., and Brackbill, Y. Etiology and covariation of obstinacy, orderliness, and parsimony in young children. *Child. Develpm., 34*, 1963, 919-943.
35. Hinde, R. A. Changes in responsiveness to a constant stimulus. *Brit. J. Anim. Behav., 2*, 1954, 41-55.
36. Hunt, J. McV. Intrinsic motivation and its role in psychological development. (In) *Nebraska Symposium on Motivation.* University of Nebraska Press, Lincoln, 1965.
37. Hylten, F. E., et al. Difficulties associated with breast feeding. *Brit. Med. J., 1*, 1958, 310-315.
38. Irwin, O. C. Amount and nature of activities of newborn infants under constant external stimulating conditions during the first ten days of life. *Genet. Psychol. Monogr., 8*, 1930, 1-92.
39. Jeliffe, D. B. *Infant Nutrition in the Subtropics and Tropics.* World Health Organization, Geneva, 1955.
40. Jones, H. E. The retention of conditioned emotional reactions in infancy. *Pedagog. Sem. and J. Genet. Psychol., 37*, 1930, 485-498.
41. Koffka, K. *The Growth of Mind.* Kegan Paul, London, 1924.
42. Lashley, K. S., and Wade, M. The Pavlovian theory of generalization. *Psychol. Rev., 53*, 1946, 72-87.
43. Levy, D. M. Experiments in the sucking reflex and social behavior in dogs. *Amer. J. Orthopsychiat., 14*, 1944, 644-671.
44. Lehner, G. F. J. A study of the extinction of unconditioned reflexes. J. Exp. Psychol., 29, 1941, 435-456.
45. Lenneberg, E. H. Speech as a motor skill with special reference to non-aphasic disorders. (In) *The Acquisition of Language. Monogr. Soc. Res. Child Develpm., 29, No. 92*, 1964.

46. Leventhal, A. S. Adaptation, pitch discrimination and sound localization in the neonate. Unpublished M.A. thesis. Brown University, 1963.
47. Ling, B. C. Form Discrimination as a learning cue in infants. *Comp. Psychol. Monogr.*, 17, No. 2, 1941.
48. Lipsitt, L. P. Learning in the first year of life. (In) *Advances in Child Development and Behavior, Vol. 1*, Lipsitt, L. P., and Spiker, C. C. (Eds.). Academic Press, New York, 1963.
49. Lipsitt, L. P., and Kaye, H. Conditioned sucking in the human newborn. Unpublished manuscript. Brown University, 1963.
50. McCandless, B. R. *Children and Adolescents*. Holt, Rinehart, and Winston. New York, 1962.
51. McGeorge, M. Current trends in breast feeding. *New Zealand Med. J.*, 59, 1960, 31-41.
52. McGraw, M. B. Maturation of Behavior. (In) *Manual of Child Psychology*, Carmichael, L. (Ed.). John Wiley, New York, 1946.
53. Madsen, C. H. Positive reinforcement in the toilet-training of a normal child. (In) *Case Studies In Behavior Modification*, Ullman, P., and Krasner, L. (Eds.). Holt, Rinehart, and Winston, New York, 1965.
54. Marinesco, C., and Kriendler, A. Des reflexes conditionnelles: L'organisation des reflexes condtionnelles chez l'enfant. *J. de Psychol.*, 30, 1933, 855-856.
55. Marquis, D. P. Learning in the neonate: The modification of behavior under three feeding schedules. *J. Exp. Psychol.*, 29, 1941, 263-282.
56. Marquis, D. P. Can conditioned responses be established in the newborn infant? *J. Genet. Psychol.*, 39, 1931, 479-492.
57. Mason, W. A., and Harlow, H. F. Formation of conditioned responses in infant monkeys. *J. Comp. Physiol. Psychol.*, 51, 1958, 58-70.
58. Meyer, H. F. Breast feeding in the U.S.: Extent and possible trends. *Pediatrics*, 22, 1958, 116-121.
59. Morgan, J. J. B., and Morgan, S. S. Infant learning as a developmental index. *J. Genet. Psychol.*, 65, 1944, 281-289.
60. Mowrer, O. H. *Learning Theory and the Symbolic Processes*. John Wiley, New York, 1960.
61. Mowrer, O. H. *Learning Theory and Personality Dynamics*. Ronald, New York, 1950.
62. Murphy, L. B. Some aspects of the first relationship. *Int. J. Psychoanal.*, 45, 1964, 31-43.
63. Papousek, H. Conditioned head rotation reflexes in infants in the first months of life. *Acta Pediatr.*, 50, 1961, 565-576.
64. Papousek, H. Conditioned motor alimentary reflex in infants. I. Experimental conditioned seeking reflexes. *Cesk. Pediatr.*, 15, 1960, 861-872.
65. Papousek, H. Conditioned motor alimentary reflex in infants. II. A new experimental method of investigation. *Cesk. Pediatr.*, 15, 1960, 981-988.
66. Papousek, H. A method of studying conditioned food reflexes in young children up to the age of six months. *Pavlov. J. Higher Nerv. Activ.*, 9, 1959, 136-140.
67. Parsons, T. *The Social System*, Free Press, New York, 1951.
68. Peckham, G. W., and Peckham, E. G. Some observations on the mental power of spiders. *J. Morph.*, 1, 1887, 383-419.
69. Peiper, A. Sinnesempfindungen des Kindes vor seiner Geburt. *Monatssche. f. Kinderhk.*, 29, 1925, 236-241.
70. Piaget, J. *The Construction of Reality in the Child*. Basic Books, New York, 1954.
71. Piaget, J. *The Origins of Intelligence in Children*. International Universities Press, New York, 1952.
72. Piaget, J. *Play, Dreams, and Imitation in Childhood*. Routledge and Kegan Paul, London, 1951.
73. Polikanina, R. I. The relation between autonomic and somatic components in the development of the conditioned reflex in premature infants. *Pavlov. J. Higher Nerv. Activ.*, 11, 1961, 51-58.
74. Prosser, C. J., and Hunter, W. S. The extinction of startle responses and spinal reflexes in the white rat. *Amer. J. Phys.*, 117, 1936, 609-618.
75. Prugh, D. G. Childhood experiences and colonic disorder. *Ann. N.Y. Acad. Sci.*, 58, 1953-54, 355-376.

76. Rendle-Short, J. The puff test. *Arch. Dis. Child., 36*, 1961, 50-57.
77. Rheingold, H. L., and Stanley, W. Developmental psychology. *Ann. Rev. Psychol., 14*, 1963, 1-28.
78. Rheingold, H. L. The Effect of environmental stimulation upon social and exploratory behavior in the human infant. (In) *Determinants of Infant Behavior*, Foss, B. M. (Ed.), John Wiley, New York, 1959.
79. Rheingold, H. L., and Bayley, N. The later effects of and experimental modification of mothering. *Child Develpm., 30*, 1959, 362-372.
80. Schaffer, H. R. Some issues for research in the study of attachment behavior. (In) *Determinants of Infant Behavior*, Foss, B. M. (Ed.), John Wiley, New York, 1961.
81. Sears, R. R. Identification as a form of behavioral development (In) *The Concept of Development.*, Harris, D. B. (Ed.), University of Minnesota Press, Minneapolis, 1957.
82. Sears, R. R., Maccoby, E. E., and Levin, H. *Patterns of Child Rearing.* Row Peterson, Evanston, 1957.
83. Sears, R. R., and Wise, G. W. Relation of cup feeding in infancy to thumb sucking and the oral drive. *Amer. J. Orthopsychiat., 20*, 1950, 123-138.
84. Shirley, N. M. The first two years, a study of twenty-five babies. Vol. 1, Postural and locomotor development. *Inst. Child Welf. Monogr. Ser. No. 6*, University of Minnesota Press, Minneapolis, 1933.
85. Simmons, M. W., and Lipsitt, L. P. An operant-discrimination apparatus for infants. *J. Exp. Anal. Behav., 4*, 1961, 233-235.
86. Spock, B. *The Pocket Book of Baby and Child Care.* Pocket Books, New York, 1950.
87. Stanley, W. C., et al. Conditioning in the neonatal puppy. *J. Comp. Physiol. Psychol., 56*, 1963, 211-214.
88. Stern, C., and Stern, W. *Die Kindersprache: Eine Psychologische und Sprachtheoretische Hirtersuchung 4th Edition.* Barth, Leipzig, 1928.
89. Walk, R. D. A study of some factors influencing the depth perception of human infants. Paper read at meetings of the Eastern Psychol. Assn., 1961.
90. Walk, R. D., and Gibson, E. A comparative and analytical study of visual depth perception. *Psychol. Monogr.*, No. 519, 75, 1961.
91. Wallach, M. A. Research on children's thinking. (In) *The Sixty-Second NSSE Yearbook, Part 1*, Stevenson, H. W. (Ed.,). University of Chicago Press, Chicago, 1963.
92. Watson, J. B., and Rayner, R. Conditioned emotional reactions. *J. Exp. Psychol., 3*, 1920, 1-14.
93. Wenger, M. A. An investigation of conditioned responses in human infants. (In) *Studies of Infant Behavior III.* Wenger, M. A., et al. (Eds.). University of Iowa Stud. Child Welf., No. 1, *12*, 1936, 7-90.
94. Wertheimer, M. Psychomotor coordination of auditory and visual space at birth. *Science, 134*, 1961, p. 1692.
95. White, R. Motivation reconsidered: The concept of competence. *Psychol. Rev., 66*, 1959, 297-333.
96. Whiting, J. W. M., and Child, I. L. *Child Training and Personality: A Cross-Cultural Study.* Yale University Press, New Haven, 1953.
97. Wickens, D. D., and Wickens, C. A. A study of conditioning in the neonate. *J. Exp. Psychol., 26*, 1940, 94-102.
98. Wohlwill, J. F. Developmental studies of perception. *Psych. Bull., 57*, 1960, 249-288.
99. Zazzo, R. Le probleme de l'imitation chez le nouveau-ne. *Enfance, 10*, 1957, 135-142.
100. Zazzo, R. Imitation. (In) *Discussion on Child Development*, Tanner, J. M., and Inhelder, B. (Eds.). Tavistock, London, 1956.

CHAPTER 5

MATURATION AND LEARNING

PROCESSES OF BEHAVIORAL ACQUISITION AND DEVELOPMENT

For purposes of this text we chose, in the preceding chapter, not to distinguish sharply between conditioning and other forms of learning. Conditioning, in its various forms, was treated as part of the totality of ways in which learning occurs. In the same way, we shall make no formal distinction between the *effects* of learning and experience. The reader should be aware, however, that just as conditioning and learning are differentiated by some psychologists with conditioning viewed as a subclass of learning, so are learning and experience differentiated. Experience is perhaps the more general concept, just as the term "learning" is more general than the term "conditioning." Experience refers to any condition of stimulation which impinges on the organism (the child) in such a way as to create a change from a previous state. The change may be a momentary startle or a cry of distress. Learning usually refers to changes caused by the formation or strengthening of the association between a stimulus and a response (a bit of behavior).

Not all experience, therefore, involves learning. Certain experiences, for instance, may serve to release behavior on a fairly innate basis. If a loud noise startles a child or causes him to cry, he may not have learned anything. No new association may have been created or strengthened. Experiences such as perceiving certain events in the environment may cause changes in the way that a child thinks. Repeatedly perceiving certain environmental events may, over time, cause changes in the child's understanding (cognitive structure) of how certain events in the world relate to each other. Although some psychologists dispute that in such cases bonds between stimuli and responses are being either formed or strengthened, other psychologists believe that this is exactly what is happening. As already stated, however, there are instances where the environment clearly can effect what the child does without learning having occurred. In such cases it is best to use the term experience since the formation or strengthening of associations is not involved.

We have already seen that both factors of physiological growth and effects of experience and learning influence the acquisition and socialization of behavior. From this point on we will begin to explore the interaction of these factors in more detail. We shall see that just as it is sometimes difficult to distinguish sharply between experience and learning, it is also difficult to distinguish between the effects of experience and innate physiological growth factors in tracing the course of development in childhood.

MATURATION

Some new behaviors can be attributed chiefly to the growth and readiness of bodily structures rather than primarily to experience or learning. Maturation is considered to be largely under genetic control. Certain behaviors develop in almost all infants and children, unless they are severely handicapped environmentally or genetically. The sequence of their development is fairly regular and takes place in about the same order in most human infants. The cause of these behaviors is largely physiological. Their course of development or rate of growth may be altered by factors of nutrition, temperature, or variations in physical stimulation, but they tend to appear despite considerable variations in environmental conditions.[3, 12, 20] Such behaviors have been termed maturational, or the result of maturation. Sitting up, crawling, walking, and infant babbling are all considered to be chiefly maturational in nature.

MATURATION AND PSYCHOLOGY

If one is interested in the *psychology* of child development, many of the behaviors due to maturation, like walking or being able to pick up a cup, are not of very much interest in themselves. They are important because they change the child's relationship to the environment. Being able to walk, for instance, extends the range of objects that the child is able to get to, examine and manipulate. It enables him to get further away from the mother and try out more things on his own. As a function of being able to walk, the scope of his learning experiences may widen sharply. The study of maturation, for its own sake, is really a problem in developmental biology and is often taken up in a book in that area or one in physiology or pediatric medicine.[19, 22]

Biological growth and the emergence of the ability to sense things, ingest foods, locomote, and make sounds have been built in by nature through evolution. Although maturation is a very important general factor in human growth, for many psychologists its importance lies chiefly in the fact that it makes much of learning possible. Maturation, taken alone, seldom produces new behaviors of great psychological significance. There is not much psychology operating in the act of walking. However, the maturation of physiological bodily structures and the development of certain bodily activities enable the child to learn behaviors which are psychologically significant. The maturation and readiness to respond of physical structures, when associated with teaching by the mother and other socializing agents, or with self-directed activity by the infant, can lead to processes of psychological importance.[8, 19, 22] Learning a specific skill often cannot begin until the organism is maturationally able to master it. Experience and self-initiated activity leading to development must sometimes await the maturation of certain bodily structures and functions.

MATURATION AND EXPERIENCE

There is often no way to separate maturational factors from conditions of extraorganismic stimulation, that is, from experience. Readiness, experience, and environment are partly reciprocal. Maturational factors constantly interact with environmental effects. Indeed, they require environmental support even to emerge. Although the tadpole begins to swim without any previous practice, it can swim farther and faster if it does get practice.[16, 17] Both the ring dove and the chimpanzee develop a better ability to discriminate between various perceptual patterns if they get certain kinds of early visual experiences. Rates of bodily growth and motor abilities in young children are partly dependent on the caloric intake of the infant, the nature of his early nutrition, and possibly such factors as climate, amount of handling by the mother, and degree of restraint by clothes.[4, 6, 11, 27] These may be important for rates of growth and are inseparable from factors of genotypic inheritance.[9] As in the case of genetics and behavior, the question to be raised is how physiological development, whatever its causes, interacts with factors of experience and learning to produce the psychological characteristics one chooses to study. In the past it had been erroneously assumed that children were not ready to develop some activity and could not grasp some concept even though no one had really arranged the proper conditions for learning.[1] Certain kinds of experiences may well speed maturational readiness and learning.[14, 23, 24, 25]

PRACTICE AND PRIVATION

An interesting result of some studies concerned with maturation has been the demonstration that unless a particular stage of physiological readiness for the performance of certain acts has been reached, a whole range of environmental stimulation may have little or no effect. Of course, in some cases, the people involved may just not have been clever enough to provide the conditions of learning that lead to early mastery.[13, 18] It has been shown for certain human behaviors, in any event, that practice at an early stage of maturation of the physical systems on which they depend does little or nothing for the child. Some functions, like vision, are ready very early and profit almost from birth from experience, whereas others profit little. Study 5.1 illustrates this point.

TRAINING BEFORE MATURATIONAL READINESS

STUDY 5.1

In two separate studies, Gesell and Thompson, and McGraw, tried to see if early training in motor skills, like walking or climbing, would enable the child to do them sooner or better. In both cases they used twins, of whom one got special training and one did not.

Gesell and Thompson tried to train one twin to climb stairs at an early age while they did not try to train the other; in fact, the untrained twin was kept away from stairs. As soon as the trained twin was able to climb up the stairs his twin was turned loose to try it also. It turned out that he could almost at once climb the stairs just as well. Since he was maturationally ready, he could climb the stairs as soon as the trained twin could. Training was largely a waste of time.

In McGraw's study one twin received no special training and the other one was trained in a variety of motor skills. In skills such as walking, the special training did little good.

Training, in both cases, did give one twin some advantage if special skills like roller skating were involved. If some particularly special skill was taught, one twin could obviously do it while the other couldn't. However, the important fact is that once an attempt to teach the untrained twin was instituted he caught up quite fast. Once a child is maturationally ready, and if early deprivation is not too long or severe, he will become the equal of others who were trained early when he is given a chance to practice and perform.

Gesell, A., and Thompson, H. Learning and growth in identical twins. *Genet. Psychol. Monogr.*, 6, 1929, 1-124. McGraw, M. B. *Growth: A Study of Johnny and Jimmy.* Appleton-Century, New York, 1935.

In addition, it has been shown that *limited* reduction in certain types of environmental stimulation does not necessarily lead to strongly adverse results in the ability to perform certain behaviors. The effects found may depend on the extent and time of the deprivations. With extensive deprivations severe incapacity may develop. The time, or critical period, of maturation during which restriction or deprivation takes place may also be crucial.[25, 28, 30] Study 5.2 shows how some restrictions on motor and social responses may have significant but minor, rather than major, effects.

PRIVATION AND MATURATION

STUDY 5.2

W. Dennis and his wife, Marsena G. Dennis raised a pair of fraternal girl twins under partially restricted conditions. They did not impose the conditions until the girls were over a month old and they removed the restrictions when they were a year and two months old. The study is partly complicated by the fact that one of the girls had a minor brain injury at birth. This may well have retarded her somewhat in some areas of development.

This was not a very well controlled study, so only tentative conclusions can be drawn from it. The restrictions included the following measures. No pictures or decorations were placed in the room where the twins were raised. The door was kept closed and the Dennises went in only to care for the twins, observe them, and experiment with them. A screen was kept between their beds. Few other people saw the twins. They were not rewarded or punished for anything they did and they were not handled much; nor were they spoken to. The Dennises did not try to teach them anything and they tried to avoid doing things the twins could imitate.

On the other hand, the environment was not barren. The twins, through a window, could see the sky and tree tops. They were fed, changed, and bathed. They could see each other when taken from their cribs and they did see other people on occasion. Although the twins were not spoken to, the Dennises talked to each other in front of them at times. There was furniture in the room to see and traffic and other noises to hear. Clearly, privation was present but stimulation was present also.

The Dennises recorded at what age (by weeks) each of the girls could do each of 50 behaviors. A sample of these includes: follow moving object (with eyes), smile at a person, grasp objects, vocalize to person, watch own hands, sit alone, rise to sitting, creep, and take a few steps alone. In general, the twins, particularly the one injured at birth, showed retardation in motor and social responses. The retardation, however, was not major and they seemed to develop their behaviors in the proper order. The restricted twins developed the behaviors that nonrestricted children have by three months, at about the same age. In behaviors developed after three months of age by normal children, they tended to be later, but did develop them. This was most clearly the case for the twin without brain damage, who followed an orderly developmental sequence. That is to say, for instance, she first sat, then crept, then walked holding on to furniture, then walked alone, as most children do.

Dennis, W. Infant development under conditions of restricted practice and minimal social stimulation. *Genet. Psychol. Monogr.*, 23, 1941, 143-189.

These early studies of maturation are not as instructive as they could be. Their conceptualization suffered from the "nature vs. nurture" type of thinking. Consciously or not, there was interest in either ascribing behavior to some sort of innate, predetermined unfolding or, conversely, in trying to show that it was really experience that counted after all. This issue was, in the past, misconceptualized. The term *maturation*, consequently, can no longer even be found in the index of one of the leading books on child development and personality.[21] Psychologists are no longer interested in fighting the war over innate determinants of behavior versus the effects of experience. They are interested in how behavior develops under conditions which include both innate and experiential determinants. The determinants may be partly innate structurally and partly the result of environment or learning. It is merely important to understand all of the factors involved.

MATURATION AND EXPERIENCE — DIFFERENT PROCESSES?

It is usually only possible to state that some behaviors, capacities, and abilities seem to owe more to a differential physical development than to environmental variations. It is even unclear what "more" means since no behavior could exist without both determinants. The distinction, as suggested above, may in fact prove, eventually, to be theoretically undesirable. It may also be unprofitable, or at least often highly difficult, to try to untangle biological from environmental effects. Racial differences in growth rates and motor development (skill in using the body) furnish a good illustration of this proposition. Study 5.3 concerns maturational differences and is presented since other studies also have shown that Negro newborns are more advanced than white newborns in early motor behavior as well as early skeletal maturation.

MENTAL AND MOTOR ABILITY FROM ONE TO 15 MONTHS

STUDY 5.3

Nancy Bayley compared the motor and mental test scores of 1409 infants aged one to 15 months. Revised forms of The Bayley Scales of Mental and Motor Development were administered to these infants in 12 cities. The population was representative of parents of young children in accordance with the 1960 census. Comparisons of the average scores for different children at each of the 15 months were made for various parts of the sample. For instance, the scores of groups of Negro children were compared with the scores of groups of white children of one month of age, two months of age, and at each month level up to 15 months of age. This is called the "cross-sectional" method. In the "longitudinal method" measurements are made on the same children, at periodic intervals, as they get older. In the cross-sectional method, each child is tested only once. Different children are tested at each of the various age levels represented. Both methods are ways of saying something about the average child at any age level.

No differences were found between Negroes and whites on the mental scale. This finding is relatively meaningless since mental test scores early in life are unstable and do not correlate, in any event, with intelligence scores later in life.

Negro babies tended to score consistently above white infants on the motor ability scale. Puerto Rican babies were identical to the whites. There were no differences in motor ability between boys and girls, in association with the education of the father, or in geographic residence. The motor superiority of the Negro infants, therefore, may well be a maturational difference; probably, but not certainly, genetically transmitted. There may, however, be some unknown environmental factor responsible for this difference. We will consider this possibility below.

> Bayley, N. Comparison of mental and motor test scores for ages 1-15 months by sex, birth order, race, geographical location and education of parents. *Child Develpm., 24,* 1965, 386-411.

The fact that Negro newborns are more advanced than white newborns in skeletal maturation at birth has been found repeatedly in many countries.[15, 26, 29] Early motor superiority may be based on this advanced skeletal maturation. This advancement, however, decreases with age, and the Negro child is usually behind the white child in skeletal maturation by three years. It has been suggested that the Negro child finally falls behind the white child due to receiving poorer nutrition.[8, 9, 10] It is a possible hypothesis that his initial advantage may be truly due to some difference in genotype.[8, 9] The maturation of teeth, to add to the hypothesis above, is also ahead in young Negro children. However, between three and four years of age this advantage is also lost and Negro children fall behind.[5, 8, 9] African Negro children from Dakar grow significantly faster at birth than European white children and do so until about nine months of age. At one year of age, however, the Negro children are growing at a slower rate than the European ones studied. By four years of age Negro children from Dakar and the white children from Europe are growing at the same rate.[8, 9]

Falkner, who has summarized the findings above, has pointed out several important points to consider if one tries to explain these findings.[8, 9] One hundred percent of Dakar infants are breast fed as against sixty percent of the babies in one of the European samples. The Dakar baby gets a different quality and quantity of caloric intake and shows changes in growth rate after weaning. The infant in Dakar remains constantly with his mother.

Let us ask some questions relating to these facts. Does more bodily contact with the mother make for early motor superiority? (African babies, in addition, are more likely to die in infancy than European ones, so only the hardier ones survive.) In the differential maturation of growth what is due to genotype, what to nutrition, and what to the fact that those who survive are the ones measured? What about the nutrition and living conditions of the Negro versus the white mother between conception and birth? Do the expectant Negro and white mothers get a similar diet? Does a mother who is always with her infant feed him more? Does the white infant learn to demand food less often? Are Negro children less confined with clothes, and would that make a difference in growth rate or motor skills at an early age? These questions are raised to show that maturational and experimental factors may interact in ways that makes separating them very difficult and perhaps not really theoretically useful. The types of studies that would have to be done to get definitive answers to such questions may not be feasible for practical, and possibly ethnical, reasons.

SUMMARY

Changes involved in development usually depend on the experiences of the child. Some of these experiences involve innate responses released by certain classes of stimuli, others cause changes in cognitive structure (understanding), and still others are involved in learning, the formation and strengthening of associations between stimuli and responses.

However, some of the new behaviors which a child acquires as he grows and changes psychologically are attributed largely to maturation rather than primarily to experience. Maturation is considered to be largely under genetic control, rather than due to learning, and it is believed to represent increments in physiologically coordinated abilities which emerge under a wide variety of environmental circumstances. Such behaviors as sitting up, walking and babbling are considered by many to be maturational in nature. Abilities considered to be maturationally caused, whatever processes best account for them, certainly change the child's relationship to his environment by allowing him greater opportunities for interaction and mastery.

It seems that certain behavioral abilities appear in a fairly regular order despite some differences in experience and are heavily dependent on physical changes. Although we saw in an earlier chapter that severe deprivation or privation can be deleterious, mild restriction, at least for limited periods, may not retard maturation seriously. However, it is worth recognizing that it is seldom possible to separate maturation from experience (environmental factors). Maturation does require a supporting environment and differential rates of maturation may be due to environmental factors which favor some children over others. It may be worth investigating, no matter what behavior is involved, if it is feasible, how maturation (innate physical) and experimental factors interact. It may not be theoretically sound to make a clear distinction between maturation and experiences, however, as causes of change any more than between genetic and environmental causes.

REFERENCES

1. Bandura, A., and Walters, R. H. *Social Learning and Personality Development.* Holt, Rinehart, and Winston. New York, 1963.
2. Bayley, N. Comparison of mental and motor text scores for ages 1-15 months by sex, birth order, race, geographical location, and education of parents. *Child Develpm., 24,* 1965, 386-411.
3. Bayley, N. The development of motor abilities during the first three years. *Monogr. Soc. Res. Child Develpm., No. 1,* 1935.
4. Bovard, E. W. The effects of early handling viability of the albino rat. *Psychol. Rev., 65,* 1958, 257-271.
5. Chagula, W. K. The age of eruption of permanent first molars in male East Africans. *Amer. J. Phys. Anthrop., 18,* 1960, 77-82.
6. Chow, K. L., and Nissen, H. W. Interocular transfer of learning in visually naive and experienced infant chimpanzees. *J. Comp. Physiol. Psychol., 48,* 1959, 229-232.
7. Dennis, W. Infant development under conditions of restricted practice and minimal social stimulation. *Genet. Psychol. Mongr., 23,* 1941, 143-189.
8. Falkner, F. (Ed.) *Human Development.* W. B. Saunders, Philadelphia, 1966.
9. Falkner, F. General considerations in human development. (In) *Human Development,* Falkner, F. (Ed.). W. B. Saunders, Philadelphia, 1966.
10. Falkner, F. et al. Some international comparisons of physical growth in the first two years of life. *Courrier, 8,* 1958, 1-11.
11. Forgus, R. H. The effects of early perceptual learning on the behavioral organization of adult rats. *J. Comp. Physiol. Psychol., 47,* 1954, 322-328.
12. Gesell, A. Maturation and infant behavior pattern. *Psychol. Rev., 36,* 1929, 307-319.
13. Gesell, A., and Thompson, H. Learning and growth in identical twins. *Genet. Psychol. Monogr., 6,* 1929, 1-124.
14. Hamburger, V. The concept of development: An issue in the study of human behavior. (In) *The Concept of Development,* Harris, D. B. (Ed.). University of Minnesota Press, Minneapolis, 1957.
15. Jones, P. R. M., and Dean, F. R. A. The effect of kwashiorkor on the development of bones of the hand. *J. Trop. Pediat., 2,* 1956, 51-68.
16. McGraw, M. B. Maturation of Behavior. (In) *Manual of Child Psychology,* Carmichael, L. (Ed.). John Wiley, New York, 1946.
17. McGraw, M. B. *The Neuromuscular Maturation of the Human Infant.* Columbia University Press, New York, 1943.
18. McGraw, M. B. *Growth: A study of Johnny and Jimmy.* Appleton Century, New York, 1935.
19. Marlow, D. R. *Pediatric Nursing.* 3rd Edition. W. B. Saunders, Philadelphia, 1965.
20. Marquis, D. G. The criterion of innate behavior. *Psychol. Rev. 37,* 1930, 334-349.
21. Mussen, P. H., Conger, J. J., and Kagan, J. *Child Development and Personality.* Harper and Row, New York, 1963.
22. Nelson, W. E. (Ed.) *Textbook of Pediatrics.* 8th Edition. W. B. Saunders, Philadelphia, 1964.

23. Rashkis, H. A. A general theory of treatment in psychiatry. *A.M.A. Arch. Neurol. and Psychiat., 78,* 1957, 491-499.
24. Scott, J. P. Critical period in the development of social behavior in puppies. *Psychosom. Med., 20,* 1958, 42-54.
25. Scott, J. P. The genetic and environmental differentiation in behavior. (In) *The Concept of Development,* Harris, D. B. (Ed.). University of Minnesota Press, Minneapolis, 1957.
26. Scott, R. B., et al. Growth and development in Negro infants. *Pediatrics, 16,* 1955, 24-29.
27. Siegel, A. I. Deprivation of visual form definition in the ring dove. *J. Comp. Physiol. Psychol., 46,* 1953, 115-119.
28. Spitz, R. A. Hospitalism: A follow-up report on investigations described in Vol. I, 1945. (In) *The Psychoanalytic Study of the Child,* Freud, A., et al. (Eds.), International Universities Press, New York, 1946.
29. Tompkins, W. T., and Wiehl, D. G. Epiphyseal maturation in the newborn as related to maternal nutritional status. *Amer. J. Obstet. Gynec., 68,* 1954, 1366-1377.
30. Yarrow, L. J. Maternal Deprivation. *Psychol. Bull., 58,* 1961, 459-490.

CHAPTER 6

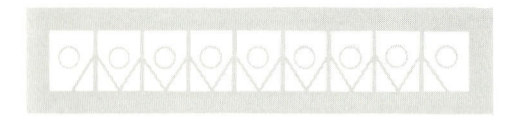

MOTIVATIONAL AND COGNITIVE PROCESSES

PART 1 — SOCIALIZATION OF MOTIVES

By age three the child is no longer a toddler. His motor functions are under control, and are no longer interesting as newly acquired stunts. The child's interests begins to turn even more toward his surroundings and "why" questions multiply on every pretext. What motives are involved in his boundless energy and curiosity? What new influences mold his reactions to people and events? It seems that the continuing socialization of motives and further growth of intellectual ability, including the use of language in problem solving, are very important developmental processes from three to six.

Motivation refers to persistent, energized, and directed patterns of behavior. The behavior is directed toward some goal. For example, the child who runs after his mother, calls to her, and reaches up his arms until he is picked up, is displaying dependency motivation. Being picked up is the goal and he shows energy, persistence, and direction (toward the mother) until that goal is reached. Dependency, sexual, aggressive, and other motives are learned. They may have innate components, but the child has to learn what the appropriate goals are and how to reach them.

SOCIALIZATION OF SEXUAL MOTIVATION

The Freudian Formulation

The child, according to this view, has gone through the *oral stage* (the baby at the breast) and the *anal stage* (the toddler on the potty) and has arrived at the *phallic stage* (the Oedipus complex) by the time he is about three years of age. Each stage is characterized by the predominance of libidinal satisfaction at a particular part of the body: oral, anal, or genital. *Libido* is supposedly a biological energy which has the aim of pleasure through reduction of sexual tension. The classic Freudian approach sees sexual motivation as derived chiefly from the libidinal drive, which is said to come into conflict with the social demands made on the child by the parents. The demands of the parents that the child learn to control his sexual, aggressive, and other impulses are said to produce typical crises which must be weathered successfully to ensure the child's continuing normal psychological development. Severe mishandling can produce serious conflicts at any stage.[20, 21, 22, 23] We shall describe Freud's theories on development in greater detail in a later chapter on stage theories of development.

This summary is of course simplified, and does not represent the complexity of this aspect of Freudian theory. Oral and anal activities are very important as the child proceeds from birth to age three, as Freud noted, but much more is going on in this age period than the Freudians describe. These other behaviors include play, exploration, manipulation, locomotion, and the acquisition of language.

Feeding and weaning behaviors and toilet training have been discussed in an earlier chapter. They are aspects of life with which every child must cope. Freudian theory emphasizes the pleasurable qualities of sucking and elimination, hence the conflicts over weaning and toilet training. The conflict over doing what the parents want occurs during a general move toward independence on the toddler's part and is probably best thought of as only one aspect of the socialization process, although an important one. Children learn much more in the first three years of life than how and what to eat and to go to the toilet. Nor is most of their time spent on these activities or in solving their conflicts about eating and toilet training.

The Oedipus complex, described by Freud, beginning sometime after three, is an abstraction from a large variety of behaviors. The boy may decide he wants to marry his mother when he grows up and is jealous of his father. He compares his anatomy with his father's and feels he can never compete. He looks at his sister or mother, the Freudians say, and wonders if their penis was taken away because they were bad, and if his might be taken away, too. Girls envy their brothers: "I'm so plain and he's so fancy." The love their father and are jealous of their mother. Many children do show many of these reactions. Children are curious about sex differences and begin to wonder where babies come from, as they notice differences in age. As we will see below, however, they are curious about many other things besides, and it seems unlikely that intrinsic sexual (or libidinal) motivation is the all-powerful determinant of childhood behavior that Freud thought it to be.

Cultural Influences on Sexuality

Long before they reach sexual maturity, children show forms of behavior that are regarded in North American society as having sexual implications. For example, fingering the genitals, exposing them to others, or looking at the genitals of others are considered to be sexual responses. There are attempts by the parents to stop such behavior. In contrast, parents in some societies regard actions of this kind as either having less sexual significance or they are more free about permitting such behavior. Chidren are allowed to run around naked, weather permitting, and parents may rub the baby's genitals to soothe him.[107] Study 6.1 gives an example of behavior in a culture relatively permissive of such behaviors in young children.

CHILDREN'S PLAY IN A SOCIETY PERMISSIVE TOWARD SEXUAL BEHAVIOR IN CHILDREN

STUDY 6.1

Three children are playing together: Marina is six, Chlorea is two, Alfonso, who joints them, is four. These children are Mixtecan Indians of Juxtlahuaca, Mexico. (Marina has playfully pushed Chlorea and Alfonso to the ground. Marina and Chlorea lie on their backs, laughing.)

Alfonso comes toward her and takes off his cotton trousers that he had on. He stands there nude and then throws his trousers over Marina. Marina gets up on her hands and feet, covered with the trousers and she cries, "Oh," from underneath them. Then she uncovers herself, sits down, and then stands up laughing. Alfonso throws himself upon her and cries. "Now I've got you," and the two children roll around on the ground kicking and laughing. Chlorea has gone a few steps away. Chlorea picks up a rock from the patio and puts it into her mouth. Marina watches, stands up and walks over to Chlorea, taking the stone away from her and hitting her on the hand, saying to her very seriously, "You shouldn't eat that." Chlorea begins to cry. Marina runs and again throws herself on Alfonso, and they whirl on the ground. A teenage girl standing on the edge of the patio says "Hurry up, Chlorea, run and hit Marina." At that moment Arelia Grusmon (mother of Marina) comes into the patio. She is carrying a basket. Marina stands up laughing, jumps on one foot, and cries "Ah, my mother's come." Arelia goes into the cook shack. Marina returns and throws herself on Alfonso, who is lying on the ground still naked. The two children roll around laughing. Marina puts her finger on Alfonso's anus and laughing hits him with the other hand. The boy pulls her hair. She squeezes the boy's testicles with her hand and cries "I'm going to hit you on the rear end." She laughs. Alfonso sits up, and also laughing, hits Chlorea lightly on the head. (Chlorea had stopped crying and had approached the other children.) The little girl starts to cry again. Marina puts her arms about her and caresses her head: then Marina looks at Alfonso as if she were angry and says, "Go on, you donkey, get up." Alfonso again throws himself on her, and the two roll around on the ground laughing.

The authors go on to say that the three children did seem more active and excited in their play than ordinarily, probably because of its sexual nature. Several adults were around, who took no steps to interfere or interrupt. They add, "Judging from other observations, it would be our guess that in about two years they will begin to ridicule behavior of this kind." Sex play is regulated in this society, but in a relatively permissive manner.

Romney, K., and Romney, R. The Mixtecans of Juxtlahuaca, Mexico. (In) *Six Cultures: Studies of Child Rearing*, Whiting, B. B. (Ed.). Yale University Press, New Haven, 1953. pp. 650-660.

American Treatment of the Sexual Motive

American parents control children's sexual motivation mainly by transmitting to their children their own anxiety reactions, which indicate disapproval of the sexual exploration, manipulation, and curiosity that inevitably occur during childhood. Parents insist that certain parts of the body be concealed even from other family members and react to exposure with evident concern. When a child manipulates his genitals or touches parts of an adult's body that has sexual significance for the child, the parent prevents the manipulative act by removing the child's hands and by presenting distracting stimuli. The mother may take the boy's hand away from his penis and place a toy into his hand instead. Another parent may remove the hand and say: "No, no." Still another may resort to striking the child's hand. Children thus learn that certain regions of the body and certain exploratory acts are taboo. Much of this negative conditioning occurs before the child is fully aware of the sexual significance of the prohibitions, so that exploration itself may seem to be the punished response. Learning modesty is an important act in childhood and becomes well established between the ages of three and six.

When children seek information about sex differences and the reproductive process, many parents give the minimum amount of information, avoid labeling body parts, give nonhuman or actually false examples (the birds and bees, the stork), exhibit considerable anxiety, and attempt to postpone explanations by saying that the child is too young to understand. This is in marked contrast to the way middle-class parents react to other of their children's questions, which are given all sorts of positive attention.[88]

For obvious reasons, experimental studies of most forms of sex behavior are practically nonexistent. The available research data come mainly from questionnaire and interview studies.[5, 47, 48, 88, 107] These studies have found that children whose fathers were permissive of nudity, permissive and nonpunitive for sex play with other children, and willing to give information about sex matters, tended to show little anxiety and guilt about sex. Children also showed little sex guilt if their mothers were nonpunitive for sex play and readily provided sex information.[6]

Deviant sexual behavior often appears to be the result of active parental encouragement and reward, such as close physical intimacy, for sexual responses inappropriate for the sex or age of the child. This was found to be the case in an example of extreme transvestitism (wearing clothes of the opposite sex) in a five-year-old boy, who constantly dressed in his mother's clothes, including cosmetics and jewelry, and had adopted a girl's name suggested to him by his mother. The grandmother and neighbors also supplied him with feminine clothes.[54]

In our culture the learning of sex rules is a complicated task for the child from three to six. He finds stimulation of his genitals pleasurable, and he is curious about differences between the sexes and between age groups. Yet in this area parents often react in unpredictable ways, with anger, evasions, and other anxiety-producing behavior. Many parents avoid labeling sex behavior as such, but call it "silly," or "dangerous," or "naughty." Parents may say, "You're feeling angry, and that's why you did that," but few parents will say, "You're feeling sexy, that's why you did that."[88] Sexual motivation is simply never allowed any direct expression by the formal arrangements of the culture until adolescence and then it is still surrounded by many prohibitions and rules. The small child is supposed to smother and ignore his genital sensations; and not even to think about them. However, parents seldom succeed in entirely supressing sexual interst and activity in children.

Other motivations are less ignored and repressed. Among these more favorably viewed motives, at least for young children, is that of dependency.

SOCIALIZATION OF DEPENDENCY MOTIVATION

The persistent seeking of nearness or physical contact, help, attention, reassurance, or approval from others is considered a sign of dependency motivation. The dependency motive is partly established by the processes of social attachment described in Chapter 4. Since the baby is born completely at the mercy of his caretakers, and only gradually learns to do things for himself, dependent behavior is highly rewarded, at least for a year or two, in most societies. The number and duration of such rewards vary considerably, however.[107, 108] Although in the United States the child is expected to learn to perform certain tasks early in childhood, he is expected to remain emotionally somewhat dependent on parents and friends. If he is not, he is likely to be considered psychologically abnormal. He is to be independent in *doing things* but reasonably emotionally dependent on his parents and older siblings. Of course, if the child shows excessive emotional dependence, he is also likely to be considered abnormal. Some middle range of emotional dependency is desired.

The amount of dependency to be shown is often a matter of cultural learning. Pejorative labels are attached to overdependent children; they are said to be clinging, demanding, attention seeking, whiney, and so on. Children who show less than the desired amount are called cold, stand-offish, withdrawn, unfriendly, or hostile. This is in marked contrast to the sexual area, where a total lack of response (identifiable by the parent as sexual) will be regarded with relief. If the child shows a lack of sexual behavior he will be considered "good" in that area of behavior. At least this is so until early adolescence when certain mild forms of sex are approved.

Some part of the differences in dependent behavior in children may be constitutional. Some boys, especially, seem never to want to be cuddled even from a very early age.[87] In general, however, the three to six year old is reasonably emotionally dependent, although more independent than younger children in doing tasks.

Moderate dependency responses elicit positive attending and ministering responses from others.[5] If they are of too high frequency or inappropriately timed, the caretaker may pretend to be unable to respond, or may pretend not to notice. If the child then proceeds to insist on attention by negative behavior such as kicking or whining, it is sometimes hard to tell whether his actions should still be classified as dependent, or as aggressive. In any case, the interaction is likely to deteriorate into a less than cordial one on both sides. Most parents agree that children should show *some* independence.[17] Children from three to six are expected to dress themselves, pick up their toys, and so on.

There are positive relationships between parental demonstrativeness and the warmth and the dependency of children.[5, 52, 85, 88] Such behaviors on the part of parents may foster dependency. Study 6.2 gives an example of such a relationship. It demonstrates that the degree of a child's dependency may well be a function of how much the parents encourage the child to be dependent.

INDIRECT EVIDENCE OF THE INFLUENCE OF PARENTAL BEHAVIOR ON DEPENDENCY IN CHILDREN

STUDY 6.2

In this study, six- to twelve-year-old children were blindfolded and asked to walk along a narrow, wobbly plank, mounted on springs, about a foot off the floor. When the child had stepped up on one end of the plank, the experimenter touched the back of his hand and waited to see if he would accept or refuse the implied help. Measures of parental behavior had been collected previously. Results showed that children who accepted the helping hand on the first trial of walking the plank tended to have child-centered parents. Such parents encouraged their children to lean on others and to some extent held them back from developing skills appropriate to their age.

Heathers, G. Emotional dependence and independence in a physical threat situation. *Child Developm.*, 24, 1953, 169-179.

Factors Affecting the Socialization of Dependency Motivation

In contrast to aggression and sex, a moderate amount of dependency in children is considered a good thing. A few experiments have been done linking the reward of dependency responses with amount of dependency shown.[14, 69] Reward for dependency results in increased dependency responses toward the rewarding agent, whereas punishment eventually leads to a decrease of such responses. Some children are rewarded more often than others when they show dependency. More frequent reward for dependency produces a stronger dependency motive. Children with a strong dependency motive are more likely to change their behavior on the basis of whether others approve of their acts or not.

Actual physical approach to others is the essential component of dependent behavior. The susceptibility to social influence can be seen as merely the tendency to approach others, interacting with level of arousal.[104] If a child becomes aroused in the presence of others and tends to approach them he can be more easily influenced.

Dependency goes along with helping others: nursery school children who often seek help and attention, also often give frequent, attentive, affectionate, protective, and reassuring responses to their peers.[25] They treat others as their parents probably treat them and such children tend to be popular. Children who interact frequently with others are remembered by other children.[56]

Early punishment of dependency is actually likely to increase the child's efforts to obtain dependency rewards, since the young child has needs which only an adult can satisfy. Eventually, however, severe rejection by the parent leads to a drop in dependency responses.[7, 109] When rejection means withholding rewards, rather than punishment, dependency may continue to increase for some time.[25, 30] This is most likely to occur if the child's past experiences have made him highly dependent[4, 8] However, if reward for dependency is withheld long enough dependent behaviors will finally drop to a very low level.

Many children from three to six are moving towards independence. They may often want to do things for themselves and will refuse help. Mastery of the environment can be most important to a child; consequently, the five and six year old does not cling as much to his mother as the younger child and can tolerate her absence for fairly long periods. Children often find being able to do things themselves highly rewarding.

SOCIALIZATION OF AGGRESSIVE MOTIVATION

It is a rare parent who has not ever heard his young child say "I hate you," or who has not been attacked by foot, fist, or teeth. Some parts of the socialization process are often frustrating for children in the United States. There are countless breakable objects to be avoided, spillable things encountered, incomprehensible rules to comply with, and a myriad of other pitfalls. The relationship between frustration and aggression will be covered in a later chapter; here it will suffice to say that frustration can lead to aggression, and this is as true for the young child as for anyone else. It should be noted that the Freudians consider aggression to be instinctual. They believe that aggression is due to an innate inner drive which must be expressed in one way or another.

Aggression is variously defined, but it is usually considered *intentional*; the aggressor is performing an action which injures another person on purpose. Bumping someone by accident is not thought of as aggressive. An intense response is more often called aggressive than a

122 MOTIVATIONAL AND COGNITIVE PROCESSES

mild one; the *intensity* is an important factor in determining whether or not it will produce injury or pain.[5]

The amount of aggression that is allowed, and the way it may be expressed, varies from one culture to the next, and usually differs for males and females.[107, 108] Next to sex, aggression is the most prohibited type of behavior for American children. The amount and type of aggression allowed is socially determined.

Study 6.3 describes the handling of aggression in young children in one Okinawan village. It shows how the expression of aggression is a function of how the people in a given culture stimulate and control it.

AGGRESSION IN THE OKINAWAN PRESCHOOL CHILD

STUDY 6.3

Aggression in children up to school age is generally tolerated although adults do not approve of such behavior. Because they feel that preschool children change their minds and moods so rapidly, adults do not interfere with their altercations. Parents laughingly explain, 'Play and fight are children's work.' Some parents attempt to channel aggression by calling a wrestling match between boys who start arguing. In this way, rock throwing and fighting with sticks are avoided, and the boys can work off their anger; but hitting and pushing, as well as rock throwing, were observed among children of this age. As the children approach school age and gain facility in language, they resort more and more to verbal aggression; however some physical aggression is carried over in the behavior of boys toward girls. At no time is aggression toward younger children tolerated.

Boys are expected to be more aggressive than girls, who are, ideally, docile, gentle, mannerly, kind, reserved, and considerate. In some ways, adults seem to train little boys to be aggressive. Beginning in infancy, they tease and bully them, holding their arms and restricting them bodily, withdrawing desired objects and pretending to scold and hit. They glean great amusement at the expense of the child if he screams and strikes out in anger. The adult expresses surprise and mock anger. Finally, when he cries, everyone will laugh while the mother responds by playfully slapping the child. Although most of this kind of teasing is restricted to male infants and young boys, female children are not entirely exempt.

Maretzki, T. W., and Maretzki, H. Taira: An Okinawan village. (In) *Six Cultures: Studies of Child Rearing*, Whiting, B. B. (Ed.). John Wiley, New York, 1963, pp. 363-539.

SOCIALIZATION OF MOTIVATED BEHAVIOR

Study 6.3 illustrates a fact that is often overlooked in the discussion of motives: they are not expressed indiscriminately. Most motives are directed by training into socially approved channels. In the United States, the small child may hug and kiss and say he loves his mother, but he is not encouraged to pat his mother's breasts, although all of these behaviors *might* be classified as sexual. A certain minimal amount of aggression is considered desirable, and encouraged. Children may be trained to fight back if they are attacked by other children, but may never be allowed to hit their parents. Yet again, a child may be encouraged to be cuddly and dependent with his parents but discouraged from attaching himself too closely to older children, and told to be wary of strangers.

The expression of motives may be specific rather than general. Often a child will act quite differently at nursery school than at home, partly because different behaviors are expected of him. The child who never talks back to his parents may joyfully boss his schoolmates. Different behaviors may be learned in one place than another and different circumstances may encourage varying responses. It is then not very meaningful to talk about an "aggressive child" without specifying under what circumstances aggressive acts appear, and what form the acts take. This kind of analysis makes the reasons for the behavior clearer and opens the way for simple environmental control of undesirable behavior. Study 6.4 illustrates one approach for the control of one girl's excessive dependency on adults and self-isolation from children in nursery school. It shows how the expression of motives may be changed or channeled.

SOCIALIZATION OF MOTIVATED BEHAVIOR

STUDY 6.4

Ann was four years four months old at the start of the study. (She was in a nursery school group of eight boys and eight girls between four and four and a half years old.) At the beginning of school, Ann interacted often with adults but seldom initiated contact with children or responded to their attempts to play with her. She did not seem severely withdrawn or scared; instead she showed a varied repertory of quite well developed physical and mental skills that drew the interest and attention of adults but failed to gain the companionship of children.

After six weeks of school, a period considered ample for adjustment to the nursery school situation, the teachers made a formal inventory of Ann's behaviors and appraised the time she spent with children, with adults, and by herself. The evaluation revealed that Ann's behavior consisted of isolating herself from children and using many and varied techniques for gaining and prolonging the attention of adults. (The teachers wanted to direct Ann's dependency motivation toward other children and partly away from adults.)

"A plan was instituted to give Ann maximum adult attention contingent on play with another child, and minimum attention upon isolate behavior or upon interactions with an adult when along.... Proximity and interaction with adults and with children were recorded at ten-second intervals.... Before reinforcement procedures were initiated, an objective record was obtained of the acutal amounts of time Ann was spending with children, adults, and alone."

After this preliminary procedure teachers were told to give Ann attention (reward) only when she interacted with children, and to give it every time she did so. As soon as Ann interacted with another child, an adult gave her indirect individual attention. A sample interaction was "Ann, you are making dinner for the whole family." When she ignored other children Ann was not given attention. When she contacted an adult she was relatively ignored (not rewarded) unless she was with another child.

Unfortunately, this approach did not work well. It was soon apparent that this approach to Ann tended somewhat to draw her away from play with children and partly center her on the attention-giving adults. The original procedures were changed. A sample amended operation was, "You three girls have a cozy house! Here are some more cups, Ann, for your tea party." Whenever Ann began to leave the group, the teacher turned away from her and became occupied with some other child or with equipment. Now Ann tended to spend more time with other children.

In order to find out whether the behavior changes effected by the above procedures had indeed been produced by the application of reward only for being with other children, procedures were reversed for five days. After this reversal, the previous pattern of reward was reinstated. Ann again was rewarded for interacting with other children. When she began spending longer periods in continuous interaction with children, adult reward of interaction was gradually made more intermittent until she received adult attention in an amount normal for the group. She no longer received special treatment.

After the last day of systematic reward of interaction, the observers recorded Ann's behavior on four days during the last month of school. The results showed that Ann's play with other children was being consistently maintained.

When the study began Ann was spending a little more than ten percent of the time interacting with children and 40 percent with adults. On day six, when Ann was first given teacher attention only when she was near children or interacting with them, an immediate change in her behavior took place. She spent almost 60 percent of that morning with children. Adult-child interaction dropped to less than 20 percent. When procedures were reversed (when she was rewarded for being with adults), she averaged less than 20 percent of mornings in interaction with children and about 40 percent in interaction with adults. (This was again reversed when training procedures were reinstated.)

This study is an example of planned reward of desired behavior. The effects were double-checked by reversing the procedure part way through and following up behavior after termination of the treatment.

Allen, K. E., et al. Effects of social reinforcement on isolate behavior of a nursery school child. (In) *Case Studies in Behavior Modification*, Ullman, L. P., and Krasner, L.: (Eds.). Holt, Rinehart and Winston, New York, 1965.

POSITIVE ASPECTS OF SOCIALIZATION

Some aspects of socialization are often overlooked; these are the pleasant aspects of the socialization procedure as contrasted to frustrating or conflict producing aspects. After all, as the child begins to master some of the behaviors required of him, he encounters increased attention and praise from adults, who tell him what a big boy he's getting to be, and who may also give him some tangible rewards. As he gets older and more adept, he is given more freedom and new privileges. If the 5-year-old has learned to assemble his own breakfast on Sunday while his parents sleep, he has a chance to choose the amounts and varieties of food he wants, without parental censorship. If he has also learned to put things away afterward, he can get away with quite an unusually satisfying and original breakfast.

A second characteristic of socialization procedures is the child's own satisfaction of mastering new tasks. Most children *want* to be like adults. Furthermore, they enjoy learning new things for their own sake. This latter motivation, as we have already seen, is variously called "competence motivation," "mastery," "curiosity," or "exploratory drive."

Competence Motivation

Development of Competence Motivation

The beginnings of competence motivation were examined in Chapter 3 when we discussed the role of optimum stimulation in development, and the problems encountered in institutionalized children. Youngsters start out with a strong disposition to see, hear, touch, and smell stimuli, to examine them from all angles, to find out all about them. If parents can adjust their pace to a child's, much of the grim quality of child "training" can be avoided, as the child perceives his own progress and enjoys his own increasing mastery of events. The notion of a separate need for competence supplements other theories of motivation. Motives based on strong stimulation, like hunger, do exist. However, there does seem to be something different operating in motives that are relatively independent of strong states of stimulation such as pain, hunger, or anger. When the child explores or manipulates objects he is often considered by adults to be at play. He is motivated but is not experiencing any strong stimulation which he needs to reduce, as in the case of pain or hunger. Such "play" may help the child to master his environment.

White characterizes this point most vividly when he says, referring to Freud's "oral stage," "The model of the feeding child does scant justice to Piaget's son, a youthful Galileo lying in his crib and dropping his celluloid swan from various positions to see where it will fall."[106] The child even under a year old does spend a good bit of time in activities other than eating. He is partly learning how the world operates. Study 6.5 quotes White's statement on competence motivation. It underscores the point that development consists partly of becoming competent in dealing with the environment.

COMPETENCE MOTIVATION

STUDY 6.5

"The concept of competence subsumes the whole realm of learned behavior whereby the child comes to deal effectively with his environment. It includes manipulation, locomotion, language, the building of cognitive maps and skilled actions, and the growth of effective behavior in relation to other people. These acquisitions are made by young animals and children partly through exploratory and manipulative play when drives such as hunger and sex are in abeyance. The directed persistence of such behavior warrants the assumption of a motivation independent of drives, here called effectance motivation, which has its immediate satisfaction in a feeling of efficacy and its adaptive significance in the growth of competence."

White, R. Competence and the Psychosexual Stages of Development. (In) *Nebraska Symposium on Motivation*, Jones, M. (Ed.). University of Nebraska Press, Lincoln, 1960, pp. 137-138.

During the second and third year, the child makes great strides both in verbal ability and in motor skills, and begins to use these talents to test his social competence. His sudden realization that it is possible to say "No" creates many crises. Often they are centered around toilet behavior, but can occur in any situation where obedience is expected. Levy calls this "oppositional behavior."[53] It is a way of resisting external influence and clearing a way for internal control of internal needs. Children who go through an intensely stubborn period are likely to be more independent later on.[33]

The third to sixth years correspond closely to Freud's "phallic stage" of psychosexual development. They also see the developments in language ability, and a marked increase in imagination and fantasy.[18] The child can begin to imagine himself as older or younger, not yet born, or married to his mother. When he can imagine himself not existing, he starts asking questions about birth and death. His curiosity expands in all areas, but is perhaps most embarrassing to the parents in the sexual area and it may seem a truly phallic stage to them, as it did to the Viennese psychoanalyst of the Freudian age. It is during this period of universal curiosity that the child begins to experience shame and guilt in an increasing number of contexts.

Competence, Shame, and Guilt

White suggests that shame is always associated with incompetence.[106] It occurs when the child cannot do something he or someone else thinks he should be able to do, and it involves belittlement and loss of respect. *Shame* is related to being exposed as inadequate in front of others. *Guilt,* on the other hand, implies having done, or thought of, something that one could do, but which the child has learned is *"wrong."* Guilt involves a concept of what is morally right or wrong which the child accepts to some extent.

Up to about seven or even eight years of age, Piaget classifies the child as still in the first stage of moral development.[74] According to Piaget, this is a stage of "moral realism;" it is the amount of damage done, the child believes, that determines his degree of culpability. There is no consideration of intent; a young child thinks that a person who breaks six glasses by accident is more to be punished than the person who broke only one glass on purpose. He regards any accidental injury after a transgression as a real punishment; God is thundering at him personally. He believes that punishment is an expiation for wrong doing, and should be severe. He has, according to Piaget, a unilateral respect for adults, whose rules are absolute. This of course is somewhat of an exaggeration, at least for children brought up in the United States. By the age of five most children seem to have learned that if they shout, "I didn't *mean* to do it!" while backing away from the irate parent, the punishment will be lighter than if they say "Ha, ha, I broke it on purpose!" A variety of social learning factors effect a child's reactions to transgression and quite a few six year olds in America think that it is worse to break one cup on purpose.

If *shame* is accepted as an emotional reaction to incompetence, then it is more or less separate from moral development and is more a cognitive recognition that what one can do does not measure up to the performance that is ideally expected under the given circumstances. This can be considered as a problem in level of aspiration, or perhaps simply of falling short of the ego ideal, as far as it is developed at this age. Freudian theory places the development of the ego ideal at this stage, so that two concepts are compatible. (The ego ideal is the child's concept of the person he would most like to be.)

Guilt can be conceptualized as involving the conscience, as distinct from ideals; it is more directly concerned with punishment for real or imagined transgressions. The learning of guilt reactions can be accounted for in terms of social learning theory. The child may say he is sorry after a transgression (breaking a social rule) and may offer to "make up" for what he has done. The parent reduces the child's anxiety about possible punishment by reacting positively to the atonement offered.[103] Alternatively, the child may learn self-criticism in the process of being punished for his transgression.[2, 3] The child's anxiety is reduced by getting the punishment over with, and his attention is drawn by the punishment to the communication of the adult about the "badness" of his act. The label of "bad" is associated strongly with the act, and also with the reduction of anxiety. Consequently, the next time the child does a similar thing, or even thinks of it, the label "bad" pops into his mind. If he does it anyway, if he criticizes himself as "bad," he feels a little better about it (less anxious) and may go to his parent and further reduce the anxiety through confession. Or, if the thought "bad" is sufficiently upsetting, he may not perform the act at all and may be said to have acquired a conscience. He may feel guilty for even having let the notion enter his mind, in which case an analyst would say that his superego or conscience was overdeveloped. The development of moral behavior and judgment as well as guilt and shame will be discussed more fully in the chapter on internalization.

SUMMARY — PART I

Children display sexual, dependency, and aggressive motivation and they have to learn to satisfy these motives in socially approved ways. Behaviors indicative of these motives are not equally tolerated. In fact, very little sexual behavior of any sort is approved of in childhood and children must suppress nudity, masturbation, looking at or touching other children who are nude, and other behaviors labeled as being "sexual." Some parents are more permissive of such forms of behavior than others are, but sexual acts by children generally make many parents who do not approve of such behavior anxious. Parental anxiety and disapproval about sexuality suppress curiosity about the body and induce guilt in the child about sexual behavior. Parental permissiveness and willingness to answer questions about sex prevent the development of anxiety or guilt about sexual matters.

Parents are generally more tolerant of expressions of dependency than of either sexuality or aggression. Although parents encourage children to accomplish more and more tasks by themselves, they often help their children and frequently enjoy it when their children want to be picked up, hugged or kissed. An average amount of dependent behavior is what most parents desire, neither too much nor too little. Neither overdependency nor underdependency are socially condoned; people dislike the clinging, shy child who always hangs onto his mother, but they equally disapprove of the cold, distant child who dislikes being with others. Aggressive behavior is seldom seen as desirable by parents, except for the child's fighting back when attacked. Fighting, swearing, and other forms of hostility are often discouraged. Generally, the child

130 *MOTIVATIONAL AND COGNITIVE PROCESSES*

has to learn under what circumstances and in what ways he can express aggression and his other motives.

As children become socialized and as they begin to master their environment they develop competence motivation, the goal of which is to be capable and effective. Competence is related to both shame and guilt. The child feels ashamed if some failure or incompetence on his part is exposed to others. Guilt feelings are partly related to knowledge about having failed to live up to some partly self-accepted standard of "moral" conduct. Feelings of guilt depend on the child learning to label as "bad" behaviors for which he was punished in the past.

PART 2 — COGNITIVE PROCESSES

INTELLIGENCE

Most people would agree that a child's competence in dealing with his environment, which largely consists of other people, depends to a considerable degree on his intelligence. Intelligence and the ability to use language become primary factors in the ability to cope with the social environment for the three to six year old.

The inventor of the concept of "intelligence" as used by most people today was Alfred Binet. He created the concept of "intelligence" when he drew up a standard list of questions to ask children, by which to rank them, according to how many they passed or failed, with other children their own age. He assumed that these questions would evaluate how well the child functioned in his everyday activities, although they covered mostly the ability to manipulate language, and, to a lesser extent, numbers. In actuality, the questions did prove to be useful in predicting success in school, and so were widely adopted. The original test came out in 1916, and was revised in 1937 and 1960 by psychologists at Stanford University.[99, 100] The revised form is called the "Stanford-Binet," and is one of the most widely used tests of child intelligence to this day. (The other is the Wechsler Intelligence Scale for Children which includes separate rates of nonverbal abilities and which will be discussed in more detail below.[105])

When a child is given the Stanford-Binet, his "raw" score on the test (number of items right) is converted first to a mental age and then to an intelligence quotient, or IQ. The test is arranged in sections by age level. For instance, at the scale level of year 13, items are found which can be passed by about 60 percent of 13 year olds. When the mental age has been computed, this is divided by the child's actual age in years and months (chronological age) to yield the IQ:

COGNITIVE PROCESSES

$$IQ = \frac{MA}{CA} \times 100$$

Thus, if the child's chronological age is five years, zero months (5.0), and he attains a mental age on the Stanford-Binet of five years, six months (5.5 years), his IQ will be $\frac{5.5}{5.0} \times 100$ or 110; somewhat better than the average IQ of children his age.

The Wechsler (WISC) does not use mental age in computing IQ. The child's score is simply compared with those of other children in his age group. The same items are given at all age levels; younger children pass fewer of the items. The WISC contains five language tests, combined in the verbal scale, and five tests of perceptual-motor organization comprising the performance scale. The verbal tests measure general information, comprehension of everyday situations, vocabulary, numerical skills, and reasoning. The perceptual-motor performance tests include wooden puzzles, speed in copying, comprehension of pictured situations, the construction of block designs, and the recognition of missing parts in pictures.

The obtained Stanford-Binet and WISC IQ scores are highly correlated.[68] The Binet is considered a somewhat better measure at the lower age levels. Table 6.1 shows that preschool IQ correlates fairly well with later IQ, especially at the older preschool ages.

This does not mean that intelligence scores may not change with age. Many children show marked changes, and many factors may influence intelligence test scores. Early IQ's (at age two or so) are particularly useful if revealing low scores (below 70), since these scores are more reliable than those in the normal or high ranges and may serve to reveal serious retardation.

THE MEANING OF INTELLIGENCE

The Binet and Wechsler measure certain aspects of general intellectual functioning; language acquisition and comprehension, imme-

TABLE 6.1 THE STABILITY OF MENTAL TEST PERFORMANCE

AGES	N	CORRELATION WITH IQ (STANFORD-BINET) AT AGE 10	CORRELATION WITH IQ (WECHSLER) AT AGE 18
2	113	.37	.31
2½	114	.36	.24
3	229	.36	.35
3½	215	.59	.42
4	211	.66	.42

After Honzik, M. P., et al. *J. Exp. Educ.*, 17, 1948, 309-324.

diate memory, and perceptual organization. Is this the only definition of "intelligence?" Some people like to draw attention to "potential" intelligence as compared with "ultimate level" of intelligence. Hebb calls these "intelligence A" and "intelligence B."[32] Intelligence A refers to a hereditary potential limiting possible intellectual development; intelligence B refers to actual observed performance at any given time. The IQ score, of course, represents intelligence B; intelligence A is a hypothetical state and, by definition, can never be measured. It may be useful, however, as a logical tool in discussing the roles of heredity and environment in intellectual functioning. We do know that the obtained IQ score is influenced by social class, the child's contact with books and abstract thoughts in conversation, and the development of the child's motivation to do well in intellectual tasks.[43, 66, 93] Some children may never approach their hypothetical hereditary potential because they have not been adequately stimulated or motivated or because they have been inadequately educated in school.

In 1940, Stoddard defined intelligence as, "the ability to undertake activities that are characterized by difficulty, complexity, abstractness, economy (speed), adaptiveness to a goal, social value, the emergence of originals, and the ability to maintain such activity under conditions that demand a concentration of energy and a resistance to emotional forces."[97] J. P. Guilford has developed a complex theoretical model to include most items included in such intelligence tests as the Binet. Intelligence is viewed by Guilford along three interacting dimensions: *contents, operations*, and *products*.[27, 28, 29]

The *contents* include four components: *semantic*, verbal concepts and meanings; *figural*, nonverbal concrete forms and spatial relationships; *symbolic*, nonverbal symbols, letters, or numbers, and *behavioral*, thoughts, feelings, and attitudes.

The *operations* manipulate the contents in five ways: *cognition*, knowing, discovering, and recognizing items of information; *memory*, retention of material or information; *convergent thinking*, productive thinking directed toward a unique solution of a problem; *divergent thinking*, creative thinking which looks for and yields multiple answers; and *evaluation*, checking and rechecking information and productions against internal and external standards.

The manipulations of the operations on the contents yield six kinds of *products: units, classes of units, relations between units, patterns or systems, transformations*, and *implications*.

Few people will possess equal ablity in all the mental contents and be equally skillful at all the operations. The model provides a way of saying that one person will be better as a tool-and-die maker (using concrete objects) and another will be better as a mathematician (using symbols) even though both would score high on a test of general intelligence like the Stanford-Binet. The model provides a method of predicting individual differences in mental skills, and of testing the nature of relationships among varied mental abilities.

Thus we see that intelligence can be defined in various ways; both the Binet and WISC measures of general intelligence will, in fact, predict later school achievement to a fair extent, when administered to a preschooler over four years of age. As specific abilities develop, it is perhaps also useful to think as Guilford does, of intelligence as a collection of interacting abilities and capacities, which produce varieties of intelligence or intellectual abilities applicable to different tasks, occupations, and avocations. Although a child's score on an IQ test says very little about his future interests and personality, it may give a good indication of his probable level of competence in school. Further, children low on general intelligence will probably find it hard to succeed on most intellectual tasks.

INTELLECTUAL DEVELOPMENT

The theories of Piaget will be more thoroughly covered in a later chapter on stage theories of development. However, material from his studies is presented here to the extent that it is pertinent to early intellectual development. The work of Piaget reminds us that to be bright or dull at age two is a very different thing than to be bright or dull at age five.[72, 73, 74, 75, 76] Somewhat different kinds of things are going on in the child's mind.

The age levels specified by Piaget for the emergence of the different ways of thinking are much less exact than he states. The *order* in which he says that various ways of thinking appear is more reliable. However, some children seem to skip an intermediate stage altogether, and children will respond at one level in one situation at one time, and at a higher or lower level on another occasion. By and large, Piaget's cognitive stages, nevertheless, do help to explain the way intelligence or thinking develops over the years.

By age two the child, according to Piaget, has emerged from the *sensorimotor period*. During the preschool years, he can be expected to progress from the substage of *preconceptual thought* (ages two to four) partly through *intuitive thought* (ages four to seven).

During *preconceptual thought*, an object gradually becomes a representative of a class of things: a toy dog will be treated like a real dog, dragged around on a leash, given its dinner, and so on. Children begin to pretend that something ordinary, like a stick, is a baseball bat, a gun, or a horse. That is, symbolic factors have entered into cognition; one thing can be a representative or symbol of something else.

Intuitive thought emerges next; the child's thinking has become more complex and partly symbolic but is still tied down to the appearance of things. He will not see that five beads close together in a short line are the same number of beads as five beads far apart in a long line. He will say the long line contains more beads, even though he watched one set of beads being changed from a short to a long line by the experimenter. Similarly, he will say that a tall, thin glass holds more water than a short, fat glass of equal volume even if he sees the water poured from one to the other. Repeated demonstrations will gradually teach him that this is not so, but an older child will know it the first time.

In another example, a child was asked to pick the "middle-sized" object from a group of three. After he learned this, he was given another group of three, of different sizes from the ones he was trained on. He could not select the middle-sized object from the new group, because he had not developed the idea of "middle-sized" as independent of the particular items he learned before.[95]

This brings us to the concept of "verbal mediation." If the child had learned the mediational concept of "middle-sized" *independent* of the particular set of items he was shown, the new problem would have been no problem at all. Does the ability to form mediational concepts emerge in an innate developmental sequence, or is it responsive to social environmental training? Will all children develop mediational concepts by a certain age, or will some arrive at maturity without getting to that stage of intellectual growth? The concept of mediation has been extensively investigated by people studying its role in the learning of verbal abilities, both in the simple learning of language, and its effect on intelligence as shown in test and school situations. It will be dealt with at some length after the general question of language acquisition has been discussed. Verbal mediation is impossible, of course, until the child has mastered language to a fair extent.

THE PROCESS OF LANGUAGE ACQUISITION

Is Language Innate?

At three, the child has developed an enormous vocabulary, and as complex a grammar as at least one team of investigators felt it was able to describe.[13] All but the severely retarded children in all cultures acquire speech. These facts, among others, lead some linguists to believe that the human child has an innate predisposition to speak, and that hearing the conversation of adults gives the child the opportunity to acquire the specific language to which he is exposed.[16, 51] They argue that it would take a child many hundreds of times the actually elapsed time to acquire all the combinations of words, variations in syntax, and other verbal refinements he exhibits during the early years of life, if language acquisition had to depend mainly on conditioning or learning. Some of these theorists speculate that there may be only one *basic* linguistic structure underlying all languages spoken in the world. They feel that since the same underlying rules of construction apply to them all, that this structure is innately represented in the brain, and not acquired through learning. They go on to say that no present learning theory can explain the acquisition of rules of grammar. Language, they feel, is acquired by a nervous system already prepared and structured to absorb the particular language of any culture.

Brown and Fraser adduce evidence for this point of view.[13] They say that the young child, without benefit of learning, is in possession of rules of construction because he overgeneralizes regularities of *inflections* and of *syntax*. In the study of inflections, a child in the first, second, or third grade is presented with a picture-book game as discussed in Study 6.6.

LANGUAGE: INNATE OR LEARNED?

STUDY 6.6

The following type of item was used with young school-age children to determine how much command of English rules of inflection the children possessed.

A bird like creature is depicted.
"This is a wug.
Now there is another one.
There are two of them.
There are two _____."

If the children can't yet read, the items can be read to them. Another example goes like this:

A man is shown swinging something about his head.
"This is a man who knows how to gling.
He glings every day.
Today he glings.
Yesterday he _____."

In this example, most adults said he "glang" glung, or "glought." Children, on the other hand, say he "glinged," showing overgeneralization of a rule they have never heard formulated, to this specific example which they could never have heard from others. One school of linguists holds that this result supports the idea of innate inflective rules possessed by all children.

> Berko, J. The child's learning of English morphology. *Word, 14*, 1958, 150-177.

The *wug* crops up again in the investigation of syntax.[12] It is used in sentences in order to elicit sentences in reply, in which the child uses the word *wug*. For example, "This is a little girl thinking about a *wug*. Can you make up what that might mean?" Here *wug* is used as a *count noun* ("a *wug*"). Or "This is a little girl who wants to *wug* something." (*Wug* is used here as a transitive verb.) Or simply, "This is a little girl thinking about some *wug*" (mass noun); ". . . thinking about something *wuggy*" (adjective). Again, young children show great comprehension of what these forms of a nonexistent word imply and can deal with them in a correct, syntactical way, even at an early age.

Reduction and Overgeneralization in Children's Speech

Brown and Fraser have concluded from their analysis of many samples of the speech of children, that child grammar is largely a reduction of adult grammar—an abbreviated or telegraphic version of familiar constructions. At the stage when children tend to omit forms of the verb "to be," as in the construction "That the cup," the average utterance of the preschool child is below 3.2 morphemes. When they are leaving out forms of "will" or "can," as in "I do it now," the average utterance is below 3.5 morphemes. (A morpheme is a meaningful unit of speech, as distinguished from a phoneme, a pronounceable unit of speech, which may or may not in itself carry meaning.)

Support is provided for the notion that children "possess" rules of grammatical construction from an early age, by studies showing that they overgeneralize regularities, using them where adults never do. However, Brown and Fraser point out that adult everyday speech often departs rather radically from the ideal recommendations of grammatical rules.[13] This seems to lead to the conclusion that children should speak more grammatically than adults; but since the rules of English grammar have so many exceptions, children only use rules more *logically*, which is not the same thing at all.

The errors in speech that children make do seem to follow a fairly regular, "telegraphic" pattern.[13, 24, 98] Children can remember only a limited number of syllables at a time, and the average length of both their spontaneous and imitative utterances are very similar and increase with age. The way the child picks words to retain from an overly long sentence is not clearly understood but may be related to emphasis in adult speech and the elimination by the child of details carrying little information. Another view suggests that the child acquires a small number of words he hears and uses often.[63] These words are called "operators" and are usually function words such as "go," "eat," or "know." These are then paired with other words to form schools of sentences, again omitting words that usually carry little information.

Followers of Chomsky believe that three year olds have all the basic structures of adult grammar, and that development through the age of seven involves the growth of *transformations.* Transformations are changes of, for instance, a statement into a question ("He went" to "Did he go?") or an active into a passive voice ("He went" to "He was sent.") Preschool children diagnosed as having infantile speech possess more generalized rules of grammar, more redundancies, and more perseverations than normal children.[13]

Is Language Learned?

Followers of Chomsky and Lenneberg do not deny that it is necessary for children to hear adult speech in order to develop speech themselves, but they do deny that learning theories are adequate to explain what is happening. They maintain that speech is elicited, not learned. The child only has to hear others speak; this elicits speech from him. The opposite point of view is also strongly held, and is discussed in the following paragraphs.

The learning of some aspects of language is very clearly outlined by D. L. Olmstead.[70] His analysis goes as follows: by six months of age, the child has learned to distinguish cries of distress from ordinary speech. By this time the sound of ordinary speech has acquired secondary reinforcing or rewarding properties (through association with the primary reinforcements of caretaking activities, stimulation, and so on). The mother who feeds the child may often talk to the child as he is fed. Therefore, he is motivated to produce speech himself since speech is associated with rewarding states. This is a further development of the theory advanced by O. H. Mowrer. This was discussed in Chapter 4, in the section on the early acquisition of verbal behavior. The more often the child hears certain sounds, the more reinforcing (rewarding) they are, and since some sounds are easier to discriminate than others, he will attempt them more often. These same sounds are easier to check by ear than when he says them himself, and so are correctly "learned" the fastest. Sounds of low discriminability will be learned late, after easier ones are mastered, and his attention is freed to turn to them. This formulation is easily tested, as Olmsted specifies "hard" and "easy" sounds to discriminate. This theory covers only the acquisition of phonology (sounds), not grammar or syntax.

Advocates of learning theory handle the acquisition of grammar and syntax in terms of discrimination among cues, with finer differentiations being learned at later ages. The child first learns the usages he hears in many different contexts, for instance, the addition of *d* or *ed* to a verb in creating a past tense. He will then add a *d* (or *ed*) to everything ("I camed downstairs") until he is corrected often enough or observes the correct usage often enough to acquire the specific past tenses of the various irregular verbs. However, such learning analysis falls short of explaining how the child acquires the complexities of language so quickly and thoroughly at such an early age. If language is learned rather than produced by a nervous system structurally primed to enable the child to acquire language once he hears it spoken, then learning theory has not yet adequately described the way in which it is learned.

LANGUAGE AND LEARNING PROCESSES

Labeling: Stimulus-Verbal Label Activity and Social Class Differences

A great deal of the early learning using language is labeling activity. An object is seen, and its name is asked. At a particular age, usually around two to three, the child suddenly realizes that things have names, and he wants to know each and every one of them. It is here that social class differences begin to influence the development of his measurable intelligence.[37, 64] Lower-class parents spend less time talking with their children for various reasons. Usually more caretakers are involved, either siblings or other adults, since the mother often works or has many other children to look after. Children who have a single mothering experience vocalize more than children who have had six to eight mother surrogates.[86] In England, and probably in America too, lower-class social language is less like written language syntactically, grammatically, and in overall sequential organization and logical progression, than is language among the middle-class.[10] Thus there is a greater gap to bridge when the child moves from home to kindergarten and schoolbooks. The middle-class child is already used to seeing picture books and to hearing people talk like the teacher does; but to the lower-class child, it may be foreign and intimidating. When the lower-class child is tested for reading readiness, such factors contribute to his often low score.

Middle-class parents tend to make finer discriminations among things they are labeling for their children than do lower-class parents. As an example of clear versus distorted or overgeneralized labeling, parents at the zoo may react in two clearly different ways to their children's questions about the animals. In one case they will say "Oh, that's an animal, and that's another animal, and that's a bird." Other parents will say, "Well, that's a zebra. See, he's like a horse, but with stripes. And that's an ostrich—look at his big feathers! Ostriches lay great big eggs. And that's a giraffe. My! Look how high he can reach!" The second type of response draws attention to details that distinguish the various species, and lead to much richer, more differentiated labeling activity.[90] This acquired distinctiveness of cues, as in learning the difference between a zebra and a horse, involves learning to respond with distinctive labels to two similar stimuli; thus increasing the cognitive difference between them. Subsequent discrimination between them is easier as a result of having labeled them differently on a previous occasion.

Practice in labeling leads to further labeling behaviors, and the child gradually acquires the habit of making mental distinctions among similar stimuli.

In symbolic terms, this is S-V activity. The child sees a stimulus and reacts with a *verbal* label. The next step will be to react to the stimulus label by producing a motor response. The child says to himself "skunk," and draws back from the animal. If he says "kitty," he will continue to approach it. If he is being trained to pick up a red square and ignore a green one, he can learn to say "red." After a certain age, this will help him to pick the right one.

The Verbal Label - Response Connection: Responding to Verbal Labels or Commands

The interrelationships among stimuli, commands, labels, and responses have been greatly clarified by the Russian psychologists working on what they call the "second signal system."[36, 55, 56, 80, 82, 91, 92] The second signal system is largely made up of language, that is to say, words.

In Luria's experiments on the role of language in behavior, children of different ages are studied to ascertain the extent to which their actions are regulated by verbalization. Study 6.7 provides a detailed summary of this series of investigations.

DEVELOPING THE V-R LEARNING SEQUENCE

STUDY 6.7

The child holds a soft rubber bulb connected to an apparatus which marks each time the child squeezes the bulb. The child is told to *press* the bulb when the blue light goes on, and *not* to press when the red light goes on. The experimenter attempts to control the child's behavior with the words "Press" or "Do not press."

Under the age of two the verbal commands have little or no effect on the child; he squeezes for either light, and finds it hard to stop, once he begins.

From two to two and a half years, on the average, the experimenter begins to exercise some control. However, the child's own speech does not regulate his behavior. Even if he *says* "Press" for blue and "Don't press" for red, he will squeeze for both.

From three to three and a half, the child heeds the command of the experimenter and can follow the previous instructions to press for blue. But he cannot inhibit his behavior by his own speech. If he is told "Press twice", he still squeezes repeatedly, though he understands the concept "twice." He *can* control his behavior if he is told to say "One!" "Two!" as he presses. (At earlier ages this technique was also ineffectual.) After some practice if the child is given a trial a few days later, without instructions to say "One!" "Two!," he still can't inhibit further pressing.

From ages three to four, if the child is trained to say "I must press" to blue and "I must not press" to red, the verbal reaction will control *only* the positive reaction to the blue light, not the negative response to red. To inhibit the reaction to red the child must be trained in a verbal response to blue, while verbally ignoring the red. However, the command of the experimenter, "Don't press," will inhibit the response to the red light at this age. The child can inhibit the response of squeezing the bulb if he is told to put his hand on his knee when he sees the red light. This is an instance of performing a response *incompatible* with the wrong one.

From four and a half to five and a half the child's own verbalization becomes more able to control his behavior completely. The child will talk, not to the experimenter, *but, to himself,* when given a task of some difficulty. He represents the environment to himself and helps to control his own responses. This becomes more covert with age, until it is completely silent and constitutes "thinking," according to the Russian theory. Once the child can tell himself what to do, he is using verbal mediation to control his own behavior.

Luria, A. R. *The Role of Speech in the Regulation of Normal and Abnormal Behavior.* Liveright, New York, 1961.

Luria, A. R. The genesis of voluntary movements. (In) O'Connor, N., (Ed.). *Recent Soviet Psychology,* Liveright, New York, 1961.

The S-V-R process: Stimulus, Verbal Label, Response

An early study illustrates the helpfulness of verbal labels in a learning task.[77] Children from two to seven years old were given the task of learning by trial and error which of five hollow objects of similar size concealed a toy. There were three experimental groups. The first group were given five different unnamed objects of approximately equal size, and proceeded to attempt the task. A second group were given the same objects, but each one was given a nonsense name, such as "Mobie," or "Pito." The third group were given objects of familiar shape for which children already knew the names, such as a cat, a dog, and so on. This last group learned much the fastest. The middle group learned better than the first group. In the middle group, 64 percent named the "correct" object as they picked it, of their own accord. In addition to learning the "correct" object, they also learned the *names* of the objects, but nevertheless, found the task easier than the group dealing with nameless objects. The names helped to distinguish each object from the others. In this process, the child sees the stimuli, reacts verbally, and then responds to the task. Similar results have been found by other researchers.[15, 94]

Another Russian experiment shows similar results, but illustrates the fact that if a word is encountered in many verbal contexts it is learned better than if it is heard in only a few contexts.[81] Ten children, 20 months old, were shown a particular doll many times. For five children, the presentation was accompanied by only three verbalizations, "Here is a doll," "Take the doll," and "Give me the doll." The other five children were exposed to *30 different* verbalizations. When asked to "pick a doll" from a row of miscellaneous toys, the second group picked *only* dolls, whereas children from the first group picked both dolls and other toys. Similar results were found using a book paired with either one or 20 *verbalizations*. Twenty books and one verbalization also proved superior results to *seeing* only one book. So seeing a variety of stimuli (20 books) of the "correct" type is also helpful in learning a concept as is having it labeled often (20 verbalizations). If children were allowed to *handle* small unfamiliar stimuli, they also learned the names faster and learned to pick them out faster than children who only saw them as they were named and were not allowed to touch them. Learing is aided by *many stimuli, many labels,* or *many responses* of the same type occurring.

There is another aspect of importance in the discrimination of stimuli through labeling. The distinctiveness of the labels themselves helps to determine the effectiveness of labeling.[84] Children learned labels for different colored lights, then learned to perform different motor responses to each light. There were four degrees of distinctiveness or ease of learning of the labels. In order of increasing distinctiveness, the labels were wug-wog (wug is a very popular nonsense syllable) zim-zam, lev-mib, and wug-zam. Wug-wog is much easier to learn than wug-zam. The more distinct (easy to learn) the label, the easier it was for the children to perform the appropriate motor response.

Labeling, however, may have some drawbacks. A verbalization may help or hinder, depending on the task.[78] A verbal label usually leaves out or distorts certain aspects of the physical stimulus which may be important: if you call all four-legged animals "Kitty," you will not notice which one is the skunk. Labeling may well proceed by successive approximations. A biologist uses a much more complicated system of labels for animals than does the average housewife. He has developed it gradually, as he learned more and more about his specialty. She, on the other hand is likely to use more different labels for soap then he does.

When a problem, easily solved on a simple stimulus-response basis, elicits many verbal responses irrelevant to the solution, bright children often do less well than younger or duller children, who have not learned to produce labels but proceed on the S-R basis. Verbal mediation is not always a help. Knowing too much may be a handicap when a simple response will do.

Reversal and Nonreversal Shifts: The Demonstration of Spontaneous Verbal Mediation

Two types of learning tasks have been found especially useful in studying the age of onset of labeling responses in children. These are the reversal and the nonreversal shift. The labeling response (V in S-V-R) is called "verbal mediation" when it abstracts a distinctive quality from physical stimuli which helps in identifying the quality as a basis on which the child can act. Examples are "middle sized," "the large one," or the "small white one."

In both reversal and nonreversal shift problems, the subject is first presented with a pair of stimuli differing on two dimensions, often *size* (large-small) and *brightness* (black-white). On the first trial he is shown the large black (LB) and small white (SW) stimuli; the LB proves to be the correct one. He may be told he is right when he picks the large black (LB) one. Next he is shown the large white (LW) and small black (SB) stimuli; the large white (LW) is now the correct one. If the subject is using S-R learning, at this point he has merely learned two separate responses, large black (LB) and large white (LW). He knows that large black is correct and so is large white. If he employs mediation, however, he has said to himself "Ah, it's the size, not the color, that counts. Large is what matters; white or black is irrelevant."

Next, in the *reversal shift*, size counts, but in the other direction. Given the same LB and SW choice, SW is correct, and given LW-SB, the SB is correct. "Aha," the person who uses verbal mediation says. "It's still size, but now it is *smaller,* not *larger.*" He has little trouble learning the new concept. The S-R learner, however, lacking a mediational response, must unlearn both LB and LW separately, and replace them with SW and SB. It takes longer for him to do this than it takes the person who uses verbal mediation to make his switch. Animals and small children do less well at this task than older children and adults.

On the other hand, the *nonreversal shift,* the criterion is changed from size to color. This involves changing only one specific "answer," however, as follows. The first part of the task is the same: of LB vs. SW, LB is correct, and of LW vs. SB, LW is correct. But in the second part, of the choice between LB and SW, SW is correct, although of LW vs. SB, LW is still correct. In this condition, the person who mediates must *unlearn "size"* and, *learn "color,"* and also that *"white" is the right color.* He must learn the concept that *specifically white color is correct.* The S-R learner has already learned LW specifically and can keep it, simply changing from LB to SW in the first pair in the second part of the task. His task is relatively simple, and in this situation he learns faster than the "mediator." He has only to learn one new response while the mediator must learn a two part concept: *"color-white."* Small children and animals here do better than older children and adults. As one would expect, lower-class children who are less likely to use verbal mediation, do better than middle-class children on such tasks, in which verbal mediation is a handicap. Table 6.2 summarizes the reversal and nonreversal learning situation requirements.

DEVELOPMENT OF MEDIATION

Children appear to change from S-R to S-V-R (mediational) learning at around five to seven years of age.[1, 44, 45, 46, 50, 96] As Jensen

TABLE 6.2 REVERSAL AND NONREVERSAL SHIFTS

		PART II	
CHOICE	PART I SOLUTION	REVERSAL SOLUTION	NONREVERSAL SOLUTION
LB vs. SW	LB	SW	SW
LW vs. SB	LW	SB	LW
Mediation task	Learn "large" Learn "size"	Unlearn "large" Learn "small"	Unlearn "size" Learn "color" Learn "white"
S-R task	Learn LB, LW	Unlearn LB, LW Learn SW, SB	Unlearn LB Learn SW

notes, interestingly enough, it is just at this age that most societies start sending children to school.[37]

As the child becomes more adept at spontaneous mediation, his mediators become more complex and varied in syntax.[38] If kindergarteners are asked to associate pairs of common objects, such as a hat and a table, they will profit by instructions to make up a phrase linking the two, to help them remember the association. Their phrases will be very simple, often a noun phrase, as "The *hat* and the *table*." By Grade 2, children were making complete sentences: "The *hat* lay on the *table*." The instructions were of increasing help in learning the associations until Grade 6, when they decreased steadily to Grade 12. Presumably the older children automatically used verbal links anyway to help remember and the instructions were not needed.

This finding is consistent with a study concerned with whether the deficiency of verbally mediated performance in early childhood is caused by a lack of labeling by the child (Production-Deficiency hypothesis); or by the fact that the labeling, although made, tends not to mediate the performance (Mediational Deficiency hypothesis).[57, 83] When children's spontaneous verbalizations were reviewed, it was found that kindergarteners are less likely than older children to spontaneously produce names in a nonverbal serial recall task, supporting the Production-Deficiency hypothesis.[19]

Intelligence Level and Verbal Mediation

The normal child can, with brief training, be made to change from an S-R to a S-V-R type of performance in discrimination learning, while retarded children show little tendency to make this transition.[11] When normal children and retarded children were compared with and without mediation instructions, both groups profited from the instructions, but the retardates were found to be about four times as slow in both conditions.[38, 40] (This study indicated that it is the IQ, not the mental age as such, that determines the ability to mediate, since the groups were matched on mental age.)

Terrell and his coworkers found that middle-class children can perform tasks quite well when the only reward is knowledge of results, whereas lower-class children need more tangible rewards.[101, 102] Are the lower-class children less bright than middle-class children? Don't they care if they are right? Or do they lack training in labeling ("that means I am right") to make them realize that they have done the right thing?

In this connection, provocative data were obtained by Jensen in studying a group of "nonverbal" high-schoolers, possessing *measured* IQ's of 50 to 75.[39] The investigation is reported in detail in Study 6.8.

MENTALLY RETARDED OR VERBALLY RETARDED?

STUDY 6.8

This study compared retarded, average, and gifted children in a nonverbal learning task. The subjects were required to push one of five buttons when one of five geometric forms was presented. Each form corresponded to one pushbutton. If the correct button was pushed, a green light went on; if the incorrect button was pushed, no light went on.

When compared with children of average IQ, those with IQ's of 50 to 75 were found to be slow learners. The experimenter then prompted them to use verbal labeling, by pronouncing the name of the geometrical form, such as "red circle," and so on. Some improved, others did not. Finally, the experimenter started saying "Good" or "Right" each time the green light went on. Learning improved greatly. Thus a nominally nonverbal task was affected greatly by verbal behavior.

The green light previously had simply not had a "reward" connotation to the retarded subjects; it *stood* for nothing. After the verbal training of associating green with "good" or "right," several learned faster than subjects of average IQ, and as well as subjects who possessed superior IQ's of 135 or more. Four of 36 "retarded" subjects scored higher than the average of the gifted group. All four of these subjects came from lower-class backgrounds. When middle-class subjects were used exclusively, in the same retarded IQ range, verbal practice did *not* help.

The experimenter concludes that the subject who has not had verbal training may do poorly even in tests of a purportedly nonverbal nature. The middle-class retardates probably have already had verbal training.

Jensen, A. R. Learning ability in retarded, average, and gifted children. *Merrill-Palmer Quart.* Behav. Develpm., *90*, 1963, 123-140.

Intelligence Level, Verbal Training, and Social Class

Some children from lower socioeconomic classes receive very little training in verbal labeling, verbal mediation, and verbal discrimination of stimuli (see References 39 and 89). When they are included in groups of "slow learners" or the "mentally retarded," they make up a very heterogeneous crew. They may have low measured IQ's because they have lacked opportunities for learning, thus keeping the mental age (MA) low. If such a child shows great improvement between a learning situation where no mediational instructions are given, and another situation where the instructor induces such mediation, it indicates that his retardation is *not organic*, but has been environmentally produced.

This kind of problem is illustrated by studies on Anglo- and Mexican-American children of low socioeconomic status.[41, 79] Mexican-American children of low *measured* IQ proved superior to Anglo-American children of the same IQ on learning tasks with little verbal mediation required, or when verbal labels were made explicit by the experimenter. In a confirming experiment, when groups of children were matched on IQ and social class and tests were given requiring verbal mediation, the performance measures of the average IQ and low IQ Mexican-Americans became practically indistinguishable. However, they remained clearly separated among the Anglo-Americans. The conclusion follows that the Mexican-American children are retarded mainly on verbal mediation, rather than organically retarded.

Similarly, when orphanage children were given special speech and language training only on weekends for a total of 92 hours, over about seven and a half months, they showed a gain of 14 IQ points over a well-matched control group. The initial average IQ of all children was about 80. The transfer of this training was quite general, and showed up in a variety of assessment procedures.[37]

Jensen consequently proposes a different kind of test for measuring a culture-free IQ level.[37] Free recall tasks are used which are relatively unaffected by mediational learning. Memory span for digits is especially useful, and Jensen advances many possible variations on such a task, which could be combined to cover most variation in intelligence, such as immediate vs. delayed recall, and so forth.[38]

BREAK FROM CHRONOLOGY

So far the development of the child has largely been presented in a chronological form. Although processes have been discussed, they have largely been presented in the context of the general age range in which they tend to appear. The next three chapters, however, are organized less chronologically.

The three chapters to follow cover *behavior genetics*, *stage theories*, and *social learning in children*. *Behavior genetics* deals with the contributions of heredity to the child's behavior; *stage theories* present a specific theoretical way of explaining the child's development as does the theory of *social learning*, although in a quite different way. Now that we have followed the child's development up to about six years of age, it is time to consider some of the broad theoretical approaches which psychologists have invoked to account for that development.

SUMMARY — PART 2

The concept of intelligence was introduced by Alfred Binet as a measure of how well children were able to function in their everyday activities. In reality, most tests of intelligence measure the ability to use verbal and numerical symbols and so are most useful in predicting performance in school where such abilities largely determine success or failure. Some psychologists have questioned the utility of a simple intelligence quotient score since they feel that children have a variety of intellectual abilities that cannot be summed up in a single measure. Intelligence can be viewed as being multidimensional, containing a variety of abilities such as being adaptive, fast, original, or having a good memory, seeing relations easily, or being able to grasp meanings. It has been argued that having one of these abilities to a high degree need not imply having all the others to a high degree also. However, such abilities are related to some extent since a factor of "general intelligence" has been found, meaning that a person high (or low) on some aspects of intelligence will tend to be high (or low) on other aspects also. Some children are more or less intelligent than others even if they do vary in some of their specific abilities.

Piaget considers intellectual development to take place in distinct stages. The first is the stage of sensorimotor intelligence which does not involve the use of symbols. Further development in cognitive skills involves the beginning of the use of symbols, although thought still remains fairly concrete. The child may be able to master concepts such as "middle sized" but can use them only if new situations resemble closely the ones in which such concepts were originally acquired.

Perhaps the child's greatest growth in cognitive ability depends on the mastery of language. There is a great deal of controversy over whether or not language is acquired in accordance with the laws of learning theory. Those who do not think it is believe it to be acquired as a result of the child's nervous system merely being stimulated by the use of language in the culture. It has been argued that concepts like classical conditioning, imitation, discrimination or reinforcement are inadequate to account for the acquisition of language by children.

No matter how the child acquires language, in time language comes to regulate a great deal of his behavior. The child can learn to control his own behavior by giving himself verbal instructions. He can literally tell himself what to do. In addition, developing mediational concepts like "middle sized," "it's the large black one," or "only small white is correct now," which are in the form of statements the child makes to himself, help the child to solve problems. Children who do not adequately develop the ability to mediate verbally are at a disadvantage in school where this is vital to mastering the subjects taught.

Certain theoretical concepts have already been introduced in this text. However, the emphasis has been on a chronological description of the developing child. Although the role of genetics and learning factors has been introduced, along with some discussion of "stage theory" there has been no sustained effort to account theoretically for the course of development. The development of the child has been traced from a state where the infant was largely a reflexive creature dependent entirely on the caretaking activities of others, to a point where the child has become able to feed himself, talk, and regulate some of his behavior in accordance with the wishes of parents and his newly developing cognitive controls. Although some explanations for this development, as just stated, have been introduced, it now seems helpful to engage in a fuller discussion of the ways in which development may be comprehended. Consequently, the next three chapters will concentrate more fully than earlier ones on the role of inheritance, on stage theories, and on the nature of social learning.

REFERENCES

1. Alberts, E., and Ehrenfreund, D.   Transposition in children as a function of age. *J. Exp. Psychol., 41*, 1951, 30-38.
2. Aronfreed, J.   The effects of experimental socialization paradigms upon two moral responses to transgression. *J. Abnorm. Soc. Psychol., 66,* 1963, 437-448.
3. Aronfreed, J.   The origins of self-criticism. *Psychol. Rev., 71,* 1964, 193-218.
4. Baer, D. M.   A technique of special reinforcement for the study of child behavior: Behavior avoiding reinforcement withdrawal. *Child Develpm., 33,* 1962, 847-858.
5. Bandura, A., and Walters, R. H.   *Social Learning and Personality Development.* Holt, Rinehart and Winston, New York, 1963.
6. Bandura, A.   Relationship of family patterns to child behavior disorders. Progress Report U.S.P.H.S. Research Grant M 1734. (In) *Social Learning and Personality Development,* Bandura, A., and Walters, R. H., Holt, Rinehart and Winston, New York, 1963.
7. Bandura, A., and Walters, R. H.   *Adolescent Aggression.* Ronald, New York, 1959.
8. Beller, E. K., and Haeberle, A. W.   Dependency and the frustration aggression hypothesis. Paper read at the meetings of the Eastern Psychol. Assn., 1961.
9. Berko, J.   The child's learning of English morphology. *Word, 14,* 1958, 150-177.
10. Bernstein, B.   Language and social class. *Brit. J. Sociol., 11,* 1960, 271-276.
11. Bialer, I.   Primary and secondary stimulus generalization as related to intelligence level. *J. Exp. Psychol., 62,* 1961, 395-402.
12. Brown, R. W., and Berko, J.   Word association and the acquisition of grammar. *Child Develpm. 31,* 1960, 1-14.
13. Brown, R. W., and Fraser, C.   The acquisition of syntax. (In) *The Acquisition of Language. Monog. Soc. Res. Child Develpm. 29,* No. 92, 1964, 43-79.
14. Cairns, R.   Antecedents of social reinforcer effectiveness, Unpublished manuscript. University of Indiana, 1962.

15. Cantor, G. N.   Effects of three types of pretraining discrimination learning in preschool children. *J. Exp. Psychol., 49*, 1955, 339-342.
16. Chomsky, N.   *Syntactic Structures.* Mouton, The Hague, 1957.
17. Emmerich, W., and Smoller, F.   The role of patterning of parental norms. *Sociometry, 27*, 1964, 382-390.
18. Erikson, E. H.   Identity and the life cycle: Selected papers. *Psychol. Issues, Monograph 1*, 1959.
19. Flavell, J. H., Beach, D. R., and Chinsky, J. M.   Spontaneous verbal rehearsal in a memory task as a function of age. *Child Develpm., 37*, 1966, 283-299.
20. Freud, S.   Character and Anal Eroticism. *Collected Papers, Vol. 2.* Basic Books, New York, 1959.
21. Freud, S.   The Infantile Genital Organization of the Libido. *Collected Papers, Vol. 2.* Basic Books, New York, 1959.
22. Freud, S.   The Predispositions to Obsessional Neurosis. *Collected Papers, Vol. 2.* Basic Books, New York, 1959.
23. Freud, S.   *Three Contributions to the Theory of Sex.* Nerv. and Ment. Dis. Pub. Co., New York, 1930.
24. Gesell, A., et al.   *The First Five Years of Life: A Guide to the Study of the Preschool Child.* Harper, New York, 1940.
25. Gewirtz, J. L.   Three determinants of attention-seeking in young children. *Monogr. Soc. Res. Child Develpm., 19*, 1956.
26. Glidewell, J. C. (Ed.)   *Parental Attitudes and Child Behavior.* Charles C Thomas, Springfield, Ill. 1960.
27. Guilford, J. P.   Development and application of tests of intellectual and special abilities. *Rev. Educ. Res., 29*, 1959, 26-41.
28. Guilford, J. P.   Intelligence: 1965 model. *Amer. Psychologist, 21*, 1965, 20-26.
29. Guilford, J. P.   *Personality.* McGraw-Hill, New York, 1959.
30. Hartup, W. W.   Nurturance and nurturance withdrawal in relation to the dependency behavior of preschool children. *Child Develpm., 29*, 1958, 191-201.
31. Hartup, W. W., and Keller, E. D.   Nurturance in preschool children and its relations to dependency. *Child Develpm., 31*, 1960, 681-689.
32. Hebb, D. O.   *A Textbook of Psychology.* W. B. Saunders, Philadelphia, 1966.
33. Hetzer, H.   Entwicklungsbedingte Erziehungsschwierigkeiten *Ztschr. Pedagog. Psychol., 30*, 1929, 77-85.
34. Honzik, M. P.   On verbal labeling and learning. (In) *Social Class, Race, and Psychological Development*, Deutsch, M., Jensen, A. R., and Katz, I. (Eds.). Holt, Rinehart and Winston, New York, In Press.
35. Honzik, M.P., MacFarlane, J. W., and Allen, L.   The stability of mental test performance between two and eighteen years. *J. Exp. Educ., 17*, 1948, 309-324.
36. Ivaschenko, F. I.   An experimental study of the relationship between words heard, seen, and pronounced. *Pavlov. J. Higher Nerv. Activ., 8*, 1958, 168-173.
37. Jensen, A. R.   Social Class and Verbal Learning. (In) *Social Class, Race, and Psychological Development.* Deutsch, M., Jensen, A. R., and Katz, I., (Eds.) Holt, Rinehart and Winston, New York, In Press.
38. Jensen, A. R., and Rohwer, W. D., Jr.   Syntactical mediation of serial paired-associate learning as a function of age. *Child Develpm., 36*, 1965, 601-608.
39. Jensen, A. R.   Learning ability in retarded, average, and gifted children. *Merrill-Palmer Quart. Behav. Develpm., 90*, 1963, 123-140.
40. Jensen, A. R. and Rohwer, W. D., Jr.   Verbal mediation in paired-associate serial learning. *J. Verb. Learn. Verb. Behav., 1*, 1963, 346-352.
41. Jensen, A. R.   Learning abilities in Mexican-American children. *Calif. J. Educ. Res., 12*, 1961, 147-159.
42. Jenkins, J. J.   Mediated associations: Paradigms and situations. (In) *Verbal Behavior and Learning: Problems and Processes*, Coper, C. N. and Musgrave, B. S. (Eds.). McGraw-Hill, New York, 1963.
43. Kagan, J., and Moss, H. A.   Parental correlates of child's I.Q. and height: a cross-validation of the Berkeley Growth Study results. *Child Develpm., 30*, 1959, 325-332.
44. Kendler, H. H., and Kendler, T. S.   Vertical and horizontal processes in problem solving. *Psychol. Rev., 69*, 1-16.

45. Kendler, H. H., and Kendler, T. S. Effect of verbalization on reversal shifts in children. *Science, 134,* 1961, 1619-1620.
46. Kendler, T. S., Kendler, H. H., and Learned, B. Mediated responses to size and brightness as a function of age. *Amer. J. Psychol., 75,* 1962, 571-586.
47. Kinsey, A. C. et al. *Sexual Behavior in the Human Female.* W. B. Saunders, Philadelphia, 1953.
48. Kinsey, A. C., Pomeroy, W. B., and Martin, C. E. *Sexual Behavior in the Human Male.* W. B. Saunders, Philadelphia, 1948.
49. Koch, H. The relation of primary mental abilities in five and six year olds to sex and characteristics of siblings. *Child Develpm., 25,* 1954, 209-223.
50. Kuenne, M. R. Experimental investigation of the relation of language to transposition behavior in young children. *J. Exp. Psychol., 36,* 1946, 89-93.
51. Lenneberg, E. H. (Ed.) *New Directions in the Study of Language.* Massachusetts Institute of Technology Press, Cambridge, 1964.
52. Levy, D. M. *Maternal Overprotection.* Columbia University Press, New York, 1943.
53. Levy, D. M. Oppositional syndromes and oppositional behavior. (In) *Psychopathology of Childhood.* Hoch, P. H., and Zubin. J. (Eds.). New York, Grune and Stratton, 1955.
54. Litin, E. M., Griffin, M. E., and Johnson, A. M. Parental influences in unusual sexual behavior in children. *Psychoanal. Quart., 25,* 1956, 37-55.
55. Luria, A. R. *The Role of Speech in the Regulation of Normal and Abnormal Behavior.* Liveright, New York, 1961.
56. Luria, A. R. The genesis of voluntary movements. (In) *Recent Soviet Psychology,* O'Connor, N. E. (Ed.). Liveright, New York, 1961.
57. Maccoby, E. E. Developmental Psychology. *Ann. Rev. Psychol. 15,* 1964, 203-250.
58. Menyuk, P. Alliteration of rules in children's grammar. *J. Verb. Learn. Verb. Behav., 3,* 1964, 480-488.
59. Menyuk, O. Comparison of grammar of children with fundamental deviant and normal speech. *J. Speech Hear. Res., 7,* 1964, 109-121.
60. Menyuk, P. Syntactic rules used by children from pre-school through first grade. *Child Develpm., 35,* 1964, 533-546.
61. Menyuk, P. Syntactic structures in the language of children. *Child Develpm., 34,* 1963, 407-422.
62. Miller, N. E. Theory and experiment relating psychoanalytic displacement to stimulus response generalization. *J. Abnorm. Soc. Psychol., 43,* 1948, 155-178.
63. Miller, W., and Ervin, S. The Development of Grammar in Child Language. (In) *The Acquisition of Language. Monogr. Soc. Res. Child Develpm., 29,* No. 92, 1964. 9-34.
64. Milner, E. A study of the relationship between reading readiness in grade one school children and patterns of parent-child interaction. *Child Develpm., 22,* 1951, 95-112.
65. Moore, S., and Updegraff, R. Sociometric status of pre-school children: related to age, sex, nurturance-group and dependency. *Child Develpm., 35,* 1964, 519-524.
66. Moss, H. A., and Kagan, J. Maternal influences on early I.Q. scores. *Psychol. Rep., 4,* 1958, 655-661.
67. Mowrer, D. H. *Learning Theory and the Symbolic Processes.* John Wiley, New York, 1960.
68. Mussen, P. H., Dean, S., and Rosenberg, M. Some further evidence on the validity of the WISC. *J. Consult. Psychol. 16,* 1952, 410-411.
69. Nelson, E. A. The effects of reward and punishment of dependency in subsequent dependency. Unpublished manuscript. Stanford University, 1960.
70. Olmsted, D. L. A theory of the child's learning of phonology. *Language, 42,* Apr.-June 1966, 531-535.
71. Osler, J. F., and Trautman, G. E. Concept attainment: II. Effect of stimulus complexity upon concept attainment at two levels of intelligence. *J. Exp. Psychol., 62,* 1961, 9-13.
72. Piaget, J. *The Child's Conception of the World.* Harcourt, Brace, New York, 1929.
73. Piaget, J. *The Child's Conception of Physical Causality.* Kegan, Paul, Trench, Trubner, London, 1930.
74. Piaget, J. *The Moral Judgment of the Child.* Free Press, Glencoe, 1948.

75. Piaget, J. *The Origins of Intelligence in Children*. International Universities Press, New York, 1952.
76. Piaget, J. *Play, Dreams, and Imitation in Childhood*, Norton, New York, 1951.
77. Pyles, M. K. Verbalization as a factor in learning. *Child Develpm., 3*, 1932, 108-113.
78. Ranken, H. B. Language and thinking: Positive and negative effects of naming. *Science, 141*, 1963, 48-50.
79. Rapier, J. Unpublished research. (In) Jensen, A. R. Learning abilities in Mexican-American children. *Calif. J. Educ. Res., 12*, 1961, 147-159.
80. Ratner, K. S. Some features of the motor conditioned reactions to verbal stimuli in man. *Pavlov. J. Higher Nerv. Activ. 9*, 1959, 441-447.
81. Razran, G. The observable unconscious and the inferable conscious in current Soviet psychology: Interoceptive conditioning, semantic conditioning, and the orienting reflex. *Psych. Rev., 68*, 1961, 81-147.
82. Razran, G. Soviet psychology and psychophysiology. *Behav. Sci., 4*, 1959, 35-38.
83. Reese, H. W. Verbal mediation as a function of age level. *Psych. Bull., 59*, 1962, 502-509.
84. Reese, H. W. Transfer to a discrimination task as a function of amount of stimulus pretraining and similarity of stimulus names. Unpublished Ph.D. dissertation. State University of Iowa, 1958.
85. Rheingold, H. L. Modification of Social Responsiveness in Institutional Babies. *Monogr. Soc. Res. Child Develpm., 21*, No. 2, 1956.
86. Rheingold, H. L., and Bayley, N. The later effects of an experimental modification of mothering. *Child Develpm., 30*, 1959, 363-372.
87. Schaffer, E. R., and Emerson, P. E. Patterns of response to physical contact in early human development. *J. Child Psychol. Psychiat., 5*, 1964, 1-13.
88. Sears, R. R., Maccoby, E. E., and Levin, H. *Patterns of Child Rearing*. Row, Peterson, Evanston, 1957.
89. Semler, J., and Iscoe, J. Comparative and developmental study of the learning abilities of Negro and white children under four conditions. *J. Educ. Psychol., 54*, 1963, 38-44.
90. Singer, M. T. Verbal labeling and conceptual clarity. Talk given at Stanford University, 1962.
91. Sin'kovskaia, K. V. The influence of verbal explanation on the time taken to reverse salivary and motor conditioned reflexes in children of school age. *Pavlov. J. Higher Nerv. Activity, 8*, 1958, 611-615.
92. Sin'kovskaia, K. V. The effect of verbal instruction on the secretory and motor conditioned reflexes of school children. *Pavlov. J. Higher Nerv. Activ., 8*, 1958. 161-167.
93. Sontag, L. W., Baker, C. T., and Nelson, V. L. Mental Growth and personality development: A longitudinal study. *Monogr. Soc. Res. Child Develpm., 23*, No. 68, 1958.
94. Spiker, C. C. Stimulus pretraining and subsequent performance in the delayed reaction experiment. *J. Exp. Psychol., 52*, 1956, 107-111.
95. Stevenson, H. W., and Bitterman, M. E. The distance effect in the transposition of intermediate size by children. *Amer. J. Psychol., 68*, 1955, 274-279.
96. Stevenson, H. W., and Iscoe, I. Overtraining and transposition in children. *J. Exp. Psychol., 47*, 1954, 251-255.
97. Stoddard, G. D. Intelligence: Its nature and nurture. *Yearbook Nat. Soc. Stud. Educ., 39*, 1940.
98. Stutsman, R. Performance tests for pre-school age. *Genet. Psychol. Monogr., 1*, 1-67.
99. Terman, L. M., and Merrill, M. A. *Measuring intelligence: a Guide to the Administration of the New Revised Stanford-Binet Tests*. Boston, Houghton-Mifflin, 1937.
100. Terman, L. M., and Merrill, M. A. *Stanford-Binet Intelligence Scale: Manual for the Third Revision, Form L-M*. Boston, Houghton-Mifflin, 1960.
101. Terrell, G. The role of incentive in discrimination learning in children. *Child Develpm., 29*, 1959, 231-236.
102. Terrell, G., Durkin, K., and Wiesley, M. Social class and the nature of the incentive in discrimination learning. *J. Abnorm. Soc. Psychol., 59*, 1959, 270-272.
103. Unger, S. M. A behavior theory approach to the emergence of guilt reactions in the child. *J. Child Psychol. Psychiat., 5*, 1964, 85-101.

104. Walters, R. H., and Parke, R. D. Social motivation, dependency and susceptibility to social influence. (In) *Advances in Experimental Social Psychology*, Vol. 2. Berkowitz, L. (Ed.) Academic Press, New York, 1966.
105. Wechsler, D. *Wechsler Intelligence Scale for Children (Manual)*. The Psychological Corporation, New York, 1949.
106. White, R. Competence and the Psychosexual Stages of Development. (In) *Nebraska Symposium on Motivation*, Jones, M. (Ed.).University of Nebraska Press, Lincoln, 1960, 137-138.
107. Whiting, B. B. (Ed.) *Six Cultures: Studies of Child Rearing*. John Wiley, New York, 1963.
108. Whiting, J. W. M., and Child I. L. *Child Training and Personality*. Yale University Press, New Haven, 1953.
109. Winder, C. L., et al. Dependency of patients, psychotherapists' responses, and aspects of psychotherapy. *J. Consult. Psychol.*, 26, 1962, 129-134.

CHAPTER 7

INHERITANCE AND PSYCHOLOGICAL PROCESSES

INTRODUCTION

It is an obvious fact that infants, children, and adults do not all behave alike, nor do they have identical capacities, aptitudes, or rates of development.

In the nineteen-twenties and nineteen-thirties a spirited battle was joined between psychologists who insisted that most of the causes of and variability in human behavior could be accounted for by variations in environmental conditions and those who believed that genetic factors could primarily account for development and individual differences.[31, 40] This was the nature vs. nurture dispute. This dispute over the source of variation, whether genetic or environmental, became ideological in nature. In effect, the environmental view became predominant and until the nineteen fifties work on genetic or innate determinants of human behavior was at an ebb.

This dichotomy of environmental versus genetic determination of development is not theoretically useful. What is really at issue is the interaction of the genetic and environmental factors producing certain characteristics in a child or groups of children, at a certain time and under given conditions.[1, 21] It may really be best, in fact, to think of various types of environments, one being a genetic environment. A child with a genotype for "fatness" may weigh less than one with genotype for "leanness" if the former gets little to eat because of the poverty of his parents and the latter is fed constantly by rich, anxious parents. The

153

question is how the internal genetic environment interacts with nutrition. It has been clearly shown that the height of children is often closely correlated with the height of the parents and that there is a considerable hereditary component in the determination of stature.[42, 43] However, children of Japanese immigrants born in America end up taller than their parents who were born in Japan. The nutritional factor of a better diet makes them grow taller.[9] There is no single solution to the nature-nurture problem. If all children had exactly the same experiences, that is the same diet, climate, amount of reward, and so forth, all differences between them would be of genetic origin. *This never happens.* If all children had the same genotype then all differences between them would be due to the external environment; this cannot occur. Only identical twins have the same genotype. *Individual differences, therefore, are always due to some interaction of biological and environmental determinants.* There are few psychological characteristics of children that are influenced heavily by genetics that are not also modified by experience; there are also many behaviors in children that are chiefly learned or produced by experience, which are influenced by the child's physiological make-up, either directly or indirectly.

Watson, the founder of American behaviorism, stated in 1924: "Give me a dozen healthy infants, well formed, and my own specified world to bring them up in, and I'll guarantee to take anyone at random and train him to become any type of specialist I might select—doctor, lawyer, artist, merchant-chief, and, yes, even beggar and thief, regardless of his talents, penchants, tendencies, abilities, vocations, or race of his ancestors."[51] Evidence now suggests that Watson could never have made good on this boast even if given a chance.

INNATE FACTORS

The reason Watson's statement was rash is that infants are either born with, or develop early, certain bodily structures that help cause behavioral predispositions that persist over time. The resulting behaviors not only persist but may be hard to change. Many of these predispositions may be related to physiological structures, which are inherited. Some may, however, be due to experiences before birth, during birth, or shortly thereafter. For example, one study found marked differences in the functioning of the neuromuscular system of young infants. The infants were classified as quiet, moderately active, and active in their behavior. The neuromuscular differences were present quite early and their effects tended to persist.[17] Infants also show reliable individual differences in sleep and feeding patterns, as well as in their responses to sensory stimulation.[11] These differences are not considered to be mainly produced by prolonged learning. Biochemical and autonomic nervous system functioning also varies reliably from infant to infant, with each baby having his own somewhat different but regular pattern.[35, 52] Study 7.1 is illustrative of the fact that infants only a few months old show persistently constant responses to the external environment and that they tend to behave the same way when they are two years old.

INTRINSIC REACTION TYPES

STUDY 7.1

Stella Chess and her coworkers studied 85 children from the time they were two to three months old until they were about two years old. They directly observed the infants for two- to three-hour periods in the home on repeated occasions. The children were also observed by their pediatrician and were given tests of development at various times. Nine categories of behavior were studied and named.

Activity — Passivity
Regularity — Irregularity
Intense reactor — Mild reactor
Approacher — Withdrawer
Adaptive — Nonadaptive
High threshold — Low threshold
Positive mood — Negative mood
Selective — Nonselective
Distractibility — Nondistractibility

In addition to direct observations they obtained detailed histories about the infants' behaviors from the parents. Histories were taken when the babies were two to three months old and then at three-month intervals in the first year, and at longer intervals after that.

Analysis of the behavior in infancy and behavior beyond the first year supported their hypothesis of the presence of "intrinsic reaction types." That is, the infants tended to show specific, individual patterns of behavior in the nine categories. These patterns were observable quite early and tended to persist. Consistency in reaction type carried through the two-year length of the study. Of course, the consistent individual differences could have formed before the second or third months and not have been inborn or innate; or they could have been due to both innate and experiential factors. The impression of Dr. Chess and her colleagues, however, is that the differences and their consistent persistence were due to innate factors and not due to learning. They assume that some children are born more active, or distractible, or irregular, and so on, than others.

They point out that surveys done on the effects of early child care practices, such as weaning the child early or late or having him on a fixed versus a demand feeding schedule, do not show any consistent effects on personality. The reason they do not, according to Dr. Chess and her colleagues, is that the very same early child care practices might have varying or even opposite effects on infants who are innately different. A "regular" infant may be easily taught to eat every four hours and thus not suffer from being on a fixed feeding schedule, while an "irregular" infant may find being made to eat exactly every four hours extremely distressing.

Chess, S., et al. Characteristics of the individual child's behavioral responses to the environment. *The Amer. J. Orthropsychiat.*, 29, 1959, 791-802.

SENSORY AND MOTOR PROCESSES

Genetic factors affect bodily structures which are involved in the acquisition of behavior. These structures include the nervous system, internal organs, and external features such as arms and legs. The more closely the behavior of children is influenced by bodily structure, the more clearly one can see the effects of heredity. Most of Dr. Chess's behavior categories like activity, high threshold, or intense reactor, are really closely tied to nervous system functions and external bodily structures. Other studies have shown that abilities like sharp hearing are dependent almost entirely on physiology and are highly dependent on heredity.[48, 49] In addition, abilities which depend mostly on the dexterity of the hands and their coordination with vision are also highly heritable (inherited). Consequently, even though the child has to be shown how to perform the tasks, his abilities at card sorting, tweezer dexterity, and mirror drawing are determined to a fair degree by largely inherited factors like hand speed and hand steadiness.[34] Activity, vigor of movements and impulsivity, which are strongly affected by nervous system activity, are largely innate, and still show the effects of inheritance at high school age.[49] There is no marked reversal in these characteristics, on the whole, even after 15 or 16 years. Study 7.1 illustrates the extremely high degree to which some learned behaviors are heavily influenced by the genetic environment which largely controls bodily structures and their functioning.

TWIN RESEMBLANCES IN MOTOR SKILLS

STUDY 7.2

Quinn McNemar, a distinguished statistician and psychometrician, early in his career became interested in the effects of heredity on motor skills, especially those which required the use of the hand and its coordination with vision.

In one study, he utilized as part of his sample 46 pairs of fraternal twins and 47 pairs of identical twins, all boys of junior high school age. Fraternal twins, although born at the same time, are genetically no more alike than any two ordinary brothers and sisters. Fraternal twins represent the fertilization of two different egg cells by two different sperm, but at about the same time. They do share some common genetic characteristics, having the same parents, but no more so than children born to the same parents a year or more apart. On the other hand, identical twins have an identical genotype. Identical twins represent the splitting of one fertilized egg cell and its consequent development into two organisms. Being genetically identical, any differences between them are due to the external environment.

If motor skills have a heavy hereditary influence, one identical male twin should do about as well in them as his identical brother. One identical twin should get about the same score as another. Fraternal twins do have a somewhat similar genotype, having the same parents. However, the genotype of one is different from that of the other to a fair extent. Consequently, even if heredity importantly influences motor skills, fraternal twins should show only a medium amount of similarity in skills in this area.

McNemar chose five measures of motor skill. The first was a pursuit rotor task which is similar to keeping a target in the sights of a gun. The second was a hand steadiness test and the third a test of hand speed. The fourth dealt with the ability to pack spools. The fifth was a test of the ability to sort playing cards.

Let us see how closely the behavior of the pairs of twins

resembled each other. The behaviors are represented in terms of correlations, with 1 representing exactly the same score in a set of twins and zero no similarity in scores at all. Correlations of 1 or zero are almost never found since measurement is not that exact. A correlation of .90 or above means very high similarity and one below .10, certainly very little. Let us look at the results:

	Identical Twins	*Fraternal Twins*
Pursuit rotor	.95	.50
Steadiness	.85	.24
Speed	.82	.43
Spool packing	.61	.49
Card sorting	.73	.50

In every case the identical twins have more similar scores (the higher the correlation the more similar the score) than the fraternal twins. If one identical twin gets a certain score, his brother gets one very close to it. The correlations of the fraternal twins are always lower but they are substantial, usually close to .50. That is the size correlation one would expect if genetic influence on some behavior was very high in the children of the same parents. If one fraternal twin gets a certain score his brother will get a score somewhat higher or lower, but not extremely different. It is clear, therefore, that genotype heavily influences motor skill of the hand and that external environmental influences in this area are less important. Although identical twins may be treated more alike than fraternal twins, that is not likely to account for the striking results found by McNemar.

McNemar, Q. Twin resemblances in motor skills. *J. Genet. Psychol.*, 42, 1933, 70-97.

ENVIRONMENTAL EFFECTS

Findings such as those of Chess and NcNemar do not mean that behavior cannot be changed by external environmental circumstances, even if it is heavily influenced by inherited physiological factors. For example, impulsivity in young children has been reduced, at least for a short period, by means of simple instructions. Nevertheless, it may well be that impulsivity is partly determined by hereditary factors. Many hereditary predispositions to behave in certain ways can be modified by suppressing them through punishment and setting counter examples, or by rewarding their opposite.[6] Left-handed children, for instance, are often trained to become right-handed. Under certain circumstances, as when a child deviates from what is thought to be the best way to behave, people intervene to alter what may be a partly inherited disposition. Study 7.3 is an illustration of the proposition that people may try to change and succeed in changing hereditary predispositions in children.

ENVIRONMENTAL PRESSURES FOR CONFORMITY

STUDY 7.3

Dr. Raymond B. Cattell and his colleagues attempted to find out the extent to which certain personality factors were due to inheritance and the degree to which they were due to environmental factors. The were able to study identical twins, nonidentical twins, ordinary brothers and sisters raised in the same family, ordinary brothers and sisters raised separately in different families, pairs of unrelated children raised together in foster families, and random pairs of children unrelated and living apart in the general population. In their study they included the various combinations which could be expected to show greater or lesser effects of both heredity and environment. Identical twins should share the greatest hereditary similarity and unrelated children in the same foster home should show the greatest effects of the external environment.

One of Cattell's most interesting findings was what he called "coercion to the biocultural norm." By this he meant that if a child deviates in one direction from a norm or average set by the biological and cultural central tendencies of his group, he will experience attempts to change him in the other direction. In other words, children who have genetically influenced behavioral tendencies not in line with those of others, will find that people will try to get them to change those behaviors. Of course, this is not always the case and, moreover, the parent or other socializers may fail. However, certain genotypes may fail to influence behavioral tendencies in children because their effects are reversible and adults may see to it that they are reversed.

Cattell also discovered what he called "coercion to the ideal." Here the adults don't want the child to be average but to conform to some ideal which may be extreme. Although parents may want their child to be average in independence and dominance in early years (coercion to the biocultural norm), they may want him to be as careful and exact as possible in doing tasks (coercion to an ideal). If a child is innately impulsive and distractible, parents or others may train him to modify these tendencies in a direction which they feel is more desirable.

> Cattell, R. B., et al. A first approximation to nature-nurture ratios for eleven primary personality factors in objective tests. *J. Abnorm. Soc. Psychol.*, *14*, 1957, 143-159.

INHERITANCE AND IQ

By 1919, it was clear that there was a substantial correlation between the intelligence test scores of children of the same parents (siblings) and also between the intelligence scores of parents and their children. The correlation was usually about .5. Several investigators found relationships of this magnitude.[10, 19, 41] These findings gave rise to the general proposition that intelligence was quite highly influenced by genotype, that is, by hereditary factors. This proposition rested on the finding that the general level of intelligence test scores was much more similar among brothers, sisters, and other family members than among randomly selected, unrelated members of the population.

Unfortunately, the studies of ordinary family members living together failed to take into account the effects of a similar home environment. Family members share a common social and physical environment. Similarities in their scores can be produced by similar experiences, including similar conditions of learning. Mating in marriages is assortative rather than random, which is to say that often "like marries like." Educated men tend to marry educated women, and people tend to marry within their own social class.[8] This results in making the home more homogeneous; children are usually exposed to parents of similar backgrounds. Since these studies did not control for the effects of a common living environment on IQ score, they failed to demonstrate anything conclusive about the role of heredity in intelligence.

STUDY OF CHILDREN IN FOSTER AND ADOPTIVE HOMES

Attempts have been made to separate the influences of experience from hereditary influences. Barbara Stoddard Burks compared the correlations between the IQ's of children living at home and those of their parents, with correlations between IQ's of foster children and their foster parents. Children living with their own parents have both genotype and environment partly in common with their parents. Children in foster homes have the environment partly in common with the foster parents, but, not being biologically related to them, have little or no genotype in common. If the common social environment is largely accountable for intelligence, the IQ's of foster children should be nearly as similar to those of their foster parents as the IQ's of children living with their natural parents are to the IQ's of their own parents. Dr. Burks found that the intelligence of children living at home correlated .45 with their father's IQ and .46 with that of their mother. This is the usual finding. On the other hand, the IQ's of foster children correlated only .07 with those of the foster father and .19 with those of the foster mother. The common social environment in the foster home seemed to have minor effects on the IQ's of the children. Burks estimated that heredity contributes about 80 percent to intelligence under ordinary fairly good conditions.[5]

Unfortunately, this study does not give us information about the correlation between the IQ's of the foster children and their natural parents. A long term study by Skodak and Skeels is more definitive, since they had a great deal of information about the natural or true parents as well as about the foster parents. Study 7.4 presents their study and also discusses the valuable "longitudinal," approach of taking repeated measurements on the same group of children. Again, This study clearly implies that heredity is an important factor in determining intelligence.

RELATIONSHIPS BETWEEN ADOPTED CHILDREN AND THEIR TRUE AND FOSTER PARENTS

STUDY 7.4

Marie Skodak and Harold M. Skeels, of the Iowa Child Welfare Research Station, did a "longitudinal" study of the development of intelligence in adopted children. A longitudinal study gathers information on repeated occasions, over a long period of time, on the same subjects. In this way, the stability of behaviors, or the ways in which they change as a function of age or other time related variables, can be studied. The mental development of the children in this study was evaluated four times: when they were two years and two months old; at four years and three months; at seven years; and when they were 13 years and six months old. All children in the study had been placed in an adoptive home under the age of six months, were given an intelligence test after one year's residence in the adoptive home, and were of white, North European background. Information was available on the true, natural parents and the adoptive parents of each of the 60 girls and 40 boys in the study.

If home environment were a very important factor in intelligence, one would expect that the foster child's IQ would be correlated with the education of the adoptive parents. Better educated parents would provide a more stimulating home environment for the child and his IQ should become higher as a result. However, no correlation was found between the educational level of the adoptive parents and the IQ's of the children they were caring for. On the last IQ test done at age 13 years, six months, the IQ of the child correlated only .02 with the education of the adoptive mother, and not at all (.00) with the education of the adoptive father.

Skodak and Skeels found that the adoptive parents were in general from a higher socioeconomic background than the true, natural parents. Consequently, the environment was working against a correlation between the IQ's of the adopted children and those of their natural parents. Not only were they away from their natural parents from the age of six months, but they were in a different, better environment. If there was a substantial correlation between the IQ's of these children and those of the parents from whom they were separated at six months of age, it would be due to genotypically controlled, hereditarily influenced factors. In fact, the actual correlation between the true, natural mothers' IQ's and the IQ's of their children brought up elsewhere by others was .44 (when the children were 13 years and six months old). This figure is near the correlation found when children live at home with their natural parents. IQ thus seemed to be heavily influenced by genotype.

Skodak, M., and Skeels, H. M. A final follow-up study of one hundred adopted children. *J. of Genet. Psychol.*, 74, 1949, 85-125.

EFFECT OF ENVIRONMENT

The fact that such studies point to the importance of hereditary factors in intelligence certainly does not mean that environmental factors are not very important. It has been reported that children placed in foster homes with intelligent, educated adults show gains in intelligence test scores while those placed in foster homes with less intelligent, less educated adults show little rise in intelligence. The "better" the foster home, in terms of environment, the higher the IQ of the children.

Children adopted early seem to benefit more from a "good" adoptive home than those adopted later. If siblings are separated before they are six months old their intelligence in later life correlates lower than if they are raised together at home. Unrelated children placed into the same home do acquire a somewhat similar level of intelligence, although the correlations range only between .25 and .37.[16] It must be noted that these and other findings are partly contradictory to the results reported in Study 7.4. Methodological and other problems make it difficult to resolve the contradictions. Children falsely considered feeble minded, when put in a beneficial environment, have later attained normal and above IQ scores. The preponderance of studies show marked environmental as well as hereditary effects.

THE STUDY OF TWINS

The study of twins provides another approach to the question of the extent of hereditary influence on intelligence. We have already seen that there are two types of twins: Identical or monozygotic (MZ) twins developing from one fertilized cell and having, therefore, almost identical genotypes and fraternal, also called dizygotic (DZ), twins developing from two different fertilized cells and having genotypes comparable to those of any two siblings (brothers or sisters). Identical (MZ) twins should be more alike than fraternal (DZ) twins in all those areas of behavior to which genetic differences contribute heavily, since MZ twins are almost identical in heredity. Studies therefore, sometimes compare fraternal to identical twins. If the MZ twins are more similar on some characteristic, the characteristic is considered to be heavily influenced by heredity. In a refinement of this method, MZ twins are studied who have been separated from each other shortly after birth. If they are still very much alike in some attribute in spite of having grown up in different environments, that attribute is likely to be heavily dependent on hereditary influences.

A caution should be introduced about the limits of the twin study method of estimating hereditary effects. There is no guarantee that identical twins are not treated more alike than fraternal twins. The parents may dress them identically and people may not be able to tell them apart. Even if identical twins are separated in childhood, child placement agencies may go out of their way to put them in similar homes. Furthermore, until recently, it was difficult to determine if twins really were identical or not. Nor has care always been properly exercised in these studies in matching for factors of age, socioeconomic position, and other pertinent variables. Many of the same criticisms can also be made of the methodology of foster or adoptive child studies.[48] Nevertheless, the findings seem to be so consistent that they cannot be ignored, despite possible methodological faults. At most, the above criticisms bear on the exact degree of the relationships found, not on their overall validity. The most cited study in this field appears in Study 7.5.

THE STUDY OF TWINS AND INTELLIGENCE

STUDY 7.5

A classical study in this field was carried out by H. H. Newman and his coworkers with the results reported in 1937. They studied three separate sets of twins: 50 pairs of identical twins and 50 pairs of fraternal twins living with their parents, and 19 pairs of identical twins separated and reared apart. The 19 pairs of identical twins were almost all separated before they were a year old and raised in different homes. Three measures of intelligence were used and the results reported in terms of correlations were highly consistent:

	Fraternal Twins	*Identical together*	*Identical reared apart*
Binet mental age	.60	.86	.64
Binet IQ	.63	.88	.67
Otis IQ	.62	.92	.73

If one looks first at the correlations in the middle column, it is clear that identical twins reared together have very similar IQ's. The correlations are very high, showing that if one identical twin had a certain IQ the other one had a highly similar, almost equivalent, one. Of course, they shared a similar home environment. The identical twins reared apart, shown in the last column, do not show correlations as high, but the correlations are substantial. This means that the different environments the separated identical twins lived in sharply affected their IQ's. Despite the same heredity, identical twins reared apart don't have equivalent IQ's, although their IQ's are still similar. They are *slightly* more similar than those of fraternal twins, whose degrees of similarity can be seen in the first column. In this study the similarity of IQ's of identical twins reared apart is greater, but only by a little, than that of fraternal twins reared together. (Of the identical twins reared apart, the ones reared in socioeconomically superior homes showed higher IQ's.)

One possible conclusion from this study is that although heredity contributes significantly to intelligence, the external environment also clearly plays a very important role. Home environment certainly modifies the IQ's of identical twins reared apart, showing that intelligence is effected significantly by life experiences.

Newman, H. H., Freeman, F. N., and Holziner, K. J. *Twins: A Study of Heredity and Environment.* University of Chicago Press, Chicago, 1937.

Other evidence from twin studies clearly supports the conclusion that heredity plays an important role in determining measured IQ, but that, within limits, the measured IQ is influenced significantly by the external environment. It is quite likely that the external environment will have a large impact if it is very good or if it is very poor. The more extreme the environment the greater its effects will be.

UNDERSTANDING HEREDITY AND ENVIRONMENT IN RELATION TO INTELLIGENCE

For some time the study of the genetic contribution to general intelligence was part of the unfortunate battle between those who claimed that heredity was all-important and those who wanted to believe that almost anything could be achieved by manipulating the environment the child lived in. The first group was certain that children were predestined to be stupid, mediocre, or brilliant and the second that children were born with minds like a blank page upon which experience would write an IQ. Rather than asking whether heredity or external environment was more responsible for intelligence, the contestants could have been asking how these two conditions interact to produce the final result. We are dealing with an interaction and not an either-or proposition.[12] It must be recognized that *intellectual ability,* which an IQ test measures only partially, is a complex ability, partly learned and partly controlled by the genotype acting through physical structures. Intelligence is too complicated to be inherited like eye color. Clearly, however, biochemical processes, brain structure, and other nervous system structures, which contribute to the development of intellectual ability, are inherited. These biological processes and structures, which can be viewed as a biological environment, heavily influence the limits of intelligence which can be achieved. The actual achieved levels, however, significantly depend on the nature of the child's experience.

Environment, in the sense of experiences, is significant in setting the level of intelligence within the limits allowed by the largely inherited capacities of an individual's central nervous system. This is seen most clearly when a group of children suffers from an extremely bad external environment. The traditional example here concerns the famous "English canal-boat children".[19] However, it has its counterpart in some of our more impoverished Negro slum children. IQ test scores on such children are quite low. To conclude that they are hereditarily retarded and born to retarded parents would be incorrect. Evidence shows that if such children are put in a good environment, under decent educational conditions, their intelligence level rises significantly. However, even under the best of conditions no group seems to produce more geniuses than any other merely because of environmental advantage. Heredity seems to set the limits of intelligence, but environment may determine whether intelligence reaches these limits or falls quite short of capacity.[38] Finally, no one knows of what the human mind is potentially capable or what the limits of intellect are. Environmental manipulations may be found, such as mnemonic devices or teaching machines, which will help children surpass what now look like hereditary limits.

MENTAL RETARDATION

The possibility of having a retarded child worries many actual or potential parents. Children with IQ's under 70 are considered retarded. There is nothing magic about this figure; it is partly arbitrary and a matter of classificatory convenience. If the child's IQ is about 50 to 70 he is termed a "moron;" an "imbecile," if the IQ is about 25 to 50; and an "idiot," if the IQ is less than 25. The classifications, although rough, do correspond to some extent to learning ability and social adequacy. An IQ of 25 is insufficient for a child to master even the simple tasks of feeding and dressing. At an age when other normal children can largely fend for themselves, such children must be cared for or they will die. With an IQ over 25, children may be able to master some of the simpler functions of taking care of themselves, but they will not be able, if they survive, to earn a living or manage outside of very sheltered conditions. An IQ over 50 makes possible both self-maintenance and the performance of quite simple tasks, for which money is paid. However, at IQ levels of 50 to 70 the child needs much help and constant supervision and will continue to need it as an adult.[50]

Factors of Inheritance in Mental Retardation

There are instances where mental deficiency is due to a biochemical defect which is inherited. However, mental deficiency can be due to brain injury before, during, or after birth. It can be the result of complex biochemical states whose origins are only partly known and which may or may not involve hereditary factors. Other causal agents whose nature is currently obscure may also be involved. The clearest case of the mental deficiency depending on genetic factors is that of *phenylketonuria*, also known as *phenylpyruvic oligophrenia*. In this case a genotype is inherited which fails to produce the enzyme needed to convert one of the amino acids, phenylalanine, into the substance, tyrosine. Consequently there is both a shortage of tyrosine and a toxic build-up of phenylalanine. As a result the child's brain will not develop normally: his ability to learn is severely restricted, and he is likely to become an inmate of an institution for the feeble-minded.[24, 30] Fortunately, it is now possible to deal with this condition. Best results are obtained if it is noticed early. The infant is fed a diet consisting of foods free of phenylalanine. With the use of the special diet, mental development improves even in older afflicted children.[3, 53] The way in which this condition is genetically transmitted is known. The parents are mentally normal but carry the dangerous genetic possibility in their chromosomal structure. By means of procedures now available, persons with a history of phenylketonuria in their families can be tested and the probability of phenylketonuric children being born to them can be predicted.[22]

Three other conditions which cause mental retardation through brain degeneration, once some development has already taken place, are of known genetic origin. These are *infantile amaurotic idiocy, juvenile amaurotic idiocy*, and *Huntington's chorea*. The first begins at a few months of age, the second between two and ten years of age, and the last anywhere from ten to 70 years of age. These are conditions of neural degeneration and the disorders may last for a long time before death sets in. The parents, although carrying the genes responsible, themselves remain normal in the case of amaurotic idiocy. In the case of Huntington's chorea one of the parents will also develop the disorder sometime in life.[33] Some genetic brain disorders with a bearing on either early development or later degeneration are probably not present at birth or even a few years later. The results of genetic action, as of environmental action, for good or ill, goes on for a lifetime. Consequently, some genetically controlled biochemical disorders leading to maldevelopment or degeneration may manifest themselves at various points in childhood or adulthood.[4, 33] Study 7.6 shows how environmental intervention in the hereditary disease of phenylketonuria can be of tremendous help. It is illustrative of the fact that when the specific nature of genetic action is known, it can often be changed.[29]

DETECTION AND PARTIAL CURE OF PHENYLKETONURIA

STUDY 7.6

Dr. Arnold R. Kaplan, of the Laboratory of Medical Genetics of the Cleveland Psychiatric Institute and Hospital, has reviewed most of the facts known about phenylketonuria.

The disorder can be detected early in life by a relatively simple test even before mental retardation begins. Detectable amounts of phenylpyruvic acid may not be found until the infant is about six weeks old. The time to do the needed test, therefore, is soon after six weeks of age, perhaps the first time the infant has a check-up by his pediatrician. Although it may be advisable for every infant to have the test, it is imperative if older brothers or sisters have had the disorder or if there is a history of it in the family.

If the disorder can be detected early, and the proper diet is instituted, severe retardation can be prevented. If the infant is treated before six months of age his intelligence, while still possibly partly retarded, will usually fall into the IQ range of 70 to 100. Treatment after two years of age is almost useless; the child will be completely untrainable.

Results are best if treatment is started at about six weeks, or even before, if the condition is picked up that early. Milk does have phenylalanine in it and a substitute is needed. Such substitute formulas are commercially available.

Unless the special diet is instituted, mental retardation is almost certain to ensue. Most children with this inherited biochemical disorder cannot communicate verbally. Oddly enough, a few children with the disorder develop a near-normal intelligence. It is unknown how or why. This is not a very widespread disorder and accounts for only one percent of institutionalized mental defectives. It has been variously estimated that somewhere between one in 10,000 to one in 40,000 infants develop it.

Kaplan, A. R. Phenylketonuria: A review. *Eugen. Quart.*, *9-10*, 1962-63, 151-160.

A much more common type of mental retardation, which may involve a genotypic component, is *mongolism*. The mongoloid infant is so characteristic in his physical appearance that the disorder is easy to spot and has been known as a distinct problem for a long time.[44] Apparently a disorder of the chromosomes is involved.[23, 32] The mongoloid child has 47 chromosomes instead of the usual 46.[15] The problem, to oversimplify, is that of too much genetic material. The degree of retardation varies, with some mongoloids limited to the idiot level of performance but some functioning at a much higher, although still retarded, level.

INHERITANCE OF MENTAL DISORDERS

Schizophrenia

Mental disorders developed in childhood, or even later, may have a hereditary component. However, in the case of mental abnormalities other than degenerative nervous system disorders, no one has yet discovered how the genes contribute to the abnormalities. It is unclear what chromosomes or genes are involved or how. It has been shown repeatedly that if one identical twin develops schizophrenia (a severe form of psychosis). There is a 76 to 86 percent chance that the other identical twin will develop it. In the case of fraternal twins or ordinary siblings, if one develops schizophrenia, the chances are only 14 percent that the other one will also develop it. No one, however, has yet found out what sort of genetic or biochemical factor is responsible, if any.[27, 28, 45]

Inheritance of Neurotic Tendencies

There has been some research which indicates the possibility that a hereditary component may be involved in some aspects of neuroses, a form of psychological abnormality less severe than the psychoses. The components of neuroticism which may be influenced by hereditary factors can sometimes be traced to the functioning of the autonomic nervous system. The autonomic nervous system influences emotional reactions. Purportedly some unknown genetic action effects the autonomic nervous system, which in turn predisposes the child, and later the adult, to acquire some behaviors which are considered to be neurotic in nature. Neurotic anxiety and depression and mild schizoid tendencies may possibly have a heritable component. Other types of neurotic tendencies show no significant heritable aspect.[20] It should be made clear that neuroses are probably mostly determined by the ways parents interact with their children and by other social environmental experiences, although heritable bodily factors may play a part.

Introversion and Extraversion

The *type of neurosis* which a child or adult develops may depend partly, it has been contended, upon whether he is more introverted or more extraverted. This viewpoint claims that a hereditary component of an unknown type may be operating in determining the degree to which a child is extraverted or introverted. Of course, normal, neurotic, and psychotic persons all vary in their degree of extraversion or introversions. Introverted neurotics are said to develop anxiety, depression, or obsessional symptoms. Extraverted neurotics become hysterics or psychopaths, disorders known for their low degree of experienced anxiety. The degree of anxiety may be a function of the autonomic nervous system.[13]

The typical extraverted child is sociable, needs people to talk to, takes chances, and is impulsive. He likes change, is carefree, and easygoing. The extraverted child has a quick temper, is somewhat unreliable, and has trouble controlling his feelings. He is hard to socialize and his disorders, *if he develops them*, tend to be ones of conduct, delinquency, aggression, acting out, and, sometimes, of an hysterical nature. The introverted child is quiet and reserved. The introvert is not impulsive, is serious, and likes things well ordered. The introverted child tends to be pessimistic, reliable, and easily socialized. His problems, *if any*, involve anxiety, depression, or social withdrawal.[14]

It is interesting to note that introverted neuroses of childhood may, in the long run, be less of a problem than those developed by extraverted children, and, of course, *many introverted or extraverted children may never develop any neuroses*. The fears or anxieties that may be at the base of introverted children's neuroses often seem to disappear with time. Children may get over their fears. Some extraverted children's basic troubles may actually arise from their inability to worry or form social concerns. Since they may becomes antisocial and undersocialized, their troubles are more likely to persist into adulthood. Of 66 children who were originally sent for psychiatric help because of their antisocial and aggressive problems (truancy, lying, defiance, cruelty, and so forth) most tended to persist in these or similar behaviors. At the age of 18 only 21 percent of them had made a satisfactory adjustment. At 18 years of age, 59 percent had failed to make any major change in their conduct and 12 of them had committed at least one crime, and 13 (20 percent) developed some form of psychosis.[37] Another study dealt with 54 adults who were sufficiently introverted (shy and withdrawn) as children to be brought to a clinic anywhere from 16 to 27 years before. It was found that two-thirds were satisfactorily adjusted. Only two of them were disturbed enough to be in a mental hospital.[36] Other studies have yielded somewhat similar findings. Whatever the genetic contribution may be to certain types of introversive and anxiety-based disturbances in childhood, the effects are clearly reversible. These emotional disturbances of childhood seem to disappear, in many cases, even without any treatment by professionals. They certainly respond to psychological treatment. It should be kept in mind that high and low anxiety possibly based on autonomic nervous system activity and introversion-extraversion are two different factors. Study 7.7 is illustrative of work in this area.

THE INHERITANCE OF EXTRAVERSION-INTROVERSION

STUDY 7.7

Professor Hans J. Eysenck, of the Institute of Psychiatry at the Maudsley Hospital of London University, set out to determine whether extraversion-introversion in children was influenced by heredity. In addition to measures of extraversion-introversion he had measures of autonomic nervous system activity and intelligence of the children.

Eysenck, who with his coworkers has done many of the studies on the heritability of neuroses, used the twin study method. He relied on the differences found between identical and fraternal twins. His sample of children was taken from four suburbs of London. He found 102 pairs of twins of whom only 56 pairs were tested. Four were then dropped to equalize the groups so that 52 pairs were actually used. They were divided into four groups of 13 pairs each. The four groups were: male identical, female identical, male fraternal, female fraternal. The children were between 13 and 14 years old.

Eysenck found that intelligence, autonomic nervous system activity, and extraversion-introversion all had a hereditary component. However, the three factors were relatively independent of each other. There could be high or low IQ extraverts, who could also vary on autonomic activity, and so on. That is, various combinations of extraversion-introversion, intelligence, or autonomic nervous system activity would be possible in a given child. Heredity was shown to play a part in the determination of each of the three.

Eysenck, H. J. The inheritance of extraversion-introversion. *Acta Psychol.*, *12-13*, 1956-58, 95-110.

INHERITANCE AND SOCIAL VALUES

It seems instructive to consider a case where a chiefly genotypically controlled state influences a child's behavior because it is related to social values. In this instance, the physical aspects which the genes control can become vital to a child's behavior predominantly because of the value people put on the physical attributes at issue. Some boys mature early physically and some boys mature late physically. In puberty and early adolescence some boys experience an early growth spurt; they become taller, heavier, more muscled, better coordinated, and develop their secondary sexual characteristics at an earlier age than other boys. Some boys do not undergo their growth spurt until later in adolescence; they may be well into high school before they get their main increases in height, weight, musculature, coordination, and secondary sexual characteristics like face and body hair.[26, 38]

The attitudes and behaviors shown by parents and their friends toward the adolescent boy—how they treat and accept him—may depend, in late junior high school and early high school, on his physical status. Early maturers have an advantage over late maturers. They are more likely to make sports teams, to be elected to school offices, and to have higher status. Adolescent boys who are physically mature at an early age are rated as being more attractive, better groomed, more matter-of-fact, more sociable and as showing more social initiative. The boys who are slower (later) in physical maturation are seen as engaging in more attention-getting behavior, being more restless, more bossy, less grown up, and less good looking than the boys who mature early.[47] Boys who are treated more like adults and who can excel at adult activities behave more like and are treated more like adults. Boys who look more like children are treated more like children and behave more like children. The advantage gained by the early maturers in adolescence persists into adulthood. In their early thirties they will be more responsible, more sociable, more dominant, and make a better impression.[25, 26] This is true despite the fact that by age 19 late maturers have caught up physically. We can see, therefore, that social, environmental variables can interact with genetic ones to cause interesting differences among children. Study 7.8 discusses some of these differences.

PHYSICAL DEVELOPMENT AND THE SOCIAL ENVIRONMENT

STUDY 7.8

Paul Henry Mussen and Mary Cover Jones hypothesized

that the boy whose physical development is slow is exposed to a social environment which will have adverse effects on his personality development.

A projective test, the Thematic Apperception Test, was the main measure of personality in this study. In this personality measure the participants are asked to look at cards showing people in various scenes or settings. (A few cards show scenes without people in them.) They are then asked to make up stories about the scenes, telling what led up to them, what is going on now, and how the story ends. They are also asked to tell what the people are feeling and thinking. The scenes are somewhat ambiguous and the participants are encouraged to exercise their imagination freely. The stories are taken to be indicative or typical of the needs, wishes, feelings, and conflicts of the person making them up. The person is said to be projecting himself into what he is writing.

The subjects in the study were 16 early maturing boys and 17 late maturing boys, all 17 years old. The types of stories told by the two groups of boys revealed that the Mussen and Jones general hypothesis was true. The late maturing boys were more likely to describe an unfavorable social environment in their stories. The data seemed to show that a more negative social world had had adverse effects on the personalities of the physically slow maturers. The stories of the late maturing boys indicated that they had had unfavorable conceptions of themselves and they felt more inadequate; that they had been and were being dominated and rejected although they still felt both dependent and rebellious toward their parents.

The early maturing boys, holders of school political office, pictures of athletic prowess and popularity, revealed a positive social environment as their lot. They felt adequate, accepted and relatively free from parental dependency and rebellion, in comparison with the late maturers. They were more self-confident, independent, and adult-like, judged from their written stories.

Mussen and Jones conclude that *rate* of physical maturing, chiefly regulated by genes, is important in personality development. However, this effect is due to the way children are treated *because of* their physique and is *not* caused directly *by* their physique.

Neither were all the boys in either of the two groups exactly alike. Individual parents' attitudes as well as other circumstances and abilities caused considerable differences.

174 *INHERITANCE AND PSYCHOLOGICAL PROCESSES*

> However, the findings held on the average for each of the two groups.
>
> Mussen, P. H., and Jones, M. C. Self conceptions, motivations, and interpersonal attitudes of late and early maturing boys. *Child Develpm.*, 28, 1957, 243-256.

We can see, therefore, that hereditary influences can effect psychological development in a variety of ways, some of them much more direct than others. Very little has been done to systematically study the interaction of hereditary and experiential factors, the nature of the mutual dependency of genetic and nongenetic environments in specific areas of inquiry. As indicated by the last sentence, it may be best not to think of heredity and environment but only of different types of environments acting on each other. There is a genetic environment, a physiological one, a physical and social one, and a psychological one. These all mutually influence each other to produce development in childhood.

SUMMARY

Although it has been customary to contrast genetic determinants with environmental ones as "causes" of development, it may be more useful to think in terms of the interaction of two or more types of environmental factors, one of them being a genetic one. Genetically produced influences interact with nongenetic ones to produce the various aspects of human behavior.

Intelligence, for instance, partly depends on biochemical and physiological capacities which are largely inherited, and life experiences, involving various types of stimulation, which are not inherited. Intelligence level is clearly constrained by inherent limits depending on biological possibilities, but the types of experiences encountered in the course of development may set the actual level of intelligent behavior which a child reaches. The genetic environment would be most important in determining intelligence if all children had the same life experiences. If their experiences were very similar, differences in IQ would chiefly be due to biological factors. Environmental effects can be most clearly seen when children have such impoverished life circumstances that almost all of them fail to reach their potential. Intelligence, as other human behavioral capacities, depends on the interaction of various influences, some of which are internal and inherited and some of which depend on the type of stimulation acting on the child.

Some children are born retarded or fail to develop normally due to biochemical or neurological defects. Certain of these defects are inherited, but their effects are reversible or may be compensated for. Other defects are not yet preventable or remediable to any significant extent and may not be heritable.

It is possible that genetic factors may play a predisposing part in the acquisition of various mental abnormalities. Biological defects of a yet unknown type may partly account for such psychoses as schizophrenia. The type of neuroses which some people develop may be influenced by the functioning of the autonomic nervous system.

Inheritance may affect the child in quite indirect ways dependent on the treatment he receives from others because of his physical characteristics. Since adults may favor certain eye or hair colors, prefer prettier children with certain physical capacities at given ages, or like children who react to stimulation in one way rather than another, *innate* physical characteristics or response tendencies may partly determine a child's social life experiences. These social experiences, in turn, will influence the childs' feelings, thoughts, and actions.

REFERENCES

1. Anastasi, A. Heredity and environment and the question "How?" *Psychol. Rev., 65*, 1958, 197-208.
2. Anastasi, A., and Foley, J. P. A proposed reorientation in the hereditary-environment controversy. *Psych. Rev., 55*, 1948, 239-249.
3. Armstrong, M. D., and Tyler, F. H. Studies on phenylketonuria. I. Restricted phenylalanine intake in phenylketonuria. *J. Clin. Invest., 34*, 1955, 565-580.
4. Burdette, W. J. (Ed.) *Metabolic Defects in Relation to the Gene.* Holden-Day, San Francisco, 1962.
5. Burks, B. S. The relative influence of nature and nurture upon mental development; a comparative study of foster parent-foster child resemblance and true parent-true child resemblance. *Yearbook Nat. Soc. Stud. Educ. Part 1, 27*, 1928, 219-316.
6. Cattell, R. B. A first approximation to nature-nurture ratios for eleven primary personality factors in objective tests. *J. Abnorm. Soc. Psychol., 54*, 1957, 143-159.
7. Chess, S., et al. Characteristics of the individual child's behavioral responses to the environment. *Amer. J. Orthopsychiat., 29*, 1959, 791-802.
8. Conrad, H. S., and Jones, H. E. A second study of family resemblances in intelligence: environmental and genetic implications of parent-child and sibling correlations in the total sample. *Yearbook Nat. Soc. Stud. Educ. Part 2, 39*, 1940, 97-141.
9. Dobzhansky, T. *Mankind Evolving.* Yale University Press, New Haven, 1962.
10. Elderton, E. M. A summary of the present position in regard to the inheritance of intelligence. *Biometrika, 14*, 1923, 378-408.
11. Escalona, S. Emotional Development in the First Year of Life. (In) *Problems of Infancy and Childhood: Sixth Conference.* Josiah Macy Foundation, New York, 1952.
12. Eysenck, H. J. The inheritance of extraversion-introversion. *Acta. Psychol., 12-13*, 1956-58, 95-110.
13. Eysenck, H. J. A dynamic theory of anxiety and hysteria. *J. Ment. Sci., 101*, 1955, 28-51.
14. Eysenck, H. J., and Rachman, S. *The Causes and Cures of Neurosis.* Knapp, San Diego, 1965.
15. Ford, C. E. Methods in human cytogenetics. (In) *Methodology in Human Genetics*, Burdette, W. J. (Ed.), Holden-Day, San Francisco, 1962.
16. Freeman, F. N., et al. The influence of environment on the intelligence, school

achievement, and conduct of foster children. *Yearbook Nat. Soc. Stud. Educ. Part 1, 27,* 1928.
17. Fries, M. E., and Woolf, P. J.   Some hypotheses of the role of congenital activity type in personality development. *Psychoanal. Stud. Child., 8,* International Universities Press, New York, 1953.
18. Gordon, H.   Mental and Scholastic Tests among Retarded Children. *Ed. Pamphlets, No. 44, Board of Control, 4th Biennial Report,* 1918-1920.
19. Gordon, H.   The influence of heredity on mental ability. *Report of the Children's Department.* State Board of Control, California, 1919.
20. Gottesman, I. I.   Differential inheritance of the psychoneuroses. *Eugen. Quart., 9-10,* 1962-63, 223-227.
21. Haldane, J. B. S.   *Heredity and Politics.* Norton, New York, 1938.
22. Hsia, D. Y-Y, et al.   Detection by phenylalanine tolerance tests of heterozygous carriers of phenylketonuria. *Nature, 178,* 1956, 1239-1240.
23. Jacobs, P. A., et al.   The somatic chromosomes in Mongolism. *Lancet, 1,* 1959, 710.
24. Jervis, G. A.   Phenylpyruvic oligophrenia: deficiency of phenylalanine oxidizing system. *Proc. Soc. Exp. Biol.,* New York, *82,* 1953, 514-515.
25. Jones, M. C.   The later careers of boys who were early or late maturing. *Child Develpm. 28,* 1957, 113-128.
26. Jones, M. C. and Bayley, N.   Physical maturing among boys as related to late behavior. *J. Educ. Psychol., 41,* 1950, 129-148.
27. Kallman, F. J.   *Heredity in Health and Mental Disorder.* Norton, New York, 1953.
28. Kallman, F. J.   The genetic theory of schizophrenia. *Amer. J. Psychiat., 103,* 1946, 309-322.
29. Kaplan, A. R.   Phenylketonuria: A review. *Eugen. Quart., 9-10,* 1962-63, 151-160.
30. Knox, W. E., and Hsia, D. Y-Y.   Pathogenic problems in phenylketonuria. *Amer. J. Med., 22,* 1957, 687-702.
31. Leahy, A. M.   Nature, nurture and intelligence. *Genet. Psychol. Monogr., 17,* 1935, 235-308.
32. Lejeune, J. et al.,   Etudes des chromosomes somatiques de neuf enfants monogolions. *C.R. Acad. Sci. Paris, 248,* 1959, 1721-1722.
33. McClearn, G. E.   Genetics and Behavior Development. (In) *Review of Child Development Research,* Hoffman, M., and Hoffman, L. W. (Eds.). Russell Sage Foundation, New York, 1964.
34. McNemar, Q.   Twin resemblances in motor skills. *J. Genet. Psychol., 42,* 1933, 70-97.
35. Mirsky, I. A.   Psychoanalysis and the biological sciences. (In) *Twenty Years of Psychoanalysis,* Alexander, F., and Ross, H. (Eds.). Norton, New York, 1953.
36. Morris, D. P., et al.   Follow-up studies of shy, withdrawn children. 1. Evaluation of later adjustment. *Amer. J. Orthopsychiat., 24,* 1954, 743-754.
37. Morris, H. H., et al.   Aggressive behavior disorders in childhood: a follow-up study. *Amer. J. Psychiat., 112,* 1955, 991-997.
38. Mussen, P., et al.   *Child Development and Personality.* Harper and Row, New York, 1963.
39. Mussen, P. H., and Jones, M. C.   Self conceptions, motivations and interpersonal attitudes of late and early maturing boys. *Child Develpm., 28,* 1957, 243-256.
40. Newman, H. H., et al.   *Twins: A Study of Heredity and Environment.* University of Chicago Press, Chicago, 1937.
41. Pearson, K.   Inheritance of physical characters. *Biometrika, 12,* 1918. 367-372.
42. Pearson, K.   On the laws of inheritance in man. II. *Biometrika, 3,* 1904, 131-190.
43. Pearson, K., and Lee, A.   On the laws of inheritance in man. I. *Biometrica, 2,* 1903, 357-462.
44. Penrose, S. L.   *The Biology of Mental Defect.* Sidgwick and Jackson, London, 1954.
45. Singer, R. D.   Organization as a unifying concept in schizophrenia. *A.M.A. Arch. Gen. Psychiat., 2,* 1960, 61-74.
46. Skodak, M., and Skeels, H. M.   A final follow-up study of one hundred adopted children. *J. Genet. Psychol., 74,* 1949, 85-125.
47. Tryon, C. M.   Evaluation of adolescent personality by adolescents. *Monogr. Soc. Res. Child Develpm. 4,* No. 4, 1939.
48. Vandenberg, S. G. (Ed.)   *Methods and Goals in Human Behavior Genetics.* Academic Press, New York, 1965.

49. Vandenberg, S. G. The hereditary abilities study: hereditary components in a psychological test battery. *Amer. J. Hum. Gen., 14*, 1962, 220-237.
50. Villee, C. A. *Biology.* W. B. Saunders, Philadelphia, 1964.
51. Watson, J. B. *Behaviorism.* Norton, New York, 1924.
52. Williams, R. V. *Biochemical Individuality.* Wiley, New York, 1956.
53. Woolf, L. I., et al. Treatment of phenylketonuria with a diet low in phenylalanine. *Brit. J. Med., 1*, 1955, 57-64.

CHAPTER 8

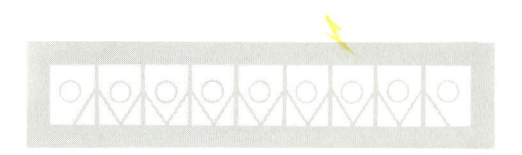

STAGE THEORIES

STAGE THEORY IN CHILD DEVELOPMENT

Some developmental psychologists believe that development takes place in a fixed, sequential order. Noting that behavior changes qualitatively, in type or nature, as well as quantitatively, some psychologists divide the course of development into periods or stages. Each period or stage is supposedly one which represents a new and different way of thinking or behaving. Stage theorists usually assume that different types of thought or behavior emerge in a fixed, sequential order. Since each type depends on the one that came before, or is somehow preordained biologically, every child is thought to go through the same stages in the same order, although not at exactly the same age. Other psychologists, whose views we will examine later, do not accept the assumptions stated above. They view behavioral development to be a changing but continuous process not readily divisible into discrete stages.

FREUD'S PSYCHOSEXUAL STAGES OF DEVELOPMENT

Sigmund Freud's theory of psychosexual development and Piaget's theories of various types of cognitive development, furnish the two best examples of stage theories.[10, 12, 26, 28] We shall examine Freud's theory first.

Freud's theory of psychosexual development is a maturational stage theory. It chiefly considers aspects of behavior classed under the concept of motivation. The forces which shape the motivation of the infant and child are conceived as deriving their power from a general undifferentiated pleasurable (sexual) energy, called the libido.[4] The libido is considered to be a quantity of sexual or pleasurable energy present at birth. The libido is thought to transfer its predominant focus from the mouth, which was the first zone for pleasurable gratification through sucking, to the anal zone, and finally to the genitals.[9] This movement of the libido is considered to take place in a series of age correlated, biologically determined, maturational shifts.[9, 10] Up to age one, the infant is regarded as chiefly an oral creature, taking his pleasure in through the mouth and secondarily through other sensory organs like the eye. From roughly one to three, libido apparently moves and resides in the anal area; pleasure is thought to be derived from eliminating or withholding feces. This is the anal period. From three to five or six, according to Freud, libido moves to and remains in the area of the genitals. Pleasure is derived from stimulation of that area or fantasies concerning it. This is called the phallic period and ends with partial resolution of the Oedipal complex, which we will not consider here. After six or so, until puberty, libido becomes inactive. This stage of inactivity is called the latent period. Latency ends, Freud said, with puberty; and, if true adult sexuality follows, libido is again vested in the genitals, giving rise to the final genital period of psychosexual development.[7, 13]

Freud considered these stages to be universal, stating that all infants and children go through them in the same order at about the same general ages. The movement of the libido can be affected by environmental factors like overindulgence or frustration but is biologically predetermined. The environmental factors decide only how much libido might remain behind in a previous zone and how much moves on to a new zone.[14, 18] Libido left behind in an earlier zone is said to be fixated there. Freudian theory, clearly, is a stage theory, the major stages being *oral*, *anal*, *phallic*, *latent*, and *genital*; it is maturational, since the libidinal movement does not depend very much on practice or experience and is considered to be biologically inherent.

Fixation

Fixation of libido was thought by Freud to be one of the major determinants of childhood and adult personality. In the Freudian view, fixation, essentially the failure of a considerable amount of libidinal energy to move on to the next zone of libidinization, occurs for either of two reasons. First, the infant or child might receive so much gratification or satisfaction at any particular stage of psychosexual maturation that he is unwilling to give up so much pleasure. This partial fixation at an earlier stage causes the child to be somewhat more infantile than one who more easily gives up pleasures typical of an earlier age. For instance, an adolescent fixated at the oral stage may take an inordinate interest in eating, drinking and smoking when he should be forming serious relationships with girls. A second cause of fixation might be too much frustration rather than too much gratification. If a child is too deprived at any stage he may continue all his life to seek after that type of gratification, trying to make up for what he missed.[7, 12, 33] According to Freudians, an adolescent (or adult) may remain orally fixated because he was either overindulged or neglected in early infancy.

Fixation and Personality and Character Types

Certain behavioral characteristics are considered to be typical of the stage of psychosexual gratification at which fixations take place. For instance, Freud originally proposed his theory of the anal character in terms of the fixation and distortion of the anal component of pregenital libido.[11] Toilet training is considered to be the crucial problem confronting the child at this stage. Anal eroticism, or pleasure from defecation, is opposed in this period, from one to three years of age, by social demands for cleanliness, continence, and regularity. The child fixated at this period, because of too lenient or too harsh toilet training demands, is supposed to become an anal character. An anal character is characterized chiefly by three traits: orderliness (overaccentuated, pedantic interest in cleanliness, reliability, and conscientiousness); parsimony (extending to collecting, hoarding, and avarice); and obstinacy (defiance, vindictiveness, and irascibility). These traits are an outcome of the conflict between child's pleasure in elimination and the punishments he gets for dirtiness, incontinence, and irregularity.[7]

In a similar way, theories about oral and phallic character have been constructed by followers of Freud.[7]

Studies on Gratification and Deprivation

Actually there is no evidence that, within reasonable limits, either too much or too little gratification in infancy and early childhood leads to any consistent differences in behavior.[18, 24] Sewell and Mussen, investigating the effects of oral gratification, compared children who were breast fed with those who were bottle fed, children fed on a demand schedule with those fed on a regular schedule, and children weaned slowly with those weaned suddenly. No relationship was found between any method of feeding or weaning and later adjustment. It is clear from studies in this area that wide differences in gratification and deprivation can occur without causing marked differences in behavior.[18, 34] Infant care practices do not tend to be good predictors of behavior or adjustment in later life.[18, 33, 34]

INTERPERSONAL RELATIONS

It seems to be more useful to view specific feeding or toilet training practices as part of the larger pattern of psychological rewards and punishments (interpersonal relationships). A study by Behrens illustrates this point.

MATERNAL ATTITUDES

STUDY 8.1

Marjorie Behrens studied the child rearing practices of families who were coming to a mental health clinic. She failed to find any relationship between feeding, weaning, toilet training, and adjustment. However, she also investigated the mother's underlying attitudes. That is, she studied the mothers' evaluations of and feelings toward their children. These attitudes probably showed themselves many times daily in the way a mother behaved toward her child. Behrens considered the mother's "character" and her observed *conduct* toward the child.

She obtained very high correlations between the mothers' underlying attitudes to their children which no doubt were highly correlated with *behavior* toward the children, and the children's adjustment. Maternal attitudes correlated between .69 and .93 with the children's adjustment at age three. A mother's observed conduct toward her child and her manner of meeting the maternal role also had a strong relationship to the child's behavior.

Behrens, M. L. Child rearing and the character structure of the mother. *Child Developm.*, 25, 1954, 225-238.

It is clear that what counts is not so much specifically what the mother does in terms of toilet training or feeding or even whether she is more or less frustrating. *How* she does it and the reasons *why* she does it may be more vital.[3] Whether the mother is warm or cold, anxious or calm, physically punitive or likely to withdraw love is more important than specific methods, their timing, or total amounts of gratification. It is the interpersonal relationship that counts. As we shall see later, social learning theory tries to translate the general term "interpersonal relationship" into the more specific and exact language of learning theory.[2] The term "interpersonal relationship" is vague but can be more exactly defined, if one so desires, in terms of learning operations or variables. One must note that social learning theorists have neglected the emotional side of human relations until recently; currently, however, they are doing work in areas such as "empathy" and "vicarious" reinforcement.

CHILDHOOD ACTIVITIES

White considers Freud to be in error for postulating a maturational, biological model based on libido and divided into stages. White believes that stress on oral, anal, and phallic stages is misleading. He does not deny the importance of feeding, toilet training, or masturbation but points out that infants and young children really spend little of their time eating, eliminating waste materials, or enjoying their genitals. White puts emphasis on the unbroken continuity of experiences by means of which the child comes to deal effectively with his internal and external environment. He feels that the Freudians have grossly neglected such vital behaviors in infancy and childhood as manipulation of objects, curiosity, locomotion, language, cognition, thinking, exploration, and manipulative play. It is these activities, which the mother may encourage or discourage, which may be crucial for many aspects of development.[37]

One should be careful, however, not to underestimate the importance of common developmental tasks which all children must face. In Western culture children must give up the bottle, learn to go to the toilet, and control their sexual, aggressive, and dependent impulses. These demands pose problems for all children and effect their feelings, thoughts, and actions. One may reject "stages," but it is not realistic to deny the saliency of the issues common to most children in our culture.

JEAN PIAGET

The Acquisition of Intellect

Modern developmental psychologists have, for various reasons, largely ignored Freud's developmental model. Of much more interest to them is the work of Jean Piaget, a Swiss developmental psychologist. One reason for this is that Freud never studied children, but constructed his theories on the basis of what adult neurotics told him in psychoanalytic treatment. He did not engage in the systematic observation of children, nor did he do experiments involving them. Jean Piaget and his co-workers, on the other hand, have spent most of their adult lives studying children through observational, interview, and more or less precise experimental methods.

Piaget's work has caught the imagination of some of the most ingenious theorists and experimenters of Europe and America, who are extending and testing his work.[16, 21, 35] He has always been familiar with Freud's work and has been influenced by his thinking. Although he has a quite different system, being chiefly interested in cognitive factors such as intelligence and modes of thinking and conceptualizing in the child, he has also been impressed by regularities in behavior at specific ages. Consequently, like Freud, he is a stage theorist, stressing order, sequence, and invariance in development.[8] Freud and Piaget were both originally trained in and worked in the biological sciences. Since physical development usually proceeds in invariant, sequential order it may be understandable that they assumed this to be the case for psychological development.

Piaget uses the term "period," rather than "stage," for large time spans of development and reserves the latter term for their subparts. He believes that the development of intellectual (or thinking) ability takes place in three large periods. The *sensorimotor period* of intelligence lasts, according to Piaget, from birth to two years of age. He sees this as a rather concrete period of rudimentary and practical dealings with the environment. During this period, he claims, simple perceptual and motor adjustments to the world take place. These have no symbolic components until the last stage.[25, 26, 28, 29] Piaget divides this sensorimotor period into six stages: stage of simple reflexes, birth to one month; coordination of reflexes, one to four months; orientation of actions to objects outside the body, four to eight months; intentional behaviors of a purposive nature, eight to 12 months; interest in novelty as a satisfaction, with attempts to do things new ways, 12 to 18 months; and symbolic representation through language and thinking beginning to replace purely trial-and-error behavior, 18 months to two years.[28]

The second large period of intellectual activity goes on, from two to 11 years of age and is a *period of concrete operations*. This period has three stages and one subperiod, the three stages take place from: years two to four; years four to five and one half; and five and one half to seven. The subperiod lasts from seven to 11 years of age. During this large subperiod the child begins, with rather rudimentary and fumbling attempts, to use symbols like words and numbers in thinking and solving problems. At 11 he has fairly systematic and stable command of linguistic and mathematical symbols to help him understand the world around him.

The third large period lasts from ages 11 to 15. At the beginning of this period the child uses symbolic thinking to deal with practical aspects of reality and the solution of concrete problems. By 15, at the end of this period, he can deal with abstractions. He can cope with imaginary issues or things that might happen or might be the case through symbolic cognitive thought, whether verbal or mathematical. The final period of adult logical and abstract thinking is then completed. This final period is called the *period of formal operations*.[27, 28, 32]

The Concept of Conservation

One of the primary intellectual events which Piaget considered to take place during the period of concrete operations was the child's discovery of the conservation of mass, weight, and volume.[8] "Conservation" means that things remain essentially the same for the child even if their *appearance* changes. In a conservation of mass problem a child is shown two balls of clay, which are exactly the same in size, shape, and weight. The child will say, of course, that both balls have an equal amount of clay. One ball is then made into a long sausage shape. The child is asked if the long clay sausage contains the same amount of clay as the other, unchanged ball. If the child says yes, he has mastered the concept of conservation of mass; if he says no, he has not. In conservation of volume, water in a flat container is poured into a tall, thin one. If the child says that there is now more water, then he has not mastered the concept of conservation of volume. It is hard for young children of three or four to conceive of conservation. If things change their appearance they are then often thought to have changed mass, weight, or volume.[5, 8, 26] Piaget contended that the discovery of the concept of conservation followed a regular developmental sequence which was correlated with age in the child. Between seven and eight, he said, conservation of mass was mastered, conservation of weight from nine to ten, and conservation of volume about eleven to twelve. The development of the concept of conservation of volume ends Piaget's period of concrete operations. Once this concept is mastered the child is ready to begin to master formal operations.

EXPERIMENTAL TESTS OF PIAGET'S THEORY OF INTELLECTUAL DEVELOPMENT

A major problem with Piaget's work is that he based his findings either on somewhat unstandardized observations and interviews with quite small numbers of children, or on somewhat loose, if ingenious, experiments which did not use adequate statistics. Because of his tendency to rely on studies of small samples of children (many of his conclusions rest on observations of his own three children), his use of a flexible and somewhat unstructured way of interviewing children, and the inexactness of his experiments, Piaget has been a source of exasperation to many modern developmental psychologists trained in America. Intrigued by his theories and findings, but uncertain of their validity, psychologists have made a concerted effort to test his work more rigorously. Study 8.2 represents one of these efforts to test some of his contentions about conservation.

CONSERVATION OF MASS, WEIGHT, AND VOLUME

STUDY 8.2

David Elkind attempted to replicate Piaget's work on conservation by using standardized procedures and a statistical evaluation of the results.

He studied 175 children in classes from kindergarten to sixth grade. He had six groups of children with average ages of: five years and eight months, six years and eight months, eight years and six months, nine years and seven months, ten years and seven months, 11 years and nine months. This is an example of the *cross-sectional* approach in which different children of different ages are studied. This approach takes less time than repeated testing of the same children as they get older. Repeated study of the same children as they grow up, as we have seen earlier, is called the "longitudinal" method.

For the measure of conservation of *mass,* children of all groups, tested one at a time, were shown two clay balls of the same size. If the child agreed that they both had the same amount of clay, one of the balls was made into a hot-dog shape. The child was then asked if they both still had the same amount of clay. A similar method was used to test for conservation of *weight* and *volume*. For weight, after the child agreed that both balls weighed the same, one was made into a hot-dog shape. The child was then asked if they both still weighed the same. In the conservation of volume test the child was asked, after one became hot-dog shaped, if they both still took up the same amount of space or room.

Elkind's results, in general, support the findings of Piaget. In the first place, the older the child was the more likely he was to have mastered the concept of conservation, whether of mass, weight, or volume. Secondly, the younger children, as Piaget would predict, could not get the conservation of volume; even at 11 years of age only 25 percent of them had mastered the concept. The conservation of weight was mastered by younger children. Seventy-three percent of nine year olds got it right, whereas only four percent of them understood conservation of volume. As Piaget has said, conservation of mass is the first and most easily understood. Seventy percent of seven year olds responded correctly in saying that there was exactly as much in the hot-dog shape as in the ball. By 11 years of age ninety-two percent of the children responded correctly.

The concept of conservation of mass did not appear in a great majority of children until ages seven to eight; the conservation of weight was not present in a large majority until ages nine to ten; and at age 11 only 25 percent of the children had mastered conservation of volume. The results tend to substantiate Piaget's claim as to the order in which children discover the conservation of mass, weight, and volume. They also tend to support his claims as to the ages when they develop.

Elkind, D. Children's discovery of the conservation of mass, weight, and volume. *J. Genet. Psychol.*, 98, 1961, 219-227.

GENERALITY OF STAGES

A closer look at Elkind's findings, which seem to support Piaget, raises at least some questions which trouble the learning theorist.[5] Although it is true that at age 11 only 25 percent of the children correctly solved conservation of volume problems, it was also true that four percent of the six, eight, and nine year olds got it right. This small percentage may be due to lucky guesses, but it may be that some children much younger than 11 years old really can get it right. If they can, even though Piaget may be correct about the general age at which conservation of volume develops, how is one to account for its presence in some younger children? Although the concept of conservation of weight is chiefly found between nine and ten, as he says, 21 percent of five year olds, 52 percent of six year olds, and 51 percent of seven year olds got it right also. How is one to account for this? Nineteen percent of the five year olds got the conservation of mass. One may speculate that some four or three year olds might get it right also and this would be under the age where Piaget would expect to find it. No children under five years of age were tested. At age six, 51 percent of the children got conservation of mass and 52 percent, almost exactly the same figure, got conservation of weight. This also needs explanation. However it should be noted that the exact age at which a given intellectual ability first appears is not a crucial part of Piaget's views. What is more important to his theorizing is the contention that these abilities (periods or stages) develop in an invariant, sequential order in every child.

STAGES AND SPECIAL EXPERIENCE

According to Piaget's theory, logical structures, such as those needed for conservation concepts, develop as a function of activity and ordinary experience. Special experiences, such as rewards for correct responses, or observing others, should make no difference. In essence, he doubts that learning has much effect on cognitive development. He feels that concepts like the conservation of volume are not acquired through socially imposed events of the external world, such as rewards, or models to imitate, or coaching, but only from the interaction of the child's own activities with external events. According to learning theory, concepts are at least partly established as a function of repeated external rewards or opportunities to imitate.[2] Despite the fact that Piaget may be right about the general time and thought sequence of intellectual development in many children, learning probably does play an important role. Some children may learn or be taught certain types of intellectual mastery either before or only after the ages specified by Piaget. There is the possibility that some of the sequences of development observed in children by Piaget are partly or considerably a function of the ages when adults teach it to them. If this turns out to be the case then development may be less sequentially invariant than Piaget assumes.

RESEMBLANCE SORTING

One more example may be helpful in understanding Piaget's stage theory of intellectual (cognitive) development. One of the things children learn is how to classify objects. At first they group or put together objects that look alike in some way. This is called "resemblance sorting." When given a whole batch of objects and asked to put those together which belong together, younger children will take those which resemble each other somehow and place them together. They may, for instance, put all the red ones together. This is typical of four year olds. Eleven year old children classify on a different basis. They may choose a single attribute such as the ability to cut and then combine the objects on that basis of what is called an inclusion relationship. This is also called "hierarchical classification." For instance, 11 year olds, from a whole pile of objects, may pick a pen knife, scissors, a razor blade, a straight razor, a kitchen knife, and a hatchet and put them together. They may give as the basis for classification the reason that all the objects put together can be used to cut things.

Ellin Kofskey, after reading various works by Piaget, came to the conclusion that there are 11 steps by which children move from resemblance sorting to hierarchical classification. Most important was the contention by Piaget that they were acquired in invariant order from step one to step 11. She studied children ranging in age from four to nine to find out if this were true. It turned out in fact that the older the child the more of 11 conceptual tasks he was able to do. The order of difficulty of the steps also turned out in the expected order with 1 the easiest and 11 the hardest.[22] However, there was no precisely invariant order of mastery. Just because a child got one of the harder steps did not mean that he could do all of the easier ones. In addition, for each step, there were no age differences among children who made different kinds of errors. That is, older children were as likely to make a certain kind of error as younger ones. Ellin Kofskey concluded that Piaget is, on the whole, right about the order in which children tend to master intellectual tasks. However, she went on to say that steps can be jumped and errors of various sorts can intrude at almost any age or type of task. The acquisition of mastery, while occurring in a general order, may be much less invariant or stage like and more flexible in order than Piaget indicates.[2, 22]

PIAGET AND THE DEVELOPMENT OF MORAL JUDGMENTS

Piaget has advanced the proposition that there are two main periods of the development of moral judgment in children in addition to an initial motor, or "ritual" period.[2, 8, 30] Moral judgment does not concern whether a child behaves morally, but how he judges or thinks about moral matters like breaking rules or committing misdeeds. Moral judgment refers to the way in which a child evaluates such issues. The first of the two main periods was thought by Piaget to last until about the age of seven, after which the child began to acquire a second way of judging moral issues. The first period has been termed one of "objective morality." Children before seven are said to evaluate the seriousness of a deviant act according to *how much* damage is done and to ignore *why* it was done. At about seven, or thereafter, children are said to judge a rule-breaker or one who causes damage or injury, by his intent, by the reasons that led to his behavior. This is the period of "subjective moral evaluation." The child is said to take into account subjective or inner factors besides what objectively happened.[19, 20]

According to Piaget, from age three to about seven or eight, the child is cognitively limited. Because of this he tends to think of manmade moral rules as unchangeable physical laws. He sees rules as permanent, unchanging things and not as conveniences made up for purposes of better human living. This has also been called "moral realism."[2] In this period the child is also said to be "egocentric" since he sees the rules only from his own perspective and not from those of others. After seven or eight, the child becomes capable, Piaget claims, of appreciating the outlook of others. This is the result of his repeated interactions in games, play, and other activities with children his own age. It emerges from respect for and feelings of sympathy and gratitude toward other children. Equality and reciprocity with same age friends develops. Children develop a feeling of justice and fairness and no longer take things just on authority. They consider the reasons for rules and can conceive of changing them. This has been called the stage of "autonomous justice."[19]

Kohlberg, who is a leading American expert on Piaget's views on moral values, says that Piaget observed 11 age-related changes in moral judgment. He considers only six of the 11 to be genuine, age-related, dimensions of development. These six are described by him as follows: The first is *intentionality*, younger children judge in terms of consequences, older ones in terms of intent to do harm; *Relativism of judgement* is the second one; the young child sees things as either all right or all wrong while the older child knows that there is more than one view of what is right or wrong. Third is the concept of *independence of sanctions;* the young child says that something must be wrong if it is punished whereas the older child knows that a person can be punished even if he is right. *Reciprocity*, the fourth concept, means that younger children are more selfish, whereas older ones are more likely to return favors. Fifth is the idea of *restitution or reform.* Younger children think that wrong-doing should be followed by harsh punishment, but older ones advocate milder punishments for the purpose of reforming the wrongdoer or having him make up for his misdeed. Sixth and finally, there is the *naturalistic view of misfortune.* Younger children think, if a person has an accident or some other misfortune after having done wrong, that he must have been punished by God. Older children do not mix up punishment with accidents. They know that misdeeds need not produce misfortune.[19, 20, 21]

Evidence Concerning Piaget's Views on Moral Judgment

The evidence seems to indicate that ways of thinking about wrong doing and related moral behaviors do indeed show changes in the direction indicated by Kohlberg and Piaget as a function of age. However, the changes do not seem to come in sudden shifts, but rather seem to happen gradually. Selfishness, for instance, is a smoothly decreasing function of age, or to put it the other way, generosity is a smoothly increasing function of age. When given a chance to give or keep a larger or a smaller share of colored seals or money, most ten year olds kept much more than half, most 11 year olds kept less than 60 percent, and 12 year olds kept only 40 percent or less than half.[15]

How rigidly children accept rules also seems to change gradually rather than taking place in jumps or stages. At least this seems to be the case in American children aged six to 12. Further, acceptance of rules is correlated with intelligence. More intelligent children know earlier in age that rules can be changed or bent.[19, 21] In addition, although many younger children do judge by results rather than intentions, 40 percent of six year olds no longer believe that large damage done by accident is worse than a small one done on purpose.[17] Subjective moral judgments, which Piaget considers to develop at about seven or eight years of age, are clearly found in many younger children. One study showed that boys and girls as young as five to six and a half were already showing a fair number of moral judgments which took intentions into account. Boys ranging in age from five to six and a half gave subjective moral judgments about 25 percent of the time and girls of the same age about 35 percent of the time.[1, 2] Older children, of course, as Piaget says, predominantly use subjective moral judgments.

It is clear that specific cultural factors, methods of child training, and intelligence level can cause children to think or judge in certain ways at earlier or later ages. Some children are capable of operating at advanced levels earlier than Piaget indicates and some may never come to think in the mode of some later period.[2, 19, 20] Piaget is probably correct about general age trends and the general order of cognitive development, but not necessarily about the specific age at which any given child will develop a certain way of thinking. This is less important than the possibilty that he is in error in assuming stages to appear in invariant order and in assuming that learning has little influence on cognitive development.

PIAGET AND LEARNING THEORY

A main problem of Piaget's system, in the view of many American psychologists, is that he has largely ignored the problem of learning, in the way that they think of learning. His is a system which uses the idea of interactive experience, rather than learning as such. Periods and stages of thought or moral judgment come about, according to Piaget, as a result of the active interaction of the child's activity with the environment.[8, 28] The key concept in Piaget is *adaptation*. The two principal factors at work in adaptation are *assimilation* and *accommodation*. Adaptation in the child is said to take place whenever a given child-environment action sequence has the effect of changing the child in such a way that further interchanges more favorable to the child will take place in the future. If the child succeeds in grasping a spoonful of food and getting some in his mouth an adaptation has taken place. He is now on the way to feeding himself, a more favorable interchange with the environment than being fed. If the child can change things in the environment so that they can be incorporated into his current state of functioning, assimilation is said to have taken place. An experience, in such a case, is assimilated into the child's way of thinking. If, on the other hand, the child has to change his behavior or way of thinking because of some experience, he is said to have accommodated. Adjustment to the world is accommodation, and changing the experience to fit the child's mind is assimilation. Both go on continually and the child adapts to the world by changing it and having it change him.[8]

Results of Adaptation

As a result of continued adaptations, particularly due to the need of the child to accommodate to changes in his life, new structures or ways of thinking appear. Periods and stages are the results of continuous needs to assimilate and especially to accommodate to new experiences. The child does not just adapt passively; he also seeks new experiences.[29] When new experiences cannot be assimilated to old ways of thinking, new intellectual structures are formed.[8] For Piaget, these are really biological examples. Adaptation by means of interaction with the environment is for him a biological principle. Piaget points out that all living organisms adapt and grow by taking in things from the outside and then placing something back into the environment. Higher organisms may also actively change their environments. For Piaget, assimilation and accommodation are basic to the functioning of all organisms. It is worth noting that Piaget was a biologist before he became a child psychologist and he at times calls cognitive development "mental embryology."[31]

Although, as we have seen, Piaget saw the child both changing and being changed by the environment, he mostly ignored learning factors such as reward and punishment (positive and negative reinforcement) and imitation. Although he, in fact, described stages of imitation and their importance in accommodation, he did not conceive of them as crucial in the development of periods of thinking and judging.[8] An experiment by Bandura and McDonald presented in Study 8.3 shows, on the other hand, the marked effects that imitation and reinforcement can have on children's moral judgments. It is illustrative of the disagreements that social learning theorists have with Piaget.

IMITATION, REINFORCEMENT AND MORAL JUDGMENTS

STUDY 8.3

The purpose of this study by Albert Bandura and Frederick J. McDonald was to show that moral judgments were less age-specific than suggested by Piaget's work. They also wanted to demonstrate the role of imitation and reward in altering the types of moral judgments made by children. In the first place they found that moral responses indicative of Piaget's subjective stage of moral development were already present in some children even at ages five to six and a half.

The first experimental group consisted of those boys and girls, five to ten and a half, who chiefly made *objective* judgments, that is, those who considered only the amount of damage done and not why. The second experimental group consisted of boys and girls of the same ages who mostly gave *subjective* judgments. They chiefly considered the intention behind the act and not how much damage was done.

The main part of the experiment, only part of which is discussed here, consisted of exposing both groups to an adult who made judgments opposite to the child's habitual way of judging. The adult, in the presence of the children, was rewarded by being told that his judgments were good. Thus, children used to making objective judgments saw an adult who made subjective ones and was praised for it. The children who mainly gave subjective judgments saw an adult who made objective judgments and was praised for it.

After exposure to the adult model, seeing someone make and be rewarded for a type of judgment the children seldom made, the children were tested again. Twelve new situations were now presented to the children to see if they still preserved their old style of judging or whether, having seen an adult judge in an opposite way, they would change their behavior.

The results were very clear cut. The children who before gave mainly objective judgments now gave about 50 percent subjective ones. The children who switched from objective to subjective moved from one Piaget period to another in less than two hours! It may be argued that they were only imitating, and not really thinking that way. But at least they were able, clearly, to give "higher level" responses consistently. If not conclusive, this study certainly suggests the need to take learning factors such as imitation and reward into account when constructing theories about the development of moral judgments.

Bandura, A., and McDonald, F. S. Influence of social reinforcement and the behavior of models in shaping children's moral judgments. *J. Abnorm. Soc. Psychol.*, 67, 1963, 274-281.

PIAGET'S CONTRIBUTION TO CHILD DEVELOPMENT AND STAGE THEORIES

Despite the criticisms made of Piaget's work, his contribution to child development has been highly significant. It is fair to say that his efforts have led to the excellent work being done today on cognition (modes of thinking) in children. He pioneered in the investigation of intellectual development, perception, and thought in the child. American developmental psychology, until interest in his work developed, tended to polarize between the psychoanalytic approach of Freud which stressed motivational factors and psychopathology, and the behavioristic tradition of Watson, which attended mainly to external behaviors.

The work of Piaget focused attention on the importance of understanding cognitive development. His emphasis on modes and stages of reasoning and problem solving, as well as on the effects of experience and the development of curiosity and exploration, helped to fill a major gap in our understanding of the nature of intellectual development in children. His work is a challenge to modern experimental and learning psychologists working in the developmental framework. They will have to find ways not only to evaluate his work but to integrate it into an overall theory of child development. It is no longer wise or possible to ignore the challenging issues he has raised about child-environment interaction and the roles of cognition (modes of thinking) and language in regulating behavior.

Piaget also helped focus attention on the question of the advisability of viewing development as being stage-like in character. He certainly thought it was. Social learning theory, as we shall see again later, largely denies this. This latter view sees development as more continuous and smooth in nature and as highly dependent on specific conditions of learning. Where behavior seems stage-like, social learning theory does not accept child environment adaptation as the ultimate explanation but looks for conditions of reinforcement and imitation, at given ages, as the key factor. The social learning theorist claims that if many children behave alike at any age level, they must all have been exposed to similar conditions of learning at that age level.[2]

IS THE STAGE CONCEPT DISPENSABLE?

Some Other Stage Theories

Freud's and Piaget's stage theories are only two among many, although they are the most prominent. E. H. Erikson, H. S. Sullivan, and others have also constructed stage theories of development. Sullivan has divided the history of development into the following stages: infancy, childhood, the juvenile era, preadolescence, early adolescence, late adolescence.[26] Erikson, who covers development from birth until death, posits eight stages: oral-sensory, muscular-anal, locomotor-genital, latency, puberty and adolescence, young adulthood, adulthood, and maturity.[6]

To a large extent, both Sullivan and Erikson feel that stages are created by what the child has to cope with, particularly the demands placed on him by society. The demands are mediated or conveyed to the child through interactions with his parents and others; that is, through interpersonal relationships. Society requires that certain tasks be mastered at certain age levels: that children be toilet trained by three, or that they be able to go to school and learn by six. As a consequence of the demand that they master particular tasks or have certain abilities by a given age, many children may face similar learning experiences and react in certain uniform ways during that general age.[2] Such theories, part of a psychoanalytic approach known as the "interpersonal" or "socioculturally determined," are a step away from Freud's biological maturational model. They stand part way between the Freudian and the social learning viewpoint.

Are Stages Fixed?

If stages were viewed in this way, they lose their aspect of inevitability or fixedness. Any change in interpersonal relations or sociocultural demands would alter the type, number, and nature of stages. Further, since not all children, at any age, face identical interpersonal relationships, and since parents differ in the timing and severity of their demands, as well as in how they reward or punish the child, the stages can only be approximate guesses at how a certain number of children will be behaving at any age period. Stages or periods become partly a matter of classificatory convenience, a bit arbitrary, but perhaps reflective of the behavior or cognitions of large numbers of parents and children of given ages, due to similar interactions or learning experiences. However, such approaches may come close to making the concept of "stage" superfluous.

Behavior is not explained by the stage. Rather the stage is a shorthand notation for the fact that many children will think or behave somewhat similarly at roughly the same ages, if they have similar interpersonal experiences, similarly behaving adults to imitate, similar social learning histories, and similar demands placed on them. Children for whom life experiences differ, at any age, will differ in their behavior. They will seem untypical of the stage they are supposed to be in for their age.

The concept of period or stage, viewed in this way, loses much of the significance it has in the work of Freud and, to a lesser extent, in that of Piaget. Attention is turned away from the period or stage, which is seen to be the product of other, causative, underlying factors, such as the social learning experiences of the child. The nature of cultural demands, social learning, or interpersonal experience becomes the issue, rather than the concept of stage, which represents only an epiphenomenon, or inexact byproduct of social and other experiences in the child's life.[2]

SUMMARY

A great deal of controversy in the domain of developmental psychology has centered about the question of whether development proceeds in stages following one another in a sequential and fixed order. Those who adhere to this view contend that development proceeds in orderly and invariant steps, one following the other in the same sequence, in each relatively normal child. Stages or substages, they feel, cannot be skipped since each succeeding point in development depends on the mastery of the one before it.

In some stage theories, such as that of Freud, the sequence of development is thought to be biologically preordained and universal since man is one species. In other stage theories, for instance, Piaget's, there is less insistence on biological inevitability, but biological analogies and concepts are sometimes used. Piaget places stress on the child's need to adapt to the world. This adaptation takes place through the active interplay of the child's activity with the environment. In his interchanges with the environment the child sometimes assimilates experiences to his current psychological state and sometimes he accommodates (changes) his psychological state to fit the experiences. If experience cannot be assimilated then accommodation must take place. Development, thus, is the result of *active* attempts to cope with experience, that is, to adapt to the environment.

As adaptation goes on, new psychological structures indicative of new ways of thinking appear. In time, each stage, that is, each way of psychologically dealing with the environment, becomes inadequate for adaptation. The child develops new mental structures for dealing with experience and proceeds to the next higher stage. First the infant deals with the environment through his senses and through muscular (motor) activity. He has no language or other symbols and has to rely on sensorimotor activity. Through a series of invariant, sequential steps, by adolescence, the child finally becomes capable, according to Piaget, of dealing with experience in terms of formal thinking involving the use of abstract symbols and deductive reasoning. Piaget and his followers have been quite successful in investigating the nature of cognitive development in the child.

Despite the enormous contribution of Piaget to the understanding of the growth of the human intellect, his system has come under considerable criticism. It has been pointed out that stages of development may not be entirely invariant. Possibly stages, or at least substages, may be skipped. Children may master some mental operations without having acquired others which his theory would dictate as necessary precursors. Certainly children do not all seem to acquire the same mental abilities at the same ages.

Perhaps the most spirited attack on Piaget has been on the basis of his neglect of the effects of learning. Piaget is interested in experience, the child's active interaction with the world, rather than with the effects of positive or negative reinforcements. He has also neglected the consideration of special attempts to teach children complex ways of thinking at relatively early ages, that is, neglected attempts at special education. Since Piaget is interested in the way in which children think, he has not been very concerned with the rewards and punishments which people administer to children. He does not really consider the establishment, strengthening, or weakening of associations (stimulus-response connections) to be crucial in determining the structure of thought.

Neither has Piaget placed much weight on the role of imitation in thinking, although he has written about imitation to a considerable extent. He has limited himself chiefly to describing imitation at various ages and to pointing out its function in helping the child to accommodate. Social learning theorists have stressed the importance of imitation and reinforcement in determining how children will think and in establishing how children will behave at any point in their lives.

If Piaget has neglected learning effects, then American social learning theorists have equally neglected the area of cognition (thinking). In the future it is quite likely that cognitive theory and learning theory will grow closer together.

REFERENCES

1. Bandura, A., and McDonald, F. J. The influence of social reinforcement and the behavior of models in shaping children's moral judgments. *J. Abnorm. Soc. Psychol.*, 67, 1963, 274-281.
2. Bandura, A., and Walters, R. H. *Social Learning Theory and Personality Development*. Holt, Rinehart and Winston. New York, 1963.
3. Behrens, M. L. Child rearing and character structure in the mother. *Child Develpm.*, 25, 1954, 225-238.
4. Cameron, N., and Margaret, A. *Behavior Pathology*. Houghton-Mifflin, Boston, 1951.
5. Elkind, D. Children's discovery of the conservation of mass, weight, and volume. *J. Genet. Psychol.*, 98, 1961, 219-227.
6. Erikson, E. H. *Childhood and Society*. W. W. Norton, New York, 1950.
7. Fenichel, O. *The Psychoanalytic Theory of the Neuroses*. W. W. Norton, New York, 1945.
8. Flavell, J. H. *The Developmental Psychology of Jean Piaget*. D. Van Nostrand, New York, 1963.
9. Freud, S. *Three Essays on the Theory of Sexuality*. Hogarth Press, London, 1953.

10. Freud, S.   Three Contributions to the Theory of Sex. *Nerv. Ment. Dis. Monogr. Ser.*, No. 7, 1930.
11. Freud, S.   *Character and Anal Eroticism. Vol. 2, Collected Papers.* Hogarth, London, 1924.
12. Freud, S.   *The Infantile Genital Reorganization of the Libido. Vol. 2, Collected Papers.* Hogarth Press, London, 1924.
13. Freud, S.   *Instincts and their Vicissitudes. Vol. 2, Collected Papers.* Hogarth Press, London, 1924.
14. Freud, S.   *The Ego and the Id.* Hogarth Press, London, 1923.
15. Handlon, B. J., and Gross, P.   The development of sharing behavior. *J. Abn. Soc. Psychol., 59,* 1959, 425-428.
16. Inhelder, B.   Patterns of inductive thinking. *Proceedings, 14th Int. Congr. Psychol.,* 1954, 217-218.
17. Janis, M.   *The Development of Moral Judgment in Preschool Children.* Yale University Child Study Cent., New Haven, 1961.
18. Kessler, J. W.   *Psychopathology of Childhood.* Prentice-Hall, Englewood Cliffs, 1966.
19. Kohlberg, L.   Development of Moral Character and Moral Idealogy. (In) *Review of Child Development Research,* Hoffman, M., and Hoffman, L. W. (Eds.). Russell Sage Foundation, New York, 1964.
20. Kohlberg, L.   Moral Development and Identification In Child Psychology. *The 62nd Yearbook of Nat. Soc. for Stud. Educ., Part 1,* University of Chicago Press, Chicago, 1963.
21. Kohlberg, L., and Ziegler, E.   The impact of cognitive maturity upon the development of sex role attitudes in the years four to eight. *Monogr. Soc. Res. Child Develpm.,* 1963.
22. Kofsky, E.   A scalogram study of classificatory development. *Child Develpm., 37,* 1966, 191-203.
23. MacRae, R., Jr.   A test of Piaget's theories of moral development. *J. Abnorm. Soc. Psychol., 49,* 1954, 14-18.
24. Orlansky, H.   Infant care and personality. *Psych. Bull., 46,* 1949, 3-12.
25. Piaget, J., and Inhelder, B.   *The Child's Conception of Space.* Routledge and Kegan Paul, London, 1956.
26. Piaget, J.   *The Construction of Reality in the Child.* Basic Books, New York, 1954.
27. Piaget, J.   *The Child's Conception of Number.* Humanities Press, New York, 1952.
28. Piaget, J.   *The Origins of Intelligence in Children.* International Universities Press, New York, 1952.
29. Piaget, J.   *Play, Dreams and Imitation in Childhood.* W. W. Norton, New York, 1951.
30. Piaget, J.   *The Moral Judgment of the Child.* Free Press, New York, 1948.
31. Piaget, J.   Du rapport des sciences avec la philosophie. *Synthese, 6,* 1947, 130-150.
32. Piaget, J., and Inhelder, B.   *Le Developpement des Quantities Chez l'Enfant.* Delchaux et Niestlé, Neuchâtel, 1941.
33. Sears, R. R.   Survey of objective studies of psychoanalytic concepts. *Soc. Sci. Res. Counc. Bull., 51,* New York, 1943.
34. Sewell, W. H., and Mussen, P. H.   Relationships among child training practices. *Amer. Soc. Rev., 20,* 1955, 137-148.
35. Smedslund, J.   The acquisition of conservation of substance and weight in children. 1. Introduction. *Scand. J. Psychol., 2,* 1961, 11-20.
36. Sullivan, H. S.   *The Interpersonal Theory of Psychiatry.* W. W. Norton, New York, 1953.
37. White, R. W.   Motivation reconsidered: The concept of competence. *Psych. Rev., 66,* 1959, 297-333.

CHAPTER 9

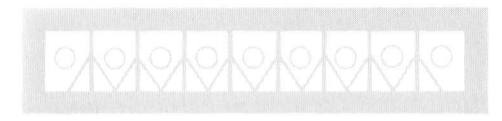

THE PROCESSES OF SOCIAL LEARNING IN CHILDREN

PART 1 — REINFORCEMENT AND IMITATION

INTRODUCTION

The infant is born with a physical system that will mature and grow, given proper conditions of nutrition, shelter, and safety. He is born with some reflexes and innate predispositions to respond to the things about him and he will also acquire some behaviors and cognitions because his nervous system is such that it will inevitably lead to interactions with the environment around him. The tendencies to look, manipulate things, to be curious, and to explore may be of semi-innate or inevitable nature.[60, 72] Much of the child's development however, is due to learning which is a result of positive and negative reinforcements (rewards and punishments) and the imitation of social models (other people). Most particularly, the child's *social behaviors* are the result, to a great extent, of learning, which is a function of the effects other people have on him.

Early in the course of his life, the child will have to learn to go to the toilet rather than soil himself. He will learn to get hungry usually three times a day. He will have to learn to button buttons, pull on socks, and to tie shoe laces. He will have to learn the names of the things around him. The child will learn what the objects in his world are for, what he can do to them, and what they are likely to do to him. He will learn concepts like "in front of me" and "behind me." He will learn the names of classes of things like "furniture" or "animals."

The child will learn, sometimes the hard way, who is likely to harm him. He will learn to be afraid or anxious of certain people and situations and also some of his own impulses, thoughts, or actions. He will learn to become angry if certain things are said to him and to be pleased if others are said. He will learn to like the company of others. All these are social behaviors, since they involve the child's reaction to others and their reactions to him.

The child will learn that he should greet adults when he sees them. He will learn whom he can hit and whom he cannot. He will learn that certain words can't be used in polite company. The child will learn when he can expect help from his mother and when he is expected to do things for himself. The child will learn that behavior acceptable at one time and place won't do at all in later years or under other circumstances.

In fact, much of the child's life is spent in learning. Some of this learning consists of acquiring formal knowledge in school. However, much of it has to do with learning the proper, successful, satisfying, and adaptive ways of conducting himself in his culture with other people. He learns, in essence, to become socialized. To a certain extent, his behavior and personality will be a result of how he learns to act, feel, and think. Although some of this learning will be self-initiated, much of it depends on what people around him do, what they reward or punish him for, and how they do it. In short, most of his behavior, and almost all of his motives, feelings, thoughts, attitudes, and values are learned. He is not born with them. He learns them in a social context. The broad end product of this learning, when successful, is an individual who is a relatively well-functioning member of some part of his culture.

THE VOCABULARY OF SOCIAL LEARNING

Before considering the nature and importance of learning in child development, it will be helpful if certain psychological terms are understood. Some of these terms are modified from their traditional usages to suit the needs of the present text. It is perhaps simplest to list these terms and their definitions so that the reader not already familiar with them can refer to them as needed.

Learning The formation or strengthening of an association between a stimulus and a response.

Stimulus An event that can be shown to affect behavior. Responses can usually be attached to such stimulus events. A word, a cookie, the mother's face, a light, can all be stimuli.

Response Any sort of *behavior*, external or internal. Laughing, hitting someone, smiling, crying, feeling anxious, and turning left are all responses (or classes of responses). Smiling is a response that often becomes attached to the stimulus of the mother's face. Behavior consists of responses whether emotional, cognitive, or overtly active in nature.

Cue Any stimulus that has acquired the function of a signal to respond. The father's angry face is a stimulus and may be a *cue* (signal) for a child to stop doing something.

Positive reinforcer or reward Anything that strengthens the association between stimuli and responses or that follows a response causing it to occur more frequently. Candy and praise are examples of favorite positive reinforcers for children. Responses (behaviors) are strengthened (occur more often) as a function of reinforcement. A child may study more often if he is repeatedly praised for doing so. Studying consists of a class of responses and is a type of behavior which reward strengthens.

Negative reinforcer Anything that a child would prefer to avoid. Negative reinforcers are sometimes called noxious or aversive stimuli. A slap in the face, or withdrawal of love are both referred to as negative reinforcers or noxious, aversive stimuli. They usually cause a child to do something less often. Negative reinforcement, when it follows given behaviors, leads to a decrease in the frequency of occurrence of those behaviors. This decrease is often attributed to the process of suppression.

Punishment Subjecting a child to negative reinforcers for behaving in certain ways. That is, subjecting him to noxious, aversive stimuli that he would prefer to avoid, when he does certain things which the parents or others dislike.

Imitation The child's reproduction of behavior which he has seen others perform. The fact that a child has learned by imitation may be shown when he performs what he has seen someone else do. This person whom he copies is sometimes called a *model*.

Performance Overt behavior after learning. A child may have formed a stimulus response association (learned something), but whether he actually does *perform* the behavior overtly may depend on a number of factors. He is more likely to perform the behaviors if the behaviors are associated with reward, for instance.

Drive reduction A decrease in drive. A drive is a very strong state of stimulation. Decreases in a drive state are often rewarding or positively reinforcing. A child may become anxious about severe punishment he expects because he has broken a lamp at home. He may confess that he broke the lamp to his parents. They, let us say, only reprimand him mildly. Consequently, his anxiety is greatly reduced and his tendency to confess strengthened. Severe hunger or pain are other strong states of stimulation which children act to reduce.

Habit Any specific, strong, persistent response or behavior attached to a class of similar stimulus situations. If confession is usually rewarding, in certain situations, the child may habitually confess when he does wrong in such situations or in similar ones.

Stimulus generalization Making the same or a similar response to similar stimuli. The child may habitually confess not only to his parents but to any authority figure like a teacher or policeman. These people are similar to his parents because they have a position of disciplinary authority over him.

Discrimination Learning to make different responses to different stimuli. A child may learn that confessing to his parents lessens the severity of punishment but that confessing to his teacher will not. He may then confess to his parents but not to his teacher.

Frustration The delay or cessation of reinforcement (reward). A child is frustrated if his weekly allowance is denied him or if there is no dessert after dinner.

Conflict The result of two incompatible and fairly equally strong responses being elicited in the same stimulus situation. A child sees a cookie (stimulus) and wants to take it (response one), but also fears being punished if he does so and so wants to leave it (response two). He is in conflict between approaching or avoiding the cookie. Both responses are of about the same strength and both cannot occur at the same time. They are incompatible.

Displacement Doing the next most likely thing or doing it *to* the next most likely person or object, if the strongest response or stimulus is blocked. A boy angry at a bigger boy he fears displaces his anger and picks on a smaller boy instead. A boy is afraid to hit his father but yells at him instead. The first example is an instance of stimulus displacement and the second of response displacement.

Classical conditioning Learning to perform an already formed and usually innate response to a new stimulus. An infant sucks (innate response) when the mother puts his bottle's nipple (stimulus) into his mouth. This is reflexive and does not have to be learned. After this occurs several times the infant may already begin to suck (innate response) when he sees the bottle (new stimulus) near his mouth. The sight of the bottle now elicits sucking because this visual stimulus was paired several times with the placement of the nipple into the mouth.

Operant learning Performing a response more frequently (at a greater rate) because it has been reinforced. (It may also involve learning to perform a response only when a specific stimulus is present.)

Instrumental learning Learning to do the things that are instrumental to getting reinforced. The child learns to pull a chair over to stand on, in order to reach the cookies. Pulling the chair over is a response or behavior instrumental to obtaining a cookie. There is no basic difference between operant and instrumental learning.

Goal The end state of a child's behavior sequence. Getting food is the goal for a hungry child. Being picked up may be the goal for a child who wants attention.

Motivation A persistent, energized tendency to perform some class of goal-oriented responses. The child may have a strong achievement motive. This means that he will persistently try to do well in situations calling for some sort of task performance.

Extinction A decrement in and final elimination of some response or behavior because reinforcement is withdrawn. If the cookie jar is always empty, the child will stop climbing on a chair to get at it.

Suppression Learning not to do something, because it has been punished. If a child has often been punished for taking money from his mother's dresser, he may, due to fear of being caught, come to suppress the impulse to touch the money. The response, however, is not extinguished. If he is certain he won't be caught, he may take some again.

Cognition Any internal representation (often in terms of language or other symbols) of experience. A cognition often regulates or mediates behavior. A cognition may take the form of a concept. A concept, such as "middle sized," which grows out of the child's experience in interacting with objects, can be used to mediate (regulate) the child's behavior in certain problem solving situations. Cognition, in general, often refers to thinking.

Affect Affect refers to emotional arousal. Fear, anger and joy are states of emotional arousal. Affect and emotion are used as completely interchangeable terms in this text.

SOCIAL NATURE OF LEARNING

Reinforcement

Learning is the most important factor in the development of social behavior. Social behavior refers to behaviors which affect or are affected by other people. Social behavior in childhood develops by being rewarded and punished, through the effects of learning by observation, and as a function of children observing what happens to others. The consequences of behavior for children, what happens when they do something, can generally be classed as either positively reinforcing (rewarding) or negatively reinforcing (aversive, or punishing). The rewarding or aversive outcome of the child's behavior depends on how other people, for instance his mother, react to it. Sometimes, however, the behavior may be positively or negatively reinforced for nonsocial reasons. Some behaviors, like exploring or playing, may carry their own reward in the pleasure they afford in themselves.[60, 72] Other behaviors may cause the child to obtain something he wants, or something he does not, as when he touches a hot stove. The results of a child's behavior on other occasions may simply be nonrewarding. Nonrewarding behavior tends to extinguish in time, and aversive stimulation (negative reinforcement) tends to suppress behavior. Positively reinforced or rewarding, pleasurable behaviors tend to get stronger and to happen more frequently. In the course of learning, whole hierarchies or sets of behaviors are built up by the child. These have varying probabilities of appearing in the types of stimulus situations in which they have led to reinforcement. A child will do something, in certain places and contexts, if he expects some sort of reward, either external or internal for it, and if the reward is worth enough to him.[5, 65] Reward may be internal when it is self-satisfying. The good feeling that comes from some physical activity may be a reinforcer. Children can also reinforce themselves by feeling that they have done well or have been good by performing some act.[11, 34, 35, 36]

It should always be kept in mind that children, as well as parents, have the power to reward and punish! Children shape their parent's behavior as well as being shaped by them. Social learning is a two-way street. Children kiss and hug their parents when the parents behave in certain ways. They also can yell "I hate you!" or cry when the parents do things the children detest.

Performance and Imitation

In childhood, when many of the patterns characteristic of personality development are acquired, it is the parents who most vitally influence the child's behavior. In order that a behavior may be rewarded, punished, or ignored, it has to be performed. It is both through observation of people and the influence of the playthings provided for them that children learn many of the behaviors they often perform.[7, 42, 61, 63] However, whether they continue to perform, and how often, depends on the consequences of the behavior. We have all seen little girls trying to sweep like their mothers do, washing toy dishes as she washes real ones, or diapering their dolls. We have all seen little boys trying to steer a toy car the way their father drives the family car, playing soldier, or throwing a baseball. Both boys and girls have probably seen and partly learned all of these behaviors. However, due to differential reinforcement (the rewarding of girls for behaviors considered feminine, and boys for those regarded as masculine), those performances approved for the specific sexes develop. To help this learning process, boys and girls are given different things to play with. Little girls are provided with dolls, tea sets, and little brooms; boys are given toy guns, soldiers, steam shovels, and footballs. Not only are boys rewarded by approval when they imitate masculine activities and girls when they copy their mothers, but they are often verbally instructed in how to behave. Such sex-typed behaviors, behaviors more appropriate for one sex than the other, will be more fully discussed in the chapter on internalization.

Children may also be given symbolic models, whom they never see, to copy, like Abraham Lincoln for boys or Florence Nightingale for girls.

Today it may more often be some sports star for boys and some glamorous TV star for girls. In any event, the parents hope that their children will model themselves after someone of whom they highly approve. Parents may often not wait for appropriate behaviors to appear by trial or error or due to natural imitation, so that they can be reinforced. Verbal instructions outlining proper models of behavior are used which describe to the child how the parent wishes him to behave, or the parent models the behavior for him; that is, shows him how to do it.[16, 42]

Dynamic Factors

It should not be assumed that behavior in childhood develops exclusively through imitation or instructions, followed by strengthening of the behavior with rewards such as praise, candy, or toys. We have already noted that some behavior is rewarding because it brings the child intrinsic satisfaction and is fun. Play is a good example. The patterns of control which parents exert over the behavior of the child also help to establish learned emotional responses such as anger, anxiety, guilt, frustration, trust, and love, which are not only behaviors in their own right, but which have effects on other emerging and developing behaviors. The frequent use of punishment by the mother for toilet accidents can lead to even more bed wetting; the use of aggression to eliminate aggression may merely serve to generate even more aggression in the child.[16, 66, 67] Children do not always perform or behave as their parents want them to. The laws of learning and performance do not always coincide with the wishes of parents. The extremely punitive parent not only provides the child with a model of aggression which the child may imitate but may also frustrate the child. Frustration itself may be anger producing, inciting the child to further impulses toward aggression.[20, 26, 48] It has also been noted that severe punishment gives rise to fear of the parents and anxiety about what they may do in the future. Fear or anxiety are unpleasant emotions, and behaviors which stop such aversive feelings will be strengthened.

The effects of punishment vary depending on its frequency, strength, and timing.[2, 13, 17] The child may internalize his parents' values and do what they want, thus avoiding anxiety over disobedience, or he may learn to avoid his parents and become secretive. If they can't see or catch him, he will be less anxious. If the child has a reasonably close attachment to his mother and father, punishment may lead him to accept their values. If he does not, he may be driven by fear and anxiety into avoiding them. Some children learn to behave well at home but displace their aggressive behavior to some other place like the school.[1, 16, 49] Others are left conflicted, behaving well at some times, but not at others.[43, 51, 52]

"Dynamic" forces such as those just discussed, prove to be important in the development of the child. They will be discussed in detail later in this chapter. Such factors as punishment, anxiety, frustration, love, anger, and conflict are called "dynamic" because they have a drive or motivating effect on the child. The child is an active participant in life as well as a passive observer and recipient of reinforcements. Further, the child experiences emotions; he has inner feelings. However, a number of different types of responses, emotional or otherwise, may be made to the stimuli of anxiety, anger, or frustration.[18, 28, 38, 39] The choice of response in fact, is itself largely socially learned. It is likely that the responses adopted in order to lower anxiety, the characteristic modes of action used to cope with frustration, and the mechanisms used to resolve conflict depend largely on how the adults seen by the children cope with such feelings and problems. It also depends on the instructions or training a child gets from the parents and on the consequences of his own behavior in the face of these emotion-laden situations. An investigation by Bandura found in Study 9.1 illustrates this point.

INFLUENCE OF PARENTS ON ANXIETY AND INHIBITION

STUDY 9.1

Albert Bandura, who is at Stanford University and an expert on imitation in childhood, studied a group of aggressive boys and a group of nonaggressive, inhibited boys of the same age and social class.

He found that parents anxious about sex had sons who were both guilty about sex and were also anxious about asking others for help. The presence of anxiety about sex, acquired from the parents, probably led to a fear of getting close to people and being dependent on them. The parents of the inhibited (nonaggressive) boys were themselves inhibited. In addition, like their sons, they were afraid of asking for help and being dependent on people. In these areas, the children seemed to be carbon copies of the parents. They probably imitated their parents' emotional and other reactions and quite possibly were approved of by their parents for doing so.

The more modest and anxious the parents were about sexual activity, the less sexual activity their children showed.

Whatever the precise combination of factors causing this state of affairs, it was undoubtedly of a socially learned nature.

Bandura, A. Relationship of family patterns to child behavior disorders. Progress Report, U.S.P.H.S. Research Grant M-1734. Stanford University, Stanford, 1960.

THE PROCESS OF IMITATION

The concepts of imitation and identification play a major role in both Freudian theory and in social learning theory. Despite a wide divergence of meanings and roles attributed to these two terms, they are recognized by most psychologists as playing a fundamental role in socialization, the acquisition of the behaviors and values of the child's culture. The early learning theory descriptions of imitation did not account for the emergence of new skills or novel behavior. Rather, they dealt with how a child learned to imitate someone else when the child already knew how to perform the behaviors involved.[50] Study 9.2 describes one of the early classical experiments in the area of this approach to imitation.

LEARNING OF IMITATION BY CHILDREN

STUDY 9.2

The following experiment is described by Neal E. Miller and John Dollard in their book, *Social Learning and Imitation*, the first major modern work in this field. Only part of the experiment is presented here.

In a room, one box was put on each of two chairs which were ten feet apart. The boxes had hinged lids on them and were closed, but could be opened.

The subjects in the study were 42 first-grade children. On each trial of the study, without the child seeing it, a gumdrop was placed into one of the boxes. The children were told that one of the boxes had a piece of candy in it. They were instructed that they would get one trial at a time and could have the candy every time they picked the right box. They were further told that on each trial only one box would have candy in it, and that they would have to guess which one.

A crucial part of the study included each child being given the information that another child would go first. This first child was instructed in secret, by the experimenters, which box the candy would be in. The first child, who knew where the candy was, would go to the box the candy was in, open the lid, and take it. The other child watched and then got his turn. The candy was always hidden for the second child in the box in which the first child found candy. In short, the children who had to find the candy first saw another child go to the right box and get candy. They saw a successful model. After the model's turn the other child had his turn. The question was whether the second child, although he did not know which box the candy was in, would imitate the successful model and go to the box in which the first child had found candy.

On the first trial, 77.5 percent of the children did not imitate. This was probably due to their thinking that if another child took something from a place, it must be gone, or that surely it would be hidden in the other box for their turn. Very quickly, however, on about the third trial, the children started to go to the box in which the model had found candy. After that, all of the children, on the remaining trials, went right to the box in which the model had found the candy. One hundred percent were then imitating the model by going to the same box.

None of the children learned any new skills. They already knew how to look, and to walk, and to open boxes. They *were* learning to copy someone in that particular situation; that is, to do what the child model had done. They learned to go to a certain *place* because the person ahead of them was rewarded there. If they went there also, they were rewarded, so they imitated or copied the first child's behavior. The place, of course, varied; it could be the one box or the other; whichever one the model went to.

Miller, N. E., and Dollard, J. *Social Learning and Imitation.* Yale University Press, New Haven, 1941.

In learning terms, the first child was under the drive of hunger. The cue was instruction of the experimenter about the correct box. The behavior was going to the box, opening it, and taking the candy. The reward was obtaining the candy, including eating it if he wanted to. The second child was also operating under the hunger drive. His cue was seeing the first child go to the correct box. The behavior was going to the same box as the first child and obtaining the candy. The candy was the reward. Simply, the second child got his reward for the behavior of imitating the first child. In this way imitative behavior was rewarded and soon became the dominant behavior.

In this account of imitation, the behavior of others provides the cue for the performance of behaviors that the child already has mastered. There is little doubt that learning of this type often takes place in children. They *learn to imitate*, because when they do they often get rewards. Especially imitating older children, who know more than they do, often gets younger children what they want. However, this does not account for how children, through imitation, learn new or novel behaviors, which they never knew or performed before. The account of imitation given above also assumes that some direct reward must be given to a child in order for him to learn. As we shall see, this may not always be the case.

OBSERVATIONAL LEARNING AND IMITATION

There is evidence for what has been called "observational learning."[7, 13, 15] In this case the child watches someone else do something, but neither he nor the person watched (the model) receives any external reward; nor does the child overtly reproduce the behaviors performed by the model while watching. Later, the experimenters see if the child will imitate what he has seen, although neither the child nor the model was directly reinforced for any of the behaviors involved. The case for observational learning without direct external reinforcement receives strong support from several studies by Albert Bandura and his associates. Part of one of these experiments is described in Study 9.3.

OBSERVATIONAL LEARNING

STUDY 9.3

In this study Bandura and his associates raised the question whether children, boys and girls of about five, would imitate models who displayed aggressive play behavior. Neither the models nor the children received any sort of external reward. The experimenters were partly interested in knowing whether the children, without external rewards, would imitate the aggressive play of live models. They also wanted to know if the children would imitate the same behaviors performed by models in a film, and the same models, in costume, portraying an aggressive cartoon character. We will discuss only the effect of observing a live model since the results of observing film or cartoon characters are highly similar.

The five-year-old boys and girls in the real life aggressive play condition were brought individually into a room in which the model (an adult) was waiting. After working with a tinker toy for a minute, the model changed behavior sharply. There was a large plastic inflated Bobo doll in the room about the size of a child, but perhaps taller and certainly rounder. The model began to aggress against the Bobo doll. He did so in novel and unusual ways, probably never before seen or used by the child. The model sat on the Bobo doll and punched it in the nose several times. The model then raised the Bobo doll and smashed it on the head repeatedly with a wooden mallet. He then threw the doll up in the air and kicked it about. While the model performed these behaviors three times, he also uttered fairly unusual words: "Sock him in the nose, hit him down, throw him in the air, kick him, pow!" All the child did was watch.

Shortly afterwards, the child was made mildly angry, by not being allowed to play with some attractive toys. The purpose of slightly angering the child was to increase the chance that, if given the opportunity, the child would do something aggressive. A calm child, having learned the aggressive acts just by watching, might not perform what he had seen. Making him a bit angry might motivate him to perform the types of aggression he had learned by watching.

The child was then left alone in the room with the Bobo doll. The room had a variety of other toys in it also, giving the child a chance to do anything he wanted to do. Although the child was alone, the experimenters, unknown to the child, were watching through a one-way mirror. The child spent 20 minutes in the room during which time all his ongoing behavior was rated by judges according to predetermined behavioral categories.

The results clearly showed that the children who observed the aggressive model learned and imitated, despite the absence of external reward. The evidence for learning came partly from comparing these children with ones who saw no model, but were also angered and allowed to do anything they wanted in the room for 20 minutes. Those who saw models not only became aggressive generally, but they tended to aggress physically and verbally *in the same way the model had.* They hit the Bobo doll with the mallet, punched it in the nose, yelled: "Kick him, pow!" and so on. They did these things just as the model had. They had probably never done these things in precisely the same way before. They imitated, and so had obviously learned, without direct external reward.

Bandura, A., et al. Imitation of film-mediated aggressive models. *J. Abnorm. Soc. Psychol.*, 66, 1963, 3-11.

Bandura and Walters contend that imitative responses in children can be learned simply by the contiguity of sensory events; that is, by watching things that follow each other in sequence.[8, 16] A child can learn new behaviors merely by observing that certain events occur together. Reward and punishment chiefly influence, they claim, where and *how often* the child will actually perform the learned behaviors. If observed behavior brings rewards to the child or to others, it will be frequently imitated. If it brings punishment, there will be little imitation. Learning depends only on attending and watching. According to social learning theory; it is *performance*, actual overt imitation, that is most affected by rewards and punishments. Bandura and his co-workers have shown this in a very clever experiment shown in Study 9.4.

LEARNING VERSUS PERFORMANCE IN CHILDREN

STUDY 9.4

Bandura and his colleagues, in this study, demonstrated the difference between learning (acquisition) and performance in children.

Children saw a film in which a person performed four different types of novel aggression. This model also used novel aggressive words and phrases. Some children saw a film in which the model was punished for the aggressive behavior. Other children saw an identical film except for the fact that the model was rewarded for the same aggressive behavior. A third group of children also saw the same film but nothing happened to the model; he was neither punished nor rewarded.

The children were then left alone, one at a time, to see

what they would do. The children who saw the film in which the model was rewarded and those who saw the film in which there were no consequences for the model's behavior tended to imitate the model's aggression to a high degree. The children who saw the model punished, even though they were left alone, showed minimal aggressive imitation.

All the children then were told that if they could do all the things they had seen the model in the film do, they would get some very attractive rewards. All differences between the groups now vanished. The children who saw the film model punished and previously had a low tendency to imitate aggression now reproduced the model's aggressive behavior as much as and as well as the other children.

Obviously they had learned as much about the model's aggressive behavior from watching the film as the others. They did not perform as aggressively at first because they had seen punishment following such behavior. Now that the behavior led to promised rewards, they imitated it overtly.

Bandura, A., *et al.*, The influence of rewarding and punishing consequences to the model on the acquisition and performance of imitative responses. Unpublished manuscript, Stanford University, Stanford, 1962.

CONDITIONS AFFECTING IMITATION

Imitation and the Model

Obviously, a child is highly likely to imitate if he expects to get something for doing so, and will imitate less if he expects to be punished for it. The expectation of reward or punishment may be based on the child's own past experience. Little girls may be rewarded by approval if they do the dishes as mommy does but not if they try to drink a martini as mommy may do. However, children can benefit from seeing what happens to others before it happens to them. This is called "vicarious reinforcement." Children are less likely to imitate something if they see someone in a movie punished for doing so.[14] They are more likely to perform imitatively if they see someone rewarded for the same behavior. Children need not be directly reinforced, positively or negatively, to affect their behavior. Through empathy or vicarious experience, their behavior is affected by seeing what happens to others.[14, 34, 35, 36] If they see other children having fun at some activity they want to do it also.

Children are more likely to imitate a model who has been warm, affectionate, and helpful to them than someone who has been cold and rejecting. The behaviors of a positive helpful person take on value for the child and he is influenced to reproduce their behaviors in his own activities. Some psychologists call this "positive identification." Two psychologists conducted an experiment in which the model behaved in a warm, friendly manner with one group of children and in a remote, non-nurturant way with another group. Children who experienced the model as being warm imitated the model's behavior to a greater extent than those children toward whom the model behaved in a cool fashion.[10] Other studies have also demonstrated the importance of affection, leading to a close attachment to the mother and others, in producing adequate learning in the infant and child.[56, 57, 66]

POWER, CONTROL, AND IMITATION

In addition to molding his behavior along the patterns of people who are good to him, the child also seems to imitate people whom he sees as controlling rewards. It has been shown that the child is likely to model himself after the image of people who have power and are the dispensers of rewards.[12, 44, 57] The child may want to grow up to be like these people who are masters of their own fate and those of others. Study 9.5 concerns parts of an important experiment in this area of inquiry.

IMITATION AND SOCIAL POWER

STUDY 9.5

Bandura and his assistants wanted, among other things, to test the proposition that the person who has power by controlling rewards is more highly imitated by children then someone who only consumes rewards. The subjects in this study were five-year-old nursery school boys and girls.

When the child was in the experimental room, a person designated as *the controller* entered carrying a box containing highly attractive toys suitable for boys and girls. The controller of resources also had a colorful, juice-dispensing fountain and a lot of cookies. There was also another adult in the room, designated to be *the consumer*. While the child watched, the controller gave the consumer, among other things, miniature pinball machines, mechanical sparkling toys, kaleidoscopes, and dolls. The controller and the consumer interacted together and the controller was helpful, supportive, and generous in giving praise, approval, and positive attention. The consumer talked about what he was getting, about how nice the things were, and showed pleasure in the situation. The consumer drank juice and ate cookies while the controller turned on a TV radio toy for the consumer to attend to. For another group of children the situation was the same, except that the consumer was a child and not an adult. All children, therefore, saw a controller of resources, someone with the power to give, and either an adult or a child who got the things and consumed some of them.

The main object of the experiment was to see which person the watching children would imitate the most. Would it be: the controller (giver), the adult consumer, or the child consumer? The results are quite clear. Regardless of whether the consumer was an adult or a child, it was the *controller* (giver) whose behaviors were imitated the most. Most particularly, boys highly imitated a male controller.

Out of the 48 children in the study, 32 also said that the model who possessed rewarding power (the controller) was more attractive than the consuming adult. The behaviors of the consumer, whether an adult or a child, were also imitated to some extent, but not as much as those of the controller. The consumer was thought to be more attractive by only a minority of the children. There is a tendency to imitate people who get things as well as people who control and give them, but not as much.

Bandura, A., et al. A comparative test of the status envy, social power, and secondary reinforcement theories of identificatory learning. *J. Abnorm. Soc. Psychol.*, 67, 1963, 527-534.

Identification with the Aggressor

With regard to imitating people with power, it is interesting to take note of the psychoanalytic (Freudian) concept of "identification with the aggressor." Identification with the aggressor refers to the tendency of someone who merely fears aggression or someone who is the real victim of aggression to act aggressively himself, in the very manner of the aggressor.[30] Freud initiated this idea by noting that the boy in the phallic or oedipal period, fearing castration or death at the hands of the father for coveting the mother, tends to identify with his father, accepting his values and copying his behavior. The real or fancied victim is seen, according to Freudian theory, as transforming himself from the object of aggression into an ally of the aggressor or an agent of aggression. In this way he can reduce his fears and feel powerful himself.

A good example of such behavior in adults is given by Bruno Bettelheim. It concerns prisoners in Nazi concentration camps who behaved in the same brutal way toward their fellow prisoners as the guards did toward them. They made makeshift uniforms, marched about, and abused other inmates of the concentration camps as if they were guards themselves.[21] In the same way, sons of brutal fathers may be found bullying other boys. Regardless of the validity of the psychoanalytic interpretation of such behavior, it is an example of imitating those in power who control rewards and punishments. Powerful people who are successful may be imitated because the child perceives consciously or unconsciously that their methods work.

Characteristics of the Child and Imitation

The already developed characteristics of the child observer are important in determining which behaviors of others he will choose to imitate and to what extent. Once boys know they are males and have some ideas of the masculine way to behave, they are particularly likely to imitate men, especially men who behave the way men should. Girls, on the other hand, are more likely to imitate women, particularly when they are behaving in a feminine way.[16] Children don't copy just anything or anyone. What the observing child is already like and how the child perceives himself or herself are important factors in controlling imitation. Children lacking in self-esteem, for instance, or children who lack competence, are more likely to model themselves in the image of others than children who have high self-esteem and feel capable.[31] Dependent children imitate more than independent ones. Obviously, also, children who have been frequently rewarded for imitating do so more often than those who have not. Finally, children are more likely to model themselves after persons they believe to be similar to themselves.[33, 41] The perception of similarity to someone else is believed by some to create a powerful impetus to imitating that person.[40]

THE REINFORCEMENT PROCESS

Reinforcement

One of the foremost principles of learning is the law of reinforcement. Stated simply, this principle holds that the strength of a behavior (habit) is a positive function of the number of times it has been reinforced (rewarded). Study 9.6 contains an illustration of this principle in children.

THE LAW OF REINFORCEMENT IN CHILDREN

STUDY 9.6

Paul S. Siegel and James G. Foshee, at the University of Alabama, set out to demonstrate that the law of reinforcement held for children. They studied boys and girls ranging from just under three years to just over five and a half years of age.

After going without food for three hours, children were taken one at a time, and placed before an apparatus equipped with a lever they could press. If they pressed the lever, candy came out. The children could eat the candy. Some children got two reinforcements (candies), some got four, some got eight, and some got 16. That is, for some children the appartus delivered candy only two times in a row for pressing the lever, whereas others got candy four, eight, or 16 consecutive times for pressing the lever.

After the first time that the child got no more candy for pressing the lever, the child was still allowed to press the lever for a period of three minutes. However, in this extinction period, no candy was given and it was up to the child whether he pressed the lever or not.

On the average, the children who got only two candies pressed the lever about 33 times in the three-minute period when they got nothing. The children who got candy four times in a row pressed the lever 41 times, on the average, in the same period of time. Eight reinforcements led to about 52 presses of the lever for no reward in the three-minute period, whereas those reinforced consecutively 16 times pressed the lever about 100 more times despite receiving nothing for it. Clearly the law of reinforcement held. The more often the children were reinforced, the more often they tended to press the lever. To put it another way, the greater the number of reinforced trials they got, the stronger their lever-pressing habit was.

Siegel, P. S., and Foshee, J. C. The law of primary reinforcement in children. *J. Exp. Psychol.*, *45*, 1953, 12-14.

Social Reinforcement

If children are rewarded for doing something, they will persist in that behavior. The behavior will occur more frequently because it pays off. Some reinforcers may serve to reduce biological or appetitive drives. Candy is a good example of a reward that can serve to lower hunger or to satisfy an appetite for sweets. Many of the reinforcers which serve to strengthen certain of the child's behavioral tendencies, however, are of a social nature. Positive *social* reinforcers refer to things that people do which seem to please the child and which cause the behaviors which they follow to occur more often, or with greater strength, or more quickly. A smile, a nod of approval, paying attention to the child, touching his body gently, saying "good boy," or "nice girl," or "that's wonderful" are all instances of social reinforcers. Much of the child's behavior is a function of which of his actions lead to positive social reinforcement by others. It should be noted that children are active and also deliver positive and negative social reinforcers to others. They can say "bad mommy," or smile sweetly at daddy.

Study 9.7 presents part of an excellent investigation on the use and effects of positive social reinforcement.

SOCIAL REINFORCEMENT OF INFANTS FOR VOCALIZATION

STUDY 9.7

Harriet L. Rheingold and her colleagues were aware of the fact that three-month-old infants are capable of a social response when adults come near them. The infant stares at the adult near him, smiles, becomes more active, and makes sounds. This sound-making or babbling is called *vocalization.* When the infant babbles, adults often "answer" him, smile at him, chuck him under the chin, or pay other attention. There is often a vocal exchange between the mother and the child, a kind of mutual baby talk. The investigators who did this study wondered if such social reinforcement, what the infant often seemed to get when he babbled or vocalized, served to increase vocalization.

During the first and second days of reinforcement, after it had been determined how much the infant ordinarily vocalized, the experimenter leaned over the crib of a three month-old-infant. (The study utilized 21 male and female three-month-old infants.) The face of the experimenter was expressionless. As soon as the infant made a sound (vocalized) the experimenter reinforced it. The way the experimenter reinforced the infant's vocalization was by quickly smiling, lightly stroking the infant's belly, and making three pleasant clucking sounds at him. Each time the infant vocalized he was quickly socially reinforced by the combination above. This was done for a three minute period, nine times a day, for two days.

The results were very clear. On the day before the social reinforcement of vocalization began, the infants vocalized about 13 times during the three nine-minute periods (27 minutes). On the first day of reinforcement they made about 19 vocalizations in the same amount of time and about 25 vocalizations on the second day of reinforcement (again in the same amount of time). Smiling at the infant, stroking him, and making a pleasant sound at him when he vocalized caused the infant to vocalize more often.

Rheingold, H. L., et al. Social conditioning of vocalization in the infant. *J. Comp. Physiol. Psychol.*, 52, 1959, 68-73.

Reinforcement Not Given by Others

It should be stressed again that reinforcement does not have to come from the outside. It does not have to be given to the child by someone else. Some activities of the children are probably positively reinforced because they feel good.[53, 72] That is, they elicit states of positive affect (emotion). The child may also be "vicariously reinforced" by seeing what happens to someone else.[14, 16] Children can also reinforce themselves; that is, they can often get and take things they want themselves or give themselves self-approval. A child who finally succeeds in tying his own shoe laces feels good. The activities which lead to the child's obtaining a reinforcer without the involvement of others, or his approving of himself, become strengthened. Playing or taking candy, or helping a friend may be instances of such activities. Behavior occurs more frequently if it is rewarding regardless of the source of the reward. Fun, seeing someone else get something nice, or self-approval can be just as reinforcing as being given something by another person.

Partial Reinforcement

It is fairly safe to say that no child is ever reinforced every time he does something. The mother often does not see what the child has done or is too busy to reward him. The child may fail to get something he wants, or the food tastes bad, or he is not satisfied with his own performance. Reinforcement, therefore, is almost always *partial* rather than continuously delivered 100 percent of the time. It is obvious that a child will learn more quickly if he is rewarded every time, or almost every time, he does something. However, he will also cease doing things quicker if he has always been rewarded for doing something and then the rewards stop. It is very clear to the child when 100 percent reward stops that what was always rewarded is no longer rewarded. If, on the other hand, he has only been rewarded once in a while, he may persist much longer if rewards later stop. Since in the past he has only occasionally been rewarded for doing something, he has had lots of experience with many nonrewarded behaviors finally being followed by a reward. He may persist for a long time, therefore, waiting for the eventual reward which finally came in the past. After some time of course, he will give up and stop. The cessation of reward and the resulting decline in behavior is called "extinction." Study 9.8 illustrates this principle.

PATTERNS OF REWARD AND RESISTANCE TO EXTINCTION IN YOUNG CHILDREN

STUDY 9.8

Sidney Bijou, a leading expert on the effects of partial reinforcement on children, compared the frequencies with which children, who were originally rewarded either 100 percent or 20 percent of the time, would do something after reinforcement ceased. He used 18 preschool children between 39 and 60 months of age as subjects.

The 18 children were divided into two groups. Each child in the first group got a small toy every time (100 percent) he put a ball in a hole. The ball rolled down and the child could put it in the hole again. Every child in the other group got a toy only 20 percent of the time he put the ball in the hole. Both groups, however, got the same number of toys — six. The first group got six trials and a small toy on each of the six trials. The second group got 30 trials, but only six toys, since they were only rewarded on some trials.

After trial six for the first group and trial 30 for the second, there were no more toy reinforcers. Remember that the children in both groups got six toys. The extinction period then began. In the extinction period they were allowed to keep placing the ball in the hole as often as they wanted to. They were allowed to do this for three and a half minutes. In this time the 100 percent reward group put the ball in the hole about *15* times on the average, but the 20 percent reward group put it in about 22 times on the average. Those who had been rewarded on only some trials were responding more often without reward than those rewarded on all trials.

If they had been allowed to go on, the group rewarded previously on every trial would have stopped putting the ball in when the partially reinforced group would still occasionally have been placing the ball in the hole. Behavior takes longer to stop if it was partially reinforced in the past.

Bijou, S. W. Patterns of reinforcement and resistance to extinction in young children. *Child Develpm.*, 28, 1957, 47-55.

REINFORCEMENT AND "ABNORMAL" BEHAVIOR

Those behaviors tend to persist which bring the child reinforcing satisfactions in life. Positive satisfactions come from material rewards, the approval of others, things which are intrinsically satisfying, and the child's self-approval. Considerable attention has been paid, however, to behaviors which seem to bring nothing but misery to the child. Why do they persist? We all know of children who behave in ways which seldom seem to be rewarded by others. Such children may behave in an excessively dependent manner or be overly aggressive, selfish, or stubborn. Although they may not be reinforced by others, such behaviors may be rewarding to the child chiefly because they cause him to feel less fearful or anxious as soon as he performs them.[53, 55] The immediate reduction of fear or anxiety is the reward.

A child who feels helpless much of the time may feel very scared whenever he has to do something. Consequently, he may regularly run to others for help. As soon as he does so, he may be reinforced by feeling better, experiencing a drop in anxiety or fear. The negative consequences of such over-dependency such as being thought a "baby" or not becoming self-reliant, come later. Negative consequences come only after going for help has already been reinforced by temporarily lowered anxiety. In the same manner a child anxious about being rejected by others may be reinforced by a reduction in anxiety when he verbally insults others before they can be nasty to him. Despite the fact that in the long run it really will cause others to reject him, he will persist in this, because it is immediately satisfying or reinforcing. Essentially, the immediate emotional reinforcing effects of some behaviors cause them to become quite strong despite the fact that they are "maladaptive" in the long run, having negative social consequences.[55]

Furthermore, behaviors which are generally considered to be socially undesirable may, as a matter of fact, be directly reinforced from time to time by others. Some people may occasionally help out the overly dependent child and the aggressive child may bully some others into being nice to him.[16] Since reinforcement for such "maladaptive" behaviors may be quite partial, they may be very hard to get rid of once they are established. Partially reinforced behaviors, as we have seen, tend to persist.

Finally, it is an unfortunate fact that it is the most outrageous behavior of children which is sometimes rewarded. A child may keep asking for something like extra ice cream and not get it. Finally, he may throw a tantrum, kicking and screaming on the floor. If the mother can't stand it she may give him more ice cream to restore peace and quiet. She is reinforcing tantrum behavior by her actions. The child has had a lesson to the effect that it is extreme behavior, unpleasant to the mother, that gets him what he wants. To give another example: a child needs help tying his shoe but his mother is busy ironing and either does not hear his plea for help or ignores him. The child gets louder and louder. Finally, in desperation and anger he pulls very hard on her dress and yanks on her arm so it hurts her a bit. The mother is somewhat angry but, now aware that she has to do something, ties his shoe. Again, a behavior which is usually socially unacceptable, but which gets the mother's attention, is reinforced. In the same vein, some mothers only pick up their young children when they cry. Since being picked up is pleasant, such children learn to cry a lot. They would cry less if often picked up when they were in a good mood. In this way, due to reinforcement effects, children can develop behaviors which are often seen as "problems." They are, in the long run, socially maladaptive, and may land the child in a psychiatric clinic, even though they may have developed simply as a result of reinforcement.[16]

THE EFFECTS OF NEGATIVE REINFORCEMENT

Negative reinforcement plays a most important role in the regulation of social (and other) behaviors in the child. Negative reinforcement is another name for punishment, *in this text*. When parents have decided that behaviors already being performed by the child are not desirable, or when he performs them when or where they don't want him to, punishment may be used in an attempt to eliminate them. The purpose of punishment, in most cases, is either to suppress or inhibit some specific response which the child is making or to prevent its occurrence in certain circumstances.[54, 66] For instance, the parents may want the child to stop stealing, stop striking his sister, or stop running across busy streets altogether. Parents may not mind swearing or nudity in the house but may not want the child to swear or to appear nude in front of company or in the school. Parents may punish physical aggression by their child toward themselves but may be lenient when he aggresses against same-age playmates.[17]

If the child finds himself in circumstances where he does not fear punishment he may again behave in ways which previously brought on punishment. Negative reinforcement (punishment) may sometimes have only limited effects. It can also have long lasting effects, however, if it leads to internalized suppression. If it does not lead to internalization, punishment alone is effective only as long as the child fears punishment. Punishment can also be effective if it is coupled with teaching the child to do something else instead of the punished behavior. Punishment can be used to suppress a behavior until the child learns to do something more constructive instead. Punishment can keep a child from running across streets until he learns to ask adults to help guide him across.

NON-REWARD

Non-reward has somewhat different effects than punishment. The failure of behavior to be followed by any satisfying consequences (non-reward or extinction) leads to its gradual decline and permanent elimination.[69, 70] Termination of positive reinforcement, however, may temporarily lead to frustration and an intensification of the behavior. The child may try very hard at first to get the reward reinstated.[46] However, if the reward continues to be absent, the behavior will gradually decline and finally stop. A report on a child by C. D. Williams discussed in Study 9.9 illustrates this point nicely.

ELIMINATION OF TANTRUM BEHAVIOR BY NON-REWARD

STUDY 9.9

C. D. Williams reported on the elimination of aggressive and demanding tantrum behavior in a 21-month-old boy. This child was quite ill for the first 18 months of his life and got lots of help, care, and attention. When he needed something, his parents supplied it.

He got better after 18 months, and his parents began to pay less attention to him and did not cater to him as much any more. The child began, rather vigorously, to try to recapture the previous state of affairs. He began to cry a lot for his parents and to loudly demand their presence and attention. This behavior was particularly strong at bed time. If made to go to bed on time he had tantrums.

His parents decided to be kind but firm. They went through a bed time routine in a calm and friendly way. Then they closed the door of his room and left him. Of course the child began to cry, scream, and carry on but the parents paid no attention and left him in his room without responding.

The first night they did this the child's screaming and other tantrum behavior went on for more than 45 minutes. The second night he was quiet. The third night he had a tantrum again but only for ten minutes. The length of his screaming was down to about two minutes by the sixth night. On the seventh, eighth, ninth, and tenth nights, there was no tantrum behavior. Since his parents would not reward the screaming tantrums by giving him attention or allowing him to stay up longer, he stopped such behavior. This report also shows the instructive power of a single case. One case will not establish a general rule or law, but can point the way to further research and substantiation.

Williams, C. D. The elimination of tantrum behavior by extinction procedures. *J. Abnorm. Soc. Psychol.*, 59, 1959, 269.

SUMMARY — PART 1

The child has to learn how to get along in a world of adults and other children. He becomes socialized, that is, he acquires ways of behaving which enable him to adapt to the requirements of the world about him. He must regulate his sexual, aggressive, and dependent behaviors, act in accordance with his sex and age, and master developmental tasks from toilet training to the social intricacies of dating behavior.

Perhaps the most important regulatory effect on the social behavior of the child consists of the positive or negative reinforcements the child receives from those about him. Other people often decide to either reward or to punish the child depending on how the child is behaving. This type of behavior is reciprocal. As the parents try to control the child the child also tries to control the behavior of the parents. Thus, an interpersonal system of mutually rewarding or punishing behaviors develop.

Children learn a lot by watching. They observe what others are doing and are able to *learn* by such observation. Later a child may *perform* what he has learned by watching. If performance leads to a reinforcing state of affairs the child's tendency to engage in the acts in question will be strengthened. If the child's imitative acts do not lead to reinforcement the child will become less and less likely to perform the acts involved. A child does not have to be reinforced in order to learn by observation, but he does need to be reinforced for doing what he has learned if he is to continue doing it.

Children are not likely to imitate, even if they have learned, if they have seen others punished for the behaviors involved. They are much more likely to imitate behaviors which they have seen to lead to rewards for others. This is called "vicarious reinforcement." The child's behavior can be effected vicariously, by his observation of the fate of others.

Children are prone to imitate people who have power and status; that is, people who control resources and can dispense them. They are also quite likely to imitate nurturant people, people who in the past have been warm and considerate to the child. The kind of child who is most likely to imitate is one who is uncertain of being able to do things well by himself. Thus, the child who often fails, one who is quite dependent, or who has low self-esteem, is very likely to copy the actions of others.

Reinforcement need not be dispensed by other people to the child. Some activities lead to a reinforcing state of affairs by themselves; the activity may be its own reward. Seeing others reinforced, as we have seen, may also be reinforcing for children. Once children have acquired certain standards they may, in addition, reward or punish themselves, depending on whether or not they act in accordance with those standards.

Both so called "normal" and "abnormal" behaviors depend largely on reinforcement effects. Certain undesired or "abnormal" behaviors exist because they may be strongly reinforced before they are punished. The reinforcement may be partial reinforcement, and behavior learned under partial reinforcement is hard to extinguish.

PART 2—DYNAMIC PROCESSES IN SOCIAL LEARNING

SUPPRESSION

Parents can't always wait for some behavior to be extinguished as a result of non-reward. They may have to employ more dynamic principles with motivating effects. When a child does dangerous things or behaves in a way injurious to others, parents may want to change his behavior rapidly. If a boy finds it rewarding to beat his sister repeatedly, some other method than extinction will probably be used by the parents to eliminate such behavior. The parents must somehow motivate him to suppress such behavior permanently or until they can teach him to do something else instead. They need a method that works fairly quickly. Punishment, as we have seen, is the method most often used and this means delivering negative reinforcement, some sort of aversive stimulation to the child. It must be made contingent on his behavior; that is, if he does what he shouldn't, punishment must follow. The effect of punishment, quite often, is to inhibit or suppress behavior.

Suppression is different from extinction, because, once expectation of punishment is gone, the child may go back to behaving just as he did before. A boy constantly hit by his father for striking his sister may be motivated to suppress such behavior when his father is about, but may beat her up when the father is gone. He will be most likely to do this if he can be certain that she will not tell the father. Suppression, however, can lead to long-lasting effects under two conditions.[2, 34] The first is if, while punishment is suppressing behavior, an alternate behavior is built up to a much higher level. The father, who by use or threat of punishment stops the boy from beating the girl, may do other things also. He may reward the boy for being nice to the sister. He may be nice to both of them and get them to do things together. He may get the sister to stop irritating the brother. If previously the sister was a stimulus that elicited aggressive behavior from the brother, she may now become a positive stimulus who elicits love, friendship, and caretaking behavior. The father no longer has to punish or threaten to punish the boy. Even when the father is not there, and even when the boy could hit his sister without being found out, he will not do so. His benevolent behaviors toward her are now stronger than his aggressive ones. Punishment can be used to suppress undesirable social behaviors until more desirable ones are established.

Suppression can also lead to fairly long-lasting effects when it is instrumental in producing some degree of internalization. When a child is punished he experiences fear and anxiety. Part of this anxiety becomes attached to his impulses to do the formerly punished act, and to the behaviors involved in doing it.[2, 3, 4] If the child begins even in a preparatory way to do what he has been punished for, he may begin to feel anxious. If he stops his incipient or preparatory movements, his anxiety will go down and this reduction in anxiety will be positively reinforcing. Since he is reinforced by a drop in anxiety for curbing his impulses and for avoiding the formerly punished behavior, the response of *not doing* will be strengthened. The reward for not doing something comes as a result of a process going on inside of him, the reduction of his own anxiety by his own behavior. Stopping himself is rewarded. In this way he internalizes self-control. An experiment by Aronfreed and Reber, part of which is presented in Study 9.10, shows how punishment can lead to internalized suppression.

INTERNALIZED BEHAVIOR SUPPRESSION DUE TO PUNISHMENT

STUDY 9.10

Aronfreed and Reber conducted a rather complex experiment, only part of which is presented here. They studied 88 boys at the fourth and fifth grade levels. We will compare only their punishment-at-initiation group with their control group, which was not punished.

In the punishment-at-initiation group, each child was run through several trials in which he had to choose one of two toys. One toy was always much more attractive than the other. Of course, on the first couple of trials the child reached for the more attractive toy. When he did so he was verbally punished in a way that was meant to make him feel anxious. The experimenter said sharply: "No—that's for older boys," and raised the fingers of his hand behind the toy as if to slightly cover it.

The experimenter's verbal disapproval always came when the boy's hand was near the toy, but before he could touch it. The experimenter then took the attractive toy away. This procedure was repeated several times. After three such verbal punishments the child no longer reached for the more attractive toy on the ensuing trials. In fact, even one punishment was sufficient to stop 21 of the 34 children from reaching for the more attractive toy. One to three punishments were sufficient to suppress reaching for the punished alternative when the experimenter was there, but how would the child behave when he was gone? This test of internalization (to be presented at the end of this study) of course is the crucial factor. Internalization, in this study, refers to the child's behavior when no one can see him.

The boys in the control group were never punished. They were just told that the nicer looking toys were more suited to older boys and that they were not to pick them up. Most of them, on most trials, did not pick them up.

After this phase of the experiment the experimenter left the room for five minutes. He left a pair of toys in front of the child, one much more attractive than the other. However, the child had never seen this *particular* pair before. The question was whether, now being completely alone, the child would pick up the more attractive toy. Things were arranged so that the experimenter could later tell whether the attractive or the unattractive toy had been moved.

The results were striking. Sixteen of the 20 boys in the control group, who had never been punished, picked up the attractive toy while the experimenter was gone. Of the 34 boys who had been verbally punished as they began to reach for the attractive toy, only nine picked up the attractive one, even when alone for the five minutes.

Aronfreed and Reber argue, convincingly, that the boys punished for reaching toward the attractive toy had attached anxiety to the impulse and response of reaching for an attractive toy. When left alone they probably felt anxious if any impulses to touch or actual small motions toward the attractive toy occurred. Most of them, (twenty-five out of thirty-four), therefore, didn't touch it in the five-minute period. Not touching it, no doubt, lowered their anxiety and rewarded not touching. Most control boys had never touched an attractive toy before either because they had been told not to. However, never having been punished, they had little or no anxiety about doing so. With the experimenter gone for five minutes, as we have seen, 16 of the 20 handled the more attractive toy.

Aronfreed, J., and Reber, A. Internalized behavioral suppression and the timing of social punishment. *J. Pers. and Soc. Psychol.*, 1, 1965, 3-16.

Adverse Effects of Punishment

It should be noted, however, that strong punishment, particularly if it is viewed as excessive, unfair, or arbitrary by the child, can have rather undesirable side-effects. That is, strong punishment, such as severe beatings, can generate fear, anger, frustration, or conflict. These strong, unpleasant emotions and disliked situations are associated with the punishing agents, usually the parents. The parents may be avoided in the attempt to escape from potential brutal punishment. If the parents thus become aversive stimuli, partly disliked and feared persons, their influence as models or sources of positive reinforcement may become greatly diminished. If physically or psychologically the child is hiding out from his parents, they will be in a weaker position to shape his behavior. Further, the child will imitate them less.[16] Strong punishment, frequently administered, leads, at best, to ambivalence; it leads to mixed feelings of love and hatred toward the parents. Punishment does not have to be physical to be strong. Withdrawal of love from a child can be a very strong form of punishment. Excessive use of withdrawal of love can also create ambivalence.

APPROACH-AVOIDANCE CONFLICT

Conflict, displacement, and frustration are further "dynamic" factors which influence the development of behavior in childhood. These terms have their origin in Freudian and general psychoanalytic theory. They were later taken over by learning theorists and given definitions within their own frameworks. Conflicts, according to social learning theory, arise when the child has acquired two or more incompatible tendencies to respond, in the same stimulus situation. There is conflict between which of the two or more possible actions he will take. Of the various forms of conflict, the one termed "approach-avoidance" is probably one of the most instructive.[43, 51] In this case the child has response tendencies both to approach (response 1) and to avoid (response 2) some person, place, or thing. Such situations arise because the child has both an excitatory response tendency to behave in a certain way associated with reward in the past, and also an inhibitory response tendency to avoid the behavior because he has also been punished for it in the past. A boy who has enjoyed eating up all the ice cream in the refrigerator may also have been strongly reprimanded for his greedy act. A little girl who has taken her older sister's doll and had fun with it may also have been hit by her sister for doing so. When stimulated by the excitatory response tendency to get at the ice cream or take the doll again, these two children will also experience an inhibitory, anxiety-laden response tendency to avoid doing so. In the terms of a leading learning theorist, they will be torn between "hope" and "fear."[53, 54]

When such conflicts are about ice cream or dolls, they may be fairly trivial in the life of the child. However, if the child has formed a strong attachment to either or both parents and then faces frequent punishment, let us say in the form of withdrawal of love, then the issue may be serious. The child will have strong tendencies to approach the parents but will also fear or have anxiety about their disapproval, giving rise to negative feelings about them. In Freudian terms, as we have seen, this is ambivalence.[6, 24] Since all parents are sources of reward and punishment, all children must experience some degree of approach-avoidance conflict or ambivalence about their parents. The outcome of approach-avoidance conflicts depends on the relative strengths of the excitatory and inhibitory tendencies. If the child is very hungry and loves ice cream and the earlier punishment for taking ice cream was not devastating, he may, after a brief hesitation near the refrigerator, open the door and proceed again to take and eat the ice cream. If the girl didn't get much fun out of playing with her sister's doll and the older sister beat her quite hard, she may well refrain from taking the doll again, despite some temptation. If the response tendencies to approach and avoid are of about equal strength there may be a lot of vacilllation, hestiation, and movement back and forth, before a decision is finally made to act one way or another.[37, 51, 52]

AVOIDANCE-AVOIDANCE CONFLICT

In some cases the child has a choice only between two negative alternatives. If the child is constrained so that he cannot avoid one or the other, he may have to respond in one of two ways, either of which he would prefer to avoid.[43] Examples could be a choice between a spanking or losing a week's allowance, or between having to go to bed early or losing a trip to the zoo the next day for staying up late. Any choice is a negative one. If he can, the child will try to get out of the sitatuion in some way that will resolve the issue more to his liking. He may argue that he deserves neither a spanking nor a loss of allowance or that he can stay up later and still be well rested and able to walk around the zoo for most of a day. However, if the parents do not give him any other choice and succeed in preventing him from "leaving the field," that is, from altering or avoiding the situation, he has to choose between two unpleasant alternatives. It is assumed that he will pick the one that is least undesirable for him.[43]

A particularly insidious, or possibly injurious, situation may arise when the child is led falsely to believe that rewards are available to him, or that, at worst, he is in an approach-avoidance situation. He may be tricked into accepting this when in reality only unpleasant outcomes are possible and he is really in a hidden avoidance-avoidance situation. Such is the case in what has been called the "double bind," a situation some have claimed can be responsible, if repeated often enough, for creating "schizophrenic behavior" in the child. Study 9.11 outlines how some believe this can happen.

A CONFLICT INTERPRETATION OF THE DOUBLE BIND

STUDY 9.11

Harold A. Rashkis and Robert D. Singer were interested in taking the double bind hypothesis of the development of schizophrenia and showing that it could be understood in terms of the conflicts a child faces. It should be noted that the double bind hypothesis is just that, a hypothesis. Although plausible, it has received very little experimental confirmation. However, there is a lot of psychiatric opinion, based on study of schizophrenic families, to support it.

Bateson defines a double bind situation as one having two or more persons present (usually a child and a mother), and having a constant repetition of the types of situations described below: a primary negative message by the mother, such as, "Don't bother me now."; a secondary message contradicting the first, such as, "Why don't you come over here?" after telling him not to bother her; and the prevention of the child's escape. As an example of the double bind, Bateson suggests the case of a child who wants a piece of candy. The mother says: "Do not eat candy or I will punish you." This represents the primary negative message. The mother then completes the double bind by somehow communicating to the child that he should go after what he wants and not be a sissy. This is the secondary message, conflicting with the first. No matter what the child does he is doing wrong. If he doesn't eat the candy he is a coward in his mother's eyes and she lets him know it. If he does eat the candy he is punished.

Repetition of such situations is alleged to lead to schizophrenia. The child's world becomes one of stress and confusion from which he withdraws. Like any small child he is in his mother's power and she is clever enough to always make him feel in the wrong. He cannot cope with this and becomes psychotic.

There is one basic prototypic situation involved in all that the mother does. The mother acts as though she loves the child, in all these situations, but she really does not. When the child approaches her she rebuffs him; when he consequently avoids her, she shows anger at him for his lack of affection and cooperation. The child is continually upset and confused because he cannot tell what he should do. He is dependent on the mother and has nowhere to turn. Schizophrenia, it is claimed, may be the eventual result.

Rashkis and Singer pointed out that the child is in an avoidance-avoidance conflict which is disguised so that the child cannot grasp the reality of the situation. Actually, no matter what he does, he is punished. His choices are only among negative alternatives. However, the mother implies that there is some way to please her, to get love, attention, food, or other rewards. There has also been a history of past punishment, so the child, for a long time, proceeds as if he were in an approach-avoidance conflict. He keeps expecting, despite fear, that his mother will relent next time. The hope is in vain.

Rashkis, H. A., and Singer, R. D. The psychology of schizophrenia. *A.M.A. Arch. Gen. Psychiat.*, 1, 1959, 406-416.
Bateson, G., et al. Toward a theory of schizophrenia. *Behav. Sci.*, 1, 1956, 251-264.

DISPLACEMENT

Displacement is usually considered to be a function of situations involving conflict. For instance, if a child has developed a fear of aggressing against his parents, he may take his aggression out on someone else instead. This is *stimulus* displacement. Instead of attacking his parents (social stimuli) at whom he is really angry, he displaces his wrath to an alternate social stimulus. The victim may be a disliked child next door whom he does not fear nearly as much as the parents.

There is *response* as well as stimulus displacement. The child who is very angry at his father may want to hit him. He may fear to do this, expecting rather nasty reprisal, and settles for sticking out his tongue at him or shouting at him instead. In this case he does attack the person at whom he is angry but does not display his preferred response of hitting; he uses an alternative aggressive response which is safer. In both kinds of displacement either the *target* of attack or the *mode* of attack will be one safer than the most preferred one.[73, 75]

When the primary goal of some behavioral tendency in the child is blocked, the behavior will most often be directed toward permissible goals, whether they are similar to the original goal object or not.[16] The boy angry at his father may attack the boy next door not chiefly because the neighbor child is anything like his father. He may hit the boy next door because no one likes that boy very much and some people feel that he may deserve a good punch now and then.[16] This is essentially the "scapegoat theory" of prejudice in a modified form. The scapegoat is a person or group already disliked. Since attacking such persons or groups may be socially approved, they are handy targets for displaced aggression.[29] If a boy has been struck by his big brother whom he fears to attack, he may be more likely to turn his aggression against a boy of a disliked minority group whom he has been encourage to hate than toward some boy very similiar to his brother, but not disliked.[1]

FRUSTRATION

Frustration is often a product of situations which involve punishment, conflict, or non-reward. Classically, frustration has been defined as the psychological result of the blocking or delay of goal-oriented activity.[16, 46] Essentially it is produced by delay or complete cessation of reinforcement. If the way to a goal is blocked, then reward (obtaining the goal) is delayed. One of the frequent consequences of frustration in childhood is the activation of response tendencies toward aggression.[20, 23] When a child is denied food or a toy, or if the parents won't pay attention to him he will not only be frustrated, but may become quite angry and lash out in some aggressive way. Aggression may well become the dominant response to frustration because it may get the child what he wants. In this sense, aggression in the face of frustration may be learned. If a child's aggressive behavior gets the parent to pay attention, or to give him the toy, the child will be rewarded both by achieving his goal and by a drop in the level of uncomfortable inner emotional stimuli associated with being frustrated.[25, 32, 59, 71]

Aggression is far from the inevitable consequence of frustration. It has been noted that in some cultures aggression is not the predominant response to frustration even in children.[18] Regression or primitivization, the child's return to older, simpler, or disorganized forms of behavior may occur as a result of frustration. Children may also be taught to respond constructively in the face of frustration with problem solving behavior. Parents can teach their children to persist or to look for new ways of obtaining goals, or to seek substitute goals when children face delay in getting what they want.[28] Children can learn not to become angry or aggressive when frustrated.[18, 28] How children behave when they have to wait, or can't get what they want at all, depends on how their parents behave in similar situations and what type of behavior, in such situations, brings them reward.[16] The emotional reponse of anger is itself capable of modification through learning. Children can learn not to become angry at what previously angered them and to become angry at what had before evoked quite different feelings.[28]

Children most easily experience emotional frustration when they feel that the deprivation of what they want is arbitrary. If they are denied in a capricious or offhand manner they are particularly likely to become angry and aggressive. As children get older they become capable of understanding the reasons why some things are denied them. If the older child feels that deprivation is reasonable and fair he is less likely to become frustrated. If he gives things up of his own accord he is less likely to become aggressive than if things are taken away from him. A child is generally less likely to become angry or aggressive if he thinks he is being treated fairly, despite deprivation, particularly if he has decided to deprive himself.[47, 58]

COGNITIVE PROCESSES

Children not only learn overt behaviors, that is actions, they also learn about the world. They do so both through direct experience and through what others tell them about the world. Children acquire a language and in doing so learn the names of things. The learn to label. With the help of language and direct experience, while also acting on and affecting the world, the child forms cognitive structures. As the child develops internal symbolic representations of the environment and his experiences he can think about what has happened to him even after the events are over. Verbal symbols, which the child uses to represent experience, help him remember. Many of the events in a child's life elicit emotional states like anxiety, anger, excitement, or joy, Parts of these emotional states become associated with some of his memories, his verbal representations of past experience. Remembering some event can thus become an emotional experience since fear or joy can now be elicited by the memory (cognitive representation) of certain past events. Many of the child's thoughts, rather than being neutral, are associated with positive or negative feelings.

In addition, the child develops mediational processes. He forms concepts like "middle sized," or develops attitudes or values which have an emotional component. These mediational factors, which are internal, often influence the overt behavior of the child. They are called mediational, as we saw in an earlier discussion on language and behavior, because they mediate or come between external stimuli and the eventual behavior. Mediational factors help determine the nature of the behavior shown by the child when he is stimulated. This is part of the process of internalization, which will be considered at length in a later chapter. The development of cognitive processes frees the child from complete dependence on what is happening to him at the moment. The regulation of his behavior, to some extent, shifts to internal control; it becomes partly determined by his "understanding" of the world. This "understanding," however, is largely a product of his past social experiences.

SUMMARY — PART 2

Punishment may bring about suppression of certain of the child's behaviors. Although suppression may be temporary, it can also lead to long-lasting effects through internalization. If the fear and anxiety experienced by the punished child become attached to forbidden acts, the child may become fearful and anxious any time he begins to carry out such an act. If he stops what he is about to do, the child feels relieved, anxiety and fear are reduced, and the child's tendency to *stop doing* or *not do* the forbidden act is reinforced. The reinforcement for "behaving properly," therefore, comes from a process going on inside the child. This represents internalization because the child feels better internally when he regulates his own behavior.

Children experience many conflicts. Obviously many of the acts for which children are punished would otherwise be rewarding. Children may be rebuked for otherwise satisfying behaviors like masturbation, taking ice cream, striking another child when angry, and so on. They sometimes do such things and are positively reinforced, other times they are chiefly punished (negatively reinforced) for these same acts. Children, therefore, may experience a great deal of approach and avoidance conflict; they may fear doing many things which are attractive to them. They may have tendencies both to approach and to avoid the same situation or the same persons. Since parents are the sources of both reward and punishment, they are both loved and feared. Psychoanalysts call this state of affairs "ambivalence," the tendency of the child at times to love and wish to approach and at the same time to fear and wish to avoid parents while harboring both positive and negative feelings towards them.

Conflict can lead to displacement. If a child is punished for a certain act or for doing something to a particular person, he may resort to some other act or attack another individual. A boy afraid to hit his father may argue with him, as a substitute. A girl afraid to vent her anger at her mother may pick instead on a neighbor girl whom nobody likes.

Situations of non-reward or conflict can lead to frustration. Although the responses to frustration are learned, a commonly acquired reaction to frustration is anger and aggression. Children are most likely to become frustrated and aggressive if they feel that they have been deprived in an arbitrary manner. It is easier for a child to tolerate a lack of reinforcement if he feels that the people depriving him are being fair.

Cognitive processes (thinking) are not often considered under the "dynamic" aspects of social learning. However, important aspects of internalization involve cognitive aspects. Emotional states like joy, anger, or anxiety can become attached to the child's cognitive representations of the world. Emotions become conditioned to memories and a child's feelings can become aroused when he thinks about past events during which he experienced strong states of affect. Such emotion-laden memories can have significant effects on the child's current behavior

REFERENCES

1. Adorno, T. W., et al. *The Authoritarian Personality.* Harper, New York, 1950.
2. Aronfreed, J. *Conduct and Conscience: The Socialization of Internalized Control over Behavior.* Academic Press, In Press.
3. Aronfreed, J. The internalization of social control through punishment: Experimental studies of the role of conditioning and the second signal system in the development of conscience. *Proceedings of the 18th Internat. Congress Psychol.,* Moscow, U.S.S.R., 1966.
4. Aronfreed, J., and Reber, A. Internalized behavioral suppression and the timing of social punishment. *J. Pers. and Soc. Psychol., 1,* 1965, 3-16.
5. Atkinson, J. W. *An Introduction to Motivation.* D. Van Nostrand, New York, 1964.

6. Bach, G. R. Father-fantasies and father-typing in father-separated children. *Child Develpm.*, 17, 1946, 63-80.
7. Bandura, A. Social learning through imitation. (In) *Nebraska Symposium on Motivation*, Jones, M. R. (Ed.). University of Nebraska Press, Lincoln, 1962.
8. Bandura, A. The influence of rewarding and punishing consequences on the acquisition and performance of imitative response. *Unpublished manuscript*. Stanford University, 1962.
9. Bandura, A. Relationship of family patterns to child behavior disorders. *Progress Report*. U.S.P.H.S. Research Grant M-1734. Stanford University, Stanford, 1960.
10. Bandura, A., and Huston, A. C. Identification as a process of incidental learning. *J. Abnorm. Soc. Psychol.*, 24, 1960, 1-8.
11. Bandura, A., and Krupers, C. J. Transmission of patterns of self-reinforcement through modeling. *J. Abnorm. Soc. Psychol.*, 69, 1964, 1-9.
12. Bandura, A., et al. A comparative test of the status envy, social power, and secondary reinformcement theories of identifactory learning. *J. Abnorm. Soc. Psychol.*, 67, 1963, 527-534.
13. Bandura, A., et al. Imitation of film mediated aggressive models. *J. Abnorm. Soc. Psychol.*, 66, 1963, 11-31.
14. Bandura, A., et al. Vicarious reinforcement and imitation. *J. Abnorm. Soc. Psychol.*, 67, 1963, 601-607.
15. Bandura, A., et al. Transmission of aggression through imitation of aggressive models. *J. Abnorm. Soc. Psychol.*, 63, 1961, 575-582.
16. Bandura, A., and Walters, R. H. *Social Learning and Personality Development*. Holt, Rinehart and Winston, New York, 1963.
17. Bandura, A., and Walters, R. H. *Adolescent Aggression*. Ronald, New York, 1959.
18. Bateson, G. The frustration aggression hypothesis and culture. *Psych. Rev.*, 48, 1941, 350-355.
19. Bateson, G., et al. Toward a theory of schizophrenia. *Behav. Sci.*, 7, 1956, 251-264.
20. Berkowitz, L. *Aggression: A Social Psychological Analysis*. McGraw-Hill, New York, 1962.
21. Bettelheim, B. Individual and mass behavior in extreme situations. *J. Abnorm. Soc. Psychol.*, 38, 1943, 417-452.
22. Bijou, S. W. Patterns of reinforcement and resistance to extinction in young children. *Child Develpm.*, 28, 1957, 47-55.
23. Buss, A. H. *The Psychology of Aggression*. John Wiley, New York, 1961.
24. Cameron, N., and Magaret, A. *Behavior Pathology*. Riverside Press, Cambridge, 1951.
25. Cowan, P. A., and Walters, R. H. Studies of reinforcement of aggression: I Effects of scheduling. *Child Develpm.*, 34, 1963, 543-552.
26. Dollard, J., et al. *Frustration and Aggression*. Yale University Press, New Haven, 1939.
27. Estes, W. K. An experimental study of punishment. *Psych. Monogr.*, 57, No. 3, 1944.
28. Feshbach, S. The function of aggression and the regulation of aggressive drive. *Psych. Rev.*, 71, 1964, 257-272.
29. Feshbach, S., and Singer, R. D. The effects of personal and shared threats upon social prejudice. *J. Abnorm. Soc. Psychol.*, 54, 1957, 411-416.
30. Freud, A. *The Ego and the Mechanisms of Defense*. International Universities Press, New York, 1946.
31. Gelfand, D., M. The influence of self esteem on rate of verbal conditioning and social matching behavior. *J. Abnorm. Soc. Psych.*, 62, 1961, 586-592.
32. Hull, C. L. *Principles of Behavior*. Appleton-Century-Crofts, New York, 1943.
33. Jackubczak, L. F., and Walters, R. H. Suggestibility as dependency behavior. *J. Abnorm. Soc. Psychol.*, 59, 1959, 102-107.
34. Kanfer, F. H., et al. Self-reinforcement as a function of degree of learning. *Psychol. Rep.*, 1962, 10, 885-886.
35. Kanfer, F. H., and Marston, A. R. Conditioning and self-reinforcing responses: An analogue to self-confidence training. *Psychol. Rep.*, 13, 1963, 63-70.
36. Kanfer, F. H., and Marston, A. R. Determinants of self-reinforcement in human learning. *J. Exp. Psychol.*, 66, 1963, 245-254.
37. Kaufman, E. L., and Miller, N. E. Effect of number of reinforcements on strength of approach in approach-avoidance conflict. *J. Comp. Physiol. Psychol.*, 42, 1949, 65-74.

38. Kaufmann, H., and Feshbach, S. Displaced aggression and its modification through exposure to antiaggressive communications. *J. Abnorm. Soc. Psychol.*, 67, 1963, 79-83.
39. Kaufmann, H., and Feshbach, S. The influence of antiaggressive communications upon the response to provocation. *J. Pers.*, 31, 1963, 428-444.
40. Kohlberg, L. A. Cognitive-Developmental Analysis of Children's Sex-Role Concepts and Attitudes. (In) *The Development of Sex Differences*, Maccoby, E. E. (Ed.). Stanford University Press, Stanford, 1966.
41. Lanzetta, J. T., and Kanareff, V. T. The effects of a monetary reward on the acquisition of an imitative response. *J. Abnorm. Soc. Psychol.*, 59, 1959, 120-127.
42. Leighton, D., and Kluckhohn, C. *Children of the People*. Harvard University Press. Cambridge, 1947.
43. Lewin, K. *A Dynamic Theory of Personality*. McGraw-Hill, New York, 1935.
44. Maccoby, E. E. Role taking in childhood and its consequence for social learning. *Child Develpm.*, 30, 1959, 239-252.
45. Marston, A. R., and Kanfer, F. H. Human reinforcement: Experimenter and subject controlled. *J. Exp. Psychol.*, 66, 1963, 91-94.
46. Marx, M. H. Some Relations between Frustration and Drive. (In) *Nebraska Symposium on Motivation.*, M. R. Jones (Ed.). University of Nebraska Press, Lincoln, 1956.
47. Maslow, A. H. Deprivation, threat and frustration. *Psych. Rev.*, 48, 1941, 364-366.
48. Miller, N. E. The frustration aggression hypothesis. *Psych. Rev.*, 48, 1941, 337-342.
49. Miller, N. E., and Bugelskil, R. Minor studies of aggression: II. The influence of frustration imposed by the in-group on attitudes expressed towards out-groups. *J. Psychol.*, 25, 1948, 437-442.
50. Miller, N. E., and Dollard, J. *Social Learning and Imitation*. Yale University Press, New Haven, 1941.
51. Miller, N. E., and Kraeling, D. Displacement: Greater generalization of approach than avoidance in a generalized approach-avoidance conflict. *J. Exp. Psychol.*, 43, 1952, 217-221.
52. Miller, N. E., and Murray, E. J. Displacement and conflict: Learnable drive as a basis for the steeper gradient of avoidance than approach. *J. Exp. Psychol.*, 53, 1952, 227-231.
53. Mowrer, O. H. *Learning Theory and Behavior*. John Wiley, New York, 1960.
54. Mowrer, O. H. *Learning Theory and the Symbolic Processes*. John Wiley, New York, 1960.
55. Mowrer, O. H. *Learning Theory and Personality Dynamics*. Ronald Press, New York, 1950.
56. Mussen, P. H. Some antecedents and consequents of masculine sex-typing in adolescent boys. *Psychol. Monogr.*, 75, No. 2, 1961.
57. Mussen, P. H., and Distler, L. Masculinity, identification and father-son relationships. *J. Abnorm. Soc. Psychol.*, 59, 1959, 350-356.
58. Pastore, N. The role of arbitrariness in the frustration-aggression hypothesis. *J. Abnorm. Soc. Psychol.*, 47, 1952, 728-731.
59. Patterson, R, G., et al. Reinforcement of aggression in children. Unpublished manuscript. University of Oregon, 1961.
60. Piaget, J. *Play, Dreams and Imitation in Childhood*. W. W. Norton, New York, 1951.
61. Powdermaker, H. *Life In Lesu*. W. W. Norton, New York, 1933.
62. Rashkis, H. A., and Singer, R. D. The psychology of schizophrenia. *A.M.A. Arch. Gen. Psychiat.*, 1959, 1, 406-416.
63. Reichard, G. A. Social life. (In) *General Anthropolgy*, Boas, F. (Ed.) D. C. Heath, Boston, 1938.
64. Rheingold, H. L. Social conditioning and vocalization in the infant. *J. Comp. Physiol. Psychol.*, 52, 1959, 68-73.
65. Rotter, J. B. *Social Learning and Clinical Psychology*. Prentice-Hall, Englewood Cliffs, 1954.
66. Sears, R. R., et al. *Patterns of Child Rearing*. Row Peterson, New York, 1957.
67. Sears, R. R., et al. Some child-rearing antecedents of aggression and dependency in young children. *Genet. Psychol. Monogr.*, 47, 1953, 135-243.
68. Siegel, P. W., and Foshee, J. G. The law of primary reinforcement in children. *J. Exp. Psychol.*, 45, 1953, 12-14.

69. Skinner, B. F. *Science and Human Behavior*. Macmillan, New York, 1953.
70. Skinner, B. F. *The Behavior of Organisms*. Appleton-Century-Crofts, New York, 1938.
71. Walters, R. H., and Brown, M. Studies of reinforcement of aggression: III Transfer of response to an interpersonal situation. *Child Develpm.*, 34, 1963, 207-214.
72. White, R. W. Motivation reconsidered: The concept of competence. *Psych. Rev.*, 66, 1959, 297-333.
73. Whiting, J. W. M., and Child, I. L. *Child Training and Personality*. Yale University Press, New Haven, 1953.
74. Williams, C. D. The elimination of tantrum behavior by extinction procedures. *J. Abnorm. Soc. Psychol.* 59, 1959, 269.
75. Wright, G. O. Projection and displacement: A cross-cultural study of folktale aggression. *J. Abnorm. Soc. Psychol.*, 49, 1954, 523-528.

CHAPTER 10

ACHIEVEMENT: THE CHILD FROM SIX TO EARLY ADOLESCENCE

SCHOOL AND ACHIEVEMENT MOTIVATION

The Need to Achieve

With the beginning of school, competition and the need to achieve are thrust upon all children. For boys, competition will be primarily centered around sports and achievement in school and secondarily about social acceptance by peers. For girls, this order may be reversed, with social achievement being a more valued goal than academic competence.[32, 41] However, depending on social class and other variables, regardless of order of importance, both social acceptance by others outside the family and tangible excellence in school performance become important factors in the life of the child. With the beginning of school, socialization and social learning move, to a significant extent, outside the home. Achievement, in whatever field, becomes the primary source of reinforcement, and success must often be earned outside the family.

Erikson has correctly noted that the beginning of the school years ushers in a time when the culture begins to focus the attention of the male child upon his eventual job of being a worker and provider for his family.[19] Particularly, the boy must learn to win recognition (success) by producing things and the girl by acquiring qualities leading to being liked and accepted.[70] Boys are chiefly reinforced for instrumental performances in sports and learning, whereas girls get more reinforcement for being "ladylike," being good-looking, friendly, and tidy. Children come to have the qualities which people want them to imitate and for which they are admired.[45] Some achievement orientation, whether in academics, sports, or in striving for an admired "personality," is almost inescapable for the American child.

Professor J. W. Atkinson has spent much of his life studying achievement motivation and has given the area its clearest definition: "Achievement motivation attempts to account for the determinants of the direction, magnitude, and persistence of behavior in a limited but very important domain of human activities. It applies only when an individual knows that his performance will be evaluated (by himself and others) in terms of some standard of excellence and the consequences of his actions will either be a favorable evaluation (success) or an unfavorable evaluation (failure)."[3,4] This definition certainly pertains to the life of the school age child. Although he was previously often accepted and loved by his parents simply for being himself, their child, he finds it is now no longer enough merely to exist. By age six he has become toilet trained and has learned to eat on schedule, dress himself, and accomplish other life tasks, so he has already been exposed to his parents' concerns about his intelligence, looks and manners. Their concern about the child's achievement does not emerge from nowhere when he becomes six. However, the onset of school, where grades are given and where the need exists to enter into play groups and face other children every day, brings achievement oriented behaviors into extra sharp focus.

Preparation for Achievement

Those cultures, social classes, and families which stress competition with standards of excellence, or insist that the child be able to perform certain tasks by himself should produce children with high achievement motivation. It is likely that the foundations for performing achievement oriented behaviors are laid by parents' demands that their children do things for themselves and master certain tasks early. As we shall see below, training in independence can help develop a need to achieve. Some parents may well go out of their way to reward early mastery-related behaviors, that is, to encourage independence. Study 10.1 describes a classical study in this area.

EARLY DEMANDS AND ACHIEVEMENT ORIENTATION

STUDY 10.1

Marion R. Winterbottom studied the relationship between the strength of the need to achieve in eight-year-old boys and mothers' standards of training in independence and mastery.

The strength of the need to achieve was measured by a projective story-telling technique. The stories told by the children were scored for the strength of the need to achieve which they revealed. The boys were divided, on the basis of the scores obtained, into those who showed a high need to achieve and those who showed a low need to achieve. The actual procedure was a bit more complex than can be described here. Information was collected only from the mothers of the ten boys who showed the highest and the ten who showed the lowest need to achieve.

The mothers of the 20 boys were given a series of questionnaires by interviewers. They were first asked to indicate their goals in training their child on 20 kinds of independence and mastery behaviors and to note the age by which these behaviors were learned by the child. Next they were presented with a list of possible reactions to these behaviors and were asked to check the kinds of responses they made when their sons fulfilled their demands and what they did when their sons did not. The mothers were asked to indicate the success of their sons in relation to their peers. They were also queried about the ages at which they would have desired their sons to reach certain goals and how they rewarded or punished in the face of their sons' successes and failures. Finally, they were asked about the types of restrictions they placed on their sons.

The results were as follows:

1. Mothers of boys who had a high achievement motivation did not make more demands on their boys than mothers with low achievement oriented sons, but they did make them *earlier*. The sons were expected to show independent mastery sooner.

2. Mothers of boys who had a high achievement orientation used all types of rewards—verbal, gifts, and physical affection—more frequently. They were particularly given to using physical affection as a reward for early mastery of tasks. Neither group of mothers punished more or less.

3. These mothers rated their sons higher on independence and mastery. Of course this is how these mothers wanted their boys to behave and we have only their word to go by.

4. Mothers of high achievement oriented boys, in general, indicated that they were not particularly more restrictive than the mothers of low achievement oriented boys. They did, it is true, impose more early restrictions up to age seven,

but still made more demands than restrictions in the early years. Restrictive training comes earlier for the high achievement oriented boys, but this is accompanied or preceded by a good deal of independence training. Again, if these boys obeyed the restrictions which were placed on them, they received a lot of physical affection as a reward.

Winterbottom, M. R. The relation of need for achievement to learning experiences in independence mastery. (In) *Motives in Fantasy, Action and Society*, Atkinson, J. W. (Ed.). D. Van Nostrand, New York, 1958.

TRAINING IN ACHIEVEMENT

Independence training and training in achievement oriented behaviors need not go hand in hand. Granting the child independence, expecting self-reliance, and giving autonomy, may sometimes indicate a lack of interest or involvement. Placing a child on his own, without setting standards to be met, and without being involved with the child in a rewarding way, is not likely to lead to achievement oriented behaviors. Achievement behavior on the part of children may be fostered by encouraging independence, but only if that is accompanied by direct achievement training.[16] In fact, achievement training, by itself, is probably the most potent factor in producing achievement oriented children. Achievement training may be defined as the product or parental behaviors which impose on the child standards of excellence in performing tasks, and as acts which make reward contingent on good performance. Parents who expect much of the child and reward him for doing well are also often models of achievement orientation themselves. They may have high self-confidence and in addition convey to the child that they believe that he can do well. Study 10.2 describes an investigation in the area of achievement training, only part of which is reported.

ACHIEVEMENT TRAINING

STUDY 10.2

Bernard G. Rosen and Roy D'Andrade were interested in the causes of achievement behavior. They set out, through observation of family interactions, to explore the relationship between achievement behaviors of the child and the child training practices of the parents. The question was: What do the parents of high achievement oriented children do to make them that way? How is achievement orientation learned?

Forty boys, age nine to 11, white, native-born, matched for I.Q. and social class, were studied along with their parents. Half of the boys had high achievement oriented scores and half low achievement oriented scores. In each achievement category, high and low, half of the boys were middle-class and half lower-class. However, achievement oriented behaviors are probably not equally distributed in all social classes. The social class variable may have been made irrelevant by the fact that low and high achivement oriented boys may have parents who behave similarly, despite their social class. That is, if you take children with high achievement needs, their parents' behaviors may be very similar regardless of the social class they are in. It is, nevertheless, quite possible that there is a greater proportion of achievement oriented parents in the middle-class than in the lower-class.

Tasks were devised for the boys which also involved the parents in the task performance. The observation of the parents' behavior as their sons engaged in these tasks provided information about the demands the parents made on them. Data were also gathered by watching the parent-son interactions, during the child's problem solving efforts. These data concerned the way in which the parents enforced their demands and the amount of autonomy or independence they gave to the child.

Some of the results are as follows:

1. Parents of a high achievement oriented boy tend to have high aspirations for him and have a high regard for his problem solving abilities. They set up a standard of excellence which they expect the boy to reach.

2. As the boy progresses toward task solution they reinforce him positively with warmth and approval or, particularly in the case of mothers, negatively, with disapproval if he is performing badly.

3. Fathers of high achievement oriented boys allow more autonomy than the mothers do. The fathers give hints rather than instructions and push less. They seem to be competent, confident men, who tend to let the boy perform.

4. Mothers of boys with high achievement orientation engage more actively in achievement training. They have higher aspirations for their sons than the mothers of boys having low achievement needs and are more concerned over their sons'

success. They are more likely both to reward and to punish than the more indifferent mothers.

5. Mothers of high achievement oriented boys allow more autonomy or independence and give their children more options about how to go about doing a task. However, they demand that it be done well.

6. The mothers of high achievement oriented boys are striving competent persons and expect their sons to be the same.

7. Social class made no difference, but this may have been due to factors discussed earlier.

Rosen, C. R., and D'Andrade, R. The psychosocial origins of achievement motivation. *Sociometry, 22,* 1959, 185-218.

The acquisition of the motivation to achieve seems to follow the principles of social learning. The parents of boys with a high need to achieve are themselves models of people who frequently engage in achievement behaviors. They set goals of excellence for their children and reward them for progress toward those goals and punish them for failure to make progress. They allow a choice of routes to excellence but do not reward lack of effort, and certainly punish failure. How to accomplish a task may be up to the boy, but he must accomplish it somehow. It is not surprising, therefore, that, for the sons of such parents, reaching standards of excellence acquires emotional value which helps to motivate them to succeed.

Effects of Achievement Training

Since the sons of achievement oriented parents often can achieve well and are rewarded for doing so, achievement can become a pleasurable activity. Of course, if the boy really cannot accomplish what is expected of him, emotional complications and a tendency to underachieve or to escape from competition may follow. Being coerced at home into working at academic tasks in the pre-school age period, for instance, can lead to developing avoidance or escape responses when confronted with homework in later years. Such children have had unpleasant emotions associated with school work.[33]

However, lack of achievement training may be a greater danger. As Verville has pointed out: "If his mother makes his bed, picks up his clothes and toys, takes him in the car to school, and does his homework, he is untrained . . . and cannot work without direction. Furthermore, he feels no obligation to do so because he has never been required to manage unpleasant or difficult tasks."[71]

Setting Achievement Levels Through Self-Reinforcement and Modeling

The levels of excellence which children set for themselves need not depend on external reinforcement. Two additional factors seem to be of salient importance. First, children may adopt, as levels of excellence to be met, the goals which they see others setting for themselves. Children in slum schools may not do very well because the other children may not try hard and the teachers may expect little of themselves either. Conversely, in upper middle-class neighborhoods, children may see most of the other children and the teachers trying very hard, setting high goals. Second, once children learn certain standards, by observation, they may reinforce themselves. If children get near their goals, they may approve of themselves and get the reward of feeling good or may feel free to indulge in certain pleasures. If children are doing poorly, they may refuse to reward themselves; feeling unworthy, they may even punish themselves by self-deprivation. The study in Study 10.3, part of which is reported, illustrates this principle.

ACHIEVEMENT, MODELING, AND SELF-REINFORCEMENT

STUDY 10.3

The subjects in this experiment, by Albert Bandura and Carol J. Kupers of Stanford University, were 80 boys and 80 girls ranging in age from seven to nine years. A male and a female adult and two nine-year-old children served as models who could be imitated.

A bowling game apparatus was used in this experiment. The middle marker was labeled, "10 points," and the two side ones were labeled, "5 points." The subject was told that whenever he or she rolled a bowling ball which hit a target, the corresponding marker would drop. The children, however, could not see the actual target area and so could not tell where the balls they threw were really striking. Consequently the experimenters could control the markers and the scores.

There was a large bowl of candies nearby and this was pointed out to each child as he or she came to play the game. Each child was permitted to eat candy at any time or to save candy to take home. There was absolutely free access to the candies at all times and this was made clear to the children.

The game was played first by a model and then by the child in the experiment. The model always played first. There were essentially two main experimental conditions: high criterion for self-reinforcement, low criterion for self-reinforcement. There was a different group of children for each of the two conditions. In the high criterion for self-reinforcement condition the model took some of the candies only when obtaining or exceeding a score of 20. Only when this happened did the model take candy and say something like: "I deserve some of those candies for that high score. That's great!" When the score was under 20, the model took no candy and would say: "I get no candy for that. That does not deserve a candy treat." In the low criterion for self-reward condition, the model behaved in the same way but adopted a criterion of much lower performance. On trials on which the score was only 10 or better the model took candy and made self-approving comments. For scores less than 10, the model took no candy and indulged in self-criticism.

The experimenter, in either condition, then left and the child, now with the model gone, was left to play 15 trials with three balls each. The child could take any amount of candy at any time. Since the scores were rigged, each child got scores similar to the ones the model scored.

The results were striking. None of the children who saw a model who set high standards took any candy for a score of five. None of the boys and only 13 percent of the girls who saw a model set high standards took candy for scores from 10 to 15. However, after having seen a model take candy for high scores, 100 percent of the boys and 87 percent of the girls took candy for scores of 20 or over. Remember that the children could have stuffed themselves with candy for any score, if they wanted to. The results above were the case when the model was an adult male. The findings were quite similar when the model was an adult female or a child. The results for girls did not differ much from the results for boys in any of the high criterion groups.

The findings in the low criterion group were also clear. Here the boys and girls had seen an adult male or female (or a boy or girl) model take candy for scores of 10 or above. In all groups, the majority of children took candy for scores of 10 or above. Having seen an adult or a child taking reward for a score of only 10, they also took rewards for 10. However, very few took candy for a score of just 5.

Clearly the children adopted the reward criterion of the person they saw and, when free to do as they wished, rewarded themselves largely only for that level of performance or above. The children's self-reward patterns depended heavily on the behaviors of those whom they saw.

Bandura, A., and Kupers, C. J. Transmission of patterns of self-reinforcement through modeling. *J. Abnorm. Soc. Psychol.,* 69, 1964, 1-9.

ACHIEVEMENT AND RISK TAKING

Fear of Failure

It has been noted that in addition to a disposition to seek success, there is in all children some general behavioral tendency to avoid failure.[3, 4] When faced with a situation where he is confronted by some demand to perform, the child may experience some degree of fear about possible failure. Tests in school are a good example of such a situation and fear about failure on examinations has been called "test anxiety." Some children have been noted to be fairly consistently and highly anxious about failure on tests while others are usually much less anxious about examinations.[57, 58, 62]

Fear of failure should affect risk taking behavior. If a child is afraid of failure he can partly mitigate its consequences in two ways. First, he can just refuse to take any risk. That is, he can set himself quite low standards. If he will set D, a barely passing grade, as his goal, he is usually certain to reach it and will not have to fear that he won't. On the other hand he can set an unrealistically high goal, which he knows he can't reach, and so engage life on some fantasy level devoid of reality. If a not too intelligent child always sets a make-believe A for his goal and constantly gets a C, he can shrug his shoulders and feel, underneath it all, that an A is an unattainable dream. It is expected that many children with a low need to achieve may also have a high fear of failure and will tend to set either goals that are too low or too high. Children who have a high need to achieve may often have a lower fear of failure.[3, 53] As a consequence, they may choose reasonable but challenging goals. They prefer goals providing a 50-50, or somewhat lower, chance of success. That is, they like challenges. Or, to put it another way, they may prefer risks of an intermediate sort.[3, 4, 42, 43]

The relationship between fear of failure and low achievement motivation may hold only when the child has been aroused to an achievement orientation by some situation like a forthcoming test or a contest. There are indications that under nonarousing conditions there may be little correlation between fear of failure and the need to achieve. Of course children are most likely to be required to set goals and decide what kind of a risk to take when the situation does have achievement arousing properties. Nevertheless, it is highly likely that there are *some* children who have a high need to achieve despite a high fear of failure, and some who have a low need to achieve and a lack of anxiety about not doing well. They may just never have had much training in acquiring an achieving orientation.[42, 43] Study 10.4 deals with the relationship between achievement motivation and risk taking. It shows that children with a high need to achieve like moderate, challenging risks, but avoid extreme risks.

RISK TAKING IN CHILDREN AND ACHIEVEMENT MOTIVATION

STUDY 10.4

David C. McClelland, of Harvard University, who pioneered in the study of achievement motivation, hypothesized that children with a high need to achieve would prefer moderate risks while children with a low need to achieve would show more variability in risk taking, choosing high or low degrees of risk.

He studied two groups of children. The first group consisted to 26 five-year-old children in kindergarten. The second group was composed of 32 eight and nine year olds in the third grade. The achievement motivation level of the children was measured and children high and low on need achievement were identified.

Four risk taking tasks were used. The kindergarten study used a ring toss game which allowed the child to choose his distance from the peg. The farther back the child stood the greater the risk, since chances for a high score would be lowered by being farther away from the target. A tilting maze board was also used with this younger group. The child indicated the score he expected to get before he rolled his ball. The farther along the maze he set his goal the higher his score could be, but his chance of failure was also increased. Two other tasks were used with the older children, a dot connection task and a word memory task. In each case the children could set their own risk level by regulating the difficulty level of the task. Of course, the more difficult the level set, the better their score could conceivably be and the greater would be the chance of failure.

The results can be reduced to the general finding that

children with a low need for achievement tended to choose extreme degrees of risk and also to show greater variance in the amount of risk they undertook. The children with a high need to achieve tended to choose moderate risks, where they might fail but where chances for success were still pretty good. This study seems to support the conclusion that the child with a high need to achieve likes a difficult but reasonable challenge that gives him a fair chance for a meaningful success.

McClelland, D. C. Risk taking in children with high and low need for achievement. (In) *Motives in Fantasy, Action, and Society*, Atkinson, J. W. (Ed.). D. Van Nostrand, New York, 1958.

CHILDREN'S ACHIEVEMENT AND SOCIAL CLASS

Social Class and Achievement Orientation

Although middle-class parents may in some ways be more permissive in terms of catering to the needs of the infant and young child, they may in some ways place the child under strong pressure for ultimate performance. The middle-class parent places great emphasis on independent task mastery in early childhood. There are more demands and expectations associated with school performance at age six and later. Middle-class children are taught to believe in success and taught to be willing to take the steps that make achievement possible.[44, 54] The results from a study by Aberle and Naegele found in Study 10.5 underline this point.

THE MIDDLE CLASS AND ACHIEVEMENT PRESSURES

STUDY 10.5

Aberle and Naegele found that midde-class child rearing is future oriented. Middle-class fathers expected their sons to have middle-class, or higher, positions in the occupational structure. They tended to want the kind of child training which would ensure achievement. Most middle-class fathers they studied were success oriented. They were interested in furthering behavior which would make for success in future oriented values. They emphasized and encourage initiative, scholastic achievement, emotional stability, and athletic prowess. They often subjected their children to evaluative comment (positive or negative verbal reinforcement for performance) because the child's present performance was thought to be indicative of his future role.

Such parents were providing clear guidelines for expected behavior, rewarded it when it occurred, and were critical when it did not. Under such circumstances children should learn the forms of behavior which their parents want them to acquire.

Aberle, D. F., and Naegele, K. D. Middle class fathers' occupational roles and attitudes toward children. *Amer. J. Orthopsychiat.*, 22, 1952, 366-378.

FAMILY STRUCTURE, SOCIAL STRUCTURE, AND ACHIEVEMENT

Family behavior, which we have seen to be correlated with social class, is one of the important determinants of achievement motivation and educational attainment.[18, 43] Many of the personal qualities and skills that enable children to meet standards of excellence in school—self-reliance, competence, judgement, problem solving ability, and a questioning mind—are learned in family parent-child interactions that provide guidance but allow the child leeway in practicing mastery and decision making.[55]

Parental dominance, the unwillingness to reinforce the child's mastery and decision making behaviors, often produces either passive dependency or negative rebelliousness. Domination is characterized by a rigidity or inflexibility of purpose, an unwillingness to admit the contribution of another's experiences, desires, and purposes." The domineering parent enforces his own judgments in determining the goals which his child is to pursue.[2, 17, 18] Such parents do not reinforce acts of independence.

Responsibility and confidence are learned through reinforced opportunities to engage in problem solving activity. Parental domination largely consists of not allowing such learning experiences. The mother's dominance over the father particularly leads to low autonomy and low academic motivation in boys. Such mother-domination, with the father not held up as a model to imitate, leads to relative dependency, lack of confidence, and incompetence in boys.[1, 2, 12] Boys in such homes do not get a chance to learn the behaviors needed to succeed outside the family setting.

Either complete subordination of the child or non-regulation of the child's behavior leads to a relative lack of achievement motivaton and skills. The highest levels of academic motivation and achievement occur in boys and girls who take part, under parental modeling and reinforcement, in decisions concerning their own activities. Dominance by either parent is prejudicial to an achievement orientation. High educational achievement is most prevalent among children raised in families where there are relatively democratic relations between the parents and democratic attitudes toward the child.[1, 2, 12]

Differences between the social classes, with the possible exception of lower-class minority groups are diminishing, as good educational opportunities become more available. Consequently, variables like parental domination become more important than social class. In Great Britain, West Germany, Northern Italy, and Mexico, equal educational opportunities are being increasingly provided, and most social classes end up highly valuing education. Equality among the sexes is also on the increase, leading to the same result.[12, 67]

For some children, however, this happy state of affairs does not exist. Good educational opportunities are unavailable for many slum children. Such children may also be living in a loosely organized matriarchy. The lower-class child is at a disadvantage because the nature of his family relationships makes it less likely that, even if good facilities and opportunities are made available (and they are seldom available), he will be able to take advantage of them.[18, 25] In Southern Italy, to give another example, paternal authoritarianism is still strong, economic conditions are poor, schools are poor, and social change is slow. Any combinations of poor educational opportunities and lack of stable and democratic family living are unfortunate.

It is not clear to what extent changes in technology, mass communication, and educational opportunity alter family patterns. Nor is it clear to what extent changes in family patterns alter society. The causation may well be a circular one. To some extent changes in the family environment also may change the level of economic progress. However, it has been shown in Mexico, for instance, that educational gains can be made despite a lack of initial social change in family structure. Once educational and economic opportunities were made available, there developed a greater interest in schooling for children. After the children had begun to go to school and people developed an elevated level of aspiration, changes in family child rearing practices began to appear. Younger, steadily employed, and more educated parents punished more lightly, allowed more play, and sent their children to school for as long as possible.[38] The answer for elevating the achievement orientation and educational aspirations of the American lower-class child may lie in providing their parents with good jobs. Economic opportunity may be the way to break the vicious circle of deprivation and lack of aspiration. A change in family behavior for other reasons might also lead to the same end.

SCHOOL DAYS—THE ABILITY TO DELAY GRATIFICATION

Delay of Gratification

For the child of six and older to cope with the demands of schools, it is not enough for him to have a repertoire of achievement related behaviors. Even with a motive to achieve, the child must have other behavioral abilities if he is to achieve satisfaction from his school activities and participation in games, hobbies, and interactions with friends. The child must be able to become interested or aroused, able to pay attention, and able to control his impulses. Related to control of impulsivity is a very important age-linked variable, the ability to delay gratification. As children get older they are increasingly able to give up the pleasure or reward of the moment in order to get a larger and more valued reward later.[46, 49] Children of two or three want what they want and they want it right away. They picture their parents as omnipotent creatures within whose power it lies to cater to any desire. If the wished for object is not forthcoming, the child will become angry with the parents and may aggress, cry, or both. As many children get older they learn not only to wait, but to give up relatively small desires of the moment for more tangible rewards later. Indeed, a good adjustment at six and later, and a satisfying future life, requires that his ability be learned fairly thoroughly.

Much of the pertinent experimental research on the ability to delay gratification has been done by Professor Walter Mischel of Stanford University, but the concept has its origins in the work of Sigmund Freud. Freud differentiated between the "pleasure principle," which involved the wish to gratify every passing impulse, and the "reality principle," which was linked to the conditions under which it was socially and personally allowable to gratify such impulses. The reality principle often dictates, according to Freud, that one must wait to indulge certain pleasures. The pleasure principle rules supreme in the young child and the reality principle emerges only with the passage of time as the result of life experiences.[23] Failure to learn to delay gratification may be involved in various sorts of psychological disorders such as psychopathic behavior, infantile or immature personality, or other "acting out" behaviors of an impulsive nature.[51]

Certainly the capacity to delay is useful to any child. It is 12 years from entrance into school until high school graduation; there is often a long wait in the outfield until a fly ball comes, not to mention the tragic wait until the next trip to the supermarket after the chocolate ice cream runs out. Some children, of course, never learn to delay very well and remain impulsive. Such children often do not do as well in school as they might because they often give snap answers without delaying and thinking first.[31] Impulsivity and the inability to delay gratification also relate to other concepts. A strategy of some children, who are highly anxious about tests and examinations, is to answer questions as fast as possible so as to be finished and, thus, to escape from the situation. Although high anxiety leads other children to go over questions and answers compulsively in the fear that they may be wrong, high anxiety motivates others to flee from disagreeable reality.[57, 58]

The ability to delay gratification is learned gradually. The presence of models who are examples of the ability to delay and who reward such delays is a help. Mischel showed in seven- and nine-year-old children that the absence of a father in the home led to a preference for immediate reinforcement. Presence of a father in the home was related to a greater ability to delay gratification at these ages.[47] In a later study Mischel showed that children with a well developed ability to wait for rewards were more socially responsible and less likely to be delinquent.[46]

Resistance to Temptation

In another chapter we will deal extensively with such factors as internalization of standards, "ego strength," and the feeling of guilt. At the present, however, we would like to explore the relationship of the ability to delay rewards to the phenomenon of cheating. To cheat or not to cheat is soon a problem for the child who enters school. This issue is taken up in an experiment by Professor Mischel discussed in Study 10.6.

DELAY OF GRATIFICATION AND CHEATING

STUDY 10.6

Mischel and Gilligan hypothesized that a preference for immediate gratification and the lack of willingness to wait for larger rewards would make it hard for children to resist temptation if cheating would bring them gratification. Conversely, children would be better at resisting temptation if they were able to wait longer for rewards.

Mischel measured both the ability of the children to delay gratification and their level of achievement motivation. The ability to delay gratification was measured by giving children a series of choices on each of which they could choose either to get a small reward at once or to wait for a much more valuable reward they could only get considerably later.

The resistance to temptation situation consisted of a

shooting gallery game. The children shot at targets with a gun. Three brightly colored sportsmen badges (marksman, sharpshooter, expert) were offered as prizes, based on the child's score. Unknown to the children, the targets were arranged so that no matter how they shot they would each get the same score. The experimenter pretended to be very busy and asked the children to keep their own score. The children, therefore, could cheat and report any score they wanted to, although each would "get" an identical score. Since the children were allowed ten shots and recorded their score for each shot, it was possible to tell on each trial whether they cheated or not. In this way is was possible to tell how soon each child started to cheat, if at all. The temptation to cheat was heightened by the fact that the game was set so that the children would get low socres, less than needed to earn the marksman, or lowest, rating.

As expected, the children low on the ability to delay gratification were more likely to cheat (report a higher score than they got) and they tended to cheat sooner. (There was not much relationship between the need to achieve and the tendency to cheat.) We conclude that children who have a need for immediate gratification may often be less resistant to temptation than children who can wait for their rewards.

Mischel, W., and Gilligan, C. Delay of gratification, motivation for the prohibited gratification, and responses to temptation. *J. Abnorm. and Soc. Psychol.*, 69, 1964, 411-417.

As long as doing well in school will represent the way to immediate parental attention, praise, and material rewards, some children will cheat. They will often be the children who are not able to resist the chance of obtaining these gratifications at once despite knowing that honest work may have a larger payoff in the long run. If quick rewards are a psychological necessity, some children will do whatever they must to achieve those rewards.

Antecedents of Causes of the Ability to Delay

Trust

Why is it that some children are more able to delay gratification than others or that a child will delay gratification in one situation and not in another? We have already suggested that the behavior of the models a child has to observe and whether the child is directly trained to delay gratification are of importance. However, there are other factors to be considered. Certainly a six-year-old boy will not choose to have a ten cent Hershey bar in two days rather than a penny Tootsie Roll at once if he does not believe that he really will get the Hershey bar later. A child who is used only to broken promises and a failure to get much of anything will not be willing to give up a bird in the hand for a phony promise in the mythical bush. A child who does not have a sense of interpersonal trust based on his experience that parents and teachers mean what they say will take what he can when he can get it. Trust based on people keeping their promises helps the child to curb his impulses of the moment.[49, 50] Delay must be rewarded if it is to persist. Trust is the result of promised rewards delivered.

Reward Value

Another factor to be taken into consideration is the value of the reward for the child. If a child knows that he can get something very important to him by waiting, rather than taking something trivial now, he may do so. Under some circumstances a lower-class child may, interestingly enough, delay gratification and wait two days to get a larger bag of marbles rather than get two marbles at once. He may choose to wait because he may have no other way of obtaining so many marbles. The middle-class child may take the two marbles now since his father will buy him a big bag of marbles any time he wants them. "Why not take anything I can get now if I can get anything I want later also?" is the sound promise of the eight year old from an affluent family.[37] Children, then, are more likely to delay gratification if they can trust or believe in the delivery of future rewards; if the rewards to be gained in the future really mean something to them; and if they can be obtained only by waiting.

Expectation of Success

Mischel has pointed out that it is seldom enough in the life of the child simply to wait. To get something the child usually has to do something. He has to be quiet or nice to his sister to get a reward, or he may have to keep his room clean for a week, get all A's on his report card, or obtain a passing grade on "conduct." Only then will the reward come. Rewards are usually contingent on such specific behaviors. Clearly, if the child expects that he can do the task required to get his reward, he may well delay gratification; if he feels that the task expected of him is beyond his ability, he may give in to his impulses of the moment. The more children succeed in school or in other areas of their lives, the more delay they can tolerate. Once they are used to success they expect that, through extended effort, reward will come. Expectation of failure, unfortunately, may produce failure. If the child expects that he can't accomplish the task which can bring what he really wants, he will indulge himself instead in some minor way and ignore the task, thereby failing. Having failed he is that much less likely to expect to succeed on a similar task and thus less willing, at some later time, to delay gratification.[50] We have already seen that many middle-class parents not only desire that their children should succeed but expect that they can. Parents who let their children know that they believe in them, when such a belief is rational, are helping them in a number of ways, including aiding them to curb impulsive behavior.

Models and Ability to Delay

Finally, the importance of the style of life of the people among whom the child lives has been experimentally validated. Children who chiefly had a delay of reward behavioral pattern shifted toward a greater preference for immediate gratification after seeing an adult who took immediate rewards. Children who tended to take immediate rewards shifted to a greater preference than before for delaying gratification, after seeing an adult who waited for delayed rewards.[7]

The grade school age child may still be quite impressionable and apt to imitate the style of behaviors of those about him. A child from a self-indulgent environment is not as likely to develop a future oriented style of life as one from an environment where people will sacrifice today for the promise of tomorrow. The success of Chinese and Jewish students in the educational system is perhaps partly due to the orientation of their parents toward sacrifice for a better future.

Arousal and Attention

In addition to having a motive to achieve and the ability to delay gratification, the child must be able to pay attention in school. Paying attention implies a certain level of arousal rather than a lethargic state. A number of studies have shown that children are more likely to learn and to imitate if they are mildly aroused.[8] To what do children pay attention? It seems that the main elicitor of attention in children is some situation or event which is slightly unusual, different, or incongruous. That is, one which arouses curiosity. If material is very familiar and fails to arouse any curiosity it will elicit indifference. If it is too strange or beyond the child's grasp, it may elicit fear, avoidance, or even hostility. A moderate amount of unfamiliarity seem so intrigue the grade school age child and hold his attention.[30] The findings in Study 10.7, reported in an article by Kagan, makes this point very well.

ATTENTION AND FAMILIARITY

STUDY 10.7

Dr. Edward Ziegler, of Yale University, asked children in grades 2, 3, 4 and 5 to look at cartoons. These cartoons required very little reading to get the point of the joke. He asked the children to tell about (explain) the cartoons. Meanwhile Ziegler had someone mark down every time each child laughed or smiled while looking at the cartoons. The older the children were, the better they were able both to understand and to explain the cartoons.

The third grade children tended to laugh and smile at the cartoons more than the second grade children did. The fourth grade children laughed and smiled even more than the third grade ones. However, the incidence of smiling and laughing went down markedly in the fifth graders. The fifth grade children understood the cartoons too well and may, at home or other places, have seen many like them. The second graders did not smile or laugh much because the material was too strange, whereas the fifth graders were not amused because it was too familiar.

Ziegler, E. Unpublished paper. (In) Kagan, J., On the need for relativism. *Amer. Psychologist, 22,* 1967, 131-142.

SCHOOL DAYS AND ANXIETY

Anxiety and Performance

It has been pointed out that most children look forward to attending school and like it once they get there, despite certain complaints.[63, 64] However, it may be hard to find any child who does not have some fears about school. We have already briefly discussed fear of failure and test anxiety. Some children high on test anxiety may be the victims of a complex relationship which is hard to untangle. The highly anxious student may not do as well in studies as one with lower anxiety.

It has often been shown that anxiety can interfere with the learning or performance of complex tasks.[44, 60, 61, 69] Of course, this need not always be the case. If it is possible to do better on a task by being slow and careful, the highly anxious child, because he is somewhat compulsive, may do better. Usually, however, anxiety interferes with complex learning and performance and the highly anxious student does less well. If he does not do well, a child may become more anxious about studies. This makes it seem as if anxiety comes first, followed by failure, followed by higher anxiety. But what engenders the anxiety in the first place? It may be that some children or even older students first being to fail or do poorly, and that this engenders the anxiety which begins the vicious circle.

School Phobia

Some children are afraid to go to school. They may be afraid of events directly associated with the school or they may simply be afraid of being separated from their mothers.[15] Fear of school or fear of separation from the mother are most common in the lower elementary grades. Girls, who usually learn to be more dependent than boys and are more attached to mother, are more likely to develop "school phobia" than boys.[34] Luckily the unwillingness to go to school is one of the problems of childhood which responds well to psychological treatment. When it is dealt with promptly most children resume going to school in a few weeks.[72] School phobia seems to lend itself to treatment by means of principles derived from learning theory. Study 10.8 shows a partial description of learning therapy with a school-phobic boy.

LEARNING THERAPY IN A SCHOOL-PHOBIC BOY

STUDY 10.8

Karl, a seven-year-old boy, went to the first grade for a few days but showed a marked dislike of doing so. By the second week he would stay in class only if one of his parents was with him. This is a case of fear of separation since Karl, even before school, would not tolerate being very far from home. He always stayed close to his mother during the day and, if playing, would often check to see if she were near.

Karl was referred to and treated at a University clinic. On the first visit he came in hanging onto his mother's coat. He was seated at a table, and his mother was seated in the doorway of the room. Karl was given toys to play with and was also engaged in play by the experimenter-therapist. The first time Karl did not look at his mother he was given some candy. And so, by not looking at his mother he was rewarded. The mother, as instructed, both praised Karl for staying in the playroom and made a fuss over him, at home, any time he played outside more than thirty minutes.

In session two the mother sat outside the playroom. When Karl let the experimenter-therapist close the door, he was given some candy and praise. He continued to get praise at home for long periods of play away from the parents. Separation from the mother and the father was, in this way, further rewarded.

In later sessions Karl allowed his parents to stay in the reception room. He was given praise for any acts of independence and activity away from home that he reported.

All the sessions involved doll play, with dolls representing various members of a family. There was a boy doll named Henry (very much like Karl) who was used in play situations where he was shown safely spending time at school and other places away from the doll parents. This procedure represents teaching through symbolic modeling.

After his tenth session Karl made his first trip to school with a special teacher who stayed with him at all times. This teacher then left him alone at school for longer and longer periods of time. After a week of going to school with the special teacher Karl was lavishly praised at home when he announced that he would go to school by himself. He did go by himself and was again praised and given attention. He then announced that the would return to school on a regular basis, and did so.

There were 23 treatment sessions in all. Three months after treatment Karl's progress in school was checked. The school reported excellent improvement in general adjustment and no signs of fear about going to school.

The basic procedure used candy and praise as rewards for being able to stay away from the mother for longer and longer distances and times. At the same time, doll play was used as a way, through symbolic modeling, to show him that being away from home could be safe and to allow him to express and reduce his fears. All the steps were gradual so that fear would never be too high.

Patterson, G. R. A learning theory approach to the treatment of the school phobic child. (In), *Case Studies in Behavior Modification*, Ullman, P. L., and Krasner, L. (Eds.). Holt, Rinehart and Winston, New York, 1965.

SCHOOL AND SOCIAL LIFE

The Early School Years

The child who enters school is still very much tied to his family. Although he is thrown together with other children in the classroom and playground, he is still quite home oriented and also may be quite attached to or in awe of the teacher.[9] Parents and teachers are still the most important sources of gratification.

The first few grades find the child still more an individual trying to gain confidence in himself than a group member very closely attached to other children. Interpersonal relations for the six, seven or eight year old are rather immature, fickle, and fleeting. Even in the ten year old, friendships are relatively unstable. Other children are still not stable and important sources of reward. Sixth graders in one study made up a list of their three best friends and again made up a list of their three best friends a few weeks later. For 60 percent of the children one of the three best friends of only a few weeks ago was off the list for some relatively trivial reason.[5]

The Teacher

Children in the early primary grades imitate the teacher. They also want the teacher's approval. There are play groups, but they serve as vehicles for fun without too great an attachment to its members. Boys of eight are not often found in clubs, and it is relatively harder to organize younger children into organized group activities than children of 12 or over.[9, 14]

Perhaps the strongest relationship a child has outside his family, in the early school years, is with the teacher. However, this attachment to the teacher may well depend on the child's being able to perceive a certain similarity between the teacher and the mother. Since most school teachers come from a middle-class background, sharing traits and values with middle-class parents, the middle-class child may find it relatively easy to accept the teacher, become attached to her, and to imitate her. The disadvantaged lower-class child may not have the same experience. The middle-class teacher and the values she holds, or tries to convey, may be alien to the lower-class child. Children tend to imitate and to like what seems appropriate to them. A study by Dr. Norma Feshbach, part of which is discussed in Study 10.9, bears on this issue.

TEACHER IMITATION IN ADVANTAGED AND DISADVANTAGED CHILDREN

STUDY 10.9

Norma Feshbach, of the University of California at Los Angeles, recognized that children learn behaviors in school through direct observation and imitation of the teacher as well as by direct reinforcement. She was interested in ascertaining if both advantaged and disadvantaged children would imitate the teacher. She was also interested in seeing if a rewarding teacher would be imitated more than a critical one.

Through the medium of films, nine- and ten-year-old boys, from both advantaged and disadvantaged backgrounds, were exposed to both a positive, rewarding teacher and a negative, critical teacher. (There were comparable boys in a control group who saw no teacher on film or otherwise.) The teachers were white and middle-class in manner as well as appearance.

After the film was viewed by the children, a situation was set up in which the children played school and teacher. This situation gave them a chance to imitate the things they had seen the teachers do in the film, if they were so inclined. Of the 33 children in the study, 21 were from an advantaged middle-class background and 12 were from a disadvantaged lower-class background.

The great majority of the imitation that occurred was done by the advantaged middle-class children and they tended to imitate the positive, rewarding teacher. One can speculate that this teacher, seen on film, whom they imitated, might have been similiar to their own mothers. The advantaged children tended to imitate the negative teacher very little.

The disadvantaged lower-class children engaged in very little imitation of either teacher whether rewarding or critical. However, Dr. Feshbach found, interestingly enough, that more disadvantaged children preferred the critical teacher than the rewarding one. Despite their failure to imitate the critical teacher any more than the rewarding one, they might have preferred her because she behaved somewhat more like women they were used to.

Feshbach, N. Variations in teachers' reinforcement style and imitative behavior of children differing in personality characteristics and social background. *CSEIP Report No. 2.*, U.C.L.A., 1967.

Similarity and Empathy

The exaggeration of differences between individuals tends to reduce empathy as well as to reduce the tendency to imitate. One way empathy can be defined is as the ability to experience an emotion similar to that of another person as a result of responding to the perception of that feeling in the other. To give a simple example: if a boy sees that another boy is frightened, and then feels afraid himself, he is responding empathically. Or, if a small girl perceives that another little girl is angry at the teacher and then becomes angry herself, this is another case of empathy.[64, 65]

Similarity helps to facilitate empathic behavior. It is easier for a child to respond emotionally to someone similar to him than to someone different. Some psychologists consider empathy to be related to imitation and identification. An emotional appreciation for the feelings of others is a basis for behaving in a similar fashion to them.[21] Again, the lower-class child in the middle-class oriented school system may be emotionally incapable of responding empathically to the teacher since the teacher may be too different from the type of people the disadvantaged child is used to.

Boys and Girls

In the first grade some degree of social segregation along sex lines has already taken place. Boys have learned that they are boys and girls that they are girls. They have also learned to behave differently to some extent. In addition each sex soon tends to prefer its own company, partly because their interest, behaviors, and values have begun to differ along sex lines. Boys are rougher and get interested in sports, whereas girls may be physically less active, more obedient, neater, and tend toward more feminine activities. The development of true differences based on the reinforcement of boys and girls by their parents and teachers for divergent ways of acting heightens the lack of empathy between the sexes. As we have pointed out, it is not easy to feel empathy with someone who is different. Study 10.10 underscores this issue in the life of the school age child.

EMPATHY AND SIMILARITY

STUDY 10.10

Dr. Norma Feshbach and Kiki Roe set out to show that boys would have more empathy for the feelings of other boys and girls more for the feeling of girls.

They used a series of slides depicting seven year olds in one of four emotional situations. There were two situations for each emotion: a birthday party and winning a TV contest, for *happiness;* a lost dog and social rejection, for *sadness;* a lost child and a frightening dog, for *fear;* a toy snatcher and a false accusation, for *anger.* There were two sets of these slides, differing only in that the children shown in one set were *all girls* and in the other they were *all boys.*

Twenty-three boys and 23 girls in the first grade saw the slides. Each child had to tell how seeing each slide made him feel and how he thought the child in the slide felt.

The results were very clear. The slides showing boys were much more likely to make the boy subjects feel the same emotion assigned to the boy in the slide by the experimenters. If a girl was in the slide the boys were less likely to report feeling the assigned emotion. The same was true for girls. If a girl appeared in a slide showing a birthday party, for instance, girls seeing it were likely to report that it made them feel happy too. If a boy appeared in a slide, girls were less likely to report feeling the emotion considered appropriate for that slide.

Boys and girls were about equally accurate (except for *fear,* in which case boys were more correct) in stating how either a boy or girl in any slide felt. The point is that boys were less likely to *feel* the same way themselves on seeing the slide if it had a girl in it, and vice-versa.

Feshbach, N., and Roe, K. Stimulus factors affecting empathic behavior in first grade children. In press.

SCHOOL DAYS AND SOCIAL TIES

New Sources of Reinforcement and Imitation from Nine to 13

The years after the first three or four primary grades are likely to be trying ones for parents and teachers. After several years of going to school and interacting with playmates, important changes take place in the life of the preadolescent child. As bonds and emotional ties are forged with other children, particularly close friends and playmates, these other children become important sources of rewards and punishments, and more influential as models to imitate. It becomes important to belong and to be accepted. The intermediate grade, preadolescent child develops a strong interest in group activity and loyalty to his circle of friends. Exclusion and betrayal are painful. These groups develop their own leaders who are imitated. The approval of the parents and teachers, at one time the only main source of reinforcement, now becomes less potent. Preadolescent children begin to reinforce each other and look to each other, as well as adults, for attention and approval.[9, 24]

Sanctions for behavior in this period from about nine to 13 come to a significant extent from the social group of which the child is a member. When group rules changes, the behavior of the child changes. By affiliating himself with other children any given child at this age is in a better position to pursue his own goals. He is helped to get his own way by the physical and moral support of his friends. They become sources of anxiety reduction, recognition, chances to excel, and other rewarding activities. The child now has a strong source of gratification outside the home and school.[56] He or she spends more time with other children, yearns for their approval, and uses them as weapons against their parents.

Peer Group and Independence

After peer group formation (informal membership and affiliation with same age children) has become established, a period of behavior relatively unacceptable to adults may set in and the child may begin to make vociferous demands. The preadolescent aspires to greater independence. He wishes to engage in activities which are rewarding for any one of a number of reasons, whether the parents favor these behaviors or not. One parent reported the following demands by her 12-year-old son. He wanted to: go to the movies at night alone, explore a nearby river and fish alone, decide what clothes should be bought for him, wear clothes his parents didn't approve of, talk to and meet adults, strange or otherwise, buy gifts for people on his own, set his own bedtime hours, and take part in family plans and decisions.[40]

Previously dependent on parents and teachers for the rewards of life, the child now sees a world of gratification, relatively free of the adult world, beckoning him. The height of unruly behavior often comes around nine years of age, particularly for boys. Nine and ten are the years for disobedience, dirtiness, disorder, and deceit. Teachers report more behavior problems in the fourth, fifth, and sixth grades than at any other time. The adolescent, whom most people think of as the prime trouble-maker, has often won his fight for independence. It is the preadolescent who is often the chief troublemaker and fighter for independence *par excellence*. By or before high school years many children have worked out these problems in one way or another.[8, 10, 29] Of course, parents usually feel they can control the ten year old and that he has time to change. The larger adolescent appears harder to control and parents have only limited time to influence him.

Is Preadolescent Turmoil a Stage?

There is nothing stage-like or predetermined about the previously described behavior patterns often seen in our culture. They are quite likely to change if certain causative variables change, or they may have changed already. If parents become very permissive and freely allow children to do as they want, if Lolita becomes the model rather than a cause for scandal, if the "teeny-bopper" is the norm of the day, the phenomena described for the years nine to 13 may vanish, or occur earlier. Children behave with a certain uniformity at certain ages because they face common conditions in the demands placed on them, common treatment, common experiences, common models to imitate, and common patterns and sources of reward and punishment. If any combination of these demands changes, the behavior of the child will change. If different social classes, races, religions, or ethnic groups present different role models and differentially reward their children, the behavior of all children will hardly be identical. If most people, on the other hand, will come to act similarly and to treat their children similarly, the children will behave more identically.

Boys and Girls

Although another chapter will deal more extensively with sex typed behavior, we should note here that what is true for the boy need not be true for the girl. Since boys and girls are not treated alike they do not behave alike. Sex typed behavior is behavior strongly associated with one sex or the other. Parents are more restrictive with girls and expect them to be better behaved. The peer groups to which a girl belongs will not sanction the types of rowdy behavior in which some groups of boys revel. School misbehavior from nine to 13 years of age is higher among boys than girls. Boys of this age end up in child guidance clinics much more often than girls do. It is during the years 16 to 17, when sexual misconduct in girls frightens the parents, that they appear in clinics with the greatest frequency.[10, 36] There may be a trend today for such sexual behavior to occur earlier. Both the stability and amount of certain behaviors shown by boys and girls depends to a large extent on which of these behaviors are seen as appropriate and tolerable at various ages by their parents and peers. Study 10.11 demonstrates this principle, drawing on just a few parts of an extremely large and complex longitudinal study by Kagan and Moss.

SEX ROLE AND BEHAVIOR

STUDY 10.11

The book *From Birth to Maturity*, by Jerome Kagan and Howard Moss, is based on more than 30 years of research by many people. It represents a summary of the comprehensive study of a population of male and females, from birth until adulthood, carried out at the Fels Institute.

Kagan and Moss point out that individuals learn to act in ways consistent with cultural expectations of how males and females should behave at various ages. The earlier chapter on social learning, in this text, outlines the learning principles through which these social expectations become a behavioral reality.

Kagan and Moss found behaviors during the years six to ten to be good predictors of adult behavior in some instances. They feel that important behavioral learning and organization goes on in these years as a function of the peer group, the mastery of achievement skills, and parental imitation. Once *certain* patterns of behavior are established from six to ten, they may persist into adulthood.

Specifically they found that dependence and passivity in girls from age six to ten was a good predictor of passivity and dependence in later years. This was much less true for boys. Since girls are kept more passive and dependent, they end up passive and dependent. Boys may be passive or dependent at six or seven years of age, but their peer group demands more independence and their parents are likely to allow and encourage more independence. Consequently, boys may change in this regard. A passive and dependent boy at age six or ten can end up an active and independent adult.

Just the opposite may be the case for sexuality. Since it is considered more permissible for boys to show sexual interest, boys who show more sexual behavior from six to ten also show more as adult males. Girls, on the other hand, are heavily discouraged from any sexual activity from six to ten. However, once married, or at some point before that, they can and do show more sexual behavior. Consequently, the lack of sexual interest or activity in a ten-year-old girl is no predictor of her future sexual conduct. Behavior shows consistency over time only if it is rewarded or punished consistently over time. Shifts in what is rewarded or punished will cause shifts in behavior.

Kagan, J., and Moss, H. A. *Birth to Maturity.* John Wiley, New York, 1962.

THE INNER WORLD OF PREADOLESCENCE

After showing such extended fidelity to the findings of empirical research and to social learning theory, it may be appropriate to cite the views of a man who probably never did an experiment, never systematically collected any data nor engaged in statistical tabulations. The psychoanalyst Harry Stack Sullivan probably understood the inner world and emotions of the child from age six to adolescence as well as anyone ever has. The following sections are based on his discussion of "the juvenile and preadolescent eras" in *The Interpersonal Theory of Psychiatry,* a book based on his unpublished lectures.[68]

Becoming Social

Sullivan held that what he called the "juvenile era", the time from entrance into school until the child finds a true friend, is of great importance. This is the time, he said, of becoming social. He felt that this is the first time when the child is given a chance to overcome some of the less desirable effects of his home life. Through the medium of a good friend and contact with other children it is now possible for a given child to enter into broader environments outside of his necessarily somewhat limiting home life. Whatever went on before in terms of interpersonal relations and the foundation of personality is now thrown open to the possibility of change through the influence of people beyond the home.

Social Subordination

Sullivan discussed both social subordination and social accommodation. In dealing with social subordination he noted that the school age child is exposed to a new type and kind of authority. Because of compulsory education the child becomes exposed to a number of teachers, all or any of whom can possibly have a good effect on the child. In addition to the teacher such other models as recreation directors, cub scout masters, den mothers, and school-crossing policemen may become important in the child's life. As Sullivan says: "In his relations with his teacher and the various other adult authority figures who appear, the juvenile is expected—as the child has begun to be by his parents—to do things on demand; and he is given rewards, punishments, and so on with respect to compliance, noncompliance, rebellion, and what not. But there are more or less formally enforced limits to each of these new authorities. At the same time, there is the possibility for the juvenile to see the interrelation of the behavior of his compeers to success or failure with the new authority figures. And in addition to the adult authorities, there are, in almost every school situation, malevolent juveniles—bullies. Part of the incredible gain in ability to live comes from one's finding a way of getting by under the episodic and destructive exercises of authority by such compeers."

Social Accommodation

He felt, however, that social accommodation, rather than subordination, was the most crucial part of the juvenile era. He saw social accommodation as a necessity arising from continual contact with children of about the same age but with a variety of personal peculiarities. Each child has to learn to cope with lots of other children who demonstrate a whole variety of interpersonal differences in their behavior. The child in the first several school years and thereafter learns a tremendous amount about other children and changes or accommodates his own behavior as a result of this knowledge. He profits by vicarious and empathic learning. He sees who parents and teachers value, who gets praised and who gets punished, and for what. He sees how children view each other and how they relate to various authority figures. He can use this knowledge to guide his own behavior.

Finding a Friend

In his discussion of preadolescence, the period after the first few primary grades, but before adolescence, Sullivan stressed the need for interpersonal intimacy, and the experience of loneliness. He saw the earliest school years as those in which the child needed many playmates like himself. Sullivan considered the need for one particular member of the same sex as a close and intimate friend as a later development of preadolescence. He thought that between eight and a half and ten a true "chum" was found. Then the thought, "What should I do to get what I want?" turned to, "What should I do to contribute to the happiness and to support the prestige and feeling of worthwhileness of my chum?" It is then that the sensitivity to what matters to another person develops and the ability to collaborate and to grasp the meaning of "our teacher" or "our team" reaches fruition.

Acceptance and Exclusion

The experience of loneliness, according to Sullivan, may have its roots in the early school years, in some bitter experience when the child is ostracized by his peers. Exclusion, or the fear of not being accepted by one or more of those age mates whom the child needs as models for learning how to become human, may begin the sharp experience of loneliness. Another hurt-provoking component of lonliness stems from the inability to find and have a chum, friend, or loved one for the type of intimate exchange and sharing that brings the satisfaction of security. Loneliness is a most unpleasant feeling, but one which most children experience at one point or another in their lives. Those who are lucky enough to be true and good friends, who are able to share and to have a feeling of collaboration, and who are accepted, are lucky indeed. It is not easy to form such relationships in our competitive culture. As the conclusion of our presentation of Sullivan's views, we may note that, unfortunately, insufficient research has been done on many of the important issues which he has raised. Let us again turn to some research findings.

THE SCHOOL AND SOCIAL ACCEPTANCE

There are three factors which characterize a child's position in the school: the child's emotional acceptance by others—do "they" like him or her?, the child's personal competence—what can he or she do and how well?, the child's social power—how much can the child influence others? These propositions are based on research findings.[24, 26, 39]

The most outstanding characteristic of the social structure of the school is its stability. The same children tend to retain their acceptance by others or lack of it, their competence in various activities or their dearth of it, and their ability to influence others or their lack of power, from school month to school month and from year to year. There is some shifting of allegiances, development or loss of skills, and emergence of new leaders and the recession of old ones. By and large, however, the pecking order among children in the classroom tends to be established early and fairly rapidly and to persist if there is not a lot of change in class memberships.[26]

The extent of the stability of the factors above is at least partly related to the number of pairs of children who are mutually attracted to each other, the number of subgroups of mutual friends in the classrooms, and the number of isolates chosen by hardly anyone as friends or persons of influence. Most elementary grade classrooms seem to have subgroups or "cliques" who interact with each other and not too much with the other children. They are composed of children of the same sex who seem to cluster together because: they have common attitudes and values, they live near each other or sit near each other in class, they think they have desirable personality traits in common, that is, they believe each other to be friendly, good-looking and cheerful.[26]

Once groups have formed, it is not easy for a newcomer to break in, nor do boys have easy access to girls' groups or girls to those of boys. The experiment reported in part in Study 10.12 is a good illustration of this point. It is not comfortable to be an outsider. It takes time to be accepted and initial encounters may not be easy.

SEX DIFFERENCES AND RESPONSES TOWARD OUTSIDERS

STUDY 10.12

Norma Feshbach was interested in seeing what would happen if a new child was introduced into an already formed pair of children.

Eighty-four middle-class, first grade children were formed into pairs. There were 20 pairs of boys and 22 pairs of girls. They were selected at random from the classroom and taken two at a time into another room. To give them a feeling of mutual togetherness they were told that they were a special club and would have attractive toys to play with. They got a club name and nice badges to wear. They were allowed to play together and told that next week they would have another club meeting.

When their club meeting came the next week, they got their badges again, were reminded of their club name, and went back to the same room. They were then told that a new child would be joining them from a classroom other than their own. Half of the original pair of boys were joined by another boy and half by a girl. Half of the original girl pairs were joined by another girl and half by a boy. Dr. Feshbach then had careful ratings made of how the pairs reacted to the newcomer and how the newcomer behaved toward the previously formed pairs.

The girls showed a cold unfriendliness toward a newcomer, especially when he was a boy. Both boys and girls made significantly more positive approach responses toward the same sex than toward opposite-sex newcomers. Many more girls than boys, on finding out that a new child was to join them, made negative, critical remarks. The newcomer was hesitant in such a situation. In fact, the newcomer made significantly fewer responses than were made by either of the other two children to him or to each other. The boys who joined an all-boy group showed more direct and indirect aggression than did newcomers in any of the other groups. Girls, in general, showed more indirect, nonphysical types of aggression. Boys in the already formed groups tended to approach a new boy more than a new girl and the already formed girl groups were more likely to approach positively a new girl.

Feshbach, N. Sex differences and modes of aggressive responses towards outsiders. In press.

DETERMINANTS OF ACCEPTANCE AND INTERPERSONAL BEHAVIOR

Glidewell and his associates have stated: "In summary, if a child is fortunate enough to be strong and healthy, intelligent, and upper-middle class, and possessing well-developed interpersonal skills, he is likely to have high self-esteem and a capacity to perceive accurately the nature of the approaches and responses of others to him. Under such conditions, he is likely to begin to initiate cautious interaction attempts with others — especially the most obviously respected children and teachers. . . . As the skillful child develops more acceptance, power, and competence in the classroom, he appears to develop still greater self-esteem. . . . The child who enters the classroom with less vigorous health, with limited intellect, inadequate interpersonal skills, from the lower classes . . . is likely to produce responses which are likely to induce responses (from other children and teachers) which are, at best, restrained embarrassment, or at worst, hostile ridicule."[26] He will receive more negative than positive reinforcements.

The process is a circular one. If the child shows competence and the ingredients which in our culture lead to acceptance and power, his road, although at first hesitant, will become smoother and his behavior more confident. He will be imitated, accepted, reinforced, and his confidence will grow. The child, starting out with less of what "counts" with others, will get more negative reinforcements, his way will be a rough one, and he may either withdraw or engage in aggressive and possibly antisocial acts. His only behavior options may be passive rejection or counteraggression.[11, 26, 35, 38]

THE TEACHER AND SOCIAL CLASSROOM BEHAVIOR

Not everything is up to the children. The teacher can be a powerful source for intervention and change in the classroom. The social power of the teacher has often been demonstrated. The behavior of the teacher is a very important source of influence in the intellectual and social climate of the classroom. We have already seen that middle-class children are very likely to imitate the teacher. The comments and other reinforcements of the teacher are quite potent in influencing the behavior of the children. For some children the teacher's behavior toward him is as important a factor as the value orientations and attitudes of the parents. The teacher can utilize and distribute her power so that children are more ready to accept each other, support each other, and interact on a positive basis. This may also be accomplished by proper delegation of teacher power in the classroom.[12, 13, 22, 27, 59] Unfortunately the use of teacher behavior and power can also be turned to destructive ends.

SUMMARY

With the beginning of school the child spends a considerable amount of time away from parents and siblings in a competitive environment. Although the child has been given tasks to do before and has been judged before, he is now more consistently compared to others and is expected to "measure up." He is judged by teachers, peers, parents, and others in terms of school work, popularity, "social adjustment," and skill at games. School engages the motive to achieve in a variety of areas.

Both before and during the school years, children acquire levels of expected performance. They internalize standards of achievement which they strive to reach. These standards may be high, low, or average, in comparison with the standards which other children have. The level of the need to achieve acquired by any child depends on the standards held by the models he has been exposed to, on direct training in achievement behavior, and on early encouragement of independence.

Children hope for success and they may also fear failure. Hope for success, often linked to a high need to achieve, leads to a preference for a moderate degree of risk; that is, a desire for challenging but attainable goals. Fear of failure, often but not always associated with a low need to achieve, tends to be linked to a desire either to avoid risk by setting low standards or a preference for taking risks so high that the results don't really count. Fear of failure leads to unrealistic goal setting, choosing the too easy or the too hard for which the child really does not try.

Day to day performance in school involves the ability to delay. The child must curb his impulses and give up what he may want to do at the moment; sometimes he gives up what he wants to do at once in order to get something he values more later. A variety of variables determines whether or not a child will delay gratification in any given situation. The child will be more likely to wait if he: *trusts* that he will get a later reward, if he is waiting for something with *high reward value* (something important), if he feels that he will be *successful* in earning the greater reward, and if he has been exposed to people who are *models* of the ability to wait.

A lack of success in school can engender fear just as fear of school helps cause failure. Some children, however, are not frightened of any specific aspect of school, rather, they are unwilling to be separated from home. A child has an easier time in school if the teacher, the teacher's expectations, and the nature of the desired behaviors are *similar* to those he has been used to at home. The school, consequently, is more comfortable for the middle-class child who finds it easier to empathize with and accept the school, which chiefly upholds middle-class values.

The preadolescent school years are ones in which the child becomes involved in acquiring friends on a more permanent and meaningful basis than previously. During the "juvenile era," children acquire "chums," have special friends of the same sex, and may experience loneliness and rejection. Acceptance and exclusion become important issues. Fairly consistently in a school group some children seem to be accepted, competent, influential, and powerful. Other children fail to show these qualities. The degree to which children show these characteristics tends to be reasonably permanent if the group does not change too much. The children who end up in the most favored positions, in the areas noted above, tend to be upper-middle class, intelligent, strong and healthy, interpersonally skillful, and usually show high self-esteem. The school situation, including the other children, favors those who have "advantages" to start with.

REFERENCES

1. Aberle, D. F., and Naegele, K. D.   Middle class fathers' occupational role and attitudes toward children. *Amer. J. Orthopsychiat, 22,* 1952, 366-378.
2. Anderson, H. H.   An examination of the concept of the dominance: an integration in relation to domination and ascendance. *Psych. Rev., 47,* 1940, 21-22.
3. Atkinson, J. W.   *An Introduction to Motivation.* D. Van Nostrand, Princeton, 1965.
4. Atkinson, J. W., and Litwin, G. H.   Achievement motive and test anxiety conceived as motive to approach success and motive to avoid failure. *J. Abnorm. Soc. Psychol., 60,* 1960, 52-63.
5. Austin, M. C., and Thompson, G. G.   Children's friendship: A study of the bases on which children select and reject their best friends. *J. Educ. Psychol., 39,* 1948, 101-116.
6. Bandura, A, and Kupers, C. J.,   Transmission of patterns of self-reinforcement through modeling. *J. Abnorm. Soc. Psychol., 69,* 1964, 1-9.
7. Bandura, A., and Mischel, W.   Modification of self-imposed delay of reward through exposure to live and symbolic models. *J. Pers. Soc. Psychol., 2,* 1965, 698-705.
8. Bandura, A., and Walters, R. H.   *Social Learning and Personality Development.* Holt, Rinehart and Winston, New York, 1963.
9. Blair, A. W., and Burton, W. H.   *Growth and Development of the Pre-adolescent.* Appleton-Century Crofts, New York, 1951.
10. Blatz, W. E., and Bott, H. M.   Studies in mental hygiene of children, *Pedagogical Seminary,* 1927, 552-582.
11. Bonney, M. E.   Popular and unpopular children: A sociometric study. *Sociom. Monogr., No. 9,* 1947.
12. Bronfenbrenner, U., and Suci, G. J.   Patterns of parental behavior in America and West Germany: A cross national comparison. *Int. Soc. Sci. J., 14,* 1962, 488-506.
13. Bronfenbrenner, U., et al.   Adults and peers as sources of conformity and autonomy. Unpublished paper. Cornell University, Ithaca, 1965.

14. Chave, E. J. *Personality Development in Children.* University of Chicago Press, Chicago, 1937.
15. Coolidge, J. C., et al. Patterns of aggression in school phobia. (In) *Psychoanalytic Study of the Child, 17*, International Universities Press, New York, 1962.
16. Crandall, V. J., et al. A conceptual formulation of some research in children's achievement development. *Child Develpm., 31*, 1960, 787-797.
17. Elder, G. H., Jr. Family structure and educational attainment: a cross sectional analysis. *American Soc. Rev., 30*, 1965, 81-96.
18. Elder, G. H., Jr. *Adolescent Achievement and Mobility Aspirations.* Inst. for Res. in Soc. Sci., Chapel Hill, 1962.
19. Erikson, E. H. *Childhood and Society.* W. W. Norton, New York, 1950.
20. Feshbach, N. Variations in teachers' reinforcement style and imitative behavior of children differing in personality characteristics and social backgrounds. *CSEIP Technical Report No. 2*, U.C.L.A., 1967.
21. Feshbach, N., and Roe, K. Stimulus factors effecting empathic behavior in first grade children. In press.
22. Flanders, N. A. Teacher-pupil contacts and mental hygiene. *J. Soc. Issues, 15*, 1959, 30-39.
23. Freud, S. *Beyond the Pleasure Principle.* Boni and Liveright, New York, 1922.
24. Gellert, E. Stability and fluctuation in power relationships of young children. *J. Abnorm. Soc. Psychol., 62*, 1961, 8-15.
25. Ginzberg, E. *The Negro Potential.* Columbia University Press, New York, 1956.
26. Glidewell, J. C., et al. Socialization and social structure in the classroom. (In) *Review of Child Development Research*, Volume 2, Hoffman, L. W., and Hoffman, M. L. (Eds.). Russell Sage Foundation, New York, 1966.
27. Henry, J. Attitude organization in elementary classrooms. *Amer. J. Orthopsychiat., 27*, 1957, 117-133.
28. Hunt, J. McV., and Solomon, R. A. The stability and some correlates of group status in a summer camp group of young boys. *Amer. J. Psychol., 55*, 1942, 33-35.
29. Jones, H. E., et al. Child development and the curriculum. *Yearbook Nat. Soc. Stud. Educ., 38*, Bloomington, 1939.
30. Kagan, J. On the need for relativism. *Amer. Psychologist, 22*, 1967, 131-142.
31. Kagan, J., et al. Information processing in the child: significance of analytic and reflective attitudes. *Psych. Monogr., 78*, 1964, 1-37.
32. Kagan, J., and Moss, H. A. *From Birth to Maturity.* John Wiley, New York, 1962.
33. Kanner, L. *Child Psychiatry* (3rd Edition) Charles C Thomas, Springfield, Ill., 1957.
34. Keller, J. W. *Psychopathology of Childhood.* Prentice-Hall, Englewood Cliffs, 1966.
35. Kuhlen, R. G., and Lee, B. J. Personality characteristics and social acceptability in adolescence. *J. Educ. Psychol., 34*, 1943, 321-340.
36. Levy, J., and Monroe, R. *The Happy Family*, Alfred A. Knopf, New York, 1938.
37. Levy, M. F. A critique of studies of tolerance for delayed gratification. Unpublished paper. New York University, New York, 1966.
38. Lewis, O. *Topotzlan: Village in Mexico.* Holt, Rinehart and Winston, New York, 1962.
39. Lippit, R., and Gold, M. Classroom social structure as a mental health problem. *J. Soc. Issues, 15*, 1959, 40-58.
40. Loomis, M. J. *The Preadolescent.* Appleton-Century-Crofts, New York, 1959.
41. Maccoby, E. E. Sex differences in intellectual functioning. (In) *The Development of Sex Differences*, Maccoby, E. E. (Ed.). Stanford University Press, Stanford, 1966.
42. McClelland, D. C. Risk taking in children with high and low need for achievement. (In) *Motives in Fantasy, Action and Society*, Atkinson, J. W. (Ed.), D. Van Nostrand, New York, 1958.
43. McClelland, D. C. *The Achieving Society.* D. Van Nostrand, New York, 1958.
44. Mandler, G., and Savason, S. B. A study of anxiety and learning. *J. Abnorm. Soc. Psychol., 47*, 1952, 166-173.
45. Mischel. W. A social learning view of sex differences in behavior. (In) *The Development of Sex Differences*, Maccoby, E. E. (Ed.) Stanford University Press, Stanford, 1966.
46. Mischel, W. Preference for delayed reinforcement and social responsibility. *J. Abnorm. Soc. Psychol., 62*, 1961, 1-7.
47. Mischel, W. Preference for delayed reinforcement: An experimental study of cultural observation. *J. Abnorm. Soc. Psychol., 56*, 1958, 57-61.

48. Mischel, W., and Gilligan, C. Delay of gratification, motivation for the prohibited gratification and responses to temptation. *J. Abnorm. Soc. Psychol.*, 69, 1964, 411-417.
49. Mischel, W., and Metzner, R. Preference for delayed reward as a function of age, intelligence, and length of delay interval. *J. Abnorm. Soc. Psychol.*, 64, 1962, 425-431.
50. Mischel, W., and Staub, E. Effects of expectancy on working and waiting for larger rewards. *J. Pers. Soc. Psychol.*, 2, 1965, 625-633.
51. Mowrer, O. H., and Ullman, A. D. Time as a determinant of integrative learning. *Psych. Rev.*, 52, 1945, 61-90.
52. Patterson, G. R. A learning theory approach to the treatment of the school phobic child. (In) *Case Studies in Behavior Modification*, Ullman, P. L., and Krasner, L. (Eds.). Holt, Rinehart and Winston, New York, 1965.
53. Raphaelson, A. C. The relationship between imaginative, direct, verbal, and physiological measures of anxiety in an achievement situation. *J. Abnorm. Soc. Psychol.*, 54, 1957, 13-18.
54. Rosen, B. C. The achievement syndrome: A psycho-cultural dimension in social stratification. *Amer. Soc. Rev.*, 21, 1956, 203-211.
55. Rosen, C. R., and D'Andrade, R. The psychosocial origins of achievement motivation. *Sociometry*, 22, 1959, 185-218.
56. Sanford, R. N. Physique, personality and scholarship. *Monogr. Soc. Res. Child Develpm.*, 8, No. 1, 1943.
57. Sarason, S. B., et al. *Anxiety in Elementary School Children*. John Wiley, New York., 1960.
58. Sarason, S. B., et al. A longitudinal study of the relation of test anxiety to performance on intelligence and achievement tests. *Child Develpm. Monogr., No. 98*, 1964.
59. Schmuck, R. A., and Van Egmond, E. Sex differences in the relationship of interpersonal perceptions to academic performance. *Psychol. in the Schools*, 2, 1965, 32-40.
60. Spence, K. W., et al. The relation of test anxiety (drive) level to performance in competitional and noncompetitional paired-associates learning. *J. Exp. Psychol.*, 52, 1956, 296-305.
61. Spence, K. W. Current interpretations in learning data and some recent developments in stimulus-response theory. (In) *Learning Theory, Personality Theory, and Clinical Research*. The Kentucky Symposium. John Wiley, New York, 1953.
62. Spielberger, C. D. (Ed.) *Anxiety and Behavior*. Academic Press, New York, 1966.
63. Stendler, C. B. Social class differences in parental attitudes toward school at grade 1 level. *Child Develpm.*, 22, 1951, 36-46.
64. Stendler, C. B., and Young, N. Impact of first grade entrance upon the socialization of the child: Changes after eight months of school. *Child Develpm.*, 22, 1951, 113-122.
65. Stotland, E., and Dunn, R. E. Empathy, self-esteem and birth order. *J. Abnorm. Soc. Psychol.*, 66, 1963, 532-554.
66. Stotland, E., and Walsh, J. Birth order in an experimental study of empathy. *J. Abnorm. Soc. Psychol.*, 66, 1963, 610-614.
67. Strauss, N. H. Conjugal power structure and adolescent personality. *Marr. and Fam. Liv.*, 24, 1962, 17-25.
68. Sullivan, H. S. *The Interpersonal Theory of Psychiatry*. W. W. Norton, New York, 1953.
69. Taylor, J. A., and Spence, K. W. The relationship of anxiety level to performance in serial learning. *J. Exp. Psychol.*, 44, 1952, 61-64.
70. Tuddenham, R. D. Studies in reputation: III. Correlates of popularity among elementary school children. *J. Educ. Psychol.*, 42, 1951, 257-276.
71. Verville, E. *Behavior Problems of Children*. W. B. Saunders, Philadelphia, 1967.
72. Waldfogel, S., et al. A program for early intervention in school phobia. *Amer. J. Orthopsychiat.*, 29, 1959, 324-333.
73. Winterbottom, M. R. The relation of need for achievement to learning experience in independence mastery. (In) *Motives in Fantasy, Action, and Society*. Atkinson, J. W. (Ed.), D. Van Nostrand, New York, 1958.
74. Ziegler, E. Unpublished paper. (In) Kagan, J. On the need for relativism. *Amer. Psychologist.*, 22, 1967, 131-142.

CHAPTER 11

THE PROCESS OF CHILD REARING

PART 1 — SPECIFIC PARENTAL BEHAVIORS

We have examined some of the behavior shown by children as they develop during the primary grade years. We have already discussed some of the theories which explain how children acquire their cognitive and social behaviors during this time. However, we have not been very specific about the techniques which parents use to raise their children or about the effects of these methods. For instance, although the process of reinforcement has been discussed, we have not had much to say about how parents actually apply it or about what they tend to reward or punish. All parents do not use either reward or punishment to the same degree. They do not all apply differential rewards for the same behaviors or to children of the same age. It is useful to understand how parents differ in raising their children and to note what effects these various parental behaviors have on children. First, we will discuss how parents treat their children and, later in the chapter, consider how these various types of treatment affect the child. After considering how parents raise their children we will look at the effects their practices have on their children's actions, thoughts, and feelings.

It is a truism that the way parents rear their children has an important effect on the conduct of the children in everyday life, both in and out of the home. Parental efforts at child rearing are certainly the most potent influences in shaping the child's social, cognitive, and emotional behaviors. The materials on stage theories and social learning, which we have already presented, and information on internalization which comes later, account, in terms of psychological processes, for the behavior of the child. The specific events which affect the child, however, and for

274

whose effects theory must account, are primarily the result of the actual behavior of parents. We do not mean to minimize the influence of friends, teachers, relatives, or other social models and social reinforcing agents. As we shall see in the next chapter, however, the family, which in our society largely means the parents, is the most important influence shaping the child's behavior.

DIMENSIONS OF CHILD REARING

Individual differences in behavior among children are easy to note. Some children are more extraverted than others, some more aggressive.[14] Some children perform many tasks on their own by the age of five; others of the same age need adult assistance with most things. Certain boys of eight or ten get into a lot of fights, whereas other boys of the same age seldom if ever fight. There are 13-year-old girls who wear blue jeans and sloppy sweaters and like to play touch football with boys, and other girls of the same age who like dancing, high heels, dresses, and prefer dating to sports. What causes these differences?

Some individual differences in behavior among children are largely due to genetic-physiological factors; others are caused by a complex interaction of unusual genetic-physiological factors with the social environment. Most are caused largely by differences in social learning in the family. For the moment, therefore, we are largely concerned with those systematic styles or patterns of behaviors of parents which lead to differences in child behavior. We are interested in the process of child rearing, the relatively consistent and important ways in which parents raise their children.

Our first task will be to identify the patterns and dimensions of the child rearing process. That is, what sorts of models, and patterns of reinforcement, do different parents furnish? What are the chief ways in which parents vary in their efforts to rear their children? Which behaviors do different parents reward or punish and how do they do it? Patterns of child rearing concern all the ways in which parents characteristically behave toward their children, including the very important matter of discipline. Discipline is a term used for the patterns of punishment (and reward) which parents dispense in order to get their children to do what they wish them to do.

The study of how parents rear their children is a difficult and fascinating one. Usually investigators can only find out how parents raise children by interviewing the parents. It is usually the mother who is asked about how she raises her child. Study 11.1 describes part of one of the most widely quoted efforts in this area, a study by Sears, Maccoby, and Levin.[26]

PATTERNS OF CHILD REARING

STUDY 11.1

Robert R. Sears, Eleanor Maccoby, and Harry Levin engaged in a large scale study on patterns of child rearing. In order that their study might be reasonably representative of and generalizable to many families, they interviewed 379 mothers of varying social and religious backgrounds. They chose the mothers so that information could be gathered about an equal number of boys and girls and so there would be information available on only, first, middle, and youngest children. Sears, Maccoby, and Levin tried to include mothers from all socioeconomic levels. The mothers had children who were about five years of age and the children were enrolled in kindergarten.

Mothers who were divorced or otherwise not living with their husband were not interviewed. Participation in the study was precluded if the child was adopted, a twin, or handicapped in some way. Mothers not born in the United States were not interviewed. Divorced women or foreign-born women may or may not rear their children differently from the way women included in the study did. The study, consequently, is reasonably comprehensive, but the results may not be applicable to all groups.

The investigators, as stated, used the interview method to get their information Only mothers were interviewed, and consequently the father's views were not represented. The method followed creates some problems concerning the validity of the results. Mothers of five year olds may not remember accurately how they really acted toward their children several years before or how their children behaved at that earlier time. There is evidence that mothers are partly inaccurate in reporting child rearing behavior, particularly in retrospect. Fathers sometimes give different reports from mothers. It is perhaps unwise to draw very rigorous conclusions solely on the report of what a mother says she does or may have done to her child, or on her impression of how her child behaves or behaved.[18]

A relatively structured type of interview was used. All mothers were asked the same questions about the same types of behavior, but the interviewers had latitude in probing further to get needed information. All the interviews were tape recorded and the answers carefully tabulated. The mothers were interviewed both about their own behavior toward their children and about how their children behaved. Areas of the investigation included: feelings the mothers had about becoming pregnant, how warm and affectionate the mothers had been since the child was actually born, and how well-adjusted the mothers were in their marriages. The investigators also asked the mothers about how and when they fed and weaned their children, and how and when they toilet trained them. They also inquired about the mothers' methods of handling the children's dependent, aggressive, and sexual behaviors. The authors, in addition, asked about the mothers' methods of disciplining their children. They were mainly interested in how the mothers got their children to "obey." The investigators, therefore, were concerned chiefly about the mothers' methods of training and disciplining their children, and, of course, in how the children behaved as a consequence.

Sears, R. R., Maccoby, E. E., and Levin, H. *Patterns of Child Rearing.* Row, Peterson, Evanston, Ill., 1957.

Warmth and Permissiveness

Sears, Maccoby, and Levin were able to find seven dimensions or patterns of child rearing, based on what the mothers had to say about raising their children. Of these seven, two dimensions are of particular interest because their importance has been confirmed by other studies. One is a general dimension which may be termed "warmth." Great warmth would define one extreme of such parental behavior, and perhaps the terms, "coldness," "hostility," or "rejection" would define the other extreme. Some have labeled this dimension *warmth coldness.* The following maternal behaviors define the *warmth* or *warmth-coldness dimension*: the warm mother affectionately interacts with the baby, tends to be demonstratively playful, often praises the child, and is accepting of dependency. In terms of discipline, she makes extensive use of reasoning in trying to get the child to obey her. Thus we see that a dimension or pattern of child rearing is an abstraction from actual behaviors engaged in by mothers which are calculated to influence their children.

A second important dimension of maternal behavior found was *permissiveness-strictness,* sometimes called *permissiveness-restrictiveness.* The strict mother does not allow her child to engage in much aggressive or sexual behavior. She wants her child to be neat, orderly, to have good table manners, and to be relatively quiet. Mothers who are rather strict or restrictive tend to use physical punishment and do not like their children to be dependent.[9, 26] The dimensions of warmth and *permissiveness-strictness* are relatively independent of each other; that is, there are mothers who are warm and permissive, but there are also mothers who are warm and restrictive. Conversely, some mothers are permissive but relatively cold to the child, and others are both strict and cold. When remembering this it is useful to consider that patterns of child rearing are abstractions referring to general patterns of behavior. Few mothers or fathers fit any pattern exactly; they only approximate "patterns" to some degree in their behavior.

Another less important dimension of child rearing found by Sears, Maccoby, and Levin was called *general family adjustment*. This relates to the amount of confidence the mother has in herself and her husband, how satisfied she is with life, how delighted she and her husband are with the child, and how much confidence versus anxiety she has about being able to raise her child adequately. Other minor dimensions described were *responsible child training orientation, aggressiveness and punitiveness, perception of husband,* and *orientation to the child's general well being*.[26] These dimensions, based on reported patterns of the mothers' behaviors, do not appear as consistently in other studies as do the *warmth-coldness* or *permissiveness-restrictiveness* dimensions.

Disciplinary Orientation

A main finding of Sears, Maccoby, and Levin involved their description of two main patterns of discipline which have also been found by other investigators. They called one pattern of child discipline *love oriented* and the other *object oriented*. Like their warmth and permissiveness-strictness dimensions, we shall see that these two general patterns of discipline, or ones very close to them, appear in a number of studies.[2, 3, 9] Almost all parents, it should be made clear, use a variety of ways of disciplining their children. The point is that many parents rely more heavily on one type of discipline than on another. The use of love oriented discipline refers both to giving the child a fairly large amount of love, affection, and attention, and sometimes depriving him of them. Mothers who tend to behave in these ways praise and reward the child for doing what they want him to do, using affection and attention as rewards for "proper" behavior. They also use withdrawal of love or attentions as a punishment. When the child misbehaves, such parents often isolate the child, thus withholding contact and attention. Sometimes they withhold love and affection until the child changes his behavior and does as they wish. Such parents use their emotional relationship with the child to socialize him.

Mothers, on the other hand, who use object oriented discipline, do not rely as heavily on the giving or withholding of affection. Rather, they utilize giving or withholding desirable objects. They tend to use toys, food, or similar incentives as positive or negative reinforcers. They may give them when the child is "good" or take them away when he is "bad." They may also deprive the child of privileges in order to socialize him. Such parents, in addition, resort more often to physical punishment; they are more likely to spank their children.[2, 26] Finally, they are also less likely to reason with their children, more likely to act without explanations. Conversely, parents who use love oriented discipline do a great deal of explaining to their children, reason with them, and generally stimulate them to cognitive activity.

Schaeffer's Dimensions

The findings of Sears, Maccoby, and Levin received support from a description of mothers' behaviors toward their children constructed by E. S. Schaeffer.[23] His model indicated two main dimensions of child rearing on the part of mothers. He called one the *love-hostility* dimension, which seems quite close to the warmth-coldness dimension already discussed. The other was labeled *control-autonomy*, which would seem to parallel strictness-permissiveness. If one takes combinations of these two dimensions of child rearing, it is possible to classify mothers into four types. For instance, a mother who shows her child considerable love and allows him to be fairly autonomous can be called a "democratic" mother. On the other hand, one who is also quite loving but is overly controlling of the child may be called "over protective." The hostile mother who nevertheless lets her child autonomously do as he wishes, might be termed "indifferent." The hostile mother, however, who does not allow her child to be autonomous, may be labeled "authoritarian" or "dictatorial."

Becker's Dimensions

Still another analysis of mothers' behaviors toward their children verifies the presence of the warmth-coldness and restrictiveness-permissiveness dimensions. However, this study introduces an additional, and highly important, dimension. W. C. Becker, who chiefly made the analysis, considers not only the overt behavior of the mother toward her child to be important, but also the degree and type of her *emotional* involvement.[9, 10, 11] At one extreme, he points out, a mother might treat her child with "calm detachment," whereas an opposite type of mother might usually interact with "anxious emotional involvement." In the case of two mothers, both of whom might be warm and quite restrictive, one might be effectively organized, since she was relatively calmly detached, whereas the other might be overprotective, as a function of being anxiously emotionally involved. The two mothers might have quite a different impact on their children, due to their differential emotionality, even though they were both equally warm and restrictive. We all know of mothers who are emotionally quite involved, fussing over every act of the child. They can be contrasted with more emotionally detached mothers, who are calmer and more detached from their children's lives.

MEASURING DIMENSIONS OF CHILD REARING

It seems reasonable to ask how psychologists have gone about constructing the various dimensions of child rearing. We already know that they rely heavily on data gathered from mothers. However, this is not inevitably the case. Fathers may also be interviewed on occasion, or data may be obtained through questionnaires or psychological tests. Among the best of the interview questionnaires or schedules is that of Baldwin and his coworkers, assembled at the Fels Institute in the middle nineteen-forties. It is suitable for questioning both mothers and fathers, as well as for asking questions about the home. The questions on home life may be general and include more than queries on maternal or paternal behavior; they may ask about objects in the home or the number of relatives in residence.[6, 7, 22] What do psychologists do with such information once they get it? Once the information is gathered, how does the psychologist proceed? He often uses a statistical device known as *factor analysis*. Factor analysis can be applied to data gathered in various ways. This complex statistical technique is used to find out which behaviors, however measured, usually seem to go together. For instance, if you find one behavior, what other behaviors are most likely to be found also? A cluster of behaviors which consistently appear together is called a factor. Once such a factor is found it can be given a name summarizing the character of the behaviors included.

THE CHILD REARING PROCESS AND PROBLEM CHILDREN

Half of the parents in a study by Becker and his coworkers had at least one child in need of psychological help. The investigators, using factor analysis, found that certain parental characteristics clustered together. Some mothers were maladjusted and uncoordinated in their handling of the child. These same mothers were also arbitrary in their discipline, which was ineffective. The child was reported to be a "conduct problem" by these mothers with evidence also present that the child's social development was retarded. If any one of the tendencies on the part of either the mother or the child listed above tended to be present the others tended to be present also. The same factor (cluster of behaviors) also appeared on the basis of interviews with the fathers. Becker and his coworkers called this cluster the *conduct problem* dimension. The appearance of the Conduct Problem dimension or factor is not surprising. Almost half of the families involved in the study had at least one child in need of psychological treatment and the children were, in fact, being given such treatment at the time of the study. The investigation discussed above is presented in greater detail in Study 11.2.

PARENTAL BEHAVIORS AND PROBLEMS OF CHILDREN

STUDY 11.2

Wesley C. Becker and four collaborators decided to investigate the factors in parental behavior and personality related to problem behavior in children. To achieve their aims, they decided to use the factor-analytic statistical procedure. In order to gather data suitable for the procedure, they conducted interviews with 32 couples whose children were normal, and 25 couples who had at least one abnormal child. The interviews were conducted separately with the mothers and fathers, and five separate psychologists rated the answers on the categories of the Fels parent behavior scales constructed by Baldwin and his associates. In addition, the parents filled out a personality inventory, the Guilford-Martin, which measures traits such as shyness, depression, introspectiveness, and masculinity. Finally, Becker knew the age, sex, IQ, and social class of the participants in the study.

All the information was coded into 46 different variables, or categories of behavior. Becker and his coworkers determined the relationship among these variables in terms of which of them tended to cluster together, forming factors. None of the data on which his study was based included firsthand observations of behavior, but, as in so many other studies, depended mainly on nonobservational data, such as interviews or tests.

The factor analysis tended to show that in families with "conduct problem" children (aggressive and uncontrollable children), both parents tended to be maladjusted, tended to erupt with uncontrolled emotionality, and were often arbitrary in their behavior toward the child. The mothers of these aggressive and uncontrolled children were often dictatorial. Further, they were thwarting, and gave many orders, and the father failed to enforce the regulations which the mother laid down. This pattern of parental behavior, the conduct problem factor, was reliably associated with antisocial behavior in the children.

Another factor emerged having to do with children who were also abnormal, but who, rather than being wild, were shy, sensitive, and felt inferior. Becker and coworkers termed these children as having "personality problems," as contrasted with the factor of conduct problems. The presence of a personality problem in the child seemed, interestingly enough, to be related chiefly to the behavior ratings of his father and to be relatively independent of the mother's ratings. The father was described as maladjusted and as frustrating to his child. Becker very strongly suggests in his article that future research in child development and on child abnormality pay much more attention to the behavior and significance of the father. It is true that many studies have ignored the father altogether, assuming that the mother is by far the greatest or the only important influence on the child. This is an unwarranted assumption.

Becker, W. C., et al. Factors in parental behavior and personality as related to problem behavior in children. *J. Consult. Psychol.*, 23, 1959, 107-117.

Becker and his coworkers extended their attempts to measure patterns of child rearing related to emergence of behavior problems in the child. In a study published in 1962 they used the interview and rating procedures of Sears, Maccoby, and Levin already discussed in this chapter.[10, 26] This time the interviews were conducted not only with mothers and fathers, but with teachers also. Again factor analysis was used to reduce the rated behaviors to clusters of behaviors which went together. Most of the Sears scales were used as well as a number of scales from the Fels Institute interview schedules. The number and types of child rearing dimensions found varied depending somewhat on whether the mothers' or the fathers' interview data were factor analyzed. Analysis of the mothers' interviews did produce the two salient dimensions of warmth vs. hostility (coldness) and permissiveness vs. restrictiveness (strictness). In all, however, ten factors or dimensions were derived from analysis of the interview data. These factors included materal relating to how the mother saw her husband, how anxious the mother was about child rearing, how responsive she was to her child, how concerned she was about status, and how much she used physical punishment. The fathers also seemed to engage in a considerable amount of behavior that could be arrayed on the warmth vs. hostility dimension. The permissiveness vs. restrictiveness dimension did not appear as strongly for fathers as for mothers. This dimension has to do with regulating neatness, order, table manners, and care of house and furniture. The mother, who is with the child during the day, is the person whose actions are most pertinent to this dimension of behavior. Fathers varied on the use of strictness vs. laxness, use of physical punishment, and opinions about their wives.

Perhaps the most striking feature of the study was the finding that parents seemed to share common patterns of child rearing. They came in pairs, to paraphrase Becker. There were some differences, as already noted, but similarities between mothers and fathers were more common. If the mother was high on warmth, permissiveness, and was relaxed about sexual matters, the father tended to act similarly. Conversely, if the father was hostile, restrictive, and anxious about sex, so, in many cases, was the mother. Five of the factors obtained were the same for mothers and fathers: warmth vs. hostility, high vs. low child rearing anxiety; high vs. low anxiety about the child's sexual behavior; high vs. low use of physical punishment; and permissiveness vs. restrictiveness.[10] (Later in this chapter we will discuss more extensively the effects of such parental behavior on the behavior of the child.) Study 11.3 presents some aspects of the investigation just discussed with a view to highlighting certain research issues.

A FURTHER INVESTIGATION OF PARENTAL BEHAVIORS AND PROBLEM CHILDREN

STUDY 11.3

Becker and his colleagues extended their work by obtaining data on 60 families. All the mothers and fathers who participated in the study had a child in kindergarten. Consequently, the children tended to be about five years old. This is important since the main device for obtaining data was the interview procedure developed by Sears and his collaborators, who also interviewed the mothers of five year olds. The Becker and Sears samples may have differed in a number of ways. We know nothing of the religious affiliations of the families Becker studied. There were 379 mothers interviewed by the Sears group, whereas only 60 mothers and fathers were interviewed in the Becker study. However, the ages of the children were the same. Therefore, if the results of the two studies match to some extent (and they do), we have an instance of a *partial replication*. Asking the same questions also helped to repeat, or replicate, the work of Sears' group. Such replications, even if partial, are vital in research. If several studies, done similarly, on similar samples come up with similar results, we can have more confidence that reliable findings have been produced. Despite the seeming weakness of relying on what parents say, many studies largely relying on interviews have produced reasonably similar results in the area of patterns of child rearing.

Two main points of interest can be found in this research. First, the study suggests that the dimension of permissiveness-restrictiveness is more complex than has often been assumed. It was found that there may well be a difference between permissiveness and just plain laxity. The former implies a general attitude toward child rearing based on some conscious or unconscious belief in allowing children a certain degree of freedom. Being lax, however, may mean that the child is given freedom merely because the parents are lazy or distracted. In the same vein, there seems to be a distinction to be made between restrictiveness and strictness. Restrictiveness may chiefly imply placing a fairly large number of demands on the child. Being strict involves the use of severe penalties to back up the demands.

We have already touched on the second main point of this study. This is the finding that there is a general similarity among the child rearing behaviors of husbands and wives, despite some differences. Several instances of this relationship are of interest. If the husband was rated as being hostile by the psychologists going over the interviews, so was the wife. In the cases of these hostile couples, if the wife said that her husband was hostile the husband also saw the wife as hostile. Hostility in such families affected the husband-wife relationship, and through it, the child. Aggression became a way of life. If the husband was rated by the psychologists as being more strict than his wife, the wife also considered the husband to be hostile and strict with the children. Conversely, if the husband was rated by the psychologists, on the basis of the interviews, as being noncoercive and lax, the wife was also rated as warm and permissive by the psychologist. The wife, as expected, would also see her husband as warm and permissive.

Many other examples could be given. What is so striking is the finding that each parent is a fairly good judge of what the other is like. Even more important is the fact that these parents tended, more often than not, to have similar or complementary child rearing attitudes and behaviors. Perhaps they had them to start with, or over the course of years of living together had evolved mutual patterns of relating to their children.

> Becker, W. C., et al. Relations of factors derived from parent interview ratings to behavior problems of five year olds. *Child Develpm.*, *38*, 1962, 509-535.

SUMMARY OF CHILD REARING DIMENSIONS

We have discussed a number of dimensions of child rearing which psychologists have derived from the behaviors which parents show toward their children. The dimension most often found is that of *warmth-coldness (hostility)*. To be warm means being accepting, affectionate, approving, and understanding. It includes the frequent use of explanations with tolerance for the child's requests for help and is also correlated with using love oriented discipline. Although some parents show extreme degrees of either warmth or coldness, most are somewhere in between, being neither extremely warm nor extremely cold or hostile to their children. Parents' behaviors may also vary somewhat from day to day, year to year, or situation to situation. Psychologists are interested in the extent and frequency with which a parent is warm or hostile over many occasions.

The second most commonly found dimension is *permissiveness-restrictiveness (strictness)*. The very restrictive parent tends to set many rules and regulations, and to be fairly strict in enforcing demands about sex play and modesty behavior. Such a parent is demanding about table manners, early toilet training, neatness, orderliness, care of furniture, and having little noise. Aggression towards siblings is seldom tolerated by restrictive parents and aggression toward themselves or playmates is also frowned upon. Restrictive parents discourage aggression in their children to a great extent.

In terms of the *emotionality* dimension, the *anxious* parent tends to react with tense emotionality to many things the child does and such parents have trouble staying calm. There is, in addition, frequent babying of the child. The emotionally over-involved parent shows an overprotective attitude and tends to worry too much about the child's health, development, and behavior. Such parents communicate anxiety to the child, along with the feeling that the world is a dangerous place.

In all these instances opposite qualities and effects may be imputed to parents at the other end of these dimensions. Again, however, let us remember that few parents fall at either extreme. Most parents are moderately warm, permissive or emotional. Finally, parental behaviors may vary from one situation to another. Some parents may be strict about toilet training and permissive about eating; they may be emotional about illness but detached when the child wins a race. Parents do show generality in their behavior toward their children but this generality is far from complete.

DISCIPLINARY PROCESSES

The ways of treating the child discussed above are also related to the specific disciplinary methods the parents use, that is, to the ways in which they reward and punish their children's conduct. We shall now treat discipline, for purposes of convenience, as a separate topic. Discipline relates to parental behavior calculated to control the child's conduct. Among patterns of child rearing one must include the chief approaches to disciplining the child. These include the punitive and rewarding activities of the parents, calculated to make the child do what they wish him to do. As we have seen, methods of discipline fall into two broad dimensions or patterns. One has been called *love oriented* and the other *object oriented*.

Love or Induction Oriented Discipline

Parents who rely more on *love oriented* methods make considerable use of praise and reasoning to induce desired behaviors in their child. When the child misbehaves or fails to respond to praise or reasoning, they resort either to a withdrawal of love or the threat of its withdrawal. They may show disappointment with the child, express displeasure, and possibly ignore him. If he accedes to their demands, they no longer threaten to withdraw their love and attention or, having withdrawn it, they reinstitute it. Love and praise are used as positive inducements to evoke desired behaviors. Reason is utilized to clarify and explain expectations and standards or to explain to the child why certain things are required of him. The parents also can and will deprive the child of attention, approval, and love as long as the child fails to "behave." This is punishment just as much as hitting a child is punishment.

This method of controlling the child's behavior has also been called an "*induction*" procedure.[2, 5] Anxiety is induced in the child as a result of the threat of withdrawal of parental love. He can lower his anxiety by approaching the parents and changing his behavior. Since he knows his mother would be disappointed or hurt if he did perform a certain act, the thought of doing the act may induce enough anxiety in the child to prevent his performance of it. This may often happen even if his mother is absent at the time.

Object Oriented or Sensitization Discipline

The other main method of discipline, the *object oriented*, consists of fairly frequent use of physical punishment, in addition to giving or withholding objects. It also includes "bawlings out," screaming, and yelling at the child. The imperative mode is often used; that is the child is given forceful commands about what to do. He may be verbally or physically threatened, often in front of others and he may be ridiculed or shamed in public. Parents who behave this way often punish their child by depriving him of things he likes. Furthermore, they seldom reason with the child. This sort of parent behavior toward the child has also been called a "sensitization" procedure.[2, 3, 5] The parents or other authority figures must be present for this method to have optimal results. The child's anxiety comes not from any possible loss of love but from seeing that mother or father is around to possibly hit him, yell at him, or deprive him of something. The child becomes sensitized to impending punishment or deprivation of physical objects if he does wrong. He is particularly sensitized in the presence of his parents or other authority figures. Again, most parents use a mixture of induction and sensitization techniques. However, some parents rely more heavily on induction techniques and others utilize sensitization methods more predominantly.

SUMMARY — PART 1

The behavior of parents in training their children falls into describable patterns. Some parents are warmer to their children, whereas others are colder or more hostile. The warmer parents spend more time praising, playing with, attending to, and reasoning with their children. There are parents who are generally permissive while other parents are stricter or more restrictive. The restrictive parent is more likely to insist on order, cleanliness, manners, and obedience from the child at a fairly early age. Some parents seem to be very emotional about their children's activities and others are more emotionally detached. These patterns of activities can come in any combination. For instance there are warm and permissive mothers, but there are also warm and restrictive mothers.

Parents discipline their children in order to get them to behave in ways approved of by society. Disciplinary activities also seem to fall into describable patterns. Most studies have revealed two patterns: one is oriented toward gaining obedience by giving and withholding love from the child as well as reasoning with him; the other chiefly relies on physical punishment and withholding of physical rewards.

These patterns of child rearing, including disciplining the child, have been derived chiefly from information gained from interviewing mothers. Mothers are asked about matters such as when and how they toilet train their children, how they act when the child becomes aggressive, when they weaned their child, what they do when the child defies them, and so on. Sometimes fathers are also interviewed, tests of various types may be administered to parents, and data gathered about the religion, age, social class, and other attributes of the parents. This information is often reduced in a way which enables it to be analyzed to reveal the factors (or patterns) which appear most consistently. Unfortunately there are few observational or experimental studies concerning patterns of child rearing. Consequently psychologists must largely rely on what parents are willing to say about their child rearing activities.

PART 2 — EFFECTS OF CHILD REARING PROCEDURES

We will now take up the issue of how different types of discipline affect the child's behavior. The most important effect of *love oriented* or *induction* procedures is that they lead both to internalization of standards and internalization of reactions to transgression. In other words, the use of love as a reward and the use of the threat of its withdrawal as a punishment tend to lead the child to accept and internalize the standards of his parents. The use of reasoning and explanation aids acceptance of rules. Induction discipline leads to anxiety about violating standards and often negative emotions like shame or guilt may arise in children raised this way if they do "misbehave."[2, 3, 15] Consequently, children living in homes where induction techniques based on giving and withholding love, approval, and attention are widely used, will come to regulate their own behavior. They do so partly to terminate or avoid feeing anxiety, shame, and guilt. Such children tend to accept parental rules and are relatively well socialized. If they do deviate or transgress they may confess, offer to make restitution, or criticize themselves.[2, 3, 15] Such corrective activities help to lower their anxiety, shame, or guilt. Further, once they internalize rules and standards living up to them makes such children feel satisfied and good.

Object-oriented or *sensitization* methods of discipline have different effects on children. Sensitization procedures do not seem to lead readily to internalization of standards or emotional reactions like guilt and shame after transgression.[2] Rather, they lead to externalized reactions to rule breaking and their main effect on the child seems to inculcate in him a fear of punishment and a feeling that other people are against him.[3, 13, 16] The child whose parents make considerable use of physical punishment or object withdrawal will spend a fair amount of time just trying to avoid or escape punishment. Rather than becoming well socialized and in control of his own behavior, he may become highly sensitized to what others are liable to do to him. Although his life may appear to him to be under the control of other people, people often seen as hostile, he does escape most of the burdens of shame and guilt. Studies 11.4 and 11.5 deal with important works in the area of discipline and transgression, and illustrate the points made above.

INDUCTION AND SENSITIZATION

STUDY 11.4

Justin Aronfreed, of the University of Pennsylvania, studied 122 12-year-old boys and girls as well as their mothers. Since he was interested in comparing patterns of discipline in the working class and the middle class, he chose subjects from both these social groups. Twenty seven boys and 33 girls came from working-class backgrounds; 34 boys and 28 girls came from middle-class backgrounds.

Aronfreed employed a projective story completion technique with the children and a questionnaire interview with the mothers. Each child was given five incomplete stories. In the beginning of each story a child becomes angry for no really good reason (by usual social standards) and then does something quite hostile or aggressive. In each story, then, a child was unreasonably aggressive. The task of the 12-year-old boys and girls was to complete the five stories. It is assumed that what the child writes relates to how he would act if he violated the social rule of not being unreasonably aggressive and how he thinks others would act toward him in such circumstances. This is called a "projective technique." Instead of asking the child specific questions, it is assumed that he will *project* himself into the stories. He is not asked about himself or his parents directly and can respond without becoming self-conscious. There is no need to distort to make a good impression, since the child is just asked to complete a story.

The mothers were interviewed at home about their disciplinary practices. The questions asked dealt with various forms of aggressive behavior, the circumstances in which they happened, and how the mother dealt with them. The questions ranged over aggressive behaviors such as the childs' throwing things or swearing. The mother was asked both about past and present behavior and emphasis was placed on the way she disciplined such behavior in her child.

Aronfreed found that he could classify the disciplinary

techniques of the mothers into two types: either "induction techniques" or "sensitization techniques." The stories written by children whose mothers used induction techniques showed that they had acquired standards indicative of conscience. Children whose parents largely employed induction techniques also showed evidence in their stories of self-criticism, and were more prone to accept personal, internal responsibility. They were less likely to believe that their misbehavior would be resolved by unpleasant external events which would come about more or less by chance. Induction techniques led to internal acceptance of standards and "conscience" formation.

The children whose parents used sensitization techniques, chiefly physical punishment, wrote stories mostly concerned with the painful external consequences which would follow being aggressive. Such children did not show signs of accepting personal responsibility in their stories. They often wrote about external punishment coming to the child in the story more or less by chance. There were considerably fewer stories about any tendency to be self-critical after transgressing aggressively. The girls whose mothers used physical punishment were also less likely to think that the children in their stories would confess. Sensitization techniques are less likely than induction methods to lead to socialization and "conscience" formation.

Aronfreed, J. The nature, variety, and social patterning of moral responses to transgression. *J. Abnorm. Soc. Psychol.*, 63, 1961, 223-239.

THE EXPERIMENTAL METHOD

Many of the studies presented in the text have used the method of experiment, often the most powerful empirical tool of the scientist. The experimental method, however, has seldom been used by psychologists investigating patterns of child rearing. When using nonexperimental techniques such as interviews, questionnaires, or observations of behavior in the home, the investigator has some serious problems. First, he has only limited control over the situation. He is not able to manipulate, change or arrange matters systematically so that he may observe the corresponding results. It is only possible, without systematic control, to conclude that if one state of affairs exists, another also exists. Without experiments, where the investigator can control and change the factors involved, it becomes extremely hard, if not impossible, to determine cause and effect. Without an experiment, it is only possible to talk of associations; two or more things regularly occurring or clustering together. No matter how obvious things may seem, without experimental test, one can never be sure about matters of cause and effect. Study 11.5 reviews one of the few experimental studies directly relating to the effects of various disciplinary methods.

AN EXPERIMENT ON TWO MORAL RESPONSES TO TRANSGRESSION

STUDY 11.5

It was noted by Aronfreed in his 1961 investigation, discussed in study 11.4, that parents who use love-oriented induction techniques tend to reason with their children, giving explanations about various rules or requests which they make. He decided, therefore, to study experimentally the effects of reason giving on the child's reactions to transgression. A transgression refers to the breaking of a rule or injunction. All the children in this experiment played a game in which they were told that *the fewer toy soldiers they knocked down the better it would be.* They were told that given the nature of the game some toy soldiers would have to get knocked down, but the fewer knocked down the better. Children in a *high reason* group, however, were told that they should be very careful and gentle, that being careful and gentle was the most important thing. The importance of carefulness and gentleness was stressed three times. Children in a *low reason* group got no explanation to the effect that it was important to be careful and gentle. The words "careful" and "gentle" were not used with them. They were just told that it was good to knock down few soldiers and not good to knock down a lot of soldiers.

Aronfreed also manipulated one other variable besides high or low reason giving. He manipulated high or low control over punishment. All of the children got a large pile of candies. In the *high control over punishment* group, the children were told that after each turn they would have to decide how many to give up. It was entirely up to each child in this condition how many of the candies he gave up, after each turn in the game, for knocking over toy soldiers. In the *low control over punishment* group, the experimenter decided how many of the candies the child lost on each turn for knocking over toy soldiers. The number of candies a child lost, that is, essentially what punishment a child got, was entirely in the child's control in one condition and entirely out of his control in the other.

There were four groups of children. One group knew just what the standards were and had control over their own punishment. A second group also knew what the standards (reasons) were but had no control over their own punishment; the experimenter controlled punishment. The third group was not explicitly told the standards but had control over their own punishment. The fourth group also lacked explicit standards and, additionally had no control over their own punishment. The four groups then were: high reason giving-high control, high reason giving-low control, low reason giving-high control, low reason giving-low control.

Besides the toy soldiers *there was a toy nurse* in the game. Her job in the game was to take care of the wounded soldiers. *The toy nurse was built so that she would break on the eleventh trial after the child had handled it.* The experimenter asked each child, in each of the four conditions: "Why do you think it (the nurse) broke?" and also, "What do you think you should do now?" The purpose of the experiment was to see how the two main variables, reason giving and control over punishment, affected the answers to these questions. Would the child be *self-critical* and accept blame for breaking the nurse, and second, would he try to make *reparations*, react to transgression by making it up? Specifically the experimental question to be answered is how does high and low reason giving and high and low control over punishment affect the tendency to be self-critical and to make reparations after transgression?

The results concerning self-criticism were very clear. High reason giving (regardless of high or low control over punishment) led to being *self-critical*; that is, those who had been clearly told to be gentle and careful were more self-critical about the nurse being broken on the eleventh trial. However, it didn't seem to matter whether on the previous ten trials the child punished herself or was punished by the experimenter as far as the tendency to be self-critical (to accept blame) was concerned. The chief effect of high control, that is punishing oneself rather than being punished by someone else, was that it led the child to make *reparations* if she had also been told to be careful and gentle. They tried in some way to make up for "breaking the nurse." Children who had been punished by the experimenter and not told to be careful and

> gentle did not try to make reparations. *Knowing the rules leads to being self-critical for transgressing them. Being made responsible for punishing oneself leads to wanting to make up for misdeeds if one understands the rules in the first place.*
>
> Aronfreed, J. The effects of experimental socialization paradigms upon two moral responses to transgression. *J. Abnorm. Soc. Psychol.*, 66, 1963, 437-448.

DISCIPLINE AND AGGRESSION

An effect of sensitization techniques is that they tend to generate tendencies toward aggression and hostility. If the child is under surveillance and is sensitized to the possibility of punishment, he may suppress his own hostile-aggressive tendencies. In other situations, where punishment isn't feared, aggression may reveal itself rather strongly. A study by Sears and his coworkers illustrated this possibility very well.[27] It was found that in a free doll play situation, where the child was away from home in a permissive atmosphere, the more punitive the mother was known to be, the more aggression the child showed. However, in school where the child knew that teachers who didn't like aggression were watching, the more punitive his mother was the less aggression the child showed. The behavior in school was the opposite of behavior in the free doll play situation.

However, the effects of punitiveness on the behavior of the child are not entirely clear from the studies available and the effects may be different for boys than for girls.[12, 25, 26, 27] However, it is possible to conclude that frustrating punitive parents, who are also models of aggression, may produce increased aggression in the child for a number of years.[8, 27] Eventually, the repeated parental punishment for aggression, among other causes, may finally serve to suppress a great deal of overt, antisocial aggression in the child. The child may then express aggression in socially approved ways or become self-punitive, turning aggression towards himself.[8, 25] It has also been shown that if the parents punish aggression harshly chiefly when directed toward themselves by the child, it may be displaced towards others and even lead to aggressive delinquent activity on the part of the child.[8]

EFFECTS OF WARMTH VS. COLDNESS (HOSTILITY) AND CHILD BEHAVIOR

Let us now see how some of the general patterns of child rearing affect the behavior of children. Warm parents do tend to use induction methods of discipline. *Warmth* leads to the child's accepting responsibility, to his acquiring guilt feelings, and to internalized reactions to wrongdoing, if it is coupled with induction disciplinary methods.[2, 3, 26] Warmth, however, seems to be related to almost all areas of child behavior.[2, 26] Children become attached to warm mothers and therefore tend to behave the way she wants them to. The child seems to learn to want whatever events regularly happen in a warm satisfying context. A strong bond is forged between the child and a warm mother, probably because she spends more time with him, rewards him more, makes things clearer and reasons with him.[9, 24, 26] Since the child gains so much from the warm mother and becomes so attached to her, the child has a great deal to gain by avoiding the possibility of losing her attention, approval, or love. The threat of actual withdrawal of love, or the fear of withdrawal, are most effective in producing compliance.

Coldness (or *hostility*) on the part of the mother seems to lead to many difficulties in the child. These include feeding problems, bed wetting, high aggression, and weak self-control.[26] There is less of a bond or attachment between the child and parent, consequently the child has little to lose when the mother does not approve, or threatens to withdraw her love. A child doesn't become anxious about losing what does not exist. Mothers who lack warmth tend not to reason with their children and their children in turn seem to lack self-control and have difficulty in accepting standards of conduct.

RESTRICTIVENESS-PERMISSIVENESS AND CHILD BEHAVIOR

Children of restrictive parents are often highly socialized.[7, 26, 28] They are expected to behave in a more adult way earlier and they learn to do so. Children who have relatively restrictive parents may develop feeding problems, but this is about the only generally socially disruptive aspect of reasonable restrictiveness.[26] If anything, restrictiveness leads to overconventionality or oversocialization. As we stated earlier, restrictiveness or permissiveness may appear in a context of warmth or coldness, with or without hostility, and with various sorts of emotional involvement. We shall consider some of these interactions shortly.

On the whole, children with restrictive parents tend to be courteous, obedient, neat, and polite; they may be a bit withdrawn, being generally somewhat inhibited. Over-restrictiveness may lead to passivity and dependency.[19, 28] Children of permissive parents tend to be assertive and expressive, on the other hand. They are less regular in their habits and are more impulsive. Children of permissive parents tend to be more active and independent than those of restrictive parents.[6, 7]

When permissiveness is coupled with hostility on the part of the parent, the child is largely on his own and has to contend with parents who dislike him. Such children tend to be aggressive and poorly controlled. The combination of laxness and hostility (with occasional erratic recourse to harsh discipline) seems to generate the antisocial juvenile delinquent. It is the combination of parental permissiveness with rejection which produces noncompliant, antisocial youngsters. These are often the children showing conduct disorders.[1, 9]

Restrictiveness on the part of parents combined with hostility or rejection seems to be one of the causes of some types of childhood neuroses. The experience of being both overcontrolled and disliked by the parents can drive the child to self-contempt, social withdrawal, and inner conflict. Suicidal tendencies and accident proneness in children have been noted as a result of the restrictive hostility of parents.[9] The child becomes oversocialized and rejects himself as his parents reject him, or aggresses against himself as his parents aggress against him. Inhibited, neurotic children tend to have more hostile constraint in their homes than delinquent children do. Lacking freedom or love, these children turn against themselves.

INTERACTION OF WARMTH WITH OTHER DIMENSIONS

The warm and permissive parent produces the independent child. Such children, although independent, seem to take reasonable responsibility for their own behavior. They are generally friendly to adults and other children. Children raised this way tend to be creative and moderately persistent; they don't give up easily, but don't persist at impossible tasks for very long either. They are, generally not destructive, probably because they aren't often frustrated and because their parents aren't models of aggression.[7, 20] They tend to be a bit undersocialized and nonconforming, without necessarily being problem children. They are socially assertive and may be bossy, but this behavior often seems to be accepted by other children.[7, 20] They are clearly more achievement-oriented in terms of independently mastering the environment and often practice behaving like adults.[7, 20, 21]

Parents can be warm and restrictive at the same time. It is too easy to slip into the mistake of assuming that to be restrictive means to be cold, rejecting, or hostile. If the parents are restrictive but warm, the child tends to be low on aggression and relatively high on conformity.[29] The child is clearly more dependent and less creative when his parents restrict him. Despite the parent's warmth and the child's conformistic behavior, the child may be somewhat frustrated by the restrictive demands placed upon him and become somewhat hostile and slightly unfriendly, although not aggressive.[9, 26, 29]

Study 11.6 summarizes many of the complex relationships discussed in this chapter. The various types of parental behavior interact to produce different effects on the behavior of the child. It may help to present the effects of four of the combinations of child rearing.

PATTERNS OF CHILD REARING AND CHILD BEHAVIOR

STUDY 11.6

Much of the previous discussion was based on an excellent survey of studies by W. C. Becker, of the University of Illinois. From the many investigations in this area he produced a summary table of the interactive effects of the *warmth-hostility (coldness)* and *restrictiveness-permissiveness* dimensions on child behavior. A summary of this table appears here, with some minor modifications and additions.

	RESTRICTIVENESS	PERMISSIVENESS
Warmth	Child is socialized, neat, polite, obedient, and dependent. He is minimally aggressive but is in favor of enforcing rules. He is dependent, not creative; compliant, but somewhat unfriendly. In short, restrictiveness fosters well-controlled socialized behavior of a submissive dependent type, but even with warmth there is fearfulness and some hostility. There is likely to be internalization of standards and experiences of guilt and shame.	Child is dominant, successfully assertive or aggressive. He is active and creative. The child engages in adult-like activities. He is achievement-mastery oriented, independent, friendly, creative, and not hostile. He is socialized perhaps less easily, but does become socialized through love, good models, and the use of reason. However, his actions concerning others may at times be overly assertive.
Hostility or Coldness	Child may possibly become neurotic. His aggression is turned toward himself. The child is socially withdrawn and shy. There is not much adult imitation or role taking. The child despises himself as he is despised.	Child is often delinquent or a conduct problem. He tends to be noncompliant and aggressive toward others.

Based on Becker, W. C. Consequences of different kinds of parental discipline. (In) *Review of Child Development Research*, Hoffman, L., and Hoffman, L. W. (Eds.). Russell Sage Foundation, New York, 1964.

SUMMARY — PART 2

Psychologists are interested in patterns of child rearing because the way in which parents treat their children affects the feelings, thoughts, and behaviors of those children. For instance love oriented or induction methods of discipline lead to the child's accepting adult standards and rules. Violation of these rules leads the child to feel responsible and to make attempts at correcting the situation. The child may feel self-critical and if he has caused injury, may try to make restitution. Object oriented or sensitization disciplinary methods usually create avoidance reactions in the child based on fear of punishment. Obedience depends not on self-regulation but on fear of retaliation. The child does not tend to feel guilty and is not likely to try to make amends unless he expects it to lead to reduced punishment. As in other patterns of child rearing, of course, we are dealing with degrees, not all or none. Most parents use all sorts of disciplinary methods, but they may use some more than others.

Warmth and restrictiveness on the part of parents usually produces a well behaved, compliant child, prone to some guilt feelings. Warmth and permissiveness leads to eventual socialization, but there is more assertiveness as well as more independence and creativity. Coldness and hostility, particularly when excessive, have undesirable effects. Coldness and permissiveness can produce the antisocial delinquent, and coldness and restrictiveness can lead to neurosis and self-hatred. Parents, again, are not always warm or cold, neither are they permissive or restrictive about everything a child does. However, parents may vary fairly systematically from each other in how they generally react towards their children on many similar occasions or in regard to similar activities on the part of their children.

REFERENCES

1. Andry, R. G. *Delinquency and Parental Pathology.* Methuen, London, 1960.
2. Aronfreed, J. *Conduct and Conscience: The Socialization of Internalized Control over Behavior.* In Press.
3. Aronfreed, J. The origins of self criticism. *Psych. Rev., 71,* 1964, 183-218.
4. Aronfreed, J. The effects of experimental socialization paradigms upon two moral responses to transgression. *J. Abnorm. Soc. Psychol., 66,* 1963, 437-448.
5. Aronfreed, J. The nature, variety, and social patterning of responses to transgression. *J. Abnorm. Soc. Psychol., 63,* 1961, 223-239.
6. Baldwin, A. I. The effect of home environment on nursery school behavior. *Child Develpm., 20,* 1949, 49-61.
7. Baldwin, A. L. Patterns of parent behavior. *Psychol. Monogr., 58,* 1945, 1-75.
8. Bandura, A., and Walters, R. H. *Adolescent Aggression.* Ronald, New York, 1959.
9. Becker, W. C. Consequences of different kinds of parental discipline. (In) *Review of Child Development Research.* Hoffman, M., and Hoffman, L. W. (Eds.). Russell Sage Foundation, New York, 1964.
10. Becker, W. C., et al. Relation of factors derived from parent-interview ratings to behavior problems of five year olds. *Child Develpm., 33,* 1962, 509-535.
11. Becker, W. C., et al. Factors in parental behavior and personality related to problem behavior in children. *J. Consult. Psychol., 23,* 1959, 107-117.
12. Bronfenbrenner, W. Some familial antecedents of responsibility and leadership in adolescents. (In) *Leadership and Interpersonal Behavior.* Petrullo, L., and Bass, B. M. (Eds.), Holt, Rinehart and Winston, New York, 1961.

13. Burton, R. V., et al. Antecedents of resistance to temptation in four year old children. *Child Developm., 32*, 1961, 689-710.
14. Chess, S., et al. Characteristics of the individual child's behavior reponses to the environment. *Amer. J. Orthopsychiat., 29*, 1959, 791-802.
15. Hill, W. F. Learning theory and the acquisition of values. *Psych. Rev., 67*, 1960, 317-331.
16. Hoffman, M. L. Child rearing practices and moral development: generalizations from empirical research. *Child Develpm., 34*, 1963, 295-318.
17. Hoffman, M. L. Power assertion by the parent and its impact on the child. *Child Develpm., 31*, 1960, 129-143.
18. Hoffman, L. W. and Lippitt, H. R. The measurement of family life variables. (In) *Handbook of Research Methods in Child Development*, Mussen, P. H. (Ed.), John Wiley, New York, 1960.
19. Kagan, J., and Moss, H. A. *Birth to Maturity.* John Wiley, New York, 1962.
20. Levin, H. Permissive child rearing and adult role behavior. (In) *Contributions to Modern Psychology.* Dulany, D. E., et al. (Eds.). Oxford University Press, New York, 1958.
21. Maccoby, E. E. The taking of adult roles in middle childhood. *J. Abnorm. Soc. Psychol., 63*, 1961, 493-503.
22. Roff, M. A. A factorial study of the Fels parent behavior scale. *Child Develpm., 20*, 1949, 29-45.
23. Schaeffer, E. S. A circumplex model for maternal behavior. *J. Abnorm. Soc. Psychol., 59*, 1959, 226-235.
24. Schaffer, H. R. Some Issues in the study of Attachment Behavior. (In) *Determinants of Infant Behavior*, Foss, B. M. (Ed.). John Wiley, New York, 1961.
25. Sears, R. R. The relation of early socialization experiences to aggression in middle childhood. *J. Abnorm. Soc. Psychol., 63*, 1961, 466-492.
26. Sears, R. R. et al. *Patterns of Child Rearing.* Row, Peterson, Evanston, Ill., 1957.
27. Sears, R. R., et al. Some child rearing antecedents of aggression and dependency in young children. *Genet. Psychol. Monogr., 49*, 1953, 135-234.
28. Symonds, P. M. *The Psychology of Parent-Child Relationships.* Appleton-Century Crofts, New York, 1939.
29. Watson, G. Some personality differences in childhood related to strict or permissive parental discipline. *J. Psychol., 44*, 1957, 227-249.

CHAPTER 12

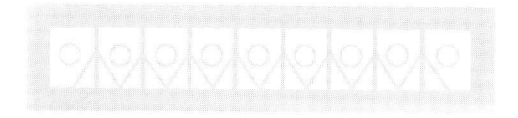

FAMILY AND SOCIAL CLASS IN THE SOCIALIZATION PROCESS

THE FUNCTION OF THE FAMILY

In most societies the neonate is born into a family, usually consisting of a mother and father, and possibly brothers and sisters; it is within this setting that child rearing takes place.

The processes of social learning and the activities of the child are largely shaped by the behavior of the parents and siblings. Compared to the influence of teachers and friends, the family is the most potent force in shaping the behavior of the child, at least in the early school years and possibly even in the adolescent period. As we shall see in the chapter on internalization, what happens during early years in the family may be a most important determinant of behavior throughout life. Behavior tendencies internalized in childhood, in the home, may persist psychologically even when the home has been left far behind in time and space.

The family has a multiplicity of functions: it serves as an outlet for the expression of love; it provides its members with affection and companionship; it becomes a source of financial security. Sexual needs are satisfied between husband and wife and it provides the intimacy in which anger and fear may be expressed. Perhaps most important of all, the family provides for the rearing of the child during his formative years. It is largely in families that social learning occurs and it is here that the neonate is taken care of and slowly becomes able to care for himself.

Early development occurs in the home. Love, companionship, economic security and expression of emotional and sexual needs can be satisfied outside the family, but there are few other possibilities in our society for the care and rearing of children.[19] One may speculate that the special demands of raising children are to a large extent responsible for the universality of the institution of the family.

One of the primary functions of the family, in almost all parts of the world, is to teach the child the rules and patterns of living of the particular segment of society into which the child is born. It may also teach him something about the ways of the wider society in which he may eventually participate.[19, 23] This process is known as acculturation or socialization: raising the child to learn and accept the ways of his particular culture or society. The family is not the only institution developed by mankind for the raising of children. However, it does seem to be the most common way of transmitting to the young the traditions and conventions they will have to learn in order to live and work adequately as adults. The learning of these standards, often so that they become the child's own, relatively independent of the presence or absence of surveillance, is called "socialization." The continuity of society depends to a fair extent on how well the family teaches the child to internalize social standards. If new ways of doing things are needed and if new patterns of behavior are required in a society, then changes in family life or attempts to change family life are likely to follow.[4, 25] The need to learn new ways of behaving may lead to changes in child rearing practices and family relationships.

THE NUCLEAR FAMILY

As we have said, most children the world over are born into a unit of society known as the family and are cared for within this unit during their formative years.[4, 19] There are exceptions to this arrangement, of course. In some parts of Israel, for example, there exists what is known as the kibbutz system of infant and child care. The kibbutz itself is usually a small rural community in which the children are often raised by trained child-care workers and the parents only visit or are visited by their children. Both the mother and father are usually at work during the day and entrust the raising of their children to the trained child-care personnel, although they do participate, to some extent, in child rearing.[30] Similar arrangements exist in Russia and other countries. In most parts of the world, however, children are reared at home from infancy until final separation from the family unit.

Most American children today are raised in a type of unit known as the "nuclear family." In this arrangement, a husband and wife live in a separate house or apartment, together with those of their children who have not yet moved to a housing unit of their own. Although in America a grandparent or even an aunt or uncle may be part of the household, having relatives in the same general housing unit is becoming the exception rather than the rule.[19, 28] This does not mean, however, that relatives have no influence on the rearing of American children. The nuclear family maintains contact with grandparents, aunts, uncles, and cousins. These may be sources of warmth and affection for the children and may influence the child rearing attitudes and practices of the parents. Relatives may also be sources of support to the nuclear family in times of need or stress. At other times they may be sources of problems and interference.[33]

The importance for the child of people other than the natural mother and father differs by social class. It may be worthwhile noting, for instance, that the grandmother is often a chief agent of child rearing in lower-class families where the mother works and the father has abandoned the home.[16] It has also been observed that relatives sometimes have more influence in the upper-class family, since they have considerable power through their wealth and social influence. The upper class has greater pride in its family name and a closely knit unit of interdependencies grow up among those high in society.[2]

The average American child spends most of his first six years, indeed much of his first seventeen or eighteen years, living at home with his mother and father, and his brothers and sisters. In addition to the genetic makeup his parents have passed on to him, other important determinants of a child's development are: how the parents stimulate him; what sort of behaviors they manifest for him to imitate; for what acts they reward and punish him; what attitudes and beliefs they have; and what kind of physical environment the parents provide for him.[3]

EXTENDED FAMILIES

The familiar is often the only thing one can imagine vividly. Life in a nuclear family may be the only one that seems natural to us, and it is easy to lose sight of the fact that many children the world over are raised under different familial circumstances. Many children in other countries, particularly in Africa and Asia, are raised in what is called an "extended family." One common feature of extended family arrangements is that the child is raised in the midst of relatives and their children, who may help to take care of the child and influence the actions of his mother. (Of course, this is not true of all extended families.) It is also characteristic of some extended families that older children have a great deal of responsibility in the rearing of younger children. Children raised under such circumstances may become attached to more people than American children.

In the United States, we are used to one man having one wife at a time, the system of monogamy. Actually, the rule is that there must be only one wife at a time, with divorce preceding remarriage. In some cultures a child is born to a mother who concurrently shares the father with one or more women who are also his wives and who may also have borne him children. Extended families may either be monogamous like our nuclear families, or polygamous. The distinctive feature of the extended family is the large number of individuals related by blood or marriage, often, but not always, living closely together and bound up in a network of mutual privileges and responsibilities.

Two Types of Extended Families

It seems worthwhile to take a brief look at two types of extended family arrangements in two different societies. One is a strictly monogamous type, and the other is one in which a husband may have several wives. In both cases, however, extended families are involved. These two societies illustrate the differences in social arrangements that are possible, while still providing for family living and child rearing responsibility. Their comparison also furnishes an example of a scientifically, relatively uncontrolled way of looking at child development but one that is intriguing and often useful, the *anthropological field study*. This approach can use a variety of methods of gathering information. It usually avoids the complexities of precise statistical measurement, and seldom are there attempts to vary environmental conditions in order to study the effects of the variation. That is to say, the experimental method is rarely used. The anthropologist, or student of human behavior from some other discipline, goes to a culture other than his own and, as systematically as he can, records how people live there. Often the observer relies on what people in the culture tell him. He usually has in mind certain aspects of the culture, such as how children are raised, which he wishes to observe and be told about in great detail. It is also possible that methods such as personality testing or interviewing, and asking similar questions of many people, will be used. The observations of people in the culture and interviews with informants usually follow a pattern determined by the social scientist in question and the aspects of the culture which interest him the most.

The two groups of people we will now specifically examine in terms of family type and child rearing arrangements are the *Rajputs* of Khalapur, India, and a *Gusii* community in Kenya, Africa. Material describing investigations of these two groups are found in Studies 12.1 and 12.2 respectively, augmenting the discussion in the main body of the text. These two cultures have been chosen from a work which includes the study of six cultures, one the study of a small town in the New England section of the United States, and the other five from parts of Kenya, India, Okinawa, Mexico, and the Philippines.[34]

The Cross-Cultural Approach

These studies were undertaken because anthropologists and psychologists have long believed that specific types of child rearing practices in early childhood lead to the formation of different types of behaviors in later childhood and adulthood.[10] If cultures can be found which vary markedly in the way adults treat their young children, and if older children and adults are found to be quite different in their behavior in each culture, then our knowledge of the effects of child rearing on behavior will be advanced.[10, 35] Each culture forms a "natural experiment" of the effects of various types of child rearing. They are not actual experiments performed by social scientists but represent fortuitous or "natural" variations provided by the cultural diversity of our world. Although in anthropological fieldwork, many methods can be and sometimes are used, the method of systematic observation is the most usual. This enables the cross-cultural observer to draw conclusions about the effects of child rearing by comparing and contrasting patterns of child rearing and their results in various cultures.

The Rajputs of India

The Rajputs of India live in the northern part of the country not very far from Kashmir. Although town dwellers, they go off most days into the nearby countryside where they own land, in order to make their living by farming and raising animals.[24] Twenty-eight out of the thirty-six Rajput families investigated were extended ones. These families included members of several generations living in the same general housing area. That is, great-grandparents and great-grandchildren might interact together every day. The most common arrangement included children, parents, grandparents, and their respective spouses, living in proximity for three generations. This means, for instance, that various brothers, the brothers' parents, the brothers' wives, and all their children would see each other and interact daily. Such an arrangement highlights opportunities for *imitation* and *mutual reinforcement*, whether positive or negative.

The Rajputs are monogamous and even within the same family unit the men and women are usually segregated. The men have their own house platform on which they often sleep, except when they are visiting with their wives. The women have their own quarters and a large courtyard which is also their territory. The courtyard is a place where the women often sleep. They also cook there and that is where they take care of the children. The courtyard is shared by women who are the wives of brothers. Also in the courtyard may be found the young children, unmarried older daughters, married sons' wives and their children.

The real point of interest is that, in a very real sense, the Rajput child's learning experiences take place in public. Many members of a large extended family can see how the child behaves and what the mother does to the child. If the mother is busy, other women, or even an old man with little to do, may care for the child. Despite the fact that each mother chiefly cares for her own child, a crying child is often picked up by any woman or older child.[24, 34] If the child does not stop crying it may be passed from one female to another and each will try to calm it. Some woman may even offer her breast as a pacifier. If it is a young child and it seems hungry, the mother-in-law or an aunt may take over the work of a mother busy at another task so that she can stop and nurse the child. Few young mothers in the United States can expect such help so naturally and regularly. The Rajput child sleeps with its own mother, who has the main responsibility for washing, dressing, and feeding it; however, when help is needed there will be ready and willing hands about. The child grows up in the hustle and bustle of a large family.[24, 34] This provides a great deal of tactual, auditory, and visual stimulation with the consequent effects discussed in earlier chapters. In addition, socialization is hastened by a variety of caretakers sharing common behavioral patterns.

ANTHROPOLOGICAL OBSERVATION AMONG THE RAJPUTS OF INDIA

STUDY 12.1

Leigh Minturn, a social psychologist, and John Hitchcock, an anthropologist, studied the Rajputs of India through the auspices of the Cornell India Project.

In utilizing the anthropological observational method the investigator is often handicapped by a language problem and the difficulty of winning the cooperation and goodwill of the people to be studied. The investigator must depend heavily on his interpreter and native informants. Minturn was helped by Gurdeep Jaspal, who knew the language and acted as her interpreter. Gurdcep Jaspal also assisted in helping her understand the Rajput culture. Hitchcock had Sri Shyam Narain Singh as an interpreter and coworker. It seems that Narain Singh was blessed with a love of the Rajput people, a penchant for hard work and a fine sense of humor. These qualities are especially useful in a part of the world that has a hot, wet, monsoon season in the summer and a dry spring, accompanied by a scorching wind from the western desert; at times the temperature is 100°. The above facts are not psychologically illuminating but may be pertinent to the realities of much of cross-cultural research.

Most interesting was the finding that Rajputs believe that children learn primarily by observing. Hence the Rajputs do little direct training of their children and expect them to learn by watching what is going on. Their opinion in this regard, as we have seen, coincides with the theories of many American developmental psychologists who also believe that children learn much by sheer observation. Minturn and Hitchcock noted that children are exposed in the common courtyard and other places to people of all ages and sexes. Consequently, they are able to observe how people behave.

Other children and adults, furthermore, are sometimes used as role models; that is, pointed out as examples of how to behave. This is seldom done, however, as a deliberate teaching device; it happens naturally. The children learn to absorb skills, customs, and values through natural observation and imitation. The extended family structure helps by furnishing plenty of people to imitate.

Minturn, L., and Hitchcock, J., Jr. The Rajputs of Khalapur, India. (In) *Six Cultures: Studies of Child Rearing*, Whiting, B. B. (Ed.)., John Wiley, New York, 1963.

The Nyansongo Gusii

Not very far from Lake Victoria in Kenya is a section known as Gusiiland. The Nyansongo Gusii live between 5000 and 7000 feet above sea level and so enjoy a relatively cool climate, for Africa. They are Bantu-speaking Negroes who are both a farming people and raisers of cattle, sheep, and goats.[22, 34] The chief living unit of the Nyansongo Gusii is a hut containing a married woman, her unmarried daughters, and sons who have not reached puberty. It is quite possible that the woman's husband lives there part of the time. However, he may have other wives and, if he does, he will live with them as much or more of the time than he does with her. The woman and her children work the land near her house. If she has sons, when they grow up and marry they will probably build houses and work land reasonably close by. Food is stored near each household and the husband has certain right over the food produced by his wives and children.[24, 34] Although not living in nearly as close proximity as the Rajputs, nor having a common courtyard or sleeping platforms, the Gusii must be considered to have an extended famly arrangement. When the sons grow up and marry, they build huts near that of their mother and bring home their wives who raise their children there. The mother and sons' families clearly consider themselves as "one household." Nevertheless, observational learning may be expected to play a less important role in this culture than in the lives of the Rajputs.

Polygamy, or a plurality of wives, is considered desirable by the men who also wish for many children. It is believed good to have as many as four wives, although almost no man seems to attain more than two. Despite the extended nature of the family, each wife has her own house. There is at least one reasonably large piece of farm or pasture land between the huts of each cowife. This helps to keep jealousy and conflict to a minimum. Some cowives get along very well but others develop bitter hatreds. It seems likely that the more greatly the wives differ in age the less jealousy there is and the better they get along together.

The Gusii Infant and Mother

The infant's closest initial relationship is with its mother and the young child may see very little of its father. The mother spends a lot of time working in the fields. Consequently a child caretaker, usually a girl six to ten years old, soon does a lot of the chores of tending to the infant and toddler. Most often the child caretaker is an older sister, but sometimes it is a younger brother or someone else's child. Attachment of the infant to an older sister caretaker may be quite strong. The family which the young Nyansongo Gusii child experiences is a much more restricted one than the teeming one which confronts the Rajput child. It was noted by Minturn and Hitchcock that the Rajput mothers agreed on many aspects of child rearing and would not do certain things for fear of what others would say. The Gusii mother, on the other hand, is more isolated and others are less likely to be concerned about or able to note what she does. Consequently, Gusii mothers vary in their child rearing methods and rely less on having the child learn by imitation. However, there are some uniformities in child rearing, particularly the use of physical punishment by mothers as Study 12.2 illustrates.

PHYSICAL PUNISHMENT OF GUSII CHILDREN

STUDY 12.2

Robert and Barbara LeVine, social scientists, lived with the chief of a Gusii community in Nyaribari in the South

Nyanza District of Kenya. They used four interpreters during their stay and in addition to observation, they utilized the interview method. Barbara LeVine interviewed the Gusii mothers and Robert LeVine interviewed older boys and girls. Besides watching and interviewing, Barbara LeVine participated in the female initiation rites, danced with the women, and took photographs of women's activities which men were not allowed to observe at close quarters. This particular cross-cultural method of observational study is called the *participant-observer technique*. The investigators participate in a culture other than their own while observing it.

Physical punishment and the consequent instilling of fear are common ways in which the Gusii mother tries to make her child conform to her wishes. Physical punishment or its threat far outweigh the giving of reward in raising children. Threats come first. The mother threatens to throw the child out of the house at night and sometimes she tells him that hyenas will eat him. She may even threaten to kill him or to tie him up and leave him or say that she will have the father punish him unmercifully.

If threats fail to make the child do as she wishes the mother resorts to striking the child with a wooden cane. She may deprive the child of food, give him hard work to do, or actually make him spend the night out of the house in the dark. It is children from three to six years of age who get hit the most. Children over six, if they are disobedient, are seen largely as lost souls not correctible by beating.

The Gusii are of the opinion that the method and amount of punishment used by a mother on her child is her own affair. It is a private matter between her and her child. Other people tend neither to aid her nor to stop her. Punishment may depend more on the mood of the mother than on general social rules or her awareness of the wishes of others. If she feels good, the children may be able to ignore her threats. The child seems to learn his mother's mood and acts accordingly. The LeVines report great variability in the severity of discipline among Nyansongo mothers. By standards of societies in general, discipline is harsh, but there is always the chance of escape. A Nyansongo Gusii child may run away for a day or so to the nearby house of one of his father's other wives and may later return to his own mother in the hope that her anger has abated. It often has.

The Nyansongo do not rely very heavily on observational learning. They believe that it is important to teach the child to be good and to do the right things early. Mothers use

> punishment to make children learn. They usually succeed, but some children seem to become our equivalent of delinquents. The children who avoid the parents and manage to escape punishment do not become well socialized.
>
> LeVine, R. A., and LeVine, B. Nyansongo: A Gussi community in Kenya. (In) *Six Cultures: Studies of Child Rearing*. Whiting, B. B. (Ed.). John Wiley, New York, 1963.

GENERALITY DESPITE DIVERSITY

We can see, therefore, that there are ways of organizing family life and arranging for the care and rearing of children which differ widely from our own. However, the principles discussed in earlier chapters hold for any culture. Similar psychological causes produce similar effects no matter where they occur. Excessive use of physical punishment in America as well as in Kenya can lead to anti-social behavior or other problems. Children raised chiefly through strong fear will often "behave" only as long as they expect punishment for not behaving properly. Since mankind is one species, we should not be surprised to find developmental laws equally valid in all cultures. The principles of social learning and the effects of patterns of child rearing have equivalent effects wherever they occur. Their use differs, not their results.

THE CURRENT STATE OF THE AMERICAN FAMILY

Let us turn now to the American family into which most of us were born. What is it like? What is its future? How does it interact with the child? Despite dire predictions, discussions about the "sexual revolution," and the complaints of alarmists upset by the high divorce rates, the American marriage and family is a going concern. It seems unlikely to vanish. Divorces, frequent as they are, tend to occur more often early in marriages rather than later, and are more frequent among childless couples. In some years, as many as two-thirds of the couples obtaining divorces have no children.[4] Those who divorce do not tend to stay divorced; they mostly get married again. Few children spend many years without a married couple in the home, even if one member may be a stepfather, or less frequently, a stepmother. The lower class may be an exception since among the very poor it is not entirely uncommon for a child to grow up in a fatherless family.

Americans seem to be as eager to marry as ever. The percentage of the population fifteen years of age and over who are married has been increasing since 1890.[4] Not only are Americans highly likely to marry, they will marry at relatively early ages; at about 23 years of age for men and 20 years for women.[4] The proportion of the population married and living with a spouse is very high, regardless of any previous divorce.

Changes in the Family

The family is not yet on the wane although it may have become less stable. It has become smaller and more specialized, but in some ways more important, since it has to meet more needs today than a hundred years ago.

In 1790 the average family had 5.7 children; today the average number of children per family is about 3.5.[4] There has been a trend to urban and suburban living and a move away from the farm and small rural towns; consequently, isolation and greater mutual husband-wife reliance is the rule. We have already discussed the tendency to exclude relatives from living with the family of today. The family, therefore, is smaller. Although separated from relatives, it is likely to be living closer to other nonrelated families and to be dependent on the amenities of urban living. Some of these include commercialized entertainments such as television, large schools for the children, and the frequent interaction of children with other children outside the family. Paradoxically, although the nuclear family is in some ways more isolated, in others it is more involved in society than ever before. It has been suggested that the institution of marriage and the family is outmoded and no longer functional. If this is true, as it may be, it certainly does not yet reflect the behavior of most Americans.

The Modern Marriage

The American family retains as its chief function the socialization of children. Human social behavior is learned, and the family is the part of society in which it is largely acquired. However, the young man and woman who marry today may not do so primarily in order to have and raise children, although this may be a secondary purpose. A basic reason for entering into marriage, to its participants, is that of satisfying their mutual affectional, security, and sexual needs.[19] Or, as they may put it, they love each other. In the past, the extended family met many of these security and affectional needs. Now, the young married couple may have to rely only on each other and their children to meet most of their needs.

Fairly severe demands, therefore, are made on the modern marriage. Partners have a great freedom of choice in deciding whom to marry. The male has less authority than formerly, and the status of women and the number of jobs open to them have increased. This means that marriage must be worked out in terms of a more equal partnership than in the past. In addition, it is now generally easier to get divorced than it was formerly. Since the married couple expects to live alone, although relatives may help financially and with advice, the couple have to satisfy each other both psychologically and physically. They have to make a living and cope with their children. In these endeavors, despite sometimes helpful cooperation and aid from relatives, they are pretty much on their own. It seems remarkable that the institution of marriage has stood up as well as it has. It is possible that new demands of modern life will eventually effect more drastic changes in the family system, producing new settings for the rearing of children.

Marriage and Children

Many married couples want to have children and particularly look forward to having their first child. The birth of the first child is both an event eagerly looked forward to, and, at the same time, somewhat of a crisis, disrupting the previous pattern of living.[14, 17] Studies 12.3 and 12.4 furnish information about both of these factors. Having children is an important part of American marriage and people who cannot have children of their own may decide to adopt a child. Ours is a society which takes a great interest in its children and concerns itself seriously with their health, behavior and education. The two studies below show that having a child is a mixed blessing; the infant is both a source of pleasure and of problems.

THE FIRST CHILD AS JOY

STUDY 12.3

D. F. Hobbs was interested in the reactions of parents to their first child. The study was done when the babies were already born and were about ten weeks old. Some people have called this the "baby honeymoon." It is a period when parents seem to be enchanted by their first child. It is possible that before the baby actually arrives, or six months to a years later, parents may not feel quite so elated. The time when an investigator collects his data may be important in studying aspects of parental attitudes toward children.

Ninety percent of the parents Hobbs investigated were white, urban-living Protestants. They were from all educational levels (illiteracy to graduate education). They were each questioned on their feelings about their first child.

Ninety-six percent of the parents reported wanting the first child. Ninety-one percent of the husbands and seventy percent of the wives indicated marriage to be more happy and satisfying since birth of the first child. None of the men and only two percent of the women said that the baby made the marriage less satisfying. Seventy percent stated that they felt "happy," "wonderful," or "lucky," when they first saw the baby and some stated that they felt more mature when they become parents. Clearly these parents were elated after the birth of their first child and were still elated ten weeks later.

We have already noted the possibility that the time the study was done, ten weeks after the birth of the child, might have been important. So might what social scientists call "the sample." We cannot be sure that Negroes, Jews, Catholics, people on farms, or unwed mothers would feel the same way about their first child. They might be happier or not, more or less elated, feel more or less mature. It is not always safe to generalize from one sample to another. What is characteristic of one group may or may not be true for another.

Hobbs used the questionnaire method to gather his data. He constructed a check list of 23 items to measure the extent of the factors associated with the birth of the first child. The parents could choose only one of three degrees (not, somewhat, very much) indicating how they reacted to each one of 23 pre-selected items. An example would be: "Since our baby was born, our marriage is — more happy and satisfying than before (not, somewhat, very much)." In this method the investigator has to rely on what the respondents choose to check, from a pre-selected array of alternatives. There is no way for the respondents to qualify their answers, degree of agreement, or to add new items.

Hobbs, D. F., Parenthood as crisis; a third study. *J. Marr. and Fam.*, 27, 1964, 367-372.

THE FIRST CHILD AS TROUBLE

STUDY 12.4

E. D. Dyer focussed on the first child as a critical event in the family. He studied both urban and suburban middle-class couples, in which at least one of the pair was college-educated and under 35 years of age. He found, as have some others, that the advent of the first child into the urban middle-class family called for a new style of living for which the previous patterns were inadequate. Giving birth, taking care of the child, and losing the freedom of being able to go anywhere anytime, plus the financial burdens added to the family budget, do make for certain difficulties.

The following are problems reported by mothers of young children and the percentage of them reporting these troubles.

Tiredness and exhaustion—87 percent
Loss of sleep in the first six to nine weeks—87 percent
Feelings of neglecting the husband to some degree—67 percent
Uncertainty about being able to be a good mother—58 percent
Trouble with being tied down to the home—35 percent

Fathers of young children reported:
Loss of sleep up to six weeks after birth of the child—50 percent
Adjustment troubles with the new responsibility—50 percent
Upset of schedules and daily routine—37 percent
Financial worries and demands on their time, some few reports.

One year after the birth of the child 40 percent of the couples still reported fairly important problems connected with the child. One major complaint of husbands and wives was that being a parent interfered with their previously established habits of doing things whenever they wanted to.

It was found that problems were less severe if the marriage was quite a happy one before the child was born. Problems were also less severe if the parents had taken a course on marriage, were married three or more years when the first child came, or if the child was "planned," that is, they had decided to have the child on purpose.

Dyer, like Hobbs, used the questionnaire method. He used a questionnaire scale on which the parents could indicate the extend to which the arrival of the first child represented a crisis to them. The items were based on the areas of marriage which previous studies indicated might suffer disruptive effects with the birth of the first child. Again, the investigator is forced to take the parents' answers at face value, and the parents responses are limited by the question asked them. The new child, then, is both a source of pleasure and of difficulties.

Dyer, E. D., Parenthood as crisis: A re-study. *Marr. and Fam. Liv.*, 25, 1963, 196-201.

SOCIAL CLASS AND THE CHILD REARING PROCESS

Social Class Differences

Parent behaviors in terms of patterns of discipline and child rearing, reviewed more systematically in the previous chapter, tend to vary mainly according to the social class of the family.[9, 11, 31, 32] However, it is sometimes useful to consider the special experiences of a given religious, racial, or ethnic group, in addition to social class alone, as a determiner of child-rearing practices. For instance, the family structure of Negroes is influenced by their social history as slaves and their history of constant persecution as well as their class position, as we shall see later. The general family patterns of Negroes are close to the general family patterns of other groups who occupy corresponding social classes.[12, 16] Nevertheless, that they came to America as slaves and that their right to have families within a stable marriage was usually denied them by their white owners is important. It is equally important that they have generally been excluded from the middle class.

The Lower Class

Sociologists divide the lower class into the upper-lower, or somewhat more skilled working class (upper-working class), and the lower-lower (lower-working class), consisting largely of the less educated, less skilled, and frequently unemployed.

The lower-class family is likely to live in less comfortable housing then the middle-class family. Employment for the lower-class male tends to bring a lower income than for the middle-class male. The family is more likely to be receiving funds from Welfare, especially Aid to Dependent Children, if the natural father is from a lower-lower-class background. The most salient characteristic of the lower-lower-class family is the relatively weak position of the father. Even though his behavior is sometimes aggressive and autocratic, the father lacks the power, respect, and prestige of his middle- and upper-class counterparts. The stresses of unemployment and poor housing seem to be correlated with frequent emotional outbursts and impulsive behavior on the part of males within an unstable household.[12, 16] The wife is likely to have to go out and work, and therefore to have relatively more economic power.[5, 6, 7] In the lower-lower class, the husband, if unable to make a living, has sometimes deserted the family. He is in a very poor position, at best, to dispense rewards. Consequently, a matriarchy may tend to develop, where the mother or grandmother is the real head of the household. The father, having little power and often absent, does not provide a model for imitation.

In much of the following discussion, the Negro lower-lower class will be used for illustrative purposes. What is true of the Negro under these conditions is true of the white under similar conditions as well. The Negro is especially cited here because of the great amount of current social interest in problems of prejudice, integration, power for, and education of the Negro lower class. Of special pertinence is the problem of identification for the Negro boy when his father has been deprived of power as a man and as a human being.

It is useful to keep in mind while discussing the Negro lower class that about 25 percent of Negroes in the Northern and Western United States and about 13 percent in the South are middle class. Many middle-class Negroes are strongly committed to the central values of white American culture, enjoy a fairly good educational and economic position, and have stable and conventional families. There is also a Negro upper class of professional and business men, which would correspond to the white upper-middle class. The nature of Negro lower-lower class family life is largely a function of the history of slavery, segregation, prejudice, exploitation, and mass migration to the North. Their behavior differs very little from the white lower-lower class. The family structure has been heavily influenced by the lack of economic opportunity for Negro males, their subordination to whites, and the relative prevention of Negro participation in political life.[12, 16] Social learning theory would predict that with powerless models, seldom able to reward, socialization would be weak at best for Negro children. As long as the white keeps Negroes economically inferior, they cannot expect socially approved behavior on the part of Negroes. Further, Negroes may have their own ideas of how to live which do not coincide with the social values of middle-class whites. Many Negroes today may not want to be like the white middle-class; they want their own culture.

Matriarchy

From the days of slavery until today, for varying reasons at different points in history, the Negro mother remained the most stable element in the Negro family. In the time of slavery there was no true Negro family. Although labor of the Negro slave supported the Southern economy, he had few privileges. The mother cared for her children and was in charge of the cabin which the natural father, black or white, was only allowed to visit. Child rearing was completely her responsibility. With the end of slavery and the ensuing confusion, dislocation, and attempts to start a new life, the mother or grandmother had to keep the children together. Negroes were now all free to marry, but the Negro lacked experience with the family as an institution since, in America, it had existed only among free Negroes and a few favored slaves. Legal marriage and family traditions were institutions in which most former slaves had not been allowed to participate. After emancipation, the dominant force in the family still tended to be the grandmother or the mother. If a Negro girl became pregnant out of wedlock and the natural father had no land or steady employment, her mother might not want her to marry him. This was particularly true of the lower-lower class in the cities. Where the Negro owned land, as in some parts of the rural South, or was otherwise able to achieve relative economic security, there were less births out of wedlock, marriage was the rule, and the husband-father most often remained permanently with his wife and children. Few whites, even today, truly understand the extent to which the tragic history of slavery has affected the lives of Negroes.

NEGRO MIGRATION AND MALE STATUS

In the early 1900's Negroes started moving in large numbers from the South to the North and from rural to urban areas. The wife found it easier to obtain work than the husband, since she was in demand for domestic work as a cook, maid, or child caretaker. The lower-lower class husband, unable to find steady work, having to depend on the wife, and at loose ends, often became demoralized. He was not held up as a model for his son to "imitate" and he had no economic power, consequently one solution was simply to leave home. Matriarchy was perpetuated, and illegitimacy and desertion of the family by the husband may have increased. Many Negro males simply couldn't afford a divorce even if they wanted one. The absence of a father or stable adult male figure in the home became a problem for many city slum Negro children, as it also was for many lower-lower class white children. This situation was exacerbated by a mother often having to prove, in order to get "welfare aid," that there was no adult male in the home. Unemployed husbands often left, or sneaked out so that the wife could qualify for "welfare."

The problem is still substantially one of the status of the male, who must depend on his ability to succeed in accordance with the rules of the larger society. White society has not allowed the Negro male to succeed. It has robbed him of his social influence in regard to his own children. When the Negro male has a skilled trade or profession and is allowed to work at it steadily, he assumes responsibility for his family, is generally disciplined, takes an interest in his children, and wants them educated.[12] The lower-lower class male, whether Negro or white, is at a disadvantage since in the eyes of his wife and children, in his own eyes, and in those of the community, he is a failure. He is a low status figure with little power. Consequently, his social reinforcement value is low; he cannot really influence the behavior of others. The wife has more power in the family if she works, and the husband has less.[6, 16] Even if the father does not desert the family, the lower-lower class boy, white or Negro, may find himself in a female dominated matriarchal home. It is consequently harder for him to learn the male role, to become oriented toward achievement or to learn how to compete with middle-class males.

THE CONVERGENCE OF CHILD REARING PATTERNS

Patterns of child rearing in the upper-lower and middle classes seem to be growing more and more alike. Parents from these classes may reward similar behaviors and model similar behaviors. It is becoming harder to make any distinctions between the upper-lower and lower-middle class. In the 1920's and 1930's the working class parents were accustomed to use a greater amount of physical punishment but were less demanding of their children. They hit them frequently but restricted them less. The middle-class parents were perhaps more restrictive toward their children, expecting higher standards of them, but likely to use love oriented disciplinary methods, such as withdrawal of approval or signs of displeasure. A partial reversal of this trend may have taken place in the 1930's, when the middle class became more permissive and less restrictive. Evidence of greater use of physical punishment by the working class had pretty much vanished by the 1950's.[9, 20, 21] The patterns of child rearing in the upper-lower and middle classes have continued to become more similar and standardized, partly as a function of wide dissemination of such works as *Baby and Child Care*, by Dr. Spock, and the U.S. Children's Bureau's *Bulletin on Infant Care*. In general, both these social classes have shown greater "permissiveness" in child rearing, a greater expression of "warmth" toward the child, predominant use of "love-oriented" methods of discipline, and a greater shift towards family democracy.

The shift towards democracy has meant more equality of function between men and women. The mother has become somewhat more of an authoritarian disciplinary figure while also showing warmth and affection. The father has come to show more warmth to his children and has become both less of an authority figure and less punitive. The modern father participates more in child rearing than fathers used to. The increased class similarities may be partly due to the success of the labor union movement and the consequent increased earning power and higher educational level of the upper-lower class. The working class has become somewhat middle class in its attitudes and behavior. If mothers and fathers in upper-lower and middle classes now share greater equality, they are in a position to be more equally potent sources of imitation and more equally powerful sources of both reward and punishment.

DIVERGENCES BETWEEN THE WORKING AND MIDDLE CLASSES

However, this is not to say that there are no important differences in family life and child behavior between the (upper-lower) working and the middle class. We can specify what is similar and what is different. Child rearing practices, we have noted, are becoming more alike. In addition, most parents in the United States, regardless of social class, stress future-oriented goals for their children.[13] That is, skilled workers' families are also providing training in achievement behavior. By and large they want their children to strive for fairly important goals which are not simple to achieve. The interests and worries of the parents revolve around child behaviors which are seen as leading to success in the role they hope the child will fill in the future. The working and middle classes, however, still differ somewhat in what behaviors they are concerned about and some of the specific goals they value. The differences between the social classes are revealed by the child behaviors that are of concern to the parents in the present as well as how they hope the child finally turns out. Study 12.5 illustrates both similarities and differences in child rearing between the working and the middle classes.

PUNISHMENT IN THE WORKING AND MIDDLE CLASSES

STUDY 12.5

Melvin L. Kohn, of the National Institute of Mental Health, investigated the proposition that: "In matters of discipline, working class parents are consistently more likely to employ physical punishment, whereas middle class families rely more on reasoning, isolation, appeals to guilt, and other methods involving a threat of loss of love." He found parts of this proposition have no validity. Working and middle-class parents reported an almost identical tendency to use physical punishment. Only a small minority of either the middle or working class parents used physical punishment frequently.

However, a reasonable proportion, though still a minority, had used it within the month preceding that study and a majority had used physical punishment within the previous six months. This was true regardless of social class. Parents of neither class had much recourse to physical punishment, according to their reports, but many parents of both classes used it from time to time. Both social classes turned to physical punishment only after other attempts to control the child's behavior proved ineffective.

Where the two social classes diverged was in the *conditions* under which they did or did not punish. These conditions in turn, were related to the goals parents set for their children. Most parents of the working class wished their children to be "respectable." Working class parents, therefore, were quite interested in how the child behaved from moment to moment. It was the immediate consequences of the childs' behavior that concerned them. If it wasn't respectable, it had to be suppressed by immediate action, including physical punishment as a last resort.

The principal aim of the middle class, on the other hand, was to have the child "internalize standards of conduct." The middle-class parent was less concerned about the exact nature or respectability of the current behavior. They were more worried about what it "meant," or what it would lead to. Middle-class parents rewarded or punished more in terms of their beliefs about the child's intent or purpose in acting as he did than on the basis of his actual current actions. They wanted the child to develop well, to accept proper values of conduct, and to act in accordance with them. The working-class parent imposed rules and expected them to be obeyed. The middle class valued the childs' self-control and self-regulation. The working class was satisfied with good behavior, and not as concerned about internal control by the child.

Kohn, M. L. Social class and the exercise of parental authority. *Amer. Sociol. Rev.*, 24, 1959, 352-366.

Middle Class Emphasis on Internalization Processes

As noted by Kohn, middle class parents think highly of internalized standards of conduct. They appreciate honesty and self-control, delay of gratification, achievement, and curiosity. They particularly value these qualities in boys.[20, 21] It is not surprising, therefore, that boys from middle-class families tend to surpass those from working-class families on self-control, achievement, responsibility, leadership, popularity, and general adjustment.[31]

Ideas about how to be a "good parent" differ in these two social classes along the same lines as their definitions of a "good child." Working-class mothers think that their main job is to make their children conform in certain ways. Middle-class mothers think more in terms of the growth and development of their children and a relationship of affection and mutual self satisfaction between the child and themselves.[7, 20] Ironically, middle-class children actually behave better and are more "respectable" since they internalize standards more than working-class children. They are better able to control themselves.

DIFFERENTIAL TREATMENT OF BOYS AND GIRLS BY SOCIAL CLASS

In the lower class, the mother is often the authority figure. She shows the most affection also, but, in addition, controls the resources at least as much as the father. She may be the only adult present. This has particular significance for boys at the lower-class levels. The lower the educational level, the more likely is the same-sex parent to indulge the opposite-sex child and punish the same-sex child. The lower class mother, therefore, is more lenient with the son and stricter with the daughter. The opposite is true at the upper levels. The upper-middle class mother is more likely to be strict with her son. The less well-educated father indulges his daughter but the upper-middle class father does not.[9] This has particular significance for upper-middle class girls. Only the better educated father is likely to punish his daughter physically more than the mother does and, conversely, the lower-class father is more likely to hit his son. There are few differences in affection, positive emotional reward, or negative emotional punishment of children between fathers of different social classes if one lumps boys and girls together. All social classes seem to be about equally emotionally involved with their children in general. However, patterns of punishment accorded to boys and girls, as we have seen, may vary by social class.[9]

In the lower-middle class the girl gets little punishment from the mother or father. She gets a large dose of both parental affection and restrictive control. This combination, as we have seen, leads to over-socialization, along with a great deal of dependency, timidity, and general inhibition. This does not happen in the upper-middle class where the father is somewhat harsher to the girl although the mother is more lenient. This moderate parental harshness makes the upper-middle class girl more independent, less inhibited, and keeps her from becoming over-socialized. She is treated more like a boy and so behaves more like a boy, wanting to go to college and often demanding a career.

For boys, the opposite seems to be the case. At upper-middle class levels, boys and girls are treated fairly much alike. Girls are no longer overprotected as they are at lower-middle class as well as working-class levels. Boys in the upper social classes are treated in an indulgent manner, as contrasted to the harshness shown to boys of the less well educated families. As a result, upper-middle class boys may *sometimes* be somewhat undersocialized, showing less responsibility and leadership.[9] The investigation discussed in Study 12.6 explores some of these trends. Emphasis is placed here on the parts of the study which underline the often overlooked importance of the father in the family and his crucial effect on children.

THE FATHER, SOCIAL CLASS, AND CHILD BEHAVIOR

STUDY 12.6

Urie Bronfenbrenner, of Cornell University, has long been interested in how patterns of parental and child behavior have varied, both by social class and over the course of time, in the United States. An important contribution in this area is his study of the differential effects of mothers and fathers on children in various social classes.

His work demonstrates that the fathers' behavior, often overlooked by developmental psychologists, may be as important as the mothers' or even more so, in determining such characteristics as responsibility and leadership. Dr. Bronfenbrenner studied 400 male and female children who were about 16 years old (tenth grade). He also studied their parents. He used the fathers' educational level as an index of social class. Fathers were divided into groups who: had some graduate work, were college graduates, were high school graduates, did not finish high school.

He found that within any social class level fathers show greater individual differences in disciplinary behaviors than the mothers do. Mothers within any social class are fairly alike in how they treat their children. Fathers are not. Differences in how children behave within a social class may, therefore, largely depend on what the fathers do or don't do. This seems to be especially true in the lower social classes. Individual differences in severity of discipline are greatest among fathers who have not graduated from high school. Some are quite strict and punish a lot and others punish hardly at all.

In families where the father has had some graduate training, fathers are more alike in their behavior.

The poorly educated fathers tend to be strict with their sons and to overprotect their daughters. The behavior of the father is particularly important in determining the behavior of his son. Boys are most responsible when the father is the main agent of discipline. The boy becomes least responsible when the mother and father wield equal authority over him. Boys seem to become more conventionally socialized in a patriarchy. If the father is not involved with the boy's rearing, then the boy is likely to show low levels of responsibility and leadership. Relative deprivation of affection from the parent of the same sex (the father, for the boy) has particularly bad effects. Especially in the middle ranges of education, fatherly discipline, combined with fatherly warmth and companionship, produces boys who are responsible leaders.

Bronfenbrenner, U. Some familial antecedents of responsibility and leadership. (In) *Adolescents in Leadership and Interpersonal Behavior*, Petrullo, L. and Bass, B. M. (Eds.). Holt, Rinehart and Winston, New York, 1961.

DIFFERENCES IN MOTHER-FATHER ROLES AND SOCIAL CLASS

Traditionally, the American society is mother-centered in its arrangements for child care. The father works outside the home and the wife takes over the child-rearing role. The main cultural concept may still largely be that child rearing, even of male children, is a feminine duty.[27, 28] The teachers in nursery school, kindergarten, and in the first six grades are mostly women. Men traditionally are given the more instrumental roles in our culture and women the more expressive ones. This means that traditionally the father's job is to make a living. He must have instrumental skills; he has those skills which are used to support the family. The expressive role, given to the female, emphasizes the emotional elements of life, those associated with the satisfactions of warmth and love.[27, 28] The father stereotypically provides economic security, the mother, emotional security.

For the reasons cited above, the father has often been ignored in studies of child rearing. However he often becomes a vital model for the boy to imitate and frequently has the greatest control over rewards. The father, again traditionally, is considered to be the head of the household. However, particularly if he is in the lower-lower class, the father segregates himself from the wife's activities. The lower-class father hangs around with his friends and relatives in his spare time. He is less available as a model and is a less potent source of reinforcement. This is much less true of the middle-class husband who spends more leisure time activities with the family.[6,7] Both the lower-class and the upper-middle-class fathers strive, in different ways, to be the chief models and sources of reward, the former by occasional exercise of verbally and physically aggressive behavior, and the latter by means of the respect gained from the economic earning power of a profession which brings social status. The middle-class father, classically, has had more success than the lower-class father. However, as social values have recently changed during adolescence, the middle-class father has also run into difficulty. The children of the affluent middle class often become models and reinforcers for each other during adolescence, at least partly rejecting their parents' standards.

CHANGING ROLE ASSIGNMENTS

In recent years there has been a gradual change, although not a reversal, in expectations about how men and women should behave. For instance, more and more women are working. The activities of males and females are becoming more alike both in the case of adults and children. The wife has more power in the family if she works. In a typical working class suburb, 40 percent of mothers work who have at least one child at home, if the child is over 11 years old. The corresponding figures are 36 percent for lower-middle class mothers and 27 percent for upper-middle class mothers.[26] The higher the social status of the husband the less likely the wife is to work. However, the higher the social status of the family, the more democratic or equalitarian the nature of the husband-wife relationship is, whether or not the wife works.

Now that many working-class and middle-class wives have attained power through earning money, the roles of men and women are less differentiated. Since a girl may well have a career in later life, she is treated from the beginning more like a boy, particularly in the upper-middle class. Since a boy, as a future modern father, may have to cope with more family duties than has been traditional, he may today, in some social classes, be treated somewhat more like a girl. Patterns of reward and punishment, therefore, may be converging for boys and girls. Consequently, the American family is becoming less internally differentiated. Mothers and fathers may be more similar models than they once were. Women work and father interact emotionally with their children. Fathers may also find themselves accepting more child raising duties. There may be a growing similarity between husbands and wives, brothers and sisters.[5,29] The daughters of working mothers have been shown to be more independent, more self-reliant, more aggressive, more dominant, and less obedient, in short, more like "traditional" boys.[29] The sons of working mothers are often more dependent, more helpful to others, and more obedient; in short, more like the "traditional" girl. Working women express themselves and have strong opinions, just as working men do.[6, 29] With the possible exception of the impoverished, jobless, sometimes father-deserted lower-class families, the American family is growing more homogeneous, males and females are becoming more similar behaviorally.

SUMMARY

Child rearing is probably the chief function of the family the world over. Families, however, may vary in size, composition, and structure. We are used chiefly to a nuclear family which consists of the parents and their children living in a separate house or apartment apart from their mutual relatives. In such a family structure child rearing during the first several years is almost the exclusive concern of only a few people. In other cutlures family arrangements may be similar to ours or they may be quite different. Child rearing may be more public or it may be largely relegated to older children; a man's other wives, the grandparents, or uncles may have more important roles to play than they do in our culture. In some countries arrangements exist which remove most of the child-rearing activities from the parents. Institutions may be created to care for and educate children. However, this is the exception rather than the rule throughout the world.

The integrity of the family unit seems to be important if children are to successfully adapt to our culture. That is, absence of the father or mother in a society of nuclear families can be a problem. Particularly if the mother has to work and is often out of the home, the absence of a father can cause difficulties in the development of boys. Such father-absence is most likely in the lower-working class.

Although they differ less than formerly, behavior still varies from social class to social class on matters of male-female relationships and patterns of child rearing. We can speak roughly of the working class and the middle class. The middle-class parent is chiefly concerned about the long range implications of child behavior and concentrates on inculcating internalized standards of conduct. The working class is more oriented towards immediate behavior, obedience, and respectability.

The working class husband spends less time with his family and more time with other male friends. Despite any blustery behavior, the working-class father, particularly if he is lower-working class, has less power than the middle-class father. Since he makes less money and has less of the attributes admired by the culture, he has less influence over his children.

There may be changes taking place in family structures and relationships. There is a tendency towards homogenization of roles with women tending to work and men helping with household chores and child rearing. In addition, except for the lower-working class "disadvantaged," parents may be becoming more similar in how they treat each other and their children.

REFERENCES

1. Baldwin, A. L. *Behavior and Development in Children.* Holt, Rinehart and Winston, New York, 1955.
2. Baltzell, E. D. *Philadelphia Gentlemen,* Free Press, Glencoe, Ill., 1958.
3. Bandura, A., and Walters, R. H. *Social Learning and Personality Development.* Holt, Rinehart and Winston, New York, 1963.
4. Barber, R. E. *Marriage and the Family.* McGraw-Hill, New York, 1953.
5. Blood, R. O. Long range causes and consequences of the employment of married women. *J. Marr. and Fam., 27,* 1965, 43-47.
6. Blood, R. O. The husband and wife relationship. (In) *The Employed Mother in America.* Nye, I. E., and Hoffmam, L. W. (Eds.). Rand McNally, 1963.
7. Blood, R. O., and Wolfe, D. M. *Husbands and Wives.* Free Press, Glencoe, Ill. 1960.
8. Bawlby, J. The nature of a child's tie to his mother. *Internat. J. Psychoanal., 39,* 1958, 173-182.
9. Bronfenbrenner. U. Some familial antecedents of responsibility and leadership. (In) *Adolescents in Leadership and Interpersonal Behavior,* Petrullo, L., and Bass, B. M. (Eds.). Holt, Rinehart and Winston, New York, 1961.
10. Child, I. L. Socialization. (In) *Handbook of Social Psychology, Volume 2,* Lindzey, G. (Ed.). Addison-Wesley, Cambridge, 1954.
11. Clausen, J. A., and Williams, J. R. Sociological Correlates of Child Behavior. (In) *Yearbook Nat. Soc. Stud. Educ., Part 1, 62,* University of Chicago Press, Chicago, 1963.
12. Drake, St. C., and Clayton, H. R. *Black Metropolis.* Harcourt Brace, New York, 1945.
13. Duvall, E. M. Conceptions of parenthood. *Amer. J. Sociol., 52,* 1946, 193-203.
14. Dyer, E. D. Parenthood as crisis: a re-study. *Marr. and Fam. Liv., 25,* 1963, 196-201.
15. Fagin, H. Social behavior of young children in the Kibbutz. *J. Abnorm. Soc. Psychol., 56,* 1958, 112-129.
16. Frazier, F. The Negro family in America. (In) *The Family, Its Functions and Destiny.* Harper Bros., New York, 1959.
17. Hobbs, D. F. Parenthood as crisis: a third study. *J. Marr. and Fam., 27,* 1965, 367-372.
18. Irvine, E. Observations on the aims and methods of child rearing in communal settlements in Israel. *Hum. Relat., 5,* 1952, 247-275.
19. Kephard, W. M. *The Family, Society and the Individual.* Houghton Mifflin, Boston, 1966.
20. Kohn, M. L. Social class and parental values. *Amer. J. Sociol., 64,* 1959, 337-351.
21. Kohn, M. L. Social class and the exercise of parental authority. *Amer. Sociol. Rev., 24,* 1959, 352-366.
22. LeVine, R. A., and LeVine B. L. Nyansongo: A Gusii community in Kenya. (In) *Six Cultures. Studies of Child Rearing,* Whiting, B. B. (Ed.), John Wiley, New York, 1963.
23. Lidz, T. *The Family and Human Adaptation.* International Universities Press, New York, 1963.
24. Minturn, L., and Hitchcock, J. The Rajputs of Khalapur, India. (In) *Six Cultures. Studies of Child Rearing,* Whiting, B. B. (Ed.), John Wiley, New York, 1963.
25. McKinley, D. G. *Social Class and Family Life.* Free Press, Collier-MacMillan, London, 1964.
26. Myers, G. C. Labor force participation of working mothers. *J. Marr. and Fam., 26,* 1964, 306-311.

27. Nash, J. The father in contemporary culture and current psychological literature. *Child Develpm., 26,* 1965, 262-293.
28. Parsons, T., and Bales R. F. *Family-Socialization and Interaction Process.* Free Press, Glencoe, 1955.
29. Siegel, A. E., et al. Dependence and independence in children. (In) *The Employed Mother in America.* Nye, I. E., and Hoffman, L. W. (Eds.) Rand McNally, 1963.
30. Spiro, M. E. *Children of the Kibbutz.* Harvard University Press, Cambridge, 1958.
31. Strodtbeck, F. L. Family interaction, values and achievement. (In) *Talent and Society,* McClelland, D., et al. (Eds.), D. Van Nostrand, Princeton, 1958.
32. Sullivan, H. S. *The Interpersonal Theory of Psychiatry.* W. W. Norton, New York, 1953.
33. Sussman, M. B. The help pattern in the middle-class family. *Sourcebook in Marriage and Family.* Houghton Mifflin, 1963.
34. Whiting, B. B. (Ed.). *Six Cultures. Studies of Child Rearing.* John Wiley, New York, 1963.
35. Whiting, J. W. M. Sorcery, sin, and the super-ego: A cross cultural study of some mechanisms of social control. (In) *Nebraska Symposium on motivation.* University of Nebraska Press, Lincoln, 1959.

CHAPTER 13

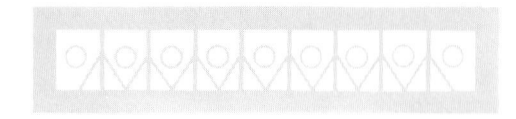

EARLY ADOLESCENCE

PART 1—GENERAL OVERVIEW OF ADOLESCENCE

COGNITIVE PROCESSES IN ADOLESCENCE

It is not possible to say exactly when adolescence begins and when it ends. It is defined culturally as much as developmentally. Two individuals at a particular so called "developmental stage" will receive widely differing patterns of reinforcement from their elders and friends for various behaviors, depending on the culture in which they live. Sexual behavior at age 12 may be sanctioned in Samoa but punished in Nebraska. Changes, however, do go on during the period generally defined as "adolescence" by the American culture. The developmental changes, associated with adolescence in America, involve the further growth of cognitive processes, including advances in the ability to think generally, abstractly, and symbolically. They include the perfection of the child's ability to consider hypothetical or imaginary cases and to assume the perspective of someone other than himself.[21, 22] This ability, called empathy or the capacity to assume the role of another, is an important aspect of social living. Intelligence continues to develop also and for many may reach its peak at late adolescence.[21, 22] The growth of intellectual, cognitive abilities facilitates advances in moral behavior, particularly the ability of the child to "behave" in order to maintain the respect of other persons as well as to avoid self-condemnation. In the realm of moral judgment, some children begin to see the value of human life as a universal human right based on community welfare, or as sacred, representing a universal human value of respect for the individual.[1, 16]

PHYSICAL PROCESSES — PUBERTY

Certainly the attainment of physical puberty plays an important part in the life of the child during what we call in this culture the "early adolescent period." Puberty represents the beginning of reproductive sexual maturity; it is during this period that physiological and biochemical changes in boys and girls make reproduction possible. These changes, following the appearance of secondary sexual characteristics such as pubic hair and breasts, include the beginning of menstruation in girls and the appearance of fertile sperm in boys. Physically, puberty occurs sometime between the ages of ten and 15, with 12 to 14 being a more common age range. Physical puberty usually takes place earlier in girls than in boys.[10] Due to nutritional and other health factors physical puberty is occurring earlier now than formerly.

Puberty certainly affects sexuality since it makes pregnancy possible, and with puberty, the child's thought and feelings about sex become more intense. Sexuality, however, begins long before puberty. Young children can obtain pleasant sensations from manipulating their own genitals or by rubbing against other people, or from active stimulation by others.[28] Children are capable of having intercourse before puberty and do so in some foreign cultures, as well as in some parts of our own.[27, 28] Sexuality, with or without intercourse, can start before reproduction is possible and can go on long beyond the age when reproduction has ceased to be possible. Nevertheless the beginning of menstruation and the production of fertile sperm, the appearance of secondary sexual characteristics, and the effects of hormone production, have a strong psychological influence on the children experiencing these changes. The specific psychological import of these biological changes however, are largely culturally defined and determined.[19, 27] These physical changes are a cause of concern to most adolescents, although there are individual differences in how children react to their bodily changes during puberty. These differences are chiefly due to how others react to the changes. Does the mother show anxiety when her daughter shows signs of becoming a woman or does she reward the daughter by showing pride? Does the father laugh at his son when the son wants to shave, or does the father buy him a razor?

SOCIAL AND INTERPERSONAL PROCESS

Friendship Formation

Much has been made of the role and power of the peer group and of defiance of parental standards in adolescence. Linked to this supposed defiance of parental standards and conformity to the behavior of peers has been the representation of adolescence as a period of stress and strain, often culminating in acts of juvenile delinquency. In fact, long before adolescence, in late middle childhood, the peer group has already become an important source of rewards and punishments, and a source of behavior to imitate.[1,6] There is no evidence of any sudden increase in friendship formation in adolescence; it seems to be a smoothly growing and smoothly consolidating phenomenon.[1,6] In many cases the friends of the adolescent are the children of his parents' friends. However, as the rewarding power of friends accumulates it becomes increasingly important and the standards of same age peers can be vital behavioral influences.

Antisocial Behavior

Despite childish escapades, the predominant peer group values can be the same as parental values. Even the so-called hedonistic behaviors of the adolescent frowned on by parents, such as fast driving, drinking, use of drugs, and sexual behavior, may often be a more or less direct imitation of either the parents' actual behavior or the parents' fantasies. Law-breaking delinquency often begins not in adolescence but in late middle childhood.[1] By adolescence, however, the child may be too independent for the parents to control, and society may punish, through the law, offenses that were previously punished by parents and teachers. The contention that early adolescence is a particular period of antisocial behavior is at least partly questionable. It is true that some adolescents may often be involved in car theft, petty larceny, drug use, or similar crimes. What may more often be the case is that the adolescent has acquired the cognitive capacity to articulate his unhappiness with parents and society in conceptual terms. He may now argue in favor of LSD, or "pot," and/or sex, or denounce his parents' generation for using the atom bomb or for being materialistic. Previously, he was limited to screaming "I hate you!", running away from home, or not doing his homework. Now he may challenge his parents' values and produce emotion provoking arguments against them due to an increased cognitive capacity.

By adolescence the child is much more able to articulate his feelings and demands which may conflict with those of the parents. However, the majority of adolescents, although largely ignored by the more sensation seeking mass media of communication, may march rather meekly down the road of socialization, while television and newspapers play up the deviants. Most adolescents accept cultural values and are on the road to academic competition, a steady job, and marriage.[5,6] For every adolescent who turns on, drops out and tunes in, a hundred to a thousand turn off, drop in and tune out. Some, of course, fall in between. Adolescence has its stresses, but so does every other period of life, from the time of toilet training to senility. (A detailed discussion of delinquency can be found in the chapter on later adolescence).

The Question of Identity

Everyone has heard about adolescent alienation, the adolescent as a marginal man, and particularly his search for values and identity. We shall have more to say about identity in the next chapter. These problems do face the early adolescent. However, the question of "Who and what am I?" begins at age two or three and not at 12.[12] The process of identity formation and the development of concepts about the self are lifelong. They may or may not become acute problems in early adolescence.[12, 30] There is evidence that as cognitive processes develop and as experience accumulates, the acquisition of selfhood or identity need not become major problems. In fact, the sense of identity and self becomes more stable and less open to fluctuation in adolescence.[32] It is worthwhile to stress the general continuity of development during adolescence rather than the sudden shifts occurring in a minority of cases. It is true, however, that the greater cognitive capacity of the young adolescent may place his formulation of questions and thoughts about his identity and selfhood on a new and more complex level. Rather than facing a *sudden* identity crisis the adolescent may be manifesting a *new way* of thinking about personal problems of many years' duration. These problems are more likely to become conscious and overt. Now, since he is capable of thinking about himself in general and abstract ways, the question of selfhood and identity may become ones which preoccupy his thoughts.

Personality

Finally, personality continues to develop in adolescence. By personality we mean the collectivity of behavioral dispositions in a child (or adult). Behavioral dispositions are more or less consistent and habitual ways of feeling, thinking, or responding in *similar* environmental situations. They are originally acquired in a context of imitation and social reinforcement. These dispositions are sometimes called "traits of personality" and many of them seem to be well developed by ten years of age or even earlier.[12, 20] It is often possible to predict many ways in which an adult will behave, what sorts of dispositions a person will have as an adult, on the basis of his traits at age ten or before.[20] Modifications take place throughout life but basic personality traits or dispositions may develop early in childhood. If they are consistently reinforced then they will tend to persist and changes will occur only if there are strong shifts in the nature of models or patterns of reward.

The adolescent has to prepare himself educationally; he has to get along with others of his age as well as adults; he has to prepare for a job or career. He has to learn to cope with his feelings of lust and desires for interpersonal intimacy. (These last two concepts are discussed in more detail in the section on Sex and Interpersonal Processes, and in Study 13.7.) Nevertheless, he may approach these new instrumental, emotional, and interpersonal problems in some of the same basic ways that he approached and dealt with earlier problems and adaptational demands.[26] Many personality changes in adolescence occur in areas and ways demanded by the culture.[12, 30] Again, for most, continuity rather than sudden transformation is the rule. Certainly there are stresses imposed on the personalities of some adolescents due to broken families, incompatible demands, the inability to adjust sexually, or to find meaning in life. The stresses may lead to personality changes, abnormal behavior, delinquency, or to new constructive solutions. The same, however, may be said for all periods of life. The need to learn new ways of behaving to meet new demands of life is a continuous condition.

ADOLESCENCE AS A SOCIAL PHENOMENON—ROLE AND STATUS

A *role* is a set of behaviors conforming to the culturally defined expectations which relate to a particular status in society. *Status* refers to a position in society defined by a network of privileges and obligations. Being a child has a certain status, as does being a father or an executive. Roles, to simplify the definition above, refer to the behaviors expected of people who have a certain status. Every status has its associated role behaviors. When people act in accordance with expected role behaviors they generally experience reward. Executives are expected to behave differently from janitors or waiters; fathers are not expected to behave like children; and grandmothers are not supposed to act like prostitutes. Adolescents have a different status from infants, toddlers, or first graders; they also have different obligations and privileges. They are expected to, and do, behave differently from either young children or adults.[27] Fourteen-year-old, middle-class adolescents are expected neither to play eight hours nor to work eight hours a day, and they do not. Role behaviors have to be learned as do other behaviors. There are models of such behaviors and deviations from expected behaviors are punished while conformity to them is rewarded.

One acquires some types of status in life by simply attaining certain ages, rather than by earning them. The status of "child" or of "adolescent" is of this nature. One does not earn this kind of status, it is "ascribed" or conferred. The roles (expected behaviors) assigned to them, however, have to be learned like any other role behaviors. Other statuses have to be earned. One has to do some very special things to be a saint, a Ph.D., an executive, or a "professional expert and consultant." Whether a status is ascribed or earned, however, the role behaviors which accompany it have to be learned. Social learning theory, as we saw earlier, describes how such learning takes place.

Adolescence as a Cultural Invention

The status and corresponding role of the adolescent is a cultural phenomenon. Americans, by and large, recognize an ambiguous period of time between childhood and adulthood and call it "adolescence." The adolescent has a certain status, not always the one he wants, and certain role behaviors are expected of him, although he may sometimes fail to fulfill them. In fact some adolescents institutionalize for themselves some statuses and roles which may be their parents' despair. The status of social critic or the role of civil disobedience doesn't please everyone. Neither does the status of "hippie," "yippie," or the role of "cultural dropout." The question is, what sorts of models will the child imitate and what will he find most reinforcing?

Some cultures define no period of adolescence. That is, they have no special statuses or roles corresponding to what we call adolescence. In parts of Africa or Asia childhood continues until sometime around physical puberty, when a special ceremony catapults the child into adulthood. Childhood may be a preparation for adulthood. A circumcision ceremony, or some other puberty rite, or rite of passage which may take only a short period of time, confers adult status. The former child is then expected to take on the obligations and behaviors of adulthood.[19]

Adolescence, therefore, is a cultural invention and exists only where it is culturally useful. In a complex, urban, industrial society a long period of education is needed. The 12 year-old would make a poor nuclear physicist and a sorry junior executive. The urban industrial society does not need the 13 year old to run its high powered machinery. Child labor is not needed. Most 15 year olds are incapable of sustaining the difficult emotional demands of modern marriage. In fact, the divorce rate of persons married at the comparatively ripe age of 17 or 18 is very high.[13] Consequently, it is culturally useful to have an extended waiting period between childhood and adulthood. Therefore, the 13 or 15 year old is often not encouraged to imitate adults and is negatively reinforced for many adult like behaviors. He is reinforced for behaviors which fall somewhere between those of the child and those of the adult.

Roles and Development in Adolescence

Even though he may be in some ways reproductively and intellectually mature, the human being from 12 to 18 has a special status in our culture, and special behaviors are expected of him. He is not given the status of the adult and yet is recognized to be beyond childhood. The adolescent is expected to go to school, to refrain from becoming pregnant, if a girl, and from impregnating females, if a boy. The adolescent is expected to *prepare* for adulthood emotionally and instrumentally. Development during adolescence is essentially the development of cognitive, emotional, interpersonal, and instrumental skills, many of which are to be used later upon assuming the adult roles of a fulltime job and marriage. Aspects of personality are further developed which are part of the behaviors rewarded in adolescence and also useful as later behaviors needed in adulthood. Some of these involve expanded interpersonal capacities such as being able to understand the feeling, attitudes, and behaviors of others while responding to them sympathetically.

Feelings of identity may also be consolidated and acquire new labels and meanings. Intimacy, friendship, peer group belonging and activity are increased and experimentation in sexual behavior occurs. Interpersonal skills are sharpened. For some, formal learning proceeds at a great rate and the ability to handle formal concepts, abstractions, and generalizations improves. The adolescent may gain greater intellectual latitude, as a result of experience and education, leading to a greater ability to question, abstract and generalize. He or she may become very religious or very agnostic, promiscuous or afraid of sex. The adolescent may become skeptical, or a blind fanatic. Or instead of experiencing great existential turmoil, many adolescents may go through the processes of socialization and internalization without too much thought or pain. It is probably a rare adolescent, however, who never questions the meaning of his life, or the validity of some of the assumptions which he has learned.

The development of the adolescent depends on his biological endowment and his social learning history, including his cognitive and emotional growth. What he becomes also depends on what is demanded of him by the culture as transmitted by the behavior of adults and peers. The interaction of all these factors determines how the adolescent resolves the issues and questions which he or she must face. In addition to responding to external models (now often his friends) and external rewards and punishments, the adolescent has acquired cognitive skills. He is able to think and to evaluate. He has also gained considerable control over his own behavior by a process called *internalization,* discussed in the next chapter.

CONFORMITY TO BEHAVIORAL DEMANDS—THE PEER GROUP

The relationship of the adolescent to adults undergoes changes as he or she is assigned new obligations and gains new privileges, that is, the behaviors for which he is rewarded or punished change as he grows older. Ties to same-age friends may become stronger, and relations to parents change as the adolescent moves closer to adult status. Parents may sometimes be frowned upon, considered old fogies, admired, feared, and loved in turn. Parents can become sources of embarrassment, pride, support, or obstruction at different times, and sometimes all at once. Their value as models or sources of social reinforcement fluctuates and changes. The peer group can become a more potent force for modeling. Fads come and go and there may be some close behavioral conformity, along certain lines, for members of the same age groups to which any adolescent informally belongs. Close friendships may be formed which can be sources of great satisfaction and much more stable than friendships at earlier ages.[27] In essence, adolescence may bring about new approaches and new orientations to interpersonal relationships, chiefly those of stability. The adolescent begins to learn to relate to others of his own age in mutually satisfying ways. In preparation for later life he learns to get his rewards from people other than the parents.

Intimacy and Sexuality

The adolescent has to learn new behaviors concerning intimacy and sexuality. Some of the restrictions placed on sexual behavior are partially lifted in adolescence as certain sexual responses are no longer suppressed. There are pressures on the adolescent girl to prove that she is sexually attractive, that she can get and hold boy friends. There are pressures on the male adolescent to prove his manhood by "making out." He may be rewarded through his popularity with girls, and attempt to engage in sexual intercourse. At the same time there are avoidance reactions due to fears about "reputation," pregnancy, venereal disease, and what is considered "right" in sexual conduct. Obviously, this area involves not just physical sexuality and feelings of lust, but also psychological behaviors involving the formation of new social bonds experienced as feelings of intimacy and sharing.[30] Social bonds, originally formed with parents and siblings, are now extended to others.

Instrumental Activities

The adolescent is expected to prepare for adult life by learning instrumental activities. For the male this means chiefly education in public school, which will gain him entrance to college or will prepare him for a good job. For the female, preparation for future roles may require both education, in order to hold a job, and learning the behavioral skills which will help her to find a husband and maintain a home and family. Of course, boys must learn family skills, but this is an informal process, and almost covert in our culture. Instrumental, money making activities are those which will later bring rewards to males, whereas females will gain their chief rewards, in most instances, from taking care of children and husbands.

Cognitive Changes

Relatively sophisticated cognitive activities are needed to engage successfully in the behaviors required in adolescence. No longer is simple behavioral responding satisfactory. The adolescent must know how his girl friend feels about him and why, if he is to influence her behavior toward him, satisfy her needs, or both. He must be able to put himself in the place of others and make complex inferences.[30] Adolescents must begin to learn to think and feel like adults, and start to assume some independent direction in their lives.

Self-Esteem

The meeting of these interpersonal demands, as noted previously, will affect the personality dispositions of the adolescent. Repeated successes in solving life problems may lead to high self-esteem, whereas continued failures may lead to low self-esteem. Self-esteem is an individual's evaluation of himself. There is no need to assume any overall single level of self-esteem. An adolescent may value himself or herself quite highly in some areas and consider himself average or poor in others.[32] He may be proud of himself as a student but feel incompetent socially. If he can judge the reactions of other people with some objectivity, the adolescent learns how they value him. These judgments of others as well as his objective successes and failures help the adolescent learn how to value himself in various areas of activity.[18] Successes lead to rewards; failures do not. This process, of course, starts early in life but becomes more firmly consolidated in adolescence as more and more events related to self-evaluation are experienced. Self-esteem may fluctuate rather markedly in earlier childhood as a result of failures and successes, acceptances, and rejections. Slowly, with the passage of time, often culminating in adolescence, a more stable level of self-evaluation or self-esteem emerges and this level of self-esteem becomes less easily influenced by momentary occurrences. If an adolescent is usually an A student, high self-regard in the area of scholastic ability does not suffer a marked lowering if one test is failed during the junior year in high school. Self-esteem largely depends on cumulative experiences of chiefly obtaining rewards or of failing to get them in various activities.

Self-esteem is only one part of the self concept. The self concept is made up of all the attitudes and cognitions a person has about himself. In time, as a child learns to label himself in certain ways, he forms cognitive conceptions of himself. That is, he knows things about himself as he knows about other people, things, and ideas. Again, a child, adolescent, or adult often has several self concepts rather than one overall self concept.[9, 32] The child learns many things about himself, whether others share these views or not. These cognitive representations which he has about himself make up his self conceptions, his understanding of who and what he is. Self-esteem is the evaluative aspect of the self concept; it represents the positive or negative value which the person places on what he believes about himself.

Conflicts in Adolescence

One of the difficulties of adolescent living arises from the fact that the culture is ambiguous about how it expects adolescents to behave. With this ambiguity are associated uncertainties and even conflicts.[27] These conflicts are largely a function of the fact that adolescents are neither rewarded or punished very consistently. The adolescent is neither child nor an adult and it is not clear when he has passed from one status to another. Our culture lacks sharp points of transition and we have no rites of passage or initiation ceremonies involving change from adolescence to adulthood.[19, 27] Parents differ in their demands and expectations and some may be inconsistent about how they expect the adolescent to behave. Consequently parents are inconsistent in what they reward and punish adolescents for. Adolescents may be expected to be dependent in some ways and independent in others. Some may be required both to earn money and to go to school. In some groups the adolescent boy may be expected to surpass his father's education, but not by too much. An adolescent may be encouraged to show independence of thought but not too many "dangerous" ideas which may frighten his parents.

The adolescent girls may be expected to be sexually desirable but not to engage in much sexual behavior. Her mother may buy her a "sexy" dress and makeup but become angry when she stays out too late. How much and what kind of sex is allowed, when, with whom, and under what circumstances, is often not clear. Some adults demand that the adolescent be idealistic but still realistic. These are only some examples of the uncertainties which adolescents must face in our culture. It is difficult for the adolescent to behave in ways which will consistently lead to reward and which will consistently allow him to escape punishment.

The status of the adolescent in terms of privileges and obligations is also confused and he can seldom be sure which behaviors are the right and expected ones. He may often be confused even about what he himself really likes and enjoys. Furthermore, since parents and peers may sometimes differ on these points, conflict may often be the lot of the adolescent.[5, 6, 10] What the parents reward his friends may not. He may have to choose between the approval of his parents or the scorn of his friends. Some students of adolescence, however, may have overemphasized the amount and severity of actual conflict and turmoil. Many adolescents do detect a general sense of what is expected of them; when the values of parents and friends are both considered they will still be closer than the values of individuals from say, a Bantu vs. a Spanish culture. A common matrix of experience exists for all persons who have grown up in the American culture, diverse as its parts may be.

PART 2—
DEVELOPMENTAL ISSUES IN EARLY ADOLESCENCE

COGNITIVE DEVELOPMENT IN EARLY ADOLESCENCE

Piaget's Period of Formal Operations

According to Piaget, at 11 or 12 years of age the "period of propositional or formal operations" begins and it is completed by age 15. At 15 years of age the child has passed from the previous "period of concrete operations" to thinking and problem solving in terms of adult logic. The chief feature of this last period of cognitive growth, according to Piaget, is the development of the ability to reason in a hypothetical way. The ability to accept data or propositions as purely hypothetical enables the adolescent to engage in hypothetico-deductive reasoning. The child between 11 and 15 develops the ability to think in terms of possible rather than "here and now actual" states of affairs.[21, 22] If he can for the moment imagine that a situation exists, then he can also begin to reason about what might follow from such a situation. That is, he can make deductions from a hypothetical state of affairs, some assumption that he entertains for the moment. This is the method of hypothetico-deductive thinking. Study 13.1 gives some examples of this new ability which is in contrast to the more concrete thinking of the younger child.

ACCEPTANCE OF HYPOTHESES

STUDY 13.1

Piaget has presented the following proposition to children at various ages: "I am very glad I do not eat onions, for if I liked them I would always be eating them and I hate unpleasant things." The child who thinks *concretely* says that this statement is wrong either because onions do not taste bad or because it is wrong to dislike onions. Children who are 13 or 14 do not quibble about the statement in this way but are able to grasp the contradiction. They can understand that there is an innate contradiction between the possibility of liking onions and the possibility that they could then be unpleasant.

The deduction from the hypothesis that onions may taste good is that they would not then be unpleasant. Piaget also points out that when eight- to 12-year-old children are allowed to experiment with a pendulum to see how it works, they do so in a haphazard way. They may vary its length or the initial push and then try to formulate any correspondence or relationships which they note. From 12 to 15, he claims, children, after a few trials, formulate all the possible hypotheses about what variables may be operating. They then use these hypotheses to set up what amounts to little experiments to test the validity of possible relationships among the variables. They no longer proceed from the actual observed results to the theoretical, but rather start with the theoretical and go on from there to verify or refute the hypotheses. The children's logic, in this case, is not just concerned with concrete events or objects, but with propositions, hypotheses, or concepts.

Piaget, J. *Logic and Psychology.* Basic Books, New York, 1957.

Piaget makes clear that the development of processes of formal thought reaches its completion during adolescence. He wrote: "The adolescent, unlike the child, is an individual who thinks beyond the present and forms theories about everything, delighting especially in considerations of what is not. . . . This reflective thought, which is characteristic of the adolescent, exists from the age of 11 to 12 years, from the time, that is, when the subject becomes capable of reasoning in a hypothetico-deductive manner, that is, on the basis of simple assumptions which have no necessary relation to reality or to the subjects' beliefs, and from the time when he relies on the necessary validity of an inference as opposed to agreement of the conclusions with experience."[22]

Piaget also considers this last period of logical thought to be the period of symbolic intelligence. He considers the development of the ability to think in terms of symbols to be one of the essential conditions for being able to operate at this formal, logical level. Real or concrete entities are now represented symbolically by the child and he can thus transcend spatial and temporal limitations. Symbols also enable him to think on a plane detached from concrete reality. He can think about temperatures on Venus or the mathematical definition of infinity.[21, 22]

The symbols of language and mathematics can be used, beginning in early adolescence, to represent what *might* be the case, what *might* happen, and what outcomes *might* be. The adolescent now can speculate about the possible outcomes of his actions or those of others, and behave accordingly.

Formal Thinking and Age

Since Piaget has so firmly tied the *beginning* of formal thinking to early adolescence, specifically age 11 to 12, it is worthwhile to look at some experimental evidence in this area. Study 13.2 outlines part of one such study.

AGE AND FORMAL THINKING IN THE VERBAL AREA

STUDY 13.2

Donald Case and J. M. Collinson were interested in finding out whether Piaget was correct in his belief that formal thinking (formal operations) is mostly absent until an age of about 11 or 12. They also wished to test his assumption that children by 15 years of age have mastered techniques of formal thinking and operations and utilize that mode of cognition when faced with the need to reason. They restricted their study to the verbal area.

Case and Collinson presented their subjects, boys and girls from ages seven to 18, with written materials in history, geography, and literature. Each child was asked questions about the material and was scored as giving an *intuitive* answer (lowest level of thinking), a *concrete* answer (next highest level), or a *formal* answer (highest level).

For instance, after reading a passage from the History of England about Dunstan (a Church reformer) to the child, the child was asked: "Was Dunstan a good man? Why? If the child merely said: "Yes, he was," and gave no reason, he was again asked, "Why?" If he then failed to reply or said something like: "Because he was a good man and did as he was told, so that made him good," the child was said to be giving an intuitive answer. Such a child had not yet reached the concrete level. If, on the other hand, the child replied: "Yes, he was a good man because he made the Church better," he was scored as giving a concrete answer. He was at the level of concrete operations, giving a very specific and concrete example of why Dunstan was good. A child was scored as having reached the level of formal operations if he or she gave an answer such as: "He was good in some ways, but not in others, because he was trying to make the Church powerful, but I don't think he was right in being cruel to those who disagreed with him." Here the child is using words which are also concepts that stand for complex behaviors. Examples of these are: "power," "cruelty," and "dissent." Such a child can understand that Dunstan was neither all good nor all bad. He can reason that although it is a legitimate aim to make the Church powerful (a hypothesis), it does not necessarily follow that it is desirable to cruelly squash dissent (deduction). Hence, the requirements for a formal answer, indicating formal thinking, are met.

The results were quite clear. Age 11 was the earliest age at which children gave more formal or concrete answers, rather than intuitive answers. (By age 11 they were also giving more concrete than intuitive ones.) Between 11 and 13 years of age the children were giving more formal answers than either intuitive or concrete. However, the combined number of intuitive or concrete answers was greater than or equal to the number of formal answers given between 11 and 13. From 14 to 18, the children overwhelmingly gave formal answers. There was, from 14 to 18, still a very small amount of intuitive and concrete thinking, but formal answers outweighed these about 11 to one.

All of the above results seem to support Piaget. However, the answers of the children from seven to ten show that they give *almost* as many formal as concrete answers. They give slightly more intuitive answers than any other kind, but their answers are fairly well distributed across intuitive, concrete, and formal. It would appear that many children are at times able to engage in formal verbal reasoning before age 11. Further, through ages seven to ten, 11, 12, 13, 14, and 15, there is a steady increase in the tendency to think formally rather than a sudden appearance of this new way of thinking. By 16 increase becomes slower since formal reasoning is about the only way of thinking used by the average adolescent of 16.

The development of the tendency to think formally, then, seems to start before age 11 and to develop gradually, but steadily, until it reaches full dominance at age 15 or 16. Piaget was right in considering the age of 11 as being somehow important in the emergence of formal reasoning. However, that may be roughly the age when it becomes a *favored* way of thinking, not when it *first* begins to develop or begins to be used. Its development may start by seven or even earlier. Formal reasoning does develop steadily until in the average adolescent it almost completely replaces other modes of reasoning.

Case, D., and Collison, J. W. The development of formal thinking in verbal comprehension. *Brit. J. Educ. Psychol., 31-32,* 1961-62, 103-111.

The young adolescent (11, 12, 13, or 14 years of age) may, therefore, depending on the occasion, think either intuitively, concretely, or formally. The older he is, the more likely he or she is to think formally. How soon formal thinking begins, or becomes predominant, may be a function not only of experience but of intelligence, social class, ethnic background, learning, and related factors. Some, taking issue with Piaget, have contended that almost any way of thinking can be taught to children at any age, after the child has learned to use language. They consider this to be particularly true if the teacher is clever and inventive enough. Psychologists of this persuasion contend that proper conditions of instruction would enable children to think symbolically and formally at an early age. An exposition of this point of view appears in Study 13.3.

TOWARD A THEORY OF INSTRUCTION

STUDY 13.3

Jerome Bruner has argued that "readiness" is a mischievous half truth. He believes that proper methods of instruction can teach the child appropriate versions of any intellectual skill at almost any age. He contends that teaching and learning must deal with continuity in change and not with the assumption of fixed ages or states of readiness. This is also essentially the social learning position.

Bruner feels that intellectual development is marked by the increasing ability to deal with several alternatives simultaneously, to attend to several sequences in the same period of time, and to allocate time and attention in a manner appropriate to multiple demands. He believes that these skills can be taught and do not have to depend on experience and maturation. In fact Bruner has devised ingenious ways to enable young children (preadolescents) to solve and understand fairly complex mathematical and spatial problems.

Bruner agrees with Piaget that intellectual growth involves an increasing capacity to say to oneself and others, by means of words and symbols, what one has done and will do. However, he feels that intellectual development depends on a systematic program where a tutor teaches a learner. Through the medium of proper inventive instruction, he contends, the learner, particularly by using language, can store a representation of events internally. This brings cognitive order into his experienced environment. To Bruner, youth is not a bar to formal reasoning: it is a challenge to be overcome by creative teaching, particularly through the utilization of visual teaching aids. Being able to visualize relationships helps the child to reason even at an early age.

Bruner, J. S. *Toward a Theory of Instruction.* Harvard University Press, Cambridge, 1966.

UNDERSTANDING THE ROLES AND PERSPECTIVES OF OTHERS IN EARLY ADOLESCENCE

Piaget believes that internalized abstract concepts become more influential than immediate concrete sense impressions as cognitive processes mature. This growing dominance of formal thought is associated with a child's ability to shift or change his thoughts from one aspect of a situation to another. The ability to shift cognitively also involves a most important process, that of being able to understand the role of another. This means that the early adolescent is now able to put himself psychologically into someone else's shoes. He is not only capable of *reacting* empathically or vicariously, an ability acquired by age five or earlier, but he can *understand* the viewpoint of another person.[8, 9, 18]

Behavioral expectations enter in an important way, into the definition of the self and the further formation of identity. The adolescent learns to represent to himself what the possible behaviors in his environment are, what his role is, what others are doing, and how they are behaving towards him. This helps to consolidate his sense of identity and selfhood.[18] He learns the expected behaviors associated with being an "adolescent," "friend," "mother," "father," "teacher," or "boss" in a more conceptual and formal way. This conceptual understanding of what behaviors are expected of him and of others allows him to predict the behavior of others. It also permits him to anticipate their actions, and to predict the possible results of his own actions. He is no longer limited to perceiving things only from his own point of view, although he may do so exclusively and passionately sometimes. Despite some strong emotional commitments to what he thinks is the right way to behave, the young adolescent can often comprehend the point of view and roles of others, even if he rejects them. He may then, at least sometimes, act accordingly.[9] Study 13.4 describes part of an investigation in this area.

COGNITIVE ASPECTS OF ROLE-TAKING IN CHILDREN

STUDY 13.4

Melvin H. Feffer and Vivian Gourevitch tested Piaget's contention that early adolescent children have reached a stage of cognitive development where they can shift both cognitive perspectives and roles. They predicted that children from about ages ten to 13 would be superior to children from ages six to nine in both the ability to structure the world cognitively and the ability to assume different social perspectives (to understand someone else's behavior from that person's point of view).

To measure the ability to understand the behavior of others they used a projective task based upon the Make a Picture Story Test. The MAPS test consists of a series of scenes into which the subject can place cut-outs of children, adults, and animals. Each child was asked to tell a story to at least two scenes after placing at least three figures into each scene. He was then asked to retell his story as it would appear from the point of view of each of the figures he used. The experimenter would say: "Now make believe you are——" (the father, sister, dog, and so forth), and then again, "Tell the story again as if you were——." The child had to change from his own perspective or point of view to that of another. He had to try to understand the behavior of other people from the points of view of these others.

A scoring scheme was made up using five categories. The categories formed a continuum from: one little change in description of the figures no matter from whose perspective it was told, to five, where at least two of the figures were presented quite differently and from the point of view of their own internal orientation. For instance, the following story scored in category five: First telling the story from the father's point of view, the child said that the mother thought the father to be unhappy because his face looked sad. The same child described the mother, from the mother's point of view, as tired because of certain things the mother had done. From the father's point of view, the child noted that the father thought that the mother didn't seem too pleased to see him. Such descriptions show a strong ability to shift perspectives.

The results showed that the ten to 13 year olds were much better at understanding the behavior of others than six to nine year olds were. That is, the young adolescents were cognitively more able to comprehend behavior through the eyes of different people than the preadolescents.

Curiously enough, however, ten to 11 year olds were better at this than 12 to 13 year olds! Further, the more verbally intelligent the child was, the better he was at shifting perspectives. Nevertheless, with intelligence partialed out (eliminated) as a factor, ten to 13 year olds showed a much better ability to understand the viewpoints of others than six to nine year olds.

Feffer, M. H., and Gourevitch, V. Cognitive aspects of role-taking in children. *J. Pers.*, 28, 1960, 383-396.

MORAL JUDGMENTS AND EARLY ADOLESCENCE — COGNITIVE ASPECTS

According to Kohlberg, moral *judgment* does not become truly moral until early adolescence. While moral *conduct* seems to develop early, morality of judgment cannot come until the child is sufficiently cognitively advanced. It is relatively easy to teach a 6 year old boy not to hit girls smaller than himself. All he has to do is identify "girls" and "smaller" and be punished for striking "smaller girls." A 6 year old girl can also be taught not to take things which are not hers. All she has to learn is that punishment follows taking what is not hers. Understanding *why* it is wrong to hurt others physically, or *why* it is wrong to steal, is much harder. The acquisition of self-accepted moral principles or an appreciation for individual rights depends on the learning of some rather complex concepts.[16] Such concepts are not acquired by very many children until about age ten, argues Kohlberg, but they seem to have been acquired by most 16 year olds. This is in accordance with Piaget's views on formal thinking. The development of moral judgment is thus seen as a special case of development of formal thought. Formal concepts, moral or otherwise, appear to be mastered between ages 11 and 16.

Kohlberg, like Piaget, believes in invariant developmental sequences. He does feel that learning, high intelligence, or an advantaged background can shorten the time it takes for a type of judgment to appear, but that the order in which the judgmental sequences occur is always the same. Kohlberg's data shows that by age 13 some children are using all of his six moral judgment types.[16] It is not entirely clear that his studies demonstrate the invariance of the sequences, although they do lend some support to that view. Kohlberg's belief that those who reach higher levels of moral judgment represent impersonal, ideal standards may owe as much to moral philosophers, as to the actual cognitive and behavioral phenomena shown by children.

Study 13.5 presents, in more detail, the invariant sequences or stages of moral judgment and behavior outlined by Kohlberg.

STAGES OF MORAL JUDGMENT AND BEHAVIOR

STUDY 13.5

A. Six age-related stages in judging the values of human life are outlined by Kohlberg. The child is believed to go through the following stages in invariant order as he grows older:
1. The value of human life is confused with the value of physical objects. The value of a person's life is based, by the child, on that person's status and physical attributes. The lives of important persons are seen as more valuable than the lives of others.
2. The value of human life is seen as instrumental to the need satisfactions of its possessor or of others. Life is to be valued because human needs can only be satisfied if one is alive.
3. The value of human life is based on empathy and affection of family members to its possessor.
4. The value of human life is seen as sacred in terms of a moral or religious order of rights and duties. Life is valuable because God created man, for instance.
5. The value of life is based on community welfare, and life is seen as a universal human right. This involves complex conceptualization, is truly moral thought, and comes with adolescence.
6. The value of human life is based on its sacredness as representing a universal human value and on respect for the individual. This is truly an abstract and general way of thinking and is unlikely to appear before adolescence.

B. Kohlberg's system of levels and types of moral behavior: These also follow a developmental sequence, although earlier types do not always drop out with increases in the child's age and the appearance of new types.

Level 1 – Premoral Behavior
  type 1 – Punishment and obedience orientation. The child tries to escape punishment by good behavior.
  type 2 – Naive instrumental hedonism. The child does whatever brings him pleasure.

Level 2 – Morality of Conventional Role – Conformity Behavior
  type 3 – Good-boy morality of maintaining good relations and approval. The child behaves to please others.
  type 4-Authority maintaining morality. The child behaves to please others.

Level 3 – Morality of Self-Accepted Moral Principles
  type 5 – Morality of contract. The child behaves because he accepts democratic rules.
  type 6 – Morality of individual principles of conscience. Moral behavior is based on inner conviction.

C. As children progress through the stages of moral thought, their reasons for conforming to adult standards change. These reasons seem to occur at fairly consistent age levels, as follows:

1. Obey rules to avoid punishment – decreases as child gets older.
2. Conform to get rewards – decreases as child gets older.
3. Conform to avoid dislike and disapproval by others – increases from age seven but levels off by 13.
4. Conform to avoid censure by authorities and to avoid guilt – increases from age seven but levels off by 13.
5. Conform to maintain respect of impartial persons – very low until ten and then increases to 16.
6. Conform to avoid self-condemnation – very low until ten and increases to 16.

Kohlberg, L. Development of Moral Character and Ideology. (In) *Review of Child Development Research*, Hoffman, M. L. and Hoffman, L. W. (Eds.). Russell Sage Foundation, New York, 1964.

SEXUAL MATURATION AND EARLY ADOLESCENCE

Sexuality, Biological, and Cultural

As we saw earlier in this chapter, adolescence is a culturally defined period rather than a developmental process based on biological maturation.[6] It is clear that both boys and girls begin to be biologically pubertal before the culture ascribes the role of adolescence to them. This fact is illustrated in Study 13.6 which shows the ages at which genital development in boys and breast bud development in girls has begun. There is a correlation of about .86 between the age of breast bud development and menarche (menstruation) in girls, although for most girls menarche begins about two years after breast bud development.[29] Development of pubic hair and development of some aspects of the uterus and vagina coincide with breast bud development.[31] About a year after the onset of testicular growth many boys show a marked increase in height. This is often called the "adolescent growth spurt." These are biological aspects of early adolescent sexuality.

BIOLOGICAL ADOLESCENT MATURATION IN BOYS AND GIRLS

STUDY 13.6

E. L. Reynolds and J. V. Wines measured genital development in boys and breast bud development in girls to get estimates of the *onset* of biological puberty or adolescence. The figures below are adapted from their studies:

Chronological age		Percent begun sexual maturation
Boys	10	5
	11	35
	12	77
	13	97
Girls	9	18
	10	34
	10.5	50
	11	70
	12	86
	13	100

We can see from these figures that, by ten and a half years of age, about half of the population of girls has begun breast bud development. If menarche (menstruation) follows in about two years, a majority of girls are capable of becoming pregnant slightly after twelve and a half years of age. Our culture, however, hardly approves of sexual intercourse for twelve and a half year old girls; in fact, our culture does not consider such girls ready for much sexual activity of any kind.

> Reynolds, E. L., and Wines, J. V. Physical changes associated with adolescence in boys. *Amer. J. Dis. Child, 82,* 1951, 529-547: Individual differences in physical changes associated with adolescent girls. *Amer. J. Dis. Child., 75,* 1948, 329-350.

The Kinsey report furnishes some interesting corroborating data. At about age 13 less than 20 percent of boys experience orgasm from masturbation or petting, and many less than 30 percent from sexual dreams, heterosexual intercourse, or homosexual activities. Less than 20 percent of 13-year-old American girls are experiencing orgasm from any of the above sources.[14, 15] Of course, percentages may well have changed since Kinsey did his studies. Although they mature earlier in biological sexual terms, girls in early adolescence experience fewer orgasms from any type of sexual activity than boys do. The difference may well be due to social learning factors. There is a double standard and girls are taught to avoid sexual behavior more strongly than boys are. Girls are taught to suppress their sexual tendencies and get less of a chance to learn and practice overt sexual behaviors. Girls are more strongly imbued with attitudes unfavorable to early sexual activity and are taught to worry about their "reputation."[14, 15] Again, this may have partly changed.

As we shall see later, sexual behavior does increase in later adolescence. This acceleration cannot be due chiefly to physical factors, since a majority of female 13 year olds and many males of 13 are capable of intercourse, as well as every other type of sexual activity leading to orgasm and pregnancy. By age 15, dating is well under way, boys and girls are often allowed out alone, and society permits a degree of sexual experimentation. The rise in frequency of sexual behavior in later adolescence is probably the result of a multiplicity of factors. They include: The partial lifting of suppression, increases in various sorts of sexual stimulation, greater freedom of mobility, relaxed parental surveillance, and ability to observe sexually active models (on double dates for instance). Such factors outweigh the influence of hormonal and other biochemical substances.[6] No one can argue that biological, sexual changes are not important in bringing about certain forms of sexual behavior. In fact, they are quite important. How, when, and with whom sexuality is expressed in overt behavior, however, depends on social learning rather than on biological determinants. The biological factors are present by age 13 when there is, in fact, relatively little sexual activity. Social learning factors determine the actual amount of adolescent sexual behavior that will appear and the forms it will take.

SEX AND INTERPERSONAL PROCESSES

Harry Stack Sullivan has been quite astute in discussing the psychological motives associated with sexuality, or as he puts it, "true genital interest," in early adolescence. He was particularly clear in differentiating among who he called: "lust," what he referred to as: "intimacy," and what he termed the "need for personal security" (the need to avoid anxiety).[30] Study 13.7 contains a brief description and explanation of some of Sullivan's views on these motives in early adolescence.

LUST, INTIMACY, AND THE NEED FOR SECURITY

STUDY 13.7

Sullivan argues that lust and the need for intimacy have, in one sense, little in common. In fact he feels that they are quite different. Intimacy involves a necessarily close relationship of mutual concern between two individuals, whereas lust chiefly involves the discharge of sexual, genital tension, through orgasm. An adolescent boy can release lust with a prostitute without intimacy. In one case an orgasm is the reward; in the other, reward depends on mutual liking. Lust and intimacy tend to collide developmentally. In early adolescence when the child is struggling to find satisfactory intimacy, often with a member of the opposite sex for the first time, the child also experiences lustful feelings. The need for shared intimacy and the need for release through orgasm do become intricately combined in adolescents' interpersonal relationships. The needs are different but may be involved in the same boy and girl relationship, thus complicating it, given our current cultural attitudes and values. The same person must serve as the source of reinforcement for a variety of behaviors or needs.

Sullivan points to a third, and more pervasive factor,

which becomes involved with behavior involving lust and intimacy. This is the need for personal security. By the need for personal security, Sullivan largely means a need for freedom from anxiety. Both behaviors oriented toward obtaining intimacy and ones directed toward obtaining orgasms may really be motivated by the need for security.

The early adolescent girl may find security (reduced anxiety) by having and holding boy friends, in being popular. Or she may want real exclusive intimacy from a boy, perhaps not having others to turn to. However, lust, on her or his part, may threaten her security and generate anxiety. If she pets heavily or engages in intercourse what will he think of her, or she of herself? What if she doesn't? Will the intimacy be threatened more by engaging in sex or not? What if others find out? Some friends may push her toward sexual behavior, some away from it. The boy may reduce anxiety and gain security if he can feel more of a man by engaging in sexual intercourse with a girl.

A need for security, rather than a feeling of lust or a need for intimacy, may be the strongest motive behind some early adolescent sexual behavior. Adolescents may gain acceptance from other boys and girls through sexual conquest. Such activity may also threaten security. Nevertheless, boys and girls have some genuine intimacy and lustful needs in early adolescence. The change from preadolescence to adolescence, Sullivan states, appears as a growing interest in the possibilities of achieving some measure of intimacy with a member of the opposite sex and a partial turning away from the same sex"chum." Sullivan aptly points out that this is very hard in our culture, because our culture does little to prepare its children for human, simple sharing with members of the opposite sex. In addition it surrounds sexuality with many complex and security-threatening rules.

Sullivan, H.S. *The Interpersonal Theory of Psychiatry.* W.W. Norton, New York, 1953.

There is empirical evidence for Sullivan's contention that early adolescence presents a threat to security through the generation of anxiety about lust and intimacy. Not only lust and intimacy are involved, but the question of acceptance by others. Insecurity (anxiety) is generated in the young adolescent over the question of how others will react to his or her sexual and other intimate behaviors with members of the opposite sex. Study 13.8 presents some empirical evidence on this point.

SEXUALITY, SOCIAL ACCEPTANCE, AND ANXIETY

STUDY 13.8

M. Powell studied 449 males and females aged ten to 30 years. He used a word association technique. Powell reasoned that the longer a person took to give a verbal association to a word representing a certain content area, the more anxiety was connected with it. Among the areas represented were religion, vocational outlook, social acceptability, and heterosexual relations. In such a technique the experimenter says words like "God," "doctor," "love," or "breast," and observes how long the subject takes to give any verbal response; for example, "God" might produce the response "*church*;" "doctor" might produce "*health*;" "love"—"*good*;" or "breast"—"*girl*." The longer the hesitancy before giving any response, the more disturbing or anxiety producing the given word, (representing an area) was taken to be.

Powell found a marked increase in anxiety in the sexual area from ages eleven to seventeen. There was also a marked rise, during the same age period, in anxiety over social acceptability. At most of the age levels from eleven to seventeen, girls showed more anxiety than boys. There was a marked increase in the anxiety of girls over sexuality at age eleven and in boys at age twelve. This is probably because girls mature earlier sexually than boys do. As children get older they do become more concerned about sexuality and social acceptability.

Powell, M Sex differences in degree of conflict within certain areas of psychological adjustment. *Psychol. Monogr., 69*, No. 387, 1955.

EARLY ADOLESCENCE AND THE NEED FOR INDEPENDENCE

As far as social behavior is concerned, there is little doubt that the eleven-year-old has limited autonomy, being closely tied to the family. The eighteen-year-old girl, on the other hand, spends more free time with friends than with her family. It is still striking that an average eighteen-year-old girl may spend 44 percent of her free time with her family and a fourteen- to sixteen-year-old girl as much as 56 percent of her free time with her family. Only four percent of eleven-year-old girls date or go steady; at ages fourteen to sixteen, 72 percent do; by age eighteen, 94 percent of all girls date or go steady. Thirty-four percent of 11-year-old girls, 56 percent of girls from 14 to 16 years old, and 60 percent of 18-year-old girls have some sort of job outside the home.[5] Obviously, there is a gain in autonomy and movement to activities outside the home after eleven years of age. The greatest gains may be from ages fourteen to sixteen. However, the increase in autonomy grows fairly steadily from eleven to eighteen and does not tend to increase in sudden spurts. Of course there are marked variations in the degree of freedom allowed by different families. The research findings in this area have been ably summarized by Elizabeth Douvan and Martin Gold. Their summary is paraphrased and explained in Study 13.9.

ADOLESCENCE AND AUTONOMY

STUDY 13.9

Contrary to the popular notion, Douvan and Gold find that most adolescents are not clamoring for freedom or for release from unjust constraint. The notion of youthful rebellion or "storm and stress," they find, stems from the unfortunate tendency to focus on delinquents, upper-middle-class neurotic children, or other interesting and newsworthy groups like "hippies." For better or worse, depending on one's values, such groups of children are not typical. Douvan and Gold do not find support in the studies available for the notion that rebellious resistance to authority is a dominant adolescent theme. This may disappoint some, but, for every overt adolescent enemy of the "establishment," there must be many, many more slowly gaining autonomy within the currently established framework of the family. (Of course this may be because parents are altering their standards and exerting less authority.)

Douvan and Gold find the modal pattern of American youth to be that of slowly and steadily gaining independence in a way defined as socially appropriate, by the prevailing values of the culture. The adolescents' requests, while often not pleasing parents and leading to some conflicts, are mostly met with reasonable consideration. The parents, whatever their ambivalence, mostly meet their children's demands for autonomy even if arguments occur. They slowly but steadily relax control and grant increased autonomy. Despite occasional arguments and emotional upheavals, the parent and the adolescent child seem to do fairly well at shifting roles and facilitating the transition from "dependent child" to "partly autonomous adolescent." Unfortunately we are most apt to read and hear about the failures in this area than about the successes.

Douvan, E., and Gold, M. Modal patterns in American adolescence. (In) *Review of Child Development Research.* Russell Sage Foundation, New York, 1966.

Someone interested in the behavior of children once wrote: "The children now love luxury; they show disrespect for elders and love chatter in place of exercise. Children are tyrants, not the servants of their households. They no longer rise when their elders enter the room. They contradict their parents, chatter before company, gobble up the dainties at the table, cross their legs, and tyrannize over their teachers." The person who wrote this was Socrates and he wrote it over 2000 years ago. Adult complaints about children, particularly adolescents, are hardly new. Nevertheless, these adolescents get older, have families, and complain about their own children in turn.

Alienation and Anomie

Despite a good deal of conformity and relative smoothness of the lives of many teenagers, there is no doubt that some of them revolt against the general values of their parents and society. Some may fail to acquire other guiding values and may suffer from feelings of alienation and anomie. We will have much more to say about this in the last chapter. "Alienation" and "anomie" refer to states of relative normlessness; a lack of internalized standards. Minority groups, the lower classes, and the uneducated are particularly likely to experience a lack of standards in which they can believe. They may lack internalized rules of behavior, acceptable to the society at large, by which they can guide themselves. They may also be aware that they are being denied the rewards which others enjoy. Their social position hinders the learning of modal cultural values some of which they may reject in any event. However, since alienation and anomie can be due to personality factors, an individual inability to find meaning and value in life, this form of suffering can also be found among the educated and the affluent. Bewilderment, pessimism, feelings of political impotence, political cynicism, and lack of life satisfactions can result from unfortunate interpersonal relationships within and outside the family. Although the actions of parents and others which lead to such states are more common in the less well-educated lower classes, they occur at all class levels.[17]

Alienation may sometimes be the result of child rearing patterns involving hostility, neglect, over-laxity, or over-restrictiveness. A poor cognitive grasp of important values is sometimes a contributing factor; anomie and alienation may be engendered by the parents' lack of joy in life or commitment to firm values. To some extent it may be the result of life in a rapidly changing society whose reward patterns are somewhat unclear and where the nature of models considered worthy of imitating may be shifting. It can stem from a belief that society is hypocritical or without meaning since it is inconsistent. Finally, it may be due to the inability of the disadvantaged to believe any longer in the promises of affluence dangled in front of them by the middle class, while they are really denied prosperity.[4, 17] Any absence, inconsistency, or inequity in reinforcement patterns can lead to alienation. The adolescent who finds himself exposed to any of these circumstances may experience outrage, anger, and a lack of meaning in life. He or she may consequently develop anomie, alienation, depression, or some form of neurosis. Adolescents may also seek for a new sense of reward through joining a subculture which has its own values, like the "hippies," while some adolescents may turn delinquent or come to depend on drugs as a way of obtaining some reward from life. New models to imitate are sought and new avenues of reward are explored in turn.

Those who experience anomie and find a way to resurrect or invent their own sense of values and meaning, alone or with others, are lucky indeed. The search for rewarding alternatives in life outside of conventional sources is hard. Unconventional solutions may be better than those of the modal culture or they may be a lot worse. Such attempts at a solution may undergo rapid change with one way quickly replacing another. No social scientist has yet empirically evaluated the current opinion of some people that alienation among the young is on the increase. It remains to be seen whether alienation from society will remain restricted to a fairly small minority of adolescents, as it has been in the past. One cannot deny the possibility that an increasing number of young people are becoming dissatisfied with the way of life they see surrounding them. It remains to be seen whether they will be able to construct more rewarding patterns of behavior than those of their parents.

SUMMARY

The greatest changes in early adolescence involve sexual development and cognitive development. Physical puberty leads to the possibility of parenthood with males producing fertile sperm and girls becoming capable of bearing children. Along with the possibility of becoming responsible for the appearance of human life, young adolescents are faced with the reality that the culture heavily discourages them from doing so. Although biologically capable of reproduction, the culture insists on a continued life of school-going, some vocational training, or perhaps light work while living at home. Marriage and family life are to be postponed for some years. The postpubertal boy or girl is asked to establish relationships with the opposite sex, on a basis short of any permanent commitment, and without social sanction for sexual intercourse.

During these years cognitive development proceeds to a full ability to use abstract symbols and to think hypothetically and deductively. At about 11 or 12 years of age, Piaget's period of formal operations commences and is brought to completion by 15 or 16 years of age. This development of thinking allows the young adolescent to put himself in the place of others and to comprehend their point of view. In addition, moral judgments become more abstract and universal than the previous concrete ideas about right and wrong. Morality begins to be based on democratic rules and inner conviction and not on the need to please others or to placate authority.

Adolescence, whether at age 12 or at age 16, is a cultural phenomenon. In our highly complex, industrialized, and urbanized society, something must be done with young people. They are not given responsible jobs or allowed to marry or live together. They are not quite children nor yet accorded adult status and are generally kept at home and in school. They begin to face the problems and satisfactions of social contact based partly on sexual attraction and the testing out of one's attractiveness, popularity, and ability to profit from male-female interpersonal relationships. Independence, although still restricted, increases and thoughts may turn to the meaning of life, ones own identity, and the general issue of values.

REFERENCES

1. Bandura, A., and Walters, R. H. *Social Learning and Personality Development.* Holt, Rinehart and Winston, New York, 1963.
2. Bruner, J. S. *Toward a Theory of Instruction.* Harvard University Press, Cambridge, 1966.
3. Case, D., and Collinson, J. M. The development of formal thinking in verbal comprehension. *Brit. J. Educ. Psychol., 31-32,* 1961-62, 103-11.
4. Cohen, A. K. The sociology of the deviant act: anomie theory and beyond. *Amer. Sociol. Rev., 30,* 1965, 5-14.
5. Douvan, E., and Adelson, J. *The Adolescent Experience.* John Wiley, New York, 1966.
6. Douvan, E., and Gold, M. Modal patterns in American adolescence. (In) *Review of Child Development Research.* Russell Sage Foundation, New York, 1966.
7. Durkheim, E. Suicide (1897). Free Press, Glencoe, Ill., 1951.
8. Feffer, M. H., and Gourevitch, V. Cognitive aspects of role-taking in children. *J. Pers., 28,* 1960, 383-396.
9. Goffman, E. *The Presentation of Self in Everyday Life.* Doubleday-Anchor, New York, 1959.

10. Horrocks, J. E. *The Psychology of Adolescence.* Houghton-Mifflin, New York, 1962.
11. Kagan, J. Acquisition and Significance of Sex Typing and Sex Role-Identity. (In) *Child Development Research,* Hoffman, M. L., and Hoffman, L. W. (Eds.), Russell Sage Foundation, New York, 1964.
12. Kagan, J., and Moss, H. A. *From Birth to Maturity.* John Wiley, New York, 1962.
13. Kephard, W. M. *The Family, Society and the Individual.* Houghton-Mifflin, Boston, 1966.
14. Kinsey, A. C., et al. *Sexual Behavior in the Human Female.* W. B. Saunders, Philadelphia, 1953.
15. Kinsey, A. C., et al. *Sexual Behavior in the Human Male.* W. B. Saunders, Philadelphia, 1948.
16. Kohlberg, L. Development of Moral Character and Moral Ideology. (In) *Review of Child Development Research. Vol. 1.* Hoffman, M. and Hoffman, L. W. (Eds.), Russell Sage Foundation, New York, 1964.
17. McClosky, H., and Scharr, J. H. Psychological dimensions of anomie. *Amer. Soc. Rev., 30,* 1965, 14-40.
18. Mead, G. H. *Mind, Self, and Society.* University of Chicago Press, Chicago, 1934.
19. Mussen, P. H., et al. *Child Development and Personality.* Harper and Row, New York, 1963.
20. Nielson, P. Shirley's babies after fifteen years: a personality study. *J. Genet. Psychol., 73,* 1948, 175-186.
21. Piaget, J. *Logic and Psychology.* Basic Books, New York, 1953.
22. Piaget, J. *The Psychology of Intelligence.* Routledge and Kegan Paul, London, 1950.
23. Powell, M. Sex differences in degree of conflict within certain areas of psychological adjustment. *Psych. Monogr., 69,* No. 387, 1955.
24. Reynolds, E. L., and Wines, J. V. Physical changes associated with adolescence in boys. *Amer. J. Dis. Child, 82,* 1951, 529-547.
25. Reynolds, E. L., and Wines, J. V. Individual differences in physical changes associated with adolescent girls. *Amer. J. Dis. Child, 75,* 1948, 329-350.
26. Roberts, K. E., and Fleming, V. V. Resistance and change in personality patterns, *Monogr. Soc. Res. Child Develpm., No. 30,* 1943.
27. Rogers, D. *The Psychology of Adolescence.* Appleton-Century-Crofts, New York, 1962.
28. Sears, R. R., et al. *Patterns of Child Rearing.* Row, Peterson, Evanston, Ill. 1957.
29. Simmons, K., and Greulich, W. W. Menarchal age and height, weight and skeletal age of girls 7 to 17 years. *J. Pediat., 22,* 1943, 513-548.
30. Sullivan, H. S. *The Interpersonal Theory of Psychiatry.* W. W. Norton, New York, 1953.
31. Tanner, J. M. *Growth at Adolescence.* Blackwell Scientific Publications Ltd., Oxford, 1962.
32. Wylie, R. *The Self Concept.* University of Nebraska Press, Lincoln, 1961.

CHAPTER 14

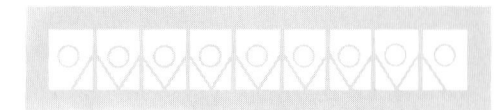

THE INTERNALIZATION PROCESS

PART 1 – INTERNALIZATION AND IDENTITY

ADOLESCENCE

Many aspects of socialization have already been covered in this book. Socialization begins almost from birth and proceeds throughout a lifetime. By the end of the early adolescent period, however, socialization is well established. Certainly all the processes involved in socialization have had a chance to act upon the child. The child has experienced various types of child rearing and disciplinary practices, has been conditioned, exposed to models, and given many rewards and punishments. He has had many interactions with the people about him. The child has experienced positive and negative emotions as a result of his activities and the responses of others to those activities. He has also experienced positive and negative emotions in conjunction with his thoughts about these actions. People have affected him and he has affected them. Language and problem solving skills have been acquired. The child has engaged in socially acceptable behaviors and has had experience with transgression and their results. He has had interactions with his family, teachers, and friends. All this has occurred by later adolescence.

We have already considered much of socialization in the chapters covering patterns of child rearing, social learning theory, and the study of the family. Before considering later adolescence we will examine internalization, which is a special, but most important, portion of socialization. Particular emphasis will be given to the internalization process in this chapter since by late adolescence considerable control over behavior has passed from outside to inside the child. Although it is true that by late adolescence much of internalization has taken place, the process is a continuing one and much consolidation and additional internalization may take place later. It should be made clear that internalization begins in early childhood and goes on for a long time. *Internalization is not a special process of adolescence.* However, since many behaviors come under internalized control by adolescence, the adolescent is often able to regulate his or her own actions without as much external supervision as the young child needs. Before discussing internalization in detail it should be useful to review the nature of socialization.

SOCIALIZATION PROCESSES

Socialization refers both to processes and to outcomes. The child's acquired ability to behave in ways generally rewarding in the segment of the culture in which he lives is an outcome of socialization processes. Socialization processes refer to the actual learning of behaviors and performances through experiencing positive or aversive outcomes dependent on the child's acts. The socialization process also pertains to observational learning, which does not depend on the consequences of the child's overt behavior.[7] The child becomes socialized both because certain of his behaviors bring him rewards, whereas others are punished, and because he can learn by observing what others are doing.[7] In general, he behaves in ways determined by his culture which bring him satisfactions. His learned patterns of behavior tend to maximize his chances of obtaining satisfactions and to minimize negative feelings or lack of satisfaction. Parents, teachers, and other children are the chief sources of both rewards and punishments and are the models who influence the child's learning. In turn, the child also serves as a model for others. He also rewards and punishes in attempts to arrange the environment to suit his own wishes.

Although the child may learn at once from observation, without performing the overt acts seen, he may perform them only at a later date. Once the overt act is performed, as we have seen, it will lead to either rewarding or aversive outcomes or merely to a lack of any sort of reinforcement. The outcome of the child's behavior will have a strong effect on the probability of their future occurrence.[7] We have already discussed under social learning and patterns of child rearing, as well as in other places, how the child's behavior is shaped or regulated by the socializing agents in his life. Most of the child's behavior is regulated by the consequences it brings and it is other people who often control the consequences.

Some of the socialization effort on the part of parents is overt and conscious. That is, parents may have in mind certain ways that they want their children to behave and the parents may then try to make the children behave that way. Children also try, and often succeed, in altering the behavior of their parents. Parents use various disciplinary techniques, verbal instructions, and symbolic models to instill the kinds of behavior they desire in their children.[7] What happens to the child is then partly contingent upon how closely he conforms to the desires of socializing agents. The socializing agents are the child's parents, siblings, teachers, and peers. Again, children are active and try to influence their socializing agents in many ways. Children can cry, plead, reason, smile, yell at parents, sulk, be cute, and do many other things to try to control their parents' behavior. They may succeed on certain occasions in controlling their parents and may have to conform only partially to their wishes.

Some of the socialization pattern is not overt or conscious. Parents and teachers may reward children, without conscious purpose or awareness. They may, without an overt plan, reward children for displaying certain kinds of behavior indicative of certain values, attitudes, or behaviors representative of certain motives. The parent may smile at a daughter when she acts "cute" or "feminine." A teacher may beam at a boy who gives a bright answer. Neither the parent or the teacher may be aware of what they are doing or why. Some parents take their children out for a special brunch after church on Sunday or let them stay up extra late at night after a Boy Scout meeting. In such ways certain behaviors important to socializing agents, perhaps because they represent patterns of behavior or motives they approve of, are reinforced without any premeditated plan.

In all cases, however, the child's behavior and those of the parents become a function of the consequences of their mutual acts. The child's and parent's actions are the *results* of the consequences of their actions. If they do one thing, one set of consequences follows; if they do another thing, something quite different may happen. These pleasant or unpleasant consequences will regulate their future behavior. Children build up quite strong habits or behavioral dispositions, but these are at first under the control of external reinforcers.

THE PROCESS OF INTERNALIZATION

At this point the term "internalization" is formally introduced to differentiate behavior chiefly under the control of internal consequences from behavior mainly under the control of external consequences. The topic of how internalization occurs in children takes up the rest of this chapter. If there is one aspect of child development which is most representative of the growing up process, it is the passing of the control of important segments of behavior from external to internal regulation. Many of the child's behaviors, in the process of socialization, undergo a change from being regulated by external consequences (rewards and punishments delivered by others) to being regulated by internal processes and consequences.[1, 3] We have already seen how the child becomes capable of approving of himself, of lowering his own anxieties, and of punishing himself. These are internal consequences.[1, 3] The dictum of many a parent of an adolescent "If we can't trust him by now, we never can," may be quite correct. Some adolescents can be trusted in certain areas of life, since they have internalized control over their behavior.

Internalization and Cognition

The child comes to understand the world. He does this by learning concepts and developing cognitive "sets," "templates," or "maps" about the environment. The world comes to be represented internally in terms of symbols, usually verbal symbols. These representations of the world enable him to predict the possible outcomes of his behavior before he acts. He can then partly regulate his own behavior on the basis of anticipation about what may or may not happen to him. The child learns to foresee *possible* external consequences and act accordingly. On the basis of his history of social learning and observation, he forms concepts about himself, his environment, and the people in it. He acquires labeling-language capacity which he can use to solve problems and to formulate an understanding of the environment for himself. In other words, he becomes capable of thinking through the use of language. He can use cognitions to *mediate* his behavior. That is, he can think first and then act, partly on the basis of how he internally represents the environment to himself.[1, 3] In this way, by adolescence, the child becomes ready for leading a relatively independent life and has a lessened need for external supervision.

Internalization, Cognition, and Emotion

Cognitive representations are seldom neutral. Affective (emotional) and evaluative responses become *attached* to the child's cognitions. The child not only knows about school, he may love it or hate it. Emotional reactions also become attached to his anticipations or impulses to engage in some behaviors. The child may not only know he wants ice cream, he may fear to take it. Cognitions, preparatory movements, and partial segments of behaviors, through a conditioning process, can all acquire emotional value. The anticipation of engaging in certain forbidden behaviors may arouse internal negative emotions like fear, shame, or guilt. Formerly rewarded behaviors may arouse hope and pleasurable excitement in the child.[45, 46] Much of behavior gradually becomes imbued with emotional meaning—so do certain impulses and thoughts. On the basis of their experiences children not only learn about themselves and aspects of the world, they also come to evaluate parts of themselves and the environment either positively or negatively.

The child also learns to respond emotionally on the basis of what is happening to others; he becomes capable of empathic and vicarious responses. He learns to behave, on occasion, in sympathetic and altruistic ways toward others. He not only comes to know what is happening to others, he learns to respond to their plight. Many of these semi-emotional processes, more rudimentary at earlier ages, come to fruition in adolescence. There is seldom a clear separation between knowledge and feeling since affective responses are continually being conditioned to cognitive representations. When a child comes to know something he often also comes to like or dislike it, to approve of it, or to reject it.

Internalization and the Outside World

Internalization, as we have said, refers to self-regulation; that is to say, to behavior due more to consequences of inner emotional change and understanding than to external consequences. Gradually, much of behavior becomes a function of internally rewarding or punishing feelings attached to thoughts and impulses rather than of external reinforcements. It is important to note, however, that behavior in children is always partly regulated by external circumstances. That is, the child's behavior, even when not dependent on external rewards and punishments, is partly dependent on the situations he finds himself in. Empathic and vicarious experiences for the child depend on either seeing how someone else feels or what type of situation the other person is in. Self-criticism may depend partly on whether the child represents the transgression he has committed as one stemming from a situation where he had some control. For instance, few children will engage in self-criticism if what occurred was not their fault. A child will not be self-critical for failure if the teacher has decided to fail the whole class because another child was "bad." A child cannot lower his guilt over having done wrong by confessing to his mother, if his parents are away on a two-week trip. Nor can a child lower moral anxiety by confession, if he is punished before he can speak. Internalization means relative independence for the child from solely external reinforcing consequences, not independence from the realities of the external world.[3]

IDENTIFICATION

The Definition of Identification

"Identification" is a name for a process which has been used to account for a number of phenomena related to internalization such as similarities between psychological aspects of children and parents, and the existence of imitation.[2, 9] It also has been used to explain the phenomena of internalized conscience, that is behaviors such as resistance to temptation or reactions following transgression. The phenomena for which it purports to account are quite real. The question at issue is whether the *one term*, "identification," is a useful one in accounting for these various phenomena and other aspects of internalization. There is good reason to think that it is not useful in this regard.[2]

Identification has not been defined with any consistency and there are many "theories" of identification.[9] Like so many other concepts relating to personality, the use of the term "identification" originated in the work of Freud.[9] He used the term, in his various writings, in at least four ways: to account for the patterning of the child's behavior after the behavior of the parents; to refer to a wish or motive on the part of the child to become like the parents; to refer to the psychological *process* involved in either of those two meanings; or, to refer to the final result, completed "identification" with the parents or other groups. This latter usage of identification implies some completed emotional tie and/or similarity to others. As one can see, these four meanings of identification are hardly identical. It is not likely that one concept can account for all the psychological factors that must be involved in these various phenomena, behaviors, motives, and processes.[14, 15, 16, 17, 18]

Is "Identification" Unitary?

Identification often implies some unitary or monolithic process of internalization taking place in a relatively short space of time. In Freudian theory, for instance, the boy of five or so, during the phallic or oedipal period, is said to internalize his perception of his father's values.[15] The evidence, on the contrary, suggests that the internalization of moral standards and behavior takes place over many, many years. It is not some wholesale borrowing of the perceived standards of a feared authority figure.[1, 3]

Moral conduct is not monolithic or consistent. A child may be "honest" in one situation but not in another; a child may be kind but a cheat; or, he may be self-critical but unlikely to confess. His parents may or may not be similar to him in these regards.[1, 3]

A child's understanding, knowledge of, or belief in certain moral values may have little to do with his actual behavior in "moral" situations; those in which he may be tempted to cheat, lie, or steal. They may bear little relationship to how his parents would behave in such cases. The relationship between "moral understanding" on one hand, and "moral behavior" on the other, is not well understood.[1, 3] It seems best, at present, not to use the term "identification" in explaining these diverse aspects of internalization.

SEX GENDER AND IDENTITY

Children, however, do develop a sense of identity and this sense of identity is internal and may regulate behavior. Children have some sense of identity well before adolescence. "Identity" may be defined as the collectivity of a child's cognitions concerning who and what he is. The adolescent may be particularly preoccupied with this issue, but his sense of identity began to develop in early childhood. The child's identity, to put it another way, consists of the attributes which he accepts and understands as being applicable to him. Put simply, identity refers to the child's beliefs about what is true about him: who, what, and how he is.

The simplest and perhaps earliest attribute which children learn to apply to themselves is either "boy" or "girl." This is called gender, sex gender, or sex concept learning. The initial aspect of identity acquired by a child may be the consciousness of being a boy or girl, and later understanding that he or she belongs to a class of boys or girls.[21] (This also implies the concept of "we children.")

This may be followed by learning to apply the attribute "male" or "female" to the self, that is, for a girl, that she is female like her mother, and for a boy that he is male like his father. The sense of identity then includes a larger class of "we females" or "we males."[48] Sexual identity becomes more crucial in adolescence but exists much earlier. "Femaleness" or "maleness" is a vital issue in adolescence because of its import for relationships between boys and girls. It becomes important for boys to feel "male" and for girls to feel "female."

Likewise, other discriminations may be internalized which involve self-labeling of attributes. These often involve the child learning his place in a category. The child may learn that he is a "son" and the girl that she is a "daughter." A boy learns that he is in the category of "sons" as other boys are. In addition to internalizing identity in terms of sexual and family categories the child also learns evaluative attributes. His identity, or attributes considered applicable to the child by himself, may come to include such emotionally evaluative labels as "smart," "good looking," "nice," and "superior," or to the contrary, "dumb," "ugly," "mean," or "inferior,"

The way in which the child acquires his identity is largely a matter of learning to accept the labels indicative of the attributes which other people apply to him. It is also a function of the types of things he learns about himself as a result of everyday experience. Identity is internal. It is the result of social learning and may be modified by it, but it is a part of the child's internal cognitive representations. Further, identity includes how the child comes to feel about (evaluate) himself. Children act in accordance with the attributes which they accept about themselves and consequently those cognitions partly regulate the child's behavior. A child who feels himself to be "dumb" is not likely to try very hard in school, whereas a child who feels very "intelligent" may overachieve. A "dumb" child probably evaluates himself more negatively than a child who considers himself to be "intelligent" and they will both behave accordingly.

Since our culture expects different behaviors and activities from boys than from girls and from males than from females, the behavior of the child becomes "sex typed." Boys learn to behave in ways expected of boys and girls in ways expected of girls.[36] The current culture, furthermore, does not give equal value to the activities of both sexes.[35] Boys are often preferred to girls and the activities of males are often more highly valued than the usual activities of females.[21] Finally, adult males and females are perceived differently by children. For instance, adult males are seen by children as being more competent and fear arousing, and adult females are seen as more nurturant.[50] All of these factors contribute to the child's sense of identity.

Gender identity is the most stable of all social identities. Psychological confusion about one's own sexual identity is usually a sign of a fairly severe mental aberration. The child's verbal learning of his own gender takes place early; it may already by established late in the second year. Two-thirds to three-quarters of three year olds correctly answer the question, "Are you a little girl or a little boy?" A fair minority, but less than half, of two and a half years olds could also answer this question correctly.[37] About two-thirds of a group of children aged 30 to 41 months (average age, three years) correctly answered the question: "Which doll looks most like you?" and, "Is it (the doll) a boy or a girl?" Attribution of sex gender is well established by four years of age and by that age most children can label six dolls correctly as "boys" or as "girls." At three years of age only about 50 percent of children can label six dolls correctly as to the sex they represent.[38]

Of course, this does not explain how children identify sex gender and what it means to them. It seems that attributes like types of clothes worn and hair style are among the main cues that children use to identify sex gender. By four years of age children tend to label gender by some such general external criterion.[38, 39] Three year olds are aware of the objects that comprise the exterior trappings of males and females in our culture.[38, 39] Since, in our culture, sex labeling and sexual behavior are not openly displayed in front of most children, a child is more likely to say that a boy is a boy because he wears pants and has short hair than because he has a penis.

Kohlberg points out that the ability of the child to label correctly the sex gender of others and self does not mean that the child "understands" that sex gender is unchangeable.[38, 39] Because of the cognitive reliance on external attributes, four to five year olds may think that sex can be changed by changing clothes and they may also believe that by doing what females do a boy can grow up to be a "mommy," or that girls can grow up to be a "daddy," by doing what men do. By six or seven, children understand that this is impossible.[38, 39] Correspondingly, some four year olds think that a cat could be a dog if it wanted to and could somehow manage to get its whiskers cut off, whereas six and seven year old know better.[38, 39] Kohlberg believes that this growing feeling of constancy, invariance, or conservation of sex gender, by six or seven, is a special case of the attainment of the concept of constancy of conservation of physical objects described by Piaget and discussed earlier in this book.[49] The few people who fail to internalize these distinctions and apply them thoroughly to themselves are considered by clinical psychologists to have "a confusion of sexual identity."

SEX PREFERENCES AND SOCIAL CLASS

It is a value of American culture that it is better to be a male than a female. However, whatever the sex of their child, parents are concerned both that their sons become "masculine" and their daughters "feminine." The lower class seems more concerned than the middle or upper classes that their sons not be "sissies" and that their daughters be "feminine." This greater concern for internalization of proper sex typed behavior by the lower class is reflected in the fact that lower-class boys adhere more closely to traditional masculine interests than do middle-class boys.[25] It is more acceptable for the sons of the rich to be interested in poetry than it is for the sons of truck drivers. Some of the points above are supported by an investigation, part of which is reported in Study 14.1.

SEX ROLE PREFERENCE BY SOCIAL CLASS

STUDY 14.1

Majorie Hall and Robert A. Keith studied 88 children who come partly from the lower social class and partly from the upper social class. They found the following:

Boys from the lower class showed a more clearcut preference for being masculine than did upper-class boys.

Boys, in general, preferred being masculine more than girls preferred being feminine.

Hall and Keith underlined the finding of a fairly rigid preference in boys for being male. Girls, on the other hand, were more flexible and had some preference for masculine ways. They feel that parents demand more restrictively that boys be boys, but that girls are treated more flexibly. It is not all right for a boy to be a "sissy," but it is tolerable between eight and ten for a girl to be a "tomboy." Of course, part of this state of affairs results from the greater prestige attached to being male. Girls may envy boys and some may wish they were boys. Finally, the lower class is clearly less tolerant of deviation of boys in the feminine direction. Of course, what is "masculine" and what is "feminine" are matters of cultural rules subject to change.

Hall, M., and Keith, R. A. Sex-role preference among children of upper and lower social class. *J. Soc. Psychol.*, *62*, 1964, 101-110.

SEX PREFERENCES AND AGE

Sex preferences begin quite early but do take time to become clearly established.[22] Even by age two there are sex differences between boys and girls in behavior and interests, including differences in the value set on toys, in activity rate, aggressiveness, and fearfulness.[28, 55] These differences may be due partly to innate differences between the sexes, but they are largely caused by differential rewards (for different behaviors) and by differential exposure to toys and playmates.[7] Young boys and girls at first value and prefer what is "theirs" or "their" way of doing things.[10, 38] Later, girls may learn to understand that masculine things and ways of behaving have greater cultural value.[39, 40] An investigation reported in Study 14.2 illustrates issues in the acceptance of sex identity.

SEX ROLE PREFERENCES IN CHILDREN

STUDY 14.2

Hartup and Zook studied 161 boys and girls going to nursery school. The ages of the children ranged from three to five years.

The age related nature of the learning of sex typed behavior was shown by the fact that girls in the four-year-old group scored as more highly feminine than three-year-old girls. Correspondingly, four-year-old boys scored as being more masculine than three-year-old boys.

Hartup and Zook say that their study demonstrates early

childhood to be an important period in sex-identity development and they also believe that sex-identity development is more complicated for girls than for boys.

They point out that in middle childhood (after five or six but before adolescence) boys prefer culturally designated masculine behavior patterns more strongly than girls prefer designated feminine behavior patterns. Even among most of their four year olds, boys showed slightly stronger masculine preferences than girls showed feminine ones. They remark that this tendency increases with age as children discover the advantage of being male.

Hartup, W. W., and Zook, E. A. Sex-role preferences in three- and four-year-old children. *J. Consult. Psychol.*, 24, 1960, 420-426.

Kohlberg has summarized many of the findings in this area.[39] He feels that, between ages three and five, children assume that things and people associated with their own sex are better, because of what he calls "egocentric-projective-identity." This simply means that similarity to the self is considered the basis for preference in early childhood. If something is like him or his kind, the young child likes it better.

THE DIMENSION OF SIMILARITY

A digression at this point is advisable, since similarity is such an important mediating variable in the life of the child, the adolescent, and the adult. Social similarity may be one of the most important variables influencing processes such as imitation, liking, preference, or the estimation of the feelings of others. The child must, for instance, be able to recognize others who are similar to him for sex gender learning to take place. People who are perceived to be similar to him are more likely to be liked, preferred, or imitated; thus they are more likely to influence his behavior.

Two experiments found in Studies 14.3 and 14.4 particularly highlight the crucial role of social similarity.

SOCIAL SIMILARITY

STUDY 14.3

Donna Gelfand and Robert D. Singer were interested in finding what kind of persons children would see as being most similar to themselves. Would fifth grade girls perceive themselves as being more similar to boys their own age or to females their mothers' age? That is, would the dimension of age ("someone my age but a boy") or the dimension of sex ("someone my sex but much older") prove to be the more important?

They reasoned that the group most generalized to, after conditioning, would be the one perceived as most similar. This argument follows from the finding of experimental psychology that if someone is conditioned to give a response to a certain stimulus, that person is most likely to give a similar response to stimuli quite close to the one to which they were originally conditioned.

The procedure used is too elaborate to report here. It involved the method of the conditioning of personality judgments, and noting the social stimuli to which they generalized. However, the findings were clear-cut and may be stated briefly. Age was a much more powerful predictor of social similarity than sex. *Girls were more likely to generalize the conditioned response to boys their own age than to women their mothers' age.* Gelfand and Singer speculated that, in our culture, girls view other children their own age, regardless of sex, as being more similar to themselves than are adults. It may come as no shock to parents that their daughters may feel more similar to other children their own age, *regardless of sex*, then they do to them. This study was repeated on late adolescent girls and identical results were obtained.

Gelfand, D. M., and Singer, R. D. Generalization of children's verbally conditioned personality judgments. *J. Clin. Psychol., 21*, 1965, 101-103.

From the findings above we may infer that the process of identity formations, an important part of internalization, may be partly regulated by similarity. For instance, it may be easier for a child to feel "empathic" with someone whom he labels as similar to himself than with someone whom he perceives as being different. It is easier to respond emotionally to someone else's feelings if he is like you. In fact, perception of social similarity may be one of the bases for the categorization of shared identity, the judgment of the child that he must share certain characteristics with someone else. If a child judges himself to be similar to other children, to boys for instance, then he may infer that they have a number of things in common. If older people are seen as different, the adolescent may feel less in common with them. Certain aspects of an experiment have been selected to illustrate the above point and are presented in Study 14.4.

THE ROLE OF SIMILARITY IN JUDGING EMOTIONS

STUDY 14.4

Seymour and Norma Feshbach frightened boys by making the boys believe that they had to serve as subjects in a medical experiment. They were shown a lot of frightening looking electronic equipment and a man in a white coat holding a hypodermic needle. (In fact, there was no medical experiment, and as soon as the study was done this was explained to the boys. The boys were then given a party including food, games, and prizes.)

After the boys were frightened they were asked to look at: pictures of boys their own age, pictures of girls their own age, pictures of women their mothers' age, and pictures of men their fathers' age. They were asked to make judgments of two sorts. First they were asked which adjective from the following list best fitted the person in the picture: mean, pleased, scared, kind, or unhappy. They then saw all the pictures again, and were asked to rate how *fearful* the person in each picture looked. Finally, exposed to the pictures the third and last time, they were asked how *malicious* (nasty) the person in each picture seemed.

Fear was maintained by keeping the frightening apparatus and the man in the white coat in view at all times. A control group, in another room, saw the same pictures and made the same ratings, but was not exposed to the equipment or the man in the white coat. The children in the control group were not led to expect any medical experiment. They remained calm. The responses of the frightened boys were compared to the responses of the calm boys in the control group.

The results showed that the frightened boys, who were scared and unhappy themselves, judged the pictures of boys their own age as being more scared and unhappy than the control group boys did. This is an instance of "projection" of their feelings. They also rated the pictures of boys their own age as looking more fearful than the control group did. The other groups of pictures, that is, those of girls their own age, or men or women their parents' age were rated similarly by both groups. Differences as to fear appeared only when the frightened boys judged pictures very similar to themselves.

Once a sense of identity exists: "I am a boy of a certain

age," then similarity can serve to mediate inferences (projection) about how others who are similar (boys of the same age) must feel.

Feshbach, S., and Feshbach, N. Influence of the stimulus object upon the complementary and supplementary projection of fear. *J. Abnorm. Soc. Psychol.*, 66, 1963, 498-502.

PERCEIVED ATTRIBUTES OF MALES AND FEMALES

Children between five and ten years of age judge the male as more competent, aggressive, and as more fear-arousing than the female. The female, however, is seen as more nurturant. The greater aggressiveness of males than of females is believed to be appropriate by children of this age, and this belief may have the effect of inducing girls to suppress impulses toward overt aggression. Since girls view overt aggression like fighting, punching, and kicking to be male attributes they may not tend to engage in such unfeminine behavior.[34] The adolescent girl, in particular, is very unlikely to fight physically. Study 14.5 illustrates some research methods and results in this area.

PERCEPTION OF PARENTAL ATTRIBUTES

STUDY 14.5

Jerome Kagan and Judith Lemkin used three ways of obtaining information about how children conceptualized parents. They studied 32 boys and 35 girls ranging in age from three years and nine months to five years and six months.

They used direct questions, indirect questions, and a picture method. In the direct questions, they asked things like: "Who are you more scared of, your mother or your father?" In the indirect questions, they asked things like: "Who is a child most scared of?" In the picture method, scenes were presented with one parent missing and the child had to say whether it was a mother or a father who was missing.

The results showed that fathers were judged to be more frightening and punitive, but also more competent than mothers. Mothers were seen as "nicer." Both boys and girls viewed parents this way.

> Boys chose fathers and girls chose mothers as the person they wanted to be like and as the person they liked best. Although girls wanted to be like the mothers, they saw the fathers as wiser and stronger. Although girls see the female role as less powerful, they do seem to perceive that they are female like the mother and wish to emulate her. The girls see the father as both affectionate and punitive and may be more ambivalent about him than the boys are. Girls are in a situation where their role model, the mother, is seen by them as weaker than the father.
>
> Kagan, J., and Lemkin, J. The child's differential perception of parental attributes. *J. Abnorm. Soc. Psychol.*, 60, 1960, 440-447.

Others have also found that American children perceive fathers as more powerful, punitive, aggressive, and fearless, but also instrumentally more competent and less nurturant, than females. These sex role stereotypes of children seem to cluster about three main factors in the perception of parents: aggression—men are tougher and more violent; exposure to danger—men are more fearless and daring; nurturance and child care—women take care of children and are more giving. Viewing child care as a female function, children also view it largely as a home function. Paternal or fatherly functions are seen as outside-the-home functions and a differentiation between the two seems to take place.[19] Adolescent males, therefore, are more overtly aggressive than adolescent girls and more interested in future vocational roles. Internalized cognitions about sex role are clearly important determinants of the social activities of boys and girls.

How children perceive parents, how they think of mothers and fathers, seems to have generality across social class and even national lines. The reasons for this are not entirely clear. It may partly originate from innate factors such as the larger size and possible greater activity level of the male. It probably has more to do with the fact that, in most cultures and social classes, the female performs the nurturant, child-care role and the father the instrumental, food and shelter providing job.[12, 32] This generally may break down as more women work, competing with males instrumentally, and as more males baby-sit, mop the floor, and take the children to the zoo. Modern roles may be less differentiated along sex lines than they used to be.

AGGRESSION AND COMPETITION—SEX TYPED BEHAVIORS

Boys show much more direct aggressive behavior than girls and adolescent girls show almost no direct fighting behavior. This is both true in everyday overt action and in play. At the age of two, boys and girls hit, scream, and cry about the same amount. Girls have to learn that hitting behavior is forbidden to them, whereas boys have to learn to cry and scream less. Since by age four much of this learning has taken place, girls get into fewer altercations by that age than boys do. Boys of four in conflict with girls are more often the overt aggressors; boys make more overt attacks on girls at this age than girls make on boys. By this age girls hit much less than boys and boys are crying and screaming less than girls. The amount of aggression in boys stays fairly constant over time; it is girls who become less overtly aggressive although they may find alternate, more subtle, and acceptable ways of expressing their hostility. Boys and girls internalize the behaviors considered suitable for their sex. This means that girls must change their level of aggression to be more feminine, and they do, internalizing suppression of overt aggression.

Preadolescent girls avoid competitive strategies which require the formation of coalitions to defeat a third member. Although adolescent girls like to avoid obvious friction, boys tend to be more overtly aggressive and exploitative in their strategy in competitive games, being more openly competitive, particularly outside the home.[30, 56] A survey of 110 cultures showed greater pressure on boys than on girls to display self-reliance and achievement striving.[8, 53] Boys and girls, for the most part, internalize these behavioral predispositions; they accept them and find behaving in these ways to be quite natural.

SEX TYPING AND INTELLECTUAL FUNCTIONING

Sex differences between boys and girls in intellectual functioning have been summed up clearly by Eleanor Maccoby and are found in Study 14.6.

SEX DIFFERENCES IN INTELLECTUAL FUNCTIONING

STUDY 14.6

1. General Intelligence: Girls get somewhat higher scores on general intelligence tests in the preschool years but boys score slightly higher in the school years.[52]
2. Verbal Ability: In preschool and early school years girls exceed boys. By age ten boys have caught up in reading skills. Girls, however, continue throughout school to be better in grammar, spelling, and word fluency.
3. Number Ability: Girls learn to count at an earlier age. In

school both are equally good at computing. Boys, however, do better at arithmetic reasoning from high school through college and adulthood.
4. Spatial Ability: In the preschool years there are no differences. From the early school years through adulthood, males do better at spatial tasks such as block design or formboards.
5. Analytic Ability: From about age seven on, boys do better than girls.[33]
6. Creativity: The findings are mixed. Girls are more creative on some types of creativity tasks, particularly if verbal productivity is involved, and boys on others, particularly if concrete instrumental matters are involved.
7. Achievement: Girls consistently get better grades even in areas where boys score higher on achievement tests. Men, however, out-achieve women in almost all areas of intellectual endeavor. Gifted boys often achieve their productive potential; gifted girls most often do not reach their productive potential.

Maccoby, E. E. Sex differences in intellectual functioning. *In the Development of Sex Differences*, Maccoby, E. E. (Ed.). Stanford University Press, Stanford, 1966.

Eleanor Maccoby lists a number of reasons why girls fall behind boys intellectually as the years go by. By the adolescent years boys are ahead on almost everything except grades. This is the case because girls become more passive, inhibited, and dependent, and boys become more bold, impulsive and independent.[43] Although there may be several causes for these behavioral differences, it is important to note that greater passivity and dependence are what the culture reinforces in girls, whereas, on the contrary, independence and activity are rewarded if shown by boys. In social learning terms, girls learn to behave in passive and dependent ways and boys learn to be more independent and active. The boy has, as a model, the more active and independent father to imitate and, as stated, is more often rewarded for independence and activity. Girls are expected to marry and are not supposed to compete with males; boys are urged to become competent in the economic world and to compete with others. Many an adolescent girl plays dumb to get and hold dates. Since girls are rewarded for obedience and "good" behavior they get good grades in school, but they are not expected to win a Nobel prize or to achieve much in areas like spatial ability or arithmetic reasoning. These latter areas are related to engineering and physics which are not seen as part of the woman's world. Girls seem to get the message fairly early in school and have it well internalized by the time they reach adolescence.

SOCIAL LEARNING INTERPRETATION OF SEX TYPED BEHAVIORAL PROCESSES

Walter Mischel has outlined the social learning approach to sex typed behavior.[44] Sex typed behavior, according to Mischel, is behavior that typically elicits different rewards for one sex than for the other. That is, the rewarding or punishing consequences vary according to the sex of the performer. A girl may be punished and a boy rewarded for the same behavior. Sex typed behavior, he contends, is acquired in exactly the same way as any other behavior. The factors affecting the learning of sex typed behavior, therefore, are: reinforcement, non-reinforcement, punishment, scheduling or patterning of reinforcement (all four of these being either *external*, *internal*, or *vicarious*), observational learning through imitation, discrimination, and generalization.[44]

Mischel points out that in addition to being exposed to the direct effects of their overt behavior, children learn concepts and labels; they do not have to rely only on doing the right thing by chance and then being rewarded. The child is told verbally how to behave by adults and such information and information from other sources tells the child what to expect if he behaves in certain ways. Children learn to infer the probable consequences of behaving like boys or girls.

Words, labels, instructions, or other symbols become associated with highly emotionally charged experiences like being given love, food, or being yelled at or struck. Verbal symbols like "sissy," "pansy," "tough," "pretty," "sweet," and "good" are associated with powerful, pleasant or unpleasant, states of affect (emotion). They act as strong rewards and punishments and have differential value for the sexes. Boys like to be called by some of them but not others. Girls prefer some that boys do not and wish to avoid ones which boys may like. These labels like "sissy" or "nice" mediate (control) behavior since they have positive or negative reinforcing value.[6] Children learn, in time, to apply these evaluative, emotionally charged labels to their own behavior and consequently, children gradually attain self-regulation, as they learn to behave as boys and girls are expected to behave.

Cognitive Effects

Cognitive theorists like Kohlberg and Kagan have, of course, emphasized cognitive factors in the acquisition of sex typed behavior.[31] According to Kagan, children internalize a sex role standard of male or female, to which they try to match their own behavior. A "sex role standard" refers to a socially learned association between selected attributes, behaviors, and attitudes on one hand, and the concepts "male" and "female" on the other. The sex role standard is really the same as the culturally approved characteristics for male and female. Kagan believes that when the child acquires the concept of being male or female, including understanding of appropriate sex role standards, the child will try to acquire behavior matching the sex role standards. The boy will try to behave in ways that he thinks are congruent with manly behavior and the girl will try to behave in ways she thinks of as feminine.

Kohlberg also believes that the desire to be masculine leads boys to imitate masculine models; for girls the desire to be feminine leads to the imitation of feminine models. Social learning theory does not deny the presence of such cognitive and motivational processes, or that boys and girls form concepts or think. Clearly, social learning theorists recognize that there are mediating cognitive processes. However, social learning theorists like Mischel contend that a child's behavior is determined by his social learning history of imitation and reinforcement, not by some abstract concept like sex gender role. Sex typed behavior, as any other, is seen by them to be a function of relevant past learning and the eliciting stimuli in current situations.[44] Mediating cognitive concepts may be recognized as part of the social learning processes, and as following the laws of learning, but they are seen as the results of learning rather than as important determiners of behavior. Their role in mediating behaviors is minimized and the role of imitation and reinforcement is stressed by theorists like Mischel.

THE INTERNALIZATION OF CONSCIENCE AND MORAL BEHAVIOR

Neither "conscience" nor "moral behavior" is a term of psychological origin. Rather they are historically derived from the field of ethics and aspects of theology. Broadly speaking, the term "moral behavior" has been applied to conduct about which the question of "right" or "wrong" can be raised. The term "conscience" is used to refer to the person's internalized system of values concerning behaviors considered by himself and/or others to be "right" or "wrong," "desirable," or "undesirable." Conscience refers to the individual's evaluative moral *standards*, including cognitions and emotional responses, concerning his acts in the area of moral *behavior*.

There is nothing psychologically unique about moral behavior since moral behavior is defined culturally and not psychologically. The acts involved are not in themselves necessarily different from other acts. For instance, the behavior of an unmarried girl engaging in sexual intercourse at age 13 is considered to fall within the realm of "moral behavior" in the United States. It has evaluative moral connotations for her and others. It may be considered by the girl or others as being "wrong" or "immoral." In Samoa such behavior may not fall within the realm of morality; it may be considered morally neutral by both the child and others. The behavior of children and adults is often influenced by whether the culture defines an act as moral, immoral, or nonmoral, but there is nothing about the behaviors as such which makes them moral or immoral. The distinction is in the acquired evaluative cognitions about the behavior, that is, what people believe about it. Hitting may be "wrong" in one situation, "right" in another, and a matter of indifference in a third. The phenomenon of hitting will be the same in all three cases, but the underlying cognitive value system of the child, which may control the behaviors, might differ. He may condemn one act of hitting and approve of another; he may learn that it is "wrong" to hit little girls but "right" to hit a larger boy who attacks him.

Aronfreed has suggested that the use of the term "conscience" might be restricted ". . . . .to those areas of conduct where substantial changes of affective (emotional) states have become attached to either actions or their cognitive representations."[3] Conscience, in this sense, refers to a child's cognitive and emotional evaluations of his conduct when his conduct affects other people. A child, then, would be showing conscience if he hit another child and then felt sorry. Aronfreed states that a liberal description of conscience ". . . . .subsumes those evaluative standards which apply to what we ordinarily call 'conduct', conduct here referring to behaviors which affect the lives of other people."[3]

This is a workable definition if one remembers that "conduct" refers only to behaviors that affect others, as distinct from evaluative judgments such as the assessment of a person being smart or pretty, or something being good art. Such evaluations are not part of conscience because they do not involve doing something to others. In our culture, there are some areas of conduct such as in athletics, when a child beats another, in a race for example, which are not considered to be in the moral realm despite the fact that people are affected. It is not possible to define exclusively either moral behavior (conduct) or conscience without some regard to cultural values about what is "right" or "wrong," what children (or adults) "ought" to feel good or bad about, or what belongs in the moral realm and what does not. Much of the child's internalization of moral conduct and of the evaluative emotional reactions referred to as conscience must follow the learning of social values and their incorporation into his evaluative cognitive structure. What the child comes to evaluate as right or wrong depends largely on what those about him evaluate as right or wrong. Finally, it should be stated again, that behaviors indicative of conscience involve emotional changes. Acting according to one's conscience leads to positive feelings, whereas transgression leads to feelings the child wishes to avoid.

MORAL VALUES AND MORAL BEHAVIOR—GENERALITY AND SPECIFICITY

Both Kohlberg and Aronfreed point out that moral judgment does not bear a very strong relationship to moral behavior. Children who can be considered *by some* as having a strong conscience, since they understand and accept certain moral standards, may often, however, break those standards. Other children may not understand or accept rules very well, which could be considered having a weak conscience, but they may behave morally. They may not cheat very much and may resist temptation well.[1, 40] Further, Kohlberg points out that the strength of conformity to a rule shown by a child bears no relation to the intensity of the guilt feelings that follow if the child violates the rule.[40] The various components of moral standards, conscience, and moral behavior may be learned in different ways and under somewhat different circumstances. Consequently the relationships among them cannot be expected to be very consistent.

This is not to say that there is *no* relationship between conscience and moral conduct or that different types of moral behavior show no association. The degree of relationship, however, tends to be low. The issue is really between the generality or the specificity of moral judgments, moral behaviors (like cheating), and reactions to transgression (like confessing). Since learning in these areas takes place gradually, in different situations, and with different socializing agents, a great deal of generality should not be expected. However, *some* generality should develop since the child does learn from some of the same people in somewhat similar circumstances.

The child's learning is not specific to each act and each situation. He can generalize from one situation to another. Parents do show some consistency in teaching their children moral values and behavior and some consistency in how they discipline the child's transgressions. The preponderant evidence shows that there is no unitary conscience, or unitary reaction to temptation, nor any high correlation between measures of the child's various types of reactions to transgression. However, there is some consistency, order and generality, not complete specificity.[11] Study 14.7 considers this issue.

GENERALITY OF HONESTY

STUDY 14.7

Robert W. Burton reconsidered and reanalyzed the classical studies of Hartshorne and May which tended to show some, but little, generality in children's behavior in the area of "honesty."[26] Hartshorne and May concluded that their "Studies in Deceit" showed no general trait of honesty in children. They believed that the small consistency children did show was a function of the situations in which they were placed, with the same children behaving similarly to the extent that the situations were alike. Similar situations were considered to be the common occasions for honest or dishonest behavior. Hartshorne and May stressed opportunities for deception or honesty across various types of situations rather than any general strength or weakness in resisting temptation in given children. They underlined the importance of different learned responses in particular settings. A child may have learned not to cheat on tests in school, but may have learned to take other people's money left lying about, or vice versa.

In reinterpreting their findings, Burton came to a slightly different conclusion. He felt that the data showed that children did have a partial underlying trait of honesty in "resistance to temptation" situations. However, he stated that Hartshorne and May were correct in rejecting some highly general "all or none" formulation about children's character. Children were neither "honest" nor "dishonest." Burton also found that in similar types of test situations children reacted somewhat similarly. The less similar any two tests of honesty were, the less consistency of honest behavior could be expected from the children.

However, he pointed out that some parents effectively teach their children that all types of cheating are to be avoided. They may point out that cheating at tests, taking money, and so on, are all dishonest. Such children, who are trained to be honest in a great *variety* of situations, may show a fairly general trait of "honest" behavior. They consistently define a variety of situations as calling for an "honest" response. Such learning comes about by rewarding or punishing the child consistently on the basis of his behavior in a wide range of clearly labeled situations.

If the child learns a similar cognitive, verbal label ("honest" or "dishonest") to all these situations, then a generality of honest behavior is facilitated. If the child in a situation of temptation can think of it as one calling for an "honest" or "dishonest" choice, the labels "honest" or "dishonest" can help control his ensuing behavior. If there is no cognitive labeling and mediation across situations—that is, if the child does not represent the various situations as all

> calling for "honest" or "dishonest" behavior, then there will be specificity. There may be an honest behavior, *as defined by others*, in one situation, and a dishonest one in another.
>
> Burton, R. V. Generality of honesty reconsidered. *Psych. Rev.*, 70, 1963, 481-499.

In summary, then, the generality and specificity of moral behavior seem to follow the laws of social learning theory. The extent of generality or specificity depends on the conditions of social learning. Children will behave the same way in situations which they have learned to recognize (label or cognize) as being similar. They will recognize them as being similar if their behavior in those situations has led to similar outcomes (almost always reward or almost always punishment), and/or if they have learned to understand that these situations are considered similar by important persons in their culture. If children do not recognize situations as being highly similar in terms of what is at issue (such as "honesty"), or if they have been inconsistently reinforced in such situations, their behavior will show little generality or consistency.

FREUDIAN APPROACH TO MORALITY

Freudians advance the concept of "superego" to stand for the general repository of internalized moral values. "Superego strength" refers to the strength and consistency or inner moral character and behavior. There is little evidence, as we have seen, for anything like a unified superego produced by "identification" or in any other way. Another personality construct proposed by the Freudians is that of the "ego" which is the reality-oriented or practical part of the human "psyche." "Ego strength" refers to the adequacy or capability of the ego in regulating behavior in accordance with the realities of the outside world. Its business is to help the child (or adult) to satisfy his instinctual needs safely. Kohlberg believes that moral character and moral behavior are more a function of ego strength than superego strength.[29, 40] Like Burton, Kohlberg feels that moral conduct is a matter of situational decision-making by the child in which the child has to assess the external world realistically. Hartshorne and May also contend that consistencies in moral conduct represent constancies in decision-making in various situations, rather than fixed behavior traits. Such contentions are in accordance with social learning theory principles. The variables Kohlberg finds correlated with moral conduct are those which reflect ability to deal with the outside world: persistence and nondistractibility, intelligence, ability to anticipate future events, ability to delay gratification, ability to maintain attention, stability of autonomic nervous system activity, low internal aggressive fantasy, and satisfaction with self and environment.[4]

Social learning theory would merely hold that calling this collection of innate reaction patterns and learned abilities ego strength is superfluous at best, and possibly misleading. To call the child's internalized moral behavior a function of ego strength tells nothing about how the factors which go to make up "ego strength" are acquired. Neither is it clear how highly the "contents" of ego strength are correlated. The ability to delay gratification and intelligence are correlated, but not very highly, and not in the same way for boys and girls. It does not seem helpful to invent terms like "superego strength" or "ego strength." What may be more to the point is an anlysis of the conditions under which children learn to internalize behavior, whether "moral" behavior or any other kind. We will turn to such an analysis in the next part of this chapter.

SUMMARY — PART 1

Internalization, a part of socialization, proceeds throughout childhood but reaches crucial proportions in the determination of behavior during adolescence. In the adolescent years, the child becomes capable of reacting more fully to his own internalized standards and values, is more likely to control his own behavior, and generally frees himself from the tyranny of immediate rewards and punishments imposed by others.

A great deal of internalization depends on cognition, on the ability to think, particularly about the possible consequences of acts. The adolescent has an enhanced understanding of his environment, its nature, rules, and possibilities, in comparison to the younger child.

The basis for internalization is the sense of identity which every person has. Fundamental to this sense of identity is the knowledge that one is a male or a female and the learning of the ways of feeling, thinking, and acting which are congruent with being male or female. There are cultural stereotypes, which can change as time goes on, concerning the behavior considered appropriate for males and females and how the personality characteristics of males and females are supposed to differ. Women, for instance are seen as being more nurturant and men as more competent and aggressive.

Children learn the socially expected behaviors which are sex gender associated and act in accordance with them. Boys come to cry less and to be more aggressive and openly competitive. Girls start to fall behind the performance of boys in school subjects which are perceived as "unfeminine," such as mathematics. Thus, behavior becomes "sex typed." There are two competing views of how this happens. Simply, social learning theory says that due to imitation and reinforcement boys learn to behave like boys and girls learn to behave like girls. Cognitive theory states that boys develop a conception of what boys are supposed to be like and girls develop a conceptualization about feminine sex identity. It goes on to contend that once these conceptions are formed, children strive to act in a way congruent or consistent with them, that is, they try to match the internalized standard.

Moral judgment and behavior depend on both learning and cognitive factors. A child's moral beliefs and acts are regulated by his past experiences of reward and punishment in situations where some of his acts may have been labeled "wrong," "bad," "immoral," or "dishonest." His future behavior will depend on a number of factors such as the generality of labeling, the nature of the explanations he was given, the similarity of the situations involved, and the consistency of the discipline utilized. In most cases affective factors are also involved since discipline arouses emotion.

PART 2 — INTERNALIZATION AND EMOTIONAL PROCESSES

PUNISHMENT AND SUPPRESSION

Children develop the ability *not to do* certain things, even though no one is around to observe them. "Suppression" is the name given to choosing not to perform some act when there is some drive, impulse, or tendency to do it. This is not to say that a child necessarily makes some conscious or deliberate choice to refrain, although sometimes he might. If a tendency to act is usually suppressed, it is because the act, in the past, has been connected with punishment which causes anxiety. The punishment of an act associates anxiety with carrying out an act. Anxiety is most powerful in bringing about suppression if it occurs at the onset of an act or is attached to cognitions associated with acting.[4, 51] The thought of doing something may then cause the child anxiety and lead him to refrain from doing it.

If a child learns not to act, when not under external control, he has internalized a bit of behavior, the behavior of stopping himself from doing something. He can reduce his own anxiety by refraining from anxiety producing activities. "Internalization" is a much broader and all-inclusive term than suppression, however. "Internalization" is the process by which a child (or adult) maintains and regulates his own behavior on the basis of affective (emotional) changes, whether negative or positive, which are often mediated by internal evaluative cognitive stimuli. Internalized behavior becomes independent of the external consequences of the behavior.[1, 3] This means that the child has internalized control over some bit of his behavior when the behavior is regulated not by immediate rewards or punishments delivered by other people, but by positive or negative feelings in himself, often as he anticipates carrying out or begins performing some act. Suppression, therefore, is part of the internalization process, but does not constitute all of it.

Attachment of Emotional Change to Behavior

Rewards or punishments cause affective (emotional) changes in the child. Usually reward induces positive feelings and punishment induces negative ones. Parts of these affective responses become conditioned to stimuli which are part of the behavior or cognitions associated with them.[45, 46] If a child is punished as he reaches for a cookie and as a result feels fear, parts of the fear response become attached to the act of reaching. If he is praised every time he begins tying his shoe laces, mild pleasure becomes attached to reaching for the laces when they need to be tied. When such pairing occurs several times, the child will feel some affect as he reaches for a cookie or his shoe laces, even if he is alone. In the cookie example, if he refrains from reaching, the act of not reaching is reinforced by a reduction in fear. This will happen even when the child is alone. In a further step, the fear responses present when he was originally punished can become attached not only to parts of acts, like reaching, but even to thinking about such behaviors. The child may no longer even consider taking a cookie. Such complete suppression is called "repression" by Freudian psychologists.

Attachment of Emotional Change to Cognition

Painful or pleasant emotions can become attached to the child's understanding or cognitive representation of a situation. If a child is punished for taking cookies he may become fearful when thinking of doing it again. Fear is an affective consequence that can become attached to cognitive stimuli, such as a child's thoughts about taking a cookie. In this way internalization can take place. As Aronfreed states ". . . .conduct is internalized to the extent that its affective consequences have been transferred from external outcomes (reward or punishment) to the intrinsic (internal) mediation of its response produced or cognitive stimulus correlates."[3] This means that the original affective consequence (fear) can be attached to either its response produced correlates (reaching for a cookie) or its cognitive stimulus correlates (thinking about reaching for a cookie). Of course the same process holds for positive or pleasurable emotional changes. These emotional attachments will facilitate behavior. If a child has often been praised by his parents for helping others he may take pleasure in doing so even if there are no adults about.

An experiment by Parke and Walters, part of which is reported in Study 14.8, illustrates the effects of the *timing* of punishment on internalized suppression. *When* the child experiences an emotional change is a very important determinant of internalization. It is hard for children to learn to regulate their own behavior if rewards and punishments were originally not closely tied to their behavior in time. Internalization is facilitated by connecting emotional changes to the beginning of acts. It is always helpful to reward or punish children for any incipient behavior, or thoughts about doing something, as soon as possible; the effects of praising or reprimanding children long after they have done something are usually considerably weaker.

TIMING OF PUNISHMENT AND INTERNALIZATION OF SUPPRESSION

STUDY 14.8

Parke and Walters studied 49 first and second grade boys with an average age of six years and 11 months. They were divided into four groups. One group was punished early but weakly, and a second, early but strongly. A third group was punished late and weakly, and the fourth, late but strongly. In effect, timing (early or late) and strength (weak or strong) of punishment were varied. Parke and Walters were interested in the effects of timing and strength of punishment on suppression. We will mainly be concerned with the effects of timing. Early punishment should lead to greater suppression since fear is attached to even beginning to do something.

To study timing of punishment, nine pairs of toys of equal attractiveness were presented to each boy on nine training trials. The subjects were run one at a time. Each boy was asked to choose one of the toys on each of the nine trials. On trials one, three, four, six, and nine, all of the children got a verbal punishment consisting of the admonition, "No, that's for the other boy!" and an unpleasant noise (for weak punishment the noise was a 65-decibel tone and for strong punishment a 96-decibel tone). The children in the early punishment condition were punished as they *started* to reach for the toy that they wanted. In the late punishment condition the children were punished *after* they had picked up the toy that they wanted.

After the punishment training, the toys that the child had been punished for, either because he reached for them (early punishment) or because he picked them up (late punishment) were left on a table. The toys were covered with a black cloth. The child was seated in front of the table and the *experimenter left the room* on a pretext of going away to get something. The child was left alone with the covered toys for 15 minutes. The child could be seen by the experimenter, who watched him from the next room through a one-way vision screen. The experimenter recorded: *how long* it took before the child lifted the cloth and picked up a toy; *how many times* the child picked up a toy; and *how much time* the child spent handling the toys.

The early-punished boys deviated (picked up a toy) less often than late-punished boys. The early-punished boys waited longer before picking up a toy than the late-punished boys. The early-punished boys did not handle the toys as long as the late-punished boys. In short, early punishment leads to greater internalization of suppression.

Parke, R. D., and Walters, R. H. Some factors influencing the efficacy of punishment training for inducing response inhibition. Experiment 2. *Monogr. Soc. Res. Child. Developm.*, 32, No. 1, 1967.

OBSERVATION OF MODELS AND AFFECTIVE CHANGE

It is worth noting again that the child does not originally have to personally experience reward or punishment in order to internalize some behavioral tendency. All he has to do is experience some emotional change in connection with an act or its cognitive representation. In this way parts of the emotion can become attached to parts of the act, preparations for performing the act, or the cognitive representation of the act. Consequently internalization can be due to the child's observation of social models. The observation of models can cause a child to experience an emotion such as joy or fear. The observation of models can result in the attachment of affective value to the perceptual responses of watching or the cognitive representation of the observed behavior.[1,3] In fact it has been suggested by Aronfreed that one reason that a child will imitate a model is that watching the model perform may cause an emotional change, for instance, make the watching child feel good. It may be pleasant or exciting for the child to see what the model is doing. Feeling good, in essence the pleasant affective part of watching, can become attached to the child's perceptions and cognitions about the model's exact behavior. When the child imitates the model's acts he may be intrinsically (internally) reinforced by again feeling some of the pleasant emotional changes which took place as he first watched and cognitively represented to himself what the model was doing.[3] The imitative behavior is internalized since it is controlled not by the external *consequences* of imitating, but by the pleasant emotional state of the child as he imitates what the model did.

IMPORTANCE OF COGNITIVE ACTIVITIES IN INTERNALIZATION

We have seen how early punishment can attach emotional states to the child's anticipations, intentions or preparatory movements. Of course, so can early rewards. Movements connected with anticipations or intentions occur before overt acts. If emotional changes of a positive or negative nature become attached to them, these affective changes can, through being conditioned to these movements, facilitate or suppress behavior. In this way the child's anticipatory or intentional movements acquire control over behavior before the overt act can take place.[3] For example, as the child begins to think about doing something he makes preparatory movements. As he does so fear is aroused, and he stops.

Perhaps a more important point is that the child's cognitive abilities — his abilities to label, verbally mediate, form concepts, symbolically represent the environment — tremendously expand internalized control over his own behavior. These cognitive functions, many of which have acquired an emotional evaluative nature, allow behavior to become fairly free of the consequences of overt acts. Cognitions are of vital importance in internalization because they allow the child to store and to represent his social experiences. The child can remember the pleasant and unpleasant things that have happened to him in the past. He begins to understand the consequences of his behavior and becomes able in time, to use such information to regulate his behavior. The child starts to conceptualize and to categorize his social experiences and becomes able to abstract common elements. He becomes able to generalize about social rules, his own behavior, the situations in which they occur, and the consequences to be expected. He acquires what may be called "cognitive structures" and these partly free him from reliance on the stimuli of the immediate situation. According to Piaget, these cognitive structures reach their highest level of development in late adolescence.

Among the consequences of the child's formation of cognitive structures concerning his conduct, for instance, is the fact that he can remember what he did some time ago and represent it to himself. If he is caught a day after a transgression and punished, he knows why; or, having done something "bad," he can keep anticipating punishment until it comes. Having done something that often brings punishment, he can do things to avoid being caught or engage in acts to reduce the severity of punishment. In addition, since he can represent to himself what he has done, punishment can still be partly effective, even if it comes days after his transgression. The emotional effects of the later punishment can become attached to his memory (cognition) of the earlier act.[3] The adolescent, thus, is not restricted to reacting to events of the moment; he can regulate his actions because he can remember the past and anticipate the future, as well as react to the present.

INTERNALIZATION AND PATTERNS OF CHILD REARING

Warmth

Parental nurturance (warmth) seems to be a prerequisite for internalization of behaviors which are part of the internalized guides to conduct expected of a well-socialized child. However, not much of relationship has been found between the *amount* of parental nurturance (warmth) and various measures of the child's internalized control of his own behavior. This may seem to be a paradox, but it really is not. It appears that a reasonable amount of warmth and nurturance is needed to establish a social attachment between the child and a socializing agent, usually the mother. Without this attachment, internalization or socialization will at best be very weak. However, beyond a point where there is a sufficiently strong tie between a child and a mother, or another socializing agent like the father, extra amounts of nurturance or warmth contribute little to internalization.[3] If there has been enough warmth to establish the tie, additional warmth is irrelevant. An investigation by Grinder, found in Study 14.9, is illustrative of the low association of *amount* of warmth with internalization of resistance to temptation.

CHILD REARING PRACTICES AND RESISTANCE TO TEMPTATION

STUDY 14.9

The subjects in this study by Robert E. Grinder were 140 children from the original 379 families investigated by Sears, Maccoby, and Levin. Each family originally studied had a child in kindergarten in a public school near Boston. Both boys and girls, of different birth orders, and from families of varying social classes, were included. At the time of the initial study the children were aged five to six. They were 11 to 12 years old when they were given a test of resistance to temptation by Grinder.

The extensive study by Sears, Maccoby, and Levin was reviewed in some detail in the chapter on patterns of child rearing (Chapter 11). From the information given by the mothers, a measure of the children's conscience development was obtained as one part of the large study. There were three conscience scales. They dealt with how readily the child confessed voluntarily, how readily the child admitted doing something wrong when asked about it, and whether the child seemed guilty and tried to make reparation after wrong doing. Of course, there were measures of the strength of the mothers' warmth and nurturance toward their children.

The resistance to temptation situation devised by Grinder was one we have already described in a study by Mischel. It was the shooting gallery game in which children could cheat, if they wanted to, in order to get a higher score and win prizes. The prizes were attractive badges.

The results clearly showed that the amount of warmth or nurturance on the part of the mother was not related to the tendency to refrain from cheating. Taken by themselves, measures of the mothers' warmth will not predict who will resist temptation and who will cheat. Grinder speculates that the mothers of most of the children in this study were sufficiently warm for their warmth to have produced whatever effects it could. All these children had sufficient social ties to their parents.

Grinder, R. E. Parental child rearing practices, conscience, and resistance to temptation in sixth grade children. *Child Develpm.*, 33, 1962, 803-820.

Withdrawal of Warmth or Love

Although the establishment of a social attachment based on warmth is a prerequisite for the acquisition of internalized behaviors like self-criticism, the crucial factor is the withdrawal of love. We have already seen that emotional changes are important in the establishment of internalization. Probably one of the most powerful sources of emotional change in the child is the withdrawal of love or the threat of removal of nurturance of warmth by the mother or father. Few acts are as emotionally powerful in arousing fear or other negative emotions in the child as the threat to the social bond that ties a child to another human being. Children become upset when their parents are angry with them or ignore them and become happy again when the parents show them affection and attention.

Self-criticism involves the child's taking love away from himself. The acquisition of self-criticism provides a good example for illustrating the role of nurturance in internalization. Self-criticism is certainly a quite internalized response because it is often made by a child to himself, in private. If self-criticism takes place in private it can have no consequences in terms of the behavior of others.[3] Sometimes, of course, self-critical remarks are made in front of others. The child may expect that being self-critical out loud may induce these others to "go easy" with him because he appears to be contrite. Self-critical responses may in such cases be reinforced by others who take such self-criticism to be a sign of the child's contrition. Study 14.10 contains a partial report of a complex experiment on the relationship between rewardingness (warmth-nurturance), withdrawal of love, and the tendency to be self-critical.

WARMTH, WITHDRAWAL OF LOVE, AND SELF-CRITICISM

STUDY 14.10

Joan Grusec studied 80 kindergarten boys and girls ranging in age from five years five months to six years 11 months. To establish *high warmth* the experimenter played with the child and was nice and friendly, asked the child questions, and was generally approving of the child. In the *low warmth* condition the experimenter mostly ignored the child. A game was used in the study. In the high warmth but *withdrawal of love* condition, after initially being warm and friendly, the experimenter commented that she was "unhappy and disappointed" with how the child was playing.

The game was rigged so as to appear that something that went wrong during the game was the child's fault. The experimenter then questioned the child as to what happened. Grusec wanted to see if the child would become self-critical, that is, to ascertain if the child would actually make self-critical remarks blaming himself. There was also a measure of generalization. The child was put in a new situation in which it was made to appear that the child had torn a picture. In this new situation the child was asked why the picture had torn. Again the aim was to find out if the child would be self-critical and blame himself. Self-critical reactions were, then, tested in an original game situation and later in a new and different situation to see if the original reaction would generalize.

The results showed that there was more self-criticism if the experimenter was warm than if the experimenter was not warm in the original game. However, generalization of self-criticism to a new situation appeared only if the experimenter was both warm and *also withdrew love*. Generalized internalization of the tendency to be self-critical appears when the child forms a social attachment to a warm human being who then *withdraws love* from the child.

Grusec, J. Some antecedents of self-criticism. *J. Pers. and Soc. Psychol.*, 4, 1966, 244-252.

Withdrawal of Love and Internalization

Once a social attachment is forged, withdrawal of love is a powerful socializing force. The child must approach the socializing agent (mother, father, teacher, friend) to get it reinstated. The reinstatement of love is contingent on the child's behaving in the way these people want him to behave. In addition, the intense negative emotions generated by withdrawal of love, such as guilt, can become associated with, reduced, or prevented by certain acts of the child. The child learns not to do certain things which can bring about the withdrawal of love, or can learn to punish himself for acts that bring it about, thus lessening the chance that he will do it again. The child may also be quite fearful and guilty while waiting for punishment. When punishment comes, the parents may also criticize him. The criticism may sometimes be correlated with the end of punishment or its diminution. Therefore, being criticized, although unpleasant, can have fear and guilt reducing value since it may be associated with the end of punishment. Later, when the child has transgressed and is feeling guilty or fearful, he may criticize himself and thus experience some reduction in these unpleasant emotions.[3]

If there is no strong social tie to the socializing figure, as in "rejected" or neglected children, there is nothing to lose. Not having love, the threat of its withdrawal, or actual withdrawal, does not really exist psychologically. In such cases little internalization can take place on this basis and the child may remain relatively unsocialized, "badly behaved," or delinquent. The child may avoid its parents and seek to escape punishment. The child can also withdraw love from the parents in an effort to control or punish them and such interactions are not uncommon in adolescence. Some parents may be very sensitive to signs of disapproval from their children.

THE SENSITIZATION PROCESSES AND INTERNALIZATION

We saw in the chapter on patterns of child rearing (Chapter 11) that sensitization procedures, in contrast to induction procedures like withdrawal of love, are relatively inefficient in bringing about internalization. In sensitization discipline the child is made to focus on what people are going to do to him here and now, often in a short space of time. They are going to hit him, yell, scream, or take away his toys, so he is forced to pay attention to the consequences of his acts in terms of what others are doing to him. Behavior remains linked to external consequences of the moment and effects remain dependent on the parents' physical presence. Withdrawal of love can be painful even when the parents are gone, whereas a slap in the face may only be effective when they are there.[1] It pays to control one's own behavior to avoid the fear generated by anticipation of the withdrawal of love. It may pay more, if a beating is at issue, to learn to stay out of the parents' way or to hide the transgression.

FEAR, GUILT, AND SHAME

Transgressions by the child are usually followed by some negative affect as a function of past punishment by the parents and violation of internalized standards. The affect experienced may be fear, guilt, or shame.[7] What the child experiences is partly determined by his cognitive structure. Fear or anxiety without guilt or shame may be experienced by the child if his only concern is the possibility of punishment. Guilt may be felt if the negative subjective feeling of the child is determined by moral evaluation of the transgression. He may feel guilty if he judges himself to have done a "bad" or "wrong" thing, particularly if his conduct has negative consequences for others. Guilt is defined by Aronfreed as the experience of anxiety in connection with the perception of the harmful consequences of a child's acts for others. Again, according to Aronfreed shame is experienced by a child after a transgression if his cognitions focus on exposure or observation. Shame is the fear or anxiety related to the possibility of having misdeeds known to others who will not approve and who may blame the child.[3]

Fear (anxiety), guilt, and shame are all unpleasant and may have the functional effect, among others, of leading to the suppression of acts and thus to internalization. Induction disciplinary techniques not only produce internalization, but they produce guilt. Guilt is often the price paid for socialization by means of love withdrawal techniques. Psychologists have long been aware of the guilt-ridden, oversocialized child who often becomes the adult neurotic. Induction techniques, like others, are best used in moderation and with an emphasis on reasoning rather than on the frequent withdrawal of love.

INTERNALIZATION AND FREEDOM

Successful socialization based on internalization may free the child partly from the tyranny of external control, but it does not free him from his own self judgments. To the contrary, he has to contend with the positive and negative feelings engendered within as a consequence of his own acts. Having internalized a variety of cognitive-evaluative reactions, he will usually act in ways that will optimize favorable internal feelings and minimize negative ones. Some of his cognitive representations to which evaluations are attached take the form of attitudes, value, and ideologies. An attitude, for instance, has both a cognitive and an evaluative component. If a child dislikes being "dishonest" it means that he has some ideas about what "dishonesty" is (cognitive) and that he disapproves of it (evaluation). If he recognizes a "dishonest" act on his own part and labels it as such, he will surely think less of himself. Internalization only gives freedom to act in accordance with one's own psychological structure.

SUMMARY — PART 2

Internalization is a process by which a child often regulates his own behavior on the basis of emotional changes which are mediated by cognitions of an evaluative nature. That is, thoughts (symbolic representations of experience) are seldom neutral, but have associated with them various states of feeling. The emotional consequences of the child's past actions, dependent on previous positive or negative reinforcements, become connected to the child's thought processes. Thinking about doing something, therefore, can cause the child to experience various feelings like interest, curiosity, and pleasure on the one hand, or fear, guilt, shame, and depression on the other. Positive feelings facilitate thoughts or behavior, whereas negative emotional states will suppress throughts or behavior.

On the basis of inner emotional changes the child's behavior comes under his own internal regulation. He does what engenders good feelings, and he avoids doing what makes him feel uncomfortable. Emotional changes can also become associated with the beginnings of motor acts, such as starting to reach for or move toward an object. Consequently, the earlier in any sequence punishment or reward comes the greater effect it will have on future internalization. The earlier in any sequence of action or thought emotional change comes the earlier in the sequence it will have its suppressing or facilitating effect.

Imitation may occur because of the positive feelings which it engenders. The observation of models can cause the attachment of affective value to the perceptual response of watching; that is, the child may like or enjoy seeing what the model is doing and so come to imitate it. Of course, all such effects depend on the development of complex cognitive structures in the child which allow him to comprehend the world and his own experiences.

Internalization often presupposes that the child is emotionally attached to one or more persons. It is the way in which these people react to him, approving his actions or being critical of them, which is often reponsible for his emotional reactions. Once emotional bonds are established as a result of being shown a certain amount of warmth and attention in infancy, the child acts to maintain those bonds. Consequently, he tries to avoid loss of love. In maintaining love and approval, the child comes to internalize adult standards as his own and thus to regulate his individual actions in conformity with internal beliefs.

REFERENCES

1. Aronfreed, J. The concept of internalization. (In) *Handbook of Internalization Theory*, Goslin, D. A., and Glass, D. C. (Eds.). Rand-McNally, New York, 1967.
2. Aronfreed, J. *Imitation and identification. An analysis of some affective and cognitive mechanisms.* Presented at meeting of the Soc. for Res. Child Develpm., New York, 1967.
3. Aronfreed, J. *Conduct and Conscience: The Socialization of Internalized Control Over Behavior.* Academic Press, New York, 1968.
4. Aronfreed, J., and Reber, A. Internalized behavioral suppression and the timing of punishment. *J. Pers. Soc. Psychol., 1*, 1965, 3-16.
5. Bandura, A., and Kupers, C. J. Transmission of patterns of self reinforcement through modeling. *J. Abnorm. Soc. Psychol., 89*, 1964, 1-9.
6. Bandura, A., and Rosenthal, T. L. Vicarious classical conditioning as a function of arousal level. *J. Pers. Soc. Psychol., 3*, 1966, 54-62.
7. Bandura, A., and Walters, R. H. *Social Learning and Personality Development.* Holt, Rinehart and Winston, New York, 1963.
8. Barry, H., and Child, I. A cross-cultural survey of some sex differences in socialization. *J. Abnorm. Soc. Psychol., 55*, 1957, 327-332.
9. Bronfenbrenner, U. Freudian theories of identification and their derivation. *Child Develpm., 31*, 1960, 15-40.
10. Brown, D. G. Sex-role preference in young children. *Psych. Monogr., 70*, No. 14, 1956.
11. Burton, R. W. Generality of honesty reconsidered. *Psych. Rev., 70*, 1963, 481-499.
12. Emmerich, W. Family role concepts of children ages six to ten. *Child Develpm., 32*, 1961, 609-624.
13. Feshbach, S., and Feshbach, N. Influence of the stimulus object upon the complementary and supplementary projection of fear. *J. Abnorm. Soc. Psychol., 66*, 1963, 498-502.
14. Freud, S. *Some Psychological Consequences of the Anatomical Distinction Between the Sexes. Collected Papers, Vol. 5*, Hogarth Press, New York, 1950.
15. Freud, S. *New Introductory Lectures on Psychoanalysis.* Norton, New York, 1933.
16. Freud, S. *The Passing of the Oedipus Complex. Collected Papers, Vol. 2.* Hogarth Press, New York, 1925.
17. Freud, S. *Mourning and Melancholia. Collected Papers, Vol. 4.* Hogarth Press, New York, 1925.
18. Freud, S. *Group Psychology and the Analysis of the Ego.* Hogarth Press, New York, 1922.
19. Gardner, R. L. An analysis of children's attributes toward fathers. *J. Genet. Psychol., 70*, 1947, 3-28.

20. Gelfand, D. M., and Singer, R. D. Generalization of children's verbally conditioned personality judgments. *J. Clin. Psychol., 21*, 101-103.
21. Gesell, A., et al. *The First Five Years of Life: A Guide to the Study of the Preschool Child.* Harpers, New York, 1940.
22. Greenberg, P. Competition in children: an experimental study. *Amer. J. Psychol., 44*, 1932, 221-248.
23. Grinder, R. E. Parental childbearing practices, conscience, and resistance to temptation in sixth grade children. *Child Develpm., 33*, 1962, 803-820.
24. Grusec, J. Some antecedents of self-criticism. *J. Pers. and Soc. Psychol., 4*, 1966, 244-252.
25. Hall, M. and Keith, R. A. Sex-role preference among children of upper and lower social class. *J. Soc. Psychol., 62*, 1964, 101-110.
26. Hartshorne, M., and May, M. A. *Studies in the Nature of Character. Studies in Deceit, Vol. 1.* Macmillan, New York, 1928.
27. Hartup, W. W., and Zook, E. A. Sex-role preferences in three and four-year-old children. *J. Consult. Psychol., 24*, 1960, 420-426.
28. Hartwick, B. A. Sex-differences in behavior of nursery school children. *Child Develpm., 8*, 1937, 343-355.
29. Hendry, L. S. Cognitive processes in a moral conflict situation: Unpublished doctoral dissertation, Yale University, New Haven, 1960.
30. Jersild, A. T., and Markey, F. V. Conflicts between preschool children. *Child Develpm. Monogr., No. 21*, 1935.
31. Kagan, J. Acquisition and significance of sex typing and sex role identity. (In) *Child Development Research, Vol. 1*, Hoffman, M. L., and Hoffman, L. W. (Eds.). Russell Sage Foundation, New York, 1964.
32. Kagan, J. The child's perception of the parent. *J. Abnorm. Soc. Psychol., 53*, 1956, 257-258.
33. Kagan, J., et al. Information processing in the child: significance of analytic and reflective attitudes. *Psych. Monogr., 78*, No. 1, 1964.
34. Kagan, J., et al. Information processing in the child: significance of analytic and reflective attitudes. *Psych. Monogr., 78*, No. 1, 1964.
35. Kagan, J., and Lemkin, J. The child's differential perception of parental attributes. *J. Abnorm. Soc. Psychol., 61*, 1960, 440-447.
36. Kagan, J., and Moss, H. A. *Birth to Maturity.* John Wiley, New York, 1962.
37. Katcher, A. The discrimination of sex differences by young children. *J. Genet. Psychol., 87*, 1955, 131-143.
38. Kohlberg, L. *Stages in Development of Children's Conceptions of Physical and Social Objects in the Years Four to Eight.* Book in preparation.
39. Kohlberg, L. A cognitive-developmental analysis of children's sex role concepts and attitudes. (In) *The Development of Sex Differences*, Maccoby, E. E. (Ed.). Stanford University Press, Stanford, 1966.
40. Kohlberg, L. Development of moral character and moral ideology. (In) *Child Development Research. Vol. 1*, Hoffman, M. L. and Hoffman, L. W. (Eds.). Russell Sage Foundation, New York, 1964.
41. Kumata, L., and Schramm, W. A pilot study of cross-cultural meaning. *Pub. Opin. Quart., 20*, 1956, 229-238.
42. Lindskoog, D. Children's differentiation of instrumental and expressive parent roles. Unpublished Master's thesis. University of Chicago, Chicago, 1964.
43. Maccoby, E. E. Sex differences in intellectual functioning. (In) *The Development of Sex Differences.* Maccoby, E. E. (Ed.). Stanford University Press, Stanford, 1966.
44. Mischel, W. A Social-Learning View of Sex Differences in Behavior. (In) *The Development of Sex Differences*, Maccoby, E. E. (Ed.). Stanford University Press, Stanford, 1966.
45. Mowrer, O. H. *Learning Theory and Behavior.* John Wiley, New York, 1960.
46. Mowrer, O. H. *Learning Theory and the Symbolic Processes.* John Wiley, New York, 1960.
47. Parke, R. D., and Walters, R. H. Some Factors Influencing the Efficacy of Punishment Training for Inducing Response Inhibition. Experiment 2. *Monogr. Soc. Res. Child Develpm., 32*, No. 1, 1967.

48. Parsons, T., and Bales, R. F. *Socialization and Interaction Process.* Free Press, Glencoe, Ill., 1965.
49. Piaget, J. *The Psychology of Intelligence.* Routledge, Kegan Paul. London, 1947.
50. Rabban, M. Sex-role identification in young children in two diverse social groups. *Genet. Psychol. Monogr., 42*, 1950, 81-85.
51. Solomon, R. L. Punishment. *Amer. Psychologist., 19*, 1964, 239-253.
52. Sontag, C. T., et al. Mental growth and personality development: a longitudinal study. *Soc. Res. Child Develpm. Monogr., 23*, No. 68, 1958.
53. Tash, R. J. The role of the father in the family. *J. Exper. Educ., 20*, 1952, 319-361.
54. Triandis, H. C., and Osgood, C. E. A comparative factor analysis of semantic structures in monolingual Greek and American college students. *J. Abnorm. Soc. Psychol., 57*, 1958, 187-196.
55. Vance, T. F., and McCall, L. T. Children's preferences among play materials as determined by the method of paired comparison of pictures. *Child Develpm., 5*, 1934, 267-277.
56. Vinacke, W. E., and Gullickson, G. R. Age and sex differences in the formation of cognitions. *Child Develpm., 35*, 1964, 1217-1231.

CHAPTER 15

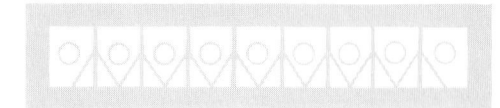

LATER ADOLESCENCE

THE ADOLESCENT SUBCULTURE

Some students of adolescence contend that there is a very definite adolescent subculture. That is, they believe that adolescents have a society with its own values and rules of behavior somehow different than the adult world. James S. Coleman feels this way and has written a book, *The Adolescent Society*, in which he states: "The adolescent lives more and more in a society of his own, he finds the family less and less satisfying as a psychological home. As a consequence, the home has less and less ability to mold him."[9] Frederick Elkin and William A. Westly feel that at least in upper-middle-class suburbia there is no separate adolescent subculture. In an article entitled, "The myth of adolescent culture," they have written: "They tend to choose friends on the basis of values they have acquired from their parents; consequently, their peer group tends to reinforce the standards of behavior of which their parents approve, and thus there is no serious conflict of generations."[13, 1] What is one to make of these conflicting views? Is there a separate social world of adolescent behavior, or is the life and activity of the adolescent a modified image of the world of his parents?

It seems that both points of view have some limited validity. In their high school years, adolescents do spend a lot of free time outside the home and associate with other adolescents who have a strong shaping influence on their behavior, atttiudes, and values. The adolescent does strive, often, to be an informal or formal member of some adolescent group or groups. Such groups, like all other groups, exact a certain degree of behavior conformity as a part of belonging and have some attitudes and values not shared by other groups.[17, 19, 43] At the same time, a great percentage of both boys and girls have reported that it would be harder for them to take parental disapproval over joining a club in school than it would be to break with their best friend over the issue; 53.8 percent versus 42.7 percent in boys, and 52.9 percent versus 43.4 percent in girls.[9] The larger figure in both cases represents the percentage stating that it would be harder to take parental disapproval over the matter; and the smaller figure is the percentage stating that it would be harder to break with their closest friend over the issue. There may be an adolescent subculture, but the adolescent is also tied to the adult one.

Clearly adolescents are not just oriented toward each other. By later adolescence, they have internalized many adult standards of conduct and conscience and there seems to be a reasonable balance of emotional ties and influence between friends and parents. Earlier internalization may, in the long run, throw the weight of influence in the parental direction despite any "generation gap." A question may be raised, in any event, about the extent to which the types of behaviors and attitudes that friends reward or punish are congruent or in conflict with those rewarded or punished by parents. The presence of two subcultures does not establish that they are at odds. Study 15.1 throws some light on this issue.

ADOLESCENT AND PARENTAL ATTITUDES AND VALUES

STUDY 15.1

James. G. Coleman offers some data on the attitudes and values of high school students and their parents. Slightly over 60 percent of both boys and girls felt that their parents would be very proud of them if they were singled out for some honor having to do with excellence in school work. About 68 percent of boys felt that their parents would be very proud of them if they made the basketball team, and 77 percent of girls felt that their parents would be very proud of them if they made cheerleader. One may accept the opinion that by high school age boys and girls have a reasonably good understanding of what their parents would be proud of. Clearly parents value athletic, social, and academic success in their children.

Parents, at least in their children's views, value all three. However, social success is seen as more highly valued for girls, and athletic success a bit more highly valued for boys than academic success. When asked what they would want to be remembered for in school, 43.6 percent of the boys said for being an athletic star, 31.3 percent said for being a brilliant student, and 25 percent said for being most popular. As far as girls were concerned, 36.1 percent listed wanting to be remembered for being a leader in activities, 35.2 percent listed being most popular, and 28.8 percent listed being a brilliant student. Fewer girls than boys care about being a brilliant student. This corresponds somewhat to the parents' view, since Coleman found that well over 70 percent of them want their sons to be outstanding students, whereas only a little more than 50 percent care so strongly about this for their daughters.

Parents seem to care less about social and athletic success for their children than do the children themselves. This establishes some conflict between the generations. When directly questioned about the issue, parents put a greater stress on academic achievement than their children did. However, Coleman notes: "But parents also want their children to be successful in the things that 'count' at school; that is, the things that count in the eyes of other adolescents. And parents know what things count. . . . Thus, even the rewards a child gains from his parents may help reinforce the values of adolescent culture—not because their parents hold these same values, but because parents want their children to be successful and esteemed by their peers."

Coleman, J. S. *The Adolescent Culture.* The Free Press, Glencoe, Ill., 1961.

It seems that parents value success and the achievement of popularity and esteem by their children. Many parents are likely to reward, or at least fail to punish, behavior on the part of their children which lead to these goals, although they may want their children to conform more to adult values or to be more scholarly. The parents themselves may want success and esteem and may encourage and tolerate whatever leads to it, although the activities adolescents must engage in to gain esteem may be somewhat at variance with parental desires. The adolescent learns that parents value success and esteem. Evaluative cognitions about the importance of success become internalized even if the meaning of success may be defined differently by the adolescent.

However, we cannot be sure, in some cases, what parents really do want. Bandura and Walters find that some fathers of adolescent delinquent boys actually tend to reinforce their sons' delinquent behaviors. This is not usually done by telling the boy "go out and steal cars," or "play truant." Rather the father seems to gain vicarious thrills by making his son tell about his sexual adventures or other antisocial activities. He may discuss his son's delinquencies with him in such ways as to tacitly, or even overtly, reinforce the boy for such activities; thus, the parents of some antisocial aggressive boys are inclined, in many ways, to encourage and condone delinquent behavior.[2] It has been pointed out that some parents gain unconscious vicarious satisfaction from their child's behavior. Despite loud protestations, parents may really admire their adolescent child for behaving as they themselves lack the courage to behave. They may reinforce such secretly envied behavior quite overtly, or, more often subtly, even if at other times it may frighten them. They may help the child keep certain "undesirable" behavior secret or they may minimize it or defend it if it becomes public.[2, 20] In some cases the adolescent may be directly following, imitating, or modeling himself after the antisocial behavior of the parents. It has been found that children are likely to imitate their fathers' criminality, particularly when the mother is also a social deviant.[25, 40]

One may tentatively conclude that there is a kind of adolescent subculture. By this is meant the existence of formal and informal group associations among adolescents. The members of these informal and formal groups have attitudes and values and consequently they reinforce certain behaviors shown by the group members, ignore some, and punish others. Since the behaviors which are approved by various adolescent groups show certain resemblances, one can speak of a subculture or subcultures.[9] Despite some differences, however, the behavior encouraged in the adolescent subculture is often not really very far from the behavior encouraged by some adults. Success, esteem, popularity, hedonism, athletic skill, a "nice personality," and education are valued by adults as well as adolescents, although perhaps not in the same order or to the same degree. Even in the case of antisocial behavior, the adolescent may be tacitly supported by a parent. In other cases the parents may have failed to behave in ways which would lead their children to accept parental values.

While there does exist an adolescent subculture, or rather, various adolescent subcultures, these are heavily influenced by the general adult culture or a specific adult subculture. The adolescent does not live just in high school or with his friends, nor do the high school and the peer group exist in some general isolation. There is continual contact, however limited in some cases, with the rest of the world. At one extreme there may be subcultures such as the "hippies," adolescent street drug addicts, or members of delinquent fighting gangs, which are quite isolated from the mainstream of adult cultural values. However, these are the exceptions, rather than the rule. Even such groups have their adult counterparts to whom they relate. The rule is probably that adolescent subcultures have some attitudes, values, and dispositions in conflict with the parental generation and many in common with them, although they are sometimes expressed in different ways. Parents may inculcate values about "freedom," "self-expression," or "complete honesty," although they have little chance to follow such values themselves. Later, parents may be very surprised to find their children actually behaving in ways consonant with values they have taught without anticipating their possible consequences.

Adolescent Values

If there are adolescent subcultures, whatever their relation to the adult world, what are some of their predominant orientations towards behavior and values? What types of behaviors and attitudes do adolescents strive for? What makes for success and acceptability in the life of the high school student?

Study 15.2 gives some answers to these questions. The data are also drawn from Coleman's book and additional comments by the present authors are included below.[9]

ATTRIBUTES OF THE LEADING CROWD

STUDY 15.2

The behaviors, attitudes, and values most acceptable to any subgroup are often those that will make for acceptance by or membership in the most admired circle of elite members of that group. Coleman asked students in several high schools what it took to get into the leading crowd.

The following answers, in order of importance were given by boys: personality, good reputation, being an athlete, good looks, good grades, having a car, having good clothes, having money, and coming from a good neighborhood. Their concept of an elite high school boy, then, would be a good-looking athlete with an attractive personality, who had not been in much trouble, who had good grades and the marks of affluence (like money, a car, clothes, and well-to-do parents). In other words, the stereotype of the middle-class dream. Substitute for "good grades" "being a good and dedicated worker," and one has the ideal middle-class adult, except that money may come to mean more than personality when there are bills to pay. The order of importance of the items may be re-ordered, but few new ones need be added.

For girls the list was: personality, good looks, clothes, good reputation, friendliness, neatness, having money, good grades, and coming from the right neighborhood. The elite high school girl is an attractive, neat, well-groomed girl with an attractive personality, who is also affluent and a reasonably able student. If one substitutes "good wife and mother" for "good grades" and places this characteristic higher on the list, one has a stereotype of the most desirable middle-class housewife.

Although middle-class values predominate, there is in the adolescent subculture a worship of "personality," athletics, and sociability in girls at the cost of solid commitment to good grades. Adolescents do not highly value a too diligent or compliant attachment to school work. The "grind" is not their ideal. However, academic achievement is still on the list of elite attributes. The notion of being able to get along with people and of being popular means more to most high school students than academic achievement. It is not clear how much of this attitude may be a verbal rebellion against the actual grade-obtaining rat race forced on high school students who face competition for college entrance.

Coleman, J. S. *The Adolescent Society.* The Free Press, Glencoe, Ill., 1961.

The student who drops out of school is usually one who fails to measure up to the behaviors that are reinforced and the attributes that are valued by the adolescent subculture. School dropouts come to a large extent from the lower classes.[34] Clearly, they can't compete in terms of cars, clothes, money, or being from the right neighborhood. The dropout is most often a poor student who gets bad grades.[10] Dropouts are not popular with their peers, do not participate in school activities, and are not very positively regarded by peers or teachers.[6] "Not making it" in terms of the prevailing values of the adolescent subculture and its middle-class values, they find school to be quite unpleasant, and leave.[3, 12] One doesn't have to come from an affluent middle-class background or be a moderately good student to "make it", although it helps. Avenues of recognition, that is, of reward and satisfaction, include good looks, athletic ability, a good reputation, or participation in social activities.

The lower-class adolescent accepts middle-class values to an amazing degree and tries to "make it" in those terms.[42] Of course, values do vary by social class, and behaviors such as a certain amount of fighting are more acceptable among lower-class boys.[23] Since the percentage of adolescents graduating from high school has been on the increase in the last few decades, more and more children are facing the need to live up to the standards of the predominantly middle-class oriented school and adolescent subculture. Those who drop out may have their own subcultural behaviors and values which may range from holding as decent a job as possible and finding meaning in life outside the middle-class framework, to engaging in antisocial delinquent acts. Those who reject middle-class behavioral patterns tend to band together furnishing models and patterns of mutual reinforcement for each other.

SEXUALITY IN LATER ADOLESCENCE

Extent of Sexuality

Between the ages of 13 and 15 the incidence of orgasm in adolescent increases sharply. By age 15 about 80 percent of adolescent boys have experienced orgasm from masturbation and about 40 percent through premarital intercourse with a female. About 50 percent of 15-year-old adolescent males have also experienced orgasm through petting, slightly over 20 percent through some homosexual-like experience, and about 40 percent while dreaming. These trends to greater sexual outlet continue to rise sharply after 15. For girls the picture is not the same at all. Petting and masturbation are the only types of sexual activity showing a marked rise for adolescent girls from the age of 13 to 15. Even so, only about 40 percent have petted at all and only 20 percent have masturbated to orgasm by age 15.

Premarital intercourse with a male is restricted to a small percentage of 15-year-old girls according to the Kinsey report. Even at age 16, 17, or 18, the percentage is low compared to males. For girls, even after 15 and throughout adolescence, petting and masturbation, rather than intercourse, homosexual activity, or dreams, furnish the chief and rather infrequent forms of sexual behavior.[21, 22] There are increasingly frequent reports about a current sexual revolution. It is not clear whether only attitudes and values about sex are changing among adolescents, or whether there is a marked rise in sexual intercourse. Indications are that there is a sexual revolution in adolescence and that it consists largely of more and earlier enjoyment of sexual intercourse by a greater percentage of girls.

Sexuality, Values and Internalization

The facts cited above are related to the values of the adult generation. There is, simply, a double standard. "Nice girls" don't engage in sexual intercourse and have to be careful about petting. "Nice boys" are also theoretically encouraged to be celibate. However, petting or sexual intercourse does not blacken an adolescent male's "reputation," and exploits as a "make out artist" may add to his self-esteem. Consequently, a lot of boys must still be having sexual activity with a relatively smaller number of adolescent girls, as well as with older females and prostitutes. However, the double standard may be weakening and sexual equality increasing.

The majority of 15- or 16-year-old adolescent girls have internalized some prohibitions against sexual behavior. By and large they still tend not to engage in promiscuous heavy petting or sexual intercourse. They tend to suppress behavioral tendencies in these directions. The direct control exercised over them by the peer group and parents helps to prevent sexual behavior by generating fear over loss of reputation and esteem. Fear of pregnancy or veneral disease may also be factors, but simple methods of birth control and antibiotics are reducing these threats. The ability to represent cognitively these possible social dangers and punishments contingent on early sexuality leads to experiencing or anticipating negative affects like anxiety. Consequently, the adolescent girl does not need constant supervision. The majority tend to avoid excessive, overt, sexual activity with males through self-control. Again, there is reason to suspect that there may be a trend toward lessened sexual inhibition due to effective birth control methods, effective curbs for venereal diseases, and changes in values concerning sexuality. Perhaps more and more adolescents today see no reason to deny themselves the innate pleasures of sexual activity. If social sanctions against premarital intercourse decline, such activity will certainly increase.

Female Adolescent Promiscuity

Atlhough there may be current trends toward earlier age of heavy petting and intercourse in girls, Lolita and the promiscuous "teeny bopper" are still the exception. Emphasis seems to be on "meaningful relationships" and sex with love. Promiscuous sexual intercourse in the adolescent girl is often a sign that the adult or usual adolescent subculture has ceased to control her behavior. The usual adolescent or adult attempts at rewarding or punishing have either been of such a rejecting nature as to prevent internalization of the usual sexual code of morality, or the adolescent girl has been exposed to antisocial models.

PREMARITAL PROMISCUOUS SEXUAL RELATIONS IN ADOLESCENT GIRLS

STUDY 15.3

Elinor Verville has summarized many of the findings in the area of promiscuous sexual behavior in adolescent girls.

She reports that unwed pregnant adolescent girls tend to have been rejected by family, peers, and friends. This has led to rebelliousness on their part and immaturity in terms of socialization and internalization of standards. The great majority of girls aged 12 to 18 sent to a reformatory had engaged in sexual intercourse. Many sexual delinquents come from homes in which promiscuity, drinking, and law violations of the parents serve as models for the child to imitate, states Verville. She finds that sexually promiscuous adolescent girls feel inferior intellectually, socially, or in physical attractiveness. Failing to acquire the rewarded attributes of the adolescent subculture, they try to use sex to gain acceptance from boys. Feeling already in disrepute and "bad," they see little reason not to indulge themselves. Having rejected such girls, the parents or the adolescent subculture can wield little control over them. Early sexual involvement with many males, Verville states, can also be the act of an angry girl set on trying to provoke, anger, and worry her parents.

Girl prostitutes, Verville finds, tend to come from broken homes in which alcoholism and paternal instability are common. When the adolescent girl is in severe economic need, the prospect of financial gain without hard work seems to be the main inducement to begin a life of prostitution.

Verville, E. *Behavior Problems of Children.* W. B. Saunders, Philadelphia, 1967.

"Promiscuity" is not a term usually applied to adolescent boys. The culture doesn't worry as much about the boy who sleeps with as many girls as he can. He is seldom very strongly condemned so long as he doesn't get the girls pregnant. His parents might not approve, but they are often unaware of his behavior since they are not particularly concerned enough to find out about it. Their censure, when they do know, is certainly less severe than if their daughters were involved in such activity. The adolescent boy who uses girls mainly for his own sexual pleasure is often not very patient or tender and may in fact lack the capacity for tenderness or intimacy. He may get sexual gratification but may be unable to have warm interpersonal relations with girls. He may even be contemptuous of the girls he sleeps with.[37]

Nonpromiscuous Sexual Intercourse in Adolescence

Premarital sexual intercourse in adolescence can be the outgrowth of a warm relationship based on mutual affection, respect, or love. Not only may there be no desire to exploit the partner, but there may be a positive desire to share a mutually enhancing and gratifying experience. Sexual relations on such a basis often grow out of steady dating where the adolescent boy and girl form a genuine social bond. They are led to sexual arousal and ultimate intercourse on the basis of continued exciting contacts and the desire for mutual gratification.

Some adolescent girls, nevertheless, also experience guilt or fear over this kind of sexual intercourse, since it may conflict with internalized standards. The adolescent boy, for similar reasons, may lose respect for the girl. Others, particularly in light of possibly changing values, have more positive than negative experiences on the basis of such sexual activities born of mutual affection. Such positive experiences may be on the increase. The determining factors bearing on satisfaction versus misery from such experiences rest on the nature of previous internalization based on their social learning experiences. One internalized value may be that sexual intercourse is desirable if the participants are convinced that strong affection, respect, and love are involved. Some may even feel that pleasure alone is all the justification needed.

The chief variable acting here may be the presence or absence of the capacity to respect one's self and others. No one has put this better than Harry Stack Sullivan. His views, with additions, are stated in Study 15.4.

SELF-RESPECT, RESPECT FOR OTHERS, AND ANXIETY

STUDY 15.4

Sullivan has stated that self-respect is necessary for the adequate respect of others. He felt that people who have a fine capacity for respecting themselves, and a remarkable capacity for living with and among others, are glad when others are able to fulfill their capacities. Sullivan points out that one of the feeblest props to feelings of self-inadequacy is the disparaging of others, a lack of respect for them. He states: "I think it has been known from the beginning of recorded time that a person who is bitter toward others, very hard on his fellow man for certain faults, is usually very sensitive to these particular faults because they are secret vices of his own. Insofar as self-respect has been permitted to grow without restrictions, because of comparatively unwarped personal development or because warp of personal development has been remedied, no hint of anxiety is connected with discovering that others have their assets and may be as worthwhile as or better than one's self."

Sullivan has also spoken about "restrictions in freedom of living." Because of the need to protect his own security, the adolescent may prefer restricted contact with others. A certain degree of isolation, and an avoidance of sexuality in order to avoid anxiety over "reputation," possible rejection, or inadequacy may be needed by the adolescent. Anxiety over breaking internalized standards can cause the adolescent to deny him or herself a great deal of useful, educative, and consensually validating experiences. This can happen in any other important area of life as well as in the sexual area. Just as some will fear indulgence in sexuality, other adolescents will avoid anxiety provoking political or religious views.

Sullivan, H. S. *The Interpersonal Theory of Psychiatry.* W. W. Norton, New York, 1953.

Adolescent Sexuality in Other Cultures

It sometimes helps up to gain perspective on our own cultures if we consider others that differ from it. We have already given examples, in other parts of the book, of child rearing practices and their effects in non-American cultures. Such illustrations underline the fact that development does not just happen and that very few behaviors are equally reinforced in all human cultures. Inevitable aspects of development usually have a strong biological basis and even these are shaped by the interpersonal context of models and rewards in which they occur. Social behavior depends on the types of social models the child is exposed to and on what social behaviors lead to satisfaction.

Kiryat Yedidim is a kibbutz in Israel. It is a village of about 500 people, mainly engaged in agricultural work. The kibbutz (a collective agricultural settlement) is marked by group living. Things are owned largely in common and the people living there work together in cooperative enterprise. People own their own personal effects such as clothes, radios, or some furniture; but land, houses, and other capital goods belong to the kibbutz, which is largely governed and run by democratically elected representatives of the members.

After birth the children born to kibbutz parents live in communal nurseries with children of the same age. Clearly, the children will be potent social influences on each others' behavior. The children move ahead with their age group, being chiefly cared for and later educated by nurses, nursery school teachers, and regular school teachers. Parents, both male and female, work and spend time with their children only in the later afternoon and early evening. From birth onward the infant belongs to the Children's Society until he or she becomes an elected member of the kibbutz. The young children, boys and girls together, are organized into small groups of about the same age and they live in cottages scattered about the kibbutz and eat in a communal kitchen. As the children grow up they move into schools with their own dormitories, eat, study, play, and live together. The boys and girls see their parents frequently but spend most of their time with each other, their caretakers and the teachers.[35]

Let us see what effect such a living arrangement has on adolescent sexual behavior. Adolescent sexual behavior in the Kiryat Yedidim kibbutz is discussed in Study 15.5

ADOLESCENT SEXUAL BEHAVIOR IN A KIBBUTZ

STUDY 15.5

The adolescents of Kiryat Yedidim have often been exposed to the bodies and consequently the sexual anatomy of the opposite sex from birth. They, as young children, bathed and went to the toilet together and slept in the same room. Consequently, they are not much interested in sexual "looking" and are not curious about sexual aspects of the body. Such curiosity has been satisfied both by exposure and sexual education, which is given in school. The children are taught that sex is neither sinful nor dirty, but that it is not terribly important either.

Everything is done together so that there is no formal dating. A boy or girl may be very fond of each other and become exclusively attached, however, so that one might say that they are going steady. Even so, they do not invite each other to social events, unless one counts their decision that they will both be there. Dances, swimming, and other aspects of recreation are open group activities.

Although sex is viewed as natural by the children and adults, the kibbutz community is opposed to sexual intercourse for adolescents and punishes such behavior by withdrawal of community approval. It is felt that sexual intercourse and the attendant focusing on sexual behavior and its interpersonal aspects would detract from education, work, and preparation for future life. Adolescent sexual intercourse would direct energies into channels other than those approved of for this stage of life.

Teachers and same age peers, both boys and girls, bring

pressure, in terms of threatened loss of love, on both male and female adolescents to not get involved in sexual affairs. There obviously is a fair amount of interest in boy-girl relationships among adolescents and much of their gossip is about just such matters. There are instances of sexual intercourse and they may become fairly open knowledge. The girls tell each other what they do with their boy friends, and adolescents show interest in the sexual life of adults, often talking about adult affairs or impending marriages.

On the whole, it has been the impression of one observer that the kibbutz adolescents have less sexual experience than American adolescents. Homosexuality is reported to be nonexistent. There seem to be preliminary forms of love play by boys and girls "going together" but instances of actual sexual intercourse seem to be rare.

The reasons given for the general nonexistence of adolescent sexual intercourse are: strong group pressures and strong adult pressures against it; and a lack of any strong sexual stimulation or salacious titillation based on unwholesome curiosity. The few who have sexual intercourse generally have it with someone outside their own peer group and seem ashamed of it. The feeling does seem to be shame, rather than fear or guilt, and stems from apprehension about having their behavior known by those who would not approve. Being closely tied to the community, loss of community approval is a potent negative reinforcer.

Spiro, M. E. *Children of the Kibbutz*. Harvard University Press. Cambridge, 1958.

If virginity is valued in our own culture (though less so than it once was) it is of even greater importance among the Mundugumor, a cannibal tribe in New Guinea. Among the Mundugumor, some girls may have affairs before marriage, but they are quick and furtive experiences surrounded by danger. If the girl is discovered, everyone will know that she is not a virgin. The exchange value of a girl who is not a virgin is low. Males are reluctant to marry a non-virgin, although if they marry a sexually experienced girl without knowing about it until after the marriage, they will keep quiet about it, fearing ridicule from others. Premarital love making is fraught with danger as this not unhumorous quote from Margaret Mead indicates: "If she receives a lover in her sleeping basket, she risks not only discovery but actual injury, for an angry father who discovers the intruder may fasten up the opening of the sleeping bag and roll the couple down the house-ladder, which is almost perpendicular and some 6 to 7 feet in height. The bag may receive a good kicking and even a prodding with a spear or an arrow before it is opened. As a result, this method of courtship, although very occasionally resorted to by desperate lovers in the wet season when the bush is flooded, is not very popular."[26] If sex is positively reinforcing, the father's action certainly is not.

What society rewards or punishes, as well as how and when, shapes the form and timing of sexual behavior. Sexual behavior is innate in the sense that pleasure can be gained from genital contact from early childhood on. The form it takes and the way it is regulated, however, are under the social control of the persons to whom the adolescent is attached by emotional bonds of various sorts. It is also under the control of his own internalized conscience formed in various social learning situations at home, school, and in the peer subculture. A final example given in Study 15.6 should underline the variety of adolescent sexual conduct possible if the culture teaches it. It may be instructive to remember, however, that some form of sexuality involving heterosexual intercourse appears in every culture. If it did not, the culture would vanish. Cultures chiefly regulate when and with whom intercourse is allowed. Of course one's culture is partly defined by those to whom one feels the closest social ties, at any given period of life. These for the adolescent, may be his friends who may reinforce him for different behaviors than his parents might.

SEX TRAINING IN WOGEO

STUDY 15.6

Wogeo is in New Guinea. In this culture, modified homosexuality is the rule among boys. The boys walk holding hands, sleep together, and engage in mutual masturbation during adolescence. These male adolescent friendships continue beyond marriage and may often be a source of irritation to the wife. The Wogeo boy must refrain from sleeping with girls before undergoing the puberty rite and this rite of passage does not come until the Wogeo adolescent is about 19 years of age or older. Male children are taught that intercourse may result in physical defects, sickness, or death, if indulged in before marriage.

It is another story for girls. Wogeo girls are actually reinforced by parents for engaging in premarital intercourse and they get social approval and gifts for heterosexual behavior.

Wogeo males, therefore, often have their first experience at intercourse through being seduced by a female.

Quite in contrast to American modal culture, heterosexuality is encouraged for girls and discouraged for male adolescents. The male adolescents, however, are allowed partial homosexual experiences.

Bandura, A., and Walters, R. H. *Social Learning and Personality Development.* Holt, Rinehart and Winston, New York, 1963. Hogbin, H. I. Marriage in Wogeo, New Guinea. *Oceania, 15,* 1945, 324-352.

All cultures regulate sexual behavior. Complete promiscuity with no rules does not exist anywhere; at least not yet. Sexual behavior becomes of major interest, in many places, after the children are old enough to become parents. This is not universally true, but it is much more often the case than not. Child bearing, child care, marriage, family lines, and property rights are closely associated in many cultures. For these reasons regulation of sexual intercourse after physical puberty often becomes a matter for close social control. The type of behavioral control over sexuality, how it is carried out, and how early it begins, varies from culture to culture. If social control through social learning changes, then there are changes in the manner, frequency, and conditions of expression of sexual behavior. A radical change in this area is sometimes called a "sexual revolution." As we have already stated, there is considerable interest over whether America is now undergoing a major sexual revolution and if so, what its exact nature is.

ADOLESCENCE AND ANTISOCIAL BEHAVIOR

Causes for Alarm

We have already seen in the last chapter that the majority of adolescents are marching down the road of socialization to high school graduation, a job, and marriage. A large minority are going to college and a majority may soon have some education beyond high school. What about the minority? Some adolescents become involved in truancy, sexual perversions, narcotics addiction, petty misdemeanors, and felonies. Some are chronic truants and others are members of fighting gangs. There is venereal disease and premarital pregnancy. Petty theft and joy riding in stolen cars are not uncommon and one hears the phrase "beyond parental control."

The adolescent has no corner on antisocial behavior although it is probably hard to find an adolescent who hasn't broken some law. Of course, it is hard to find an adult who hasn't broken one either if one counts adultery, income tax evasion, driving while intoxicated, going through a stop sign, spitting on the subway, catching one fish too many, shoplifting or sneaking in an extra bottle of rum from a visit to Mexico.

Breaking of laws by adolescents seems often to be of major concern to adults even though we have seen that such behavior may often start before adolescence. Why is this so? It is possible to speculate that law breaking or other misbehavior by younger children are seen as childish pranks, serious perhaps, but behavior that the parents feel they can control. Ten year olds do not seem very dangerous and people feel that parents should correct their behavior. But adolescents are nearing adulthood, are larger, seen as vested with more responsibility, and harder to control. Being near the usual age for separation from the family, and possibly able to successfully run away from home, there is a feeling that little time is left to change their behavior. The combination of the increasing power of adolescents, the decrease of adult control over them, and the shortness of the time left in which to take corrective action makes adults apprehensive about their misconduct. Adolescent delinquency, or even law abiding but antisocial behavior, may be seen by parents and society as signs of a future life of permanent crime, failure, or personal misery. It may well be that in a future oriented middle-class culture, adolescent delinquency immediately suggests possible lifelong problems and, therefore, arouses considerable anxiety. There is evidence that certain classes of law breaking by minors are on the increase, with adolescent crime becoming more important as a social problem. The publicity given to adolescent groups who are rejecting their parents' values is also causing increased concern among adults dedicated to modal social conventions.

Law Breaking and Psychology

There are many laws and many ways to violate them. Breaking the law can range from draft card burning to smoking marijuana, and from car theft to failing to move on when told to do so by a policeman. It includes murder and stealing a pack of chewing gum, failing to have car insurance in some states and having sexual intercourse with someone legally defined as too young. Consequently, the question of why some adolescents break the law, in the sense of looking for some simple answer, is relatively meaningless as a single psychological question.[31]

An adolescent or an adult who almost never breaks a law may be seen as oversocialized in middle-class values. He may be considered to have a rigid conscience and a rigid code of conduct. An adolescent or adult who repeatedly breaks the law in certain ways may be seen as undersocialized by middle class standards and as having failed to sufficiently internalize modal social rules of conscience and conduct. The average adolescent or adult breaks laws occasionally but not very often.

There are neurotic adolescents who break the law to get even with parents. There are psychopathic or asocial ones who either can't control their impulses or see no reason to. Such adolescents are not very much influenced by punishment. There are minority-group, disadvantaged, impoverished adolescents for whom stealing is the surest way to obtain what they want. There are adolescent drug addicts who must support their habits. There are members of gangs who are forced into gang activity and who are threatened by other gang members if they do not break the law. There are irresponsible upper-class adolescents who feel above the law; they may break laws for fun. Some adolescents break a law without knowing they are breaking one. Some adolescents are well socialized, but into a subculture in which law breaking is common and hatred of the police a well internalized value. Other adolescents break certain laws in the name of higher values and a higher morality, or in attempts to change the law.

Although laws are broken for many reasons it is a psychologically meaningful question to ask why one particular adolescent broke a particular law on one occasion, or why he breaks one or many on several occasions. It is also meaningful to ask why certain groups or types of adolescents frequently violate certain kinds of laws. It is certainly valid to ask how and why such groups form. The general question of why delinquency exists, on the other hand, is without any single psychological, or one suspects, any other kind of simple answer. The law is obeyed or broken for a variety of psychological and other reasons.

Who Breaks the Law?

Study 15.7 treats the question of who lawbreakers are.

ARE WE ALL GUILTY?

STUDY 15.7

Dorothy Rogers has summarized some findings in this area. She reports on one study in which 2049 delinquent boys who had appeared before juvenile courts were compared to 337 college boys who had not. The college boys, per capita, actually *seemed* to have committed more offenses. Their offenses, which they themselves reported, were as serious as those for which the other boys ended up in court. However, the college boys came from economically more privileged backgrounds and had managed to avoid court for the offenses they reported.

> Another study reviewed by Rogers revealed that 91 percent of a random sample of the population had committed offenses for which they could possibly have gone to jail. If serious driving violations are included, the percentage rises to 99. One may assume that the other one percent were lying or included unheralded paragons of virtue.
>
> Rogers, D. *The Psychology of Adolescence.* Appleton-Century-Crofts, New York, 1962.

It has been shown that rates of juvenile delinquency are high among adolescent minority group members from lower-class backgrounds. This is particularly true if they live in urban slum areas. That is, *repeated* delinquency is correlated with social class and consequently with certain ethnic and racial groups falling largely within that class. As one sociologist has stated: "It is our conclusion, by no means novel or startling, that juvenile delinquency and the delinquent subculture in particular are overwhelmingly concentrated in the male, working-class sector of the juvenile population."[8] All boys break some laws, but male adolescents from low socio-economic backgrounds, living in large cities, break the law in serious ways and *more often* than boys from nonpoverty backgrounds.[41] The college students cited in Study 15.7 were asked to remember *all* the delinquencies they had *ever* committed in 55 different categories of crime. The known delinquencies of the boys charged in court, however, included only the actions for which they were taken before the court. No one found out how many of the offenses in the 55 categories they had ever committed and how often.[30] Only the offense for which they were caught was known. Probably they had, over the years, engaged in more crime than the college boys.

There is reason to believe that in some cities police may be more ready to arrest and charge lower-class minority group members. On the other hand, evidence shows that many acts of lawbreaking on the part of such disadvantaged boys are never reported. In at least one city, it seems that adolescents from higher income areas are more likely to have to face the court for delinquency than boys from poorer areas.[32] This may be a rarity, but it should warn against overgeneralizing. One must conclude that delinquency is a form of behavior in which all adolescents, at least all male ones, engage to some extent. However, delinquency, in terms of frequency of occurrence, is much more heavily concentrated at the lower end of the socioeconomic scale. At least, this is true if one looks particularly at certain types of delinquencies such as antisocial gang activity, assault and battery, rape, and armed robbery. One must remember, however, that *all* social classes have their adolescent, as well as adult, lawbreakers.

Causes of the Concentration of Delinquency in Poverty Areas

Two main theories have been advanced to account for the prevalence of adolescent and adult crime in areas of poverty. One may be called the "delinquent subculture" theory and the other the "opportunity structure" theory. It may be noted that both assume that there is a delinquent subculture and that serious delinquency is more frequent among lower and working class adolescents.[7, 8] The first theory, that of the delinquent subculture, holds that juvenile crimes are largely a way of satisfying the needs of the adolescent for status; that is, recognition. Adolescents indulge in breaking the law, it is argued, to avoid isolation and opprobrium. The chief point is that "the gang is a separate, distinct, and often irresistible focus of attraction, loyalty, and solidarity."[8] Everyone, it is pointed out, wants to be a member in good standing of some groups, and to be recognized as occupying some definite roles. In other words, everyone needs to obtain rewards from life. Consequently, the antisocial delinquent seldom stands alone. He needs others as mutually reinforcing models.

Those adolescents who have similar problems of adjustment with society, those who cannot derive rewards from school, who aren't accepted by the lights of middle-class values, or who have suffered violence, rejection, and discrimination, band together to form delinquent subcultures, often in the form of gangs or close associates. Having received punishment (negative reinforcement) from others, they band together. Delinquency appeals to such adolescents to a greater extent than the other solutions which society has to offer. These other solutions do not seem to offer them chances for gratification. Once they form associations with each other, they become models for each other and reinforce mutual delinquent acts. They punish those who deviate from the group's antisocial norms and behavioral expectancies. Thus a subculture is formed, in which the expected behaviors are the antithesis of proper middle-class behavior, although the very same social learning factors are operating. An adolescent subculture exists in which the members are socialized into antisocial behavior and among whom there is an internalization of an antisocial morality and antisocial conduct.[8] It is antisocial, at least, in terms of traditional values held by the majority in the general culture.

The opportunity structure theory chiefly concerns itself with the fate of adolescents whose legitimate means to success are restricted. These are the adolescents for whom it is hard if not impossible to reach middle-class goals, whether they be good grades, affluence, athletic prowess, attractiveness, or popularity. This viewpoint holds that those adolescents whose chances for success by means of culturally approved methods are restricted will reject the culturally approved ways of reaching those goals and instead turn to methods of attaining them disapproved by most of society. In the view of the proponents of this theory, delinquent subcultures form among lower-class adolescents when there is a discrepancy between culturally induced aspirations and the possibility of achieving them by legitimate means.[7] For instance, adolescents in urban slums may not see how they can ever have a decent life. The usual social norms cease to govern the behavior of such adolescents because they do not enable them to get what they have learned to need or want. Why go to school and learn if only a menial job is at the end of the road? They, instead, may band together into gangs or less formal delinquent subgroups and within this subculture pursue money, pleasure, success, or other goals through illegal means. Middle-class or upper-working-class adolescents have a lower rate of certain types of delinquency because they have relatively better and easier chances of achieving their aspirations. They may break certain laws but be less likely to steal for a profit. Hence, they are less likely to band together in delinquent subcultures which will furnish antisocial models and reinforcements for illegal activities. They can usually gain their rewards through approved methods and when they do break laws be more likely to act alone or with different people at various times.

Both theories, which partly differ but are largely complementary, are in accord with social learning theory. Aside from the reasons for the initial formation of delinquent subcultures in the opportunity structure theory, they are chiefly theories of socialization into certain forms of deviant behavior. The socialization into deviant behavior depends on other antisocial models to imitate, reinforcements for antisocial behavior, punishment of noncompliance in delinquent activities and little chance of reward for prosocial activities. Those who can't "make it" within the rules of the modal cultural value system are driven to try to make it in ways outside of that system.

Adequacy of "Delinquent Subculture" Theories

The two theories just outlined do account to a reasonable degree for much of adolescent delinquent behavior. However, they do little to account for middle-class delinquency. There are psychological reasons for antisocial behavior which have little or nothing to do with delinquent subcultures or the lack of opportunities for employment.[33]

Delinquency is "violation of the law or municipal ordinances by children or youths of juvenile court age, or conduct so seriously antisocial as to interfere with the rights of others or to menace the welfare of the delinquent himself or the community."[39] It is clear that no single point of view can account for all the reasons why adolescents would break laws and ordinances, or interfere with the rights of others, or become a menace to themselves and other people.

Behaviors of the sort mentioned above, for instance, have been linked to anomie, a condition of normlessness supposedly relatively common in modern societies. Anomie has been considered to arise when people are encouraged to have and to fulfill as many economic and other needs as possible. Greed and gain become rampant, and restraints and limits on how to achieve success are weakened. With the weakening of restraints on how to achieve the goals of success, people have few solid values they can hang on to; there is a lack of firm rules. Consequently, for some the struggle seems futile, life loses value, and they experience anomie. Social rules and laws are unclear and also seem futile. They very goals of affluence, power, and success may become devoid of meaning in a meaningless society.[24] The adolescent afflicted with anomie may be ripe for lawbreaking. Study 15.8 makes some telling points about the psychological dimensions of anomie and its existence regardless of social class.

PSYCHOLOGICAL DIMENSIONS OF ANOMIE

STUDY 15.8

McClosky and Schaar have found that less intelligent persons and persons of low occupational status experience anomie to a greater extent than more intelligent persons and those of a higher socioeconomic level.

However, when the effects of intelligence and level of occupation are eliminated as variables, psychological reasons were found to account for much of anomie among the intelligent, the affluent, and the less fortunate.

McClosky and Schaar argue that anomic feelings result when the social learning of standards of conduct is impeded. Some reasons for the failure of the learning and internalization of such norms are sociological, but others are personal and psychological. They point out that some persons prone to high anxiety, hostility, and other chronic, strongly aversive affective (emotional) states have an inability to become socialized and to internalize modal social rules. They perceive the world as hostile and anxiety ridden. They have a poor and restricted interaction with others, whom they do not trust, and so reduce their chances for learning and accepting the rules of conduct and conscience which do exist. Such people are rigid, hostile, anxious, somewhat paranoid, guilt ridden, submissive, and intolerant.

Although the authors do not dwell on the probable antecedents of anomie among the more intelligent and affluent, some of it may be related to certain of the patterns of child rearing discussed in a previous chapter. Repeated experiences with overly permissive but neglecting parents, who may or may not also engage in sporadic but violent forms of punishment, could lead to such a result. A pattern of very restrictive treatment by cold, hostile parents may also produce anomie. Such patterns may be more common in the lower social classes and among the less intelligent, but they appear in all classes of society.

McClosky, H., and Schaar, J. H. Psychological dimensions of anomie. *Amer. Sociol. Rev.*, 30, 1965, 14-40.

Certain patterns of child rearing may produce neurotic and psychopathic children whose violations of the law constitute part of their maladjustment. The psychopathic adolescent is marked by a lack of internalized constraint over his impulses. He has trouble empathizing with others and is not very good at suppressing his desires even if indulging them means a violation of laws or social rules. Such adolescents do not seem to benefit from punishment.[28]

Other adolescents who break laws may be described as somewhat undersocialized but not particularly neurotic, not psychopathic, and not very attached to delinquent subcultures. They may not be victims of anomie either. They may merely fall in the border area of somewhat weak internalization of modal rules of conscience and conduct. They may be relatively ineffective at delaying gratification or impulses and may be infrequent, sporadic lawbreakers and occasional violators of social conventions.

A REVIEW OF THE CAUSES OF ADOLESCENT DELINQUENCY

The causes for lawbreaking or social rule violation are many. Whether seen as chiefly social or mainly psychological, however, they can be generally explained by social learning theory. As one outstanding study on the causes of delinquency puts it: "Evidence from the Cambridge Youth Study gives support to a theoretical formulation of delinquency causation. . . .The findings of interactive effects demonstrate that explanation in terms of direct causal relationships is inadequate. Delinquent behavior is the consequence of learning a pattern . . . that supports the violation of law, and there is variation in outcome according to the content learned. . .and the nature of experiences by which the culture is learned. . . .Lack of parental supervision increases the influence of companions on the street. . . . These theoretical considerations have focused on the transmission through the family and the gang of an orientation toward delinquent and nondelinquent behavior. . . ."[36]

In other words, one has to look to the conditions and effects of social learning inside the home and in the peer group if one wants to understand either prosocial or antisocial behavior. Just as one set of principles can count for normal and abnormal behavior, one set of principles can account for prosocial and antisocial behavior. The causes of law breaking are many but that does not mean that one needs many theories of behavior. Adolescents may become delinquent for many reasons but we believe that all the reasons are subsumable under the conditions of social learning.

ADOLESCENCE AND ORIENTATION TOWARD THE FUTURE

Major Concerns about the Future

Most adolescents are not habitual delinquents and are oriented toward the future. The adolescent boy may look ahead to high school graduation, then perhaps to college and graduate or professional school. Regardless of his educational aspirations the boy looks forward to a job; some sort of work, position, profession, artistic expression, or career in life. He knows that he is going to have to work and that further education, practical experience, or other forms of direct job training are linked to his future life as a wage earner and productive human being. Adolescent boys are more concerned about their future vocations than about any other issue. Girls are also aware of and concerned about vocational choices, but it is clear that marriage is the major goal of adolescent girls. Almost all adolescent girls want to get married regardless of any other vocational aspirations that they may have.[12] Study 15.9 summarizes some of the findings concerning the future goals of adolescent boys and girls.

PLANS FOR THE FUTURE

STUDY 15.9

Elizabeth Douvan and Joseph Adelson gathered information on male and female adolescents through two national interview studies. Three thousand and fifty adolescent boys and girls were interviewed, 1045 boys aged 14 to 16 and 2005 girls ranging from 12 to 18 years in age. The interviews with the adolescents were arranged through schools with various religious and social classes represented. The data did not include interviews with school dropouts or adolescents in mental hospitals or reform schools. Children with very severe problems or those who drop out of school, those who are not following the modal socialization patterns of the culture were therefore not represented in the findings. The study, however, was fairly representative of adolescent boys and girls found in public, parochial, and private schools. Each adolescent was interviewed individually and all children of the same sex were asked the same questions, with one interview form used for boys and a somewhat different one for girls.

Eighty-six percent of the boys referred directly to some decision they had already made about work or about the armed forces (enlistment or the draft). They felt that, although for many of them an actual full-time job was some years away, it was important for them to begin making tentative choices. Most boys between 14 and 16 years of age already had an idea of whether or not they were going to go on to college and in addition they had already narrowed the range of jobs from which they felt their final vocational choices would come. Seventy-five percent of the 14- to 16-year-old boys were aware of important decisions about their education that they would have to make in the next few years.

Training for a life of work is what most concerned these adolescent boys about the future and the great majority wanted to do as well as or better than their fathers. If one eliminates the boys whose fathers had jobs so good that their sons could hardly do better and boys whose fathers' jobs were so bad that their sons could hardly do worse, then a majority, 52 percent, wanted better positions than their fathers had. The male adolescent is achievement oriented but realistic. The boys' choices were dispersed over a wide range. Boys seem to have a reasonable idea of the training they will need for the type of position they want and are also flexible; they realize that it is not entirely possible to be certain of the exact job they will actually obtain after school.

Adolescent girls, for obvious reasons, were less concerned with work for its own sake or as a career. They were interested in jobs which would be socially pleasant, where they could make friends, and meet possible future husbands. Girls tended to be vague or undecided about job plans. Their tentative occupational choices were much narrower than those of boys; 34 percent were interested in being secretaries,

21 percent in being nurses, and 17 percent in being teachers. Girls want to get married, job or no job, and they want to marry someone who will make a good living in a white collar job. Only seven percent of girls wished to marry someone with a blue collar job such as a factor worker or carpenter. Fifty-eight percent of the girls clearly wanted a husband who would have middle-class status, an office worker, manager, businessman or professional. Physical appearance and the religion of a future husband did not seem as important to girls as the following: a close interpersonal relationship in marriage, cooperation in the home, skill in social situations, autonomy, stable job performance, a good job, respect for marriage and the family, and the ability to control negative impulses. (Many girls, it is safe to say, will not get the sort of husbands they want.)

Douvan, E., and Adelson, J. *The Adolescent Experience.* John Wiley, New York, 1966.

Problems of Adolescent Girls

It is clear that many adolescents are future oriented and are also reasonably well-socialized. At least most of those who do not drop out of school have to some extent accepted middle-class values: modal values of the American culture such as achievement, success, human considerateness, marriage, and stability. Social learning has influenced those adolescents who remain in school so that they often value the types of behaviors of which the majority of society approves. The current situation, one may note, may be more difficult for girls than boys. Many of them will marry men whose occupational status is lower than the status they would ideally like their husbands to have. Many girls will be forced to work at jobs other than that of secretary, nurse, teacher, or other, more glamorous choices. Many of them will spend some periods of time as filing clerks or typists, or will work in a factory or behind the counter in a store. One may speculate that many girls are in for considerable disappointments in life unless their roles as wives and mothers prove to be interpersonally satisfying.

The state of affairs reflects the fact that role expectations and their associated behaviors are more complex, ambiguous, and more conflict ridden, for adolescent girls than for adolescent boys. The culture encourages the girl to develop her own skills and to become educated but she must also be prepared to sacrifice some of these skills. She has to be prepared to subordinate the career potentials provided by her abilities and education in favor of marital responsibilities. Marriage may prove to be a situation requiring work outside the home, not for the sake of pursuing satisfying work or a career, but to bring in additional income, sometimes only for limited periods. She may have to struggle hard to realize a satisfying work life outside of marriage or accept the fact that her best skills and potentials will not be put to use. Understanding husbands and good baby sitters are not always easy to come by and many working wives feel guilty about neglecting the welfare of their family. Even if they decide voluntarily not to work after marriage, some females may later feel that they have missed something by not having a fair chance at a career.[27, 38] It is rare to find a married woman nowadays who has never felt any conflict between her personal work or creative ambitions and her obligations to husband and children.

Influences on Future Goals — Types of School

The type of school attended by the adolescent may have a marked influence on his or her behaviors and future goals. Regardless of the child's home and social background, the school will furnish him with new models to imitate. It may be a source of patterns of reward and punishment differing from previously experienced patterns of reinforcement. The adolescent may be exposed to new attitudes, values, and ideas, particularly in high school. In smaller cities and rural areas, the high school draws from a quite wide area and is not a neighborhood school and even in larger cities some high schools have children of varied backgrounds. The high school may expose the child to patterns of socialization and social learning experiences not encountered previously in his more homogeneous grammar school.

It has been shown that when high schools are classified according to the average socioeconomic status of the student body, the aspirations of individual students tend to change toward those of the majority. Working class students in chiefly middle-class high schools plan to attend college more frequently than working-class students in mainly working-class high schools. Conversely, middle-class students who attend high schools where the majority come from a working-class background are less likely to plan to attend college.[5] Large metropolitan high schools, drawing students mostly from the same social background, have only minor effects on the students. They merely reinforce the behaviors the students have already acquired. Teachers in predominantly working-class schools expect less from the students and teach in accordance with these expectations. For instance, less homework is assigned by teachers in slum area schools, accentuating the already acquired tendency of working-class students to do less homework.[5] However, when students of varied backgrounds are thrown together, the school, which includes the influence of other students and the teachers, becomes an important factor in establishing new patterns of behavior.[9] Some high schools give the students a better education, expect more from them, and exert informal pressure on the students to aim at higher goals. These are schools where the middle-class values of the teachers and/or students are likely to prevail.

Analysis of Variables Influencing Aspirations and Goals

The type of high school attended is only one variable influencing the adolescent's aspirations and choice of goals. The high school itself is not anything like a unitary variable since it consists of many people interacting and mutually influencing each other in complex ways. It is really an oversimplification to say that the high school influences behavior, when what is meant is that behavior is altered by a variety of occurrences in the school.

At least ten factors have been shown to influence the aspirations of adolescents: social class of parents, parents' aspirations, intelligence of the adolescent, emotional adjustment, social status of friends, early school performance, social mobility of the parents, special talent for sports and an admired personality, a high need for achievement, and, as we have seen, social class composition of the school.[4] Study 15.10 discusses, with some added explanations, the reduction of these ten factors into four broader categories.

CATEGORIES OF INFLUENCE OF ADOLESCENT ASPIRATIONS

STUDY 15.10

Gerald D. Bell has constructed four categories to account for the level of aspiration of adolescents. He calls the first set of factors "direct aspirational stimulus." He includes in this category direct motivation or reinforcement of aspirations by parents, friends, or school mates. The specific aspirations which will be reinforced vary according to social class.

Bell terms the second category "susceptibility to direct stimulus." Here he places factors of emotional adjustment. These would include such mediating psychological variables as level of anxiety, hostility, or the ability to pay attention and use symbols. These are mediating variables since they do not affect aspirations directly but help to determine how much and what kinds of effects the direct stimuli will have.

The third catergory is called the "desire to excel." It is

largely a function of the direct stimuli which have acted on the adolescent and of the mediating variables described above. This is a motivational variable, according to Bell, and refers mostly to the strength of the need to achieve. It does not, however, refer to the direction or nature of the goals which the adolescent will choose to pursue.

The final category is called the "perceived likelihood of success." Early school performance, level of intelligence, and current performance tell the adolescent something about his chances for success and so influence his aspirations.

The direct and detailed stimuli of Bell's first category determine the nature and goals of aspiration. It is from his parents, friends, and teachers that the child or adolescent learns *what* he should value and pursue. The form his aspirations take are heavily influenced by these direct stimuli from other people.

Bell, G. D. Process in the formation of adolescents' aspirations. *Social Forces*, 42, 1963, 179-186.

SELF AND IDENTITY

Certainly the types of goals which an adolescent sets for himself are partly indicative of how he thinks of himself. E. H. Erikson has written: "Adolescence is the age of final establishment of a dominant positive...-identity. It is then that a future within reach becomes part of a conscious life plan. It is then that the question arises whether or not the future was anticipated in earlier expectations....What the...growing, rebelling, maturing youths are now primarily concerned with is who and what they are in the eyes of a wider circle of significant people..."[15, 16]

We have already discussed the question of identity, the aggregate of labels (cognitive beliefs) which a person applies to himself or herself. The term "identity," however, has also been used in more pervasive and subjective ways. Erikson has used it to refer to "The subjective sense of an invigorating sameness and continuity; something which can be experienced as identical in the core of the individual and yet also identical in the core of a common culture; complementarily of an inner synthesis in the individual and/or role integration in the group."[15, 16] These conceptualizations define identity as a kind of stability of the adolescent's personality as seen by himself and the social groups to which he formally or informally belongs. It is his or her answer to the question "Who am I?"

This sense of identity does seem to be fairly stable in adolescence. One study on the self-concepts of 172 adolescents showed very high stability over a two-year period. That is, the way they saw themselves when first measured correlated .78 with the way they saw themselves two years later.[14] At least one study seems to indicate that this sense of stability about who and what one is may not be restricted to adolescence since it may appear at an earlier age. This study compared the stability of self-concept among third, sixth, and tenth graders; that is, for children at about ages nine, 12, 16. The measures were taken about four months apart and the correlations were, in general above .70 with no significant differences by age level. The self-concepts of third graders, in this study, were about as stable as those of adolescents.[29] Douvan and Gold conclude: "These data indicate that self-concept does not fluctuate widely through adolescence. Adolescents undergo drastic maturational changes, are subject to some sharp changes in social roles, and many experiment with different personal styles; but all this change seems to fall short of touching the core of their self-descriptions."

Related to the adolescents' identity and self-concept, as we have noted earlier, is the adolescents' self-esteem. Douvan and Gold state: "To summarize, self-esteem crystallizes at adolescence around respectable display of those characteristics which lie at the core of self-definition. Centrality depends heavily on society's prescriptions of what an adolescent should be, and American society conditions this prescription most heavily according to sex. Those youngsters who do not measure up may become anxious and show signs of disturbance. Most adolescents, however, learn to measure up, and many who are unable to, manage to conceal their shortcomings from themselves so that the modal level of self-esteem is comfortably high."[12]

METHODOLOGICAL NOTE AND CONCLUSION

The reader may have noted that not one *experiment* has been cited in this chapter. The studies reported here rely almost exclusively on interviews, questionnaires, projective tests, surveys, analyses of collected statistics, and measure of self-description. Consequently, it is hard to pin down the question of causality. In nonexperiemental studies it is not always clear what behaviors are a function of what variables, consequently it is not easy to make predicitons about the adolescent behaviors to be expected if certain environmental conditions should change. These variables may be changing with attendant changes in the behavior of adolescents.

Experimentally oriented developmental psychologists have tended to concentrate on the earlier years. One reason for this is that many processes such as perceptual development, language development, or imitational ability, are well established before adolescence. Furthermore, important types of learning, such as classical or operant conditioning, begin to take place well before adolescence; some, even in the first days of life. Important aspects of personality, some of which have stability over long periods of time, also seem to develop quite early in life.

Parents start to teach, train, and discipline their children well before adolescence. Intrigued by these early phenomena, processes, and practices, experimental developmental psychologists have tended to concentrate on the earlier years. Some are not certain that processes of crucial importance to human growth appear after the last stages of cognitive development described by Piaget. Although the chief *processes* involved in development may appear by early adolescence development is clearly a lifelong process. Until sound experimental studies concerning themselves with the adolescent and later years emerge, we will have to depend on knowledge gained from methods of inquiry which can tell us little about causation.

The reader may also note that most of the references in this chapter appeared in sociological or educational journals. This is partly because of the nature of the topics and studies selected for inclusion, but not entirely. Although some developmental psychologists have been interested in adolescence, many more sociologists and educators have been concerned with this age group. Since adolescence is largely defined by social factors rather than by phenomena of psychological development, the study of adolescence has, to a considerable extent, become the province of the sociologist and the educator. Since adolescence encompasses junior high school and high school years, educators and educational psychologists have a heavy investment in studying this age group. It is to be hoped that developmental psychologists will begin to pay more attention to the phenomena of adolescence and that they will include the experimental method as one avenue of investigation.

SUMMARY

Later adolescence is the period before society confers full adulthood. In fact adolescence shades into early adulthood without any particular ceremony or ritual. It is an indefinite and ambiguous period which stops at some point when the adolescent leaves home, graduates college, gets a job, marries, or achieves some other state recognized by most as an emblem of adulthood. Later adolescence, therefore, is a time of preparation for full participation in society. During this time, therefore, boys are largely concerned with preparation for a life of work in some occupation and girls with the social and other skills needed in marriage. Although it may look to adults as if adolescents were chiefly interested in having a good time, a great deal of their preoccupation deals with how they want to lead their lives.

Adolescents partly internalize the values of their parents and partly create a world of their own with its own subcultural activities and values differing from those of the previous generation. They have, in any event, to cope with decisions about sexuality, relationship to legal and other rules, problems of identity, and plans for the future.

By later adolescent years boys and girls are sexually mature in the biological sense and have reached the highest stage of cognitive development. Consequently, development in later adolescence is largely a matter of cultural factors. That is, psychological mechanisms of perception, learning, cognition, and those of physical maturation are fully developed by sixteen or seventeen years of age. The boy or girl will continue to change and to mature as a result of experience and the need to take on additional responsibilities. However, these experiences and responsibilities are largely dependent on his position in society such as his age, social class, or education.

Most adolescents are future oriented and take their place in society without undue turmoil. Some, however, may experience a great deal of difficulty in doing so. They may become involved in illegal activities if they are unable to succeed in the usually accepted ways. Others may find the future life held out to them to be unattractive and may strive to find more meaningful alternatives.

Adolescence, particularly its later years, has been neglected by developmental psychologists. There are almost no experimental studies of psychological development during this age period. Late adolescence has chiefly been investigated by educators, sociologists, and psychoanalysts. Thus, in this book we moved from biological considerations, to issues of learning and cognition. Then we proceeded to consider socialization and internalization, which have both psychological and social aspects. We end finally with adolescence, an almost purely social phenomenon.

REFERENCES

1. Bandura, A., and Walters, R. H. *Social Learning and Personality Development.* Holt, Rinehart and Winston. New York, 1963.
2. Bandura, A., and Walters, R. H. *Adolescent Aggression.* Ronald Press, New York, 1959.
3. Becker, H. S. Social-class variations in the teacher-pupil relationship. *J. Educ. Sociol.,* 25, 1952, 451-465.
4. Bell, G. D. Process in the formation of adolescents' aspirations. *Social Forces, 42,* 1963, 178-186.
5. Boyle, R. P. The effects of high school on students' aspirations. *Amer. J. Sociol., 71,* 1966, 628-639.
6. Cervantes, L. F. *The Dropout.* University of Michigan Press, Ann Arbor, 1965.
7. Cloward, R. A., and Ohlin, L. E. *Delinquency and Opportunity.* Free Press, Glencoe, Ill., 1960.
8. Cohen, A. K. *Delinquent Boys.* Free Press, Glencoe, Ill., 1955.
9. Coleman, J. S. *The Adolescent Society.* Free Press, Glencoe, Ill., 1961.
10. Cook, E. S. An analysis of factors related to withdrawal from high school prior to graduation. *J. Educ. Res., 50,* 1956, 191-196.
11. Douvan, E., and Adelson, J. *The Adolescent Experience.* John Wiley, New York, 1966.

12. Douvan, E., and Gold, M. Modal Patterns in American Adolescence. (In) *Review of Child Development Research, Vol. 2.* Hoffman, L. W., and Hoffman, M. L. (Eds.) Russell Sage Foundation, New York 1966.
13. Elkin, F., and Westley, W. A. The myth of adolescent culture. *Amer. Soc. Rev., 20,* 1955, 680-684.
14. Engle, M. The stability of the self concept in adolescence. *J. Abnorm. Soc. Psychol., 58,* 1959, 211-215.
15. Erikson, E. H. The concept of identity in race relations: notes and queries. *Daedalus,* Winter, 1966, 145-171.
16. Erikson, E. H. *Childhood and Society.* W. W. Norton, New York, 1950.
17. Festinger, L. Informal social communication. *Psychol. Rev., 57,* 1950, 271-282.
18. Festinger, L., et al. *Social Pressures in Informal Groups.* Harper, New York, 1950.
19. Hogbin, H. I. Marriage in Wogeo, New Guinea. *Oceania, 15,* 1945, 324-352.
20. Johnson, A. M., and Szurek, S. A. The genesis of anti social acting out in children and adults. *Psychoanal. Quart., 21,* 1952, 323-343.
21. Kinsey, A. C., et al. *Sexual Behavior in the Human Female.* W. B. Saunders, Philadelphia, 1953.
22. Kinsey, A. C., et al. *Sexual Behavior in the Human Male.* W. B. Saunders, Philadelphia, 1948.
23. Maas, H. S. The role of members in clubs of lower-class and middle-class adolescents. *Child Develpm., 25,* 1954, 241-251.
24. McClosky, H., and Schaar, J. H. Psychological dimensions of anomie. *Amer. Sociol. Rev., 30,* 1965, 14-40.
25. McCord, J., and McCord, W. The effects of parental role models on criminality. *J. Soc. Issues., 14,* 1956, 66-74.
26. Mead, M. *From the South Seas.* William Morrow, New York, 1939.
27. Merton, R. K. *Social Theory and Social Structure.* Free Press, Glencoe, Ill., 1958.
28. Morse, W. C. The education of socially maladjusted and emotionally disturbed children. (In) *Education of Exceptional Children and Youth.* Cruickshank, W. M., and Johnson, G. O. (Eds.). Prentice-Hall, Englewood Cliffs. 1958.
29. Piers, E. V., and Harris, D. B. Age and other correlates of self-concept in children. *J. Educ. Psychol., 55,* 1964, 91-95.
30. Porterfield, A. L. *Youth in Trouble.* Leo Potishman Foundation, Austin, 1946.
31. Rogers, D. *The Psychology of Adolescence.* Appleton-Century-Crofts, New York, 1962.
32. Schwarz, E. E. A community experiement in the measurement of juvenile delinquency. (In) *Yearbook of the National Probation Association,* New York, 1945.
33. Short, J. F., and Rivera, R. Perceived opportunities, gang membership, and delinquency. *Amer. Sociol. Rev., 30,* 1965, 56-67.
34. Sofokidis, J. H., and Sullivan, E. *A new look at school dropouts.* U.S. Dept. of Health, Education, and Welfare. Indicators. April, 1964.
35. Spiro, M. E. *Children of the Kibbutz.* Harvard University Press, Cambridge, 1958.
36. Stanfield, R. E. The interaction of family variables and gang variables in the actiology of delinquency. *Social Problems, 13,* 1966, 409-417.
37. Sullivan, H. S. *The Interpersonal Theory of Psychiatry.* W. W. Norton, New York, 1953.
38. Turner, R. H. *The Social Context of Ambition.* Chandler Publishing, San Francisco, 1964.
39. U.S. Department of Health Education and Welfare. Juvenile Court Statistics. Children's Bureau. Statistical Service, No. 47, 1958.
40. Verville, E. *Behavior Problems of Children.* W. B. Saunders, Philadelphia, 1967.
41. Wattenberg, W. W., and Balistrieri, J. J. Gang membership and juvenile misconduct. *Amer. Soc. Rev., 15,* 1950, 746.
42. Weckler, N. L. Social class and school adjustment in relation to character reputation. (In) *Adolescent Character and Personality.* Havighurst, R. J., and Taba, H. John Wiley, New York, 1949.
43. Westley, W. A., and Elkin, F. The protective environment and adolescnet socialization. *Social Forces, 35,* 1956, 243-349.
44. Wilson, A. B. Residential segregation of social classes and aspirations of high school boys. *Amer. Sociol. Rev., 24,* 1959, 836-845.

Index of Authors Cited

Aberle, D. F., 247
Adelson, J., 416
Allen, K. E., 125
Amatruda, C. S., 94
Ambrose, J. A., 51
Aronfreed, J., 225, 289, 291, 375, 376
Atkinson, J. W., 238

Baldwin, A. L., 280
Bandura, A., 8, 191, 205, 208, 210, 212, 243, 396, 408
Bateson, G., 229
Bayley, N., 110
Becker, W. C., 279, 280, 283, 296
Behrens, M., 181
Bell, G. D., 420
Berko, J., 136
Bijou, S., 218
Binet, A., 130
Brackbill, Y., 51
Breckenridge, M. E., 96
Brontenbrenner, U., 320
Brown, R. W., 135
Bruner, J., 340
Burton, R. W., 376

Caldwell, B. M., 57
Cantor, G. N., 65
Cattell, R. B., 159
Chase, D., 338
Chess, S., 155
Chomsky, N., 137
Coleman, J. S., 394, 395, 398
Collinson, J. M., 338
Cooley, J. A., 63

D'Andrade, R., 240
Dennis, M. G., 107
Dennis, W., 107
Dollard, J., 206
Douvan, E., 351, 416, 422
Dyer, E. D., 311

Elkin, F., 394
Elkind, D., 185
Erikson, E. H., 193, 237, 421
Eysenck, H. J., 171

Falkner, F., 110
Fantz, R., 67
Farber, I. E., 52
Feffer, M. H., 342
Feshbach, N., 259, 261, 268, 368
Feshbach, S., 368
Foshee, J. C., 215
Fraser, C., 135
Freeman, F. N., 165
Freud, S., 18, 115, 126, 178, 193, 250

Gelfand, D., 366
Gesell, A., 94, 106
Gewirtz, J. L., 68
Gilligan, C., 251
Glidewell, J. C., 269
Gold, M., 351, 422
Gourevitch, V., 342
Gray, P., 55
Grinder, R. E., 385
Grusec, J., 388
Guilford, J. P., 132, 133

Hall, M., 364
Harlow, H. F., 58-60
Hartshorne, M., 376, 378
Hartup, W. W., 365
Heathers, G., 120
Hitchcock, J., 304
Hobbs, D. F., 310
Holziner, K. J., 165
Hunt, J. McV., 92, 93

Jensen, A. R., 144, 145, 146
Jones, M. C., 172

Kagan, J., 255, 264, 369, 373
Kaplan, A. R., 168
Keith, R. A., 364
Kinsey, A. C., 347, 400
Kofskey, E., 187
Kohlberg, L., 189, 343, 363, 373, 376, 378
Kohn, M. L., 317
Kupers, C. J., 243

Lemkin, J., 369
Lenneberg, E. H., 137
Levin, H., 275-280
LeVine, B., 306
LeVine, R., 306
Levy, D. M., 79
Lipsett, L. P., 87
Luria, A. R., 139

Maccoby, E. E., 275-280, 371
Madsen, C. H., 82
Maretzki, H., 123
Maretzki, T. W., 123
May, M. A., 376, 378
McClelland, D. C., 246
McClosky, H., 414
McDonald, F. J., 191
McGrade, B. J., 46
McGraw, M. B., 94, 106
McNemar, Q., 157
Miller, N. E., 206
Minturn, L., 304
Mischel, W., 250, 251, 373, 374
Moss, H., 264
Mowrer, O. H., 89, 137
Mussen, P. H., 172, 180

Naegle, K. D., 247
Newman, H. H., 164

Olmstead, D. L., 137

Papousek, H., 86
Parke, R. D., 382
Patterson, G. R., 258
Piaget, J., 18, 88, 90, 91, 92, 126, 128, 133, 147, 182, 193, 336
Powell, M., 350

Rashkis, H. A., 228
Rayner, R., 85
Reber, A., 225
Reynolds, E. L., 346
Rheingold, H. L., 63, 85, 216
Roe, K., 261
Rogers, D., 410
Romney, K., 117
Romney, R., 117
Rosen, B. G., 240

Salzen, E., A., 49, 50
Schaar, J. H., 414
Schaeffer, E. S., 279
Sears, R. R., 79, 275-280
Sewell, W. H., 180
Siegel, P. S., 215
Simmons, M. W., 87
Singer, R. D., 228, 366
Skeels, H. M., 161
Skodak, M., 161
Spiro, M. E., 406
Spock, B., 94
Stanley, W. C., 63, 85
Stoddard, G. D., 132
Sullivan, H. S., 193, 265-267, 348, 403

Thompson, H., 106

Verville, E., 242, 401
Villee, C., 34
Vincent, E. L., 96

Walters, R. H., 8, 382, 396, 408
Watson, J. B., 85, 154
Watson, J. S., 51
Wertheimer, M., 84-85
West, L. J., 52
Westly, W. A., 394
White, B. L., 51
White, R., 126, 127
Williams, C. D., 221
Wines, J. V., 346
Winterbottom, M. R., 238

Wise, G. W., 79
Wolff, P. H., 47, 49

Yarrow, L. J., 79

Ziegler, E., 255
Zook, E. A., 366

Index

Abnormal behavior, child development and, 10-11
Achievement, early demands for, 238-240
  family structure and, 248-249
  from six to early adolescence, 237-271
  middle class pressures and, 247
  modeling and, 243
  need for, 237
  preparation for, 238
  risk taking and, 245-247
  school and, 237-240
  self-reinforcement and, 243
  social class and, 247-248
  social structure and, 248
  training in, 240-245
Adaptation, as primitive learning, 84
Adolescence, alienation during, 352
  antisocial behavior during, 328, 408
  as cultural invention, 331
  early, 326-354
    cognitive development in, 332-341
    developmental issues during, 336-354
    independence and, 350-353
    moral judgments during, 343
    sexual maturation and, 346
  friendship formation during, 327
  future orientation and, 416-421
  identity and, 329, 421-422
  internalization process and, 356-357
  later, 394-424
    sexuality in, 400-408
  overview of, 326-336
  parental values and, 395
  self-concept and identity during, 421-422
  self-esteem during, 334
Age, sex preferences and, 365-366
Aggression, competition and, as sex-typed behaviors, 370-371
  discipline and, 293
  in Okinawan preschool child, 122
  socialization and, 121-123
Alienation, during early adolescence, 352
Anomie, during early adolescence, 352
  psychological dimensions of, 414

Anxiety, and insensitivity to pain, 52-53
  influence of parents on, 205
  performance and, 255
  respect and, 403
  school and, 255-261
  sexuality and, 350
Appetitional conditioning, 86
Approach-avoidance conflict, 227-228
Arousal, optimal, vs. stimulus privation, in infant behavior, 67-68
Aversive conditioning, 83, 85
Avoidance-avoidance conflict, 228-230

Behavior(s), abnormal, child development and, 10-11
    reinforcement and, 219
  acquisition of, 103-104
  adolescent, 328, 408
  antisocial, adolescence and, 328, 408
  child, child development and, 4-5
    restrictiveness-permissiveness and, 294-295
    understanding of, from scientific viewpoint, 6-7
  classroom, teacher and, 269
  cognitive development and, 232
  conformity of, during adolescence, 332-336
  dynamic factors and, 204
  effects of environment on, 158-160
  effects of warmth and hostility on, 293-294
  empathic, and sex differences, 260
  exploratory, in infants, 62-64, 92
  genetic factors and, 26-27, 38-39
  imitative, characteristics of child and, 214
    conditions affecting, 211
    in early childhood, 87-89
    motor recognition and, 90
  infant, arousal vs. privation in, 67-68
  innate differences in, 154-155
  internalized, punishment and, 225

431

Behavior(s) *(Continued)*
  interpersonal, acceptance and, 269
  intrinsic reaction types of, 155
  maternal, 181
  means-end, and problem solving, 91
  moral, Freudian approach to, 378-379
    internalization of, 374-376
    moral values and, 376-378
    stages of, 344
  motivated, socialization of, 123-125
  negative reinforcement of, 220
  nonpromiscuous, in adolescence, 402
  non-reward and, 221
  parental, and dependency motive, 120
    problems of children and, 281, 283
    specific, 274-288
  paternal, social class and, 320
  preadolescent, as a stage, 263
  reinforcement and, 202
  sex role and, 264
  sex-typed, 263
    aggression and, 370-371
    social learning interpretation of, 373
  sexual, adolescent, in kibbutz, 405
    children's play and, 116
    cultural influences on, 116
    Freudian formulation of, 114-115
    intimacy and, during adolescence, 333
    socialization of, 114-118
  social, learning of, 202-206
  suppression of, due to punishment, 225
  tantrum, non-reward of, 221
  vocal, early acquisition of, 88
Behavioral phenomena, 15-16

Cell reproduction, 29-31
Cheating, gratification in school and, 251
Child(ren), adopted, intelligence quotient and, 160
  true and foster parents and, 161
  advantaged and disadvantaged, imitation of teacher and, 259
  and perception of male-female role, 369-370
  as object of study, 3-4
  as person, 5-6
  foster, intelligence quotient and, 160
  institutionalized, 68-70
  law of reinforcement and, 214-219
  play of, sexual behavior and, 116
  problems of, parental behavior and, 281, 283
  study of, approaches and methods of, 18-19
  understanding of, 1-13
Child development, 1-3
  abnormality and, 10-11
  acquisition of behavior and, 103-104
  child behavior and, 4-5

Child development *(Continued)*
  chronological approach and, 20-21
  early, processes of, 42-76, 77-99
  explanatory approaches to, 16
  maternal deprivation and, 68-70
  mental retardation and, 166-169
  non-chronological approach to, 21-22
  psychology and, 11-12
  science and, 22-23
  social learning theories of, 17
  stage theories of, 17, 178-196
  stimulus deprivation and, 68-70
  study of, contributions of Piaget to, 193
Child psychology, changes in, 14-15
Child rearing, 274-297
  different types of, effects of, 288-297
  dimensions of, 275-280
    interaction of warmth and, 295-296
  experimental method of, 290-293
  internalization in, 318, 385-389
  patterns of, 276
    convergence of, 316-317
  problem children and, 280-285
  social change and, 9-10
  social class and, 313, 317
Chromosomes, human, 30
Chronology, child development and, 20-21
Cognitive development, 130-148
  behavior and, 232
  early, 89-98
  formal thought and, 338
  in adolescence, 326-327
  in early adolescence, 336-341
  internalization and, 384-385
  moral judgments and, 343
  role taking in children and, 342
Competence motivation, 126-130
Competition, aggression and, as sex-typed behaviors, 370-371
Conditioning, appetitional, 86
  classical, 83
  aversive, 83, 85
  operant, 86
Conflict(s), approach-avoidance, 227-228
  avoidance-avoidance, 228-230
  during adolescence, 335
  interpretation of, 228
Conformity, behavioral, during adolescence, 332-336
  environmental pressures for, 159
Conscience, internalization of, 374-376
Conservation, concept of, 184
Culture, adolescence as invention of, 331
  genetics and, 27
  influence of, on sexual behavior, 116

Delinquency, adolescent, causes of, 415-416
  in poverty areas, causes of, 412
  subculture of, 413

Dependency, emotional, and socialization, 119-120
Deprivation, maternal, and development, 68-70
Development, child. See Child development.
  cognitive, 89-98
  emotional, in infancy, 48-52
  intellectual, 133-134
    experimental tests of, 184-186
    mental and motor, in infancy, 109
    neonatal, individual differences of, 46-48
  perceptual, 89
  physical, social environment and, 172
  prenatal, 26-41
    embryo and, 31-33
    fetus and, 33-34
  psychological, heredity and, 38-39
  psychosexual stages of, 178
Developmental psychology, aims and organization of, 14-23
  applications of, 7-9
  contributions of, to general psychology, 12-13
  education and, 11
  theoretical limitations and, 19-20
Discipline, aggression and, 293
  orientation of, in child rearing, 278
  processes of, 286-287
Displacement, conflict and, 230

Education, developmental psychology and, 11
Embryo, and prenatal development, 31-33
Emotion(s), change of, models and, 383-384
  in infancy, 48-54
  internalization and, 380-391
Empathy, sex differences and, 260
Environment, behavior and, 158-160
  heredity and, 165-166
  intelligence and, 162, 165-166
  pressures of, for conformity, 159
  social, physical development and, 172
Evaluation, of scientific approach, to children, 7
Extraversion, 170

Failure, fear of, achievement and, 245
Family, American, current state of, 308-313
  extended, 301-308
  function of, in socialization, 299-300
  nuclear, 300-301
  social class and, in socialization process, 299-324
Family structure, achievement and, 248-249

Fear. See also Phobia.
  internalization and, 389
  of failure, achievement and, 245
Feeding and weaning, socialization and, 78-79
Fetus, and prenatal development, 33-34
Fixation, development and, 179
Freedom, internalization and, 390
Friendship, formation of, during adolescence, 327
Frustration, learning and, 230

Genetic(s), behavior and, 26-27, 38-39
  culture and, 27
Genotypes, 38
Gratification, delay of, school and, 250
Guilt, competence and, 128
  internalization and, 389

Habituation, as primitive learning, 84
Heredity, 27-29
  behavior and, 38-39
  environment and, 165-166
  intelligence and, 160, 165-166
  mental disorders and, 169-174
  mental retardation and, 167
  neurotic tendencies and, 169
  phenylketonuria and, 168
  psychological processes and, 153-175
  schizophrenia and, 169
  sensory and motor processes and, 156
Hostility, effect of, on child behavior, 293-294

Identification, 360-362
  with aggressor, 213
Identity, adolescence and, 329, 421-422
  internalization and, 356-380
  sex gender and, 362-364
Imitation, characteristics of child and, 214
  conditions affecting, 211-214
  during preadolescence, 261
  in early childhood, 87-89
  learning and, before or after attachment, 87
  moral judgments and, 191
  motor recognition and, 90
  observational learning and, 208
  of teacher, by advantaged and disadvantaged children, 259
  performance and, 203
  process of, 206-208
  reinforcement and, 191, 198-223
  social power and, 212

Imprinting, and the social attachment, 54-56
Independence, during early adolescence, 350-353
  during preadolescence, 262
Induction oriented discipline, 286, 289
Infancy, emotional responses in, 52-54
  exploratory behavior in, 62-64
  levels of stimulation in, 65-70
  maternal deprivation in, 68-70
  mental and motor ability in, 109
  stimulation deprivation in, 68-70
Infant behavior, exploratory, 62-64
  levels of stimulation of, 65-70
  premature, response processes of, 34-38
Inherited behavior, 38-39
Institutionalized children, maternal deprivation and, 68-70
Intelligence, acquisition of, 182
  cognitive process and, 130-131
  development of, 133-134
    experimental tests of, 184-186
    preconceptual thought and, 133
  environment and, 165-166
  functioning of, sex typing and, 371-373
  heredity and, 165-166
    of twins, 163-165
  intuitive thought and, 133
  level of, and social class, 145
    and verbal mediation, 144
  meaning of, 131-133
Intelligence quotient, heredity and, 160
  of adopted and foster children, 160
Intercourse, sexual, in adolescence, 402
Internalization, 356-391
  adolescence and, 356-357
  cognitive activities in, 384-385
  emotional processes and, 380-391
  fear and, 389
  freedom and, 390
  guilt and, 389
  identity and, 356-380
  of conscience and moral behavior, 374-376
  parental warmth and, 385-388
  patterns of child rearing and, 385-389
  punishment and, 225
  self-criticism and, 387
  sensitization and, 389
  shame and, 389
Interpersonal relations, 180-182, 269, 327-330
  sex and, 348-350
Introversion-extraversion, inheritance of, 171

Judgment, development of, 188-190
  during adolescence, 343

Labeling, language learning and, 138
Language. *See also* Speech.
  acquisition of, 134-138
  and motor process, consolidation of, 98
  early, 88
  comprehension and expression of, distinction between, 89
  learning process and, 138-143
    verbal label-response connection and, 139
Law breaking. *See also* Delinquency.
  moral response to, 291
  psychology and, 409
Law of reinforcement, children and, 214-219
Learning, adaptation as, 84
  approach-avoidance conflict and, 227-228
  avoidance-avoidance conflict, 228-230
  frustration and, 230
  habituation, as, 84
  in early childhood, by imitation, 87-89
  language, 138-143
    acquisition of, 134-138
    labeling and, 138
    social class and, 138
    verbal label-response and, 139
  law of reinforcement and, 214
  maturation and, 103-112
  mediational, development of, 143-146
  neonatal, 83-87
  observational, and imitation, 208
  reinforcement process and, 214
  social, 198-233
    dynamic processes in, 223-233
    vocabulary of, 199-202
  social nature of, 202-206
  socialization and, 82-89
  verbal label-response and, 139
  vs. performance, in children, 210
Learning theory, Piaget and, 190
Limitations, theoretical, and developmental psychology, 19-20
Locomotion, early cognitive behavior and, 94
Love oriented discipline, 286
Lust, and need for security, 348

Male-female role, as perceived by children, 369-370
Marriage, children and, 310
  modern, 309
Maternal behavior, 181
  social attachment and, 57-58
Maternal deprivation, development and, 68-70
Matriarchy, child rearing and, 314

Maturation, 104
  biological, in adolescents, 346
  experience and, 105, 109
  learning and, 103-112
  privation and, 107
  psychology and, 104-105
  readiness for, training before, 106
  sexual, and early adolescence, 346
Mediation, verbal, and intelligence level, 144
Mental ability, in infancy, 109
Mental disorders, heredity and, 169-174
Mental retardation, verbal retardation and, 145
Methodology, science and child development, 22-23
Middle class, internalization and, 318
  pressures of, achievement and, 248
  punishment in, 317
Modeling, and achievement, 243
Models, delay of gratification and, 254
  emotional change and, 383-384
Moral behavior, Freudian approach to, 378-379
  internalization of, 374-376
  stages of, 344
Moral judgment, development of, 188-191
  during adolescence, 343
  imitation and, 191
  moral values and, 376-378
Mother, substitute, and social attachment, 58-60
Mother-father role, social class and, 321
Mother-infant attachment, socialization and, 77-78
Motivation, achievement, school and, 237-240
  aggressive, socialization of, 121-123
  cognitive processes and, 114-148
  competence, 126-130
  dependency, socialization of, 119-121
  parental behavior and, 120
  sexual, American treatment of, 117
  socialization of, 114-130
Motor ability, in infancy, 109
Motor processes, early cognitive behavior and, 93
  language and, consolidation of, 98
  sensory and, 156-158
Motor skills, finer, development of, 95

Negative reinforcement, 220
Negro migration, child rearing and, 315
Neonate, early response processes of, 42-45
  individual differences of, 46-48
  physical characteristics of, 42, 43
Neurosis, heredity and, 169
Nonchronological approaches, to child development, 21-22

Non-reward, 221
  of tantrum behavior, 221
Nyansongo Gusii, as extended type of family, 305

Object oriented discipline, 287
Operant conditioning, 86
Optimal arousal, vs. stimulus privation, in infant behavior,,67-68

Pain, insensitivity to, 52-53
Parent(s), behavior of, 274-288
  and children's problems, 281, 283
  influence of, on anxiety, 205
  warmth of, internalization and, 385-388
Peer group, demands of, during adolescence, 332-336
  during preadolescence, 262
Perceptual development, 89
Performance, anxiety and, 255
  imitation and, 203
  vs. learning, in children, 210
Permissiveness, in child rearing, 277
Personality, development of, during adolescence, 329
Phenomena, behavioral, of childhood, 15-16
Phenotypes, 38
Phenylketonuria, detection and partial cure of, 168
Phobia, of school, 256
Physical processes, of puberty, 327
Play, children's, sexual behavior and, 116
Power, social, and imitation, 212
Preadolescence, behavior of, as stage, 263
  inner world of, 265
  peer group and, demands of during, 262
  reinforcement during, 261
Preconceptual thought, and intellectual development, 133
Premature infant, response processes and, 34-38
Prenatal development, 26-41
  embryo, 31-33
  fetus, 33-34
Privation, functional, 68
  maturation and, 107
  total, 68
Problem children, child rearing and, 280-285
Problem solving, early cognitive behavior and, 91
Promiscuity, female, adolescent, 401
Psychology, child, changes in, 14-15
  developmental, applications of, to values and action, 7-9

Psychology *(Continued)*
  general, contributions of developmental psychology to, 12-13
  inheritance and, 153-175
Psychosexual development, stages of, 178
Puberty, physical processes of, 327
Punishment, adverse effects of, 226
  in working and middle classes, 317
  internalized behavior suppression and, 226
  suppression and, 380
  timing of, 382

Rajputs of India, as extended type family, 304
Recognition, motor, and imitation, 90
Reflexes, of neonate, 42-45
Reinforcement, 202
  abnormal behavior and, 219
  by self, 217, 243
  differential, 203
  during preadolescence, 261
  imitation and, 198-223
  law of, in children, 215
  learning and, 214
  moral judgment and imitation and, 191
  negative, effects of, 220
  partial, 217
  social, 216
Research, presentation of, 23
Resemblance sorting, and cognitive development, 187
Respect, anxiety and, 403
Response(s), emotional, in infancy, 48-54
  moral, to transgression, 291
  of neonate, 42-45
  premature infant and, 34-38
  smiling, 49-52
  stimulation and, 61-62
Response displacement, 230
Restrictiveness-permissiveness, child behavior and, 294-295
Retardation, mental, 166-169
  and heredity, 167
Retardation, mental vs. verbal, 145
Reward, ability to delay gratification and, 253
  patterns of, in children, 218
Risk taking, achievement and, 245-247
Role(s), changing assignments of, 322-323
  in early adolescence, 341-343
  male-female, as perceived by children, 369-370
  mother-father, social class and, 321
  of adolescent, 330-332
Role taking, cognitive aspects of, in children, 342

Schizophrenia, double bind hypothesis and, 229
  heredity and, 169
School, achievement in, delay of gratification and, 250
  achievement motivation and, 237-240
  anxiety and, 255-261
  attention and familiarity in, 255
  early years, 258
  social life and, 258-261
  social ties and, 261-265
  teacher and, 258
School phobia, 256
Science, and methodology, and child development, 22-23
Scientific viewpoint, understanding children from, 6-7
Security, need for, lust and, 348
Self-concept, adolescence and, 421-422
Self-criticism, and withdrawal of love, in internalization process, 387
Self-esteem, during adolescence, 334
Self-reinforcement, 217, 243
Sensitization, internalization and, 389
Sensitization orientation discipline, 289
Sensorimotor period, and intellectual development, 133
Sensory processes, and motor processes, 156-158
Sex, interpersonal processes and, 348-350
Sex differences, intellectual functioning and, 371-373
  response to outsiders and, 268
Sex preferences, age and, 365-366
  social class and, 364-365
Sexuality, anxiety and, 350
  during adolescence, 333
  extent of, 400
  in other cultures, 404-408
  during later adolescence, 400-408
Shame, competence and, 128
  internalization and, 389
Similarity, social dimensions of, 366-369
Skills, manual, development of, 95
  motor, finer, development of, 95
  twin resemblances and, 157
Social acceptance, determinants of, interpersonal behavior and, 269
  school and, 267-269
  sexuality and, anxiety about, 350
Social change, child rearing and, 9-10
Social class, achievement and, 247-248
  family and, in socialization process, 299-324
  intelligence level and, 145
  language learning and, 138
  mother-father roles and, 321
  paternal behavior and, 320
  sex differential treatment by, 319-321
  sex preferences and, 364-365
  verbal training and, 145

Social dimensions of similarity, 366-369
Social learning theories, of child development, 17
Social life, school and, 258-261
Social power, and imitation, 212
Social reinforcement, 216
Social structure, achievement and, 248
Social ties, school and, 261-265
Social values, inheritance and, 172
Socialization, dynamic processes in, 223-233, 357
  family and, 299-324
  feeding and weaning and, 78-79
  imprinting and, 54-55
  in children, 198-233
  in early development, 77-82
  in higher animals, 56-57
  interpersonal behavior and, 327-330
  learning process and, 82-89
  maternal behavior and, 57-58
  mother-infant attachment and, 77-78
  of motives, 114-130
  of sexual motivation, 114-118
  positive aspects of, 125-129
  school and, 258-261
  social attachment and, 54-61
  social class and, 299-324
  substitute mothers and, 58-60
  toilet training and, 80-81
  vocabulary of, 199-202
Speech. *See also* Language.
  children's, overgeneralization in, 136
  reduction in, 136
Stage theories, contribution of Piaget to, 193
  dispensability of, 193
  of child development, 17, 178-196
  special experience and, 187
Status, of adolescent, 330-332
Stimulation, levels of, in infants, 65-70
  response processes and, 61-62
Stimulus, deprivation of, development and, 68-70
  displacement of, 230
  privation of, vs optimal arousal, in infant behavior, 67-68
Stimulus-verbal label-response, 141

Study, child as object of, 3-4
Subculture, adolescent, 394-400
Substitute mothers, 58-60
Success, expectation of, and delay of gratification, 253
Suppression, 223-227
  punishment and, 380

Teacher, and classroom behavior, 269
  imitation of, in advantaged and disadvantaged children, 259
Theories, social learning, 17
  stage, 17
Therapy, learning, school phobia and, 256
Thumbsucking, 79
Toilet training, crash program of, 81-82
  socialization and, 80-81
Training, in achievement, 240-245
Trust, ability to delay gratification and, 252
Twin(s), intelligence of, heredity and, 163-165
  resemblances of, in motor skills, 157

Value(s), adolescent, 398
  parental, adolescents and, 395
  sexual, internalization and, 400
Verbal label-response, and language learning, 139
Verbal retardation, mental retardation and, 145
Vocabulary, of social learning, 199-202
Vocal behavior, early acquisition of, 88

Warmth, effect of, on child behavior, 293-294
  in child rearing, 277
  other child rearing dimensions and, 295-296
  parental, internalization and, 385-388
Weaning, socialization and, 78-79
Working class, punishment in, 317